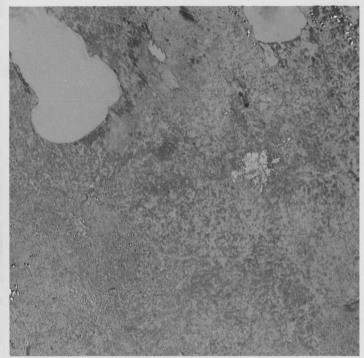

5. WINNIPEG (MANITOBA)
Radiating road and rail routes make Winnipeg a most important transportation hub. The urban area appears as a blue-grey color because of its relative lack of vegetation; fields planted in crops are bright red; land left fallow shows as blue-green.

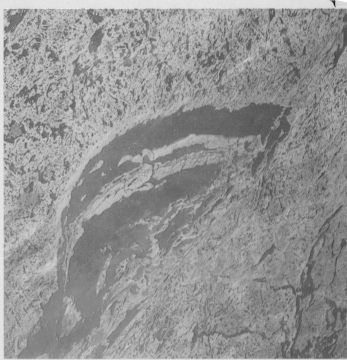

6. GREAT SLAVE LAKE (NORTHWEST TERRITORIES)
The eastern reaches of Great Slave Lake are contained by a huge fault shown as a diagonal feature on the image. Greenish-colored patches of vegetation indicate areas recently burned over by forest fires.

7. ROCKY MOUNTAINS (BRITISH COLUMBIA)
This is an area of high precipitation, much of which falls as snow that covers the high mountains in this image, emphasizing the drainage pattern. The conspicuous straight valley bisecting the area is part of the Rocky Mountain Trench, a great fault zone that extends from Alaska to Montana.

8. VANCOUVER (BRITISH COLUMBIA)
The rugged relief of the Western Cordillera extends to include Vancouver Island. Snow is visible on the peaks of the Coastal Mountains. The low-lying delta of the Fraser River appears in the north-east, with metropolitan Vancouver occupying a portion of it.

Gage Atlas of the World

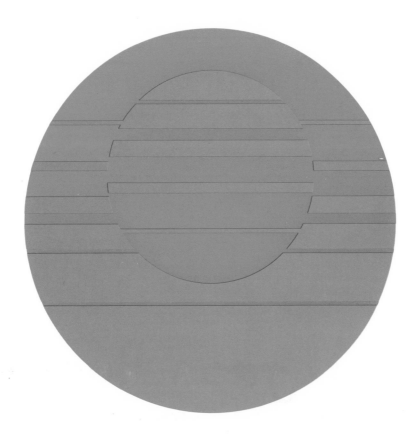

Consultants

Ines A. Farmer
Social Studies Consultant, Calgary Board of Education

John E. Koegler
(Formerly) Geography Consultant, Waterloo County Board of Education

Gary T. Whiteford
Professor, Faculty of Education, University of New Brunswick

gage EDUCATIONAL PUBLISHING COMPANY
A DIVISION OF CANADA PUBLISHING CORPORATION
TORONTO ONTARIO CANADA

Name Anna jean Burdey! ♡!

Maps and Index
© **1985 George Philip and Son Ltd., London**

This edition © 1985 Gage Educational Publishing Company

A Division of Canada Publishing Corporation

Toronto   Ontario   Canada

ISBN 0−7715−8162−9

Cover Design: William Fox/Associates
Maps and index edited by Bill Willett, George Philip and Son, Ltd.

Photo Credits: Pages 46–47. All photos from NFB Photothèque, with the exception of the Canadian Shield Lowlands which was supplied by Barry Griffiths/Network Stock Photo File.

  2 3 4 5   BP 89 88 87 86

Printed and Bound in Canada

Preface

In a country as technologically advanced as Canada, people are constantly called upon to identify, to interpret, and to organize the vast quantities of information available to them. Whether it refers to the physical, the social, or the economic world, this data can only be made meaningful by creating order within it. Maps are useful tools for accomplishing much of this, because they represent a simplified reality: data has been selected to yield the most specific and graphic illustration.

An atlas must provide for several purposes: among them, to enable users to understand the complex relationship between human beings and the environment, and to appreciate the implications of this throughout the world; also, to structure the knowledge needed for assessing local, regional, and global issues.

The **Gage Atlas of the World** attempts to achieve these goals by providing the following: topographic maps at a variety of scales; thematic maps; satellite images; photographs; diagrams; bar, circle, and line graphs; climatic data; tables of statistics; an index; and explanatory text.

The first part of the atlas explores world patterns, both physical and human. A summary of the forces that shaped the surface of the earth is followed by particulars of how its resources are made use of, and with what results. This section offers generalizations that can be examined on a regional scale.

Continental and regional studies form the second section of the **Gage Atlas of the World**. The characteristics of each continent are investigated in a systematic fashion and illustrated with regional topographic maps. These pages are devoted to the significant patterns of human interaction with the physical environment that define each individual part of the globe. As befits an atlas intended for Canadian users, thematic maps, graphs, photographs, and tables of statistics for Canada provide greater depth of coverage of this country.

Following the map section, there are tables of climatic statistics and numerical data for the countries of the world. A lengthy Canadian statistics section gives a profile in detail of this country's economic and social personality. A comprehensive index is included that lists latitude and longitude co-ordinates for approximately 11 000 places.

Spellings of Canadian names are consistent with those given in the *Gazetteer of Canada* by the Canadian Permanent Committee on Geographic Names and in the *Répertoire Géographique du Québec* by the Commission de Géographie. Other names generally agree with the rules of the Permanent Committee on Geographical Names and the United States Board on Geographic Names.

Contents

Contents

SETTLEMENTS

Settlement symbols in order of size

◧ LONDON   ▪ Stuttgart   ◉ Sevilla   ◉ Bergen   ◉ Bath   ○ Biarritz   ○ Srikolayatji
◧ MONTRÉAL   Hamilton   Moose Jaw   Prince Rupert   Gaspé   Banff   Miquelon

Settlement symbols and type styles vary according to the scale of each map and indicate the importance of towns on the map rather than specific population figures

∴ Sites of Archæological or Historical importance

BOUNDARIES

⸺ International Boundaries

⸺ ⸺ International Boundaries (Undemarcated or Undefined)

⸺ Internal Boundaries

International boundaries show the *de facto* situation where there are rival claims to territory

▱ ⬭ National and Provincial Parks

COMMUNICATIONS

═══ Freeways

┅┅ Freeways under construction

━○━ Trans-Canada Highway

─── Principal Roads

～～ Other Roads

⌇⌇ Tracks and Seasonal Roads

～ Principal Railways

⌒ Other Railways

⌁ Railways under construction

⊣---⊢ Railway Tunnels

⊣---⊢ Road Tunnels

⏝ Passes

⌇⌇⌇ Principal Canals

┼──┼ Principal Oil Pipelines

_ *3386* _ Principal Shipping Routes (Distances in Nautical Miles)

─── Principal Air Routes

✈ ✛ ✿ Airports

PHYSICAL FEATURES

～ Perennial Streams

⌁ Seasonal Streams

▲ 8848 Spot Height in metres

⬭ Seasonal Lakes, Salt Flats

⁖⁖ Swamps, Marshes

▼ 8050 Sea Depths. in metres

▭ Permanent Ice

᠊ Wells in Desert

1134 Height of Lake Surface Above Sea Level, in metres

Height of Land Above Sea Level in metres

Land Below Sea Level

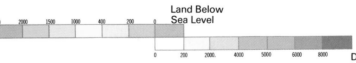

Depth of Sea in metres

Some of the maps have different contours to highlight and clarify the principal relief features

Abbreviations of measures used   mm Millimetres   m Metres   km Kilometres   °C Degrees Celsius   mb Millibars

As the Earth is spherical in shape, it cannot be represented on a plane surface without some distortion. The map projection is a system for attempting to represent the sphere on a two-dimensional plane. A projection has certain properties: the representation of correct area, true shape, or true bearings. The preservation of one property can only be secured at the expense of the other qualities.

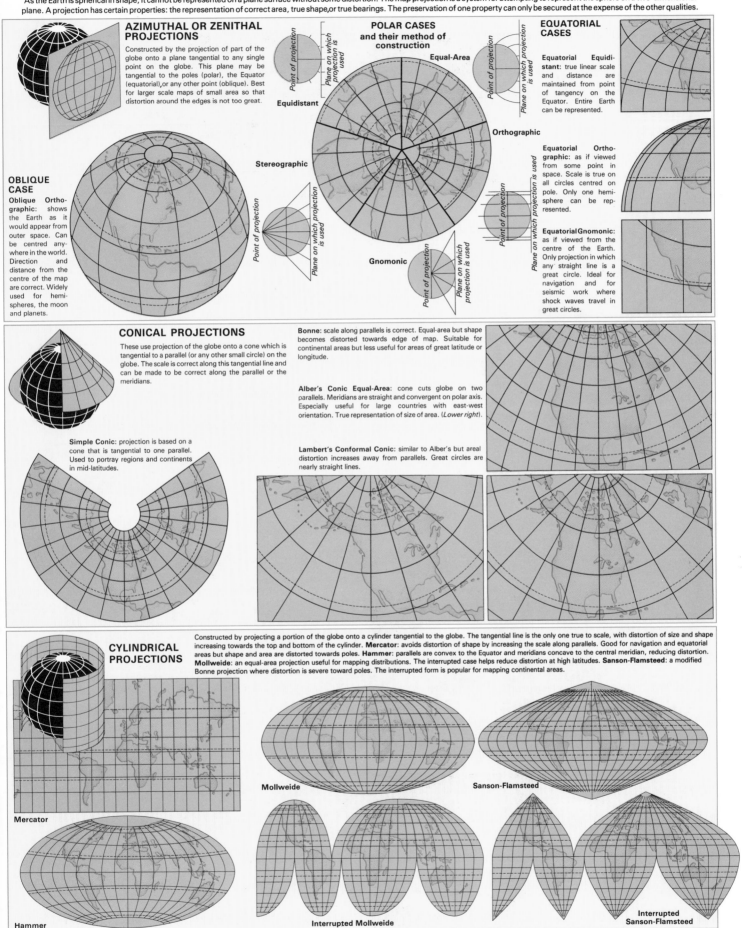

AZIMUTHAL OR ZENITHAL PROJECTIONS

Constructed by the projection of part of the globe onto a plane tangential to any single point on the globe. This plane may be tangential to the poles (polar), the Equator (equatorial), or any other point (oblique). Best for larger scale maps of small area so that distortion around the edges is not too great.

POLAR CASES and their method of construction

Equal-Area

Equidistant

Stereographic

Gnomonic

EQUATORIAL CASES

Equatorial Equidistant: true linear scale and distance are maintained from point of tangency on the Equator. Entire Earth can be represented.

Equatorial Orthographic: as if viewed from some point in space. Scale is true on all circles centred on pole. Only one hemisphere can be represented.

Equatorial Gnomonic: as if viewed from the centre of the Earth. Only projection in which any straight line is a great circle. Ideal for navigation and for seismic work where shock waves travel in great circles.

Point of projection / Plane on which projection is used

Orthographic

Point of projection / Plane on which projection is used

OBLIQUE CASE

Oblique Orthographic: shows the Earth as it would appear from outer space. Can be centred anywhere in the world. Direction and distance from the centre of the map are correct. Widely used for hemispheres, the moon and planets.

CONICAL PROJECTIONS

These use projection of the globe onto a cone which is tangential to a parallel (or any other small circle) on the globe. The scale is correct along this tangential line and can be made to be correct along the parallel or the meridians.

Simple Conic: projection is based on a cone that is tangential to one parallel. Used to portray regions and continents in mid-latitudes.

Bonne: scale along parallels is correct. Equal-area but shape becomes distorted towards edge of map. Suitable for continental areas but less useful for areas of great latitude or longitude.

Alber's Conic Equal-Area: cone cuts globe on two parallels. Meridians are straight and convergent on polar axis. Especially useful for large countries with east-west orientation. True representation of size of area. (*Lower right*).

Lambert's Conformal Conic: similar to Alber's but areal distortion increases away from parallels. Great circles are nearly straight lines.

CYLINDRICAL PROJECTIONS

Constructed by projecting a portion of the globe onto a cylinder tangential to the globe. The tangential line is the only one true to scale, with distortion of size and shape increasing towards the top and bottom of the cylinder. **Mercator:** avoids distortion of shape by increasing the scale along parallels. Good for navigation and equatorial areas but shape and area are distorted towards poles. **Hammer:** parallels are convex to the Equator and meridians concave to the central meridian, reducing distortion. **Mollweide:** an equal-area projection useful for mapping distributions. The interrupted case helps reduce distortion at high latitudes. **Sanson-Flamsteed:** a modified Bonne projection where distortion is severe toward poles. The interrupted form is popular for mapping continental areas.

Mercator

Mollweide

Sanson-Flamsteed

Hammer

Interrupted Mollweide

Interrupted Sanson-Flamsteed

The Solar System is a minute part of one of the innumerable galaxies that make up the universe. Our Galaxy is represented in the drawing to the right and The Solar System (S) lies near the plane of spiral-shaped galaxy, but 27 000 light-years from the centre. The System consists of the Sun at the centre with planets, moons, asteroids, comets, meteors, meteorites, dust and gases revolving around it. It is calculated to be at least 4 700 million years old.

The Solar System can be considered in two parts: the Inner Region planets- Mercury, Venus, Earth and Mars - all small and solid; the Outer Region planets Jupiter, Saturn, Uranus and Neptune - all gigantic in size,and on the edge of the system the smaller Pluto.

Our galaxy

Inner region planets

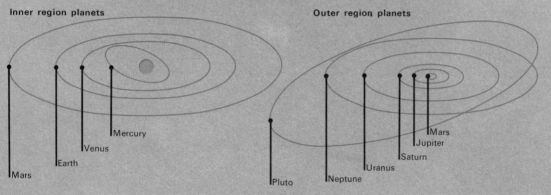

Mercury
Venus
Earth
Mars

Outer region planets

Mars
Jupiter
Saturn
Uranus
Neptune
Pluto

The planets

All planets revolve round the Sun in the same direction, and mostly in the same plane. Their orbits are shown (left) - they are not perfectly circular paths.

The table below summarizes the dimensions and movements of the Sun and planets.

The Sun

The Sun has an interior with temperatures believed to be of several million °C brought about by continuous thermo-nuclear fusions of hydrogen into helium. This immense energy is transferred by radiation into surrounding layers of gas the outer surface of which is called the chromosphere. From this "surface" with a temperature of many thousands °C "flames" (solar prominences) leap out into the diffuse corona which can best be seen at times of total eclipse (see photo right). The bright surface of the Sun, the photosphere, is calculated to have a temperature of about 6 000 °C, and when viewed through a telescope has a mottled appearance, the darker patches being called sunspots - the sites of large disturbances of the surface.

Total eclipse of the sun

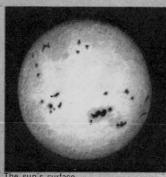
The sun's surface

	Equatorial diameter in km	Mass (earth=1)	Mean distance from sun in millions km	Mean radii of orbit (earth=1)	Orbital inclination	Mean sidereal period (days)	Mean period of rotation on axis (days)	Number of satellites
Sun	1 392 000	332 946	—	—	7°	—	25.38	—
Mercury	4 878	0.05	57.9	0.38	7°	87.9	58.6	0
Venus	12 104	0.81	108.2	0.72	3°23'	224.7	243	0
Earth	12 756	1.00	149.6	1.00	—	365.2	0.99	1
Mars	6 794	0.10	227.9	1.52	1°50'	686.9	1.02	2
Jupiter	142 800	317.9	778.3	5.20	1°18'	4332.5	0.41	14 ?
Saturn	120 000	95.1	1 427	9.53	2°29'	10759.2	0.42	11
Uranus	52 000	14.5	2 869	19.17	0°46'	30684.8	0.45	5
Neptune	48 400	17.2	4 496	30.05	1°46'	60190.5	0.67	2
Pluto	3 000 ?	0.001	5 900	39.43	17°1'	91628.6	6.38	1 ?

The Sun's diameter is 109 times greater than that of the Earth.

Distances from sun in millions km

Mercury
Venus
Earth
Mars

Jupiter

Saturn

Uranus

Neptune

Pluto

Mercury is the nearest planet to the Sun. It is composed mostly of high density metals and probably has an atmosphere of heavy inert gases.

Venus is similar in size to the Earth, and probably in composition. It is, however, much hotter and has a dense atmosphere of carbon dioxide which obscures our view of its surface.

Earth is the largest of the inner planets. It has a dense iron-nickel core surrounded by layers of silicate rock. The surface is approximately $\frac{3}{8}$ land and $\frac{5}{8}$ water, and the lower atmosphere consists of a mixture of nitrogen, oxygen and other gases supplemented by water vapor. With this atmosphere and surface temperatures usually between $-50°C$ and $+40°C$, life is possible.

Mars, smaller than the Earth, has a noticeably red appearance. Photographs taken by the Mariner probes show clearly the cratered surface and polar ice caps, probably made from frozen carbon dioxide.

The Asteroids orbit the Sun mainly between Mars and Jupiter. They consist of thousands of bodies of varying sizes with diameters ranging from metres to hundreds of kilometres.

Jupiter is the largest planet of the Solar System. Photographs taken by Voyager I and II have revealed an equatorial ring system and shown the distinctive Great Red Spot and rotating cloud belts in great detail.

Saturn, the second largest planet consists of hydrogen, helium and other gases. The equatorial rings are composed of small ice particles.

Uranus is extremely remote but just visible to the naked eye and has a greenish appearance. A faint equatorial ring system was discovered in 1977. The planet's axis is tilted through 98° from its orbital plane, therefore it revolves in a retrograde manner.

Neptune, yet more remote than Uranus and larger. It is composed of gases and has a bluish green appearance when seen in a telescope. As with Uranus, little detail can be observed on its surface.

Pluto. No details are known of its composition or surface. The existence of this planet was firstly surmised in a computed hypothesis, which was tested by repeated searches by large telescopes until in 1930 the planet was found. Latest evidence seems to suggest that Pluto has one satellite, provisionally named Charon.

Time measurement

The basic unit of time measurement is the day, one rotation of the earth on its axis. The subdivision of the day into hours and minutes is arbitrary and simply for our convenience. Our present calendar is based on the solar year of $365\frac{1}{4}$ days, the time taken for the earth to orbit the sun. A month was anciently based on the interval from new moon to new moon, approximately $29\frac{1}{2}$ days - and early calendars were entirely lunar.

Rotation of the Earth

Night and day

As the earth rotates from west to east the sun appears to rise in the east and set in the west: when the sun is setting in Shanghai on the directly opposite side of the earth New York is just emerging into sunlight. Noon, when the sun is directly overhead, is coincident at all places on the same meridian with shadows pointing directly towards the poles.

Kms	Berlin	Bombay	Buenos Aires	Cairo	Calcutta	Caracas	Chicago	Copenhagen	Darwin	Hong Kong	Honolulu	Johannesburg	Lagos	Lisbon
Berlin														
Bombay	6288													
Buenos Aires	11909	14925												
Cairo	2890	4355	11814											
Calcutta	7033	1664	16524	5699										
Caracas	8435	14522	5096	10203	15464									
Chicago	7084	12953	9011	3206	12839	4027								
Copenhagen	357	6422	12067	9860	7072	8392	6840							
Darwin	12946	7257	14693	11612	6047	18059	15065	12903						
Hong Kong	8754	4317	18478	8150	2659	16360	12526	8671	4271					
Honolulu	11764	12914	12164	14223	11343	9670	6836	11407	8640	8921				
Johannesburg	8870	6974	8088	6267	8459	11019	13984	9225	10639	10732	19206			
Lagos	5198	7612	7916	3915	9216	7741	9612	5530	14222	11845	16308	4505		
Lisbon	2311	8018	9600	3794	9075	6501	6424	2478	15114	11028	12587	8191	3799	
London	928	7190	11131	3508	7961	7507	6356	952	13848	9623	11632	9071	5017	1588
Los Angeles	9311	14000	9852	12200	13120	5812	2804	9003	12695	11639	4117	16676	12414	9122
Mexico City	9732	15656	7389	12372	15280	3586	2726	9514	14631	14122	6085	14585	11071	8676
Moscow	1610	5031	13477	2902	5534	9938	8000	1561	11350	7144	11323	9161	6254	3906
Nairobi	6370	4532	10402	3536	6179	11544	12883	6706	10415	8776	17282	2927	3807	6461
New York	6385	12541	8526	9020	12747	3430	1145	6188	16047	12950	7980	12841	8477	5422
Paris	876	7010	11051	3210	7858	7625	6650	1026	13812	9630	11968	8732	4714	1454
Peking	7822	4757	19268	7544	3269	14399	10603	7202	6011	1963	8160	11710	11457	9668
Reykjavik	2385	8335	11437	5266	8687	6915	4757	2103	13892	9681	9787	10938	6718	2948
Rio de Janeiro	10025	13409	1953	9896	15073	4546	8547	10211	16011	17704	13342	7113	6035	7734
Rome	1180	6175	11151	2133	7219	8363	7739	1531	13265	9284	12916	7743	4039	1861
Singapore	9944	3914	15879	8267	2897	18359	15078	9969	3349	2599	10816	8660	11145	11886
Sydney	16096	10160	11800	14418	9138	15343	14875	16042	3150	7374	8168	11040	15519	18178
Tokyo	8924	6742	18362	9571	5141	14164	10137	8696	5431	2874	6202	13547	13480	11149
Toronto	6497	12488	9093	9233	12561	3873	700	6265	15498	12569	7465	13374	8948	5737
Wellington	18140	12370	9981	16524	11354	13122	13451	17961	5325	9427	7513	11761	16050	19575

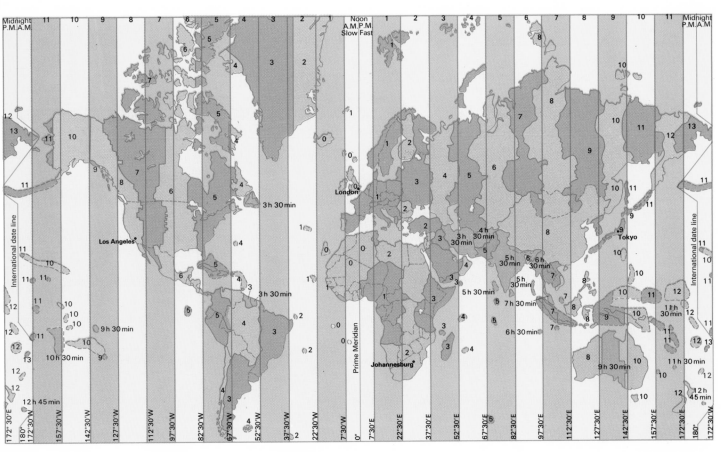

Time Zones

	Zone 1		Zone 2		½ hour zones

The world is divided into 24 time zones, each centred on meridians at 15° intervals which is the longitudinal distance the sun appears to travel every hour. The meridian running through Greenwich passes through the middle of the first zone. Successive zones to the east of Greenwich zone are ahead of Greenwich time by one hour for every 15° of longitude, while zones to the west are behind by one hour.

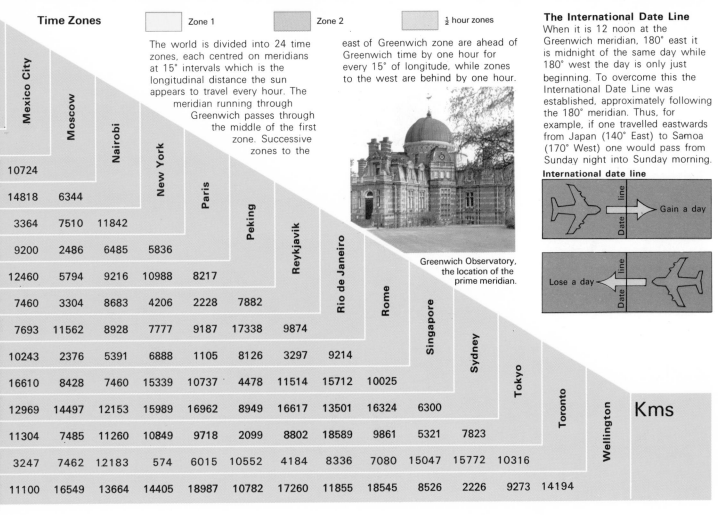

Greenwich Observatory, the location of the prime meridian.

The International Date Line

When it is 12 noon at the Greenwich meridian, 180° east it is midnight of the same day while 180° west the day is only just beginning. To overcome this the International Date Line was established, approximately following the 180° meridian. Thus, for example, if one travelled eastwards from Japan (140° East) to Samoa (170° West) one would pass from Sunday night into Sunday morning.

International date line

	Mexico City	Moscow	Nairobi	New York	Paris	Peking	Reykjavik	Rio de Janeiro	Rome	Singapore	Sydney	Tokyo	Toronto	Wellington	Kms
	10724														
	14818	6344													
	3364	7510	11842												
	9200	2486	6485	5836											
	12460	5794	9216	10988	8217										
	7460	3304	8683	4206	2228	7882									
	7693	11562	8928	7777	9187	17338	9874								
	10243	2376	5391	6888	1105	8126	3297	9214							
	16610	8428	7460	15339	10737	4478	11514	15712	10025						
	12969	14497	12153	15989	16962	8949	16617	13501	16324	6300					
	11304	7485	11260	10849	9718	2099	8802	18589	9861	5321	7823				
	3247	7462	12183	574	6015	10552	4184	8336	7080	15047	15772	10316			
	11100	16549	13664	14405	18987	10782	17260	11855	18545	8526	2226	9273	14194		

Asai

HEIGHT OF LAND
in metres

Above 6 000
4 000–6 000
2 000–4 000
1000–2 000
200–1000
0–200
Below Sea-Level

DEPTH OF SEA
in metres

0–200
200–4000
4000–8000
Below 8000

ARCTIC OCEAN

N. Cape
Novaya Zemlya
Severnaya Zemlya
New Siberian Is.

Scandinavia
Baltic Sea
North European Plain
Ural Mts.
Ob
Yenisey
Lr. Tunguska
Lena
Aldan
West Siberian Plain
Siberia
Stanovoy Ra.
Sea of Okhotsk
L. Ladoga
Volga
Don
Angara
Sayan Mts.
L. Baikal
Amur
Sakhalin
Alps
Carpathians
Danube
Apennines
Balkan Pen.
Black Sea
Caucasus
Elbrus 5633
Aral Sea
Caspian Sea
Altai
Gobi
Hokkaido
Anatolia
Elburz Mts.
Syr Darya
Amu Darya
Tien Shan
Nan Shan
Hwang-ho
North China Plain
Sea of Japan
Honshu
Fujiyama 3776
Mediterranean Sea
Euphrates
Tigris
Hindu Kush
Pamirs
Karakoram
Kunlun
Plateau of Tibet
Yangtse-kiang
Yellow Sea
East China Sea
PACIFIC
Libyan Desert
Nile
Red Sea
Sulaiman Ra.
Indus
Thar Desert
Himalaya
Mt. Everest 8848
Ganges
Si-kiang
Taiwan
OCEAN
Tibesti
Arabia
Rub'al Khali
Arabian Sea
W. Ghats
Deccan
E. Ghats
Bay of Bengal
Hainan
Mariana Is.
Wake I.
L. Chad
Socotra
C. Guardafui
C. Comorin
Ceylon
South China Sea
Philippine Is.
Guam
Caroline Islands
Marshall Is.
Cameroon Pk. 4070
Uele
(Congo)
Zaire
Ethiopian Highlands
L. Turkana
Mt. Kenya 5199
Str. of Malacca
Kinabalu 4101
Sumatra
Borneo
Celebes Sea
Moluccas
Celebes
Nauru
Gilbert Is.
Victoria
Kilimanjaro 5895
L. Tanganyika
INDIAN
Seychelles
Java Sea
Banda Sea
New Guinea
Bismarck Arch.
Solomon Is.
Ellice Is.
Cubango
L. Malawi
Comoro Is.
OCEAN
Java
Timor
Torres Str.
C. York
Coral Sea
New Hebrides
Fiji Is.
Zambezi
Mozambique Chan.
Madagascar
Mauritius
Réunion
Cocos or Keeling Is.
Kalahari Desert
Orange
Drakensberg
Hamersley Ra.
Macdonnell Ra.
Great Victoria Desert
Great Dividing
Gt. Barrier Reef
New Caledonia
C. of Good Hope
Crozet Is.
C. Leeuwin
Great Australian Bight
Darling
Murray
Australian Alps
Mt. Kosciusko 2230
North I.
Kerguelen Is.
Tasmania
Bass Str.
New Zealand
Mt. Cook 3764
South I.

SOUTHERN OCEAN

Enderby Land
Queen Mary Coast
Wilkes Land
Adélie Land
South Magnetic Pole
Victoria Land
en Maud Land

from Greenwich

The origin of the earth is still open to much conjecture although the most widely accepted theory is that it was formed from a solar cloud consisting mainly of hydrogen. Under gravitation the cloud condensed and shrank to form our planets orbiting around the sun. Gravitation forced the lighter elements to the surface of the earth where they cooled to form a crust while the inner material remained hot and molten. Earth's first rocks formed over 3500 million years ago but since then the surface has been constantly altered.

Until comparatively recently the view that the primary units of the earth had remained essentially fixed throughout geological time was regarded as common sense, although the concept of moving continents has been traced back to references in the Bible of a break up of the land after Noah's floods. The continental drift theory was first developed by Antonio Snider in 1858 but probably the most important single advocate was Alfred Wegener who, in 1915, published evidence from geology, climatology and biology. His conclusions are very similar to those reached by current research although he was wrong about the speed of break-up.

The measurement of fossil magnetism found in rocks has probably proved the most influential evidence. While originally these drift theories were openly mocked, now they are considered standard doctrine.

The jigsaw
As knowledge of the shape and structure of the earth's surface grew, several of the early geographers noticed the great similarity in shape of the coasts bordering the Atlantic. It was this remarkable similarity which led to the first detailed geological and structural comparisons. Even more accurate fits can be made by placing the edges of the continental shelves in juxtaposition.

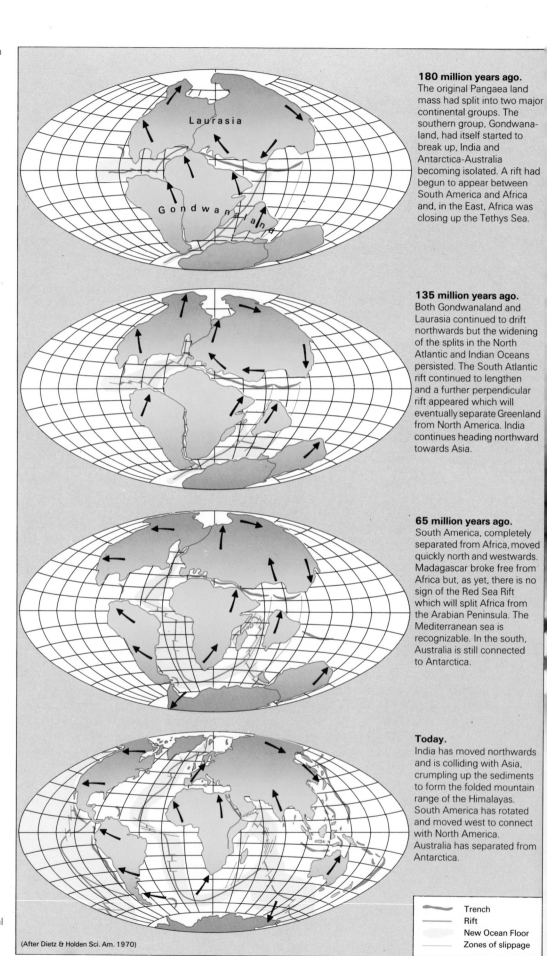

180 million years ago.
The original Pangaea land mass had split into two major continental groups. The southern group, Gondwanaland, had itself started to break up, India and Antarctica-Australia becoming isolated. A rift had begun to appear between South America and Africa and, in the East, Africa was closing up the Tethys Sea.

135 million years ago.
Both Gondwanaland and Laurasia continued to drift northwards but the widening of the splits in the North Atlantic and Indian Oceans persisted. The South Atlantic rift continued to lengthen and a further perpendicular rift appeared which will eventually separate Greenland from North America. India continues heading northward towards Asia.

65 million years ago.
South America, completely separated from Africa, moved quickly north and westwards. Madagascar broke free from Africa but, as yet, there is no sign of the Red Sea Rift which will split Africa from the Arabian Peninsula. The Mediterranean sea is recognizable. In the south, Australia is still connected to Antarctica.

Today.
India has moved northwards and is colliding with Asia, crumpling up the sediments to form the folded mountain range of the Himalayas. South America has rotated and moved west to connect with North America. Australia has separated from Antarctica.

(After Dietz & Holden Sci. Am. 1970)

	Trench
	Rift
	New Ocean Floor
	Zones of slippage

The earth's surface is slowly but continually being rearranged. Some changes such as erosion and deposition are extremely slow but they upset the balance which causes other more abrupt changes often originating deep within the earth's interior. The constant movements vary in intensity, often with stresses building up to a climax such as a particularly violent volcanic eruption or earthquake.

The crust *(below and right)*
The outer layer or crust of the earth consists of a comparatively low density, brittle material varying from 5 km to 50 km deep beneath the continents. This consists predominately of silica and aluminium; hence it is called 'sial'. Extending under the ocean floors and below the sial is a basaltic layer known as 'sima', consisting mainly of silica and magnesium.

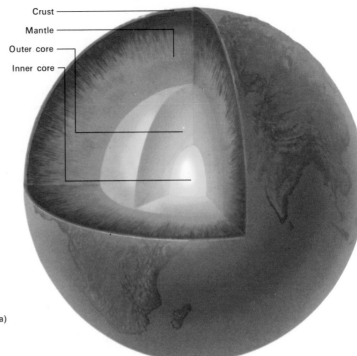

Crust
Mantle
Outer core
Inner core

Continental crust   Ocean crust

Sediment
Granite rock (sial)
Basaltic layer (sima)
Mantle

Volcanoes *(right, below and far right)*
Volcanoes occur when hot liquefied rock beneath the crust reaches the surface as lava. An accumulation of ash and cinders around a vent forms a cone. Successive layers of thin lava flows form an acid lava volcano while thick lava flows form a basic lava volcano. A caldera forms when a particularly violent eruption blows off the top of an already existing cone.

The mantle *(above)*
Immediately below the crust, at the mohorovicic discontinuity line, there is a distinct change in density and chemical properties. This is the mantle - made up of iron and magnesium silicates - with temperatures reaching 1 600 °C. The rigid upper mantle extends down to a depth of about 1 000 km below which is the more viscous lower mantle which is about 1 900 km thick.

The core *(above)*
The outer core, approximately 2 100 km thick, consists of molten iron and nickel at 2 000 °C to 5 000 °C possibly separated from the less dense mantle by an oxidised shell. About 5 000 km below the surface is the liquid transition zone, below which is the solid inner core, a sphere of 2 740 km diameter where rock is three times as dense as in the crust.

Shield volcano   **Cinder cone**   **Hornit cone**   **Caldera**

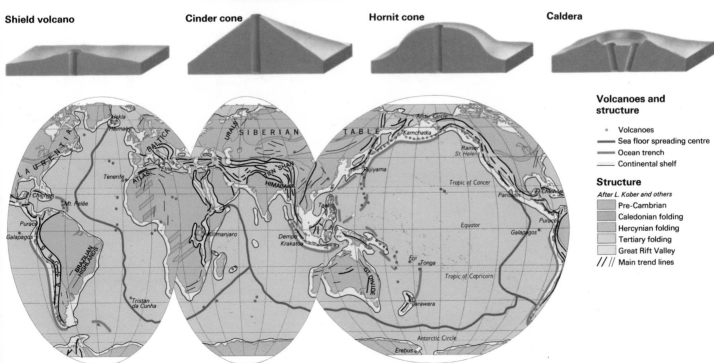

Volcanoes and structure

· Volcanoes
— Sea floor spreading centre
— Ocean trench
— Continental shelf

Structure
After L. Kober and others
Pre-Cambrian
Caledonian folding
Hercynian folding
Tertiary folding
Great Rift Valley
/ / / Main trend lines

Projection: *Interrupted Mollweide's Homolographic*

The making of landscape

The major forces which shape our land would seem to act very slowly in comparison with man's average life span but in geological terms the erosion of rock is in fact very fast. Land goes through a cycle of transformation. It is broken up by earthquakes and other earth movements, temperature changes, water, wind and ice. Rock debris is then transported by water, wind and glaciers and deposited on lowlands and on the sea floor. Here it builds up and by the pressure of its own weight is converted into new rock strata. These in turn can be uplifted either gently as plains or plateaux or more irregularly to form mountains. In either case the new higher land is eroded and the cycle recommences.

A Peneplain

Uplifted peneplain

Rivers

Rivers shape the land by three basic processes: erosion, transportation, and deposition. A youthful river flows fast eroding downwards quickly to form a narrow valley (1). As it matures it deposits some debris and erodes laterally to widen the valley (2). In its last stage it meanders across a wide flat flood plain depositing fine particles of alluvium (3).

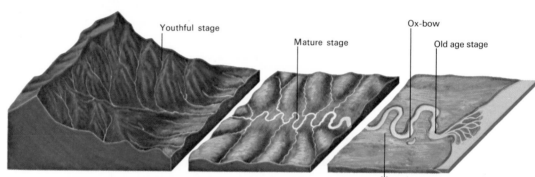

Youthful stage

Mature stage

Ox-bow

Old age stage

Meanders

Underground water

Water enters porous and permeable rocks from the surface moving downward until it reaches a layer of impermeable rock. Joints in underground rock, such as limestone, are eroded to form underground caves and caverns. When the roof of a cave collapses a gorge is formed. Surface entrances to joints are often widened to form vertical openings called swallow holes.

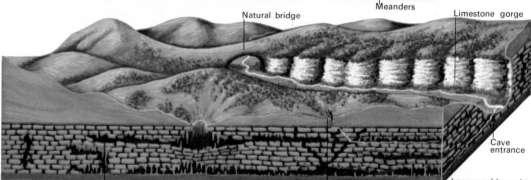

Natural bridge

Limestone gorge

Cave entrance

Cave with stalactites and stalagmites

River disappears down swallow hole

Impermeable rocks

Wind

Wind action is particularly powerful in arid and semi-arid regions where rock waste produced by weathering is used as an abrasive tool by the wind. The rate of erosion varies with the characteristics of the rock which can cause weird shapes and effects (right). Desert sand can also be accumulated by the wind to form barchan dunes (far right) which slowly travel forward, horns first.

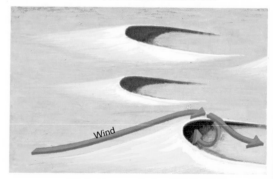

Wind

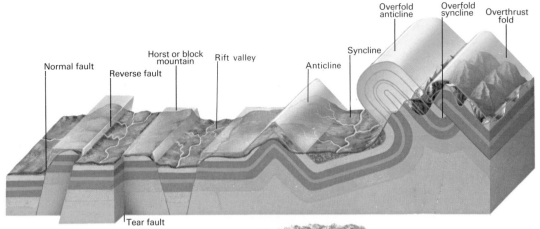

Normal fault | Reverse fault | Horst or block mountain | Rift valley | Anticline | Syncline | Overfold anticline | Overfold syncline | Overthrust fold | Tear fault

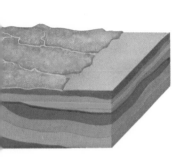

Folding and faulting

A vertical displacement in the earth's crust is called a fault or reverse fault; lateral displacement is a tear fault. An uplifted block is called a horst, the reverse of which is a rift valley. Compressed horizontal layers of sedimentary rock fold to form mountains. Those layers which bend up form an anticline, those bending down form a syncline : continued pressure forms an overfold.

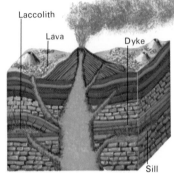

Laccolith | Lava | Dyke | Sill

Volcanic activity

When pressure on rocks below the earth's crust is released the normally semi-solid hot rock becomes liquid magma. The magma forces its way into cracks of the crust and may either reach the surface where it forms volcanoes or it may collect in the crust as sills, dykes, or laccoliths. When magma reaches the surface it cools to form lava.

Waves

Coasts are continually changing, some retreat under wave erosion while others advance with wave deposition. These actions combined form steep cliffs and wave cut platforms. Eroded debris is in turn deposited as a terrace. As the water becomes shallower the erosive power of the waves decreases and gradually the cliff disappears. Wave action can also create other features (far right).

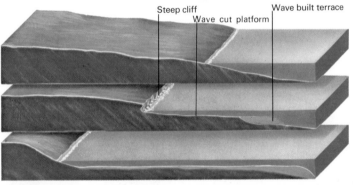

Steep cliff | Wave cut platform | Wave built terrace

Ice

These diagrams (right) show how a glaciated valley may have formed. The glacier deepens, straightens, and widens the river valley whose interlocking spurs become truncated or cut off. Intervalley divides are frost shattered to form sharp arêtes and pyramidal peaks. Hanging valleys mark the entry of tributary rivers and eroded rocks form medial moraine. Terminal moraine is deposited as the glacier retreats.

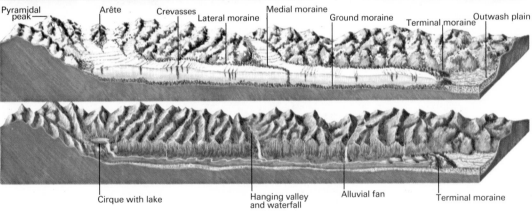

Pyramidal peak | Arête | Crevasses | Lateral moraine | Medial moraine | Ground moraine | Terminal moraine | Outwash plain

Cirque with lake | Hanging valley and waterfall | Alluvial fan | Terminal moraine

Subsidence and uplift

As the land surface is eroded it may eventually become a level plain - a peneplain, broken only by low hills, remnants of previous mountains. In turn this peneplain may be uplifted to form a plateau with steep edges. At the coast the uplifted wave platform becomes a coastal plain and in the rejuvenated rivers downward erosion once more predominates.

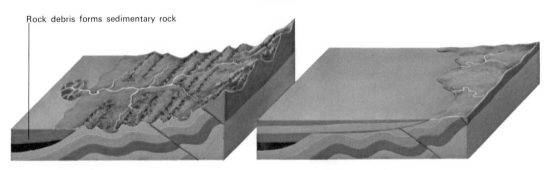

Rock debris forms sedimentary rock

Climate graphs

Weather is the condition of the atmosphere at any place at a specific time with respect to temperature, sunshine, pressure, winds, clouds, fog, and precipitation. Climate, on the other hand, is the average of the weather elements, particularly temperature and precipitation over many years. Each graph shows the climatic conditions experienced in a location for each month of the year. Stations marked with an asterisk are marginal and show the characteristics of two or more regions.

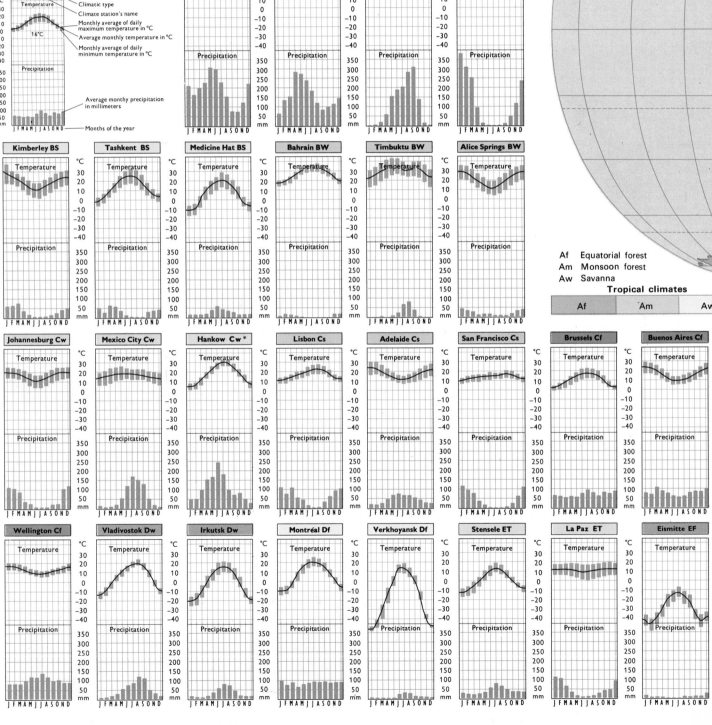

Af   Equatorial forest
Am   Monsoon forest
Aw   Savanna

Tropical climates

| Af | Am | Aw |

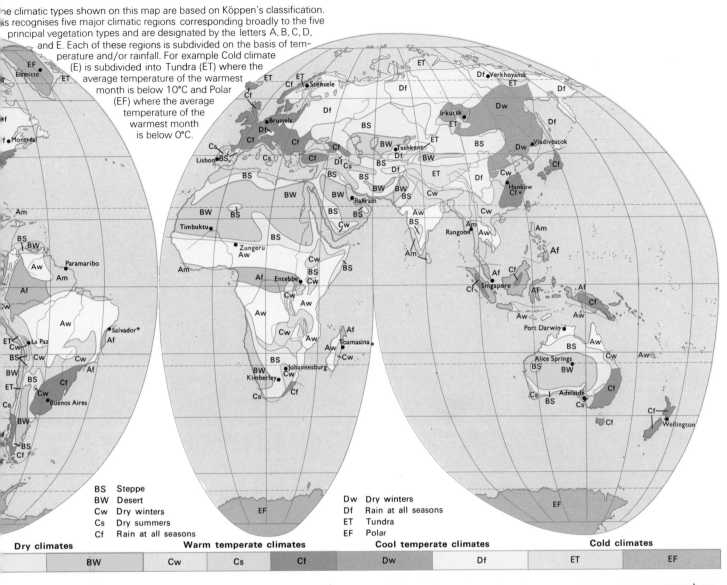

The climatic types shown on this map are based on Köppen's classification. This recognises five major climatic regions corresponding broadly to the five principal vegetation types and are designated by the letters A, B, C, D, and E. Each of these regions is subdivided on the basis of temperature and/or rainfall. For example Cold climate (E) is subdivided into Tundra (ET) where the average temperature of the warmest month is below 10°C and Polar (EF) where the average temperature of the warmest month is below 0°C.

BS	Steppe		Dw	Dry winters
BW	Desert		Df	Rain at all seasons
Cw	Dry winters		ET	Tundra
Cs	Dry summers		EF	Polar
Cf	Rain at all seasons			

Dry climates — BW — **Warm temperate climates** — Cw Cs Cf — **Cool temperate climates** — Dw Df — **Cold climates** — ET EF

Tropical storm tracks *below*
A tropical cyclone, or storm, is designated as having winds of gale force (16 m/s) but less than hurricane force (33 m/s). It is a homogenous air mass with upward spiralling air currents around a windless centre, or eye. An average of 65 tropical storms occur each year, over 50% of which reach hurricane force. They originate mainly during the summer over tropical oceans.

Extremes of climate & weather *right*
Tropical high temperatures and polar low temperatures combined with wind systems, altitude and unequal rainfall distribution result in the extremes of tropical rain forests, inland deserts and frozen polar wastes. Fluctuations in the limits of these extreme zones and extremes of weather result in occasional catastrophic heat-waves and drought, floods and storms, frost and snow.

Hurricane devastation ; Darwin

Hot desert ; Morocco

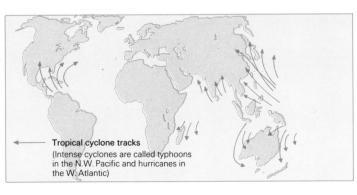

→ Tropical cyclone tracks
(Intense cyclones are called typhoons in the N.W. Pacific and hurricanes in the W. Atlantic)

Tornado ; South East U.S.A.

Polar climate ; Greenland

1:190 000 000

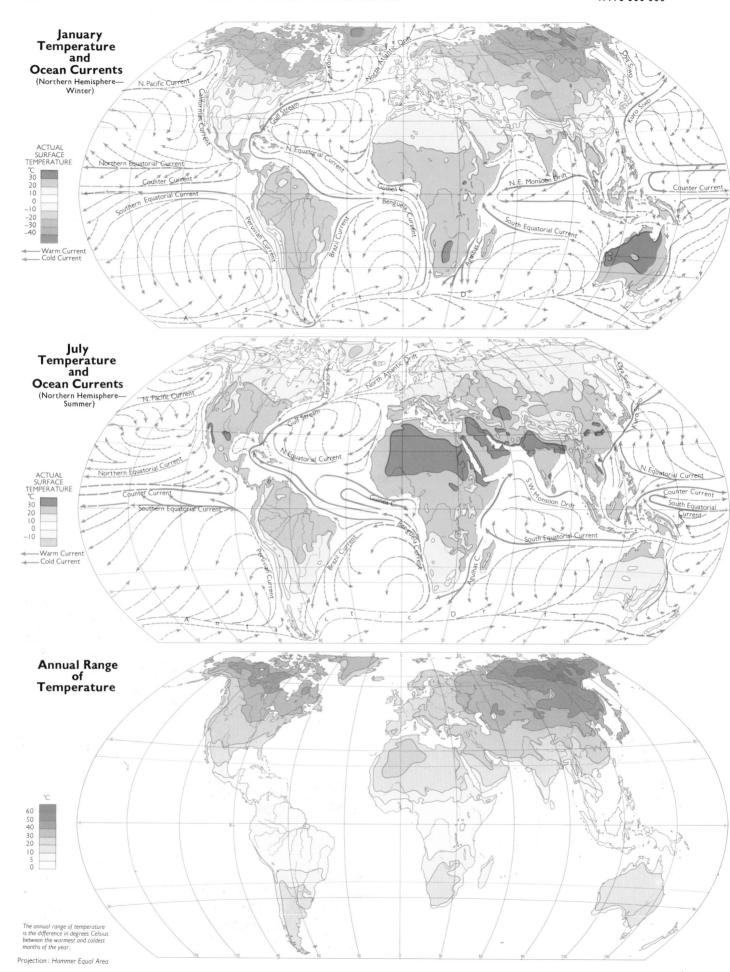

January Temperature and Ocean Currents
(Northern Hemisphere— Winter)

ACTUAL SURFACE TEMPERATURE
°C
30
20
10
0
-10
-20
-30
-40

Warm Current
Cold Current

N. Pacific Current
Californian Current
Labrador C.
North Atlantic Drift
Gulf Stream
N. Equatorial Current
Northern Equatorial Current
Counter Current
Guinea C.
Southern Equatorial Current
Benguela Current
Brazil Current
Peruvian Current
Agulhas C.
N.E. Monsoon Drift
South Equatorial Current
Counter Current
Kuro Siwo
Oya Siwo
Antarctic Drift

July Temperature and Ocean Currents
(Northern Hemisphere— Summer)

ACTUAL SURFACE TEMPERATURE
°C
30
20
10
0
-10

Warm Current
Cold Current

N. Pacific Current
Labrador C.
North Atlantic Drift
Gulf Stream
N. Equatorial Current
Northern Equatorial Current
Counter Current
Southern Equatorial Current
Guinea C.
Benguela Current
Brazil Current
Peruvian Current
Agulhas C.
S.W. Monsoon Drift
South Equatorial Current
N. Equatorial Current
Counter Current
South Equatorial Current
Kuro Siwo
Oya Siwo
Antarctic Drift

Annual Range of Temperature

°C
60
50
40
30
20
10
5
0

The annual range of temperature is the difference in degrees Celsius between the warmest and coldest months of the year.

Projection: Hammer Equal Area

1:190 000 000

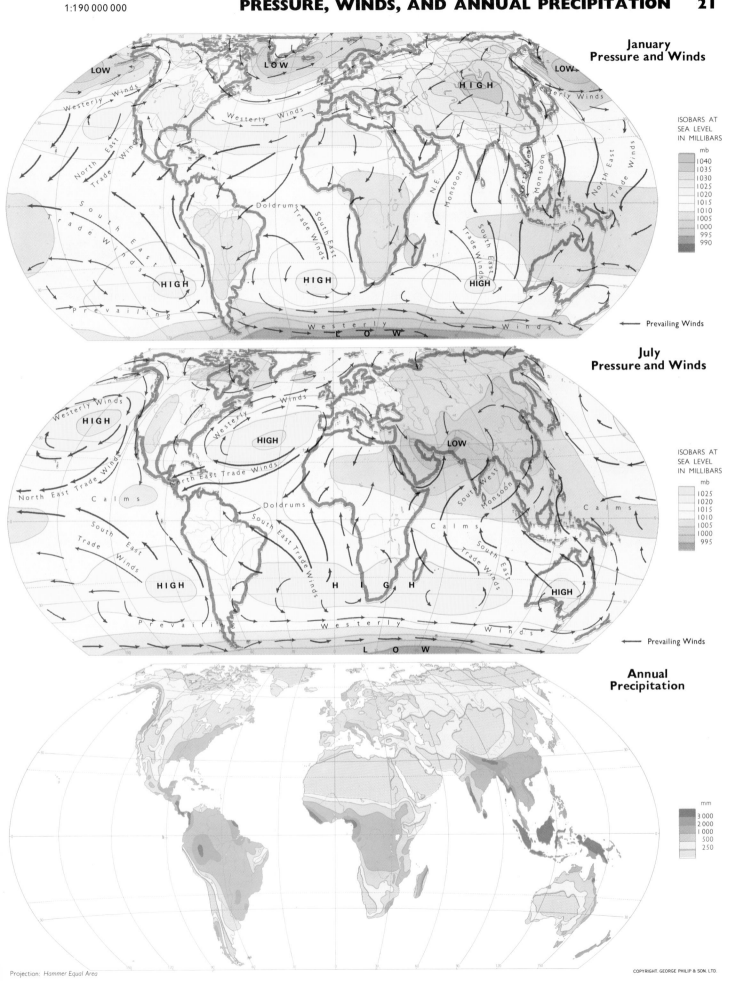

January Pressure and Winds

LOW

LOW

LOW

HIGH

Westerly Winds

Westerly Winds

Westerly Winds

North East Trade Winds

North East Trade Winds

South East Trade Winds

Doldrums

South East Trade Winds

N.E. Monsoon

North West Monsoon

South East Trade Winds

HIGH

HIGH

HIGH

Prevailing

Westerly

Winds

L O W

ISOBARS AT SEA LEVEL IN MILLIBARS

mb
1040
1035
1030
1025
1020
1015
1010
1005
1000
995
990

⟵ Prevailing Winds

July Pressure and Winds

HIGH

HIGH

LOW

HIGH

HIGH

Westerly Winds

Westerly Winds

North East Trade Winds

North East Trade Winds

Calms

Calms

Calms

South East Trade Winds

Doldrums

South East Trade Winds

South West Monsoon

South East Trade Winds

Trade Winds

H I G H

Prevailing

Westerly

Winds

L O W

ISOBARS AT SEA LEVEL IN MILLIBARS

mb
1025
1020
1015
1010
1005
1000
995

⟵ Prevailing Winds

Annual Precipitation

mm
3 000
2 000
1 000
500
250

Projection: *Hammer Equal Area*

Its surface

Highest point on the earth's surface: Mt. Everest, Tibet - Nepal boundary - 8 848 m
Lowest point on the earth's surface: The Dead Sea, Jordan below sea level 395 m
Greatest ocean depth,: Challenger Deep, Mariana Trench 11 022 m
Average height of land 840 m
Average depth of seas and oceans 3 808 m

Dimensions

Superficial area	510 000 000 km²
Land surface	149 000 000 km²
Land surface as % of total area	29·2 %
Water surface	361 000 000 km²
Water surface as % of total area	70·8 %
Equatorial circumference	40 077 km
Meridional circumference	40 009 km
Equatorial diameter	12 756·8 km
Polar diameter	12 713·8 km
Equatorial radius	6 378·4 km
Polar radius	6 356·9 km
Volume of the Earth	1 083 230 x 10⁶ km³
Mass of the Earth	5·9 x 10²¹ tonnes

The Figure of Earth

An imaginary sea-level surface is considered and called a geoid. By measuring at different places the angles from plumb lines to a fixed star there have been many determinations of the shape of parts of the geoid which is found to be an oblate spheriod with its axis along the axis of rotation of the earth. Observations from satellites have now given a new method of more accurate determinations of the figure of the earth and its local irregularities.

Land and Sea Hemispheres.

About 85% of the total land area is contained in the hemisphere centred on a point between Paris and Brussels.

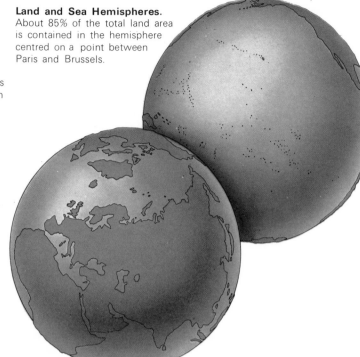

Oceans and Seas
Area in 1000 km²

Pacific Ocean	165 721	North Sea	575
Atlantic Ocean	81 660	Black Sea	448
Indian Ocean	73 442	Red Sea	440
Arctic Ocean	14 351	Baltic Sea	422
Mediterranean Sea	2 966	The Gulf	238
Bering Sea	2 274	St. Lawrence, Gulf of	236
Caribbean Sea	1 942	English Channel & Irish Sea	179
Mexico, Gulf of	1 813	California, Gulf of	161
Okhotsk, Sea of	1 528		
East China Sea	1 248		
Hudson Bay	1 230		
Japan, Sea of	1 049		

Lakes and Inland Seas
Areas in 1000 km²

Caspian Sea, Asia	424·2	Lake Ontario, N.America	19·5
Lake Superior, N.America	82·4	Lake Ladoga, Europe	18·4
Lake Victoria, Africa	69·5	Lake Balkhash, Asia	17·3
Aral Sea (Salt), Asia	63·8	Lake Maracaibo, S.America	16·3
Lake Huron, N.America	59·6	Lake Onega, Europe	9·8
Lake Michigan, N.America	58·0	Lake Eyre (Salt), Australia	9·6
Lake Tanganyika, Africa	32·9	Lake Turkana (Salt), Africa	9·1
Lake Baikal, Asia	31·5	Lake Titicaca, S.America	8·3
Great Bear Lake, N.America	31·1	Lake Nicaragua, C.America	8·0
Great Slave Lake, N.America	28·9	Lake Athabasca, N.America	7·9
Lake Nyasa, Africa	28·5	Reindeer Lake, N.America	6·3
Lake Erie, N.America	25·7	Issyk-Kul, Asia	6·2
Lake Winnipeg, N.America	24·3	Lake Torrens (Salt), Australia	6·1
Lake Chad, Africa	20·7	Koko Nor (Salt), Asia	6·0
		Lake Urmia, Asia	6·0
		Vänern, Europe	5·6

Longest rivers

	km.
Nile, Africa	6 690
Amazon, S.America	6 280
Mississippi-Missouri, N.America	6 270
Yangtze, Asia	4 990
Zaïre, Africa	4 670
Amur, Asia	4 410
Hwang Ho (Yellow), Asia	4 350
Lena, Asia	4 260
Mekong, Asia	4 180
Niger, Africa	4 180
Mackenzie, N.America	4 040
Ob, Asia	4 000
Yenisei, Asia	3 800

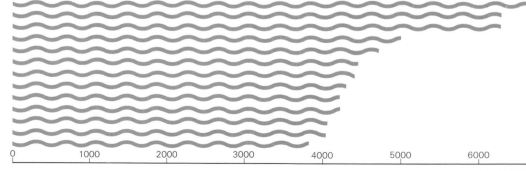

0 1000 2000 3000 4000 5000 6000

The Highest Mountains and the Greatest Depths.

Mount Everest defied the world's greatest mountaineers for 32 years and claimed the lives of many men. Not until 1920 was permission granted by the Dalai Lama to attempt the mountain, and the first successful ascent came in 1953. Since then the summit has been reached several times. The world's highest peaks have now been climbed but there are many as yet unexplored peaks in the Himalayas some of which may be over 7 600 m.

The greatest trenches are the Puerto Rico deep (9 200m.). The Tonga (10 822 m) and Mindanao (10 497 m) trenches and the Mariana Trench (11 022 m) in the Pacific. The trenches represent less than 2% of the total area of the sea-bed but are of great interest as lines of structural weakness in the Earth's crust and as areas of frequent earthquakes.

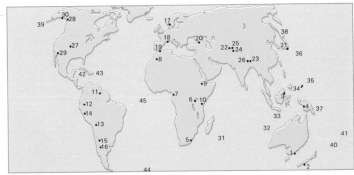

High mountains

Mountain heights in metres

E. Indies & Oceania — Africa — South America — Europe and Asia — North America

1 Kosciusko 2 230
2 Mt. Cook (N.Z.) 3 764
3 Kinabalu 4 101
4 Jaya (Irian) 5 029
5 Mt. aux Sources 3 299
6 Ruwenzori 5 109
7 Cameroon peak 4 070
8 Dj. Toubkal 4 165
9 Ras Dashen 4 620
10 Kilimanjaro 5 895
11 Roraima 2 810
12 Chimborazo 6 267
13 Illimani 6 462
14 Huascaran 6 768
15 Ojos del Salado 6 863
16 Aconcagua 6 960
17 Galdhøpiggen 2 469
18 Mont Blanc 4 807
19 Mulhacen 3 478
20 Elbrus 5 633
21 Fujiyama 3 776
22 Communism peak 7 495
23 Kanchenjunga 8 598
24 K2 8 611
25 Muztagh 7 723
26 Everest 8 848
27 Mt. Elbert 4 399
28 Mt Logan 6 050
29 Mt Whitney 4 418
30 Mt. McKinley 6 194

Bathyscaphe

Ocean depths in metres

Indian Ocean — Pacific Ocean — Atlantic Ocean

Sea level

31 Mauritius basin 6 400
32 W. Australian basin 6 459
33 Java trench 7 450
34 Mindanao trench 10 497
35 Mariana trench 11 022
36 Japan trench 10 554
37 Bougainville deep 9 140
38 Kuril trench 10 542
39 Aleutian trench 7 822
40 Kermadec trench 10 047
41 Tonga trench 10 822
42 Cayman trough 7 680
43 Puerto Rico trough 9 200
44 S. Sandwich trench 8 428
45 Romanche deep 7 758

Waterfall

Notable Waterfalls
heights in metres

Angel, Venezuela	980
Tugela, S. Africa	853
Mongefossen, Norway	774
Yosemite, California	738
Mardalsfossen, Norway	655
Cuquenan, Venezuela	610
Sutherland, N.Z.	579
Reichenbach, Switzerland	548
Wollomombi, Australia	518
Ribbon, California	491
Gavarnie, France	422
Tyssefallene, Norway	414
Krimml, Austria	370
King George VI, Guyana	366
Silver Strand, California	356
Geissbach, Switzerland	350
Staubbach, Switzerland	299
Trümmelbach, Switzerland	290
Chirombo, Zambia	268
Livingstone, Zaïre	259
King Edward VIII, Guyana	256
Gersoppa, India	253
Vettifossen Norway	250
Kalambo, Zambia	240
Kaieteur, Guyana	226
Maletsunyane, Lesotho	192
Terui, Italy	180
Kabarega, Uganda	122
Victoria, Zimbabwe-Zambia	107
Cauvery, India	97
Boyoma, Zaïre	61
Niagara, N.America	51
Schaffhausen, Switzerland	30

Dam

Notable Dams
heights in metres

Africa

Cabora Bassa, Zambezi R.	168
Akosombo Main Dam Volta R.	141
Kariba, Zambezi R.	128
Aswan High Dam, Nile R.	110

Asia

Nurek, Vakhsh R., U.S.S.R.	317
Bhakra, Sutlej R., India	226
Kurobegawa, Kurobe R., Jap.	186
Charvak, Chirchik R., U.S.S.R.	168
Okutadami, Tadami R., Jap.	157
Bratsk, Angara R., U.S.S.R.	125

Oceania

Warragamba, N.S.W., Australia	137
Eucumbene, N.S.W., Australia	116

Europe

Grande Dixence, Switz.	284
Vajont, Vajont, R., Italy	261
Mauvoisin, Drance R., Switz.	237
Contra , Verzasca R., Switz.	230
Luzzone, Brenno R., Switz.	208
Tignes, Isère R., France	180
Amir Kabir, Karadj R., U.S.S.R.	180
Vidraru, Arges R., Rom.	165
Kremasta, Acheloos R., Greece	165

North America

Mica, Columbia R., Can.	242
Oroville, Feather R.,	235
Hoover, Colorado R.,	221
Glen Canyon, Colorado R.,	216
Daniel Johnson, Can.	214
New Bullards Bar, N. Yuba R.	194
Mossyrock, Cowlitz R.,	184
Shasta, Sacramento R.,	183
W.A.C. Bennett, Canada.	183
Don Pedro, Tuolumne R.,	178
Grand Coulee, Columbia R.,	168

Central and South America

Guri, Caroni R., Venezuela.	106

Water resources and vegetation

Fresh water is essential for life on earth and in some parts of the world it is a most precious commodity. On the other hand it is very easy for industrialized temperate states to take its existence for granted, and man's increasing demand may only be met finally by the desalination of earth's 1250 million cubic kilometres of salt water. 70% of the earth's fresh water exists as ice.

The hydrological cycle

Water is continually being absorbed into the atmosphere as vapour from oceans, lakes, rivers, and vegetation transpiration. On cooling the vapour either condenses or freezes and falls as rain, hail, or snow. Most precipitation falls over the sea but one quarter falls over the land of which half evaporates again soon after falling while the rest flows back into the oceans.

Distribution of water

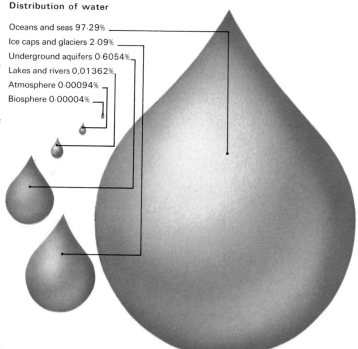

Oceans and seas 97·29%
Ice caps and glaciers 2·09%
Underground aquifers 0·6054%
Lakes and rivers 0,01362%
Atmosphere 0·00094%
Biosphere 0·00004%

Tundra

Mediterranean scrub

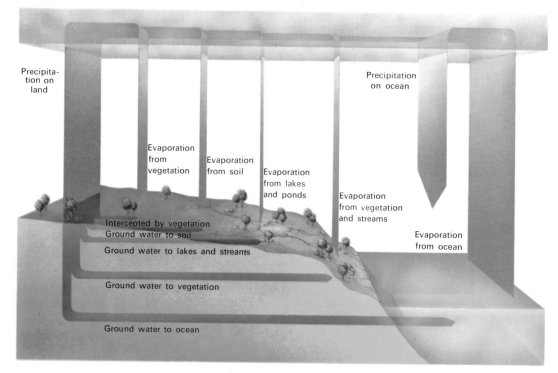

Precipitation on land

Precipitation on ocean

Evaporation from vegetation

Evaporation from soil

Evaporation from lakes and ponds

Evaporation from vegetation and streams

Evaporation from ocean

Intercepted by vegetation
Ground water to soil

Ground water to lakes and streams

Ground water to vegetation

Ground water to ocean

Domestic consumption of water

An area's level of industrialization, climate and standard of living are all major influences in the consumption of water. On average Europe consumes 636 litres per head each day of which 180 litres is used domestically. In the U.S.A. domestic consumption is slightly higher at 270 litres per day. The graph (right) represents domestic consumption in the U.K.

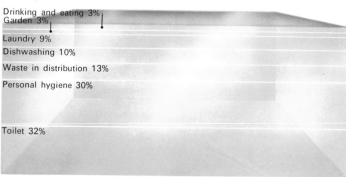

Drinking and eating 3%
Garden 3%
Laundry 9%
Dishwashing 10%
Waste in distribution 13%
Personal hygiene 30%
Toilet 32%

Coniferous forest

Broad-leaved forest

Tropical rain forest

Monsoon forest

Grassland

Savanna

Semidesert

Desert

Natural vegetation

Tundra & ice
Coniferous forest
Broadleaf forest
Mediterranean scrub
Grassland
Savanna
Sub tropical forest
Dry tropical scrub & thorn forest
Monsoon forest
Tropical rain forest
Scrub, steppe, and semidesert
Desert

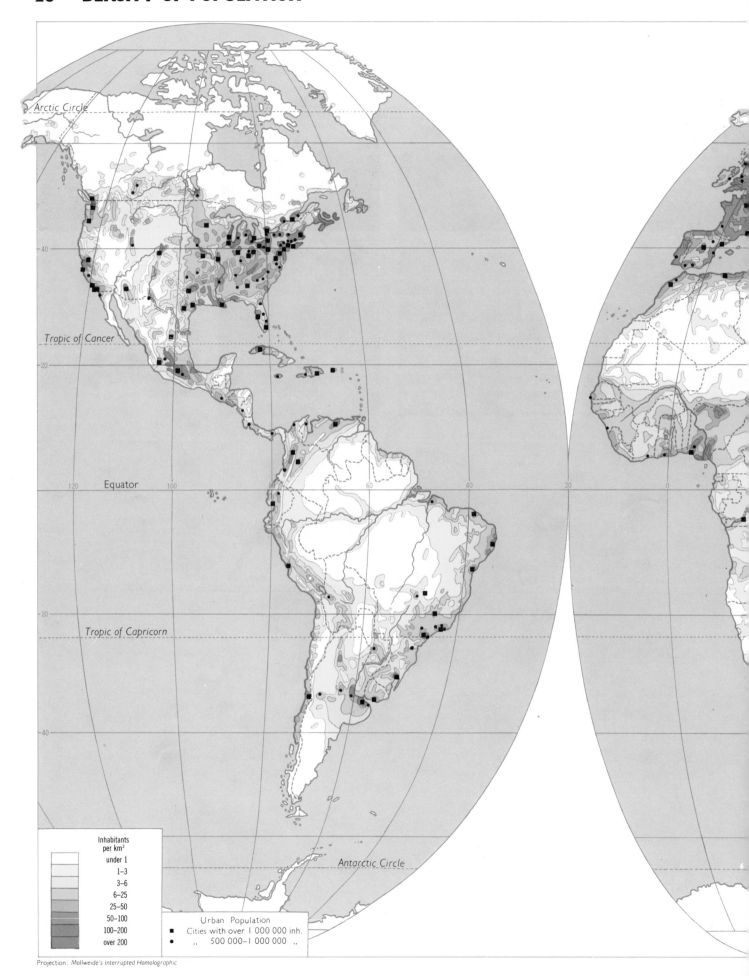

Inhabitants
per km²
under 1
1–3
3–6
6–25
25–50
50–100
100–200
over 200

Urban Population
■ Cities with over 1 000 000 inh.
● ,,   500 000–1 000 000 ,,

Arctic Circle

Tropic of Cancer

Equator

Tropic of Capricorn

Antarctic Circle

120   100   80   60   40   20   0

40

20

20

40

Projection: Mollweide's interrupted Homolographic

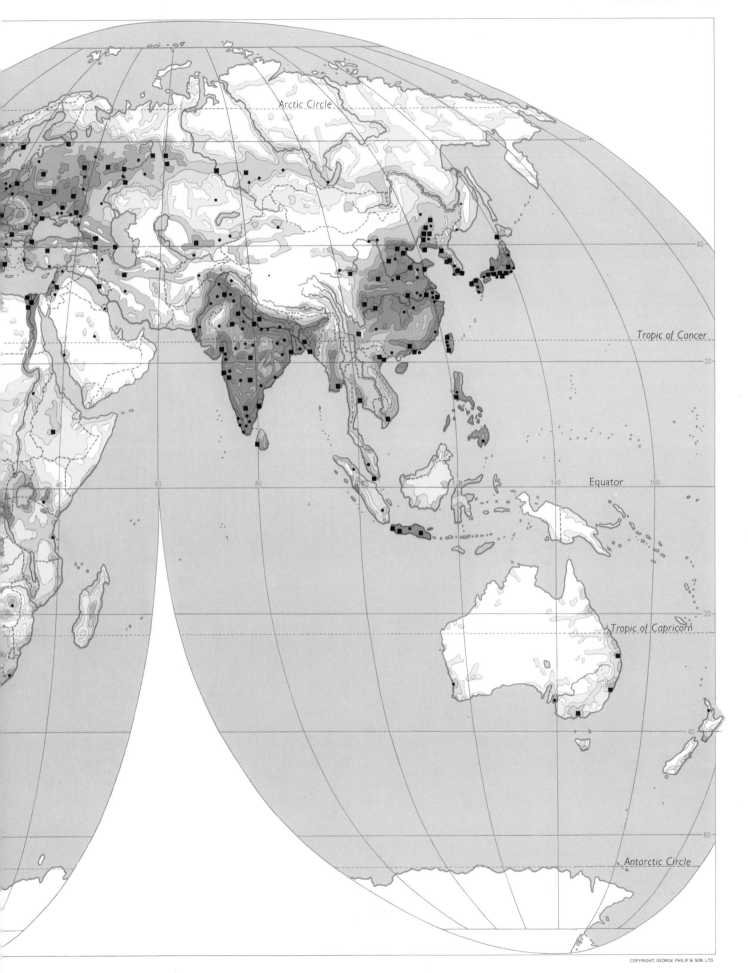

Arctic Circle

Tropic of Cancer

Equator

Tropic of Capricorn

Antarctic Circle

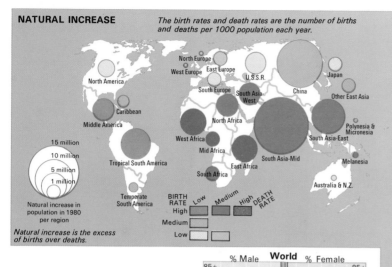

NATURAL INCREASE

The birth rates and death rates are the number of births and deaths per 1000 population each year.

Natural increase in population in 1980 per region

Natural increase is the excess of births over deaths.

15 million
10 million
5 million
1 million

BIRTH RATE — Low, Medium, High
DEATH RATE — High, Medium, Low

FAMILY SIZE

Family size is the total number of children an average woman will bear in her lifetime, for each region. In 1980 the world average was 3.6 children; in 2000 it is expected to be 2.8 children.

Family Size 1980 — 2 4 6 8 no. of children

2·8 World

North Europe 1·8, West Europe 1·8, East Europe 2·3, U.S.S.R. 2·1, North America 2·1, South Europe 2·0, Japan 2·0, China 2·0, East East Asia 3·8, Micronesia 3·8, Melanesia
Middle America 3·2, Caribbean 2·9, North Africa 3·9, South Asia-West 3·8, South Asia-Mid 3·0, South Asia-East 2·6, Australia & N.Z. 2·5
West Africa 5·4, Tropical South America 3·3, Mid Africa 4·9, East Africa 5·3
South Africa 4·2, Temperate South America 2·4

4·2 Expected family size 2000

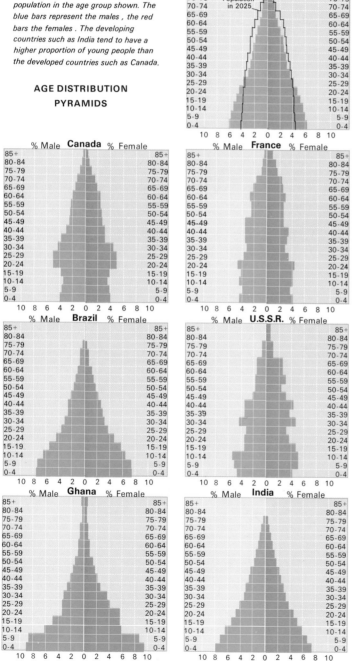

The bars represent the percentage of the population in the age group shown. The blue bars represent the males, the red bars the females. The developing countries such as India tend to have a higher proportion of young people than the developed countries such as Canada.

AGE DISTRIBUTION PYRAMIDS

World
% Male / % Female — Population in 2025

Canada
France
Brazil
U.S.S.R.
Ghana
India

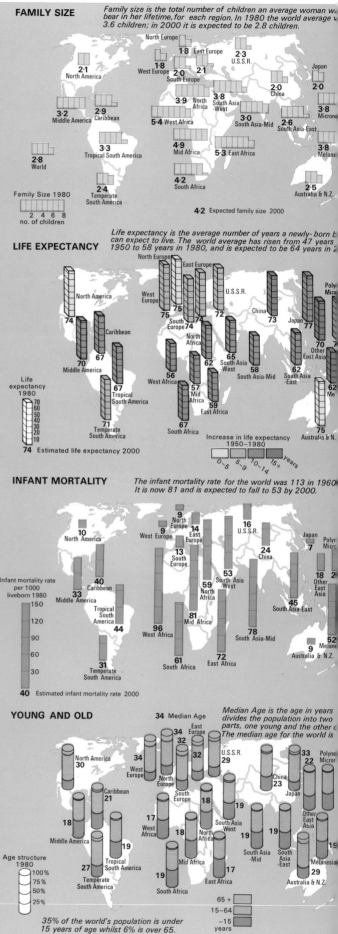

LIFE EXPECTANCY

Life expectancy is the average number of years a newly-born baby can expect to live. The world average has risen from 47 years in 1950 to 58 years in 1980, and is expected to be 64 years in 2000.

Life expectancy 1980

74 Estimated life expectancy 2000

Increase in life expectancy 1950–1980 — 0–5, 5–9, 10–14, 15+ years

INFANT MORTALITY

The infant mortality rate for the world was 113 in 1960. It is now 81 and is expected to fall to 53 by 2000.

Infant mortality rate per 1000 liveborn 1980 — 150, 120, 90, 60, 30

40 Estimated infant mortality rate 2000

YOUNG AND OLD

34 Median Age

Median Age is the age in years which divides the population into two parts, one young and the other old. The median age for the world is

Age structure 1980 — 100%, 75%, 50%, 25%

65+, 15–64, –15 years

35% of the world's population is under 15 years of age whilst 6% is over 65.

See page 31 for maps of Population Growth and Urbanization.

ILATION BY COUNTRY

The most populous country (China) contains a quarter of the world's population. The four most populous countries (China, India, U.S.S.R., and U.S.A.) contain half, and the first eighteen (all those countries named in larger type on the map) contain over three-quarters of the world's population. The remaining 150 countries contain only one quarter.

p on pages 26-27
ater detail.

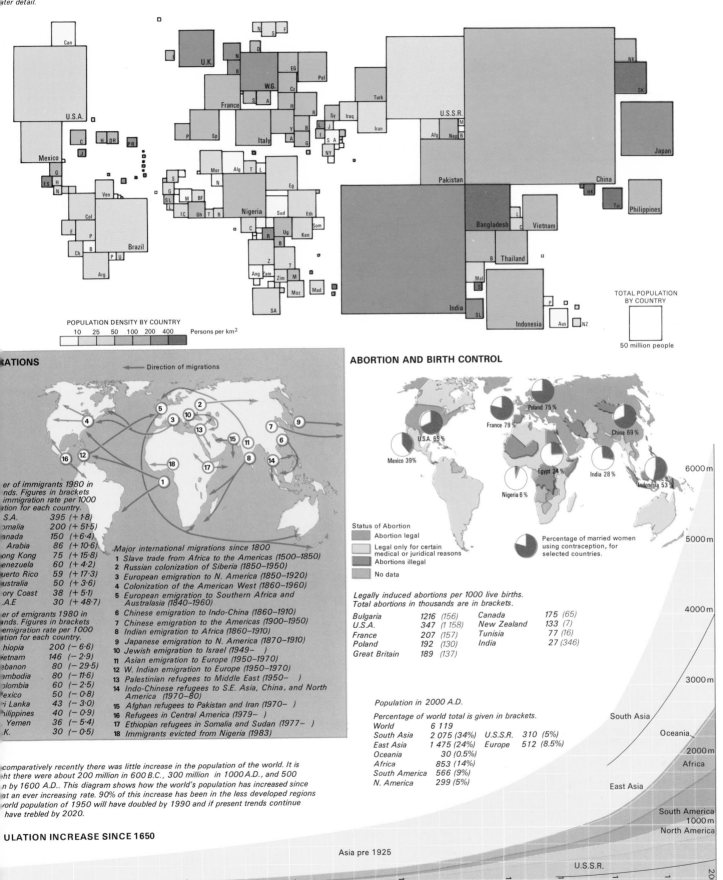

POPULATION DENSITY BY COUNTRY

| 10 | 25 | 50 | 100 | 200 | 400 | Persons per km² |

TOTAL POPULATION BY COUNTRY

50 million people

RATIONS

← Direction of migrations

er of immigrants 1980 in
nds. Figures in brackets
immigration rate per 1000
ation for each country.

.S.A.	395	(+ 1·8)
omalia	200	(+ 51·5)
anada	150	(+ 6·4)
Arabia	86	(+ 10·6)
ong Kong	75	(+ 15·8)
enezuela	60	(+ 4·2)
uerto Rico	59	(+ 17·3)
ustralia	50	(+ 3·6)
ory Coast	38	(+ 5·1)
.A.E	30	(+ 48·7)

er of emigrants 1980 in
ds. Figures in brackets
emigration rate per 1000
ation for each country.

hiopia	200	(− 6·6)
ietnam	146	(− 2·9)
ebanon	80	(− 29·5)
ambodia	80	(− 11·6)
olombia	60	(− 2·5)
exico	50	(− 0·8)
i Lanka	43	(− 3·0)
hilippines	40	(− 0·9)
Yemen	36	(− 5·4)
K.	30	(− 0·5)

Major international migrations since 1800
1 *Slave trade from Africa to the Americas (1500–1850)*
2 *Russian colonization of Siberia (1850–1950)*
3 *European emigration to N. America (1850–1920)*
4 *Colonization of the American West (1860–1960)*
5 *European emigration to Southern Africa and*
Australasia (1840–1960)
6 *Chinese emigration to Indo-China (1860–1910)*
7 *Chinese emigration to the Americas (1900–1950)*
8 *Indian emigration to Africa (1860–1910)*
9 *Japanese emigration to N. America (1870–1910)*
10 *Jewish emigration to Israel (1949–   )*
11 *Asian emigration to Europe (1950–1970)*
12 *W. Indian emigration to Europe (1950–1970)*
13 *Palestinian refugees to Middle East (1950–   )*
14 *Indo-Chinese refugees to S.E. Asia, China, and North*
America (1970–80)
15 *Afghan refugees to Pakistan and Iran (1970–   )*
16 *Refugees in Central America (1979–   )*
17 *Ethiopian refugees in Somalia and Sudan (1977–   )*
18 *Immigrants evicted from Nigeria (1983)*

ABORTION AND BIRTH CONTROL

U.S.A. 65 %
France 79 %
Poland 75 %
China 69 %
Mexico 39%
Egypt 24 %
India 28 %
Nigeria 6 %
Indonesia 53 %

Status of Abortion
Abortion legal
Legal only for certain medical or juridical reasons
Abortions illegal
No data

Percentage of married women using contraception, for selected countries.

Legally induced abortions per 1000 live births.
Total abortions in thousands are in brackets.

Bulgaria	1216	(156)	Canada	175	(65)
U.S.A.	347	(1 158)	New Zealand	133	(7)
France	207	(157)	Tunisia	77	(16)
Poland	192	(130)	India	27	(346)
Great Britain	189	(137)			

Population in 2000 A.D.

Percentage of world total is given in brackets.

World	6 119			
South Asia	2 075	(34%)	U.S.S.R.	310	(5%)
East Asia	1 475	(24%)	Europe	512	(8.5%)
Oceania	30	(0.5%)			
Africa	853	(14%)			
South America	566	(9%)			
N. America	299	(5%)			

comparatively recently there was little increase in the population of the world. It is
ht there were about 200 million in 600 B.C., 300 million in 1000 A.D., and 500
n by 1600 A.D.. This diagram shows how the world's population has increased since
at an ever increasing rate. 90% of this increase has been in the less developed regions
vorld population of 1950 will have doubled by 1990 and if present trends continue
have trebled by 2020.

IULATION INCREASE SINCE 1650

6000 m
5000 m
4000 m
3000 m
2000 m
1000 m

South Asia
Oceania
Africa
East Asia
South America
North America

Asia pre 1925
U.S.S.R.
Europe pre 1925
Europe

1700 1750 1800 1850 1900 1925 1950 1975 2000

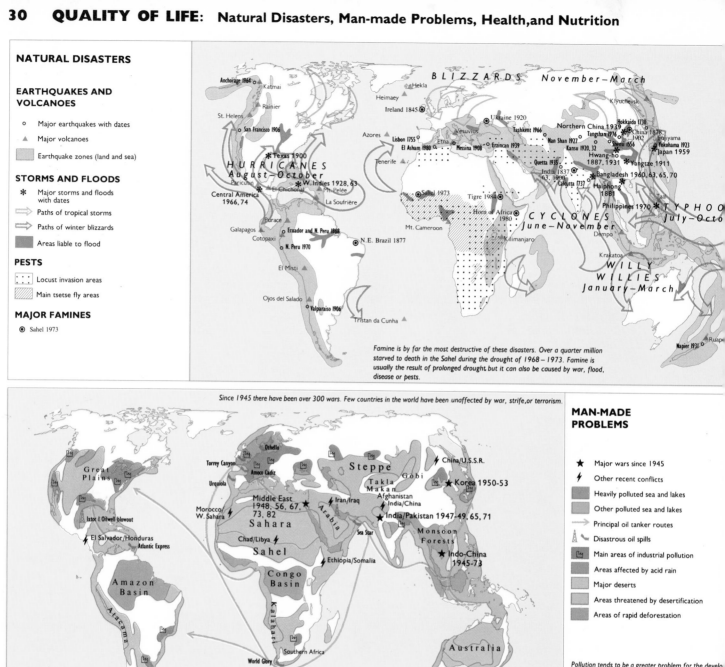

NATURAL DISASTERS

EARTHQUAKES AND VOLCANOES

- ○ Major earthquakes with dates
- ▲ Major volcanoes
- Earthquake zones (land and sea)

STORMS AND FLOODS

- * Major storms and floods with dates
- Paths of tropical storms
- Paths of winter blizzards
- Areas liable to flood

PESTS

- Locust invasion areas
- Main tsetse fly areas

MAJOR FAMINES

- ◉ Sahel 1973

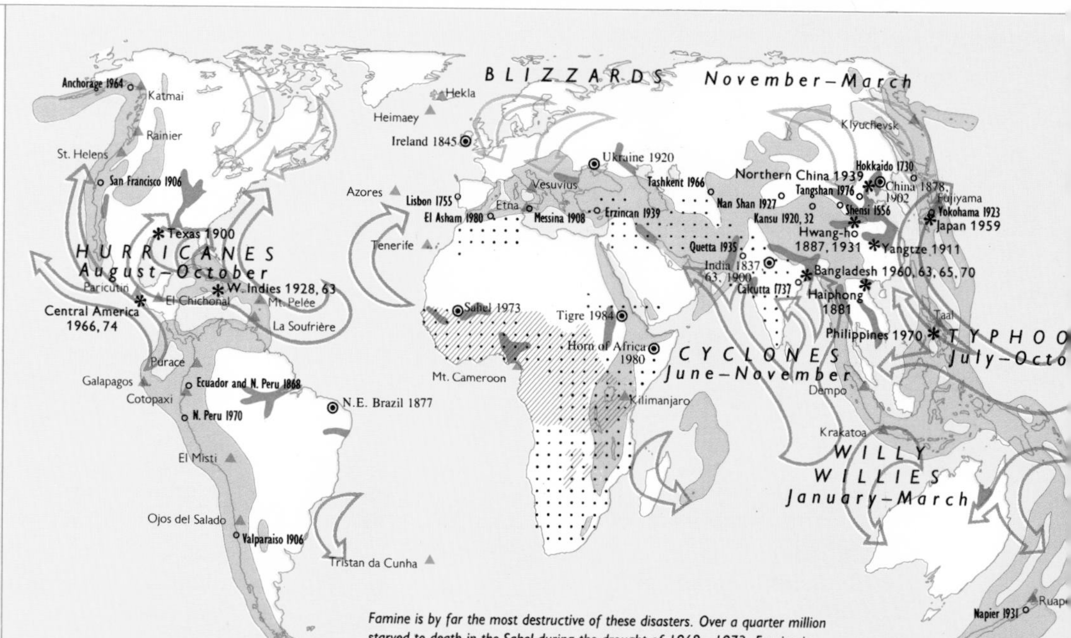

BLIZZARDS November–March
HURRICANES August–October
CYCLONES June–November
TYPHOONS July–October
WILLY WILLIES January–March
Anchorage 1964
Katmai
Rainier
St. Helens
San Francisco 1906
Texas 1900
Paricutin
El Chichonal
W. Indies 1928, 63
Mt. Pelée
La Soufrière
Central America 1966, 74
Purace
Galapagos
Ecuador and N. Peru 1868
Cotopaxi
N. Peru 1970
N.E. Brazil 1877
El Misti
Ojos del Salado
Valparaiso 1906
Tristan da Cunha
Hekla
Heimaey
Ireland 1845
Azores
Lisbon 1755
El Asham 1980
Etna
Vesuvius
Messina 1908
Erzincan 1939
Tenerife
Ukraine 1920
Tashkent 1966
Sahel 1973
Tigre 1984
Horn of Africa 1980
Mt. Cameroon
Kilimanjaro
Northern China 1939
Nan Shan 1927
Tangshan 1976
Kansu 1920, 32
Shensi 1556
Hwang-ho 1887, 1931
Quetta 1935
India 1837 63, 1900
Calcutta 1737
Bangladesh 1960, 63, 65, 70
Haiphong 1881
Yangtze 1911
Hokkaido 1730
China 1878, 1902
Fujiyama
Yokohama 1923
Japan 1959
Klyuchevsk
Philippines 1970
Taal
Dempo
Krakatoa
Napier 1931
Ruapehu

Famine is by far the most destructive of these disasters. Over a quarter million starved to death in the Sahel during the drought of 1968 – 1973. Famine is usually the result of prolonged drought, but it can also be caused by war, flood, disease or pests.

Since 1945 there have been over 300 wars. Few countries in the world have been unaffected by war, strife, or terrorism.

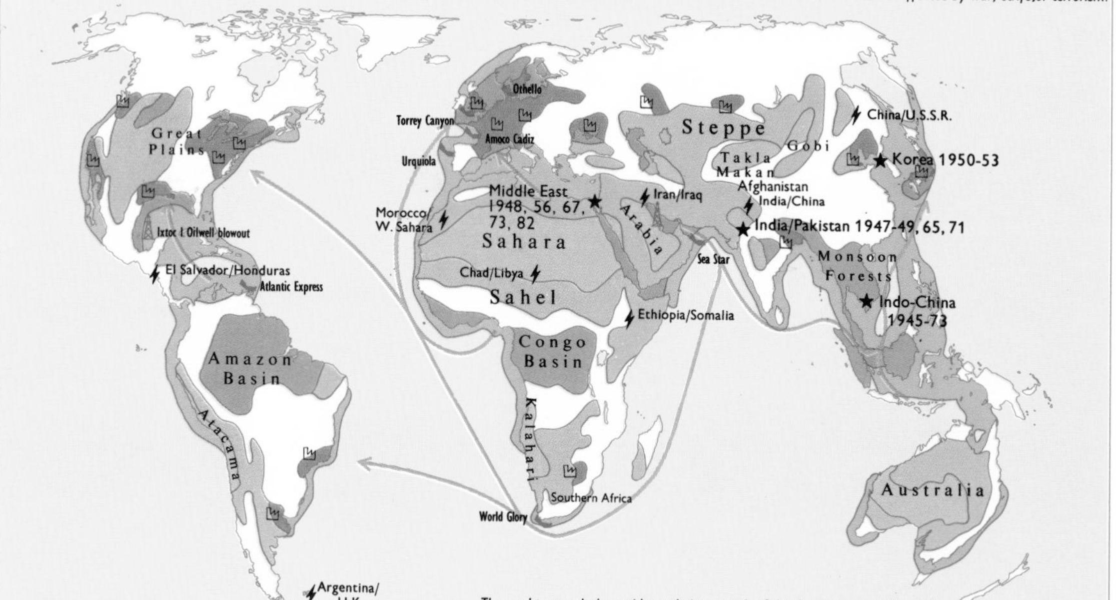

Great Plains
Torrey Canyon
Othello
Amoco Cadiz
Urquiola
Morocco/W. Sahara
Middle East 1948, 56, 67, 73, 82
Iran/Iraq
Sahara
Chad/Libya
Sahel
Arabia
Sea Star
Ixtoc I Oilwell blowout
El Salvador/Honduras
Atlantic Express
Amazon Basin
Atacama
Congo Basin
Ethiopia/Somalia
Kalahari
Southern Africa
World Glory
Argentina/U.K.
Steppe
Gobi
Takla Makan
Afghanistan
India/China
India/Pakistan 1947-49, 65, 71
China/U.S.S.R.
Korea 1950-53
Monsoon Forests
Indo-China 1945-73
Australia

The need to match the rapid population growth of the developing countries with increased production of food and fuel has led to overfarming and the destruction of the vegetation cover and the soil.

MAN-MADE PROBLEMS

- ★ Major wars since 1945
- ϟ Other recent conflicts
- Heavily polluted sea and lakes
- Other polluted sea and lakes
- Principal oil tanker routes
- Disastrous oil spills
- Main areas of industrial pollution
- Areas affected by acid rain
- Major deserts
- Areas threatened by desertification
- Areas of rapid deforestation

Pollution tends to be a greater problem for the develo[ped] countries with their intensive industry and agricult[ure]. Prevailing winds can carry air pollution a long way be[fore] it falls as acid rain, which is now a serious problem [in] Canada and Scandinavia. Traces of pollution have [been] discovered in the ice of Antarctica.

MEDICAL CARE

Persons per doctor in each country

- over 25000
- 10000 – 25000
- 5000 – 10000
- 1000 – 5000
- less than 1000

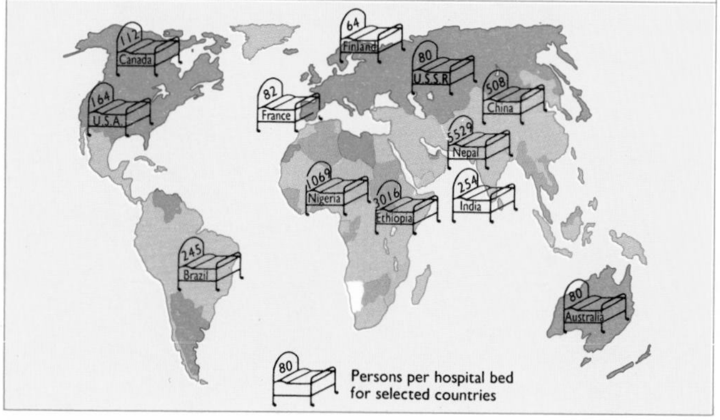

112 Canada
164 U.S.A.
64 Finland
80 U.S.S.R.
82 France
508 China
5529 Nepal
1069 Nigeria
3016 Ethiopia
254 India
245 Brazil
80 Australia

Persons per hospital bed for selected countries

NUTRITION

Calorie intake as a percentage of needs per person

- less than 80%
- 80 – 90%
- 90 – 100%
- 100 – 110%
- 110 – 120%
- over 120%

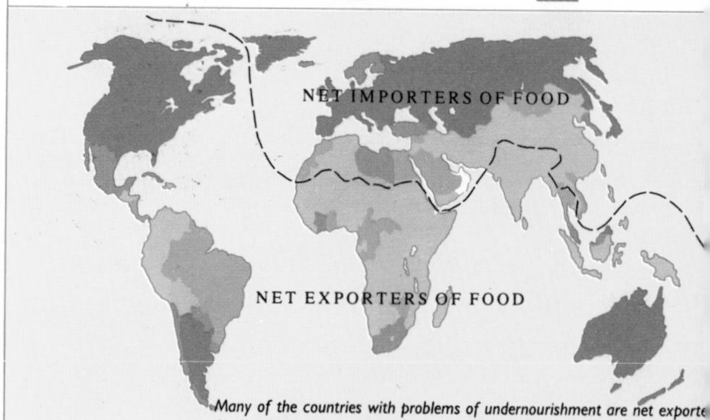

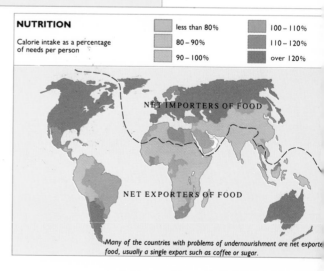

NET IMPORTERS OF FOOD
NET EXPORTERS OF FOOD

Many of the countries with problems of undernourishment are net exporte[rs of] food, usually a single export such as coffee or sugar.

STANDARDS OF LIVING

RICH

Countries with more than four times the world's average income

Countries with more than twice the world's average income

Countries with incomes just above the world's average

POOR

Countries with incomes just below the world's average

Countries with less than half of the world's average income

Countries with less than one quarter of the world's average income

Data not available

world's average income is just under 2200 US$ per ... The richest country on a per capita basis is ... with an income over 200 times that of the poorest ..., Mali.

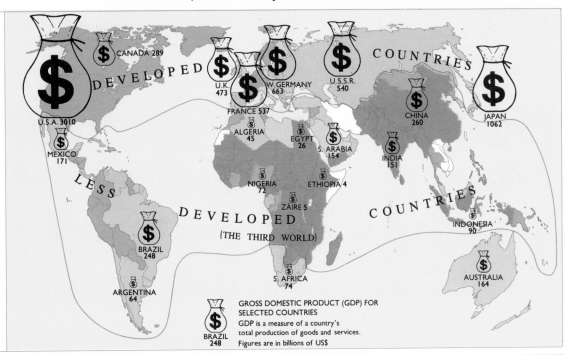

CANADA 289
U.K. 473
W. GERMANY 663
U.S.S.R. 540
CHINA 260
JAPAN 1062
U.S.A. 3010
FRANCE 537
ALGERIA 45
EGYPT 26
S. ARABIA 154
INDIA 151
MEXICO 171
NIGERIA 72
ETHIOPIA 4
ZAIRE 5
INDONESIA 90
BRAZIL 248
S. AFRICA 74
AUSTRALIA 164
ARGENTINA 64

DEVELOPED COUNTRIES
LESS DEVELOPED COUNTRIES
(THE THIRD WORLD)

GROSS DOMESTIC PRODUCT (GDP) FOR SELECTED COUNTRIES

BRAZIL 248

GDP is a measure of a country's total production of goods and services. Figures are in billions of US$

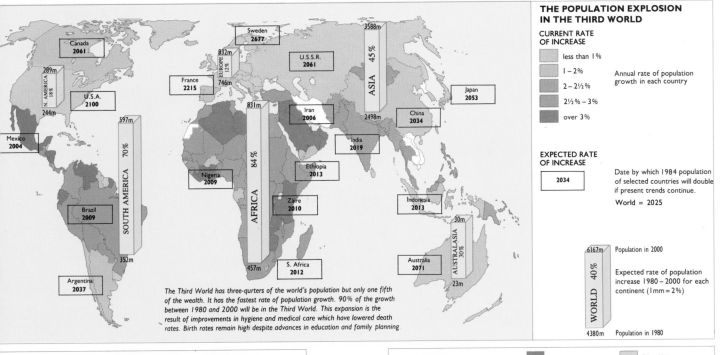

Canada 2061
Sweden 2677
U.S.S.R. 2061
ASIA 45%
3588m
N. AMERICA 18% 289m
U.S.A. 2100 244m
France 2215
EUROPE 12% 832m
746m
Japan 2053
Mexico 2004
597m
Iran 2006 831m
China 2034 2498m
India 2019
SOUTH AMERICA 70%
Nigeria 2009
AFRICA 84%
Ethiopia 2013
Brazil 2009
Zaire 2010
Indonesia 2013
Argentina 2037
352m
S. Africa 2012 457m
Australia 2071
AUSTRALASIA 30% 30m
23m

The Third World has three-qurters of the world's population but only one fifth of the wealth. It has the fastest rate of population growth. 90% of the growth between 1980 and 2000 will be in the Third World. This expansion is the result of improvements in hygiene and medical care which have lowered death rates. Birth rates remain high despite advances in education and family planning.

THE POPULATION EXPLOSION IN THE THIRD WORLD

CURRENT RATE OF INCREASE

less than 1%
1 – 2%
2 – 2½%
2½% – 3%
over 3%

Annual rate of population growth in each country

EXPECTED RATE OF INCREASE

2034

Date by which 1984 population of selected countries will double if present trends continue.

World = 2025

6167m — Population in 2000

WORLD 40%

Expected rate of population increase 1980 – 2000 for each continent (1mm = 2%)

4380m — Population in 1980

URBANIZATION

Percentage of population living in towns and cities in each country

75 – 100%   25 – 50%
50 – 75%   0 – 25%

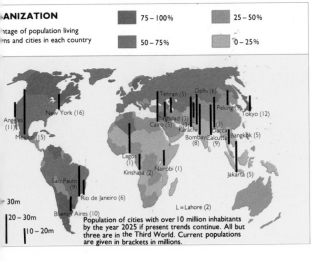

Tehran (5)
Delhi (6)
New York (16)
Peking (7)
Tokyo (12)
Angeles (11)
Baghdad (3)
Mexico (15)
Cairo (5)
Karachi (5)
Dacca (3)
Bangkok (5)
Bombay (8)
Calcutta (9)
Lagos (1)
Kinshasa (2)
Nairobi (1)
Jakarta (5)
Sao Paulo (9)
Rio de Janeiro (6)
Buenos Aires (10)
L = Lahore (2)
30m
20 – 30m
10 – 20m

Population of cities with over 10 million inhabitants by the year 2025 if present trends continue. All but three are in the Third World. Current populations are given in brackets in millions.

ILLITERACY

Percentage of population in each country who are illiterate

80 – 100%   20 – 40%
60 – 80%   0 – 20%
40 – 60%

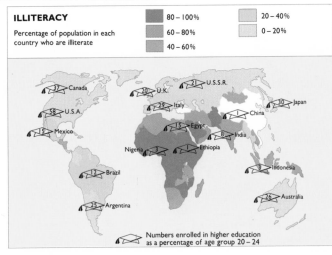

37 Canada
21 U.S.S.R.
20 U.K.
30 Japan
29 Italy
1 China
58 U.S.A.
15 Egypt
8 India
5 Mexico
3 Nigeria
1 Ethiopia
12 Brazil
3 Indonesia
25 Argentina
16 Australia

Numbers enrolled in higher education as a percentage of age group 20 – 24

1:105 000 000

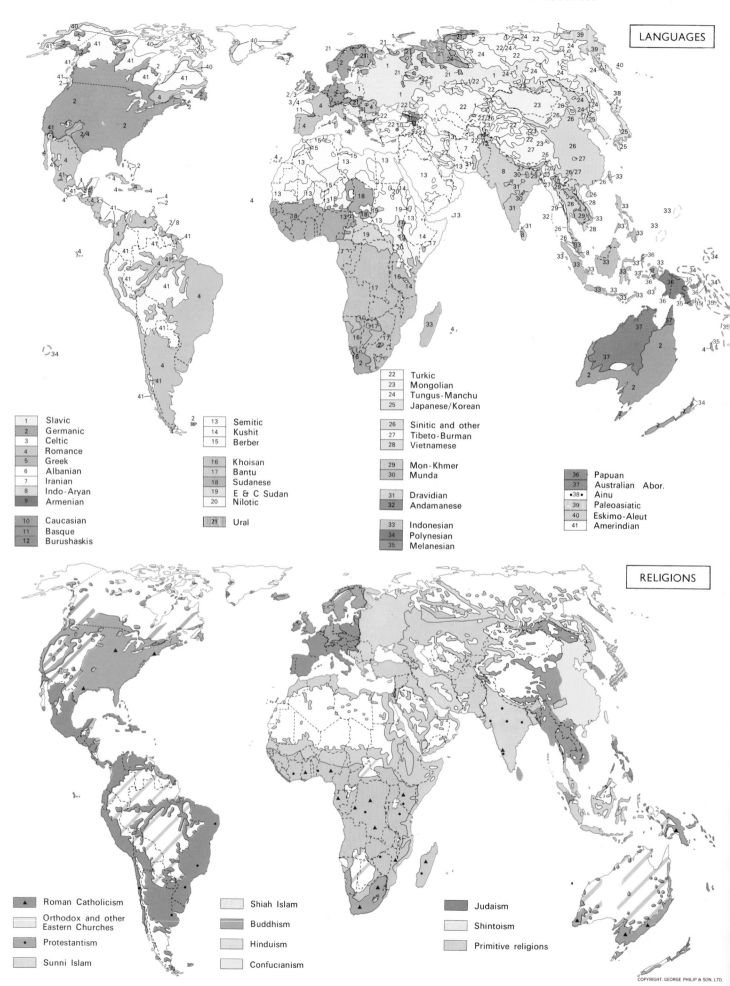

LANGUAGES

22	Turkic
23	Mongolian
24	Tungus-Manchu
25	Japanese/Korean

26	Sinitic and other
27	Tibeto-Burman
28	Vietnamese

| 29 | Mon-Khmer |
| 30 | Munda |

| 31 | Dravidian |
| 32 | Andamanese |

33	Indonesian
34	Polynesian
35	Melanesian

1	Slavic
2	Germanic
3	Celtic
4	Romance
5	Greek
6	Albanian
7	Iranian
8	Indo-Aryan
9	Armenian

10	Caucasian
11	Basque
12	Burushaskis

13	Semitic
14	Kushit
15	Berber

16	Khoisan
17	Bantu
18	Sudanese
19	E & C Sudan
20	Nilotic

| 21 | Ural |

36	Papuan
37	Australian Abor.
•38•	Ainu
39	Paleoasiatic
40	Eskimo-Aleut
41	Amerindian

RELIGIONS

| Roman Catholicism |
| Orthodox and other Eastern Churches |
| Protestantism |
| Sunni Islam |

| Shiah Islam |
| Buddhism |
| Hinduism |
| Confucianism |

| Judaism |
| Shintoism |
| Primitive religions |

1:90 000 000

Structure of Employment
(for selected countries)

The countries have been selected on the grounds of size of working population and to illustrate the contrasting structures of employment

Unclassified Agriculture

Services Mining

Manufacturing

Proportion employed in

The area of the circle is in proportion to the total working population of a country.

———— 100 million
———— 50 million
———— 30 million
———— 20 million
———— 10 million
———— 5 million
———— 2 million

The figures following the countries' names show the percentage of the population who are economically active (World 1982 = 40%)

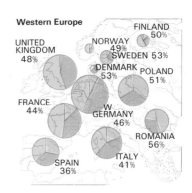

Western Europe

UNITED KINGDOM 48%
NORWAY 49%
FINLAND 50%
SWEDEN 53%
DENMARK 53%
POLAND 51%
FRANCE 44%
W. GERMANY 46%
ROMANIA 56%
SPAIN 36%
ITALY 41%

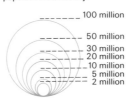

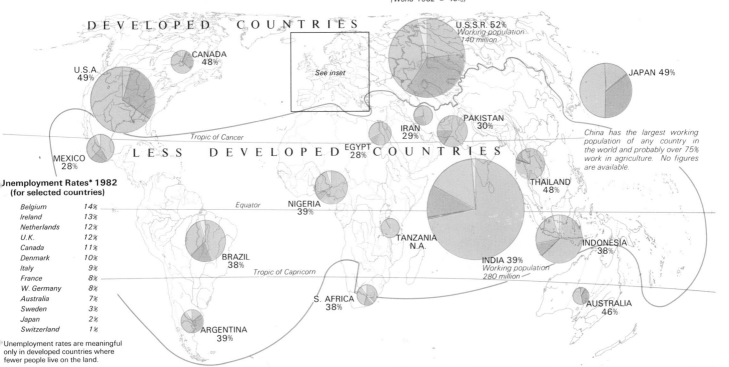

D E V E L O P E D   C O U N T R I E S

U.S.S.R. 52%
Working population 140 million

CANADA 48%

U.S.A. 49%

JAPAN 49%

See inset

Tropic of Cancer

MEXICO 28%

L E S S   D E V E L O P E D   C O U N T R I E S

IRAN 29%
PAKISTAN 30%
EGYPT 28%

China has the largest working population of any country in the world and probably over 75% work in agriculture. No figures are available.

THAILAND 48%

Unemployment Rates* 1982
(for selected countries)

Belgium	14%
Ireland	13%
Netherlands	12%
U.K.	12%
Canada	11%
Denmark	10%
Italy	9%
France	8%
W. Germany	8%
Australia	7%
Sweden	3%
Japan	2%
Switzerland	1%

Unemployment rates are meaningful only in developed countries where fewer people live on the land.

Equator

NIGERIA 39%

TANZANIA N.A.

BRAZIL 38%

Tropic of Capricorn

INDIA 39%
Working population 280 million

INDONESIA 38%

S. AFRICA 38%

ARGENTINA 39%

AUSTRALIA 46%

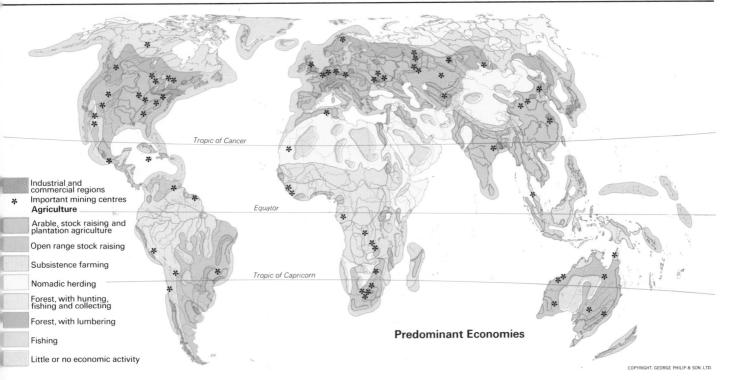

Tropic of Cancer

Equator

Tropic of Capricorn

Industrial and commercial regions

* Important mining centres

Agriculture

Arable, stock raising and plantation agriculture

Open range stock raising

Subsistence farming

Nomadic herding

Forest, with hunting, fishing and collecting

Forest, with lumbering

Fishing

Little or no economic activity

Predominant Economies

Wheat

The most important grain crop in the temperate regions though it is also grown in a variety of climates e.g. in Monsoon lands as a winter crop.

U.S.S.R. China U.S.A. India Others

World production 1983
493.3 million tonnes

Oats

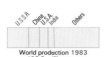

Widely grown in temperate regions with the limit fixed by early autumn frosts. Mainly fed to cattle. The best quality oats are used for oatmeal, porridge, and breakfast foods.

U.S.S.R. U.S.A. Canada Poland Australia Others

World production 1983
44.5 million tonnes

Wheat
Oats
1 dot represents
2 million tonnes

Rye

The hardiest of cereals and more resistant to cold, pests, and disease than wheat. An important foodstuff in Central and E. Europe and the U.S.S.R.

U.S.S.R. Poland E. Germany W. Germany Others

World production 1983
33.1 million tonnes

Maize (or Corn)

Needs plenty of sunshine, summer rain, or irrigation and frost free for 6 months. Important as animal feed and for human food in Africa, Latin America, and as a vegetable and breakfast cereal.

U.S.A. China Brazil Others

World production 1983
337.5 million tonnes

Rye
Maize
1 dot represents
2 million tonnes

Barley

Has the widest range of cultivation requiring only 8 weeks between seed time and harvest. Used mainly as animal-feed and by the malting industry.

U.S.S.R. U.K. W. Germany France Others

World production 1983
169.3 million tonnes

Rice

The staple food of half the human race. The main producing areas are the flood plains and hill terraces of S. and E. Asia where water is abundant in the growing season.

China India Indonesia Others

World production 1983
435.7 million tonnes

Barley
Rice
1 dot represents
2 million tonnes

Millets

The name given to a number of related members of the grass family, of which sorghum is one of the most important. They provide nutritious grain.

India China Nigeria Others

World production 1983
29.6 million tonnes

Potatoes

An important food crop though less nutritious weight for weight than grain crops. Requires a temperate climate with a regular and plentiful supply of rain.

U.S.S.R. Poland China U.S.A. Others

World production 1983
258.7 million tonnes

Millets
Potatoes
1 dot represents
2 million tonnes

Vegetable oilseeds and oils

Despite the increasing use of synthetic chemical products and animal and marine fats, vegetable oils extracted from these crops grow in quantity, value and importance. Food is the major use- in margarine and cooking fats.

Groundnuts are also a valuable subsistence crop and the meal is used as animal feed. Soya-bean meal is a growing source of protein for humans and animals. The Mediterranean lands are the prime source of olive oil.

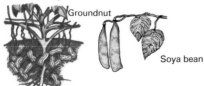
Groundnut
Soya bean

Sunflower

Groundnuts
Soya beans
Sunflower seed
1 dot represents
1 million tonnes

Tea and cacao

Tea requires plentiful rainfall and well-drained, sloping ground, whereas cacao prefers a moist heavy soil. Both are grown mainly for export.

Cacao

Tea

Coffee

Prefers a hot climate, wet and dry seasons, and an elevated location. It is very susceptible to frost, drought and market fluctuations.

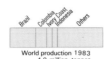

World production 1983
4.9 million tonnes

Brazil · Colombia · Ivory Coast · Indonesia · Others

- □ Tea
- · Cacao
- ● Coffee

1 dot represents
100 000 tonnes

Sugar beet

Requires a deep, rich soil and a temperate climate. Europe produces over 90% of the world's beets mainly for domestic consumption.

U.S.S.R. · France · U.S.A. · W. Germany · Others

World production 1983
287.3 million tonnes

Sugar cane

Also requires deep and rich soil but a tropical climate. It produces a much higher yield per hectare than beet and is grown primarily for export.

Brazil · India · Cuba · China · Mexico · Others

World production 1983
892.5 million tonnes

- · Sugar beet
- · Sugar cane

1 dot represents
10 million tonnes

Fruit

With the improvements in canning, drying and freezing, and in transport and marketing, the international trade and consumption of deciduous and soft fruits, citrus fruits, and tropical fruits has greatly increased. Recent developments in the use of the peel will give added value to some of the fruit crops.

Fish

Commercial fishing requires large shoals of fish of one species within reach of markets. Freshwater fishing is also important. A rich source of protein, fish will become an increasingly valuable food source.

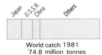

Japan · U.S.S.R. · China · Others

World catch 1981
74.8 million tonnes

- Temperate fruit
- Citrus fruit
- Principal fishing grounds

Beef cattle

Australia, New Zealand and Argentina provide the major part of international beef exports. Western U.S.A. and Europe have considerable production of beef for their local high demand.

India · U.S.A. · Brazil · U.S.S.R. · Others

World production 1983
1100.1 million head

Dairy cattle

The need of herds for a rich diet and for nearby markets result in dairying being characteristic of densely-populated areas of the temperate zones - U.S.A., N.W. Europe, and S.E. Australia.

U.S.S.R. · India · Brazil · U.S.A. · France · Others

World production 1983
228.3 million head

- · Cattle

1 dot represents
10 million head

- Dairy produce

Sheep

Raised mostly for wool and meat, their skins and the cheese from their milk are important products in some countries. The merino yields a fine wool and crossbreeds are best for meat.

U.S.S.R. · Australia · China · N.Z. · Others

World production 1983
1144.3 million head

Pigs

Can be reared in most climates from monsoon to cool temperate. They are abundant in China, the Corn Belt of the U.S.A. N.W. and C. Europe, Brazil and U.S.S.R.

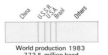

China · U.S.S.R. · U.S.A. · Brazil · Others

World production 1983
773.5 million head

- · Sheep
- · Pigs

1 dot represents
10 million head

Production of ferro-alloy metals

Steel is refined iron with the addition of other minerals and ferro-alloys. The ferro-alloys give the steel their own special properties; for example resistance to corrosion (chromium and nickel), hardness (tungsten and vanadium), elasticity (molybdenum), magnetic properties (cobalt), high tensile strength (manganese), and high ductility (molybdenum).

Chromium
South Africa | U.S.S.R. | Albania Zimbabwe Turkey India Others
World production 4.2 million tonnes

Nickel
U.S.S.R. | Canada | New Caledonia Australia | Others
World production 623 000 tonnes

Manganese
U.S.S.R. | S. Africa | Brazil Gabon Australia India
World production 11.1 million tonnes

Tungsten
China | U.S.S.R. | Canada Australia Bolivia | Others
World production 46 000 tonnes

Molybdenum
U.S.A. | Chile Canada U.S.S.R. Others
World production 91 000 tonnes

Vanadium
S. Africa | U.S.S.R. | U.S.A. Finland Others
World production 33 100 tonnes

Production of non-ferrous metals and diamonds

Tin
Malaysia Indonesia Bolivia Thailand U.S.S.R. Others
World production 222 500 tonnes

Gold
South Africa | U.S.S.R. | Canada | Others
World production 1 396 tonnes

Copper
Chile U.S.A. U.S.S.R. Philippines Zambia Canada Zaire Peru Others
World production 8.7 million tonnes

Zinc
Canada U.S.S.R. Australia Peru U.S.A. Others
World production 6.5 million tonnes

Silver
Peru U.S.S.R. Mexico Canada U.S.A. Australia Poland Others
World production 11 531 tonnes

Lead
U.S.S.R. U.S.A. Australia Canada Others
World production 3.57 million tonnes

Bauxite
Australia Guinea Jamaica U.S.S.R. Brazil Others
World production 78.2 million tonnes

Diamonds
U.S.S.R. South Africa Zaire Botswana Angola Namibia Others
World production 41.9 thousand carats

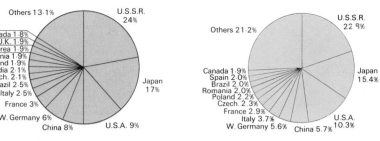

World production of pig iron and ferro-alloys

World production 451 million tonnes 1982

Others 13.1%
Canada 1.8%
U.K. 1.9%
S. Korea 1.9%
Romania 1.9%
Poland 1.9%
India 2.1%
Czech. 2.1%
Brazil 2.5%
Italy 2.5%
France 3%
W. Germany 6%
China 8%
U.S.A. 9%
Japan 17%
U.S.S.R. 24%

World production of steel

World production 645 million tonnes 1982

Others 21.2%
Canada 1.9%
Spain 2.0%
Brazil 2.0%
Romania 2.0%
Poland 2.2%
Czech. 2.3%
France 2.9%
Italy 3.7%
W. Germany 5.6%
China 5.7%
U.S.A. 10.3%
Japan 15.4%
U.S.S.R. 22.8%

World production of iron ore (Fe content).

World production 480 million tonnes

U.S.S.R. 30% | Australia 12% | Brazil 9% | China 8% | India 5% | U.S.A. 5% | Canada 4% | S. Africa 3% | Liberia 3% | Sweden 2% | Venezuela 2% | Others 17%

Growth of world production

■ Pig iron and ferro-alloys
□ Steel

m tonnes
800
700
600
500
400
300
200
100

1938 1946 1951 1961 1971 1981

World steel production per capita

	tonnes/capita
Belgium	1.01
Japan	0.84
W. Germany	0.59
U.S.S.R.	0.55
Canada	0.49
Poland	0.46
Australia	0.42
France	0.39
U.K.	0.18
China	0.04

Tropic of Cancer
Equator
Tropic of Capricorn

Principal sources of iron ore and ferro-alloys

■ Iron ore
◨ Chromium
⌂ Cobalt.
□ Manganese
◹ Molybdenum
● Nickel
+ Tungsten
◿ Vanadium
⟶ Iron ore trade flow

Principal sources of non-ferrous metals and other minerals

Base metals
▲ Antimony
▲ Copper
▲ Lead
● Mercury
● Tin
◆ Zinc

Light metals
● Bauxite
▾ Beryllium
■ Lithium
▼ Titanium
Rare metals
◆ Uranium

Precious metals
▲ Gold
△ Platinum
▽ Silver
Precious stones
▲ Diamonds

Mineral fertilizers
● Nitrates
● Phosphates
◆ Potash
◆ Sulphur
□ Pyrites

Other industrial minerals
■ Asbestos
△ Mica

Structural regions

Pre-Cambrian shields
Sedimentary cover on Pre-Cambrian shields
Primary (Caledonian and Hercynian) folding
Sedimentary cover on Primary folding

Secondary folding
Sedimentary cover on Secondary folding
Tertiary (Alpine) folding
Sedimentary cover on Tertiary folding

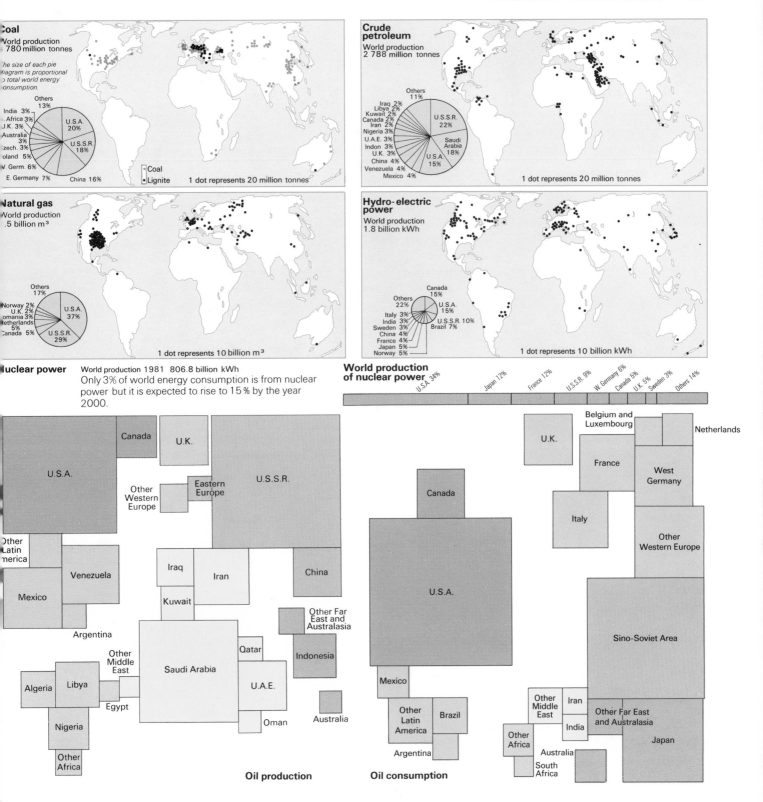

Coal

World production 780 million tonnes

The size of each pie diagram is proportional to total world energy consumption.

Others 13%
India 3%
S. Africa 3%
U.K. 3%
Australia 3%
Czech. 3%
Poland 5%
W. Germ. 6%
E. Germany 7%
China 16%
U.S.A. 20%
U.S.S.R. 18%

■ Coal
● Lignite   1 dot represents 20 million tonnes

Crude petroleum

World production 2 788 million tonnes

Others 11%
Iraq 2%
Libya 2%
Kuwait 2%
Canada 2%
Iran 2%
Nigeria 3%
U.A.E. 3%
Indon 3%
U.K. 3%
China 4%
Venezuela 4%
Mexico 4%
U.S.S.R. 22%
Saudi Arabia 18%
U.S.A. 15%

1 dot represents 20 million tonnes

Natural gas

World production 5 billion m³

Others 17%
Norway 2%
U.K. 2%
Romania 3%
Netherlands 5%
Canada 5%
U.S.A. 37%
U.S.S.R. 29%

1 dot represents 10 billion m³

Hydro-electric power

World production 1.8 billion kWh

Canada 15%
Others 22%
Italy 3%
India 3%
Sweden 4%
China 4%
France 4%
Japan 5%
Norway 5%
U.S.A. 15%
U.S.S.R. 10%
Brazil 7%

1 dot represents 10 billion kWh

Nuclear power

World production 1981 806.8 billion kWh

Only 3% of world energy consumption is from nuclear power but it is expected to rise to 15% by the year 2000.

World production of nuclear power

U.S.A. 34% | Japan 12% | France 12% | U.S.S.R. 9% | W. Germany 6% | Canada 5% | U.K. 5% | Sweden 3% | Others 14%

Oil production

Oil consumption

Oil's new superpowers

The diagrams above show the relative size of each major country's oil production and consumption. When the countries are represented like this they take on new dimensions. Thus Canada, which is much larger than the United States in area, appears much smaller in the diagram because the oil production and consumption of Canada are considerably less than that of the United States. The major producers of oil are the U.S.S.R., Saudi Arabia, and the United States. There are also significant supplies in Mexico, North Africa, and the other Middle East countries. The Middle East, with 55% of the world's reserves, produces 22% of the world's supply but consumes only 3%. However most countries consume more oil than they produce. The United States for example produces 18% of the world's supply but consumes 25% of the total: therefore millions of tonnes of oil have to be imported.

The economies of many countries depend upon energy supplies from a handful of oil exporting countries such as Saudi Arabia. There was a fall in the demand for oil in the early 1980s due largely to the world recession but this has been offset by reduced production in the Middle East as a result of the war between Iran and Iraq.

Polar Routes

Pacific
Routes

Pacific
Routes

N.Y.

S.F.

B.A.

R.J.

C.T.

Principal Air Routes
Distances in km

GREENLAND

ICELAND

UNITED
KINGDOM
Gla
IRELAND

Queen Elizabeth Is.

Victoria I.

Baffin I.

Anchorage

Churchill

Hudson
Bay

Newfoundland

Edmonton

Vancouver

C A N A D A

Calgary

Winnipeg

Québec

Seattle

Montréal

Chicago

Toronto
Boston

Detroit

San Francisco

Denver

St. Louis

New York

UNITED STATES

Washington

PORTUGAL

Lisbon

Azores

Los Angeles

Dallas

M
E
X
I
C
O

New Orleans

Houston

Gulf of
Mexico

Miami

BAHAMAS

Casablanca

Canary Is.

W. SAHARA

A T L A N T I C

Tropic of Cancer

Hawaiian
Islands
(U.S.)

Mexico

Havana

C U B A

West Indies

JAMAICA HAITI

BELIZE

GUATEMALA   HONDURAS

EL SALVADOR

NICARAGUA

DOMINICAN REP.
PUERTO
RICO

Caribbean
Sea

MAURITAN

C. Verde Is.

SENEGAL

GAMBIA

GUINEA-BISSAU

GUINEA

SIERRA
LEONE

LIBERIA

COSTA
RICA

PANAMA

Caracas

VENEZUELA

Palmyra Is.
(U.S.)

Tabuaeran

Kiritimati

P A C I F I C

Bogota

COLOMBIA

GUYANA

SURINAM

FR.
GUIANA

O C E A N

Ascension
(Br.)

Equator

Galapagos Is.
(Ecuador)

Quito

ECUADOR

Belém

Phoenix Is.

Manaus

B R A Z I L

Recife

Tokelau Is.
(N.Z.)

PERU

Lima

St. Hele
(Br.)

O C E A N

Salvador

Samoan Is.

Brasilia

Tonga

Society Is.
(Fr.)

Tuamotu
Archipelago
(Fr.)

La Paz

BOLIVIA

Rio de Janeiro

Tubuai Is.
(Fr.)

PARAGUAY

São Paulo

Tropic of Capricorn

Easter I.

Asunción

Trist
Cu
(B

Kermadec Is.
(N.Z.)

C
H
I
L
E

A
R
G
E
N
T
I
N
A

URUGUAY

Santiago

Montevideo

Buenos
Aires

Chatham Is.
(N.Z.)

Falkland Is.

S. Georgia

Tierra del Fuego

FALKLAND IS. DEPENDENCIES (Br.)

Political Associations

ROSS DEPENDENCY

BRITISH ANTARCTIC TERRITORY

West from G

Arab League

NATO

Warsaw Pact

Principal Sea Routes
Distances in km

Pacific Routes

Pacific Routes

ARCTIC OCEAN

Novaya Zemlya
New Siberian Is.

SWEDEN
FINLAND
Arkhangelsk
Helsinki
Leningrad
UNION   OF   SOVIET   SOCIALIST   REPUBLICS
Stockholm
Copenhagen
Moscow
Sverdlovsk
Novosibirsk
POLAND Warsaw
Berlin
Vienna
Kiev
Irkutsk
ROMANIA
Bucharest
YUGOSLAVIA
BULGARIA
Baku
Tashkent
Ulan Bator
MONGOLIA
Vladivostok
Sapporo
Bering Sea
GREECE
Athens
TURKEY
Istanbul
SYRIA
Baghdad
Tehran
AFGHANISTAN
Kabul
Islamabad
Lahore
Peking
Lu-ta
KOREA
JAPAN
Tokyo
Mediterranean Sea
ISRAEL
IRAQ
IRAN
PAKISTAN
NEPAL
Delhi
BANGLA-DESH
Dacca
Chungking
S. KOREA
Pusan
Osaka
Tripoli
Alexandria
Cairo
EGYPT
Baghdad
JORDAN
Karachi
Ahmadabad
INDIA
Calcutta
BURMA
Shanghai
LIBYA
SAUDI
U.A.E.
Mecca
ARABIA
OMAN
Bombay
Rangoon
Bay of Bengal
Madras
LAOS
TAIWAN
Hong Kong
PACIFIC
Tropic of Cancer
Wake I. (U.S.)
Red Sea
YEMEN
SOUTH YEMEN
Arabian Sea
THAILAND
Hue
VIETNAM
Northern Marianas
OCEAN
NIGER
CHAD
Khartoum
SUDAN
DJIB.
Bangkok
CAM-BODIA
Manila
Kano
Ndjamena
Addis Ababa
SOMALI REP.
ETHIOPIA
Colombo
SRI LANKA
Phnom Penh
Ho Chi Minh City
PHILIPPINES
Marshall Is.
CAMEROON
CENTRAL AFRICAN REPUBLIC
Douala
Mogadishu
Maldives
MALAYSIA
Federated States of Micronesia (U.S. Trust Territory)
GABON
UGANDA
KENYA
Nairobi
Kuala Lumpur
Singapore
Equator
Kiribati
CONGO
ZAIRE
RWANDA
BURUNDI
Mombasa
TANZANIA
Padang
Sumatra
Borneo
INDIAN
Seychelles
INDONESIA
New Guinea
PAPUA NEW GUINEA
Solomon Is.
Kinshasa
Dar-es-Salaam
Jakarta
Surabaya
Tuvalu (Ellice Is.)
ANGOLA
ZAMBIA
OCEAN
Darwin
Coral Sea
Vanuatu
NAMIBIA
Harare
ZIMBABWE
MOZAMBIQUE
Antananarivo
MADAGASCAR
Mauritius
New Caledonia (Fr.)
BOTSWANA
Johannesburg
SWAZ.
Alice Springs
AUSTRALIA
Tropic of Capricorn
SOUTH AFRICA
LES.
Durban
Perth
Cape Town
Adelaide
Sydney
Canberra
Auckland
Melbourne
NEW ZEALAND
Crozet Is. (Fr.)
Kerguelen Is. (Fr.)
Tasmania
Hobart
Christchurch
Dunedin

SOUTHERN   OCEAN

DEPENDENCY
AUSTRALIAN   DEPENDENCY
ADELIE LAND
Greenwich

Economic Associations

OPEC is the Organisation of Petroleum Exporting Countries.
LAIA is the Latin American Integration Association.
Venezuela and Ecuador are also members of LAIA.
OECD is the Organisation for Economic Co-operation and Development.
COMECON is the Council for Mutual Economic Assistance.

OPEC
LAIA
OECD
COMECON
• Colombo Plan Nations

Projection: *Hammer Equal Area*
COPYRIGHT. GEORGE PHILIP & SON. LTD.

1:35 000 000

400 0 400 800 1200 km

Oceans and Seas
ARCTIC OCEAN
PACIFIC OCEAN
ATLANTIC OCEAN
Gulf of Mexico
Caribbean Sea
Beaufort Sea
Bering Sea
Baffin Bay
Hudson Bay
James Bay
Gulf of Alaska
Gulf of California
Gulf of Campeche
Gulf of Honduras

Regions and Landmasses
Asia
Greenland
Iceland
Queen Elizabeth Islands
Axel Heiberg Land
Sverdrup Is.
Parry Is.
Ellesmere I.
Devon I.
Banks I.
Victoria I.
Prince of Wales
Somerset
Southampton I.
Baffin Island
Melville Pen.
Boothia Pen.
Ungava Peninsula
Labrador
Newfoundland
Nova Scotia
Alaska Pen.
Alaska Range
Brooks Range
Alexander Archipelago
Queen Charlotte Islands
Vancouver I.
Rocky Mountains
Coast Range
Cascade Range
Sierra Nevada
Great Basin
Colorado Plateau
Grand Canyon
Wasatch Mountains
Llano Estacado
Great Plains
Mexican Plateau
Western Sierra Madre
Eastern Sierra Madre
Isthmus of Tehuantepec
Yucatán Peninsula
Cuba
Hispaniola
Jamaica
Greater Antilles
Florida
Bahama Islands
Appalachian Mts.
Allegheny Mts.
Blue Ridge
Cumberland Plateau
Ozark Plateau
Laurentian Plateau
Andes

Rivers and Lakes
Yukon
Porcupine
Mackenzie
Great Bear L.
Great Slave L.
Athabasca
Reindeer L.
L. Winnipeg
L. Athabasca
Peace
Finlay
Fraser
Columbia
Snake
Great Salt Lake
Colorado
Gila
Rio Grande
N. Platte
S. Platte
Missouri
Arkansas
Red
Mississippi
Mississippi Delta
L. Superior
L. Michigan
L. Huron
L. Erie
L. Ontario
Niagara Falls
Nelson
Churchill
Saskatchewan
N. Saskatchewan
S. Saskatchewan
Back
Dubawnt
Eastmain
St. Lawrence
Hudson
L. Nicaragua
L. Maracaibo
Coco

Cities
Seattle
Portland
San Francisco
Los Angeles
Denver
Kansas City
St. Louis
Minneapolis
Chicago
Detroit
Toronto
Ottawa
Montréal
Québec
New York
Philadelphia
Washington
Boston
Memphis
Atlanta
Dallas
Houston
New Orleans
Winnipeg
Regina
Calgary
Edmonton
Vancouver
Havana
Guadalajara
México
Monterrey
Puebla
Santiago
Guatemala
Halifax
Saint John
St. John's
Julianehab
Godthab
Thule
Port-au-Prince

Mountain Peaks
Mt. McKinley 6194
Mt. St. Elias 5489
Mt. Logan 6050
Mt. Waddington 3994
Mt. Robson 3954
Mt. Rainier 4392
Mt. Shasta 4317
Mt. Whitney 4418
Mt. Elbert 4399
Blanca Pk. 4378
Mt. Washington 1917
Orizaba 5700
Popocatepetl 5452
Gunnbjörn Fjeld 3700
Mt. Forel 3360

Straits, Passages, Sounds
Bering Strait
Alaska Pen.
M'Clure Strait
Viscount Melville Sound
Lancaster Sound
Gulf of Boothia
Foxe Channel
Foxe Basin
Hudson Strait
Cumberland Sound
Frobisher Bay
Davis Strait
Denmark Strait
Juan de Fuca Strait
Queen Charlotte Sound
Florida Strait
Yucatán Strait
Belle Isle Strait
Gulf of St. Lawrence
Chesapeake Bay

Ocean Floor / Seascarps
Mendocino Seascarp
Murray Seascarp
Clarion Fracture Zone
Cayman Trough
Yucatán Basin
Colombian Basin
Guatemala Trench
Panama Canal

Tropic of Cancer
Arctic Circle

Revilla Gigedo Is.
Bermuda

Projection: Bonne
West from Greenwich

Elevation scale (m)
4000
2000
1000
400
200
0
0
200
2000
4000
6000
8000

1 : 35 000 000

400   0   400   800   1200 km

C	CONNECTICUT
D.	DELAWARE
D.C.	DISTRICT OF COLUMBIA
M.	MARYLAND
MASS.	MASSACHUSETTS

N.H.	NEW HAMPSHIRE
N.J.	NEW JERSEY
R.I.	RHODE ISLAND
VER.	VERMONT
SPM	ST. PIERRE ET MIQUELON

Projection: *Bonne*

West from Greenwich

1:32 000 000

400   0   400   800   1200 km

LAND USE

- Arable land
- Arable land with grazing
- Market gardening, fruit trees, bushes, and orchard land
- Permanent pasture
- Woods and forests
- Woods and forests with grazing land
- Rough grazing
- Non-productive land

LIVESTOCK

- Beef cattle
- Sheep
- Dairy cattle

CROPS

- Bananas
- Citrus fruits
- Coffee
- Cotton
- Fruit
- Groundnuts
- Maize
- Olives
- Rice
- Sisal
- Soybeans
- Sugar cane
- Tobacco
- Vegetables
- Wheat
- Principal fishing areas

MINERALS

- Asbestos
- Bauxite
- Copper
- Gold
- Iron ore
- Lead
- Lead and Zinc
- Mica
- Phosphate
- Silver
- Uranium
- Zinc

Sb Antimony
Co Cobalt
Mg Magnesium
Hg Mercury
Mo Molybdenum
Ni Nickel
Ti Titanium

POWER

- Coalfields
- Gasfields
- Oilfields
- HEP

LAND USE
(million hectares)

- Arable land and permanent crops 271.5
- Permanent pasture 346.7
- Other land 803.9
- Woods and forests 718.3

Total land area 2 140.5 million hectares

Arctic Circle

Prudhoe Bay
Mayo
Mo
Pine Point
Flin Flon
Edmonton
Vancouver
Mo
Seattle
Winnipeg
Shoshone
Salt Lake City
Bingham
San Francisco
Hg
Mo
St. Louis
Chicago
Detroit
New York
Washington
Los Angeles
San Diego
Dallas
Hurricane Creek
New Orleans
Houston
San Antonio
Mg
Monterrey
Sb
Veracruz
Guadalajara
Mexico
Chiapas Tabasco
Havana
Mesabi
Timmins
Co
Ni
Toronto
Niagara
Montréal
Ti
Schefferville
Wabush
Ti

Tropic of Cancer

West from Greenwich

Projection: Polyconic

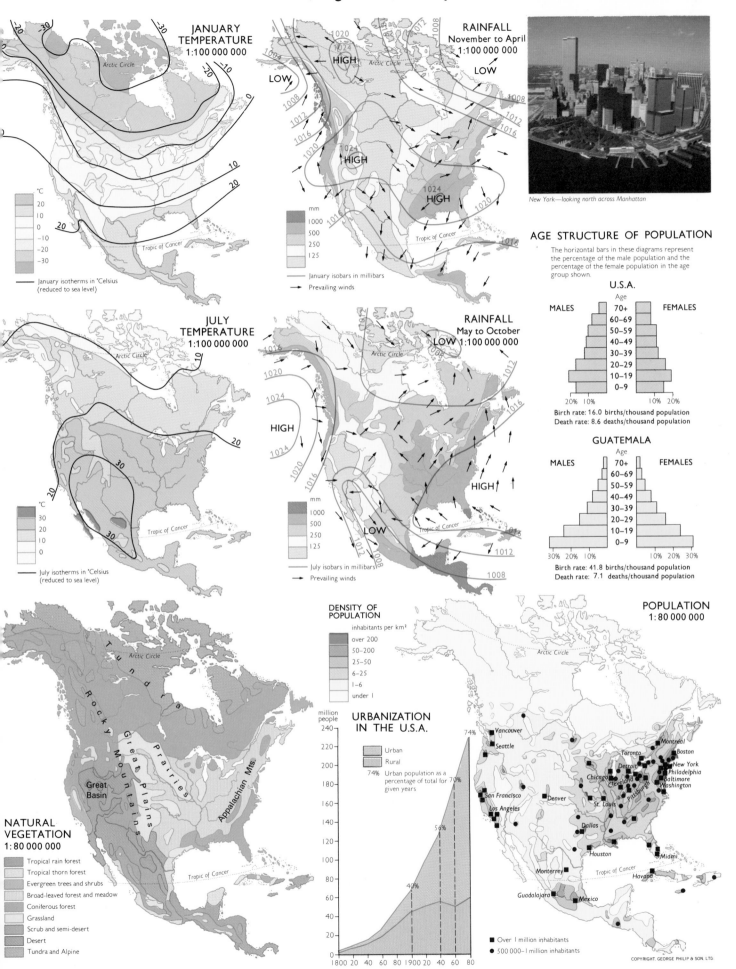

JANUARY TEMPERATURE
1:100 000 000

Arctic Circle

Tropic of Cancer

°C
20
10
0
-10
-20
-30

— January isotherms in °Celsius
(reduced to sea level)

RAINFALL
November to April
1:100 000 000

HIGH
LOW
LOW
HIGH
HIGH

Arctic Circle

Tropic of Cancer

mm
1000
500
250
125

— January isobars in millibars
→ Prevailing winds

New York—looking north across Manhattan

AGE STRUCTURE OF POPULATION

The horizontal bars in these diagrams represent
the percentage of the male population and the
percentage of the female population in the age
group shown.

U.S.A.

Age
MALES   70+   FEMALES
60–69
50–59
40–49
30–39
20–29
10–19
0–9

20% 10%   10% 20%

Birth rate: 16.0 births/thousand population
Death rate: 8.6 deaths/thousand population

GUATEMALA

Age
MALES   70+   FEMALES
60–69
50–59
40–49
30–39
20–29
10–19
0–9

30% 20% 10%   10% 20% 30%

Birth rate: 41.8 births/thousand population
Death rate: 7.1 deaths/thousand population

JULY TEMPERATURE
1:100 000 000

Arctic Circle

HIGH
HIGH

Tropic of Cancer

°C
30
20
10
0

— July isotherms in °Celsius
(reduced to sea level)

RAINFALL
May to October
LOW 1:100 000 000

HIGH
LOW
HIGH

Arctic Circle

Tropic of Cancer

mm
1000
500
250
125

— July isobars in millibars
→ Prevailing winds

NATURAL VEGETATION
1:80 000 000

Tundra
Rocky Mountains
Great Plains
Prairies
Great Basin
Appalachian Mts.

Arctic Circle

Tropic of Cancer

Tropical rain forest
Tropical thorn forest
Evergreen trees and shrubs
Broad-leaved forest and meadow
Coniferous forest
Grassland
Scrub and semi-desert
Desert
Tundra and Alpine

DENSITY OF POPULATION

inhabitants per km²
over 200
50–200
25–50
6–25
1–6
under 1

URBANIZATION IN THE U.S.A.

million people

Urban
Rural

74% Urban population as a
percentage of total for
given years

240
220
200
180
160
140
120
100
80
60
40
20

74%
70%
56%
40%

1800 20 40 60 80 1900 20 40 60 80

POPULATION
1:80 000 000

Arctic Circle

Vancouver
Seattle
Montreal
Toronto
Boston
Detroit
New York
Chicago
Cleveland
Philadelphia
Baltimore
Washington
Pittsburgh
San Francisco
Denver
St. Louis
Los Angeles
Dallas
Houston
Miami
Monterrey
Havana
Guadalajara
Mexico

Tropic of Cancer

■ Over 1 million inhabitants
● 500 000–1 million inhabitants

COPYRIGHT. GEORGE PHILIP & SON. LTD.

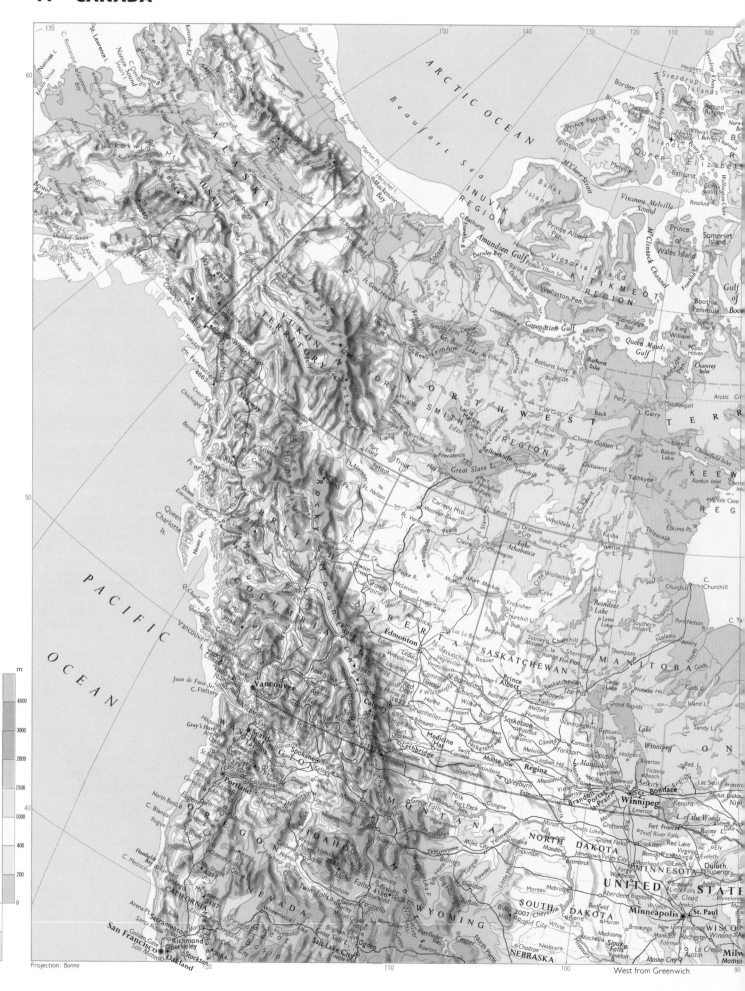

Projection: Bonne

West from Greenwich

NORTH AMERICA : GEOLOGY
1:50 000 000

RECENT	Quaternary
TERTIARY	Cainozoic
SECONDARY	Mesozoic
	Cretaceous
	Triassic
PRIMARY	Palaeozoic
	Permian
	Carboniferous
	Devonian
	Lower Palaeozoic
ANCIENT	Pre-Cambrian
IGNEOUS	Volcanic
	Intrusive
	Permanent Ice Cap

GREENLAND

Arctic Circle

Canadian Shield

Rocky Mountains

Great Plains

Appalachians

Tropic of Cancer

Baffin Bay

Melville Bay

Hudson Strait

Foxe Basin

Foxe Channel

Cumberland Peninsula

Cumberland Sd.

Frobisher Bay

Resolution I.

Ungava Bay

James Bay

Hudson Bay

NEW

QUEBEC

LABRADOR

NEWFOUNDLAND

St. John's

ATLANTIC OCEAN

St. Lawrence (St-Laurent)

Gulf of St. Lawrence

PR. EDWARD I.

NOVA SCOTIA

NEW BRUNSWICK

Cape Breton I.

ST. PIERRE & MIQUELON (Fr.)

MONTRÉAL

Québec

Ottawa

Hull

Toronto

Halifax

Saint John

Fredericton

Boston

NEW HAMPSHIRE

MAINE

VERMONT

MASS.

CONN.

R.I.

NEW YORK

Buffalo

Rochester

Syracuse

Albany

Springfield

Providence

Hartford

DETROIT

Windsor

Cleveland

Toledo

Lake Erie

Lake Ontario

Lake Huron

Georgian Bay

Sudbury

North Bay

Grand Rapids

London

Hamilton

Niagara Falls

Sault Ste. Marie

Timmins

Cochrane

Sherbrooke

Chicoutimi

Trois-Rivières

Atlantic Ocean

COPYRIGHT. GEORGE PHILIP & SON. LTD.

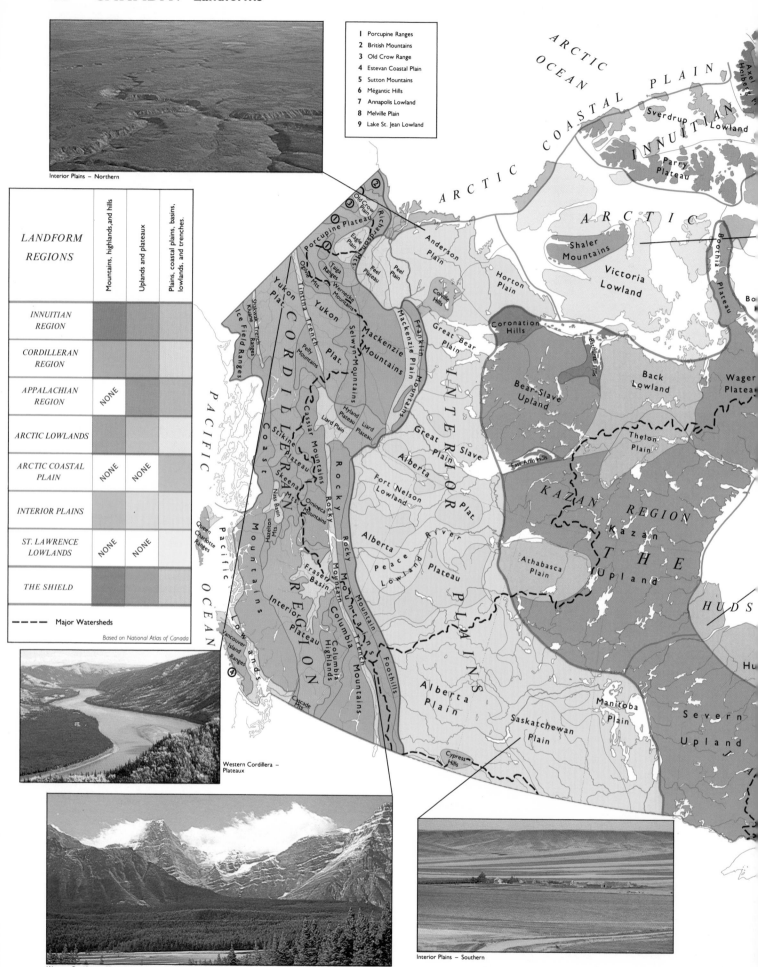

Interior Plains – Northern

	1	Porcupine Ranges
	2	British Mountains
	3	Old Crow Range
	4	Estevan Coastal Plain
	5	Sutton Mountains
	6	Mégantic Hills
	7	Annapolis Lowland
	8	Melville Plain
	9	Lake St. Jean Lowland

LANDFORM REGIONS	Mountains, highlands, and hills	Uplands and plateaux	Plains, coastal plains, basins, lowlands, and trenches
INNUITIAN REGION			
CORDILLERAN REGION			
APPALACHIAN REGION	NONE		
ARCTIC LOWLANDS			
ARCTIC COASTAL PLAIN	NONE	NONE	
INTERIOR PLAINS			
ST. LAWRENCE LOWLANDS	NONE	NONE	
THE SHIELD			

- - - - Major Watersheds

Based on National Atlas of Canada

Western Cordillera – Plateaux

Western Cordillera – Mountains

Projection: Bonne

Interior Plains – Southern

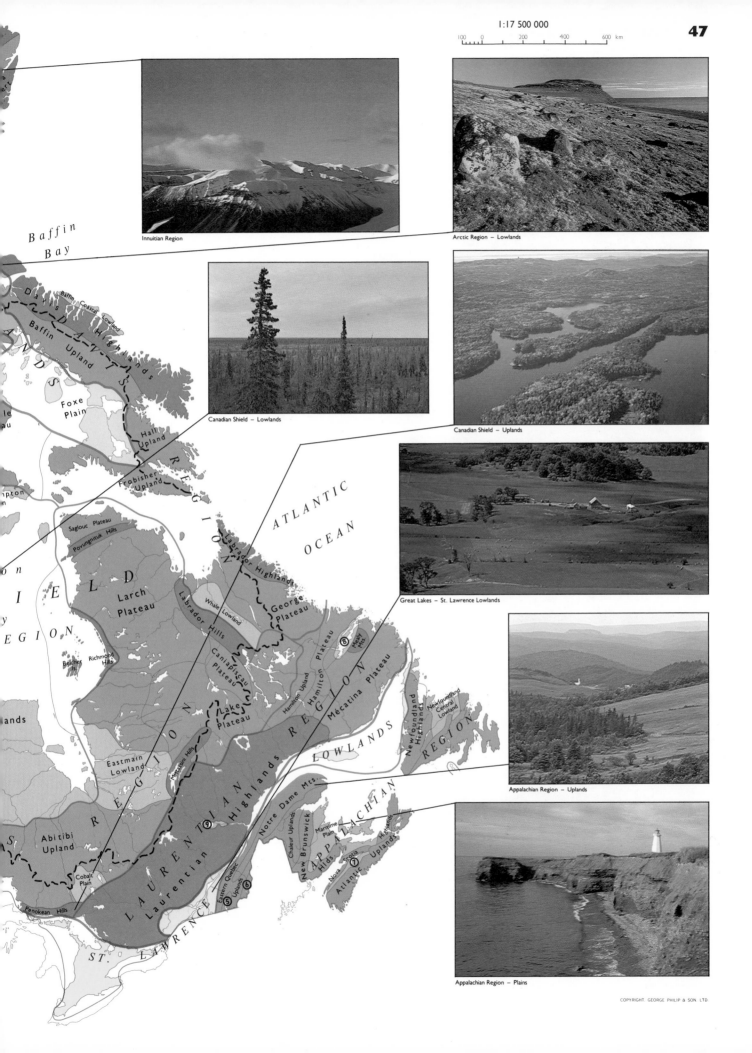

1:17 500 000

Innuitian Region

Arctic Region – Lowlands

Canadian Shield – Lowlands

Canadian Shield – Uplands

Great Lakes – St. Lawrence Lowlands

Appalachian Region – Uplands

Appalachian Region – Plains

1:30 000 000

200 0 200 400 600 800 1000 km

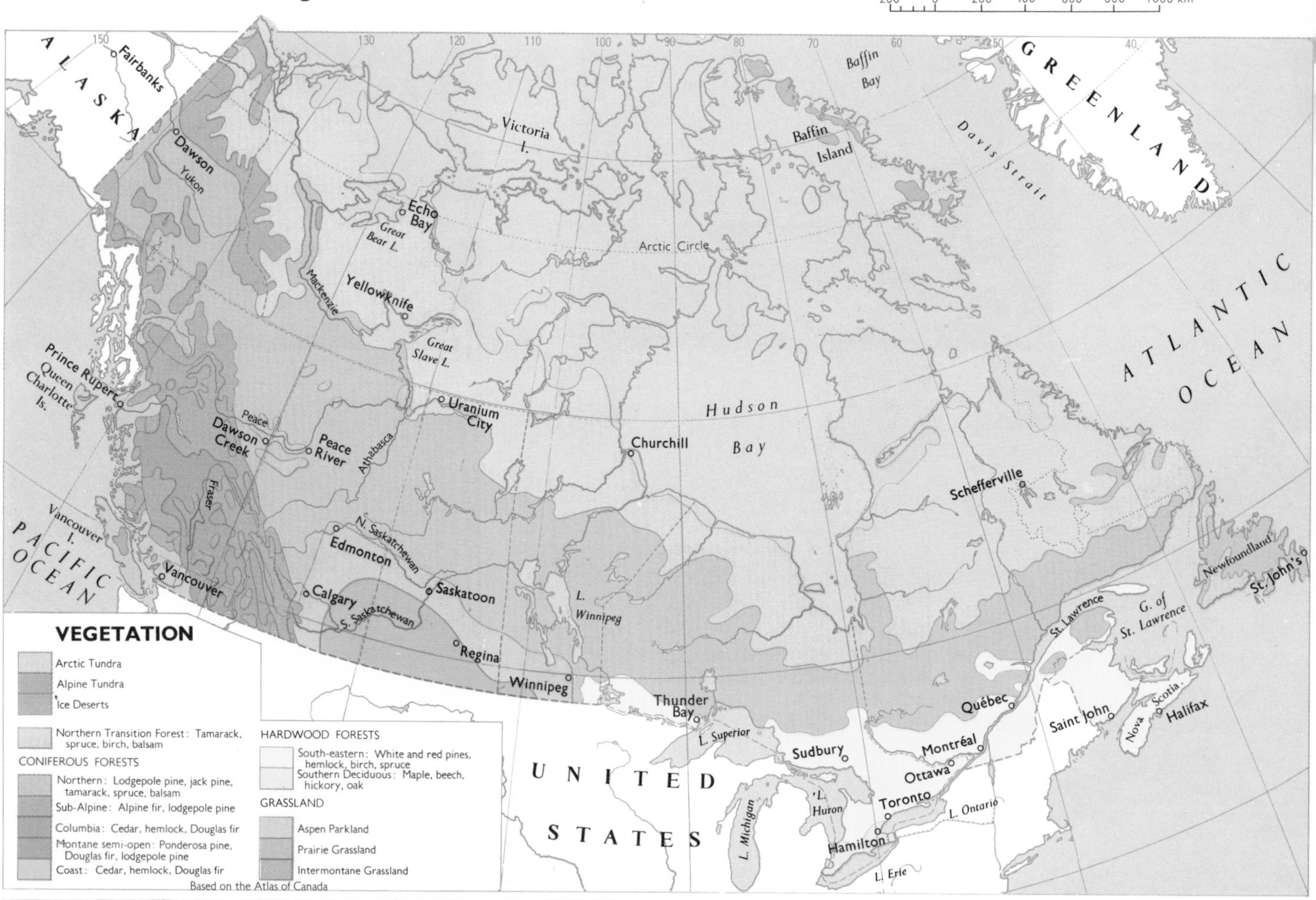

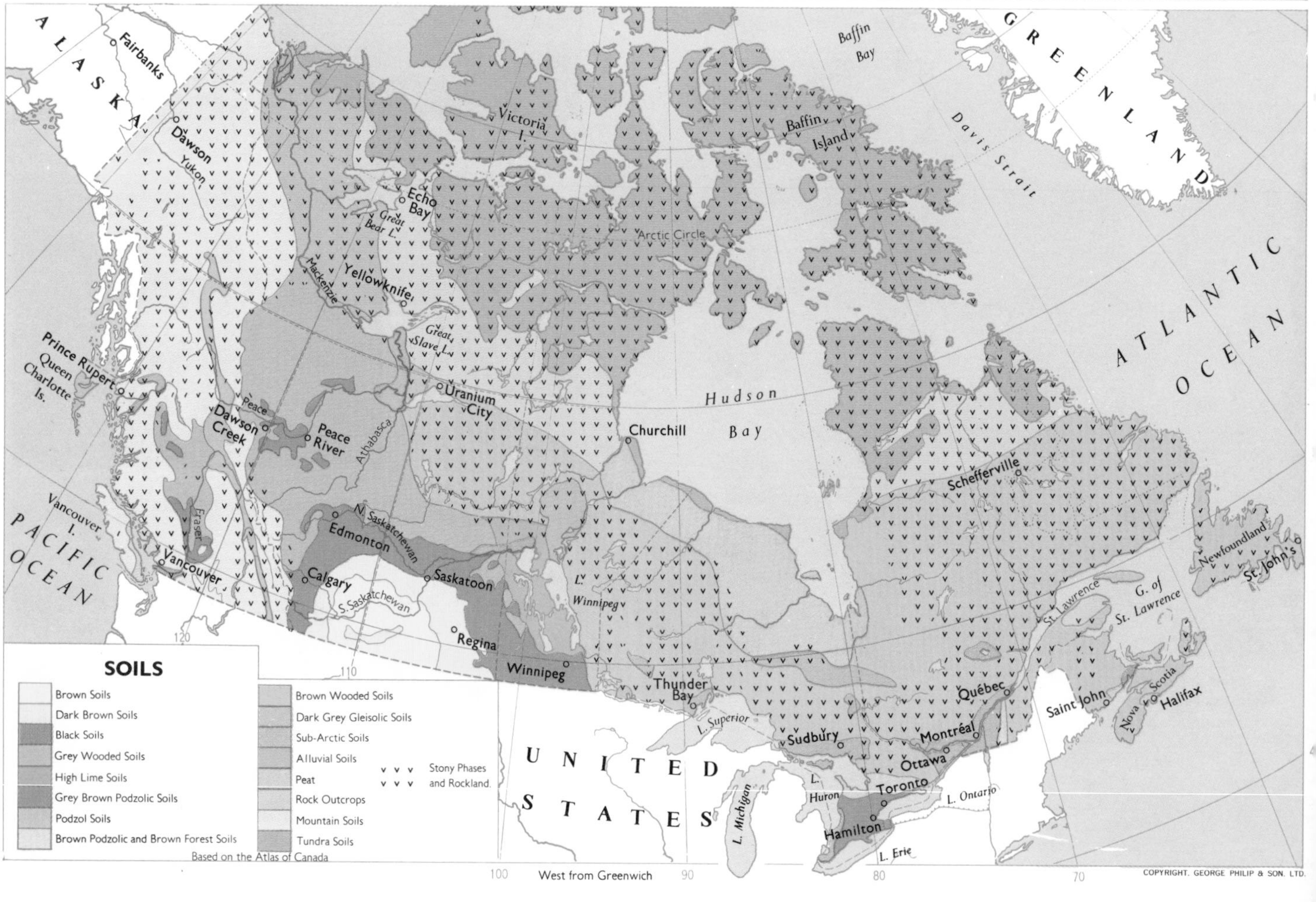

VEGETATION
Arctic Tundra
Alpine Tundra
Ice Deserts
Northern Transition Forest: Tamarack, spruce, birch, balsam
CONIFEROUS FORESTS
Northern: Lodgepole pine, jack pine, tamarack, spruce, balsam
Sub-Alpine: Alpine fir, lodgepole pine
Columbia: Cedar, hemlock, Douglas fir
Montane semi-open: Ponderosa pine, Douglas fir, lodgepole pine
Coast: Cedar, hemlock, Douglas fir
HARDWOOD FORESTS
South-eastern: White and red pines, hemlock, birch, spruce
Southern Deciduous: Maple, beech, hickory, oak
GRASSLAND
Aspen Parkland
Prairie Grassland
Intermontane Grassland
Based on the Atlas of Canada
ALASKA
GREENLAND
UNITED STATES
PACIFIC OCEAN
ATLANTIC OCEAN
Hudson Bay
Baffin Bay
Davis Strait
Baffin Island
Victoria I.
Arctic Circle
Fairbanks
Dawson
Yukon
Echo Bay
Great Bear L.
Mackenzie
Yellowknife
Great Slave L.
Uranium City
Prince Rupert
Queen Charlotte Is.
Peace
Dawson Creek
Peace River
Athabasca
Fraser
Vancouver I.
Vancouver
N. Saskatchewan
Edmonton
Calgary
S. Saskatchewan
Saskatoon
Regina
L. Winnipeg
Winnipeg
Churchill
Schefferville
Newfoundland
St. John's
St. Lawrence
G. of St. Lawrence
Thunder Bay
L. Superior
Sudbury
Québec
Montréal
Ottawa
Saint John
Nova Scotia
Halifax
L. Michigan
L. Huron
Toronto
L. Ontario
Hamilton
L. Erie

SOILS
Brown Soils
Dark Brown Soils
Black Soils
Grey Wooded Soils
High Lime Soils
Grey Brown Podzolic Soils
Podzol Soils
Brown Podzolic and Brown Forest Soils
Brown Wooded Soils
Dark Grey Gleisolic Soils
Sub-Arctic Soils
Alluvial Soils
Peat
Rock Outcrops
Mountain Soils
Tundra Soils
Stony Phases and Rockland
Based on the Atlas of Canada
ALASKA
GREENLAND
UNITED STATES
PACIFIC OCEAN
ATLANTIC OCEAN
Hudson Bay
Baffin Bay
Davis Strait
Baffin Island
Victoria I.
Arctic Circle
Fairbanks
Dawson
Yukon
Echo Bay
Great Bear L.
Mackenzie
Yellowknife
Great Slave L.
Uranium City
Prince Rupert
Queen Charlotte Is.
Peace
Dawson Creek
Peace River
Athabasca
Fraser
Vancouver I.
Vancouver
N. Saskatchewan
Edmonton
Calgary
S. Saskatchewan
Saskatoon
Regina
L. Winnipeg
Winnipeg
Churchill
Schefferville
Newfoundland
St. John's
St. Lawrence
G. of St. Lawrence
Thunder Bay
L. Superior
Sudbury
Québec
Montréal
Ottawa
Saint John
Nova Scotia
Halifax
L. Michigan
L. Huron
Toronto
L. Ontario
Hamilton
L. Erie
West from Greenwich

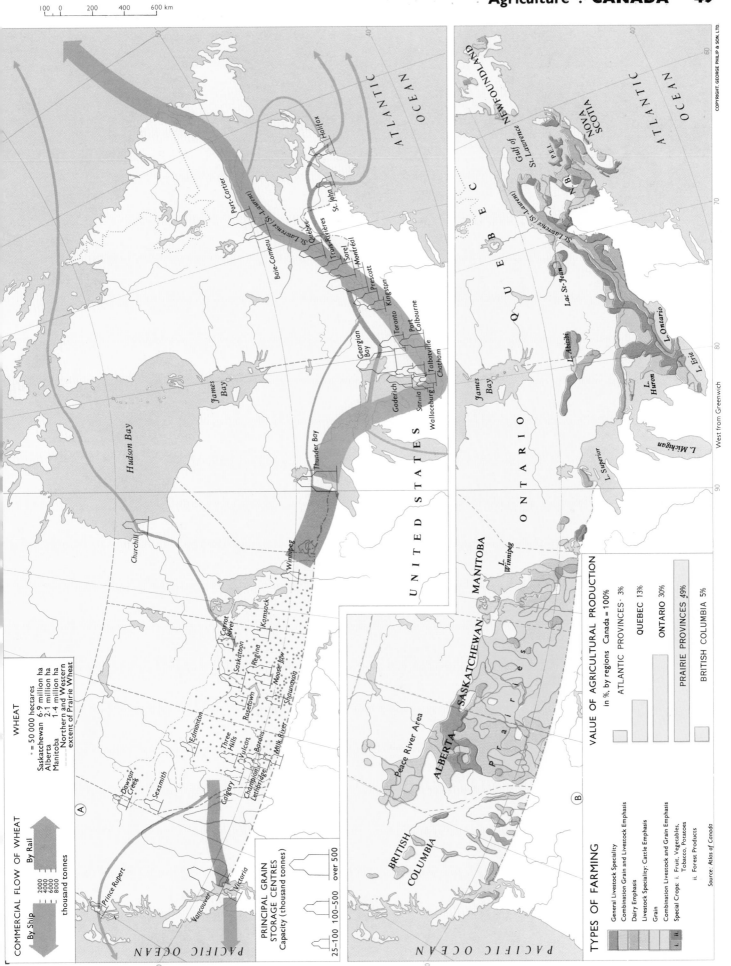

COPYRIGHT. GEORGE PHILIP & SON, LTD.

1:22 500 000

100 0   200   400   600 km

ATLANTIC OCEAN

ATLANTIC OCEAN

West from Greenwich

Halifax

Port-Cartier

St. Laurent (S.)

Baie-Comeau

Québec

Trois-Rivières

Sorel

Montréal

St. John

Prescott

Kingston

Toronto

Port Colbourne

Georgian Bay

Talbotville

Chatham

Goderich

Sarnia

Wallaceburg

Thunder Bay

Winnipeg

James Bay

Hudson Bay

Churchill

UNITED STATES

James Bay

L. Winnipeg

ONTARIO

QUEBEC

NEWFOUNDLAND

NOVA SCOTIA

N.B.

P.E.I.

Gulf of St. Lawrence

St. Lawrence (S.)

Lac St-Jean

L. Abitibi

L. Ontario

L. Erie

L. Huron

L. Michigan

L. Superior

MANITOBA

SASKATCHEWAN

ALBERTA

BRITISH COLUMBIA

Peace River Area

P r a i r i e s

Carrot River

Kamsack

Saskatoon

Regina

Moose Jaw

Rosetown

Shaunavon

Edmonton

Three Hills

Vulcan

Barons

Milk River

Champion

Lethbridge

Calgary

Dawson Creek

Sexsmith

Prince Rupert

Vancouver

Victoria

PACIFIC OCEAN

PACIFIC OCEAN

WHEAT

* = 50 000 hectares

Saskatchewan 6.9 million ha
Alberta   2.1 million ha
Manitoba   1.4 million ha
------ Northern and Western
extent of Prairie Wheat

COMMERCIAL FLOW OF WHEAT

By Rail

By Ship

thousand tonnes

2000
4000
6000
8000

Ⓐ

PRINCIPAL GRAIN STORAGE CENTRES

Capacity (thousand tonnes)

25–100   100–500   over 500

Ⓑ

VALUE OF AGRICULTURAL PRODUCTION

in %, by regions   Canada = 100%

ATLANTIC PROVINCES: 3%

QUEBEC 13%

ONTARIO 30%

PRAIRIE PROVINCES 49%

BRITISH COLUMBIA 5%

TYPES OF FARMING

General Livestock Speciality

Combination Grain and Livestock Emphasis

Dairy Emphasis

Livestock Speciality: Cattle Emphasis

Grain

Combination Livestock and Grain Emphasis

Special Crops: i. Fruit, Vegetables,
Tobacco, Potatoes
ii. Forest Products

i. ii.

Source: Atlas of Canada

CANADA : Forestry and Timber Industries

1:22 000 000

100 0 200 400 600 800 km

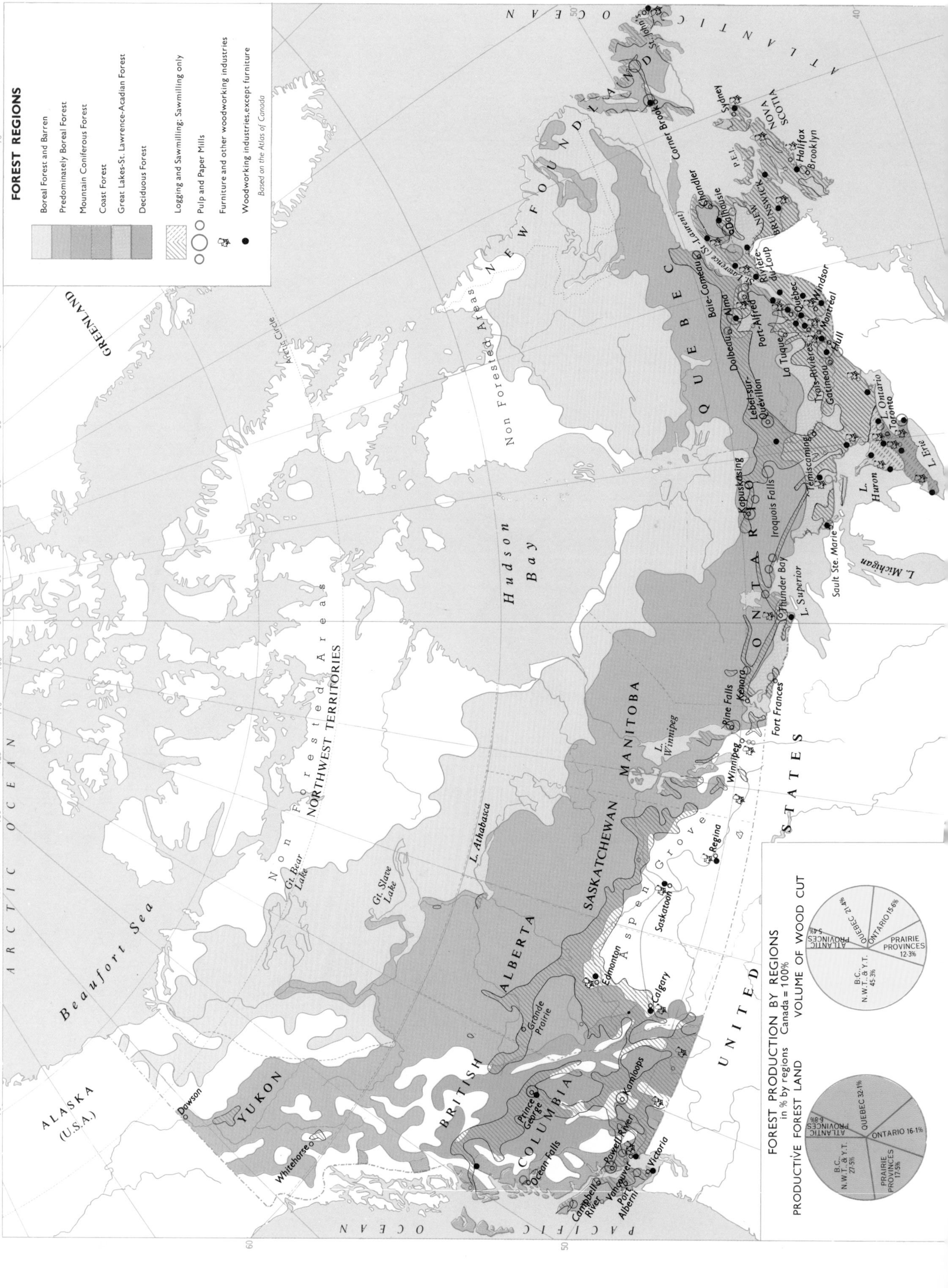

FOREST REGIONS
Boreal Forest and Barren
Predominately Boreal Forest
Mountain Coniferous Forest
Coast Forest
Great Lakes-St. Lawrence-Acadian Forest
Deciduous Forest
Logging and Sawmilling; Sawmilling only
Pulp and Paper Mills
Furniture and other woodworking industries
Woodworking industries, except furniture
Based on the Atlas of Canada
FOREST PRODUCTION BY REGIONS
in % by regions Canada = 100%
PRODUCTIVE FOREST LAND
QUEBEC 32·1%
ONTARIO 16·1%
PRAIRIE PROVINCES 17·5%
B.C. N.W.T. & Y.T. 27·5%
ATLANTIC PROVINCES 6·8%
VOLUME OF WOOD CUT
QUEBEC 21·4%
ONTARIO 15·6%
PRAIRIE PROVINCES 12·3%
B.C. N.W.T. & Y.T. 45·3%
ATLANTIC PROVINCES 5·4%
ARCTIC OCEAN
Beaufort Sea
ATLANTIC OCEAN
PACIFIC OCEAN
Hudson Bay
GREENLAND
ALASKA (U.S.A.)
UNITED STATES
YUKON
NORTHWEST TERRITORIES
BRITISH COLUMBIA
ALBERTA
SASKATCHEWAN
MANITOBA
ONTARIO
QUEBEC
NEWFOUNDLAND
NEW BRUNSWICK
NOVA SCOTIA
P.E.I.
Non Forested Areas
Aspen Grove
Arctic Circle
Gt. Bear Lake
Gt. Slave Lake
L. Athabasca
L. Winnipeg
L. Superior
L. Michigan
L. Huron
L. Erie
L. Ontario
St. Lawrence (St-Laurent)
Dawson
Whitehorse
Prince George
Kamloops
Ocean Falls
Powell River
Campbell River
Vancouver
Port Alberni
Victoria
Grande Prairie
Edmonton
Calgary
Saskatoon
Regina
Winnipeg
Pine Falls
Kenora
Fort Frances
Thunder Bay
Sault Ste. Marie
Iroquois Falls
Kapuskasing
Temiscaming
Toronto
Hull
Gatineau
Montreal
Trois-Rivières
La Tuque
Quebec
Windsor
Lebel-sur-Quevillon
Dolbeau
Alma
Port-Alfred
Baie-Comeau
Rivière-du-Loup
Dalhousie
Chandler
Halifax
Brooklyn
Sydney
Corner Brook
St. John's

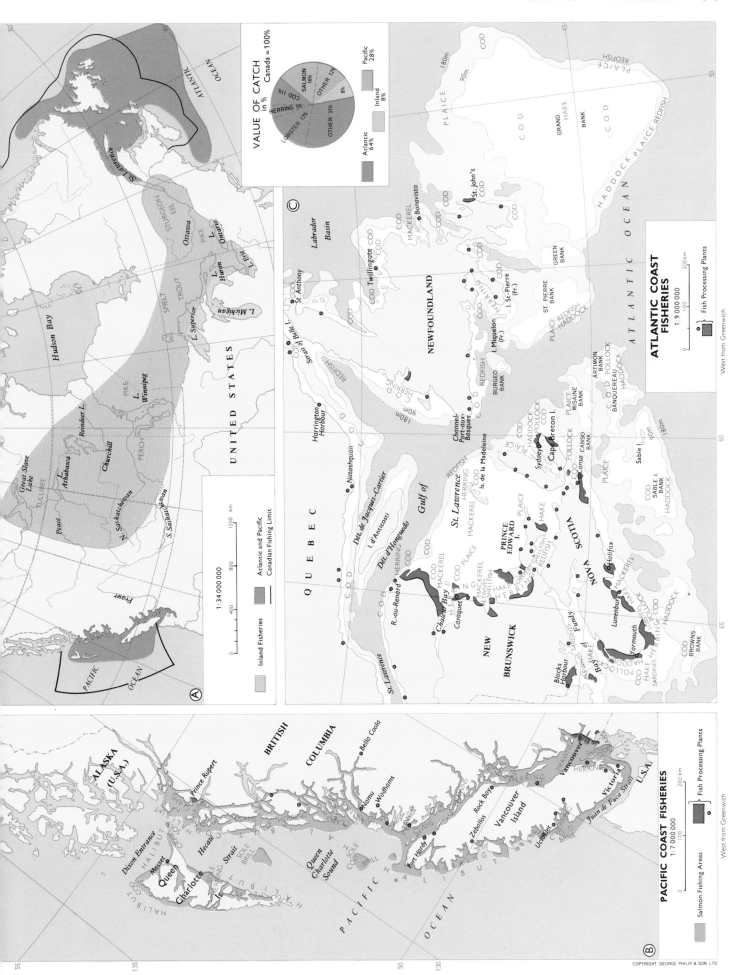

VALUE OF CATCH
in % Canada = 100%

Pacific 28%
Inland 8%
Atlantic 64%

SALMON 16%
OTHER 12%
COD 11%
HERRING 5%
LOBSTER 17%
OTHER 31%

ATLANTIC COAST FISHERIES
1:9 000 000
0   200 km
● Fish Processing Plants
West from Greenwich

1:34 000 000
0   400   800   1200 km
Inland Fisheries
Atlantic and Pacific
Canadian Fishing Limit

PACIFIC COAST FISHERIES
1:7 000 000
0   200 km
■ Salmon Fishing Areas
■ ● Fish Processing Plants
West from Greenwich

COPYRIGHT GEORGE PHILIP & SON LTD

1 : 22 000 000

100 0 200 400 600 800 km

Legend:

▷ Asbestos		Date of Discovery		*1903*
■ Salt		Date of First Production		1913
◁ Gypsum		Date of Expansion		**1910**
◆ Fluorine				
+ Sulphur from Natural or Smelter Gas				
◖ Sodium Sulphate				
◗ Silica				
◨ Potash				

■ Iron Ore	M Molybdenum		
U Uranium	C Columbium		
+ Gold	Mg Magnesium		
◆ Silver	Ta Tantalum		
◀ Zinc	Sn Tin		
◖ Lead			
◨ Copper			
◗ Nickel			
◔ Platinum			
T Cobalt			
◗ Ilmenite			

Place names (selected):

NEWFOUNDLAND
Belle-Verte
Springdale
Buchans 1945
Gull Lake
Daniel's Harbour 1975
Flat Bay
Little Bay
Baie-Verte 1972

NOVA SCOTIA
Cape Breton
Narrows
Louisbourg
Pugwash
East
Sn Kemptville 1983
Windsor
P.E.I.
NEW BRUNSWICK
Murdochville 1955
Bathurst 1910-15
Lac Allard
Asbestos 1878
Thetford 1880
Stratford

QUEBEC
Schefferville 1954
Labrador City 1962
Wabush
Fermont
Gagnon 1961
Chibougamau 1958
Chapais 1964
Matagami
Amos
Val-d'Or 1934
Noranda 1927
Quebec
Montréal 1880
Ottawa OKA
Haley Mg

LABRADOR

ONTARIO
Detour Lake
Timmins 1911
Kirkland 1913 Lake
Sudbury 1883
Elliot Lake
Cobalt 1903
Marmora
L. Huron
Toronto
L. Ontario
Sarnia
Windsor
Manitouwadge
Hemlo 1980
Wawa
Batchawana
Steep Rock 1944 1960
Red Lake 1925
Werner Lake
Thierry 1976

MANITOBA
Lynn Lake 1954
Thompson 1961
Snow Lake 1949
Flin Flon 1930-40
Gypsumville
Winnipeg
Bernic Lake Ta

SASKATCHEWAN
Uranium City - Eldorado 1955
Key Lake 1975
La Ronge
Saskatoon 1963
Esterhazy 1962
Regina
Belle-Plaine 1964
Chaplin
Ormiston
Estevan
Gladmar

NORTHWEST TERRITORIES
Little Cornwallis Island 1982
Nanisivik
Melville Sound
Echo Bay Camsell River 1930-60
Yellowknife
Pine Point 1964
Zama
Rainbow Lake
Arctic Circle

ALBERTA
Edmonton
Fort McMurray
Fort Nelson 1974
Fort St. John
Lindbergh
Metiskow
Calgary
Turner Valley

BRITISH COLUMBIA
Afton 1978
Kimberley
Trail - Renoe
Peachland
Benson Lake
Vancouver I.
Vancouver
Tasu Sound
Bralorne
Endako
Babine Lake
Kitsault Lake
Stewart 1967

YUKON
1896 Gold Rush
Dawson
Keno Hill 1921
Faro 1969
Whitehorse-Carcross
Cassiar

ALASKA
U.S.A.

Asbestos Hill 1970

Hudson Bay

James Bay

St. Laurent (St. Laurent)

UNITED STATES

VALUE OF PRODUCTION
in %, by region   Canada = 100%

	Metals	Industrial Minerals
ATLANTIC PROVINCES	13%	
QUEBEC	18%	
ONTARIO	28%	
PRAIRIE PROVINCES	20%	
BRITISH COLUMBIA	14%	
YUKON AND N.W.T.	7%	

1:22 000 000

100 0 200 400 600 800 km

▲ Oilfield
▲ Oil Refinery
□ Oil Pipeline
Interprovincial, Edmonton–Duluth completed 1950
Duluth–Sarnia completed 1953
Duluth–Sarnia via Chicago completed 1975
Sarnia–Toronto completed 1957
Toronto–Montreal completed 1976
Trans-Mountain Pipeline completed 1953
Petroleum Products Pipeline
Actual or Potential Oil or Gasfields
Natural Gas
Natural Gas Pipeline
Westcoast Transmission Pipeline completed 195,
Trans-Canada Pipeline. North of L. Superior completed 1958
Trans-Canada Pipeline, South of L. Superior & L. Huron completed 1975
Coalfield

■ Thermal Power Plant 50MW and over
□ Thermal Power Plant under 50MW
● Hydro-Electric Power Plant
○ Hydro-Electric Power Plant under construction
⊕ Nuclear Power Plant

Value of Fuel Production
Volume of Electricity Production
in % by regions   Canada =100%

ATLANTIC PROVINCES
QUEBEC
ONTARIO
PRAIRIE PROVINCES
BRITISH COLUMBIA AND NORTHWEST TERRITORIES

90
80
70
60
50
40
30
20
10

Commercial 23%
Losses and for Unaccounted 9%
Pulp and Paper Industry 10%
Mineral Industry 6%
Other Industries 23%
Residential and Farm 29%

PRINCIPAL USES
OF ELECTRIC ENERGY
IN CANADA

ARCTIC OCEAN

Queen Elizabeth Islands
Ellesmere I.
Devon I.
Banks
Melville I.
Prince of Wales I.
Somerset I.
Boothia Pen.
Victoria I.
Baffin Island
Southampton I.
Melville Pen.
Frobisher Bay

Beaufort Sea
Prudhoe Bay
Atkinson Pt.
Inuvik
Norman Wells
Mackenzie
Great Bear Lake
Yellowknife
Great Slave L.

ALASKA (U.S.A.)
Arctic Circle

YUKON
Dawson
Carmacks
Whitehorse
Watson Lake
Fort Nelson
Pointed Mountain

NORTHWEST TERRITORIES

Hudson Bay
Hudson Strait
James Bay

QUEBEC
La Grande Complex
Churchill Falls
Cat Arm Project
Anticosti
St. Lawrence
NEWFOUNDLAND
St. John's
Cape Breton I.
Sydney
Venture
NOVA SCOTIA
Halifax
P.E.I.
NEW BRUNSWICK
Moncton
Portland

Montréal
Beauharnois
Trois-Rivières
Québec
Ottawa
L. Ontario
Toronto
L. Erie
Sarnia
Douglas Point
L. Huron
Michipicoten
Thunder Bay
Sault-Ste-Marie
L. Superior
Nipigon
Chicago
Duluth
St. Paul
Minneapolis

ONTARIO
TRANS–CANADA
INTER-PROVINCIAL

MANITOBA
Winnipeg
L. Winnipeg
Pine Falls
Island Falls
Brandon
Estevan

SASKATCHEWAN
Prince Albert
Saskatoon
Kamsack
Regina
Moose Jaw
Medicine Hat

ALBERTA
L. Athabasca
Athabasca Tar Sands
Fort McMurray
Rainbow Lake
Zama
Peace River
Grande Prairie
Dawson Creek
Bonnyville
Lloydminster
Wainwright
Edmonton
Calgary
Turner Valley

BRITISH COLUMBIA
Prince Rupert
Kitimat
Kamloops
Trail
Columbia
Vancouver
Victoria

WESTCOAST TRANSMISSION
TRANS-MOUNTAIN

UNITED STATES
West from Greenwich

PACIFIC OCEAN
ATLANTIC OCEAN

ELECTRICITY TRANSMISSION LINES
1:78 000 000

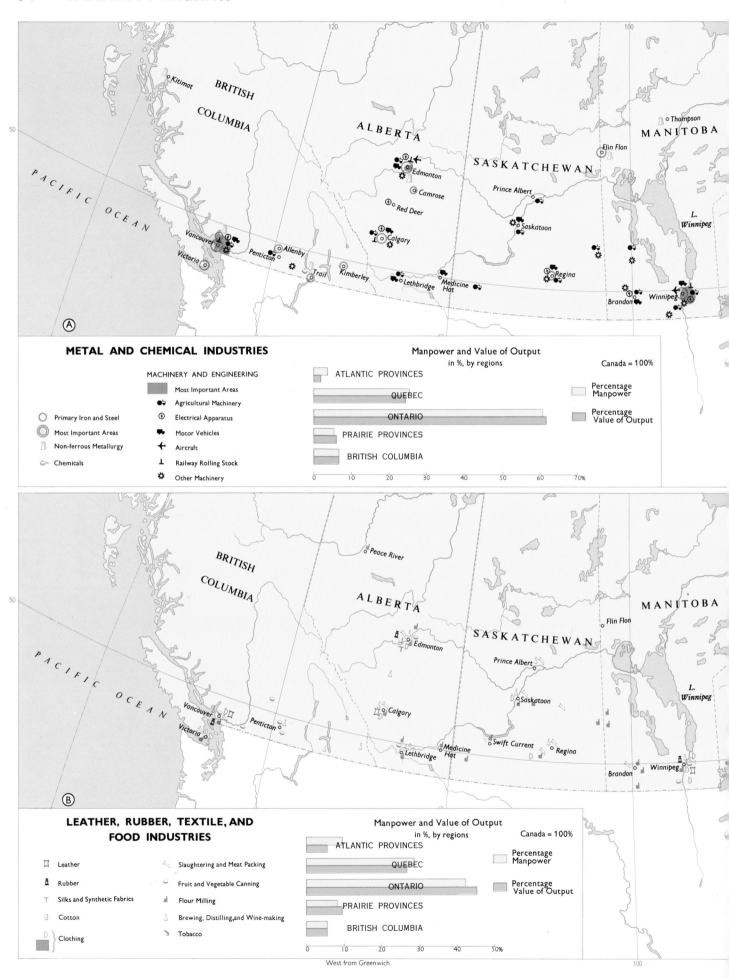

METAL AND CHEMICAL INDUSTRIES

Manpower and Value of Output
in %, by regions

Canada = 100%

MACHINERY AND ENGINEERING

- Most Important Areas
- Agricultural Machinery
- Electrical Apparatus
- Motor Vehicles
- Aircraft
- Railway Rolling Stock
- Other Machinery

- ◯ Primary Iron and Steel
- ◎ Most Important Areas
- Non-ferrous Metallurgy
- Chemicals

ATLANTIC PROVINCES
QUEBEC
ONTARIO
PRAIRIE PROVINCES
BRITISH COLUMBIA

Percentage Manpower

Percentage Value of Output

0 10 20 30 40 50 60 70%

LEATHER, RUBBER, TEXTILE, AND FOOD INDUSTRIES

Manpower and Value of Output
in %, by regions

Canada = 100%

- Leather
- Rubber
- Silks and Synthetic Fabrics
- Cotton
- Clothing

- Slaughtering and Meat Packing
- Fruit and Vegetable Canning
- Flour Milling
- Brewing, Distilling, and Wine-making
- Tobacco

ATLANTIC PROVINCES
QUEBEC
ONTARIO
PRAIRIE PROVINCES
BRITISH COLUMBIA

Percentage Manpower

Percentage Value of Output

0 10 20 30 40 50%

West from Greenwich

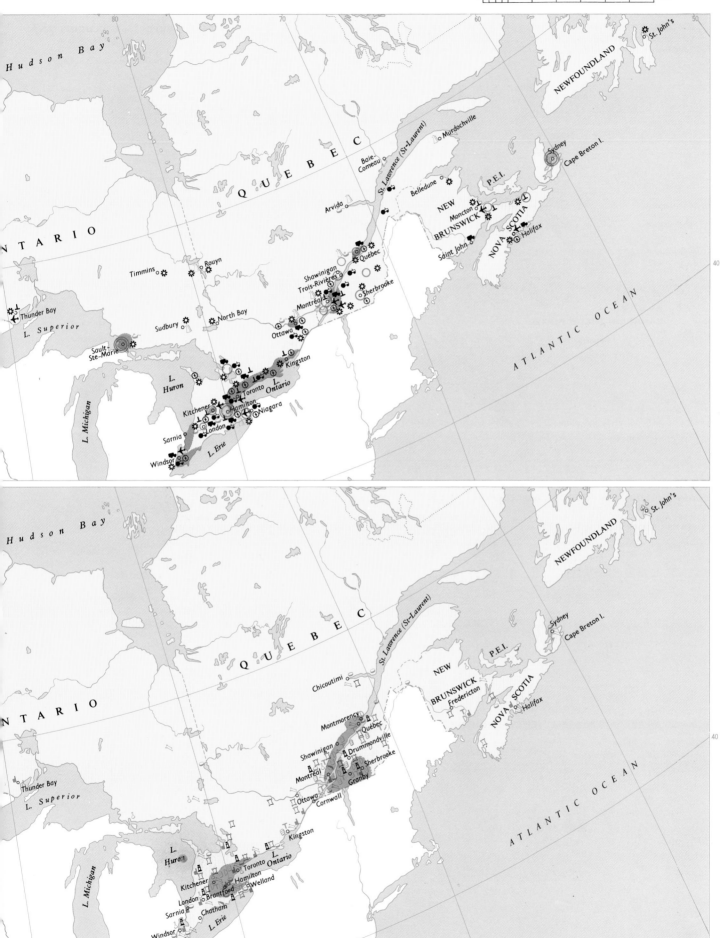

1:15 000 000

100 0 100 200 300 400 500 600 km

Top map labels:

Hudson Bay

QUEBEC

ONTARIO

NEWFOUNDLAND

St. John's

Murdochville

Baie-Comeau

St. Lawrence (St-Laurent)

Arvida

Belledune

P.E.I.

Sydney

Cape Breton I.

NEW BRUNSWICK

NOVA SCOTIA

Moncton

Saint John

Halifax

Timmins

Rouyn

Shawinigan

Trois-Rivières

Québec

Sherbrooke

Montréal

Thunder Bay

L. Superior

Sudbury

North Bay

Ottawa

Sault-Ste-Marie

L. Huron

Kingston

L. Ontario

Toronto

L. Michigan

Kitchener

Hamilton

Niagara

Sarnia

London

Windsor

L. Erie

ATLANTIC OCEAN

40

Bottom map labels:

Hudson Bay

QUEBEC

ONTARIO

NEWFOUNDLAND

St. John's

St. Lawrence (St-Laurent)

Chicoutimi

P.E.I.

Sydney

Cape Breton I.

NEW BRUNSWICK

Fredericton

NOVA SCOTIA

Halifax

Montmorency

Québec

Shawinigan

Drummondville

Sherbrooke

Montréal

Granby

Thunder Bay

L. Superior

Ottawa

Cornwall

Kingston

L. Huron

L. Ontario

Toronto

L. Michigan

Kitchener

Hamilton

Welland

London

Brantford

Sarnia

Chatham

Windsor

L. Erie

ATLANTIC OCEAN

40

90   80   West from Greenwich   70

COPYRIGHT. GEORGE PHILIP & SON. LTD.

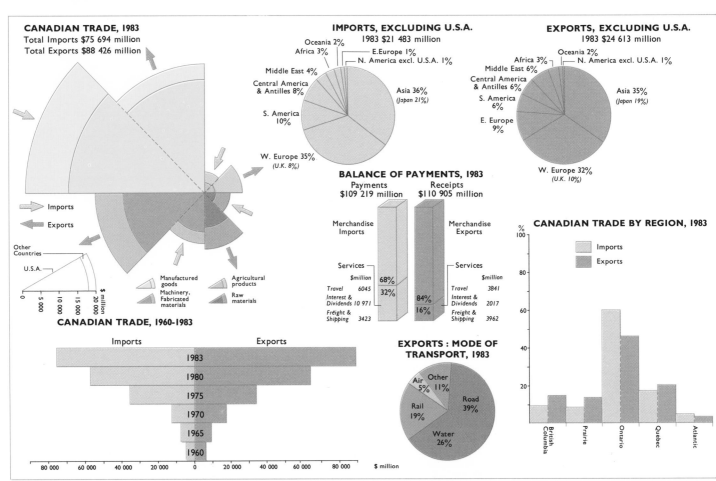

CANADIAN TRADE, 1983
Total Imports $75 694 million
Total Exports $88 426 million

Imports
Exports

Other Countries

U.S.A.

$ million
0 5 000 10 000 15 000 20 000

Manufactured goods
Machinery, Fabricated materials
Agricultural products
Raw materials

IMPORTS, EXCLUDING U.S.A.
1983 $21 483 million

Oceania 2%
Africa 3%
E.Europe 1%
N. America excl. U.S.A. 1%
Middle East 4%
Central America & Antilles 8%
S. America 10%
W. Europe 35% (U.K. 8%)
Asia 36% (Japan 21%)

EXPORTS, EXCLUDING U.S.A.
1983 $24 613 million

Oceania 2%
Africa 3%
N. America excl. U.S.A. 1%
Middle East 6%
Central America & Antilles 6%
S. America 6%
E. Europe 9%
W. Europe 32% (U.K. 10%)
Asia 35% (Japan 19%)

BALANCE OF PAYMENTS, 1983
Payments $109 219 million
Receipts $110 905 million

Merchandise Imports
Services
68%
32%

Merchandise Exports
Services
84%
16%

	$million			$million
Travel	6045		Travel	3841
Interest & Dividends	10 971		Interest & Dividends	2017
Freight & Shipping	3423		Freight & Shipping	3962

CANADIAN TRADE, 1960-1983
Imports   Exports
1983
1980
1975
1970
1965
1960

80 000 60 000 40 000 20 000 0 20 000 40 000 60 000 80 000 $ million

EXPORTS : MODE OF TRANSPORT, 1983
Air 5%
Other 11%
Rail 19%
Road 39%
Water 26%

CANADIAN TRADE BY REGION, 1983
%
100
80
60
40
20

Imports
Exports

British Columbia
Prairie
Ontario
Quebec
Atlantic

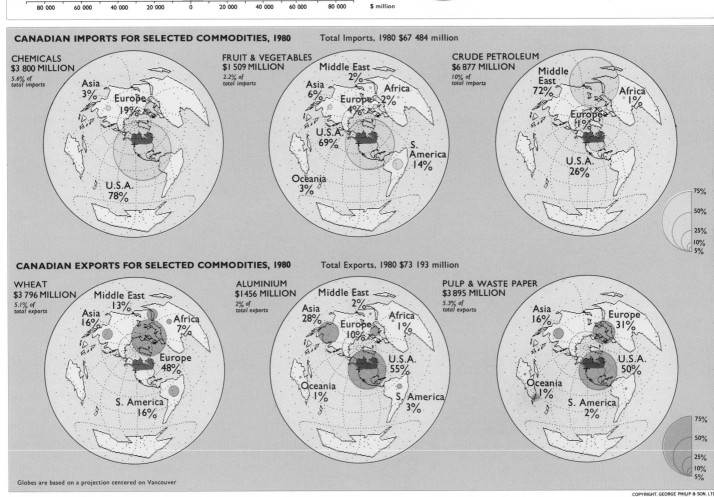

CANADIAN IMPORTS FOR SELECTED COMMODITIES, 1980
Total Imports, 1980 $67 484 million

CHEMICALS $3 800 MILLION
5.6% of total imports
Asia 3%
Europe 19%
U.S.A. 78%

FRUIT & VEGETABLES $1 509 MILLION
2.2% of total imports
Middle East 2%
Asia 6%
Africa 2%
Europe 4%
U.S.A. 69%
S. America 14%
Oceania 3%

CRUDE PETROLEUM $6 877 MILLION
10% of total imports
Middle East 72%
Africa 1%
Europe 1%
U.S.A. 26%

CANADIAN EXPORTS FOR SELECTED COMMODITIES, 1980
Total Exports, 1980 $73 193 million

WHEAT $3 796 MILLION
5.1% of total exports
Middle East 13%
Asia 16%
Africa 7%
Europe 48%
S. America 16%

ALUMINIUM $1456 MILLION
2% of total exports
Middle East 2%
Asia 28%
Africa 1%
Europe 10%
U.S.A. 55%
Oceania 1%
S. America 3%

PULP & WASTE PAPER $3 895 MILLION
5.3% of total exports
Asia 16%
Europe 31%
U.S.A. 50%
Oceania 1%
S. America 2%

75%
50%
25%
10%
5%

Globes are based on a projection centered on Vancouver

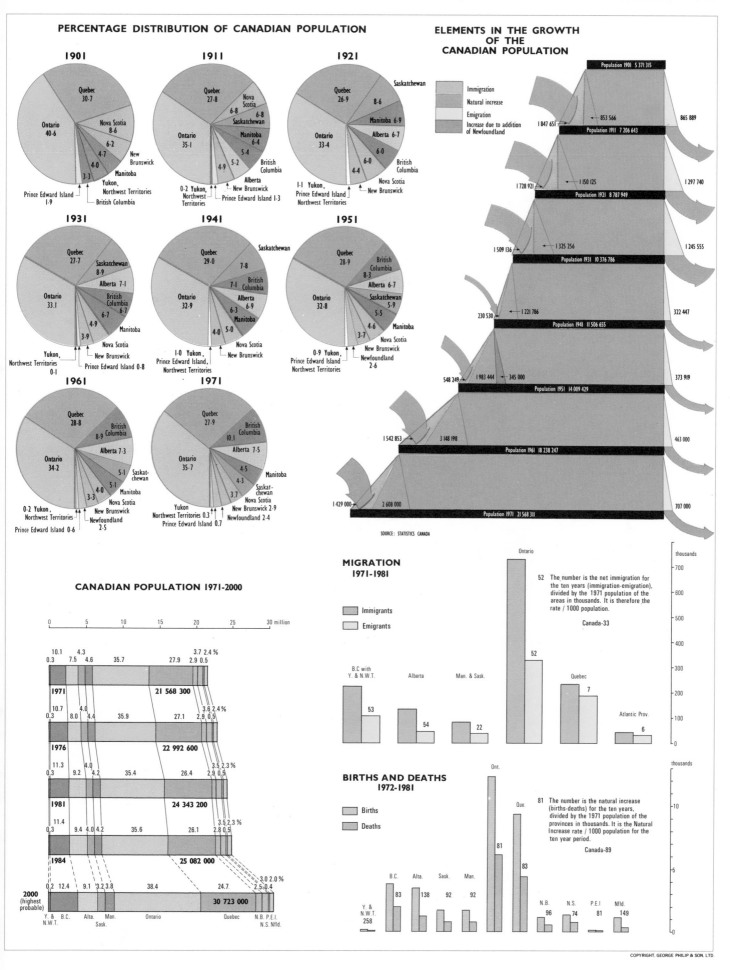

PERCENTAGE DISTRIBUTION OF CANADIAN POPULATION

ELEMENTS IN THE GROWTH OF THE CANADIAN POPULATION

1901

Quebec 30·7
Ontario 40·6
Nova Scotia 8·6
6·2
4·7
4·0
3·3
New Brunswick
Manitoba
Yukon, Northwest Territories
Prince Edward Island 1·9
British Columbia

1911

Quebec 27·8
Nova Scotia 6·8
Saskatchewan 6·8
Ontario 35·1
Manitoba 6·4
5·4
4·9
5·2
Alberta
New Brunswick
0·2 Yukon, Northwest Territories
Prince Edward Island 1·3
British Columbia

1921

Saskatchewan 8·6
Quebec 26·9
Manitoba 6·9
Alberta 6·7
Ontario 33·4
6·0
4·4
British Columbia
Nova Scotia
New Brunswick
1·1 Yukon, Prince Edward Island Northwest Territories

1931

Quebec 27·7
Saskatchewan 8·9
Alberta 7·1
Ontario 33·1
British Columbia 6·7
6·7
4·9
3·9
Manitoba
Nova Scotia
New Brunswick
Yukon, Northwest Territories 0·1
Prince Edward Island 0·8

1941

Quebec 29·0
Saskatchewan 7·8
British Columbia 7·1
Ontario 32·9
Alberta 6·9
6·3
5·0
4·0
Manitoba
Nova Scotia
New Brunswick
1·0 Yukon, Northwest Territories
Prince Edward Island 0·8

1951

Quebec 28·9
British Columbia 8·3
Alberta 6·7
Ontario 32·8
Saskatchewan 5·9
5·5
4·6
3·7
Manitoba
Nova Scotia
New Brunswick
0·9 Yukon, Prince Edward Island Northwest Territories
Newfoundland 2·6

1961

Quebec 28·8
British Columbia 8·9
Alberta 7·3
Ontario 34·2
5·1
5·1
4·0
3·3
Saskatchewan
Manitoba
Nova Scotia
New Brunswick
0·2 Yukon, Northwest Territories
Prince Edward Island 0·6
Newfoundland 2·5

1971

Quebec 27·9
British Columbia 10·1
Alberta 7·5
Ontario 35·7
4·5
4·3
3·7
Manitoba
Saskatchewan
Nova Scotia
New Brunswick 2·9
Yukon, Northwest Territories 0·3
Prince Edward Island 0·7
Newfoundland 2·4

Immigration
Natural increase
Emigration
Increase due to addition of Newfoundland

Population 1901 5 371 315
865 889
1 847 651 ← 853 566
Population 1911 7 206 643
1 297 740
1 728 921 ← 1 150 125
Population 1921 8 787 949
1 245 555
1 509 136 ← 1 325 256
Population 1931 10 376 786
322 447
230 530 → 1 221 786
Population 1941 11 506 655
373 919
548 249 ← 1 983 444 → 345 000
Population 1951 14 009 429
463 000
1 542 853 ← 3 148 198
Population 1961 18 238 247
707 000
1 429 000 → 2 608 000
Population 1971 21 568 311

SOURCE: STATISTICS CANADA

CANADIAN POPULATION 1971-2000

0 5 10 15 20 25 30 million

10.1 4.3 3.7 2.4 %
0.3 7.5 4.6 35.7 27.9 2.9 0.5
1971 **21 568 300**

10.7 4.0 3.6 2.4 %
0.3 8.0 4.4 35.9 27.1 2.9 0.5
1976 **22 992 600**

11.3 4.0 3.5 2.3 %
0.3 9.2 4.2 35.4 26.4 2.9 0.5
1981 **24 343 200**

11.4 4.0 3.5 2.3 %
0.3 9.4 4.2 35.6 26.1 2.8 0.5
1984 **25 082 000**

3.0 2.0 %
0.2 12.4 9.1 3.2 3.8 38.4 24.7 2.5 0.4
2000 (highest probable) **30 723 000**
Y. & N.W.T. B.C. Alta. Man. Ontario Quebec N.B. P.E.I.
Sask. N.S. Nfld.

MIGRATION 1971-1981

Immigrants
Emigrants

52 The number is the net immigration for the ten years (immigration-emigration), divided by the 1971 population of the areas in thousands. It is therefore the rate / 1000 population.

Canada-33

Ontario
B.C with Y. & N.W.T. 53
Alberta 54
Man. & Sask. 22
Quebec 7
Atlantic Prov. 6

thousands
700
600
500
400
300
200
100
0

BIRTHS AND DEATHS 1972-1981

Births
Deaths

81 The number is the natural increase (births-deaths) for the ten years, divided by the 1971 population of the provinces in thousands. It is the Natural Increase rate / 1000 population for the ten year period.

Canada-89

Ont.
Que.
B.C. 83 Alta. 138 Sask. 92 Man. 92 81 83 N.B. 96 N.S. 74 P.E.I. 81 Nfld. 149
Y. & N.W.T. 258

thousands
10
5
0

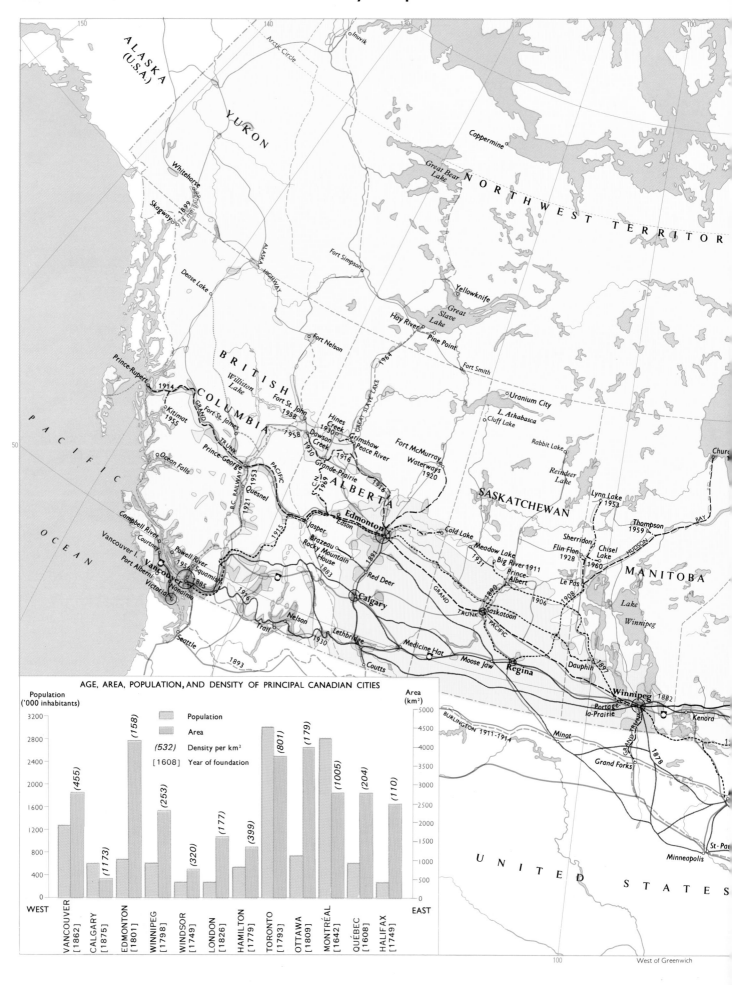

ALASKA (U.S.A.)

YUKON

Arctic Circle

Inuvik

Coppermine

NORTHWEST TERRITORY

Whitehorse

Skagway 1899 0.4 mm Gauge

Great Bear Lake

Dease Lake

Fort Simpson

Yellowknife

Hay River

Great Slave Lake

Pine Point

ALASKA HIGHWAY

Fort Nelson

Fort Smith

1964

BRITISH COLUMBIA

Williston Lake

Fort St. John 1958

Hines Creek 1930

Grimshaw Peace River

Fort McMurray

Uranium City

L. Athabasca

Cluff Lake

Prince Rupert 1914

Kitimat 1955

Fort St. James

GRAND TRUNK

1958

Dawson Creek 1930

Grande-Prairie 1916

Waterways 1920

Rabbit Lake

Ocean Falls

Prince George

1953

PACIFIC

ALBERTA

Reindeer Lake

SASKATCHEWAN

Lynn Lake 1953

B.C. RAILWAY

Quesnel 1921

Edmonton

Edson

Cold Lake

Meadow Lake 1937

Sherridon

Flin Flon 1928

Chisel Lake 1960

Thompson 1959

MANITOBA

HUDSON BAY

Church

CN 1969

Jasper

Brazeau

Rocky Mountain House 1883

Big River 1911

Prince Albert

Le Pas

1915

Campbell River

Courtney

Powell River 1958

Squamish

Vancouver I. Vancouver

Port Alberni

Victoria

Nanaimo

1885

1916

Red Deer

GRAND

1890

1906

1908

Saskatoon

Lake Winnipeg

Calgary

TRUNK

1891

PACIFIC

Dauphin

1891

Seattle

Nelson

Trail

1893

1930

Lethbridge

Medicine Hat

Moose Jaw

Regina

Winnipeg 1882

Portage-la-Prairie

Kenora

Coutts

BURLINGTON 1911-1914

Minot

GRAND TRUNK

1878

Grand Forks

Minneapolis

St-Pa

UNITED STATES

PACIFIC OCEAN

150

140

130

20

110

100

50

100

West of Greenwich

AGE, AREA, POPULATION, AND DENSITY OF PRINCIPAL CANADIAN CITIES

Population ('000 inhabitants)

Area (km²)

Population	Area

(532) Density per km²

[1608] Year of foundation

WEST

EAST

VANCOUVER [1862] (455)

CALGARY [1875] (1173)

EDMONTON [1801] (158)

WINNIPEG [1798] (253)

WINDSOR [1749] (320)

LONDON [1826] (177)

HAMILTON [1779] (399)

TORONTO [1793] (801)

OTTAWA [1809] (179)

MONTRÉAL [1642] (1005)

QUÉBEC [1608] (204)

HALIFAX [1749] (110)

1:15 000 000

100 0 100 200 300 400 500 600 km

RAILWAYS

CANADIAN NATIONAL (C.N.)

———————— National Transcontinental
– – – – – – – – Canadian Northern

Intercolonial
Grand Trunk
Great Western (merged with Grand Trunk in 1882)
Grand Trunk Pacific
Prince Edward Island railway
Hudson Bay railway (merged with C.N. in 1929)
Newfoundland railway (merged with C.N. in 1949)

Merged to form the Canadian National between 1917 and 1923

– · – · – · – Lines constructed by the C.N. since 1923

———————— CANADIAN PACIFIC (C.P. Rail)
(which built the first transcontinental route in 1885)

———————— OTHER INDEPENDENT ROUTES

· · · · · · · · OTHER INDEPENDENT ROUTES UNDER CONSTRUCTION

———————— NORTHERN ALBERTA (C.N. and C.P.)

– – – – – – – BURLINGTON (railway line from U.S.A.)

ROADS

Trans-Canada Highway
Freeways
Other roads
Roads in sparsely populated areas
Roads under construction in sparsely populated areas
Ferries

POPULATION OF CITIES

Over 2 000 000 inhabitants
1 000 000–2 000 000 ,,
500 000–1 000 000 ,,
250 000–500 000 ,,
100 000–250 000 ,,

POPULATION

Density per km²

Under 1 inhabitant
1–5 inhabitants
5–25 inhabitants
25–50 inhabitants
over 50 inhabitants

© GEORGE PHILIP & SON LTD.

Hudson Bay

Deception Bay

Kuujjuaq

LABRADOR

NEWFOUNDLAND

Schefferville 1954

QUEBEC NORTH SHORE AND LABRADOR

Labrador City 1960

Fermont

Lac Allard

NEWFOUNDLAND

St. John's

Corner Brook 1897

James Bay

Fort George

Radisson

QUEBEC

Gagnon 1961

QUEBEC CARTIER MINING Co.

Havre-St-Pierre

Port-Cartier

Sept-Iles

Port-aux-Basques

ONTARIO

Moosonee 1932

Chibougamau

Baie-Comeau

Gaspé

Sydney

Cape Breton I.

TRANSCONTINENTAL 1913

Hearst

Matagami 1957

1959

ONTARIO 1908

Dolbeau

Lac Saint-Jean

St. Lawrence

INTERCOLONIAL 1876

Prince Edward I.

1955

Chicoutimi

NEW

Moncton 1874

1964

1915

Beattyville

St-Félicien

Chambord

Port-Alfred

BRUNSWICK

Truro 1858

Cochrane

HUDSON BAY

NORTHLAND

1936

Québec

1905

Saint John

Hantsport

Halifax

Michipicoten

ALGOMA CENTRAL

Trois-Rivières

Sherbrooke

1890

NOVA SCOTIA

Superior

Sudbury

North Bay

Sorel

GRAND TRUNK

Sault-Ste-Marie

Montréal

Yarmouth

L. Huron

Little Current

Ottawa

Prescott

Portland 1853

Collingwood 1854

1887

Oshawa 1856

Picton

AMTRAK 1972

Goderich

L. Huron

Toronto

Ontario

GRAND TRUNK

Kitchener

Hamilton

St. Catharines

Sarnia

GT. WESTERN

London

Port Colborne

1854

Détroit

L. Erie

Windsor

New York

L. Michigan

ATLANTIC OCEAN

1:7 000 000

50 0 50 100 150 200 250 300 km

A T L A N T I C   O C E A N

H U D S O N   S T R A I T

Edgell I.
Resolution I.
Hatton Headland
Button Is.
C. Chidley
Killinek I.
Black Rock Pt.
North Aulatsivik I.
Seven Islands B.
Nachvak Fd.
Ryans B.
Ramah B.
Ronah
Torngat Mts.
Karoc
Saglek B.
C. Uivak
Hebron
Napartok B.
North
Nutok
Okak
Okak Is.
Cod I.
C. Kiglapait
South Aulatsivik I.
High I.
Paul I.
Noin
Voiseys B.
Tunungayualuk I.
Davis Inlet
Nunaksaluk I.
Hopedale
Big Bay
Nanok B.
C. Harrison
Holton
Indian Harbour
Grosswater B.
Cartwright
Sandwich B.
Paradise
River
Table B.
Mary's Harbour
Battle Harbour
Red Bay
St-Paul
Alexis
Island of Ponds
Square Islands

COAST OF LABRADOR

Str. of Belle Isle
Belle Isle
Mealy Mts.
Happy Valley
Goose Bay
Grand L.
North-West River
Rigolet
Kanairiktok
Naskapi
Seal L.
Nipishish L.
Michikamau Lake
Harp L.
Ossokmanuan
Ashuanipi
Churchill
Atikonak L.
Burnt L.
Emeril
Lac Joseph
Petit Lac Manicouagan
Schefferville
Menihek
Menihek Lakes
Labrador City
Wabush
Esker
Ashuanipi

Q U E B E C

N O U V E A U – Q U É B E C

U N G A V A   B A Y

Akpatok I.
C. Hopes Advance
Payne B.
Hopes Advance B.
Gyrfalcon Is.
B. aux Feuilles
Dry B.
Diana B.
Koartac

U N G A V A   P e n i n s u l a

Mts. de Povungnituk
Mts. St-Louis
C. Wolstenholme
Fj. Deception
C. de Nile-France
Douglas Hr.
Joy B.
C. Smith
Mosquito B.
Lac Klotz
Lac Nantais
Lac Couture
Lac Peters
Lac Nattual
Lac Tasiujaq
Lac la Potherie
Lac Faribault
Lac Minto
Lac Guillaume-Delisle
Nastapoka
L. à l'Eau Claire
Petite Baleine
L. Bienville
L. Nanagoat
Grande Baleine
Clearwater L.

George
Tunulic
Kaniapiskau
Wheeler
Sandy
Wabush

H U D S O N   B A Y

Ottawa Is.
Mansel I.
Digges Is.
Smith I.
Cape Smith
Povungnituk
Belcher Islands
Flaherty I.
Kugong I.
North Belcher Is.
South Sleeper Is.
Hopewell Is.
King George Is.
Baker's Dozen Is.
Tukarak I.
Innetalling I.
Merry I.
Long I.
Nastapoka Is.
Poste-de-la-Baleine

J A M E S   B A Y

North Twin I.
South Twin I.
Weston I.
Trodely I.
Charlton
Rupert B.
Eastmain
Fort George
Fort Rupert
Nemiscau
Mistassini
L. Mistassini
L. Albanel
L. Chibougamau

Manicouagan
Outardes
Betsiamites
Sept-Îles
Ste-Marguerite
Moisie
Natashquan
Aguanus
Nabisipi
Romaine
St-Jean
Magpie
Mingan
Magpie L.
Olomane
Musquaro
Kegaska
Gethsemani
Natashquan
St-Augustin
Baie-du-Poste

m   1500 1000 400 200

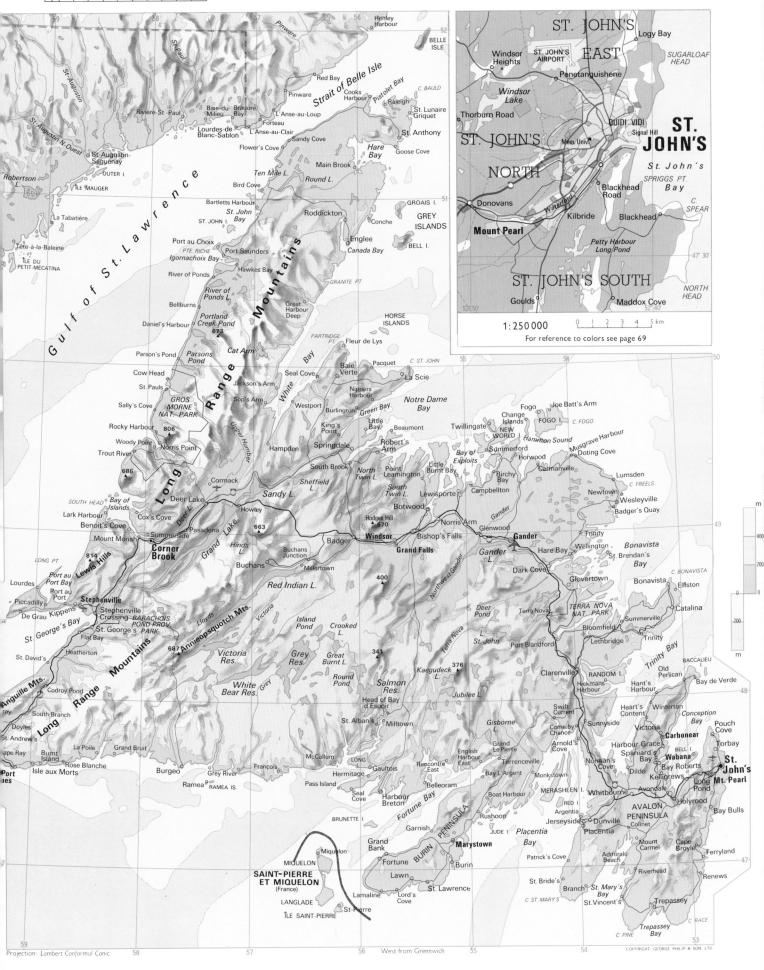

1:2 500 000

10 0 10 20 30 40 50 60 70 80 90 100 km

ST. JOHN'S inset

ST. JOHN'S
EAST

Logy Bay

SUGARLOAF
HEAD

Windsor
Heights

ST. JOHN'S AIRPORT

Penetanguishene

Windsor
Lake

QUIDI VIDI

Thorburn Road

ST. JOHN'S
NORTH

Mem. Univ.

Signal Hill

**ST.
JOHN'S**

St. John's
Blackhead
Road

SPRIGGS PT.

Donovans

Waterford

Blackhead

C.
SPEAR

Mount Pearl

Kilbride

Petty Harbour
Long Pond

ST. JOHN'S SOUTH

Goulds

Maddox Cove

NORTH
HEAD

1:250 000   0 1 2 3 4 5 km

For reference to colors see page 69

Main map labels

Henley
Harbour

BELLE
ISLE

Pinware

Red Bay

C. BAULD

Forteau
Pinware
L'Anse-au-Loup

Cooks
Harbour
Pistolet Bay

Raleigh

St. Lunaire
Griquet

Rivière-St-Paul

Baie-du-
Milieu
Bradore
Bay

L'Anse-au-Clair

Sandy Cove

St. Anthony

Lourdes-de-
Blanc-Sablon

Forteau

Flower's Cove

Goose Cove

Hare
Bay

St-Augustin-
Séguenay

OUTER I.

Ten Mile L.

Main Brook

Robertson
L.

ÎLE MAUGER

Bird Cove

Round L.

GROAIS I.

La Tabatière

Bartletts Harbour

Roddickton

Conche

GREY
ISLANDS

Tête-à-la-Baleine

St. John
Bay
ST. JOHN I.

Englee

BELL I.

ÎLE DU
PETIT-MÉCATINA

Port au Choix
PTE. RICHE
Igornachoix Bay

Port Saunders

Canada Bay

Bellburns

River of Ponds

GRANITE PT.

Daniel's Harbour

River
of Ponds L.

HORSE
ISLANDS

Portland
Creek Pond

673

PARTRIDGE
PT.

Fleur de Lys

Parson's Pond

Parsons
Pond

Cat Arm

Pacquet

C. ST. JOHN

Cow Head

Jackson's Arm

Baie
Verte

La Scie

St. Pauls

Seal Cove

Nippers
Harbour

Sally's Cove

GROS
MORNE
NAT.
PARK

Sop's Arm

White

Bay

Westport

Burlington

Green Bay

Notre Dame
Bay

Rocky Harbour

806

Little
Bay

Beaumont

Twillingate

Change
Islands

Fogo

Joe Batt's Arm

FOGO I.

C. FOGO

Woody Point

King's
Point

Springdale

NEW
WORLD I.

Hamilton Sound

Musgrave Harbour

Norris Point

Hampden

Robert's
Arm

Summerford

Horwood

Carmanville

Doting Cove

Trout River

686

Upper Humber

South Brook

Point
Leamington

Bay of
Exploits

Birchy
Bay

Cormack

North
Twin L.

Little
Burnt Bay

Lewisporte

Lumsden

Deer Lake

Sheffield
L.

South
Twin L.

Campbellton

Newtown

C. FREELS

SOUTH HEAD

Bay of
Islands

Howley

Hodges Hill
570

Botwood

Norris Arm

Gander

Wesleyville

Lark Harbour

Cox's Cove

Deer L.

Pasadena

663

Badger

Windsor

Bishop's Falls

Glenwood

Badger's Quay

Benoit's Cove

Summerside

Grand Falls

Gander
L.

Trinity

Mount Moriah

Hinds
L.

Buchans
Junction

Hare Bay

Wellington

Bonavista
Bay

814

**Corner
Brook**

Grand Lake

Millertown

Northwest Gander

Dark Cove

St. Brendan's
Bay

LONG PT.

Lewis Hills

Buchans

Glovertown

Bonavista

Port au
Port Bay

400

Red Indian L.

Deer
Pond

Elliston

Port au
Port

Island
Pond

TERRA NOVA
NAT. PARK

C. BONAVISTA

Piccadilly

Stephenville

Victoria

Crooked
L.

Terra Nova

Summerville

Catalina

De Grau
Kippens

Stephenville
Crossing

BARACHOIS
POND PROV.
PARK

341

L.
St. John

Port Blandford

Bloomfield

St. George's Bay

St. George's
PARK

Lloyds

Grey
Res.

Great
Burnt L.

Kaegudeck
376

Lethbridge

Trinity

Flat Bay

687

Annieopsquotch Mts.

Clarenville

Trinity Bay

BACCALIEU

St. David's

Heatherton

Victoria
Res.

Round
Pond

Salmon
Res.

Jubilee L.

RANDOM I.

Old
Perlican

Anguille Mts.

White
Bear Res.

Grey

Hickmans
Harbour

Bay de Verde

Codroy Pond

Head of Bay
d'Espoir

Swift
Current

Heart's
Content

Winterton

Conception
Bay

Pouch
Cove

South Branch

St. Alban's

Milltown

Gisborne
L.

Come by
Chance

Sunnyside

Victoria

Torbay

Doyles

Grand
Le Pierre

Arnold's
Cove

Carbonear

St. Andrew's

La Poile

Grand Bruit

English
Harbour
East

Terrenceville

Harbour Grace
Spaniard's
Bay

BELL I.

Wabana

Ray

Burnt
Island

Rose Blanche

McCallum

LONG

Gaultois

Rencontre
East

Bay L'Argent

Monkstown

Norman's
Cove

Dildo

Bay Roberts

**St.
JOHN'S**

Mt. Pearl

Isle aux Morts

Burgeo

Grey River

François

Hermitage

Boat Harbour

MERASHEEN I.

Kelligrews

Long
Pond

Port
es

Ramea
RAMEA IS.

Pass Island

Seal
Cove

Harbour
Breton

Belleoram

RED I.

Whitbourne

Avondale

Holyrood

Bay Bulls

Fortune Bay

BRUNETTE I.

Rushoop

JUDE I.

Placentia
Bay

Argentia

AVALON
PENINSULA

Garnish

Jerseyside

Dunville

Placentia

Mount
Carmel

Cape
Broyle

Grand
Bank

BURIN
PENINSULA

Marystown

Colinet

Ferryland

MIQUELON

Miquelon

Fortune

Burin

Patrick's
Cove

Admirals
Beach

Riverhead

Renews

**SAINT-PIERRE
ET MIQUELON**
(France)

Lawn

St. Lawrence

St. Bride's

Branch

St. Mary's
Bay

Trepassey

LANGLADE

Lamaline

Lord's
Cove

St. Vincent's

C. ST. MARY'S

ÎLE SAINT-PIERRE

St-Pierre

C. PINE

C. RACE

Trepassey
Bay

Gulf of St. Lawrence

Strait of Belle Isle

Long Range Mountains

Long Range Mountains

Projection: Lambert Conformal Conic

West from Greenwich

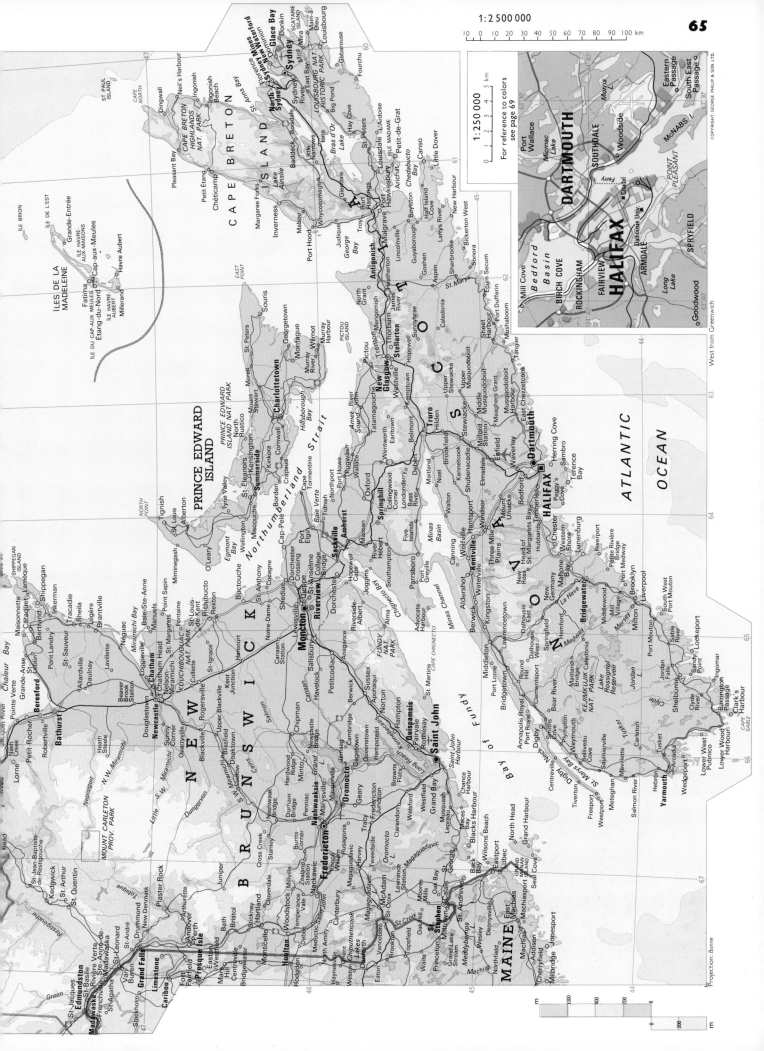

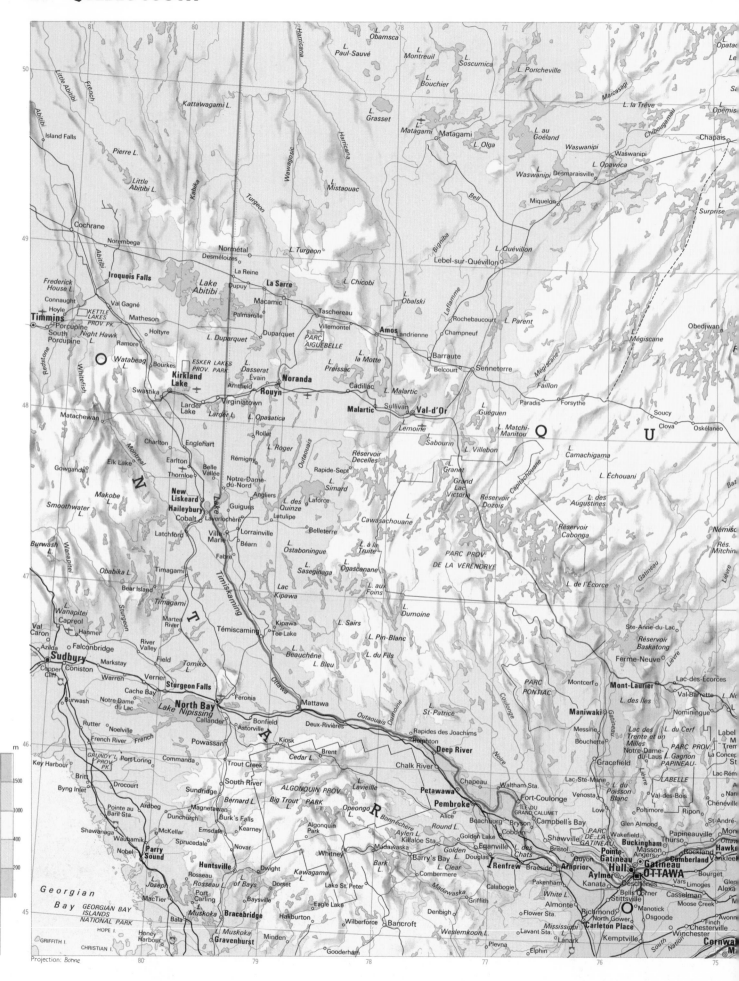

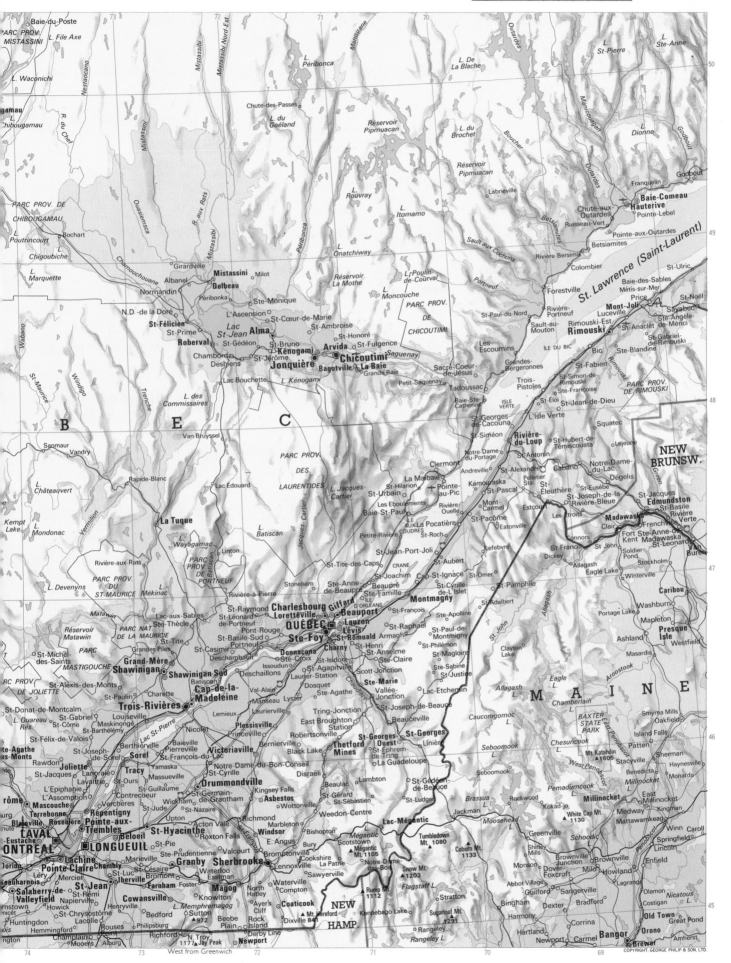

1:2 500 000

10 0 10 20 30 40 50 60 70 80 90 100 km

ARC PROV.
MISTASSINI
L. File Axe
Baie-du-Poste
L. Waconichi
amau
hibougamau
R. du Chef
Nestaocana
Mistassibi Nord-Est
Mistassibi
Ouasiemsca
L. Péribonca
L. du Goéland
Manouane
Réservoir
Pipmuacan
L. De
La Blache
L.
St-Pierre
L.
Ste-Anne
Outardes
50
PARC PROV. DE
CHIBOUGAMAU
Bochart
Poutrincourt
Chigoubiche
Manicouagan
Réservoir
Pipmuacan
L. du
Brochet
Boucher
L.
Dionne
Godbout
Franquelin
Godbout
Chute-des-Passes
L.
Rouvray
Itomamo
Labrieville
Baie-Comeau
Hauterive
Chute-aux-
Outardes
Pointe-Lebel
Ruisseau-Vert
Pointe-aux-Outardes
Betsiamites
49
Betsiamites
L.
Marquette
Chamouchouane
Girardville
Mistassini
Dolbeau
Milot
Réservoir
La Mothe
L.
Moncouche
L. Poulin-
de-Courval
Portneuf
Sault aux Cochons
Rivière-Bersimis
Colombier
St-Ulric
St. Lawrence (Saint-Laurent)
Forestville
Métis-sur-Mer
Des-Sables
Price
Sayabec
Mont-Joli
St-Noël
N.D.-de la Doré
Péribonka
Ste-Monique
St-Cœur-de-Marie
PARC PROV.
DE
CHICOUTIMI
St-Paul-du-Nord
Rivière-
Portneuf
Sault-au-
Mouton
Les
Escoumins
Rimouski-Est
Rimouski
St-Anaclet-
de-Mérici
Ste-Angèle-
de-Mérici
St-Gabriel-
de-Rimouski
St-Félicien
St-Prime
L'Ascension
St-Honoré
Grandes-
Bergeronnes
ÎLE DU BIC
Bic
Ste-Blandine
Roberval
St-Gédéon
Alma
St-Bruno
St-Ambroise
St-Fulgence
Sacré-Cœur-
de-Jésus
Trois-
Pistoles
St-Simon-de-
Rimouski
St-Fabien
Lac
St-Jean
Kénogami
Arvida
Saguenay
Petit-Saguenay
Baie-Ste-
Catherine
Tadoussac
Ste-Françoise
PARC PROV.
DE RIMOUSKI
Chambord
Desbiens
St-Jérôme
Jonquière
Chicoutimi
Bagotville
La Baie
Grands-Bais
St-Éloi
St-Jean-de-Dieu
48
Lac Bouchette
L. Kénogami
ISLE
VERTE
L'Isle Verte
Squatec
St-Georges-
de-Cacouna
L. des
Commissaires
St-Siméon
Notre-Dame-
du-Portage
Rivière-
du-Loup
St-Hubert-de-
Témiscouata
Lejeune
NEW
BRUNSW.
Van Bruyssel
Clermont
St-Antonin
Cabano
Notre-Dame-
du-Lac
B E C
Sanmaur
Vandry
PARC PROV.
DES
LAURENTIDES
La Malbaie
Andreville
St-Alexandre
St-Pascal
Pelletier
Sta.
St-Eusèbe
Dégelis
Rapide-Blanc
L. Jacques-
Cartier
St-Hilarion
Pointe-
au-Pic
Kamouraska
Mont-
Carmel
St-Éleuthère
St-Joseph-de-la-
Rivière-Bleue
St-Jacques
Edmundston
L. Châteauvert
Lac Édouard
St-Urbain
Les Éboulements
Baie-St-Paul
Rivière-
Ouelle
St-Pacôme
Estcourt
Les Étroits
Clair
St-Basile
Rivière-
Verte
Kempt
Lake
Mondonac
Vermilion
La Tuque
L.
Batiscan
ÎLE AUX
COUDRES
La Pocatière
Petite-Rivière-
St-Roch
Eatonville
Connors
Madawaska
Frenchville
Fort Ste-Anne-de-
Kent Madawaska
St-Léonard
Buren
L. Wayagamac
PARC
PROV.
DE
PORTNEUF
Rivière-à-Pierre
St-Jean-Port-Joli
Lefebvre
St-Francis
St. John
Soldier
Pond
Dickey
Stockholm
47
L. Devenyns
PARC PROV.
DU
ST-MAURICE
Mékinac
Linton
Stoneham
Ste-Anne-
de-Beaupré
St-Tite-des-Caps
St-Joachim
Cap-St-Ignace
St-Omer
St-Cyrille-
de-L'Islet
St-Aubert
CRANE
Allagash
Eagle Lake
Winterville
Caribou
RC PROV.
DE JOLIETTE
L. Ouareau
Rés.
St-Raymond
Lac-aux-Sables
St-Léonard
de-Portneuf
Ste-Thècle
St-Tite
Charlesbourg
Giffard
Loretteville
Beauport
St-François
Ste-Famille
Beaupré
ÎLE
D'ORLÉANS
St-Raphaël
Ste-Apolline
St-Paul-de-
Montminy
Montmagny
St-Adalbert
St. John
Allagash
Eagle
L.
Washburn
Portage Lake
Mapleton
Presque
Isle
Westfield
Réservoir
Matawin
PARC NAT.
DE LA MAURICIE
St-Casimir
Pont-Rouge
QUÉBEC
Lévis
Lauzon
St-Romuald
Ste-Foy
Charny
St-Henri
St-Anselme
St-Philémon
St-Magloire
Clayton
Lake
Masardis
Ashland
St-Michel-
des-Saints
PARC
MASTIGOUCHE
St-Tite
St-Basile-Sud
Portneuf
Deschambault
Donnacona
Ste-Croix
St-Isidore
Scott-Jonction
Ste-Claire
Ste-Sabine
St-Justine
Eagle
L.
Chamberlain
M A I N E
Grand-Mère
St-Léonard
Shawinigan
Shawinigan-Sud
Laurier-Station
St-Agapitville
Ste-Marie
Vallée-
Jonction
Lac-Etchemin
St-Alexis-des-Monts
Batiscan
Val-Alain
Manseau
Lyster
Ste-Agathe
St-Joseph-de-Beauce
Allagash
Caucomgomoc
L.
St-Paulin
Charette
Cap-de-la-
Madeleine
Dosquet
Laurierville
Beauceville
Caucomgomoc
L.
BAXTER
STATE
PARK
Smyrna Mills
Oakfield
St-Donat-de-Montcalm
St-Gabriel
St-Côme
Trois-Rivières
Lemieux
Tring-Jonction
St-Georges
St-Georges-
Ouest
Linière
Seboomook
L.
Chesuncook
L.
Island Falls
46
St-Félix-de-Valois
Maskinongé
St-Barthélemy
L. St-Pierre
Nicolet
Plessisville
Princeville
Robertsonville
East Broughton
Station
La Guadeloupe
Thetford
Mines
St-Ephrem-
de-Tring
Seboomook
Pemadumcook
L.
Mt Katahdin
1605
Stacyville
Sherman
Benedicta
Patten
Berthierville
Pierreville
St-François-du-Lac
Notre-Dame-du-Bon-Conseil
St-Cyrille
Bernierville
Black Lake
Haynesville
Joliette
Yamaska
Massueville
Disraëli
Lambton
St-Gédéon-
de-Beauce
Brassua
L.
Rockwood
West Penobscot
Monarda
Millinocket
East
Millinocket
Rawdon
St-Jacques
Lanoraie
Lavaltrie
St-Ours
St-Guillaume
Wickham
Drummondville
St-Germain-
de-Grantham
Kingsey Falls
Asbestos
Beaulac
St-Gérard
St-Sébastien
St-Ludger
Kokad-jo
White Cap Mt.
1130
Medway
Kingman
Winn
rôme
L'Épiphanie
L'Assomption
Contrecœur
Verchères
St-Jude
St-Nazaire
Richmond
Marbleton
Bishopton
Wottonville
Weedon-Centre
Lac-Mégantic
Jackman
Moosehead
L.
Greenville
Schoodic
L.
Mattawamkeag
Mascouche
Terrebonne
Repentigny
Rosemère
Pointe-aux-
Trembles
St-Hyacinthe
Upton
Acton Vale
Roxton Falls
Windsor
E. Angus
Bury
Mégantic
Scotstown
Mégantic
Mt. 1105
Tumbledown
Mt. 1080
Coburn Mt.
1133
Shirley
Mills
Monson
Brownville
Junction
Dover-
Foxcroft
Milo
Howland
Lincoln
Enfield
LAVAL
ONTREAL
LONGUEUIL
Lachine
Chambly
St-Luc
St-Pie
Ste-Prudentienne
Valcourt
Bromptonville
Cookshire
La Patrie
Notre-Dame-
des-Bois
Snow Mt.
1203
Stratton
Flagstaff L.
Rockwood
Brownville
Abbot Village
Guilford
Sangerville
Dexter
Corinna
Bradford
Lagrange
Olamon
Nicatous
L.
45
Pointe-Claire
Mercier
St-Jean
Iberville
Granby
Sherbrooke
Bromont
Foster
Waterloo
Eastman
Lennoxville
Waterville
Compton
Sawyerville
Rump Mt.
1112
Sugarloaf Mt.
1291
Bingham
Harmony
Carmel
Old Town
Great Pond
eauharnois
Salaberry-de-
Valleyfield
St-Rémi
Napierville
L'Acadie
Cowansville
Knowlton
Magog
North Hatley
Ayer's
Cliff
Coaticook
Mt Hereford
840
Kennebago Lake
Rangeley
Sugarloaf Mt.
1291
Dover-
Foxcroft
Newport
Carmel
Bangor
Brewer
Amherst
Huntingdon
Hemmingford
Howick
St-Chrysostôme
Lacolle
Rouses
Point
Bedford
Philipsburg
Sutton
972
Beebe
Plain
Rock
Island
Derby Line
Dixville
NEW
HAMP.
Newport
Champlain
Mooers
Alburg
Richford
N. Troy
1177 Jay Peak
Newport
Rangeley L.
Hartland
Newport
74
West from Greenwich
73
72
71
70
69
COPYRIGHT. GEORGE PHILIP & SON. LTD.
68

1:250 000

5 4 3 2 1 0   5   10 km

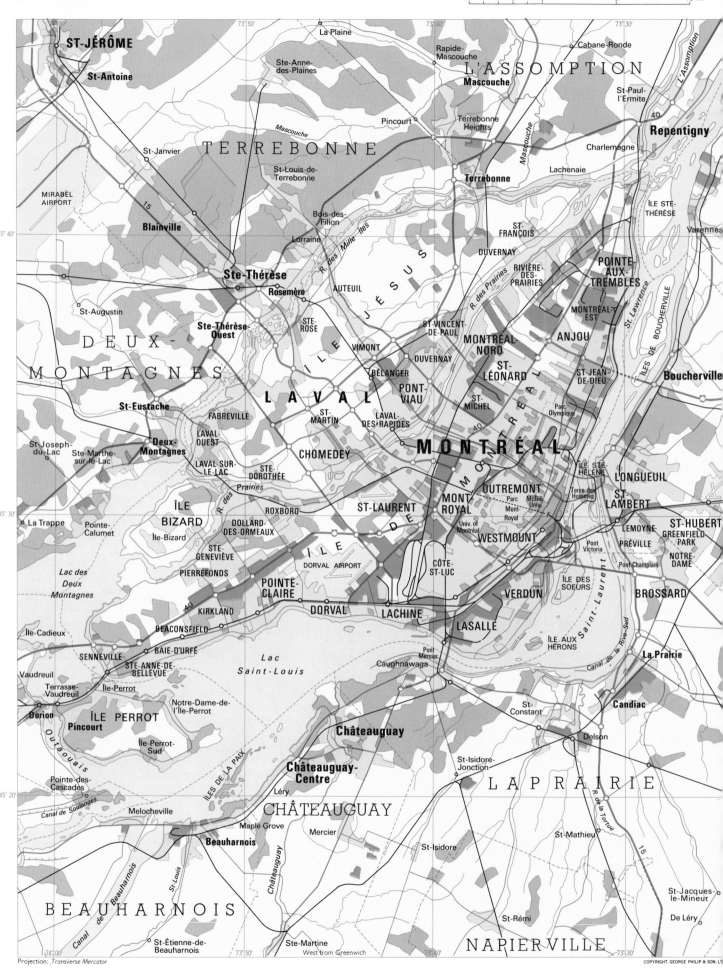

ST-JÉRÔME
St-Antoine

La Plaine

Rapide-
Mascouche

Cabane-Ronde

L'ASSOMPTION

Mascouche

Ste-Anne-
des-Plaines

St-Paul-
l'Ermite

40

Mascouche

Pincourt

Terrebonne
Heights

Charlemagne

Repentigny

St-Janvier

TERREBONNE

St-Louis-de-
Terrebonne

Terrebonne

Lachenaie

ÎLE STE-
THÉRÈSE

MIRABEL
AIRPORT

Varennes

Blainville

Bois-des-
Filion

ST-
FRANÇOIS

45° 40'

Lorraine

R. des Mille Îles

DUVERNAY

Ste-Thérèse

Rosemère

AUTEUIL

ÎLE JÉSUS

R. des Prairies

RIVIÈRE-
DES-
PRAIRIES

POINTE-
AUX-
TREMBLES

St-Augustin

Ste-Thérèse-
Ouest

STE-
ROSE

VIMONT

ST-VINCENT-
DE-PAUL

MONTRÉAL-
NORD

MONTRÉAL-
EST

ÎLE DE BOUCHERVILLE

ÎLES DE

ANJOU

DEUX-

BÉLANGER

DUVERNAY

ST-
LÉONARD

ST-JEAN-
DE-DIEU

Boucherville

MONTAGNES

LAVAL

PONT-
VIAU

ST-
MICHEL

St-Eustache

FABREVILLE

ST-
MARTIN

LAVAL-
DES-RAPIDES

Parc
Olympique

St-Joseph-
du-Lac

LAVAL-
OUEST

Deux-
Montagnes

CHOMEDEY

MONTRÉAL

Ste-Marthe-
sur-le-Lac

STE-
DOROTHÉE

MONT-
ROYAL

OUTREMONT

Parc
Mont-
Royal

McGill
Univ.

ÎLE STE-
HÉLÈNE

L'ONGUEUIL

LAVAL-SUR-
LE-LAC

Prairies

La Trappe

ÎLE

ROXBORO

ST-LAURENT

Univ. of
Montréal

ST-
LAMBERT

45° 30'

Pointe-
Calumet

BIZARD

DOLLARD-
DES-ORMEAUX

Terre des
Hommes

ST-HUBERT

Île-Bizard

WESTMOUNT

LEMOYNE

Pont
Victoria

GREENFIELD
PARK

STE-
GENEVIÈVE

ÎLE

CÔTE-
ST-LUC

PRÉVILLE

NOTRE-
DAME

Lac des
Deux
Montagnes

PIERREFONDS

DORVAL AIRPORT

Pont Champlain

Île-Cadieux

POINTE-
CLAIRE

VERDUN

ÎLE DES
SOEURS

BROSSARD

KIRKLAND

DORVAL

LACHINE

Senneville

BEACONSFIELD

LASALLE

ÎLE AUX
HÉRONS

Saint-Laurent

Vaudreuil

BAIE-D'URFÉ

Lac
Saint-Louis

Pont
Mercier

La Prairie

Terrasse-
Vaudreuil

STE-ANNE-DE-
BELLEVUE

Caughnawaga

Dorion

Île-Perrot

Canal de la Rive-Sud

Pincourt

ÎLE PERROT

Notre-Dame-de-
l'Île-Perrot

St-
Constant

Candiac

Île-Perrot-
Sud

Châteauguay

Delson

Outaouais

Châteauguay-
Centre

Léry

St-Isidore-
Jonction

LA PRAIRIE

Pointe-
des-
Cascades

ÎLES DE LA PAIX

Melocheville

CHÂTEAUGUAY

St-Mathieu

Canal de Soulanges

Maple Grove

Mercier

R. de la Tortue

Beauharnois

St-Isidore

Canal de Beauharnois

Châteauguay

St-Rémi

15

St-Jacques-
le-Mineur

BEAUHARNOIS

St-Louis

St-Étienne-de-
Beauharnois

Ste-Martine

NAPIERVILLE

De Léry

45° 20'

73° 50'   West from Greenwich   73° 40'

Projection: Transverse Mercator

1:250 000

5 4 3 2 1 0   5   10 km

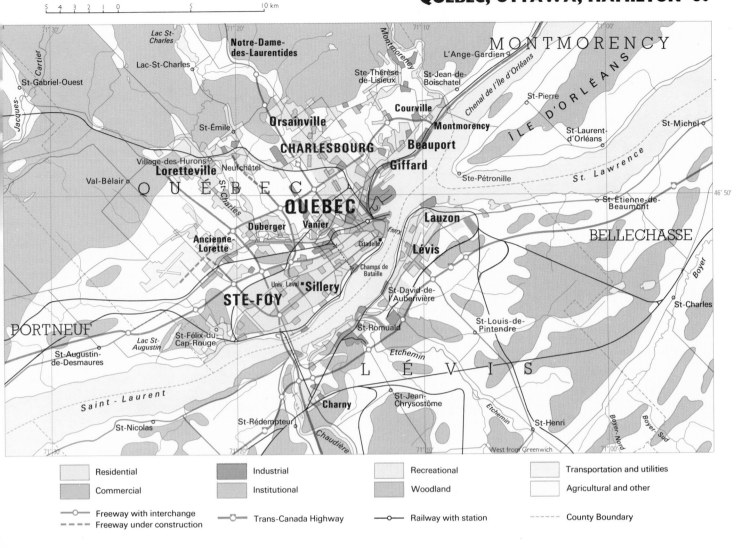

Residential	Industrial	Recreational	Transportation and utilities
Commercial	Institutional	Woodland	Agricultural and other

— Freeway with interchange   — Trans-Canada Highway   — Railway with station   - - - County Boundary

- - - Freeway under construction

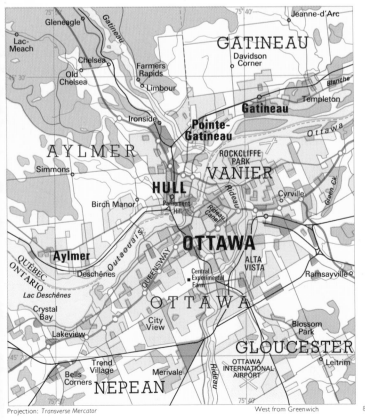

Projection: Transverse Mercator   West from Greenwich

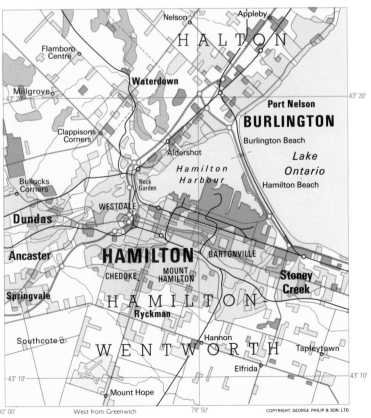

West from Greenwich

Projection: Bonne

- - - - - - Ferry routes

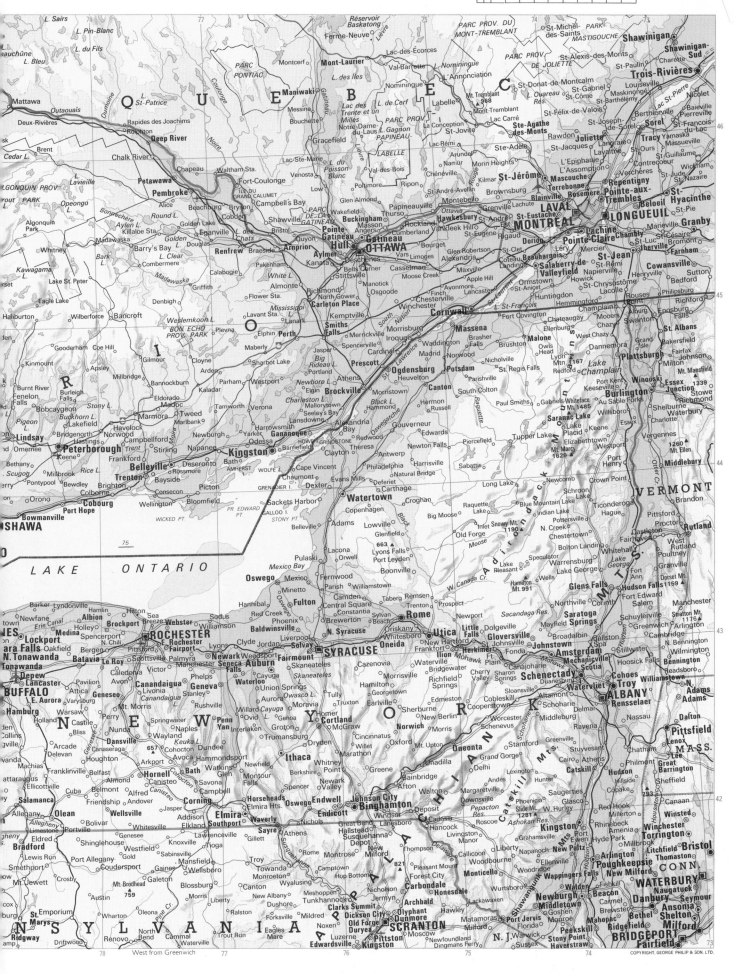

L. Sairs
L. Pin-Blanc
L. du Fils
L. Bleu
auchûne
Mattawa
Outaouais
Deux-Rivières
sk
Brent
Cedar L.
ALGONQUIN PROV.
PARK
rout L.
Opeongo L.
Algonquin Park
Whitney
Kawagama L.
Lake St. Peter
Eagle Lake
Haliburton
den

QUEBEC

L. St-Patrice
Rapides des Joachims
Rolphton
Deep River
Chalk River
Chapeau
Waltham Sta.
Petawawa
Pembroke
Alice
Beachburg
Cobden
Bryson
Campbell's Bay
Bristol

Réservoir Baskatong
Ferme-Neuve
Lièvre
Montcerf
Mont-Laurier
Val-Barrette
L. des Îles
Maniwaki
Messine
Bouchette
Gracefield
L. du Poisson Blanc
Val-des-Bois
L. des Trente et un Milles
Notre-Dame-du-Laus
PARC PROV.
PAPINEAU-
LABELLE
Ripon
Poltimore
Low
Venosta
Wakefield
Campbell's Bay
PARC DE-LA-GATINEAU
Shawville
Quyon
Aylmer
Pointe-Gatineau
Gatineau
Buckingham
Masson
Angers
Thurso
Papineauville
Montebello

L. Nominingue
Nominingue
L'Annonciation
Labelle
Mt. Tremblant
Mont-Tremblant
La Conception
Lac Carré
Ste-Agathe-des-Monts
St-Jovite
Arundel
Kilmar
Namur
Chéneville
St-André-Avellin

PARC PROV. DU MONT-TREMBLANT
St-Michel-des-Saints
MASTIGOUCHE
PARC PROV. DE JOLIETTE
St-Alexis-des-Monts
St-Paulin
St-Donat-de-Montcalm
St-Gabriel
L. Ouareau Rés.
St-Côme
Rawdon
St-Félix-de-Valois
St-Jérôme
St-Joseph
Morin Heights
Ste-Adèle
St-Jacques
L'Assomption

Shawinigan
Shawinigan-Sud
Charette
Trois-Rivières
Loujseville
Nicolet
Yamaska
St-Pierre
Pierreville
Berthierville
Massueville
Sorel
St-François-du-Lac
Joliette
Lanoraie
Tracy
Contrecœur
St-Ours
Wickham
L'Épiphanie
St-Jude
St-Nazaire
Lavaltrie
St-Guillaume

46

Mascouche
Terrebonne
Repentigny
Rosemère
Pointe-aux-Trembles
Blainville
Beloeil
St-Hyacinthe
Brownsburg
Montebello
Grenville
Lachute
LAVAL
Hawkesbury
St-André
Rockland
Cumberland
Yankleek Hill
Rigaud
Dorion
St-Eustache
MONTREAL
LONGUEUIL
Granby
St-Césaire
Bromont
Chambly
St-Luc
Iberville
Marieville
Farnham
Pointe-Claire
Lachine
Beauharnois
Léry
Mercier
St-Jean
St-Rémi
Cowansville
Sutton
Bedford
Salaberry-de-Valleyfield
Napierville
Howick
Henryville
St-Clet
Côteau Landing
Ormstown
St-Anicet
Huntingdon
Lacolle
Philipsburg
Ottawa
Rockland
Alexandria
Maxville
Apple Hill
Avonmore
Lancaster
L. St-François
Fort Covington
Chateaugay
Ellenburg
Champlain
Mooers
Rouses Point
Richford
Enosburg Falls
Swanton
St. Albans

OTTAWA
Hull
Deschênes
Kanata
Bells Corner
Stittsville
Manotick
Osgoode
Metcalfe
Vars
Limoges
Casselman
Moose Creek
Winchester
Chesterville
Finch
Cornwall
Massena
Brasher Falls
Bangor
Nicholville
St. Regis Falls
Malone
Owls Head
Lyon Mtn.
Dannemora
Redford
Chazy
West Chazy
Plattsburgh
Milton
Mt. Mansfield

Renfrew
Arnprior
Braeside
Pakenham
Almonte
Richmond
North Gower
Kemptville
Mountain
Morrisburg
Iroquois
Waddington
Madrid
Norwood
Louisville
Lawrence
Ogdensburg
Heuvelton
Potsdam
South Colton
Paul Smiths
Parishville
Gabriels
Saranac Lake
Au Sable Forks
Willsboro
Burlington
Winooski
Essex Junction
Richmond
Waterbury
Shelburne
Charlotte

45

Carleton Place
Lanark
Lavant Sta.
Smiths Falls
Merrickville
Spencerville
Cardinal
Prescott
Ogdensburg
Black L.
Hammond
Russell
Hermon
Gouverneur
Edwards
Mt. 1485
Lake Placid
Keene
Elizabethtown
Westport
Mt. Ellen

Perth
Elphin
Maberly
Jasper
Newboro L.
Athens
Brockville
Morristown
Heuvelton
Canton
Pierrefield
Tupper Lake
Mt. Marcy
1629
Port Henry
Middlebury

Bon Echo Prov. Park
Plevna
Sharbot Lake
Big Rideau L.
Portland
Charleston L.
Mallorytown
Seeley's Bay
Alexandria Bay
Redwood
Theresa
Antwerp
Newton Falls
Sabattis
Long Lake
Newcomb
Crown Point
VERMONT

Bancroft
Wilberforce
Gooderham
Coe Hill
Gilmour
Cloyne
Arden
Parham
Verona
Westport
Kaladar
Harrowsmith
Yarker
Gananoque
Clayton
Cape Vincent
Philadelphia
Harrisville
Natural Bridge
Raquette Lake
Blue Mountain Lake
Indian Lake
Ticonderoga
Hague
Brandon
Pittsford

Eldorado
Madoc
Tweed
Marlbank
Newburgh
Odessa
Barriefield
Howe I.
Grindstone
Wolfe I.
Evans Mills
Deferiet
Carthage
Croghan
Pottersville
Schroon Lake
Chestertown
N. Creek
Castleton
Proctor
Rutland

44

Lindsay
Bobcaygeon
Buckhorn L.
Lakefield
Bridgenorth
Napanee
Bath
Amherst I.
Chaumont
Dexter
Watertown
Copenhagen
Adams
Lowville
Glenfield
Big Moose
Old Forge
Inlet
Snowy Mt.
1190
Bolton Landing
Whitehall
Wells
Lake George
Fort Ann
West Rutland
Poultney
Dorset Mt.
1260

Peterborough
Keene
Belleville
Deseronto
Rossmore
Bayside
Picton
Trenton
Bloomfield
Wellington
Consecon
Sackets Harbor
Belleville
Mexico Bay
Pulaski
Lacona
Orwell
Lyons Falls
Port Leyden
Boonville
Speculator
Warrensburg
Lake Pleasant
Glens Falls
Hudson Falls
1169

Cobourg
Port Hope
Bowmanville
SHAWA
O
LAKE ONTARIO
WICKED PT.
PR. EDWARD PT.
GALLOO I.
STONY PT.
663
Boonville
Copenhagen
Mt. 991
Hamilton
W. Canada Cr.
Northville
Corinth
Glens Falls
Fort Edward
Salem
Manchester

43

Barker
Lyndonville
Hamlin
Hilton
Sea Breeze
Webster
Sodus
Red Creek
Oswego
Mexico
Fernwood
Parish
Williamstown
Camden
Central Square
Constantia
Taberg
Remsen
Prospect
Trenton
Newport
Sacandaga Res.
Mayfield
Saratoga Springs
Schuylerville
Greenwich
Arlington
Cambridge
N. Bennington
Wilmington

Albion
Brockport
Holley
Medina
Spencerport
N. Chili
Hannibal
Minetto
Fulton
Phoenix
Baldwinsville
N. Syracuse
Brewerton
Sylvan Beach
Oneida
Rome
Oriskany
Whitesboro
Utica
Little Falls
Dolgeville
Gloversville
Johnstown
Broadalbin
Ballston Spa
Stillwater
Mechanicville
Hoosick Falls

ROCHESTER
E. Rochester
Fairport
Pittsford
Scottsville
Lyons
Clyde
Jordan
Liverpool
Solvay
SYRACUSE
Fairmount
Oneida
N. Hartford
New Hartford
Frankfort
Ilion
Mohawk
Herkimer
Ft. Plain
Fonda
Amsterdam
Mohawk
Scotia
Schenectady
Watervliet
Troy
Cohoes
Williamstown
N. Adams
Adams

Bergen
Batavia
Le Roy
Oakfield
Caledonia
Avon
Manchester
Seneca Falls
Waterloo
Auburn
Skaneateles
Cazenovia
Morrisville
Waterville
Bridgewater
Cherry Valley
Sharon Springs
Cobleskill
Sloansville
Altamont
Schoharie
Duanesburg
Delmar
Nassau
Dalton
Pittsfield
Lenox

Tonawanda
Depew
Lancaster
E. Aurora
Pavilion
Warsaw
Attica
Varysburg
Victor
Canandaigua
Geneva
Phelps
Stanley
Rushville
Skaneateles Falls
Hamilton
Georgetown
Earlville
Sherburne
New Berlin
Worcester
Middleburg
Ravena
Stuyvesant
Chatham
Lee
MASS.

BUFFALO
Hamburg
Holland
Castile
Bliss
Mt. Morris
Geneseo
Livonia
Canandaigua L.
Springwater
Naples
Penn Yan
Interlaken
Ovid
Genoa
Willard
Cayuga
Aurora
Union Springs
Owasco L.
Moravia
Tully
Truxton
Georgetown
Edmeston
Cooperstown
New Berlin
Schenevus
Greenville
Cairo
Catskill
Hudson
Great Barrington
Sheffield

NEW
YORK
Arcade
Delevan
Perry
Nunda
Wayland
Cohocton
Dundee
Keuka L.
Himrod
Dresden
Trumansburg
Ithaca
Dryden
Cincinnatus
Willet
Homer
Cortland
McGraw
Marathon
Norwich
Morris
Oxford
Mt. Upton
Oneonta
Grand Gorge
Delhi
Andes
Lexington
Hunter
Phoenicia
Margaretville
Downsville
Saugerties
Hillsdale
Copake
793

Machias
Franklinville
Ellicottville
Arkport
Avoca
Hammondsport
Naples
Wayne
Bath
Savona
Campbell
Newfield
Spencer
Newark Valley
Berkshire
Whitney Point
Greene
Bainbridge
Afton
Walton
Roscoe
Livingston Manor
Grahamsville
Napanoch
New Paltz
Rhinebeck
Amenia
Millbrook
Winsted
Torrington

Arcade
Delevan
657
Dansville
Canaseraga
Houghton
Nunda
Hornell
Canisteo
Almond
Alfred
Andover
Wellsville
Whitesville
Elkland
Corning
Elmira
Southport
Horseheads
Elmira Hts.
Oswego
Endwell
Johnson City
Endicott
Binghamton
Windsor
Deposit
Hancock
Cadosia
Pepacton Res.
Ashokan Res.
W. Hurley
Hurley
Kingston
Hyde Park
Poughkeepsie
Wappingers Falls
Litchfield
Thomaston
Bristol
CONN.

Salamanca
Allegany
Olean
Allegany
Portville
Bolivar
Eldred
Bradford
Lewis Run
Smethport
Mt. Jewett
Crosby
Austin
759
Emporium
St. Marys
Ridgway
Driftwood

42

Olean
Cuba
Friendship
Belfast
Hornell
Bath
Corning
Addison
Elkland
Lawrenceville
Knoxville
Westfield
Sabinsville
Gaines
Wellsboro
Mansfield
Tioga
Blossburg
Canton
Troy
Towanda
Monroeton
Wyalusing
Camptown
New Albany
Dushore
Laporte
Muncy
Hughesville

Elmira
Waverly
Sayre
Athens
Nichols
Great Bend
Hallstead
Susquehanna Depot
Lanesboro
New Milford
Thompson
Forest City
Carbondale
Honesdale
Hawley
Lackawaxen
Port Jervis
Matamoras
Milford
Dingmans Ferry

PENNSYLVANIA
Coudersport
Galeton
Gold
Shinglehouse
Port Allegany
Roulette
Renovo
N. Bend
Cammal
Trout Run
Waterville
Ralston
Liberty
Canton
Monroeton
Meshoppen
Tunkhannock
Nicholson
Factoryville
Clarks Summit
Dickson City
Olyphant
Archbald
Jermyn
Mayfield
SCRANTON
Dunmore
Moscow
Pittston
Duryea
Avoca
Old Forge
Kingston

APPALACHIAN
Deposit
Hancock
Callicoon
Liberty
Monticello
Woodbourne
Ellenville
Wurtsboro
Middletown
Goshen
Monroe
Warwick
Sussex
N.J.
Newburgh
Beacon
Wappingers Falls
Walden
Fishkill
Peekskill
Haverstraw
Stony Point
Carmel
Brewster
Mahopac
Ridgefield
Danbury
Bethel
Ansonia
Shelton
Seymour
Naugatuck
WATERBURY
Waterbury
New Milford
Arlington
Poughkeepsie
BRIDGEPORT
Fairfield

73

1:250 000

5 4 3 2 1 0 5 10 km

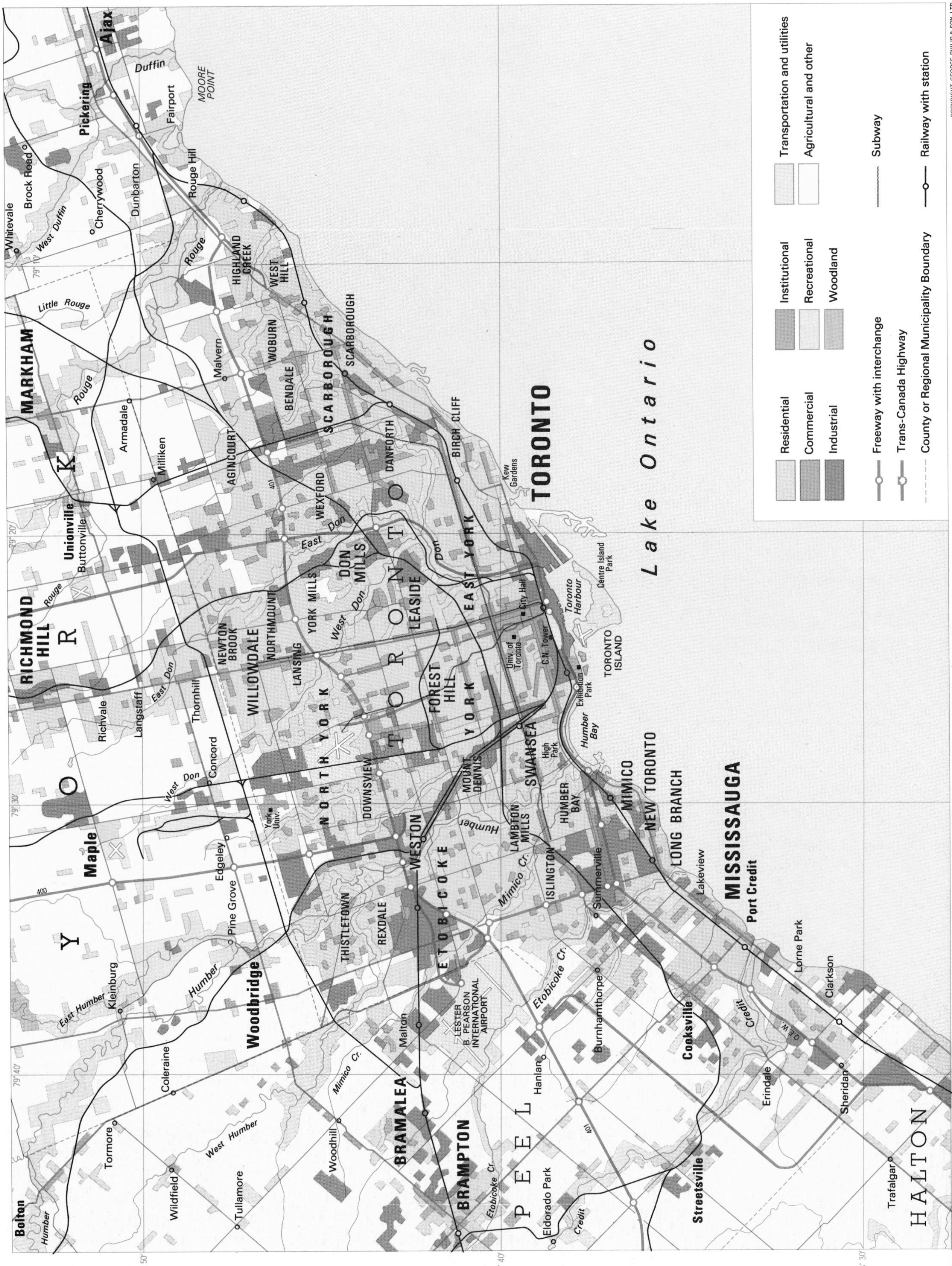

Legend:

Transportation and utilities
Agricultural and other

Institutional
Recreational
Woodland

Residential
Commercial
Industrial

Freeway with interchange
Trans-Canada Highway
County or Regional Municipality Boundary

Subway
Railway with station

Lake Ontario

MARKHAM

RICHMOND HILL

Whitevale
Brock Road
West Duffin
Cherrywood
Dunbarton
Duffin
MOORE POINT
Fairport
Pickering
Ajax

Little Rouge
Rouge
Rouge Hill
HIGHLAND CREEK
WEST HILL

Armadale
Milliken
Malvern
WOBURN
BENDALE
SCARBOROUGH
SCARBOROUGH

Unionville
Buttonville
AGINCOURT
WEXFORD
DANFORTH
BIRCH CLIFF

Richvale
Langstaff
Thornhill
NEWTON BROOK
LANSING
YORK MILLS
Don
LEASIDE
EAST YORK
Kew Gardens

NORTH YORK
WILLOWDALE
NORTHMOUNT
West Don
DON MILLS
City Hall
TORONTO HARBOUR
Centre Island Park

Concord
West Don
DOWNSVIEW
FOREST HILL
Univ. of Toronto
C.N. Tower
Exhibition Park
TORONTO ISLAND

Maple
Edgeley
York Univ.
MOUNT DENNIS
YORK
SWANSEA
High Park
Humber Bay
MIMICO

Pine Grove
WESTON
Humber
LAMBTON MILLS
ISLINGTON
Summerville
NEW TORONTO
LONG BRANCH
Lakeview
MISSISSAUGA
Port Credit

Woodbridge
THISTLETOWN
REXDALE
ETOBICOKE
Etobicoke Cr.
Burnhamthorpe
Lorne Park
Clarkson

East Humber
Kleinburg
Humber
Malton
LESTER B. PEARSON INTERNATIONAL AIRPORT
Hanlan
Burnhamthorpe
Cooksville
Credit
Erindale
Sheridan

Coleraine
Mimico Cr.
Woodhill
Eldorado Park
Credit
Streetsville
Trafalgar

Bolton
Humber
Tormore
Wildfield
Tullamore
West Humber
Etobicoke Cr.
BRAMALEA
BRAMPTON
P E E L
HALTON

Y
O
R
K

79° 50'
79° 40'
79° 30'
79° 20'

43° 50'
43° 40'
43° 30'

400
401

1:600 000

Projection: Transverse Mercator

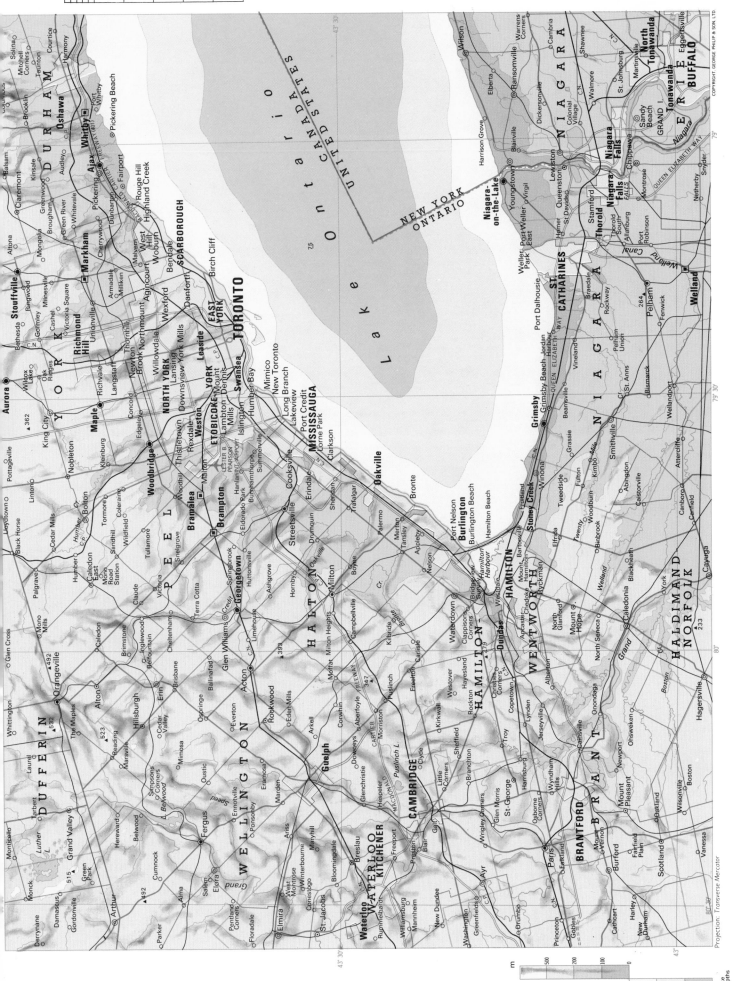

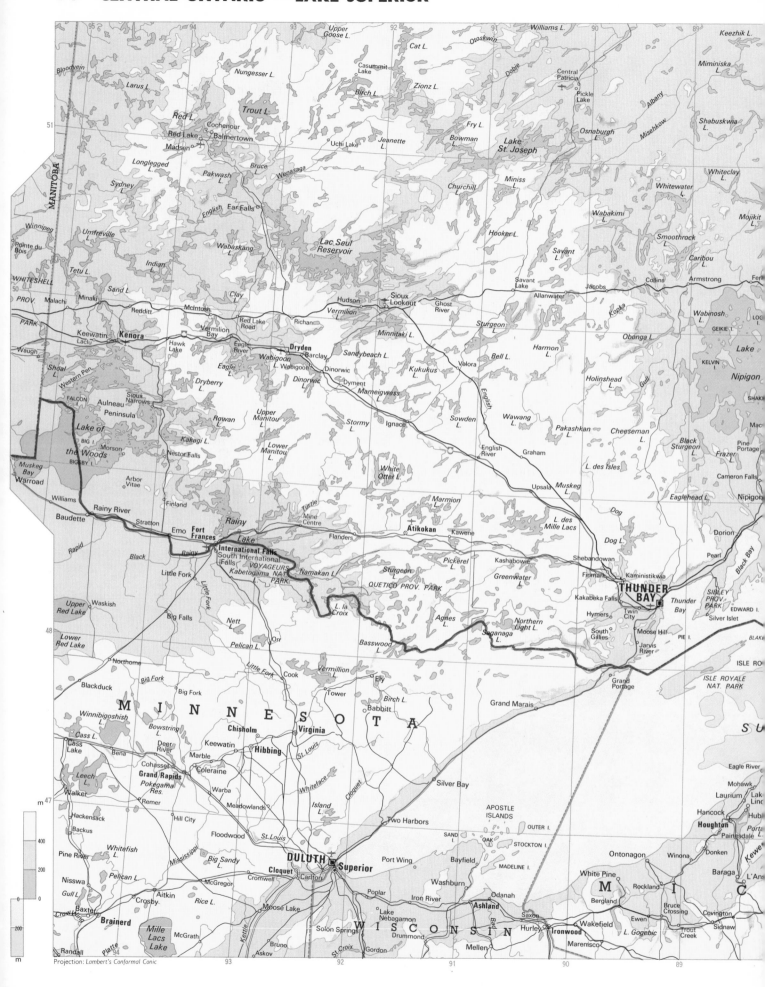

1 : 2 500 000

10 0 10 20 30 40 50 60 70 80 90 100 km

James Bay

Moosonee
Moose Factory
Galeton
51
Renison
Cheepash Moose River
Onakawana
Ranoke
Otter Rapids
Foxville
Fraserdale
Island Falls
50
Smoky Falls
Little Abitibi
Abitibi
French

Wabassi
Albany
Ogoki
Eabamet Washi L.
Makokibatan L.
Atikameg
Albany
Cheepay
Jaab L.
Sandbank
Pledger
Ridge
Pivabiska
Kinoje Lakes
Kinoje
Stooping
Kwataboahegan
Missinaibi
Mattagami
North French
Partridge

Dusey
gianagami
kotongwa
Ogoki L.
Ara L.
Abamasagi L.
O'Sullivan
Esnagami L.
Kowkash Nakina
Little Current
Drowning
Wabimeig
Kenogami
Otasawian
Kenogami
Shannon L.
Calstock
Hallebourg Mattice
Lowther
Harty
Valrita
Opasatika L.
Fauquier
Saganash L.
REMI LAKE PROV PK
Moonbeam
Smooth Rock Falls

Onaman Burrows
Wildgoose L. Geraldton
Jellicoe
Parks
Barbara
Wintering
Long L.
Caramat
Pagwachuan
Flint L.
Oshawin
Stevens
McKay L.
Kagiano L.
Killala L.
Pic
Manitouwadge
Obakamiga L.
Nagagami
Hillsport
Nagagamisis
Hornepayne
Kabinakagami L.
Cameron Oba
Akron
Oba L.
Mosher
Brunswick L.
Fire River
Dunkin
Elsas
Peterbell
Foleyet
Palomar
Kapuskasing
Opasatika
Jogues
Hearst
Pagwa River
Ogahalla
Chipman
Longlac

Rossport
Schreiber
Terrace Bay
Marathon
Heron Bay Struthers
White L.
White River
Amyot
Esnagi L.
Franz
Missanabie
Dalton
Dog L.
Wabatongushi L.
Missinaibi L.
MISSINAIBI LAKE PROV PARK
Racine
Nemegosenda
Horwood
Timmins Porcupine
Schumacher South Porcupine
Redstone
Groundhog
Mattagami L.
48
SLATE IS.
PIC I.
SIMPSON
Pukaskwa
White
University
Magpie
PUKASKWA NAT PARK
OBATANGA PROV PARK
Wawa
Michipicoten
Hawk Junction
Windermere
SHOALS PROV PARK
Chapleau
Nagasin L.
Borden
Sideburned
Kormak
Sultan
Rush L.
Gogama
Jerome
Westree
Ruel
Biscotasing
Biscotasi L.

UNITED STATES
CANADA
MICHIPICOTEN ISLAND
LEACH I.
MONTREAL I.
Michipicoten Bay
LAKE SUPERIOR PROV PARK
Agawa
Montreal
Wenebegon
Ranger L.
Goulais
White Owl L.
Ramsey L.
Onaping L.
Mazhabong
Pogamasing
Benny
Cartier
Levack Val Caron
Capreol
Azilda
Onaping
Chelmsford
Sudbury
Copper
Whitefish
Cliff
Lively
Naughton
Panache
Nairn
Espanola

Harbor
MANITOU I.
CARIBOU I.
Batchawana Bay Batchawana Bay
Whitefish Point
Paradise
Whitefish Bay
Sault Sainte Marie
Echo Bay
Searchmont
Wakomata L.
Mississagi
Little White
MISSISSAGI PROV PARK
Big Basswood
Iron Bridge
Matinenda
Blind River
Spragge
Elliot Lake
Webbwood
Whitefish Falls
Massey

Marquette
Negaunee
Au Sable Pt.
Grand I.
Grand Marais
Brimley
Sault Sainte Marie
ST. JOSEPH I.
Desbarats
Hilton Beach
Thessalon
Spanish

Gwinn Skandia Munising Chatham Shingleton Seney Newberry McMillan Hulbert Strongs Corners Dafter Rudyard

West from Greenwich

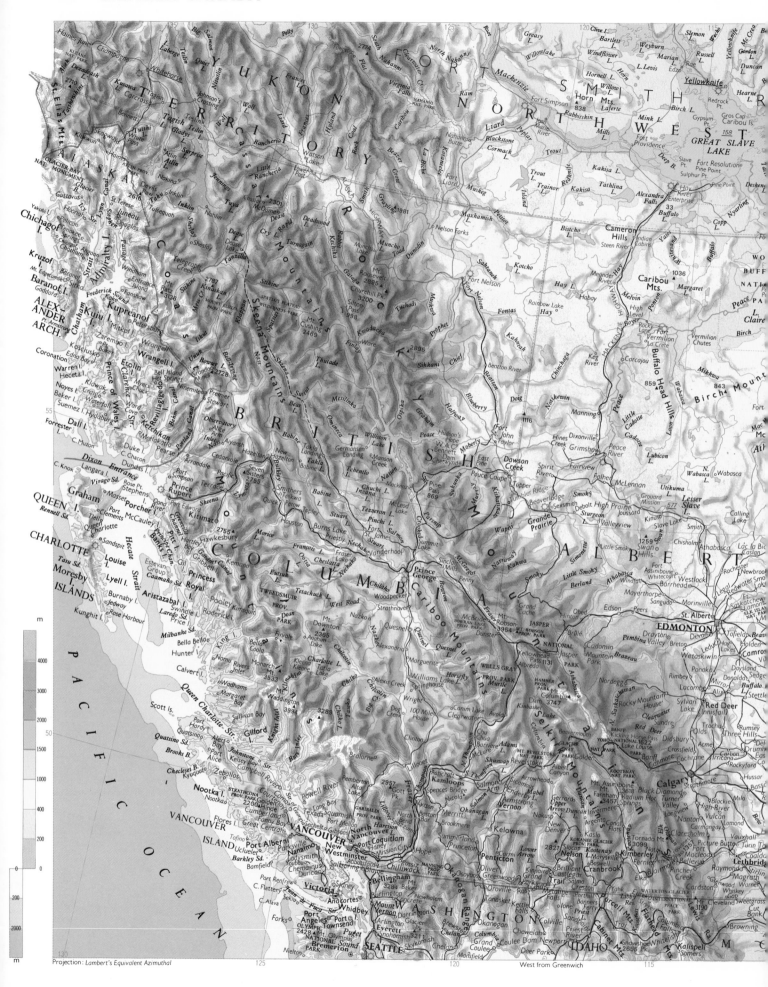

1:7 000 000

50 0 50 100 150 200 250 300 km

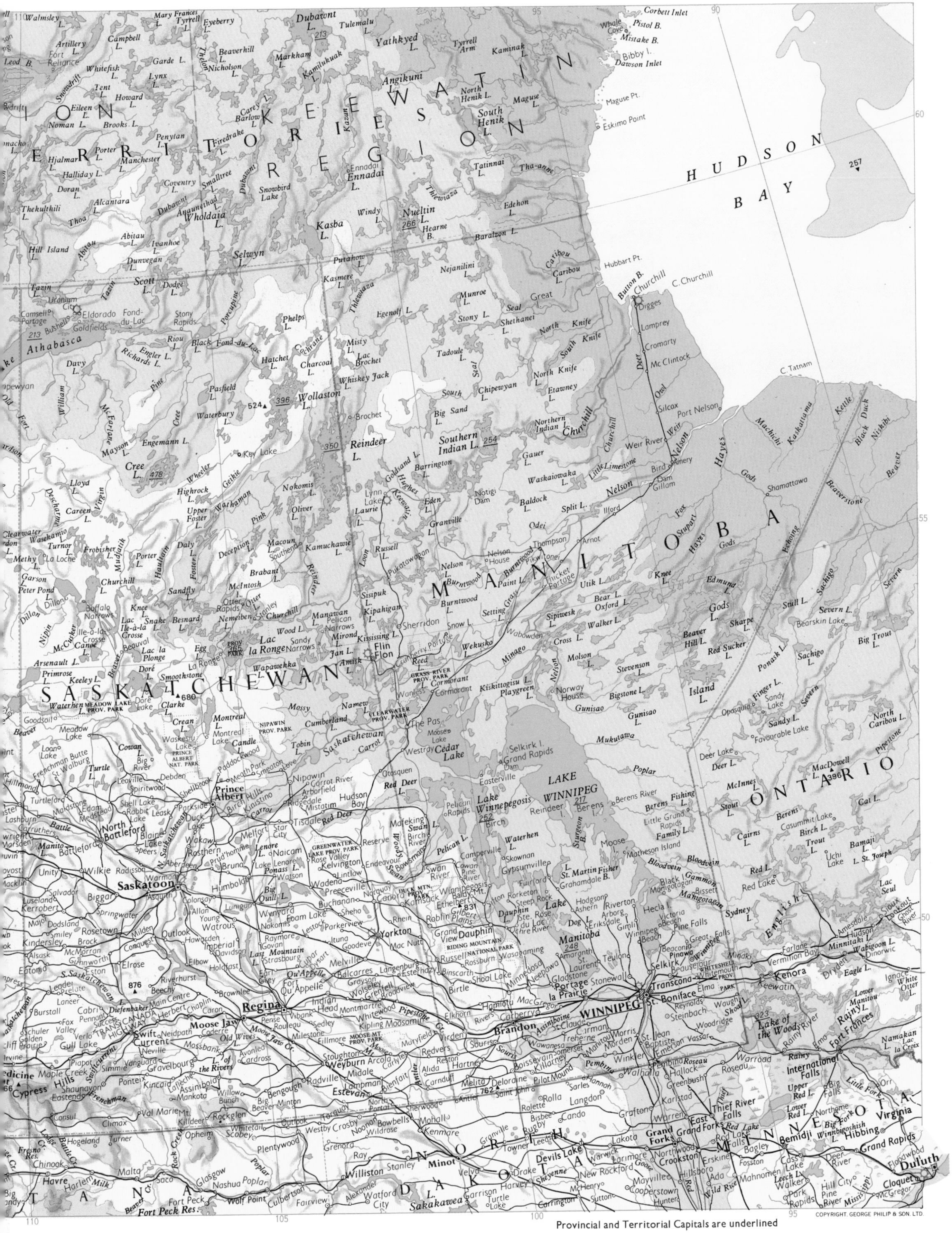

HUDSON BAY

TERRITORIES
KEEWATIN REGION

MANITOBA

SASKATCHEWAN

ONTARIO

Athabasca

Churchill

Southern Indian L.

Reindeer L.

Wollaston L.

Cree L.

Lac la Ronge

LAKE WINNIPEG

Lake Winnipegosis

Cedar Lake

Cross L.

Island L.

Gods L.

Saskatoon

Prince Albert

Regina

Moose Jaw

Swift Current

Medicine Hat

Brandon

WINNIPEG

Portage la Prairie

Selkirk

Dauphin

Yorkton

The Pas

Flin Flon

Kenora

Fort Frances

Lake of the Woods

Churchill

Port Nelson

Eskimo Point

NORTH DAKOTA

MINNESOTA

Duluth

Minot

Grand Forks

Bemidji

Williston

Devils Lake

International Falls

Provincial and Territorial Capitals are underlined

COPYRIGHT GEORGE PHILIP & SON LTD

110 105 100 95 90

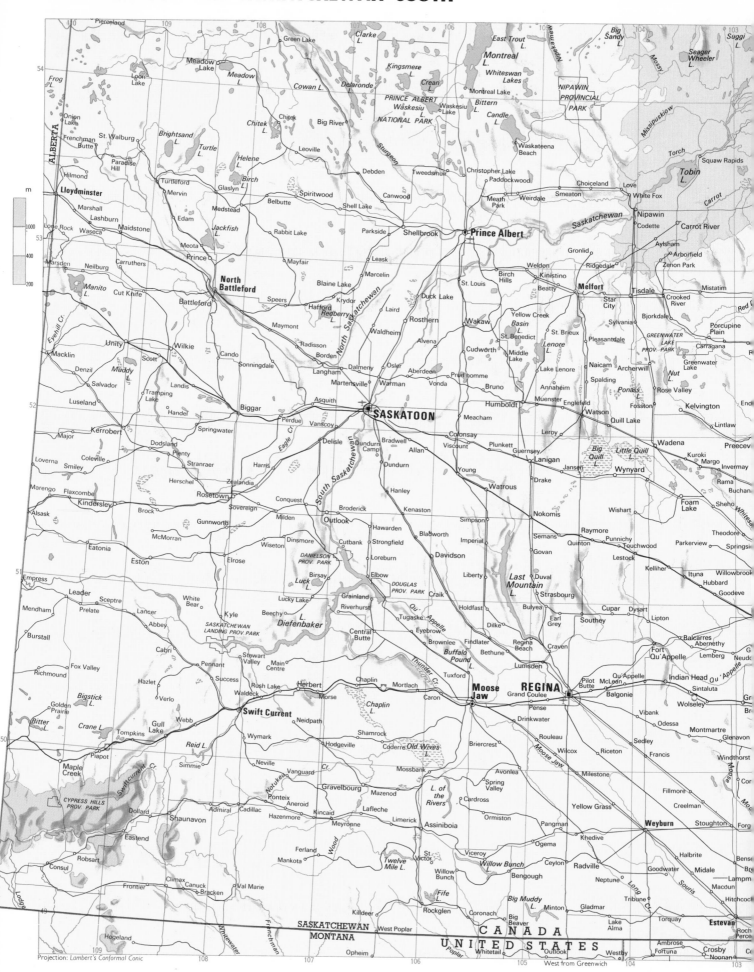

Projection: Lambert's Conformal Conic

West from Greenwich

1 : 2 500 000

10 0 10 20 30 40 50 60 70 80 90 100 km

ONTARIO

MINNESOTA

MANITOBA

NORTH DAKOTA

WINNIPEG

LAKE WINNIPEG

Lake Winnipegosis

Lake Manitoba

Brandon

Portage La Prairie

St. James

St. Boniface

St. Norbert

Transcona

Selkirk

Steinbach

Dauphin

The Pas

CLEARWATER PROV. PARK

DUCK MOUNTAIN PROV. PARKS

RIDING MOUNTAIN NATIONAL PARK

SPRUCE WOODS PROV. PARK

TURTLE-MT PROV. PARK

HECLA PROV. PARK

NOPIMING PROV. PARK

WHITESHELL PROV. PARK

Cedar L.

Red Deer L.

Swan L.

Moose Lake

COPYRIGHT. GEORGE PHILIP & SON. LTD.

1:2 500 000

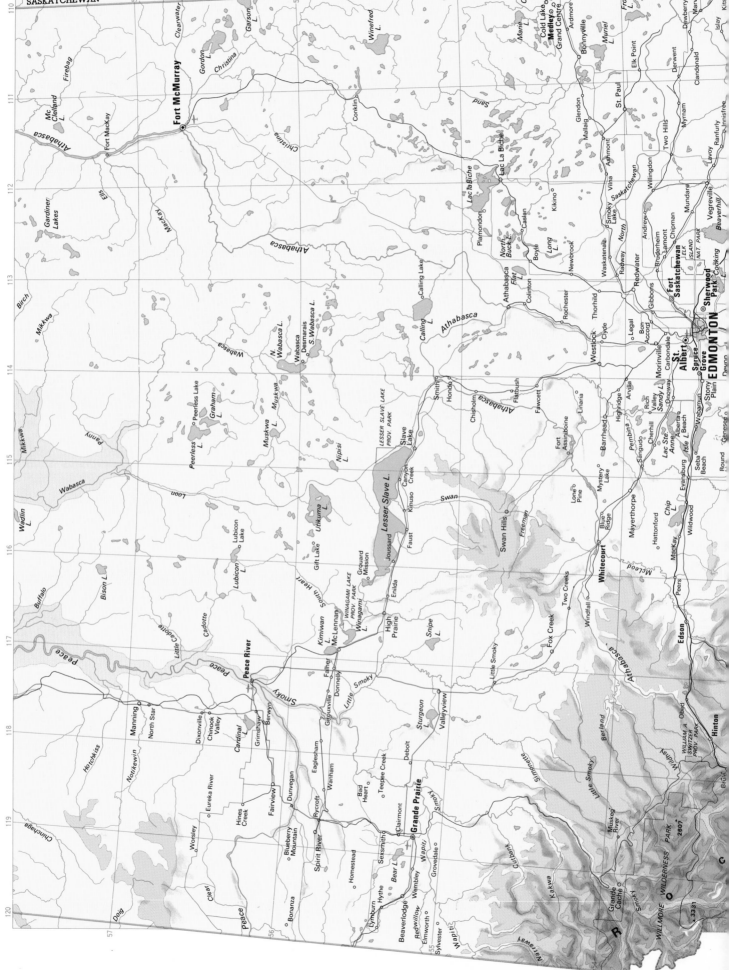

SASKATCHEWAN

Projection: Lambert's Conformal Conic   West from Greenwich

1:250 000

5 4 3 2 1 0   5   10 km

WINNIPEG map

Rosser · Gordon · Rivercrest · Pine Ridge · Manlius · Middlechurch · Birds Hill · Donan · Red · Oakbank · WEST KILDONAN · Murdock · Red River Floodway · Springfield · LORD SELKIRK · EAST KILDONAN · BROOKLANDS · ST. JOHNS · MARCONI · WINNIPEG INTERNATIONAL AIRPORT · CENTENNIAL · TRANSCONA · MIDLAND · **WINNIPEG** · Dugald · St. Charles · ST. JAMES-ASSINIBOIA · Leg. Bldgs · Seine · Headingley · KIRKFIELD PARK · Assiniboine · ST. BONIFACE · Deacon · ROBLIN PARK · ASSINIBOINE · FORT ROUGE · Navin · Charleswood · TUXEDO · Searle · FORT GARRY · ST. VITAL · Fort Whyte · Univ. of Manitoba · Red River Floodway · Elm Grove · 49° 50' · Red · Grande Pointe · Seine · Oak Bluff · St. Norbert · West from Greenwich

50° 00' · Sturgeon Cr. · Assiniboine · 97° 20' · 97° 10' · 97° 00' · 96° 50'

Legend

Residential	Industrial	Recreational	Transportation and utilities
Commercial	Institutional	Woodland	Agricultural and other

—o— Freeway with interchange   —o— Trans-Canada Highway   —o— Railway with station   ----- City Boundary

REGINA map

Brora · 104° 40' · 104° 30' · Zehner · Condie Reservoir · Boggy Cr. · Boggy Cr. · 50° 30' · UPLANDS · Wascana Cr. · NORMANVIEW · CITY VIEWS · **REGINA** · REGENT PARK · ROSS INDUSTRIAL PARK · MOUNT ROYAL · ROSEMONT · GLENCAIRN · Wascana Lake · Parl. Bldgs. · LAKEVIEW · Regina Univ. · ALBERT PARK · HILLSDALE · Richardson · Wascana Cr. · 50° 20' · Rowatt

Projection: Transverse Mercator · 104° 40' · West from Greenwich · 104° 30'

SASKATOON map

Clark's Crossing · South Saskatchewan · Saskatchewan · 106° 40' · 106° 30' · Edzel · SASKATOON AIRPORT · LAWSON HEIGHTS · 52° 10' · Forestry Farm & Animal Park · CONFEDERATION PARK · WESTMOUNT · University of Saskatchewan · SUTHERLAND · RIVERSDALE · NUTANA · **SASKATOON** · FAIRHAVEN · WILDWOOD · AVALON · Engen · YORATH ISLAND · WILSON ISLAND · Grasswood · Floral · Duro · Moon Lake · YOUNG ISLAND · 52° 00' · 106° 40' · West from Greenwich

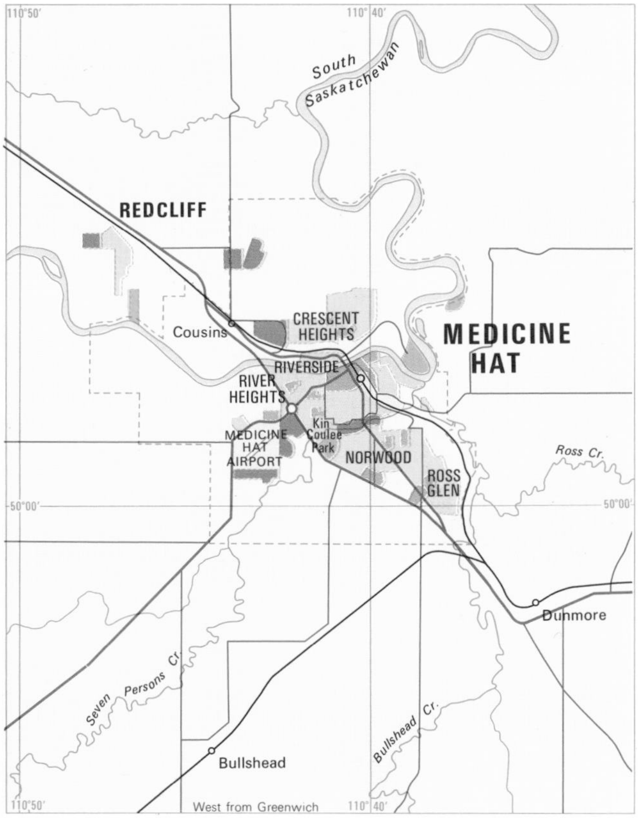

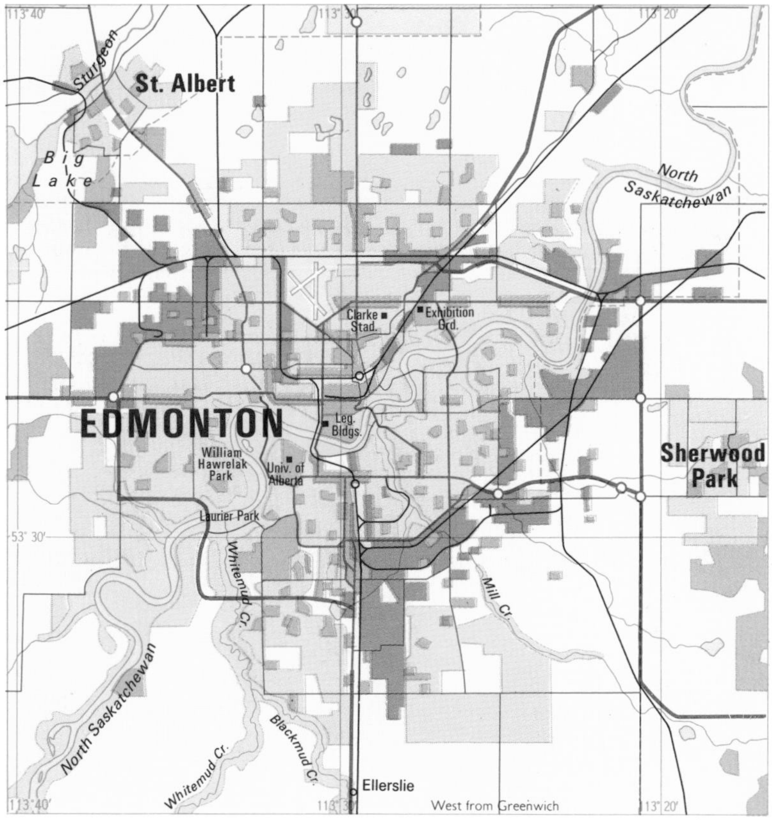

1:250 000

5 4 3 2 1 0   5 km

Medicine Hat map:

110°50'
110°40'

South Saskatchewan

REDCLIFF

Cousins

CRESCENT HEIGHTS

RIVERSIDE

RIVER HEIGHTS

MEDICINE HAT

Kin Coulee Park

MEDICINE HAT AIRPORT

NORWOOD

ROSS GLEN

Ross Cr.

50°00'
50°00'

Dunmore

Seven Persons Cr.

Bullshead Cr.

Bullshead

110°50'   West from Greenwich   110°40'

Edmonton map:

113°40'
113°30'
113°20'

Sturgeon

St. Albert

Big Lake

North Saskatchewan

Clarke Stad.

Exhibition Grd.

EDMONTON

Leg. Bldgs.

William Hawrelak Park

Univ. of Alberta

Sherwood Park

53°30'
53°30'

Laurier Park

Whitemud Cr.

Mill Cr.

North Saskatchewan

Blackmud Cr.

Whitemud Cr.

Ellerslie

113°40'   113°30'   West from Greenwich   113°20'

Legend:

Residential
Commercial
Industrial
Institutional
Recreational
Woodland
Transportation and utilities
Agricultural and other

Freeway with interchange
Trans-Canada Highway
Railway with station
City Boundary

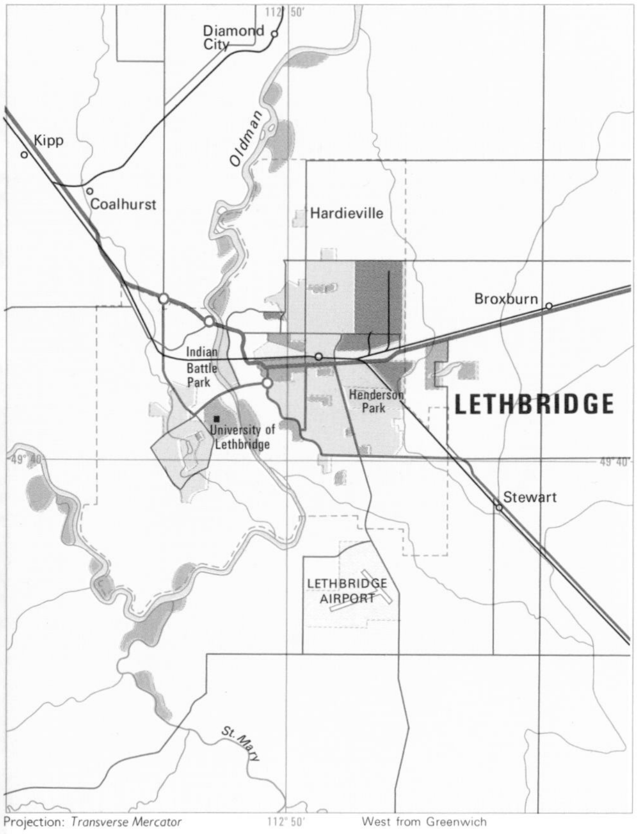

Lethbridge map:

112°50'

Diamond City

Kipp

Oldman

Coalhurst

Hardieville

Broxburn

Indian Battle Park

Henderson Park

LETHBRIDGE

University of Lethbridge

49°40'
49°40'

Stewart

LETHBRIDGE AIRPORT

St. Mary

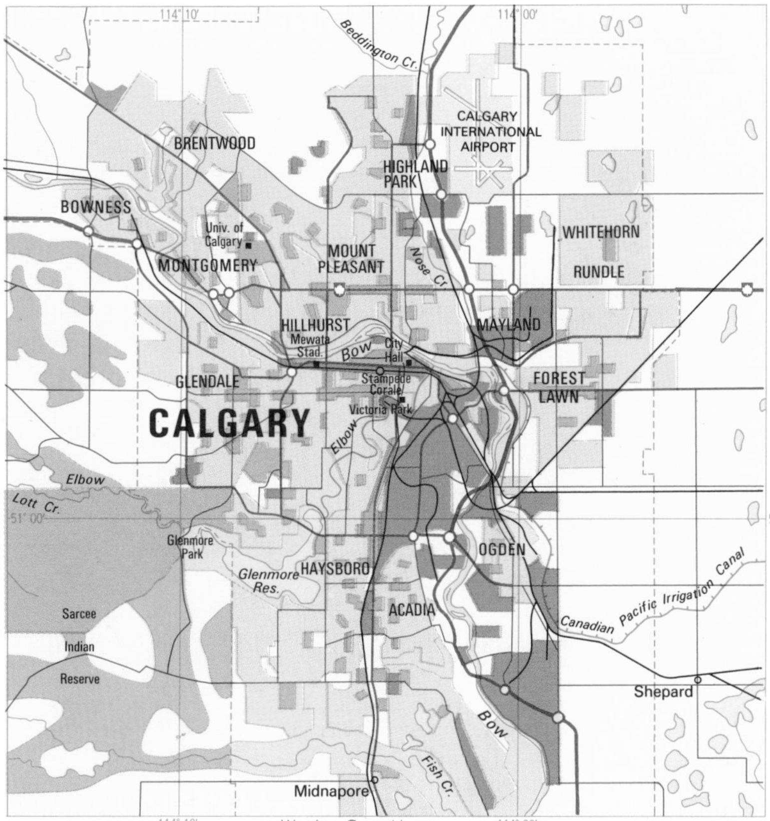

Projection: Transverse Mercator   112°50'   West from Greenwich

Calgary map:

114°10'
114°00'

Beddington Cr.

BRENTWOOD

CALGARY INTERNATIONAL AIRPORT

HIGHLAND PARK

BOWNESS

Univ. of Calgary

MONTGOMERY

MOUNT PLEASANT

Nose Cr.

WHITEHORN

RUNDLE

HILLHURST

Mewata Stad.

Bow

City Hall

MAYLAND

GLENDALE

Stampede Corral

Victoria Park

FOREST LAWN

CALGARY

Elbow

Elbow

Lott Cr.

51°00'
51°00'

Glenmore Park

Glenmore Res.

HAYSBORO

OGDEN

Canadian Pacific Irrigation Canal

Sarcee

Indian

Reserve

ACADIA

Shepard

Bow

Fish Cr.

Midnapore

114°10'   West from Greenwich   114°00'

COPYRIGHT. GEORGE PHILIP & SON. LTD.

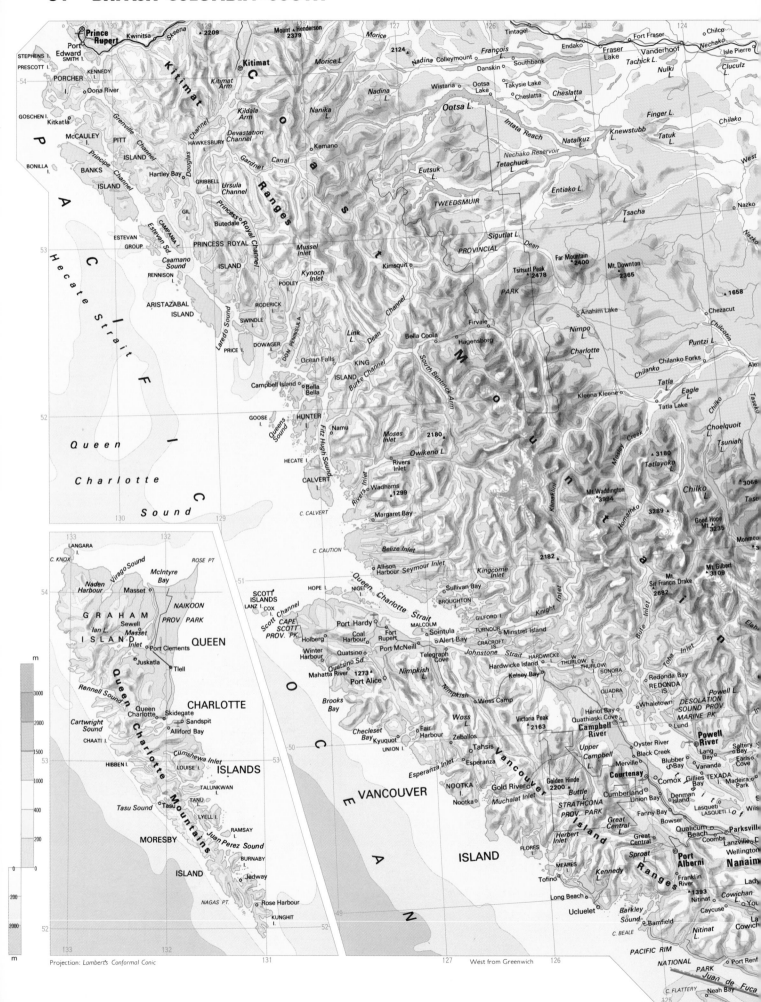

STEPHENS I.
PRESCOTT I.
PORCHER
GOSCHEN I.
Kitkatla
BONILLA I.
McCAULEY
BANKS ISLAND
PITT ISLAND
Port Edward SMITH I.
Prince Rupert
Kwinitsa
Skeena
▲2209
Mount Henderson 2379
Morice
2124
Nadina Colleymount
François
Tintagel
Endako
Fraser Lake
Fort Fraser
Vanderhoof
Chilco
Isle Pierre
Nechako
Cluculz L.

Kitimat
Kitimat Arm
Kildala Arm
Kemano
Nanika
Morice L.
Nadina
Nadina L.
Wistaria
Ootsa Lake
Takysie Lake
Cheslatta
Cheslatta
Danskin
Southbank
Tachick L.
Nulki L.

PORCHER
Oona River
Kitimat Arm
Kildala Arm
Devastation Channel
HAWKESBURY
GRIBBELL
Ursula Channel
GIL I.
Hartley Bay
Douglas Channel
Gardner Canal
Ootsa L.
Intata Reach
Natalkuz
Knewstubb
Tatuk L.
Finger L.
Chilako L.

Hecate Strait
CAMPANIA I.
ESTEVAN GROUP
Caamano Sound
RENNISON
ARISTAZABAL ISLAND
Princess Royal Channel
PRINCESS ROYAL ISLAND
Mussel Inlet
Kynoch Inlet
Kimsquit
Eutsuk L.
Tetachuck
Nechako Reservoir
Entiako L.
Tsacha L.
Nazko

Estevan Sd.
SWINDLE
RODERICK
DON PENINSULA
POOLEY
Link L.
Dean Channel
Bella Coola
Firvale
PROVINCIAL
Sigutlat L.
Dean
Far Mountain 2400
Tsitsutl Peak 2478
Mt. Downton 2365
▲1658

Laredo Sound
PRICE I.
DOWAGER
Ocean Falls
KING ISLAND
Burke Channel
Hagensborg
South Bentinck Arm
PARK
Anahim Lake
Nimpo L.
Charlotte L.
Chilanko Forks
Chilanko
Tatla L.
Chilko
Eagle L.
Ale

Campbell Island
Bella Bella
GOOSE I.
HUNTER I.
Namu
Moses Inlet
Owikeno L.
▲2180
Kleena Kleene
Tatla Lake
Choelquoit L.
Tsuniah L.

Queens Sound
Fitz Hugh Sound
HECATE I.
CALVERT I.
Rivers Inlet
Wadhams ▲1299
MOUNTAINS
▲3180
Tatlayoko L.
Chilko L.
▲3066
Tase

Margaret Bay
C. CALVERT
Klinaklini
Mt. Waddington 3994
Homathko
▲3289
Good Hope Mt. 3235
Monmou

C. CAUTION
Belize Inlet
Allison Harbour
Seymour Inlet
Kingcome Inlet
▲2182
Mt. Sir Francis Drake 2682
Mt. Gilbert 3109

HOPE I.
NIGEI
Sullivan Bay
BROUGHTON
Knight Inlet
Bute Inlet
Toba Inlet
Elaho

SCOTT ISLANDS
LANZ I.
COX I.
Scott Channel
CAPE SCOTT PROV. PK.
Port Hardy
Coal Harbour
Fort Rupert
Port McNeill
Sointula
Alert Bay
MALCOLM
GILFORD I.
Minstrel Island
TURNOUR
CRACROFT
HARDWICKE
W THURLOW
E THURLOW
SONORA
Redonda Bay
REDONDA IS
Powell L.
DESOLATION SOUND PROV. MARINE PK.

Holberg
Winter Harbour
Quatsino
Mahatta River
Quatsino Sd.
Port Alice
▲1273
Nimpkish L.
Telegraph Cove
Johnstone Strait
Hardwicke Island
Kelsey Bay
QUADRA
Whaletown
Heriot Bay
Quathiaski Cove
Lund

Brooks Bay
Nimpkish
Woss Camp
Woss L.
Victoria Peak ▲2163
Campbell River
Oyster River
Black Creek
Blubber Bay
Lang Bay
Saltery Bay
Earls Cove

Checleset Bay
Fair Harbour
Kyuquot
Zeballos
Tahsis
Upper Campbell L.
Merville
Golden Hinde ▲2200
Courtenay
Comox
Gillies Bay
TEXADA
Madeira Park
Powell River

UNION I.
Esperanza Inlet
Esperanza
VANCOUVER
NOOTKA
Nootka
Gold River
Muchalat Inlet
Buttle L.
STRATHCONA PROV. PARK
Cumberland
Union Bay
Fanny Bay
Denman Island
Lasqueti I.
LASQUETI
Qualicum Beach
Coombs

Great Central L.
Herbert Inlet
FLORES
MEARES I.
Great Central
Bowser
Lanzville
Wellington
Nanaim

Tofino
Kennedy L.
Franklin River
Sproat L.
Port Alberni
Parksville
Lady

Long Beach
Ucluelet
Barkley Sound
Bamford
Nitinat L.
▲1393
Caycuse
Cowichan
Yo

C. BEALE
PACIFIC RIM NATIONAL PARK
Nitinat
Cowich

C. FLATTERY
Neah Bay
Port Ren
Juan de Fuca

PACIFIC OCEAN

Queen Charlotte Sound

Inset map (lower left):

LANGARA
C. KNOX
ROSE PT
Naden Harbour
Virago Sound
McIntyre Bay
NAIKOON PROV PARK
GRAHAM ISLAND
Ian L.
Sewell
Masset Inlet
Masset
Port Clements
Juskatla
Tlell
QUEEN
CHARLOTTE
Skidegate
Sandspit
Alliford Bay
Rennell Sound
Cartwright Sound
Queen Charlotte
CHAATI I.
HIBBEN I.
LOUISE I.
Cumshewa Inlet
ISLANDS
TALUNKWAN
Tasu Sound
TANU
Tasu
LYELL I.
RAMSAY I.
Juan Perez Sound
MORESBY
BURNABY I.
Jedway
Nagas Pt.
Rose Harbour
KUNGHIT
Queen Charlotte Mountains

Projection: Lambert's Conformal Conic

West from Greenwich

1:2 500 000

10 0 10 20 30 40 50 60 70 80 90 100 km

VICTORIA (inset)

Royal Oak
GORDON HEAD
Colquitz
SAANICH
Lake Hill
Mt. Tolmie
Cadboro Bay
Langford
Craigflower
Belmont Park
Colwood
VICTORIA
ESQUIMALT
OAK BAY
DISCOVERY I.
MACAULAY PT.
Victoria Harb.
Beacon Hill Park
CLOVER PT.

1:250 000

0 1 2 3 4 5 km

For reference to colors
see page 88

ce George
nelley
neview
nd Rock
stoner
Woodpecker
Hixon
Strathnaver
Dunkley
Moose Heights
esnel
Graham
665
Riske Creek
nceville
Chilcotin
g Creek
Penny
Dome Creek
•2074
Bowron
Crescent Spur
Lamming Mills
McBride
Dunster
BOWRON LAKE PROV. PARK
Mitchell L.
WILLMORE WILDERNESS PARK
•2697
•3331
Mt. Robson 3954
MT. ROBSON
Red Pass
PROV.
Lucerne
Yellowhead Pass
PARK
ROCKY
Valemount
•3505
Albreda
Blue River
HAMBER PROV. PARK
Mt. Columbia 3747
3491
BANFF 3612
NATIONAL
Bow Pass
Mt. Chapman 3075
Mt. Sir Sandford 3522
Beavermouth
Donald
Kicking Horse Pass
YOHO NATIONAL PARK
3312
Lake Louise
Vermilion Pass
MOUN
Kinbasket Lake
Mica Dam
Mica Creek
1783
Wells
Kersley
Alexandria
Castle Rock
Marguerite
Macalister
Meldrum Creek
Springhouse
Wright
Likely
Quesnel
Horsefly L.
Horsefly
Hobson L.
Azure L.
WELLS GRAY
Mitchell L.
Clearwater
PROVINCIAL PARK
Murtle L.
Hendrix Lake
Mahood L.
Murphy L.
Canim L.
Mahood Falls
Clearwater
•2577
North Thompson
Avola
Adams
L. 2303
Columbia
Seymour Arm
Shuswap L.
MT. REVELSTOKE NAT'L PARK
Revelstoke
GLACIER NAT'L PARK
Glacier
Albert Canyon
Columbia
Golden
Parson
Mt. Templeman 3070
BUGABOO GLACIER PROV. PARK
3468
Duncan
Toby Creek
Williams Lake
150 Mile House
Lac la Hache
Forest Grove
Buffalo Creek
Canim L.
Clearwater
Birch Island
Vavenby
Chu Chua
Barrière
Louis Creek
McLure
Chase
Sicamous
Canoe
Hupel
Mabel L.
MONASHEE PROV. PARK
2972
Trout Lake
Gerrard
100 Mile House
Sheridan L.
Little Fort
Salmon Arm
Enderby
Armstrong
Cherryville
Sugar L.
Arrowhead
Upper Arrow Lake
New Denver
Slocan
Silverton
Kaslo
Riondel
Lone Butte
Dog Creek
70 Mile House
Bonaparte L.
Black Pines
Rayleigh
Westsyde
Kamloops
SILVER STAR PROV. PARK
Vernon
Mabel L.
Sugar L.
Nakusp
Burton
Fauquier
Edgewood
Marblehead
Duncan Dam
KOKANEE GLACIER PROV. PARK
Gang Ranch
Big Bar Creek
•2243
Chasm
Clinton
Cache Creek
Walhachin
Savona
Kamloops
South Thompson
Chase
Enderby
Armstrong
Oyama
Arrow Park
Procter
Boswell
•2877
Carpenter
Shalalth
Lilloet
•2329
Ashcroft
Cherry Creek
Savona
Kamloops
Vernon
Cherryville
Slocan
Nelson
Kootenay L.
Bralorne
Anderson L.
Seton Portage
Seton L.
Birken
Spences Bridge
Thompson
Lower Nicola
Nicola
Nicola L.
Valleyview
Oyama
Wilson Landing
Kelowna
Okanagan Mission
Carmi
Kettle R.
Renata
H. Keenleyside Dam
Brilliant
Castlegar
Kinnaird
Salmo
Pemberton
Lillooet L.
•2385
Skihist Mt. 2944
Lytton
Merritt
Aspen Grove
Okanagan L.
Peachland
OKANAGAN MOUNTAIN PROV. PARK
Summerland
Penticton
Beaverdell
Granby R.
Eholt
Greenwood
Christina L.
Warfield
Rossland
Trail
Fruitvale
Montrose
Alta Lake
GARIBALDI
Mt. Garibaldi 2678
PROV. PARK
North Bend
Boston Bar
Brookmere
Carmi
Coalmont
Princeton
Hedley
Simikameen
Oliver
•2304
Greenwood
Rock Creek
Midway
Grand Forks
WASHINGTON
Northport
Metaline Falls
IDAHO
ndale
Squamish
Britannia Beach
GOLDEN EARS PROV. PARK
Harrison Lake
Spuzzum
Yale
Hope
Keremeos
Osoyoos
Osoyoos L.
Oroville
Columbia
Ione
Priest L.
ore So
Bowen Island
Pitt L.
Stave L.
Harrison Hot Springs
Agassiz
Laidlaw
Cheam View
Silvertip Mt. 2606
MANNING PROV. PARK
Manning Park
CATHEDRAL PROV. PARK 2593
Usoyoos
Rock Creek
Kettle Falls
Colville
IBIER
Port Moody
Port Coquitlam
North Vancouver
VANCOUVER
New Westminster
Langley
Haney
Mission City
Fort Langley
Chilliwack
Sardis
Rosedale
Yarrow
Lindell Beach
Tonasket
Republic
Chewelah
White Rock
Blaine
Sumas
Lynden
Abbotsford
Maple Falls
Mount Baker
Mt. Baker 3284
NORTH CASCADES
Ross L.
Chewack Creek
Mazama
Riverside
Newport
nus
Mayne
Saturna
East Sound
Ferndale
Bellingham
Whatcom
Shannon L.
Newhalem
NATIONAL
•2703
Conconully
Pend Oreille
ple
Fulford Harbour
Sidney
Friday Harbor
Orcas
LOPEZ
SAN JUAN I.
LUMMI
Sedro Woolley
Burlington
Mount Vernon
Concrete
Marblemount
Rockport
PARK
Hamilton
Tonasket
Mazama
Winthrop
Twisp
Carlton
Malott
Okanogan
Omak
Nespelem
Springdale
VICTORIA
Oak Harbor
WHIDBEY
Coupeville
CAMANO
Stanwood
Arlington
Darrington
Glacier Peak 3211
Holden
Lucerne
Stehekin
Chelan
Okanogan
Columbia
Omak

COPYRIGHT. GEORGE PHILIP & SON, LTD.

ARCTIC OCEAN

Beaufort Sea

Borden I.
Brock I.
Prince Patrick I.
Mackenzie King I.
Parry Isla
Mould Bay
Eglinton I.
Kellett Str.
Blue Hills
1067
Liddon Gulf
Melville I.
C. Wrottesley
M'Clure Strait
Dundas Pen.
C. Hay
C. Prince Alfred
Viscount Soun
Banks Island
Storkerson B.
Prince Albert Pen.
Wynniatt Bay
Hadley Bay
C. Kellett
Sachs Harbour
Prince of Wales Str.
Passage Pt.
Stefa
Thesiger Bay
C. Lambton
750
Amundsen Gulf
C. Bathurst
Holman
Victoria Island
KITI
Prince Albert Sd.
C. Baring
Dolphin & Union Str.
Read Island
Wollaston Pen.
Coronation Gulf
Kent Pen.
Coppermine
Bluenose L.
Bathurst Inlet
Hornaday
Bathurst Inlet
Takiyuak L.
Burnside
Pel
Contwoyto L.

Colville
Pt. Franklin
Barrow
Pt. Barrow
C. Halkett
Umiat
Prudhoe Bay
Kaktovik
Martin Pt.
Permanent Polar Ice
Brooks Range
Mt. Doonerak 2350
Endicott Mts.
Evansville
Wiseman
Mt. Isto 2761
Arctic Village
Herschel I.
British Mts.
Richards I.
Mackenzie Bay
Liverpool Bay
Franklin Bay
Darnley Bay
Paulatuk
Alatakaket
Stevens
Beaver
Fort Yukon
Porcupine
Old Crow
Aklavik
Tuktoyaktuk
Eskimo Lakes
Inuvik
INUVIK REGION
L. Maunoir
Horton L.
Livengood
Fairbanks
ALASKA (U.S.A.)
Yukon
Ft. McPherson
Arctic Red River
Aubry L.
Colville Lake
Tanana
Eagle
Clinton Creek
Richardson Mts.
Peel
Ft. Good Hope
NORTHWEST
L. Belot
L. des Bois
Delta Junction
Dawson
Klondike
Mackenzie
Franklin Mts.
Smith Arm
Dease Arm
Coppermine
Mt. Sanford 4949
Beaver Creek
Stewart River
Elsa
Keno Hill Mts.
Mayo
Norman Wells
Ft. Franklin
Gt. Bear Lake
157
Echo Bay (Port Radium)
Wrangell Mts.
Pelly Crossing
Ft. Norman
Great Bear
Keith Arm
Mt. Steele 5011
Kluane L.
Carmacks
Hottah L.
Point L.
Snare Lakes
L. de Gras
Mt. Logan 6051
Burwash Landing
Destruction Bay
YUKON TERRITORY
Ross River
Pelly
2965
Rae Lakes
Mt. Kennedy 4238
Haines Junc.
Ford
Mackenzie Mountains
S. Nahanni
2743
Wrigley
L. la Martre
Lac la Martre
Aylmer L.
Clinton Colden L.
Mt. St. Elias 5489
KLUANE NAT. PARK
Whitehorse
Mackenzie
FORT SMITH
Yakutat
Kluane
Carcross
Jakes Corner
Johnsons Crossing
Tungsten
NAHANNI NAT. PARK
Ft. Simpson
Jean Marie River
Rae-Edzo
Yellowknife
Reliance
Mt. Fairweather 4663
Skagway
Bennett
Atlin
Teslin
Nahanni Butte
Liard
Detah
Yellowknife
Cross Sd.
Chichagof I.
Douglas
Juneau
Cassiar Mts.
Upper Liard
Watson Lake
Nahanni Butte
Ft. Liard
Ft. Providence
156
Rae
Great Slave L.
Rocher River
Snowdrift
Nonacho L.
Admiralty
Sitka
Baranof I.
Dease Lake
Cassiar
Dease
Fort Liard
Trout L.
Trout Lake
Hay River
Enterprise
Fort Resolution
Pine Point
Stikine
Telegraph Creek
Mt. Lloyd George 3292
ALASKA HIGHWAY
Ft. Nelson
Nelson
Petitot
WOOD BUFFALO NAT. PARK
Caribou Mts.
Ft. Smith
Wholdaia L.
Meander River

Projection: Bonne

1:10 000 000

100   0   100   200   300   400 km

G R E E N L A N D

(DENMARK)

United States Range

Barbeau Pk. 2604

C. Thomas Hubbard

Nansen Sd.

Princess Margaret Range

2140 ▲ Axel Heiberg I.

Greely Fd.

Eureka

Fosheim Pen.

Victoria and Albert Mts.

Kennedy Str.

Kane Basin

Humboldt Glacier

Inglefield Land

Knud Rasmussen Land

Smith Sound

Inglefield Gulf

Thule (Qanaq)

C. Parry

Wolstenholme Fjord

Dundas (Thule)

C. York

Melville Bay

Kraulshavn

Upernavik

Proven

Svartenhuk Peninsula

Umanak

Nugssuaq Pen.

Disko B.

Jakobshavn

Disko I.

Godthavn

Resolution I.

Holsteinsborg

B a f f i n   B a y

D a v i s   S t r a i t

Sverdrup Is.

drup Is.

Amund Ringnes I.

Norwegian Bay

Cornwall I.

Graham I.

Belcher Channel

Magnetic

Elizabeth

Penny Str.

E l l e s m e r e   I s.

Simmons Pen.

Grise Fiord

Treuter Mts. 1887

Lady Ann Str.

Coburg I.

Hyde Inlet

C. Cockburn

Jones Sound

Devon I.

C. Warrender

Lancaster Sound

Barrow Str.

Resolute

Wellington Chan.

Cornwallis I.

Russell

hurst I.

Somerset I.

R E G I O N

C. Crauford

Nanisivik

Arctic Bay

Borden Peninsula

2134 ▲ Bylot I.

Eclipse Sd.

Pond Inlet

C. Liverpool

Nova Zembla I.

C. Jameson

C. Hunter

Scott Inlet

C. Hewett

Clyde River

C. Raper

C. Henry Kater

Home B.

Kivitoo

Broughton Island

Padloping Island

Cape Dyer

Prince of Wales I.

Brodeur Peninsula

Admiralty Inlet

Prince Regent Inlet

Ft. Ross

C. Farrand

F F I N

Franklin Str.

Boothia Peninsula

Gateshead I.

Bernier B.

B a f f i n

Barnes Icecap

Bruce Mts.

AUYUITTUQ Penny Highland NAT. PARK 2591 ▲

Cumberland Peninsula

Pangnirtung

Hoare B.

C. Mercy

E O T

Gulf of Boothia

573 ▲

Steensby Inlet

Baird Pen.

I s l a n d

Cumberland Sound

Lemieux Islands

Thom Bay

Spence Bay

C. Englefield

Fury & Hecla Str.

Igloolik

Rowley I.

Hall Beach

Foley I.

Air Force I.

Prince Charles I.

Netilling L.

Frobisher Bay

Hall Pen.

King William I.

Gjoa Haven

Simpson Pen.

Pelly Bay

Melville Peninsula

Wales Peninsula

Foxe Basin

C. Dominion

Amadjuak L.

C. Mercy

Adelaide Pen.

Chantrey Inlet

Committee B.

Rae Isthmus

Repulse Bay

C. Dorchester

Foxe Pen.

Amadjuak

Lake Harbour

Everett Mts.

Resolution I.

Frobisher Bay

O N

Gulf

Macdougall L.

Arctic Circle

Vansittart I.

Foxe Channel

Cape Dorset

Big I.

C. Chidley

T E R R I T O R I E S

Wager L.

Wager B.

Torsill Mts.

Salisbury I.

H u d s o n   S t r a i t

arry L.

Roes Welcome Sd.

Southampton I.

Coral Harbour

Bell Pen.

Nottingham I.

Nottingham Island

C. Hopes Advance

Akpatok I.

Port Burwell

Baker Lake

Baker L.

Chesterfield Inlet

Fisher Strait

Coats I.

Digges Is.

Wolstenholme

Sagloue

Koartac

Maricourt (Wakeham)

Ungava Bay

K E E W A T I N

Chesterfield Inlet

Mansel I.

C. Wolstenholme

Ivugivik

St. Louis Mts.

Bellin (Payne)

Port Nouveau-Québec (George R.)

Dubawnt L.

R E G I O N

Rankin Inlet

Whale Cove

Arnaud (Payne)

Yathkyed L.

Kaminak L.

Tavani

Cape Smith

Payne L.

Koksoak

Kuujjuaq

Padle

Eskimo Point

Povungnityk

Feuilles (Leaf)

Mélèzes (Larch)

Cantapiscau

Nueltin L.

Thlewiaza

H u d s o n   B a y

Ottawa Is.

Inoucdjouac (Port Harrison)

Portland Promontory

L. Minto

COPYRIGHT. GEORGE PHILIP & SON. LTD.

Territorial Capitals are underlined

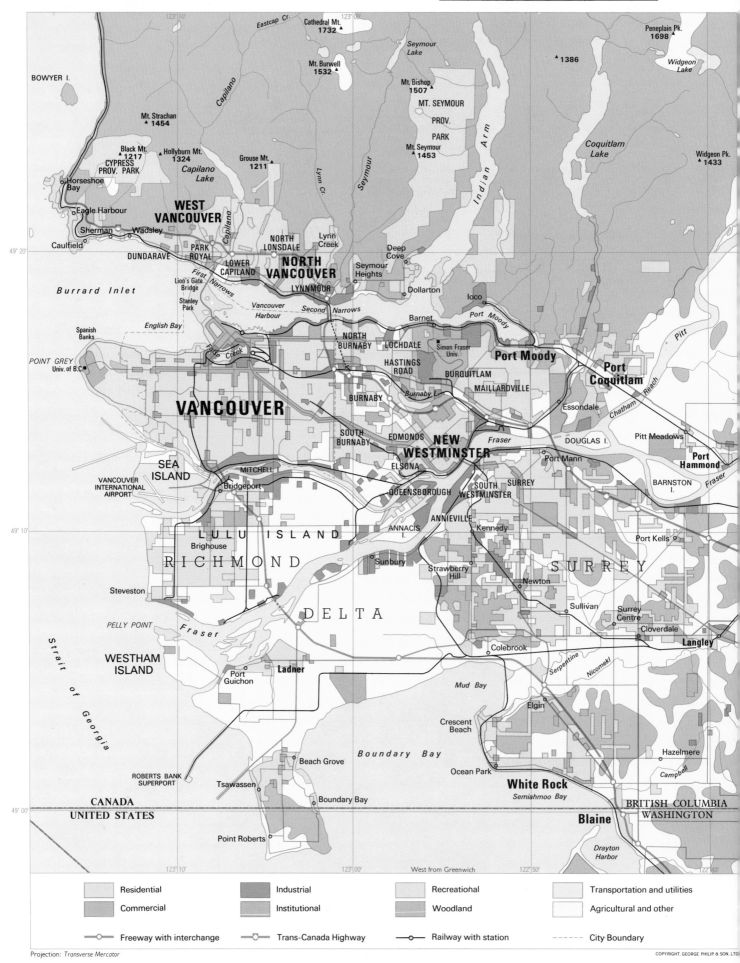

1 : 250 000

5 4 3 2 1 0   5   10 km

BOWYER I.

Eastcap Cr.

Cathedral Mt. 1732

Seymour Lake

Peneplain Pk. 1698

Mt. Burwell 1532

▲ 1386

Widgeon Lake

Mt. Bishop 1507

Capilano

MT. SEYMOUR

Mt. Strachan ▲ 1454

PROV.

Coquitlam Lake

Black Mt. ▲ 1217

Hollyburn Mt. 1324

Grouse Mt. 1211 ▲

PARK

CYPRESS PROV. PARK

Capilano Lake

Mt. Seymour ▲ 1453

Widgeon Pk. ▲ 1433

Horseshoe Bay

Lynn Cr.

Seymour

Indian Arm

Eagle Harbour

WEST VANCOUVER

Sherman   Wadsley

Caulfield

DUNDARAVE

Capilano

PARK ROYAL

LOWER CAPILANO

NORTH LONSDALE

Lynn Creek

NORTH VANCOUVER

Deep Cove

First Narrows

Lion's Gate Bridge

Seymour Heights

Dollarton

Pitt

Burrard Inlet

Stanley Park

Vancouver Harbour

LYNNMOUR

Second Narrows

Barnet

Port Moody

Ioco

English Bay

Spanish Banks

False Creek

NORTH BURNABY

LOCHDALE

Simon Fraser Univ.

Port Moody

Port Coquitlam

POINT GREY Univ. of B.C. ■

HASTINGS ROAD

BURQUITLAM

Chatham Reach

VANCOUVER

BURNABY

Burnaby L.

MAILLARDVILLE

Essondale

SOUTH BURNABY

EDMONDS

NEW WESTMINSTER

Fraser

DOUGLAS I.

Pitt Meadows

SEA ISLAND

ELSONA

Port Hammond

VANCOUVER INTERNATIONAL AIRPORT

MITCHELL I.

Bridgeport

QUEENSBOROUGH

SOUTH WESTMINSTER

SURREY

Port Mann

BARNSTON I.

Fraser

LULU ISLAND

ANNACIS I.

ANNIEVILLE

Kennedy

Port Kells

Brighouse

RICHMOND

Sunbury

Strawberry Hill

SURREY

Steveston

Newton

Sullivan

Surrey Centre

DELTA

Cloverdale

PELLY POINT

Fraser

Colebrook

Serpentine

Langley

WESTHAM ISLAND

Port Guichon

Ladner

Mud Bay

Nicomekl

Elgin

Campbell

Hazelmere

ROBERTS BANK SUPERPORT

Beach Grove

Crescent Beach

Tsawassen

Boundary Bay

Ocean Park

White Rock

Semiahmoo Bay

BRITISH COLUMBIA

WASHINGTON

CANADA

UNITED STATES

Blaine

Point Roberts

Drayton Harbor

Strait of Georgia

Boundary Bay

West from Greenwich

49° 20'

49° 10'

49° 00'

123° 10'   123° 00'   122° 50'   122° 40'

123° 10'   123° 09'

| | Residential | | Industrial | | Recreational | | Transportation and utilities |
| | Commercial | | Institutional | | Woodland | | Agricultural and other |

⊙——⊙ Freeway with interchange   ⊙——⊙ Trans-Canada Highway   ●——● Railway with station   - - - - City Boundary

Projection: Transverse Mercator

COPYRIGHT. GEORGE PHILIP & SON. LTD

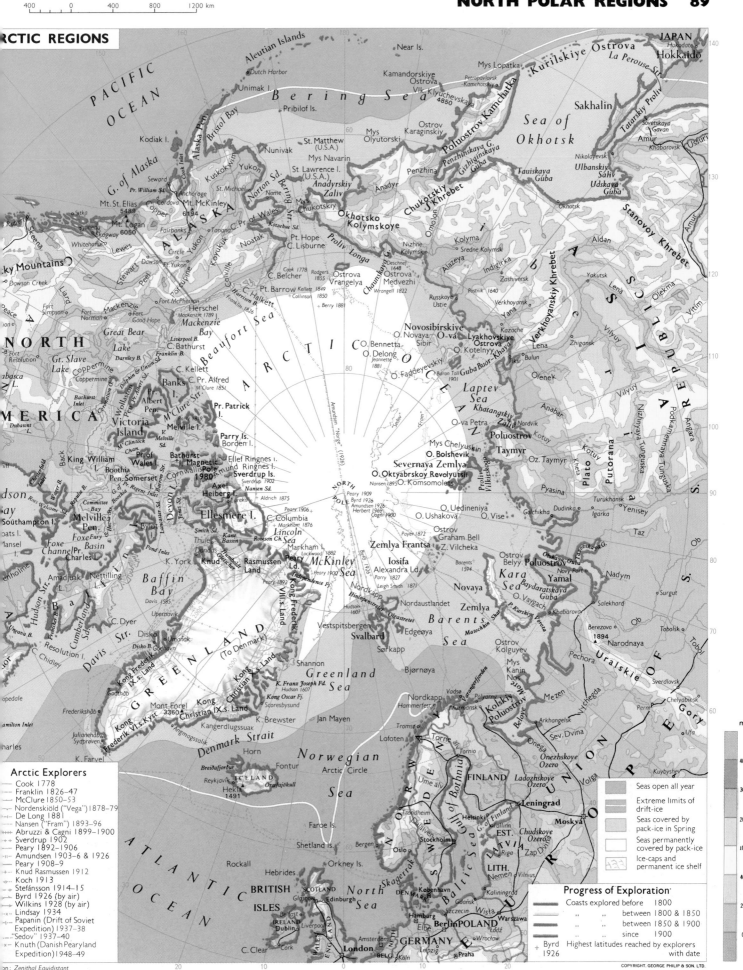

1:35 000 000

400   0   400   800   1200 km

PACIFIC OCEAN

Aleutian Islands

Near Is.

JAPAN
Hokkaido
Hakodate

Kuriliskiye Ostrova
La Perouse Str.

Mys Lopatka

Kamandorskiye Ostrova

Petropavlovsk Kamchatskiy

Sakhalin

Sea of Okhotsk

Bering Sea

Pribilof Is.

Dutch Harbor

Unimak I.

Bristol Bay

St. Matthew (U.S.A.)

Nunivak

Mys Olyutorskiy

Mys Navarin

Poluostrov Kamchatka

Vlk. Klyuchevskaya 4850

Nikolayevsk

Tatarskiy Proliv

Sovetskaya Gavan

Amur
Khabarovsk

Ussuri

Kodiak I.

G. of Alaska

Seward

Anchorage

Pr. William Sd.

Cook Inlet

St. Lawrence I. (U.S.A.)

Nome

Norton Sd.

St. Michael

Bering Str.

Mys Chukotskiy

Anadyrskiy Zaliv

Anadyr

Penzhina

Gizhiginskaya Guba

Penzhinskaya G.

Tauiskaya Guba

Okhotsk

Ulbanskiy Zaliv

Udskaya Guba

Stanovoy Khrebet

Aldan

Mt. St. Elias 5489

Mt. Logan 6050

Cordova
Copper

Mt. McKinley 6194

Fairbanks
Tanana

ALASKA

Yukon

Kuskokwim

C. Pr. of Wales

Kotzebue Sd.

Pt. Hope
C. Lisburne

Proliv Longa

Okhotsko Kolymskoye

Chukotskiy Khrebet

Omolon

Kolyma

Nizhne Kolymsk

Sredne Kolymsk

Alazeya

Indigirka

Zashiversk

Verkhoyansk

Yakutsk

Lena

Olekma

Vitim

Juneau

Sitka

Skagway

Whitehorse

Lewes

Circle

Yukon

Koyukuk

Noatak

Cook 1778

Rodgers 1855

C. Belcher

Kellett 1849
Collinson 1850

Ostrova Vrangelya
Wrangell 1822

Chaunskaya G.

Ostrova Medvezhi

Russkoye Ustie

Yana

Kazache

Zhigansk

Vilyuy

Vilyuysk

Yakutsk

ARCTIC

Verkhoyanskiy Khrebet

S.   S.   R.

Rocky Mountains

Dawson Creek

Stewart

Liard

Fort Nelson

Peace

Fort Resolution

Fort Simpson

Fort Norman

Fort Good Hope

Mackenzie

Fort McPherson

Herschel I.

Mackenzie 1789

Mackenzie Bay

Liverpool B.

C. Bathurst

Darnley B.

Franklin B.

Franklin 1826

Pt. Barrow

C. Halkett

Harrison B.

Berry 1881

Beaufort Sea

ARCTIC   OCEAN

O. Bennetta

O. Delong
Jeannette 1881

Novosibirskiye O-va

O. Novaya Sibir

Lyakhovskiye Ostrova

O. Kotelnyy

Baron Toll 1901

Guba Buor-Khaya

Tiksi

Bulun

Olenek

Zhigansk

Lena

Anabar

NORTH

Great Bear Lake

Coppermine

Gt. Slave Lake

Athabasca L.

Dubawnt L.

Fort Resolution

Coppermine

Dolphin & Union Str.

Darnley B.

C. Kellett

Banks I.

C. Pr. Alfred

M'Clure 1851

M'Clure Str.

Pr. Patrick I.

Melville I.

Borden I.

Parry Is.

Ellef Ringnes I.

Amund Ringnes I.

Axel Heiberg I.

Sverdrup Is.

Sverdrup 1902

Nansen 1895

O. Faddeyevskiy

Laptev Sea

Khatangskiy Zaliv

O-va Petra

Nordvik

Kotuy

Mys Chelyuskin

O. Bolshevik

Severnaya Zemlya

O. Oktyabrskoy Revolyutsii

O. Komsomolets

Poluostrov Taymyr

Oz. Taymyr

Pyasina

Kheta

Plato Putorana

Kotuy

Khatanga

AMERICA

Victoria Island

King William I.

Boothia Pen.

Somerset I.

Bathurst I.

Cornwallis I.

Devon I.

Ellesmere I.

Eureka

Aldrich 1875

Nansen 1896

Peary 1906

C. Columbia

Markham 1876

Lincoln Sea

Robeson Ch.

Kane Basin

Smith Sd.

Magnetic Pole 1980

Pr. of Wales I.

M'Clintock Chan.

Melville Sd.

Pr. Regent Inlet

Bathurst Inlet

Committee Bay

Repulse B.

Boothia

Pr. Albert Pen.

Wollaston Pen.

NORTH POLE

Peary 1909
Byrd 1926
Amundsen 1926
Cagni 1900
Herbert 1969

O. Ushakova

O. Vise

Ostrov Graham Bell

Z. Vilcheka

Payer 1872

Zemlya Frantsa Iosifa

Alexandra Ld.

Parry 1827

Leigh Smith 1871

O. Uedineniya

Ostrov Belyy

Novyy Port

Ostrova Belyy Poluostrov

Dikson

Golchikha

Dudinka

Igarka

Turukhansk

Yenisey

Taz

Ob

Berezovo

Narodnaya

Uralskie Gory

Ob

Surgut

Nadym

Salekhard

Ob

Tobol

Tobolsk

Chelyabinsk

Sverdlovsk

Perm

Ufa

Kuybyshev

Hudson Bay

Southampton I.

Melville Pen.

Foxe Channel

Foxe Basin

Fury

Pr. Charles I.

Mansel I.

Nettilling L.

Amadjuak L.

Baffin Island

Cumberland Sd.

Resolution I.

C. Dyer

Davis Str.

Frobisher B.

Ungava B.

C. Chidley

Hudson Str.

Markham I.

Lockwood 1882

McKinley Sea

Peary 1900

Peary Ld.

Rasmussen Land

Knud Rasmussen

Thule

K. York

Pond Inlet

Disko

Godhavn

Upernavik

Umanak

GREENLAND
(To Denmark)

Mont Forel 3360

Kong Frederik IX.s Land

Kong Christian IX.s Land

Kong Christian X.s Kyst

Kong Frederik VI.s Kyst

Peary 1892

Independence Fj.

Kong Frederik VIII.s Land

Nordostrundingen

Hinlopenstret

Olgastretet

Nordaustlandet

Nordkapp

Vestspitsbergen

Svalbard

Edgeøya

Sørkapp

Bjørnøya

Barents Sea

Zemlya

Novaya

Kara Sea

O. Vaygach

Matochkin Shar

P. Karskiye Vorota

Baydaratskaya Guba

Yamal

Khabarovo

Barents 1594

Novaya

1894

Pechora

Mys Kanin Nos

Mezen

Sev. Dvina

Arkhangelsk

Onega

Onezhskoye Ozero

Ladozhskoye Ozero

Svir

Volga

Vychegda

Nichegda

Pechora

Kolskiy Poluostrov

Belove

Murmansk

Polyarny

Vardö

Vadsö

Varangerfjorden

Nordkapp

Hammerfest

Tromsö

Narvik

Lofoten

Kangerdlugssuak

Angmagssalik

Scoresbysund

K. Brewster

Shannon

Kong Oscar Fjord

K. Frans Joseph Fd.

Hudson 1607

Jan Mayen

Greenland Sea

Denmark Strait

K. Farvel

Sydprøven

Julianehåb

Frederikshåb

Godthåb

Frederiksdal

Breiðafjörður

Reykjavík

Hekla 1491

Öræfajökull

ICELAND

Horn

Fontur

Norwegian Sea

Arctic Circle

Torne

Torneå

Tornio

Umeälv

SWEDEN

NORWAY

FINLAND

Oulu

Ladozhskoye Ozero

Leningrad

Moskvá

Chudskoye Ozero

EST.

LATVIA

Riga

LITH.

Vilnius

Nemen

Kaliningrad

Helsinki

Gulf of Finland

Stockholm

Gulf of Bothnia

Oslo

Bergen

Ångermanälven

Faroe Is.

Shetland Is.

Orkney Is.

SCOTLAND

Glasgow
Edinburgh

Belfast

IRELAND
Dublin
Liverpool

ENGLAND

BRITISH ISLES

Rockall

Hebrides

C. Clear

Cork

ATLANTIC OCEAN

North Sea

Skagerrak

Kattegat

DENMARK

København

Hamburg

Amsterdam

London

BELG.

GERMANY

Berlin

POLAND

Warszawa

Gdańsk

Szczecin

Wrocław

Łódź

Köln

Elbe

Praha

Leipzig

EUROPE

Kuybyshev

S.   S.   R.

Wisła

UNION OF

Arctic Explorers

— Cook 1778
— Franklin 1826–47
— McClure 1850–53
— Nordenskiöld ("Vega") 1878–79
— De Long 1881
— Nansen ("Fram") 1893–96
— Abruzzi & Cagni 1899–1900
— Sverdrup 1902
— Peary 1892–1906
— Amundsen 1903–6 & 1926
— Peary 1908–9
— Knud Rasmussen 1912
— Koch 1913
— Stefánsson 1914–15
— Byrd 1926 (by air)
— Wilkins 1928 (by air)
— Lindsay 1934
— Papanin (Drift of Soviet Expedition) 1937–38
— "Sedov" 1937–40
— Knuth (Danish Pearyland Expedition) 1948–49

Projection: Zenithal Equidistant

Progress of Exploration

Coasts explored before 1800
    "   " between 1800 & 1850
    "   " between 1850 & 1900
    "   " since 1900
+ Byrd 1926 Highest latitudes reached by explorers with date

Seas open all year
Extreme limits of drift-ice
Seas covered by pack-ice in Spring
Seas permanently covered by pack-ice
Ice-caps and permanent ice shelf

m
4000
3000
2000
1000
400
200
0

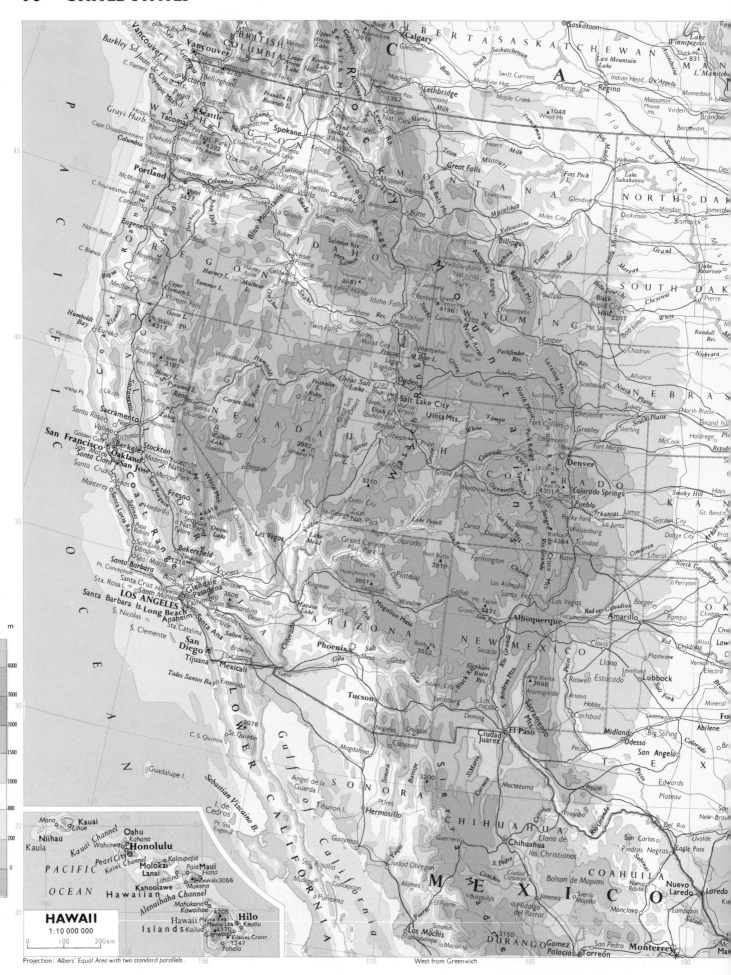

HAWAII

1:10 000 000

0   100   200 km

Projection: Albers' Equal Area with two standard parallels.

West from Greenwich

1:12 000 000

100 0 100 200 300 400 500 km

CANADA

QUEBEC MAINE NEW BRUNSWICK

Winnipeg Lake Superior Lake Huron Lake Michigan Lake Erie Lake Ontario

MINNESOTA WISCONSIN MICHIGAN NEW YORK VERMONT NEW HAMPSHIRE MASSACHUSETTS

Minneapolis St. Paul Duluth MONTREAL Ottawa TORONTO Buffalo Boston

IOWA ILLINOIS INDIANA OHIO PENNSYLVANIA NEW JERSEY CONN.

Des Moines CHICAGO DETROIT Cleveland Pittsburgh NEW YORK PHILADELPHIA

Council Bluffs MISSOURI Indianapolis Cincinnati WEST VIRGINIA MARYLAND Baltimore Washington D.C. DEL.

Kansas City St. Louis Louisville KENTUCKY VIRGINIA Richmond Norfolk

ARKANSAS TENNESSEE NORTH CAROLINA Raleigh

Little Rock Memphis Nashville Chattanooga Charlotte Columbia SOUTH CAROLINA

MISSISSIPPI ALABAMA GEORGIA Atlanta Savannah Charleston

Shreveport Jackson Birmingham Montgomery Columbus

LOUISIANA New Orleans Baton Rouge Mobile Jacksonville FLORIDA

Houston Galveston GULF OF MEXICO

Tampa St. Petersburg Orlando West Palm Beach

Miami Key West

ATLANTIC OCEAN

BAHAMAS Gt. Abaco Eleuthera I. Andros I.

QUEBEC

ONTARIO

NEW YORK

PENNSYLVANIA

MICHIGAN

OHIO

INDIANA

WEST VIRGINIA

VIRGINIA

MARYLAND

NEW JERSEY

DELAWARE

VERMONT

NEW HAMPSHIRE

MASS.

WISCONSIN

LAKE SUPERIOR

LAKE HURON

LAKE ERIE

LAKE ONTARIO

Georgian Bay

Chesapeake Bay

MONTREAL

OTTAWA

TORONTO

DETROIT

CHICAGO

MILWAUKEE

CLEVELAND

PITTSBURGH

COLUMBUS

CINCINNATI

INDIANAPOLIS

BUFFALO

NEW YORK CITY

PHILADELPHIA

BALTIMORE

WASHINGTON D.C.

BOSTON

RICHMOND

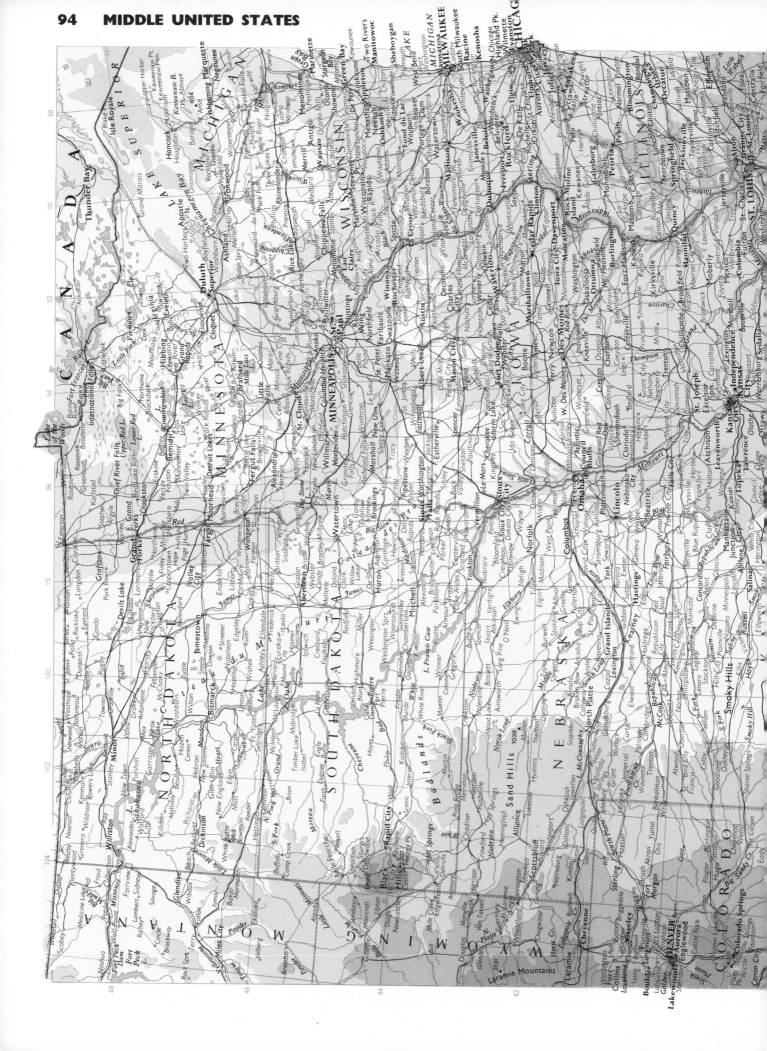

1:6 000 000

0 50 100 150 200 250 km

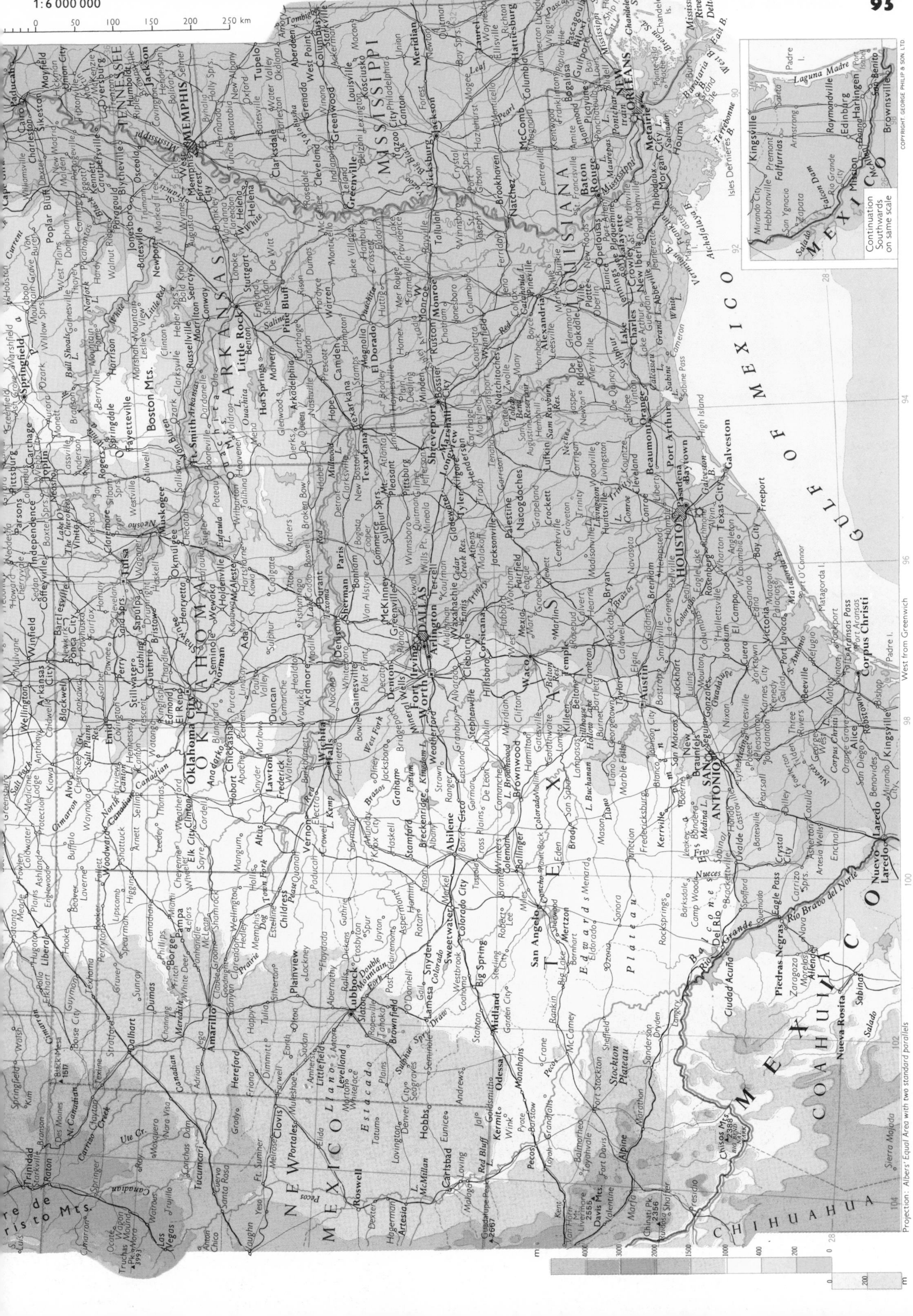

Laguna Madre

Padre I.

MEXICO

Continuation Southwards on same scale

Projection: Alber's Equal Area with two standard parallels

West from Greenwich

TENNESSEE

MISSISSIPPI

ARKANSAS

LOUISIANA

OKLAHOMA

TEXAS

NEW MEXICO

COAHUILA

CHIHUAHUA

MEXICO

GULF OF MEXICO

MEMPHIS

NEW ORLEANS

Baton Rouge

Little Rock

Shreveport

DALLAS

Fort Worth

Arlington

Irving

HOUSTON

SAN ANTONIO

Austin

Waco

Corpus Christi

Amarillo

Lubbock

Abilene

Oklahoma City

Tulsa

San Angelo

Del Rio

Nuevo Laredo

Laredo

Piedras Negras

Ciudad Acuña

Nueva Rosita

Rio Grande

Rio Bravo del Norte

Pecos

Edwards Plateau

Llano Estacado

Stockton Plateau

Chisos Mts.

Davis Mts.

Guadalupe Pk.

Boston Mts.

Ouachita Mts.

Mississippi R.

Sangre de Cristo Mts.

1:6 000 000

50 0 50 100 150 200 250 km

SASKATCHEWAN

ALBERTA

BRITISH COLUMBIA

CANADA

MONTANA

WYOMING

IDAHO

WASHINGTON

OREGON

NEVADA

CALIFORNIA

VANCOUVER

Seattle

Tacoma

Olympia

PORTLAND

Salem

Eugene

Spokane

Boise

Helena

Butte

Great Falls

Billings

Bozeman

Salt Lake City

Ogden

Provo

Reno

Casper

Bighorn Mountains

Medicine Bow Mts.

Yellowstone

Bitterroot Range

Lemhi Range

Salmon River Mountains

Sawtooth Ra.

Clearwater Mountains

Cabinet Mountains

Lewis Range

Big Belt Mts.

Little Belt Mts.

Crazy Mts.

Absaroka Range

Wind River Range

Uinta Mountains

Great Salt Lake

Columbia Plateau

Snake

Blue Mountains

Wallowa Mts.

Cascade Range

Olympic Mts.

Coast Range

Klamath Mts.

Warner Range

Great Sandy Desert

Alvord Desert

Harney Basin

Santa Rosa Ra.

Independence Mts.

Ruby Mts.

Juan de Fuca Strait

PACIFIC OCEAN

GULF OF MEXICO

Tropic of Cancer

UNITED STATES

MEXICO

GUATEMALA
BELIZE
HONDURAS
EL SALVADOR
NICARAGUA

Gulf of Campeche

Yucatan

Isthmus of Tehuantepec

PANAMA CANAL
1:1 000 000
0   10   20 km

JAMAICA
1:5 000 000
0   50 km

TRINIDAD AND TOBAGO
1:5 000 000
0   50 km

LEEWARD ISLANDS
1:5 000 000
0   50 km

WINDWARD ISLANDS
1:5 000 000
0   50 km

Projection: Bonne

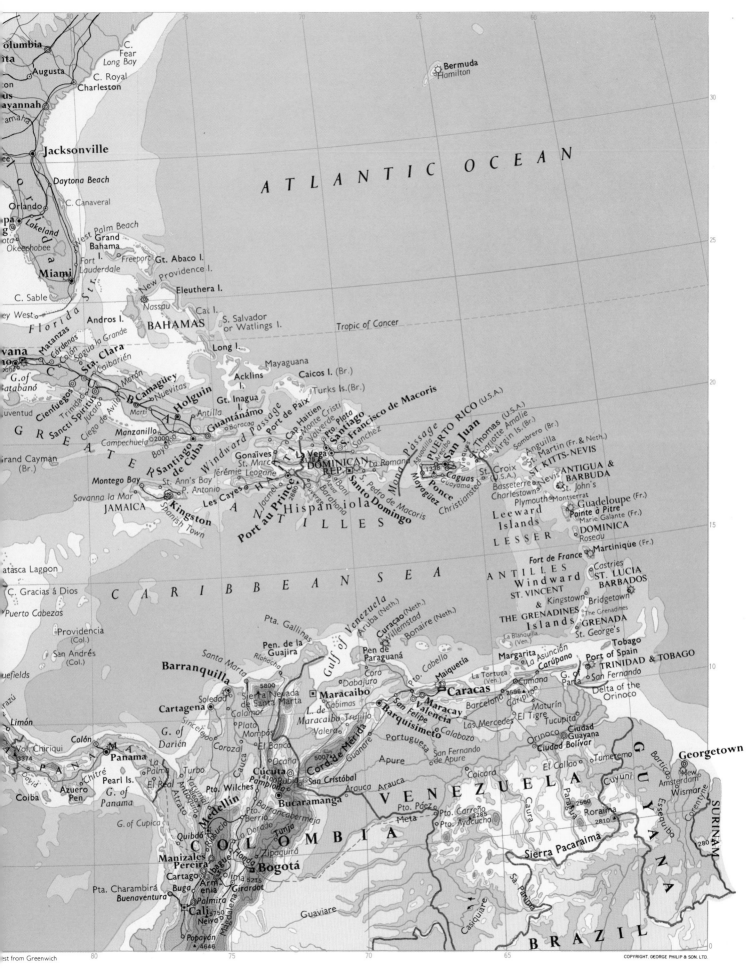

1:30 000 000

200   0   200   400   600   800   1000 km

5994

ATLANTIC OCEAN

Sa. Nevada de Santa Marta
Barranquilla
▲5800
Maracaibo
G. of Darien
Panama Canal
Margarita
Tobago I.
Caracas
Trinidad
L. Maracaibo
Cord. de Mérida
Orinoco
Medellín
Bogotá
Cordillera Occidental
Cordillera Central
Cordillera Oriental
Magdalena
Llanos
Georgetown
Guiana Highlands
2810 ▲ Roraima
Sierra Pacaraima
Serra de Tumucumaque
C. Orange
Cali
C. de San Francisco
Quito
Cotopaxi 5897
Chimborazo 6267
Guayaquil
G. of Guayaquil
Napo
Putumayo
Japurá
Negro
Equator
Amazon
Pará
Marajó I.
Belém
Pta. Pariñas
Pta. Aguja
Marañón
Juruá
Purus
Madeira
Amazon
Fortaleza
São Roque
Lobos Is.
Selvas
Ucayali
Manaus
C. Branco
Huascarán 6768
Andes
Madre de Dios
Aripuanã
Roosevelt
Tapajós
Xingu
Tocantins
Plateau of Borborema
Recife
Lima
Guaporé
Tocantins
Plateau of Mato Grosso
São Francisco
Chincha Is.
Mamoré
Araguaia
Brazilian Highlands
Salvador
Peru Trench
L. Titicaca
Ancohuma & Illampu 6550
La Paz
Bolivian Plateau
Paraguay
Brasília
Abrolhos Bank
Belo Horizonte
Serra da Mantiqueira
▲2890 Pico da Bandeira
L. Poopó
Paraná
PACIFIC OCEAN
Tropic of Capricorn
8050
Ojos del Salado 6863
Tucumán
Salado
Gran Chaco
Pilcomayo
Asunción
Iguaçu Falls
São Paulo
Rio de Janeiro
C. Frio
S. Félix
S. Ambrosio
Salinas Grandes
Córdoba
L. Mar Chiquita
Sierra de Córdoba
Aconcagua 6960
Uspallata Pass
Valparaíso
Santiago
Rosario
Paraná
Entre Ríos
Uruguay
Serra do Mar
Pôrto Alegre
Lagoa dos Patos
Arch. de Juan Fernández
Buenos Aires
La Plata
Montevideo
Rio de la Plata
SOUTH
Pta. Mogotes
Colorado
Negro
Bahía Blanca
ATLANTIC
G. of San Matias
Valdés Peninsula
OCEAN
Chiloé I.
Argentine Basin
Chonos Archipelago
Patagonia
G. of San Jorge
Taitao Peninsula
▲4058 S. Valentin
G. of Peñas
6212 ▼
Wellington
Madre de Dios I.
Falkland Islands
West Falkland
East Falkland
Magellan's Strait
Santa Inés
Cockburn Chan.
Magellan's Strait
Tierra del Fuego
Staten I.
Beagle Chan.
C. Horn

Chile Rise

Chile

Peru

m
6000
4000
3000
2000
1000
400
200
0
0
200
2000
4000
6000
8000
m

1:30 000 000

Projection: *Lambert's Equivalent Azimuthal*

West from Greenwich

1:30 000 000

200 0 200 400 600 800 1000 km

LAND USE
(million hectares)

Other land 283.5

Arable land and permanent crops 104.1

Permanent pasture 441.8

Woods and forests 924.3

Total land area 1 753.7 million hectares

Maracaibo
● Caracas
Oficina
Cerro Bolivar
◎ Bogotá
Moengo
Mn Serra do Navio
Equator
◎ Quito
◎ Recife
Cr
Cerro de Pasco
◎ Lima
Marcona
Ni
● Brasília
La Paz
Colquiri
Toquepala
Sb Potosi
Mn Urucúm
Itabira
Morro Velho
Chuquicamata
Mn
Tropic of Capricorn
Rio de Janeiro
Itaipú
São Paulo
Asunción
El Romeral
Santiago
Mo
El Teniente
Buenos Aires Montevideo
Concepción
El Chocón
Comodoro Rivadavia

LAND USE
- Arable land
- Fruit trees, vineyards, and plantations
- Permanent pasture
- Woods and forests
- Rough grazing
- Non-productive land

LIVESTOCK
- /// Cattle
- /// Sheep

CROPS
- ♪ Bananas   ◇ Sugar cane
- o Cacao   ▲ Tea
- ◆ Citrus fruits T Tobacco
- o Coffee   ▽ Vines
- ♠ Cotton   ⌇ Wheat
- ‖ Maize
- ○ Rice   ⟶ Fisheries

MINERALS
- ◎ Bauxite   **Cr** Chrome
- ▲ Copper   **Mn** Manganese
- ◇ Diamonds   **Mo** Molybdenum
- △ Gold   **Ni** Nickel
- ◆ Iron ore   **POWER**
- ◈ Lead and zinc ▲ Coalfields
- ◈ Saltpetre   ▣ Oilfields
- ▽ Silver   ▣ Gasfields
- ● Tin   ▣ Hydro-electric power stations
- **Sb** Antimony

Projection: Lambert's Equivalent Azimuthal

West from Greenwich

COPYRIGHT. GEORGE PHILIP & SON. LTD.

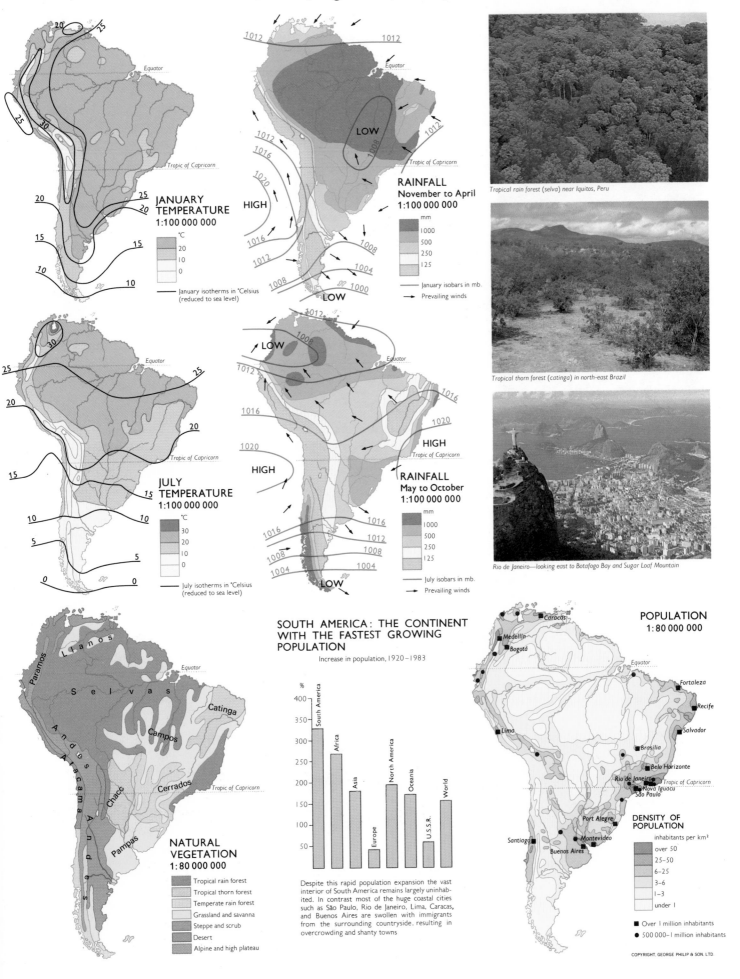

JANUARY TEMPERATURE
1:100 000 000

°C
20
10
0

— January isotherms in °Celsius (reduced to sea level)

RAINFALL
November to April
1:100 000 000

mm
1000
500
250
125

— January isobars in mb.
→ Prevailing winds

Tropical rain forest (selva) near Iquitos, Peru

JULY TEMPERATURE
1:100 000 000

°C
30
20
10
0

— July isotherms in °Celsius (reduced to sea level)

RAINFALL
May to October
1:100 000 000

mm
1000
500
250
125

— July isobars in mb.
→ Prevailing winds

Tropical thorn forest (catinga) in north-east Brazil

Rio de Janeiro—looking east to Botafogo Bay and Sugar Loaf Mountain

NATURAL VEGETATION
1:80 000 000

Paramos
Llanos
Selvas
Andes
Atacama
Chaco
Campos
Cerrados
Catinga
Pampas

- Tropical rain forest
- Tropical thorn forest
- Temperate rain forest
- Grassland and savanna
- Steppe and scrub
- Desert
- Alpine and high plateau

SOUTH AMERICA: THE CONTINENT WITH THE FASTEST GROWING POPULATION
Increase in population, 1920–1983

%
400
350
300
250
200
150
100
50

South America
Africa
Asia
Europe
North America
Oceania
U.S.S.R.
World

Despite this rapid population expansion the vast interior of South America remains largely uninhabited. In contrast most of the huge coastal cities such as São Paulo, Rio de Janeiro, Lima, Caracas, and Buenos Aires are swollen with immigrants from the surrounding countryside, resulting in overcrowding and shanty towns

POPULATION
1:80 000 000

Caracas
Medellín
Bogotá
Fortaleza
Recife
Lima
Salvador
Brasília
Belo Horizonte
Rio de Janeiro
Nova Iguaçu
São Paulo
Port Alegre
Santiago
Montevideo
Buenos Aires

DENSITY OF POPULATION
inhabitants per km²

over 50
25–50
6–25
3–6
1–3
under 1

■ Over 1 million inhabitants
● 500 000–1 million inhabitants

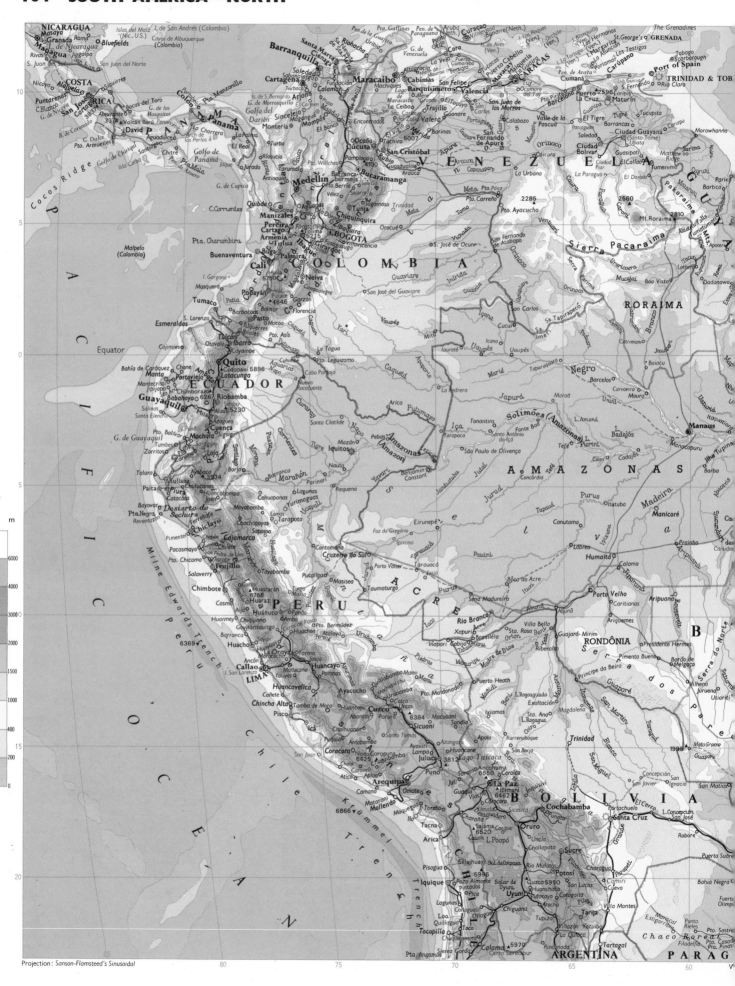

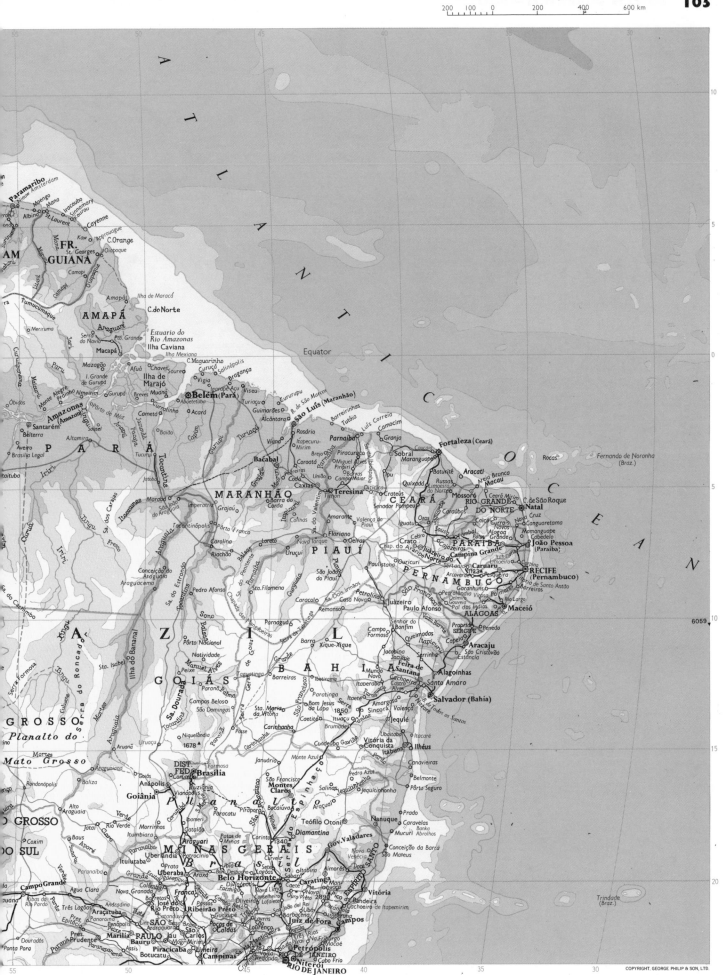

200 100 0 200 400 600 km

A T L A N T I C   O C E A N

Paramaribo
Nieuw Amsterdam
Moengo Mana Iracoubo
Albina St. Laurent Sinnamary Kourou
Cayenne

C. Orange

FR.
GUIANA

St. Georges
Oiapoque

Amapá
AMAPÁ
Araguari
C. do Norte

Estuario do
Rio Amazonas
Ilha Caviana
Macapá   Ilha Mexiana

Equator

Ilha de
Marajó
Belém (Pará)

Amazonas
(Amazon)
Santarém

P A R Á

São Luís (Maranhão)

Parnaíba
Fortaleza (Ceará)
Sobral

Rosário

Teresina

MARANHÃO

CEARÁ

Natal
RIO GRANDE
DO NORTE

PARAÍBA
João Pessoa
(Paraíba)

Campina Grande
Caruaru
RECIFE
(Pernambuco)

PIAUÍ

PERNAMBUCO

Petrolina
Juàzeiro
Paulo Afonso

Maceió
ALAGOAS

SERGIPE

B R A Z I L

BAHIA

Feira de
Santana

Aracaju

Salvador (Bahia)

GOIÁS

Vitória da
Conquista

Ilhéus

DIST.
FED. Brasília

Anápolis

Goiânia

MATO
GROSSO
Planalto do
Mato Grosso

MINAS GERAIS

Belo Horizonte

Vitória
ESPÍRITO
SANTO

Campo Grande

GROSSO
DO SUL

SÃO
PAULO

Ribeirão Preto

Campinas

Juiz de Fora

Petrópolis
RIO DE JANEIRO
Niterói

1:16 000 000

200 100 0   200   400   600 km

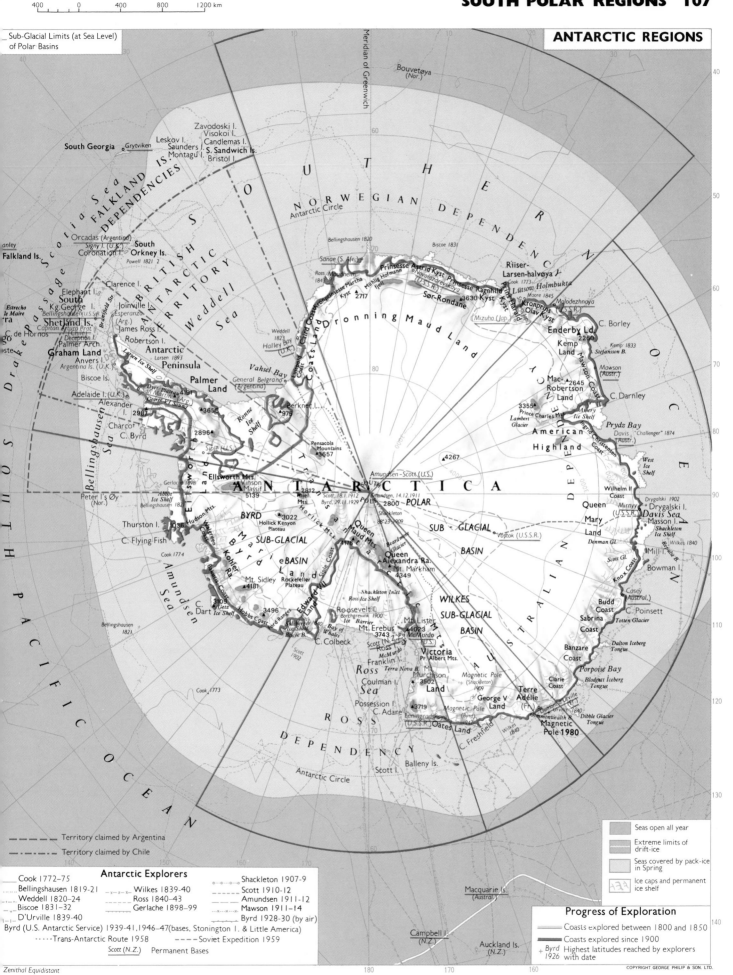

ANTARCTIC REGIONS

1:35 000 000

400 0 400 800 1200 km

Sub-Glacial Limits (at Sea Level) of Polar Basins

Territory claimed by Argentina
Territory claimed by Chile

Antarctic Explorers

Cook 1772–75
Bellingshausen 1819–21
Weddell 1820–24
Biscoe 1831–32
D'Urville 1839–40
Wilkes 1839–40
Ross 1840–43
Gerlache 1898–99
Shackleton 1907–9
Scott 1910–12
Amundsen 1911–12
Mawson 1911–14
Byrd 1928–30 (by air)

Byrd (U.S. Antarctic Service) 1939–41,1946–47(bases, Stonington I. & Little America)
Trans-Antarctic Route 1958
Soviet Expedition 1959
Scott (N.Z.) Permanent Bases

Zenithal Equidistant

Seas open all year
Extreme limits of drift-ice
Seas covered by pack-ice in Spring
Ice caps and permanent ice shelf

Progress of Exploration

Coasts explored between 1800 and 1850
Coasts explored since 1900
Byrd 1926 Highest latitudes reached by explorers with date

COPYRIGHT GEORGE PHILIP & SON. LTD.

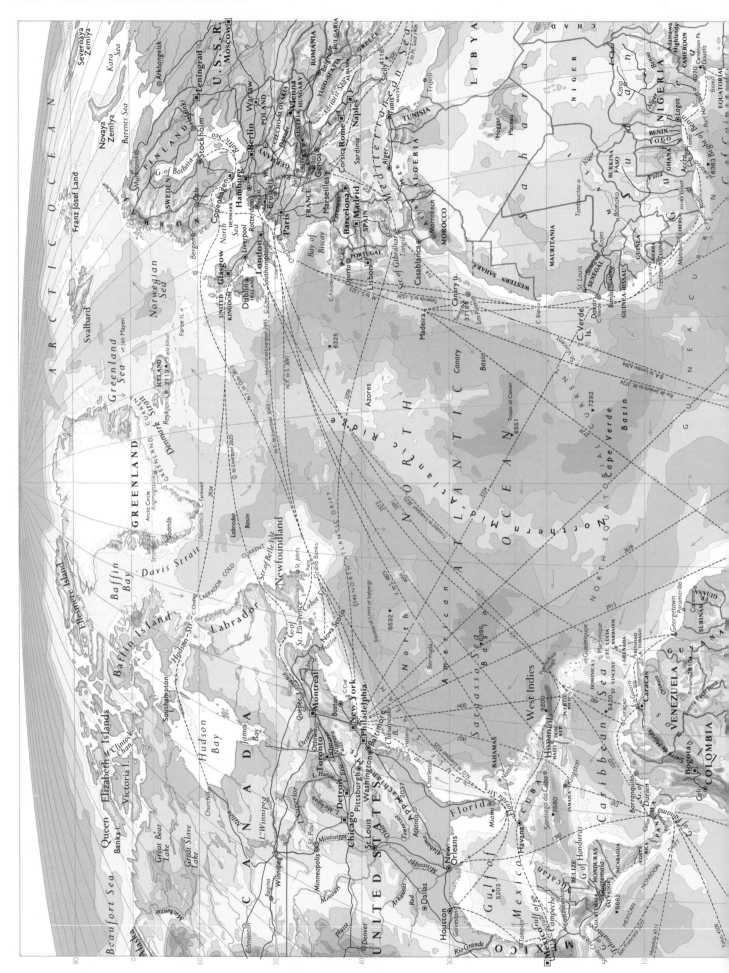

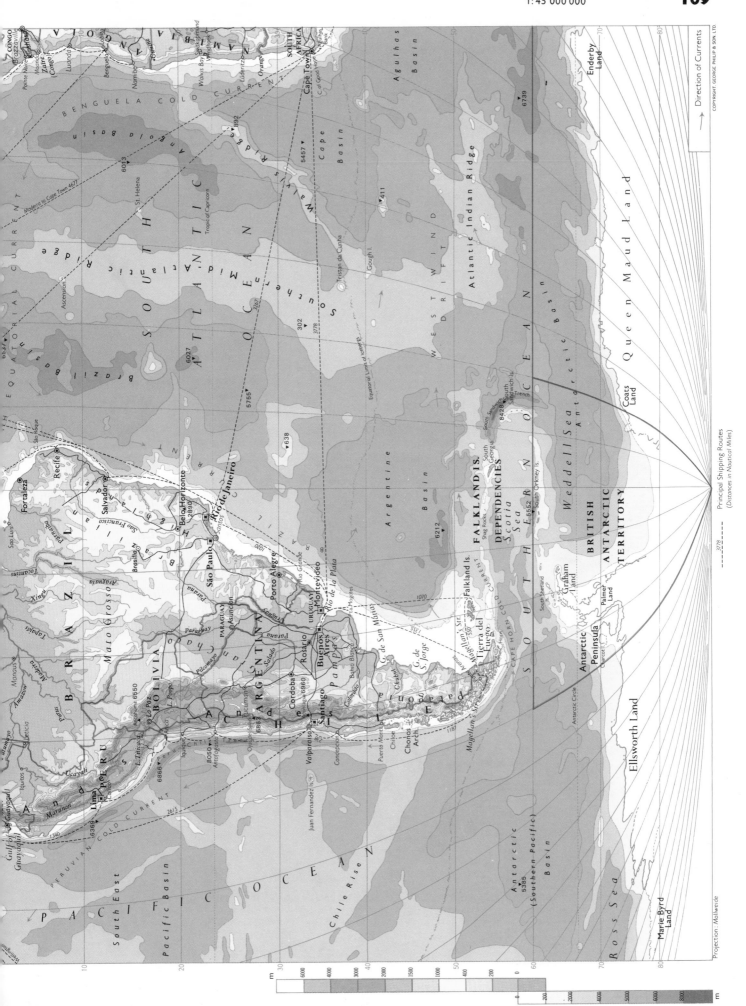

Direction of Currents

COPYRIGHT GEORGE PHILIP & SON LTD.

Projection: Mollweide

Principal Shipping Routes
(Distances in Nautical Miles)

3778

CONGO
Brazzaville
Pointe Noire
Cabinda
Matadi
Zaïre
(Congo)

A N G O L A
Luanda
Lobito
Benguela
Namibe
Walvis Bay
Swakopmund
Windhoek

N A M I B I A
Lüderitz

Orange

SOUTH
AFRICA
Cape Town
C. of Good Hope
Agulhas
Bank

BENGUELA COLD CURRENT

Madeira to Cape Town 4671

EQUATORIAL CURRENT

Ascension

St Helena

Tropic of Capricorn

Walvis Ridge

Angola Basin

Brazil Basin

Mid-Atlantic Ridge

S O U T H   A T L A N T I C   O C E A N

Southern

Cape
Basin

Agulhas
Basin

Atlantic Indian Ridge

892

5457

411

6013

6027

5755

638

302

3778

2267

Tristan da Cunha

Gough I.

Equatorial Limit of icebergs

W E S T   W I N D   D R I F T

6739

8428

South
Georgia

South Sandwich Is.

South Orkney Is.

South Shetland Is.

South
Sandwich
Trench

5552

Scotia
Sea

FALKLAND IS.

DEPENDENCIES

Antarctic

Argentine
Basin

6212

Snag Rocks

Weddell Sea

Antarctic Basin

S O U T H E R N   O C E A N

Enderby
Land

Q u e e n   M a u d   L a n d

Coats
Land

BRITISH
ANTARCTIC
TERRITORY

Antarctic
Peninsula

Graham
Land

Palmer
Land

Ellsworth Land

Marie Byrd
Land

Ross Sea

Antarctic Circle

Charcot I.

São Roque
Recife
Fortaleza
São Luís
São Francisco
Parnaíba

Manaus
Amazon
Madeira
Purus
Juruá
Tapajós
Xingu
Tocantins
Araguaia

B R A Z I L
Brasília

Belo Horizonte
Rio de Janeiro
São Paulo
Santos
Porto Alegre
Rio Grande

Salvador

Mato Grosso
Paraná

Pilcomayo

B O L I V I A
La Paz
L. Titicaca
L. Poopó
Illampu 6550
Sajama 6860
Illimani

P E R U
Lima
Callao
Ucayali
Marañón
Iquitos

Guayaquil
Gulf of
Guayaquil

Leticia

2890
6027

1080

1340

2615

6369

6866

8050

6960
Aconcagua 6960
6881

A R G E N T I N A
Córdoba
Rosario
Buenos Aires
Santa Fe
Santiago
Valparaíso
Concepción
Chillán

C H I L E
Antofagasta
Iquique
Arica

P A R A G U A Y
Asunción
URUGUAY
Montevideo
Río de la Plata
Bahía Blanca
Paraguay
Paraná
Salado
Colorado
Negro
Chubut

P a t a g o n i a
Pampas
Gran Chaco

Chiloé
Chonos
Arch.
Puerto Montt
G. de S. Jorge
G. de San Matías
Tierra del
Fuego
Magellan's Str.

CAPE HORN COLD CURRENT

PERUVIAN COLD CURRENT

Juan Fernandez Is.

Chile Rise

P A C I F I C   O C E A N

South East
Pacific Basin

Antarctic
(Southern Pacific)
Basin
5385

Galápagos

550

1355

118

1070

6212

Andes

J u a n   F e r n a n d e z

S O U T H   A M E R I C A

1:20 000 000

200   0   200   400   600   800 km

ATLANTIC OCEAN

NORWEGIAN SEA

NORTH SEA

BALTIC SEA

BLACK SEA

CASPIAN SEA
−28

ADRIATIC SEA

MEDITERRANEAN SEA

Tyrrhenian Sea

Ligurian Sea

Ionian Sea

Aegean Sea

Sea of Marmara

Sea of Azov

White Sea

Gulf of Bothnia

Gulf of Finland

Gulf of Riga

Skagerrak

Kattegat

English Channel

Irish Sea

Bay of Biscay

St. of Otranto

Str. of Messina

Str. of Bonifacio

Strait of Gibraltar

Ob

Ural

Volga

Volga

Volga

Kama

Pechora

Mezen

N. Dvina

Onega

Don

Dnepr (Dnieper)

Danube

Danube

Danube

Rhine

Elbe

Weser

Ems

Seine

Loire

Garonne

Gironde

Dordogne

Rhône

Saône

Po

Tiber

Oka

Odra (Oder)

Wisła (Vistula)

Tisza

Prut

Dnistr (Dniester)

Bug

Niemen

W. Dvina

Neva

Terek

Kuban

Manych

Kura

Rion

Araks

Euphrates

Kızıl Irmak

Tsimlyansk Res.

Rybinsk Res.

L. Ladoga

L. Onega

L. Chudskoye

L. Peipus

L. Vänern

L. Vättern

L. Mälaren

L. Siljan

L. Inari

L. Van

L. Urmia

Ural Mountains

Tundra

Obshchiskiy

Volga Uplands

Central Russian Uplands

Ukraine

North European Plain

Finland

Lapland

Scandinavia

Kjølen

Caucasus

5633

Armenia

Kurdistan

Anatolia

Taurus Mts.

3370

Pindus

Morea

Balkans

Balkan Pen.

Rhodope

Walachia

Transylvanian Alps

Carpathians

2655

Plain of Hungary

Alps

4807

Dinaric Alps

Apennines

Gran Sasso
2914

Vesuvius
1277

Etna
3263

Sicily

Sardinia

Corsica

Balearic Is.

Maritime Alps

Central Massif

Mt. Dore
1886

Cévennes

G. of Lions

Pyrenees
3404

Pico de Aneto

Cantabrian Mts.

Old Castile

New Castile

Iberian Peninsula

Sierra Morena

Andalusia

Sa. Nevada
3478

Guadalquivir

Douro

Plateau of the Shotts

Maritime Atlas

C. St. Vincent

C. Trafalgar

C. Spartel

Sudetes

Erz Geb.

Black For.

Harz
1142

Bohemian For.

Moravian Heights

Vosges

Ardennes

Netherlands

Helgoland

Dogger Bank

Fisher Bank

Rockall

Faroe Is.

Shetland Is.

Orkney Is.

Hebrides

British Isles

Great Britain

Ireland

Ben Nevis
1347

Snowdon
1085

Land's End

Valentia

C. Clear

Brittany

Thames

Iceland

Hekla
1491

Vatna Jökull
2119

Drangajökull

Jan Mayen
3734

Lofoten

Vesterålen

North Cape

Nordkinn

Kola Peninsula

Kanin Peninsula

Galdhøpiggen
2469

Kebnekaise
2123

Sarektjåkko

Leinahti

Sulitjelma
1914

Tornio

Torne

Ume

Indals

Gotland

Öland

Bornholm

C. Matapan

C. Bon

Cyprus
1951

Ida
1766

Krym (Crimea)

Sea of Kerch

Str. of Kerch

Bosporus

Pripyat

Pripyat Marshes

Mt. Blanc
4807

Pelvoux

Iberian

2211

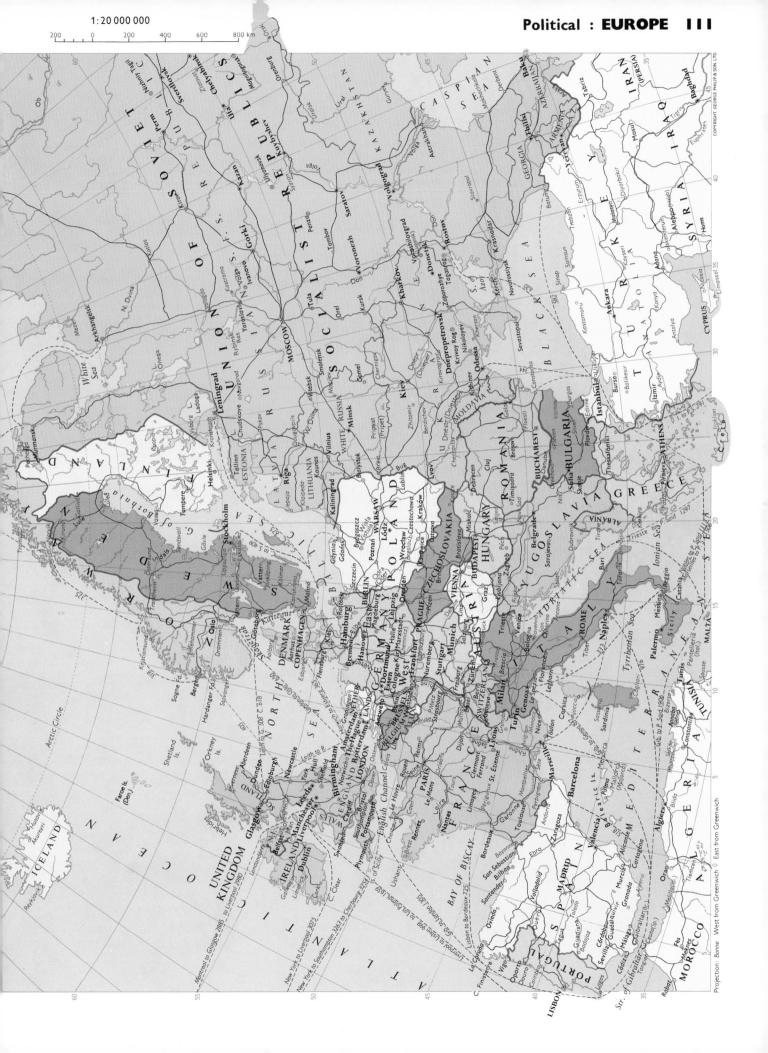

1 : 20 000 000

Projection: Bonne   West from Greenwich 0 East from Greenwich

1 : 20 000 000

200 0 200 400 600 800 km

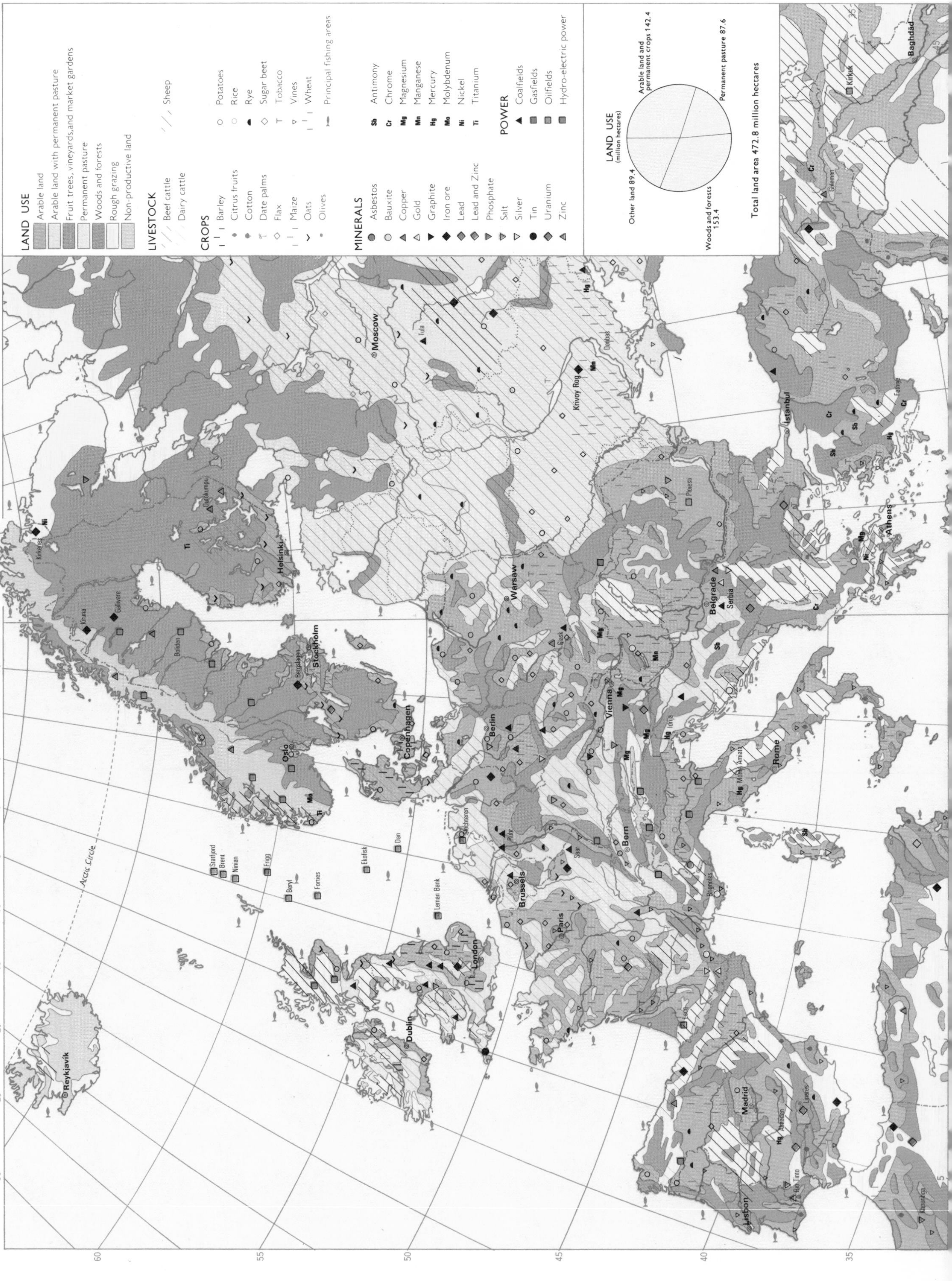

LAND USE
- Arable land
- Arable land with permanent pasture
- Fruit trees, vineyards, and market gardens
- Permanent pasture
- Woods and forests
- Rough grazing
- Non-productive land

LIVESTOCK
- Beef cattle
- Dairy cattle
- Sheep

CROPS
- Barley
- Citrus fruits
- Cotton
- Date palms
- Flax
- Maize
- Oats
- Olives
- Potatoes
- Rice
- Rye
- Sugar beet
- Tobacco
- Vines
- Wheat
- Principal fishing areas

MINERALS
- Sb Antimony
- Cr Chrome
- Asbestos
- Bauxite
- Copper
- Gold
- Graphite
- Iron ore
- Lead
- Lead and Zinc
- Mg Magnesium
- Mn Manganese
- Hg Mercury
- Mo Molybdenum
- Ni Nickel
- Ti Titanium
- Phosphate
- Salt
- Silver
- Tin
- Uranium
- Zinc

POWER
- Coalfields
- Gasfields
- Oilfields
- Hydro-electric power

LAND USE
(million hectares)

Arable land and permanent crops 142.4

Permanent pasture 87.6

Other land 89.4

Woods and forests 153.4

Total land area 472.8 million hectares

Moscow
Helsinki
Stockholm
Oslo
Copenhagen
Berlin
Warsaw
Vienna
Belgrade
Serbia
Rome
Bern
Brussels
Paris
London
Dublin
Reykjavik
Madrid
Lisbon
Athens
İstanbul
Baghdad
Kirkuk
Krivoy Rog

Arctic Circle

Statfjord
Brent
Ninian
Frigg
Beryl
Forties
Leman Bank
Ekofisk
Dan

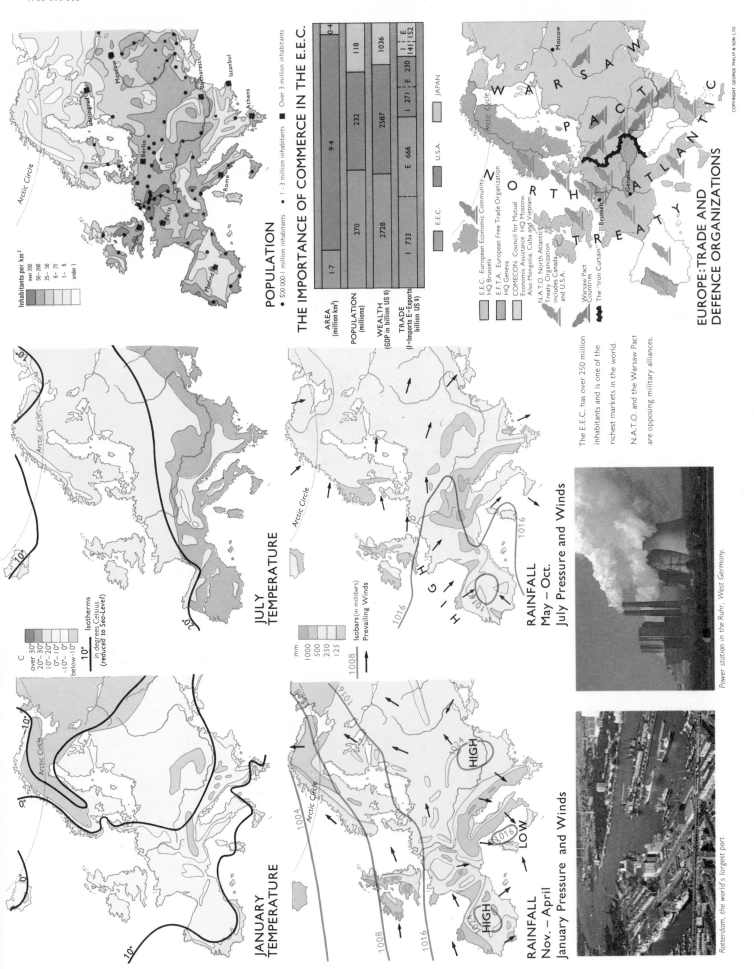

POPULATION

Inhabitants per km²
- over 200
- 50–200
- 25–50
- 6–25
- 1–6
- under 1

• 500 000–1 million inhabitants ● 1–3 million inhabitants ■ Over 3 million inhabitants

Leningrad · Moscow · Bucharest · Istanbul · Athens · Berlin · Rome · Paris · London · Madrid

THE IMPORTANCE OF COMMERCE IN THE E.E.C.

	E.E.C.	U.S.A.	JAPAN
AREA (million km²)	1·7	9·4	0·4
POPULATION (millions)	270	232	118
WEALTH (GDP in billion US $)	2728	2587	1036
TRADE (I=Imports E=Exports billion US $)	I 733 E 666	I 271 E 230	I 141 E 152

EUROPE: TRADE AND DEFENCE ORGANIZATIONS

W A R S A W   P A C T

N O R T H   A T L A N T I C   T R E A T Y

Moscow · Geneva · Brussels

- **E.E.C.** European Economic Community HQ Brussels
- **E.F.T.A.** European Free Trade Organization HQ Geneva
- **COMECON** Council for Mutual Economic Assistance HQ Moscow. Also Mongolia, Cuba and Vietnam
- **N.A.T.O.** North Atlantic Treaty Organization includes Canada and U.S.A.
- Warsaw Pact Countries
- ◇◇◇ The "Iron Curtain"

The E.E.C. has over 250 million inhabitants and is one of the richest markets in the world.

N.A.T.O. and the Warsaw Pact are opposing military alliances.

JULY TEMPERATURE

°C
- over 30°
- 20–30°
- 10–20°
- 0–10°
- -0–10°
- below -10°

Isotherms in degrees Celsius (reduced to Sea-Level) —10°

JANUARY TEMPERATURE

RAINFALL May – Oct. July Pressure and Winds

mm
- 1000
- 500
- 250
- 125

1008 Isobars (in millibars) Prevailing Winds

HIGH 1016

RAINFALL Nov. – April January Pressure and Winds

1004 · 1008 · 1016 · 1024

HIGH · LOW · HIGH

Power station in the Ruhr, West Germany.

Rotterdam, the world's largest port.

COPYRIGHT GEORGE PHILIP & SON. LTD.

1:4 000 000

50   0   50   100   150 km

Orkney Is.
Westray
N. Ronaldsay
Sanday
Stronsay
Mainland
Hoy Kirkwall
South Ronaldsay
Pentland Firth
Thurso
Wick

Shetland Is.
Unst
Yell
Mainland
Lerwick
Foula
Fair I.

SCOTLAND
North West Highlands
Grampian Mts.
Pentland Firth
Thurso
Wick
Lairg
L. Shin
Golspie
Moray Firth
Lossiemouth
Elgin
Banff
Fraserburgh
Peterhead
Invergordon
Dingwall
Nairn
Inverness
L. Ness
Kingussie
Ballater
Balmoral
Dee
Aberdeen
Stonehaven
Ben Nevis 1343
Fort William
Ballachulish
Blair Atholl
Forfar
Montrose
Arbroath
Mallaig
Stornoway
Lewis
Harris
North Uist
Benbecula
South Uist
Barra
St. Kilda
Outer Hebrides
North Minch
Skye
Kyle of Lochalsh
Portree
Rhum
Eigg
Coll
Tiree
Mull
Staffa
Iona
Oban
Colonsay
Firth of Lorn
Loch Linnhe
Jura
Islay
Inner Hebrides

ATLANTIC OCEAN

L. Tay
Crieff
Dundee
Firth of Tay
Perth
Cupar
St. Andrews
Stirling
Kinross
Leven
Forth
Alloa
Dunfermline
Kirkcaldy
Edinburgh
Leith
Dunbar
Haddington
Berwick-on-Tweed
Helensburgh
Dumbarton
Greenock
Paisley
Rothesay
Glasgow
Hamilton
Motherwell
Peebles
Galashiels
St. Boswells
Kilmarnock
Saltcoats
Irvine
Prestwick
Ayr
Selkirk
Jedburgh
Arran
Kintyre
Firth of Clyde
Campbeltown
North Channel
Loch Fyne
Loch Lomond
Moffat
Hawick
Cheviot Hills
Alnwick
Sanquhar
Nith
Dumfries
NORTH SEA

NEWCASTLE
Tynemouth
South Shields
Gateshead
Sunderland
Durham
Hartlepool
Tyne
Carlisle
Appleby
Stockton
Darlington
Middlesbrough
Whitby
N. York Moors
Northallerton
Scarborough
Pennine Range
Cumbrian Mts.
978
Whitehaven
St. Bee's Hd.
Windermere
Kendal
Lancaster
Morecambe Bay
Ribble
Ripon
York
Beverley
Hull
Flamborough Hd.
Spurn Hd.
Grimsby

Solway Firth
Kirkcudbright
Wigtown
Mull of Galloway
Isle of Man
Douglas
IRISH SEA

Malin Hd.
Tory I.
Portrush
Coleraine
Antrim Mts.
Larne
Derryveagh Mts.
Letterkenny
Lifford
Ballymena
Donegal
Donegal Bay
Bundoran
Sligo
Enniskillen
Omagh
L. Neagh
Belfast
Bangor
Lisburn
Downpatrick
Dundrum
NORTHERN IRELAND
Armagh
Newry
Mourne Mts.
Greenore
Dundalk
Killala Bay
Ballina
Erris Hd.
Achill
Clare I.
Castlebar
Westport
L. Conn
L. Mask
Connemara
Galway
Galway Bay
Aran I.
L. Corrib
Roscommon
Longford
Mullingar
Athlone
Tullamore
Monaghan
Clones
Cavan
Leitrim
Carrick-on-Shannon
Ceanannus Mór
An Uaimh
Boyne
Drogheda
Balbriggan
IRELAND
Birr
Port Laoise
Naas
Dublin (Baile Átha Cliath)
Dun Laoghaire
Bray
Athy
Wicklow Mts.
Wicklow
Arklow
Ennis
Nenagh
Thurles
Limerick
Golden Vale
Tipperary
Clonmel
Carrick-on-Suir
Kilkenny
Carlow
Enniscorthy
New Ross
Wexford
Rosslare
Listowel
Rath Luirc
Tralee
Killarney
Macgillycuddy's Reeks 1040
Cahirciveen
Castletown Bere
C. Clear
Mallow
Fermoy
Blackwater
Dungarvan
Youghal
Cork
Cobh
Cork Harbour
Kinsale
Bandon
Lee
Bantry
Blarney
Shannon
Loop Hd.
Kilrush
L. Derg
Roscrea

Anglesey
Holyhead
Beaumaris
Caernarfon Bay
Caernarfon
1085 Snowdon
Cardigan Bay
Pwllheli
Dolgellau (Dolgelley)
Barmouth
Aberystwyth
Cardigan
Fishguard
St. David's Hd.
Haverfordwest
Milford Haven
Pembroke
Cambrian Mts.
WALES
Denbigh
Ruthin
Rhyl
Llandudno
Conway
Colwyn Bay
Llangollen
Welshpool
Montgomery
Rhayader
Llandrindod Wells
Presteign
Brecon
Llanelli
Swansea
Port Talbot
Rhondda
Merthyr Tydfil
Newport
Cardiff
Monmouth
Hereford
Worcester

Blackpool
Preston
Burnley
Blackburn
Bolton
Liverpool
Birkenhead
St. Helens
Salford
Manchester
Stockport
Macclesfield
Crewe
Wrexham
Chester
Stoke-on-Trent
Leeds
Bradford
Halifax
Huddersfield
Wakefield
Barnsley
Oldham
Rotherham
Sheffield
Doncaster
Scunthorpe
Lincoln
Chesterfield
Mansfield
Derby
Nottingham
Newark
Trent
Sleaford
Boston
The Wash
Skegness
Shrewsbury
Stafford
Wolverhampton
Walsall
Birmingham
Kidderminster
Coventry
Leicester
Oakham
Rugby
Corby
Warwick
Leamington
Stratford-on-Avon
Peterborough
The Fens
March
Ely
Huntingdon
Wellingborough
Northampton
Bedford
Cambridge
Bury St. Edmunds
Ipswich
ENGLAND
Gt. Yarmouth
Lowestoft
Norwich
Kings Lynn
Ouse
Nene
The Naze
Harwich
Colchester
Chelmsford
Buckingham
Aylesbury
Oxford
Cotswolds
Gloucester
Cheltenham
Chiltern Hills
Luton
Hertford
St. Albans
Watford
Slough
Windsor
Reading
Swindon
Thames
LONDON
Southend
Thames
Chatham
Gillingham
Margate
Canterbury
Maidstone
Guildford
Reigate
N. Downs
Dover
Folkestone
Ashford
Bristol
Bath
Weston-super-Mare
Trowbridge
Wells
Salisbury Plain
Salisbury
Wilton
Winchester
Basingstoke
Aldershot
The Weald
South Downs
Lewes
Hastings
Eastbourne
Brighton
Worthing
Newhaven
Chichester
Portsmouth
Southampton
Poole
Bournemouth
Isle of Wight
Newport
Needles
Weymouth
Dorchester
Yeovil
Taunton
Exe
Exeter
Axminster
Bristol Channel
Lundy I.
Ilfracombe
Exmoor
Barnstaple
Hartland Point
Bude
Dartmoor
Devonport
Plymouth
Dartmouth
Torquay
St. Austell
Truro
Camborne
Penzance
Falmouth
Land's End
Lizard
Scilly Is.
Start Pt.

ENGLISH CHANNEL
Dieppe

St. George's Channel
Carnsore Pt.

West from Greenwich   East from Greenwich

Projection: Conical with two standard parallels

COPYRIGHT. GEORGE PHILIP & SON. LTD.

m
1000
600
400
200
100
0
100
200
400
m

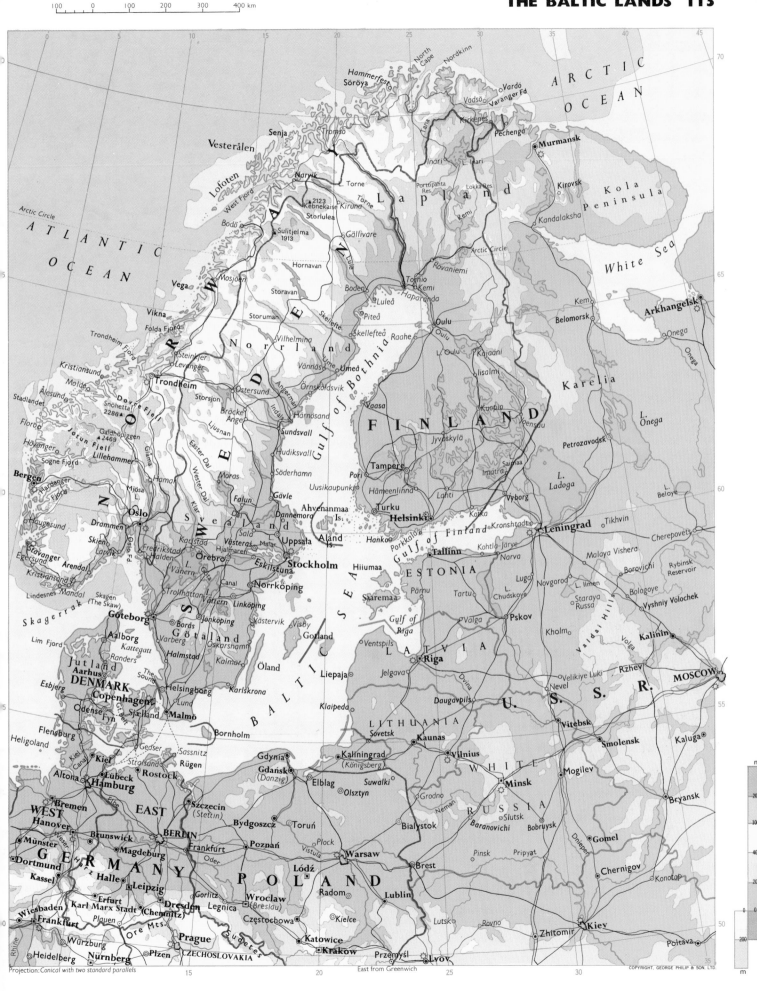

1:10 000 000

100   0   100   200   300   400 km

ARCTIC OCEAN

North Cape · Nordkinn
Hammerfest · Söröya
Senja · Tromsö
Vesterålen
Lofoten
Narvik · L. Torne
2123 ▲ Kebnekaise · Kiruna
Storlulea
Sulitjelma 1913
Gällivare

Vardö
Vadsö · Varanger Fd
Kirkenes
Pechenga · Murmansk
Inari · L. Inari
Porttipahta Res. · Lokka Res.
Kirovsk
Kola Peninsula
Kandalaksha

ATLANTIC OCEAN

Arctic Circle

Vega
Vikna
Folda Fjord
Trondheim Fjord
Kristiansund
Molde
Ålesund
Stadlandet
Florö
Hövanger
Sogne Fjord
Bergen
Hardanger Fjord
Haugesund
Stavanger
Egersund
Kristiansand
Lindesnes · Mandal

Bodö
Mosjöen

NORWAY

SWEDEN

Steinkjer
Levanger
Trondheim
Östersund
Storsjön
Bräcke
Ange
Snöhetta 2286 ▲
Dovre Fjell
Galdhöpiggen 2469 ▲
Jotun Fjell
Lillehammer
Glama
Gjövik
Mjösa L.
Oslo
Drammen
Skien
Larvik
Fredrikstad
Halden
Örebro
L. Vänern
Göteborg
Borås
Varberg
Halmstad
Jönköping
Skagen (The Skaw)
Kattegatt
Aalborg
Randers
Jutland
Aarhus
Esbjerg
DENMARK
Flensburg
Heligoland
Copenhagen
Odense
Fyn
Sjælland
Malmö

Vilhelmina
Norrland
Storavan
Storuman
Hornavan
Hudiksvall
Söderhamn
Gävle
Falun
Dannemora
Sala
Uppsala
Västerås
Mälar
Eskilstuna
Stockholm
Norrköping
Linköping
L. Vättern
Canal
Oskarshamn
Kalmar
Öland
Visby
Gotland
Västervik
Karlskrona
Helsingborg
Lund
Bornholm

Skellefte
Umeå
Örnsköldsvik
Vännäs
Ångerman
Härnösand
Sundsvall
Indal
Ljusnan
Moras
Easter Dal
Wester Dal
Klar
Hjalmaren
Hamar
Karlstad
Trollhättan
Halmstad

BALTIC SEA

Gulf of Bothnia

Tornio · Kemi
Haparanda
Oulu
Raahe
L. Oulu
Kajaani
Rovaniemi
Arctic Circle

FINLAND

Vaasa
Pori
Tampere
Jyväskylä
Iisalmi
Kuopio
Joensuu
Saimaa
Imatra
Hämeenlinna
Lahti
Turku
Helsinki
Kotka
Hanko
Porkkala
Ahvenanmaa Is.
Åland
Hiiuma
Saaremaa

Karelia
Belomorsk
Kem
Onega · L. Onega
Petrozavodsk
L. Ladoga
L. Beloye
Vyborg
Kronstadt
Leningrad
Tikhvin
Cherepovets

Gulf of Finland

ESTONIA
Tallinn
Narva
Kohtla-Järve
Pärnu
Tartu
Valga
Pskov
L. Chudskoye
Gulf of Riga
Riga
Jelgava
Ventspils
LATVIA
Liepaja
Klaipeda
Sovetsk
LITHUANIA
Kaunas
Kaliningrad (Königsberg)
Vilnius

Luga
Novgorod
L. Ilmen
Staraya Russa
Kholm
Valga

White Sea

Arkhangelsk

Onega

Borovichi
Maloya Vishera
Rybinsk Reservoir
Vyshniy Volochek
Bologoye
Valdai Hills
Volga
Kalinin
MOSCOW
Rzhev
Velikiye Luki
Nevel
Vitebsk
Smolensk
Kaluga

U.S.S.R.

Daugavpils
Dvina
WHITE RUSSIA
Minsk
Mogilev
Bryansk
Gomel
Chernigov
Konotop

Poltava
Kiev
Zhitomir
Lvov
Przemyśl

Gdynia
Gdańsk (Danzig)
Elblag
Suwalki
Olsztyn
Grodno
Bialystok
Neman
Baranovichi
Slutsk
Bobruysk
Pinsk
Pripyat
Dnieper

POLAND
Szczecin (Stettin)
Bydgoszcz
Toruń
Poznań
Plock
Vistula
Warsaw
Brest
Lódź
Radom
Lublin
Lutsk
Rovno
Wrocław (Breslau)
Legnica
Częstochowa
Katowice
Kraków
Kielce
Oder
Plauen

GERMANY
WEST
Hanover
Bremen
Brunswick
Münster
Dortmund
Kassel
Wiesbaden
Frankfurt
Würzburg
Heidelberg
Nürnberg
EAST
Berlin
Frankfurt
Magdeburg
Halle
Leipzig
Erfurt
Karl Marx Stadt (Chemnitz)
Dresden
Görlitz
Plzen
Prague
CZECHOSLOVAKIA
Ore Mts.
Sudetes
Rhine
Weser
Elbe

Kiel
Kiel Canal
Altona
Hamburg
Lübeck
Rostock
Stralsund
Sassnitz
Rügen
Gedser

Skagerrak

East from Greenwich

Projection: Conical with two standard parallels

COPYRIGHT. GEORGE PHILIP & SON. LTD.

m
2000
1000
400
200
0
200
m

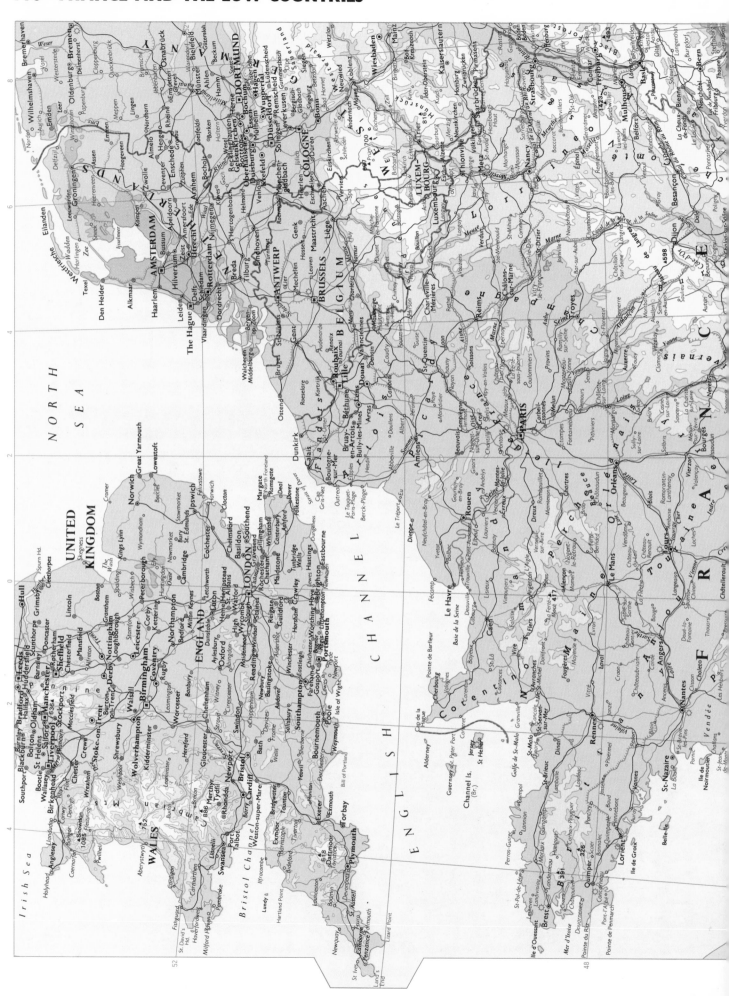

1:4 000 000

20 0 20 40 60 80 100 120 km

COPYRIGHT GEORGE PHILIP & SON. LTD.

Corsica
Cap Corse · Bastia · Cervione · Calvi · Mt. Cinto 2710 ▲ · Corte · Aléria · L'Île-Rousse · Porto-Vecchio · Ajaccio · Propriano · Sartène · Bonifacio

ITALY
TURIN · Col du Mt. Cenis · Mont Blanc 4807 · Maritime Alps · MONACO · Monte-Carlo · NICE · Antibes · Cannes · 3051 · Mt Pelat 3037 · L'Argentera

MEDITERRANEAN SEA

Grenoble · St-Étienne · Lyons · Roanne · Vichy · Clermont-Ferrand · Puy de Dôme 1465 · Puy de Sancy · Mont Ventoux 1909 · Valence · Montélimar · Avignon · Aix-en-Provence · Marseilles · Toulon · Hyères · Îles d'Hyères

Gulf of Lions

Nîmes · Montpellier · Sète · Béziers · Narbonne · Perpignan · Carcassonne · Canal du Midi · Toulouse · Albi · Castres · Rodez · Mende · Mt Lozère 1699 · Mt Aigoual 1565

Central Massif · Limoges · Brive · Périgueux · Angoulême · Bordeaux · Agen · Montauban · Garonne · Pau · Tarbes · Lourdes · Bayonne · Biarritz · St-Jean-de-Luz

ANDORRA · Pic d'Aneto · Mt Perdu 3355 · 3298 · Pyrenees · Figueras · Gerona · Barcelona · Sabadell · Tarrasa · Manresa · Lérida · Reus · Tarragona · Tortosa

Bay of Biscay · OCEAN

La Rochelle · Île de Ré · Île d'Oléron · Rochefort

San Sebastián · Bilbao · Vitoria · Pamplona · Logroño · Navarra · Basque Provinces · Santander · Burgos

SPAIN · Zaragoza · Ebro · Huesca · Teruel 2019 · Valencia · Sagunto · Castellón · Villarreal

New Castile · Guadalajara · Alcalá de Henares · **MADRID** · Getafe · Aranjuez · Toledo · Old Castile · Soria · Cuenca

Balearic Islands · Minorca · Majorca · Palma · Ciudadela · Mahón

m 4000 3000 2000 1500 1000 400 200 0 m

Projection: Conical with two standard parallels

West of Greenwich · East of Greenwich

NORTH SEA

BALTIC

NETHERLANDS

BELGIUM

FRANCE

LUX.

SWITZERLAND

ITALY

WEST GERMANY

EAST GERMANY

LOWER SAXONY

NORTH RHINE WESTPHALIA

RHINE LAND

PALATINATE

SAARI

LORRAINE

BADEN-WÜRTTEMBERG

BAVARIA

BOHEMIAN FOREST

CZECHOS...

AUSTRIA

UPPER AUSTRIA

LOWER AUSTRIA

TYROL

SALZBURG

STYRIA

CARINTHIA

BURGENLAND

FRIULI-VENEZIA GIULIA

VENETO

LOMBARDY

PIEDMONT

DAUPHINE

PROVENCE

FLANDERS

ARDENNES

EIFEL

HARZ Mts.

Thuringian Forest

ADRIATIC SEA

Gulf of Venice

Gulf of Genoa

Major cities and towns:
Flensburg, Schleswig, Kiel, Kiel Bay, Rendsburg, Neumünster, Lübeck, Rostock, Stralsund, Rügen, Sassnitz, Szczecin (Stettin), Hamburg, Bremen, Bremerhaven, Wilhelmshaven, Emden, Groningen, Oldenburg, Leeuwarden, Den Helder, Alkmaar, Haarlem, Amsterdam, The Hague, Leiden, Utrecht, Rotterdam, Dordrecht, Breda, Tilburg, Eindhoven, Antwerp, Ghent, Bruges, Ostend, Brussels, Lille, Roubaix, Tournai, Mons, Charleroi, Namur, Liège, Aachen, Bonn, Cologne, Düsseldorf, Essen, Dortmund, Duisburg, Krefeld, Wuppertal, Bochum, Gelsenkirchen, Hamm, Münster, Osnabrück, Bielefeld, Herford, Hanover (Hannover), Brunswick, Magdeburg, Berlin, Potsdam, Charlottenburg, Spandau, Brandenburg, Dessau, Halle, Leipzig, Erfurt, Jena, Gera, Dresden, Karl Marx Stadt (Chemnitz), Zwickau, Plauen, Hof, Bayreuth, Prague (Praha), Plzeň (Pilsen), Brno (Brünn), Liberec, Ústí nad Labem, Hradec Králové, Pardubice, Görlitz, Cottbus, Frankfurt, Kassel, Göttingen, Fulda, Frankfurt, Wiesbaden, Mainz, Darmstadt, Mannheim, Heidelberg, Ludwigshafen, Worms, Trier, Luxembourg, Kaiserslautern, Saarbrücken, Metz, Nancy, Strasbourg, Karlsruhe, Pforzheim, Stuttgart, Esslingen, Heilbronn, Ulm, Würzburg, Bamberg, Nuremberg (Nürnberg), Fürth, Erlangen, Regensburg, Ingolstadt, Augsburg, Munich (München), Freising, Landshut, Passau, Linz, Vienna (Wien), Wiener Neustadt, Graz, Klagenfurt, Salzburg, Innsbruck, Ljubljana, Zagreb, Rijeka, Trieste, Venice (Venezia), Padua (Padova), Verona, Vicenza, Treviso, Udine, Bolzano, Trento, Brescia, Bergamo, Milan (Milano), Como, Novara, Turin (Torino), Pavia, Cremona, Mantua (Mantova), Parma, Reggio, Modena, Bologna, Ferrara, Ravenna, Rimini, Forlì, Genoa (Genova), Spezia, Savona, San Remo, Nice, Cannes, Monaco & Monte Carlo, Marseilles, Nîmes, Avignon, Valence, Grenoble, Chambéry, Annecy, Geneva (Genève), Lausanne, Bern, Basle, Zürich, Luzern, St. Gallen, Chur, Davos, Lugano, Besançon, Dijon, Lyons, St. Étienne, Mâcon, Bourg, Mulhouse, Belfort, Freiburg, Colmar, Épinal, Châlons sur Marne, Reims, Troyes, Auxerre, Château Thierry, Soissons, Laon

Mt. Blanc 4807, Matterhorn 4478, Monte Rosa 4634, Gran Paradiso 4061, Mt. Viso 3841, Gr. Glockner 3797, Ortles 3899, Marmolada 3342, Adamello 3554, Brocken 1142, Rothaar G. 840, Vogels Berg 772, Fichtel Geb. 1051, Feldberg 1493

Projection : Conical with two standard parallels   East from Greenwich

m
4000
3000
2000
1500
1000
400
200
0
200
m

1:5 000 000

50   0   50   100   150   200 km

Inset map (Central Europe Political):

DENMARK — Copenhagen — Amsterdam — Hamburg — Berlin — POLAND — Warsaw — U.S.S.R. — Kiev — BELGIUM — Brussels — WEST GERMANY — EAST GERMANY — Bonn — LUX. — Prague — CZECHOSLOVAKIA — Lvov — FRANCE — Bern — SWITZ. — Liechtenstein — AUSTRIA — Vienna — Budapest — HUNGARY — ROMANIA — ITALY — Trieste — Bucharest — Monaco — Rome — San Marino — Belgrade — YUGOSLAVIA — BULGARIA — Sofia

Main map:

Gdańsk Bay — Zelenogradsk — Kaliningrad — Chernyakhovsk — Vilnius — LITHUANIA S.S.R. — Alitus — Varena — Gdynia — Sopot — Gusev — Pregel — Elblag — Braniewo — Lyna — Suwałki — Augustów — Lida — Novogrudok — WHITE RUSSIA S.S.R. — Malbork — Olsztyn — Ketrzyn — Gizycko — 309 — Grodno — Mosty — Neman — Volkovysk — Slonim — Shchara — Starogard — Grudziadz — Masurian Lakes Plateau — Sokółka — 238 — Bialystok — Bereza — Zhabinka — Chelmno — Wabrzeżno — Mlawa — Ciechanów — Ostrów Mazowiecka — Brańsk — Hajnówka — Czeremcha — Torun — Rypin — Lipno — Lomza — Ostroleka — Pripyat — Ostróda — Wlocławek — Plock — Wisła (Vistula) — Puitus — Bug — Brest — Biala Podlaska — Miedzyrzec — Dubrovitsa — 316 — Uzh — Desna — Warsaw (Warszawa) — Pruszków — Minsk Mazowiecki — Siedlce — Luków — Włodawa — Sarny — Pripyat Marshes — Korosten — Konin — Koło — Kutno — Łowicz — Żyrardów — Skierniewice — Otwock — Chelm — Kovel — Styr — Sluch — Radomyshl — Lódź — Pilica — Radom — Lublin — Bug — Pripyat — Teterev — Kiev — Borispol — Kalisz — Zdunska Wola — Pulawy — Krasnik — Zamość — Vladimir Volynski — Lutsk — Rovno — Novograd Volynski — Zhitomir — Fastov — Piotrków — Wieluń — Warta — Radomsko — Kielce — Ostrowiec — Sandomierz — Sokal — Dubno — Ostrog — Shepetovka — Berdichev — Belaya Tserkov — Opole — Tarnowskie Góry — Częstochowa — Jedrzejów — Pinczów — Tarnobrzeg — 390 — Radekhov — Brody — Kremenets — Starokonstantinov — Kazatin — Zabrze — Bytom — Sosnowiec — Zawiercie — San — Przeworsk — Kamenka Bugskaya — Zolochev — Khmelnitskiy — 384 — Vinnitsa — Gliwice — Chorzów — Katowice — Krakow — Wieliczka — Tarnów — Dabrowa Tarnowska — Rzeszów — Jaroslaw — Gorodok — Lvov — Ternopol — UKRAINE S.S.R. — Zhmerinka — Uman — ostrava — Cieszyn — Bielsko — Nowy Sacz — Jaslo — Krosno — Sanok — Przemysl — 471 — U.S.S.R. — Frydek — Mistek — Český Těšín — 1725 — Dukla P. — Sambor — Drohobych — Stry — Buchach — Chortkov — Kamenets Podolski — Mogilev-Podolski — Pervomaisk — Jablunka P. — 550 — West Beskids — Beskid — 4380 — Borislav — Turka — Ivano-Frankovsk — Zaleschiki — Bug — Zilina — High Tatra — 2655 — Ruzamberok — Presov — Uzhgorod — Nadvornaya — 1881 — Kolomyia — Snyatyn — Khotin — Kotovsk — Low Tatra — Mukachevo — 931 — Chernovtsy — SLOVAKIA — Košice — Beregovo — Khust — 2061 — Storozhinets — Yedintsy — Soroki — Kremnica — Banská Bystrica — Slovakian Ore Mts. — Satoraljaujhely — Bodrog — Dorohoi — Beltsy — Nitra — Zvolen — Banská Stiavnica — Lučenec — Sajo — Nyiregyháza — Sighet — Baia Mare — Radauti — Botosani — MOLDAVIA — N. Zámky — Hron — Miskolc — Tokaj — Satu Mare — 2305 — Vatra Dornei — Suceava — Komárno — Eger — Mezőkövesd — Hajdúböszörmény — Carei — Pietrosul — Bistrita — 429 — Kishinev — Tiraspol — Gyór — Vác — Gyöngyös — Hatvan — Jászbereny — Debrecen — Def — 2102 — Pietrosu — Roman — Iasi — Bendery — Tatabánya — Ujpest — Karcag — Cluj — Bistrita — Piatra Neamt — Vaslui — Esztergom — BUDAPEST — Szolnok — Oradea — Turda — Tirgu Mures — Praid — Miercurea Ciuc — Bacau — Belgorod Dnestrovski — Odessa — Cegléd — Nagykörös — Mezőtúr — Salonta — Crisu — Odorheiu — Barlad — Székesfehérvár — Kecskemét — Békéscsaba — Gyula — Black — 1848 — Mt. Bihor — Abrud — Aiud — Medias — Sighisoara — Bretcu — Tecuci — Kiskunfélegyháza — Dunaujvaros — Kiskunhalas — Csongrad — HUNGARY — Hódmezővásárhely — Makó — White Crisu — Brad — Alba-Iulia — Sibiu — Fagaras — Focsani — Kagul — Kalocsa — Szekszárd — Szeged — Arad — Mures — Deva — Simeria — Transylvanian Alps — Brasov — Ramnicu Sarat — Galati — Izmail — Chilia Mouth — Bataszek — Baja — Senta — Kikinda — ROMANIA — Hunedoara — Lugoj — Red Tower P. — Mt. Negoiu — 2535 — Mt. Omu — 2507 — Buzau — Braila — 467 — Tulcea — Sulina Mouth — Pécs — Mohacs — Subotica — Timisoara — Banat — Caransebes — 1848 — Petrosani — 350 — Cimpulung — Cimpina — St. Gheorghe's Mouth — Osijek — Novi Sad — Resita — Porta Orientalis — Pelega — 2518 — Paringul Mare — 2609 — Ploesti — Portitei Mouth — Odzak — Sremska Mitrovica — Petrovaradin — Tirgu-Jiu — Ramnicu Valcea — Tirgoviste — Ialomita — Dobrogea — Vrsac — Bela Crkva — Mehadia — Iron Gate — Orsova — Turnu-Severin — Jiu — Pitesti — Arges — Bucharest (Bucuresti) — Cernavoda — BLACK — Bijeljina — Pancevo — Dimbovita — Calarasi — Constanta — Tuzla — Belgrade (Beograd) — Smederevo — Pozarevac — Craiova — Statina — Olt — Silistra — Trajan Wall — SEA — Sava — Valjevo — 1346 — Negotin — Timok — Vedea — Ruse (Ruschuk) — Mangalia — GOSLAVIA — Sarajevo — Titovo Uzice — Cacak — Kragujevac — Zajecar — Vidin — Danube — Turnu Magurele — Giurgiu — Corabia — Zimnicea — BULGARIA — Talbukhin

Projection: Conical with two
standard parallels.

West from Greenwich   0   East from Greenwich

1:10 000 000

100   0   100   200   300   400 km

POLAND
Poznan
Plock
Warsaw
(Warszawa)
Łódź
Wisła (Vistula)
Brest
Pinsk
Pripyat Marshes
Chernigov
Desna
Sumy
Belgorod
Kazanskaya
Volgograd

Wrocław
Radom
Lublin
Bug
Pripyat
Konotop
Nezhin
Kharkov
Kazanskaya

Chorzow
Krakow
Tarnów
Kielce
Lutsko
Rovno
Zhitomir
Kiev
Pereyaslav-Khmelnitski
Poltava
Slavyansk
Artemovsk
Voroshilovgrad
(Lugansk)
Shakhty
Tsimlyansk
Reservoir

Ostrava
Cieszyn
Przemysl
Kamenets Podolski
Mogilev-Podolski
Uman
Pervomaysk
Kremenchug
(Dnieper)
Dneprodzerzhinsk
Pavlograd
Gorlovka
Makeyevka
Donetsk
Novocherkassk
Don
Manych

Bratislava
Miskolc
Košice
Kolomyia
Prut
Botoșani
Iași
Chernovtsy
MOLDAVIA
Kishinev
Bendery
Tiraspol
Voznesensk
Nikolayev
Melitopol
Berdyansk
Rostov
L. Manych
Gudilo

Budapest
Debrecen
Oradea
Cluj
ROMANIA
Sibiu
Brașov
(Orașul Stalin)
Galati
Brăila
Odessa
Belgorod-
Dnestrovski
Kherson
Perekop
Sea of Azov
Kerch
& Str.
Yeisk
Tikhoretsk
Stavropol
Armavir
Maykop

HUNGARY
Kecskemét
Szeged
Hódmezővásárhely
Arad
Timișoara
Negoiu
2535
Transylvanian Alps
Iron Gate
Turnu-Severin
Pitești
Bucharest
(București)
Constanța
G. of Karkinitsk
C. Tarkhankut
Yevpatoriya
Simferopol
Crimea
Feodosiya
Novorossiysk
Tuapse
Sukhumi
Poti

Subotica
Novi Sad
Belgrade
Craiova
Danube
Ruse
Tolbukhin
Varna
Sevastopol
Yalta
Balaklava
2211

BLACK SEA

Batumi
Rize

BULGARIA
Sofia
Plovdiv
Edirne
Istanbul
Üsküdar
Sea of Marmara
Bursa
Ankara
TURKEY

CYPRUS
Nicosia
Famagusta
Larnaca
Limassol

SYRIA
Al Ladhiqiyah
(Latakia)
Hamah
Homs

LEBANON
Beirut
Damascus

ISRAEL
Tel Aviv-Jaffa
Jerusalem
JORDAN
Amman

MEDITERRANEAN SEA

EGYPT
Alexandria
CAIRO
Port Said
Suez
Ismailia

LIBYA
Benghazi
Cyrenaica
Tobruk

------ Division between Greeks and Turks in Cyprus; Turks to the North.

1:40 000 000

400   0   400   800   1200   1600 km

ATLANTIC OCEAN

British Isles

Bay of Biscay

Carpathians

Aral Sea

Alps
Mt. Blanc 4807
Pyrenees
Apennines
Dinaric Alps
Adriatic Sea

Black Sea

Caucasus
Elburus 5633

Caspian Sea

Iberian Peninsula

Corsica

Sardinia

Anatolia

6578

Madeira

Str. of Gibraltar

Middle Atlas
High Atlas
Saharan Atlas
High Plateaus

Mediterranean Sea

C. Bon
Malta
5121
Sicily
Crete
Cyprus

Levant

Mesopotamia
Tigris
Euphrates

Syrian Desert

The Gull

Bahrain

Canary Is.
3718
Tenerife

Anti Atlas
Toubkal 4165
Dra

Chott Djerid
G. of Gabes
G. of Sidra

Tripolitania

Cyrenaica

Siwa

Arabian Desert
Sinai 2642

Nile

Red Sea

Hejaz

Arabia

Tropic of Cancer

Ras Nouadhibou

Igidi

Sahara

El Djouf

Tuat

Tasili Plateau

Fezzan

Libyan Desert

Egypt

Kufra

El Kharga
1st Cat.

Nubian Desert

Nubia

3rd Cat.
4th Cat.
5th Cat.

6th Cat.

Rub' al Khali

Perim I.
Str. of Bab el Mandeb
Gulf of Aden
Ras Asir

Soco

Hoggar

Air

Bilma

Tibesti
3415

Adrar

Atbara

Ras Dashan
4620
L. Tana

Ethiopian Highlands

C. Vert
Senegal
Senegambia
Gambia
Fouta Djalon

Niger (Joliba)

Niger

Volta

L. Chad

Chari

Wadai

Darfur

Kordofan

White Nile
Blue Nile

Somali Peninsula

Sudan

Guinea

Grain Coast
Gold Coast
Ivory Coast
Slave Coast
C. Palmas

Bight of Benin

Benue
Adamawa Highlands
Cameroon Peak 4070
Bioko
6363

Dar Banda

Bahr el Ghazal

Bahr el Ghazal
Bahr el Jebel

Uele

Congo

L. Mobutu Sese Seko

Chutes Boyoma
Ruwenzori 5109

Elgon 4321
Kenya 5199

Turkana

Juba
Shibeli

Equator

Gulf of Guinea
Principe
São Tomé
Annobón
C. Lopez

Bight of Bonny

Ogoue

Zaire (Congo)

Basin

L. Edward
L. Kivu

L. Victoria

Kilimanjaro 5895

INDIAN OCEAN

Pemba
Zanzibar

Ascension

St. Helena

ATLANTIC OCEAN

Kwanza

Zaire (Congo)

Pool Malebo

Kasai

Sankuru

Lualaba

Kasai

L. Tanganyika

Lukuga

Rungwe 2961
Mweru
L. Nyasa
Ruvuma

Aldabra Is.

C. Delgado

Comoro Is.

Bié Plateau

Cuango

Cuanza

Cunene

C. Fria

Shaba
L. Mweru
L. Bangweulu
Luapula

Malawi

Mulanje 3000

Victoria Falls

Zambezi

Zambezi

Shire

Mozambique Channel

Madagascar
2643

Réu

Walvis Bay

Namib Desert

Orange

Kalahari

Limpopo

Tropic of Capricorn

Delagoa Bay

High Veld

Compass B. 2505
Nieuveldberge
Gt. Karoo
Swartberg

Vaal

Orange
3482
Drakensberg

Algoa Bay

C. of Good Hope
C. Agulhas
Agulhas Bank

m
4000
3000
2000
1500
1000
400
200
0
0
200
2000
4000
6000
m

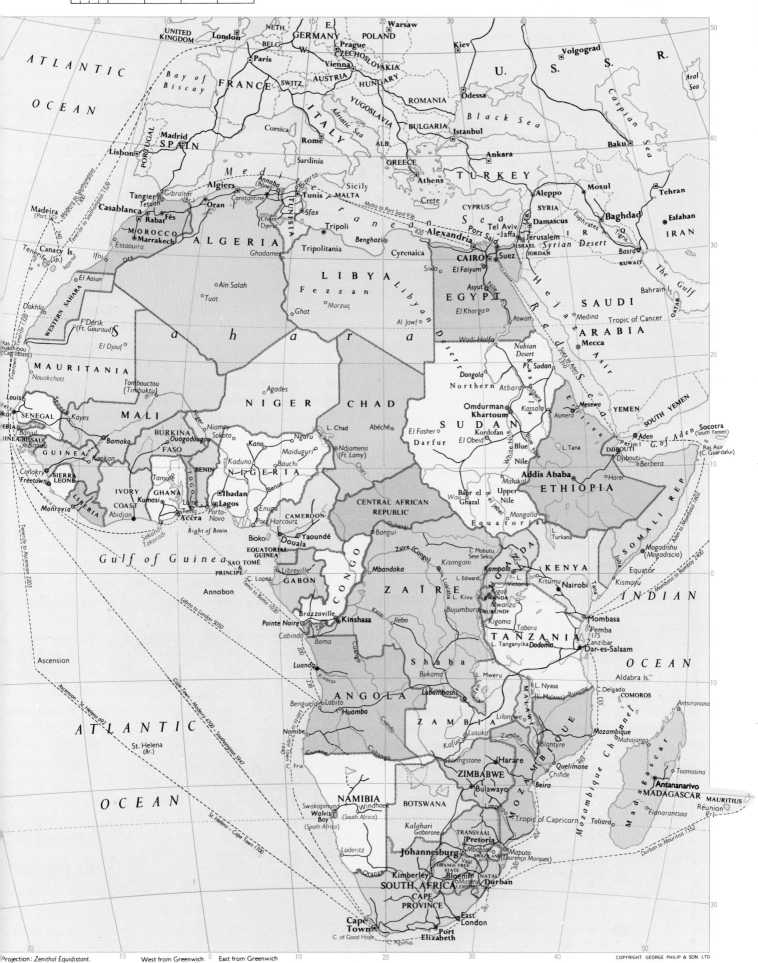

1:40 000 000

400   0   400   800   1200   1600 km

ATLANTIC

OCEAN

UNITED KINGDOM London NETH. GERMANY E. POLAND Warsaw
BELG. Prague CZECHOSLOVAKIA
Paris W. Vienna AUSTRIA HUNGARY
FRANCE SWITZ. Kiev Volgograd
Bay of Biscay ITALY YUGOSLAVIA ROMANIA U. S. S. R.
Corsica Rome Adriatic Sea BULGARIA Odessa Black Sea Caspian Sea
Madrid SPAIN Sardinia GREECE Istanbul Ankara Baku Aral Sea
Lisbon PORTUGAL Athens TURKEY 40
Sicily Crete CYPRUS Aleppo Mosul Tehran
Madeira (Port.) Tangier Algiers Annaba (Bône) Tunis MALTA SYRIA Damascus Baghdad Esfahan
Tetuán Gibraltar (Br.) Constantine Sfax Malta to Port Said 936 Tel Aviv-Jaffa IRAN
Casablanca Oran TUNISIA Tripoli Port Said JERUSALEM ISRAEL Syrian Desert Basra
Canary Is. MOROCCO Rabat Fès Benghazi Alexandria Port Said JORDAN KUWAIT Bahrain I.
Tenerife (Sp.) Marrakech Essaouira Ghadames Tripolitania Cyrenaica CAIRO Suez The Gulf QATAR
Ifni ALGERIA LIBYA Siwa EGYPT SAUDI Medina Tropic of Cancer
El Aaiún Aïn Salah Fezzan El Faiyum Asyut Aswan ARABIA Mecca
Dakhla WESTERN SAHARA Tuat Ghat Al Jawf El Kharga Wadi Halfa Nubian Desert Pt. Sudan
F'Dérik (Ft. Gouraud) S a h a r a Libyan Desert Dongola Northern Atbara Mesewa YEMEN
El Djouf MAURITANIA Nouakchott Tombouctou (Timbuktu) Agades Khartoum Omdurman Kassala Asmera Aden SOUTH YEMEN
Louis SENEGAL Kayes MALI NIGER CHAD SUDAN Kordofan Blue L. Tana DJIBOUTI Socotra (South Yemen)
Banjul Bamako Niamey L. Chad Abéché El Fasher Darfur El Obeid Nile Djibouti Berbera Ras Asir (C. Guardafui)
GUINEA-BISSAU Bissau BURKINA Ouagadougou Sokoto Nguru Ndjamena (Ft. Lamy) White Addis Ababa Harer
GUINEA Kankan FASO BENIN Kano Maiduguri Bauchi Malakal Harer
SIERRA LEONE Conakry Freetown Tamale TOGO Kaduna Chari Bahr el Ghazal Upper ETHIOPIA SOMALI REP.
IVORY Kumasi GHANA NIGERIA Ibadan CENTRAL AFRICAN Wau Nile Mongalla L. Turkana Mogadishu (Mogadiscio)
LIBERIA COAST Accra Lagos Enugu CAMEROON REPUBLIC Bangui Equatoria KENYA Equator
Monrovia Abidjan Sekondi Takoradi Porto-Novo Port Harcourt Yaoundé Bangui L. Mobutu Sese Seko UGANDA Kisumu Nairobi Kismayu
EQUATORIAL GUINEA Douala Bioko Zaïre (Congo) Kisangani Kampala L. Victoria Mombasa
SÃO TOMÉ & PRINCIPE Libreville GABON CONGO Mbandaka L. Edward RWANDA Kigali Mwanza Pemba
Annobon C. Lopez Brazzaville ZAÏRE L. Kivu BURUNDI Bujumbura Tabora Zanzibar
Pointe Noire Kinshasa Ilebo Kasai Kigoma TANZANIA Dodoma Dar-es-Salaam
Cabinda Boma Shaba L. Tanganyika INDIAN OCEAN
Luanda Kwango Bukama L. Mweru Aldabra Is.
ATLANTIC Kwanza ANGOLA Lubumbashi L. Nyasa (L. Malawi) Ruvuma C. Delgado COMOROS Antsiranana
Benguela Lobito ZAMBIA Lilongwe Mozambique Mahajanga
Namibe Huambo Cunene Cuando Lusaka MALAWI Blantyre Quelimane
OCEAN Kafue Zambezi Chinde MOZAMBIQUE Beira MADAGASCAR
St. Helena (Br.) Cubango Livingstone Harare Antananarivo
NAMIBIA ZIMBABWE Bulawayo Toamasina MAURITIUS
Ascension Swakopmund Windhoek BOTSWANA Limpopo Tropic of Capricorn Réunion (Fr.)
Walvis Bay (South Africa) Kalahari Gaborone TRANSVAAL Toliara Fianarantsoa
Lüderitz NAMIBIA Pretoria Maputo (Lourenço Marques)
Johannesburg SWAZILAND Mbabane
Kimberley ORANGE FREE STATE Vaal NATAL Durban
SOUTH AFRICA Bloemfontein Maseru LESOTHO
CAPE PROVINCE East London
Cape Town Port Elizabeth
C. of Good Hope C. Agulhas

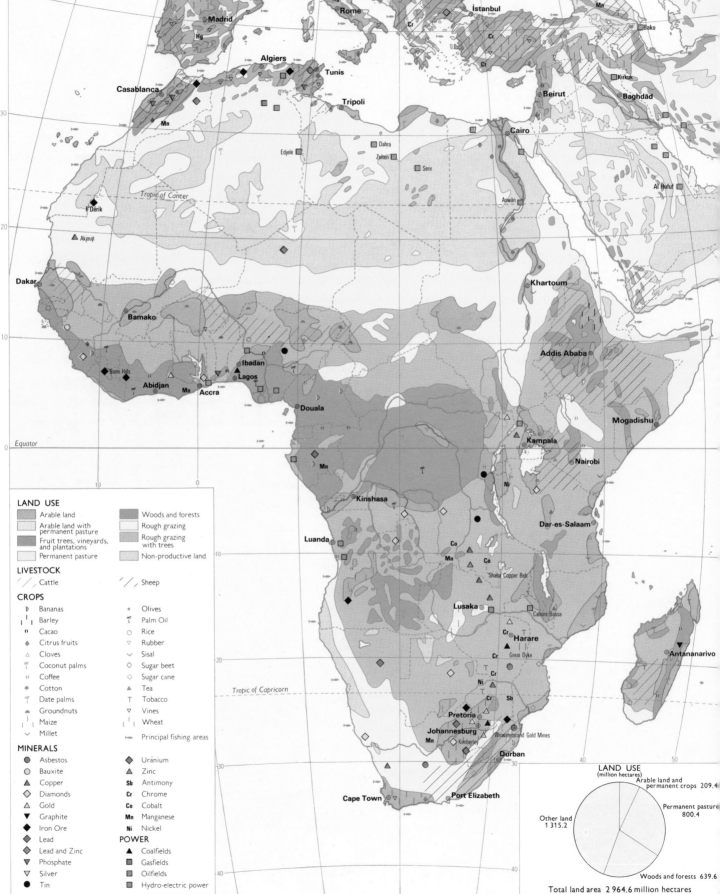

1 : 40 000 000

400   0   400   800   1200   1600 km

LAND USE

Arable land	Woods and forests
Arable land with permanent pasture	Rough grazing
Fruit trees, vineyards, and plantations	Rough grazing with trees
Permanent pasture	Non-productive land

LIVESTOCK

/// Cattle   /// Sheep

CROPS

ⅅ	Bananas	•	Olives
ⅼ ⅼ	Barley	ⅇ	Palm Oil
o	Cacao	o	Rice
◆	Citrus fruits	▽	Rubber
△	Cloves	⌄	Sisal
ⅇ	Coconut palms	◇	Sugar beet
o	Coffee	◇	Sugar cane
ⅇ	Cotton	▲	Tea
ⅇ	Date palms	T	Tobacco
⌐	Groundnuts	▽	Vines
ⅼ ⅼ	Maize	ⅼ ⅼ	Wheat
⌄	Millet	⟼	Principal fishing areas

MINERALS

●	Asbestos	◆	Uranium
○	Bauxite	▲	Zinc
▲	Copper	Sb	Antimony
◇	Diamonds	Cr	Chrome
△	Gold	Co	Cobalt
▼	Graphite	Mn	Manganese
◆	Iron Ore	Ni	Nickel
◆	Lead		
◆	Lead and Zinc	**POWER**	
▼	Phosphate	▲	Coalfields
▽	Silver	■	Gasfields
●	Tin	■	Oilfields
		■	Hydro-electric power

LAND USE
(million hectares)

Arable land and permanent crops 209.4

Permanent pasture 800.4

Other land 1 315.2

Woods and forests 639.6

Total land area 2 964.6 million hectares

Projection: *Zenithal Equidistant*   West from Greenwich 0 East from Greenwich

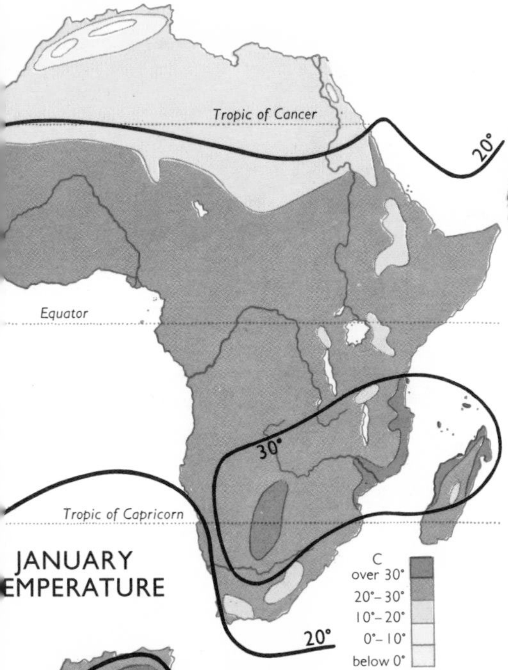

1 : 100 000 000

JANUARY TEMPERATURE

C
- over 30°
- 20° – 30°
- 10° – 20°
- 0° – 10°
- below 0°

30° Isotherms in degrees Celsius (reduced to Sea-Level)

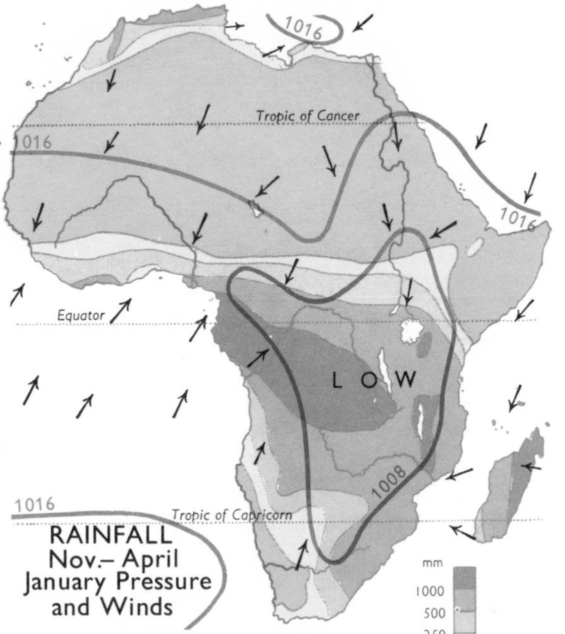

RAINFALL
Nov. – April
January Pressure and Winds

LOW

mm
- 1000
- 500
- 250
- 125

1016 Isobars (in millibars)
→ Prevailing Winds

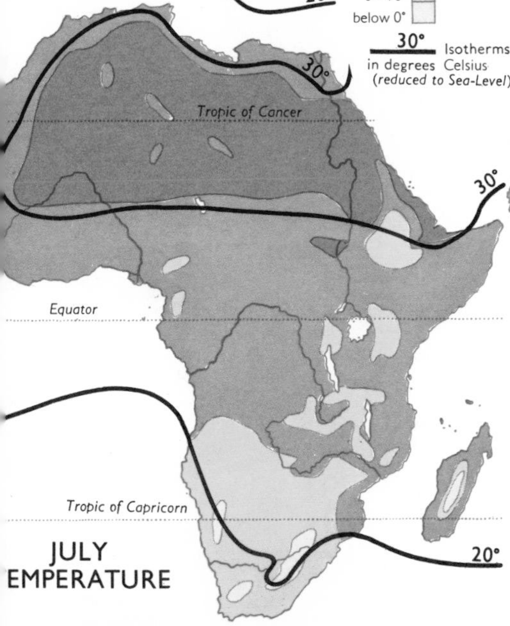

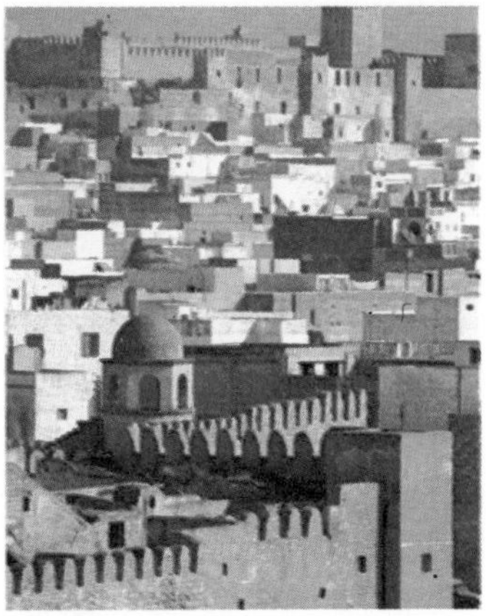

The ancient town of Sousse in Tunisia.

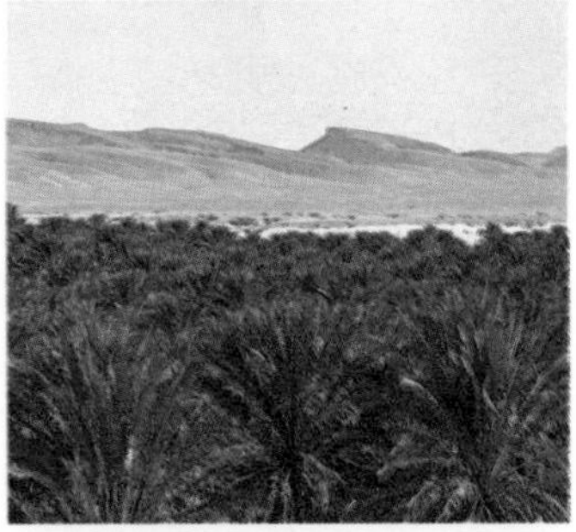

Palm groves in Morocco.

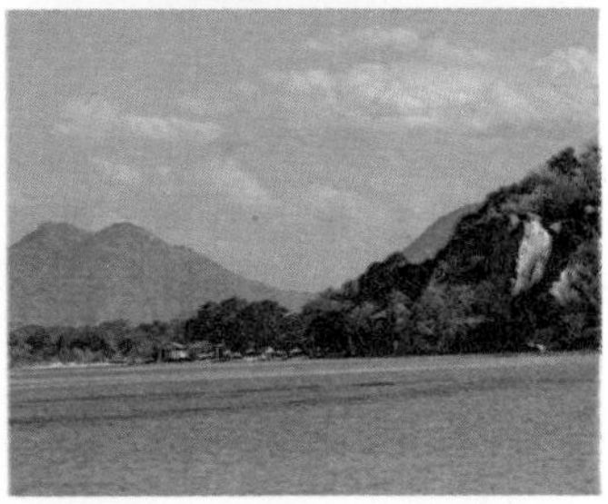

JULY TEMPERATURE

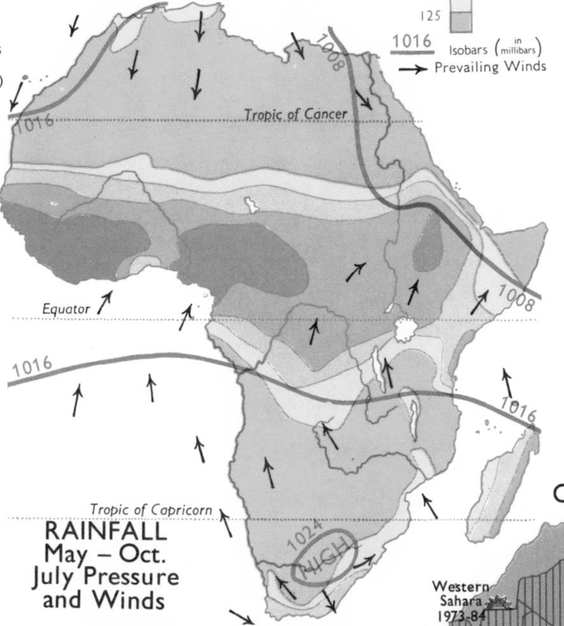

RAINFALL
May – Oct.
July Pressure and Winds

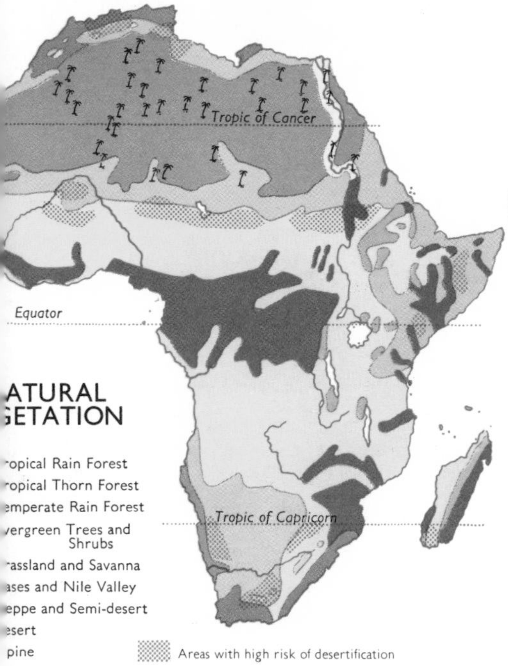

HIGH

Lake Malawi.

CONFLICT IN POST-COLONIAL AFRICA

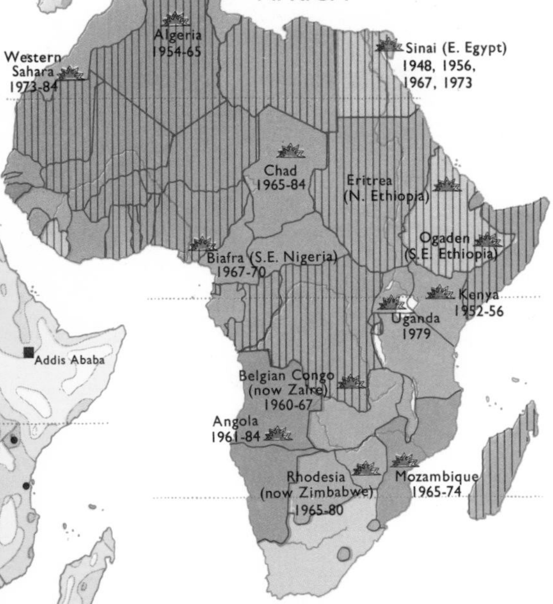

Western Sahara 1973-84
Algeria 1954-65
Sinai (E. Egypt) 1948, 1956, 1967, 1973
Chad 1965-84
Eritrea (N. Ethiopia)
Ogaden (S.E. Ethiopia)
Biafra (S.E. Nigeria) 1967-70
Kenya 1952-56
Uganda 1979
Belgian Congo (now Zaïre) 1960-67
Angola 1961-84
Rhodesia (now Zimbabwe) 1965-80
Mozambique 1965-74

NATURAL VEGETATION

- Tropical Rain Forest
- Tropical Thorn Forest
- Temperate Rain Forest
- Evergreen Trees and Shrubs
- Grassland and Savanna
- Oases and Nile Valley
- Steppe and Semi-desert
- Desert
- Alpine

Areas with high risk of desertification

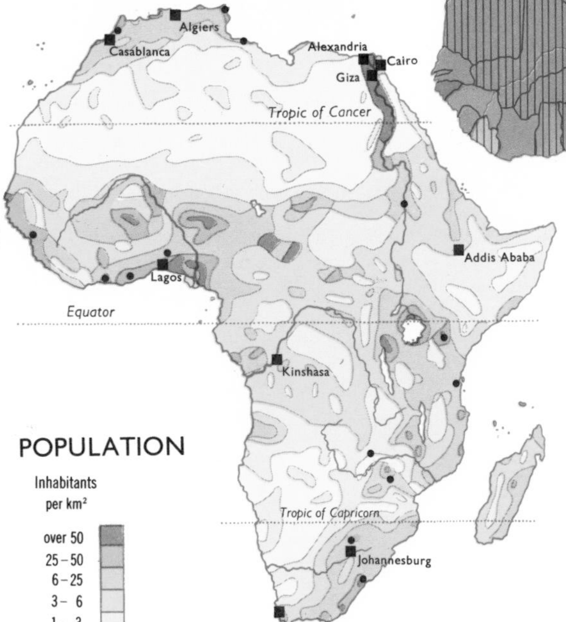

POPULATION

Algiers
Casablanca
Alexandria
Cairo
Giza
Addis Ababa
Lagos
Kinshasa
Johannesburg

Inhabitants per km²

- over 50
- 25 – 50
- 6 – 25
- 3 – 6
- 1 – 3
- under 1

● 500 000 – 1 million inhabitants
■ 1 – 3 million inhabitants

DATE OF INDEPENDENCE
- Before 1949
- 1950 - 59
- 1960 - 69
- since 1970

States currently under military rule.

Major civil wars and conflicts since 1945

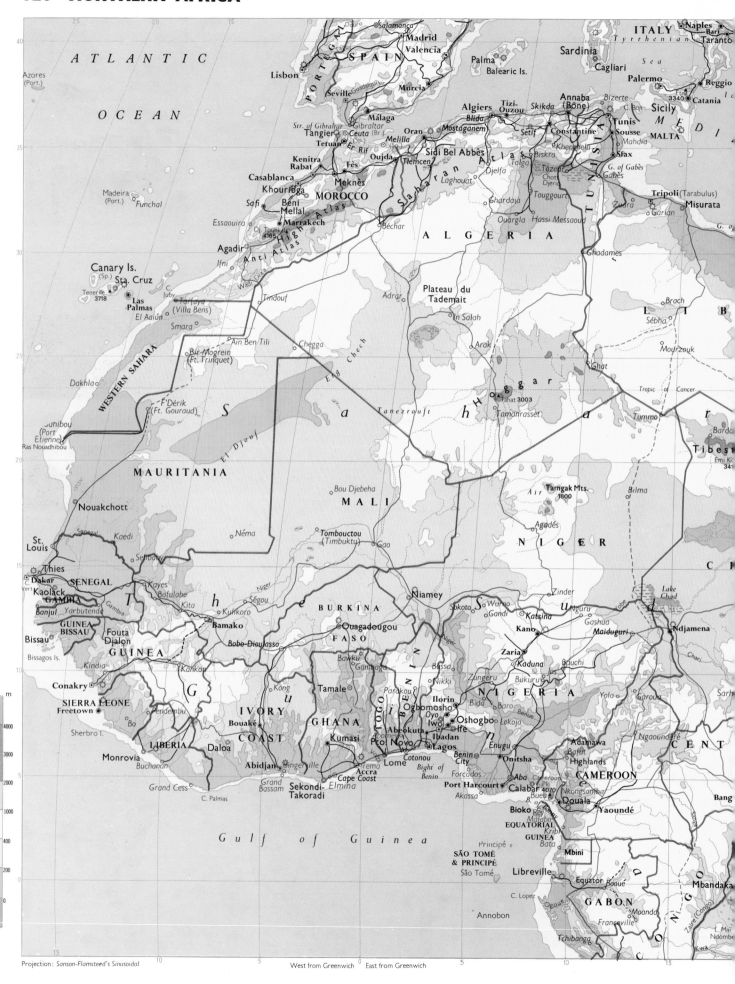

ATLANTIC

OCEAN

Azores
(Port.)

Madeira
(Port.) *Funchal*

Canary Is.
(Sp.) *Sta. Cruz*
Tenerife
3718
Las
Palmas

Dakhla

Cahibou
(Port.
Etienne)
Ras Nouadhibou

ITALY
Tyrrhenian
Naples
Bari
Taranto
Sardinia
Sea
Cagliari
Palermo
Reggio
Sicily
Etna
3340
Catania
MEDITER

PORTUGAL
SPAIN
Lisbon
Madrid
Valencia
Seville
Guadalquivir
Murcia
Palma
Balearic Is.
Málaga
Str. of Gibraltar
Tangier   Ceuta (Sp.)
Tetuan   Er Rif   Melilla
Gibraltar (Br.)
Algiers   Tizi-
Ouzou   Skikda   Annaba
(Bône)   Bizerte
Blida   Setif   Constantine   Tunis
Oran   Mostaganem   Sousse
Sidi Bel Abbès   Khenchela   Sfax
Kenitra   Oujda   Tlemcen   Saharan Atlas   Biskra   Tozeur   G. of Gabès
Rabat   Fès   Talga   Chott   Gabès
Casablanca   Meknès   Djelfa   Laghouat   Djerid
Khouribga   Ghardaia   Touggourt   Tripoli (Tarabulus)
Safi   Béni   MOROCCO   Zuara   Misurata
Mellal   Béchar   Ouargla   Hassi Messaoud   Garian   G.
Essaouira   Marrakech   High Atlas   ALGERIA   Ghadames
Dj. Toubkal   Anti Atlas
4165   Agadir   Brach
Ifni   Wadi Draa   Adrar   Plateau du   Sébha   LIB
Tindouf   Tademait   In Salah
Tarfaya
(Villa Bens)   Ain Ben Tili   Chegga   Arak   Ghat   Mourzouk
El Aaiún   Smara   Eg   Chech
WESTERN SAHARA   Bir Mogrein   Tanezrouft   Tropic of Cancer
(Ft. Trinquet)   S   Tahat 3003   Tummo
F'Dérik   a   h   a   Tibes
(Ft. Gouraud)   El Djouf   Tamanrasset   Barda
Hoggar   Emi Ko
MAURITANIA   a   r   34
Nouakchott   Bou Djebeha   Air   Bilma   Tibesti
MALI   Tamgak Mts.
1800
St.   Kaedi   Néma   Tombouctou   Agadès   N I G E R   Lake   Cha
Louis   Senegal   (Timbuktu)   Gao   Chad
Thies   Kayes   Zinder   Nguru
Dakar   Ségou   Niamey   Sokoto   Wurno   Gashua   Ndjamena
SENEGAL   Bafulabe   Niger   Gandi   Katsina   Maiduguri
Kaolack   Kita   Koulikoro   BURKINA   Kano
GAMBIA   T   h   e   Zaria   Chari
Banjul   Yarbutenda   Bamako   Ouagadougou   Bida   Kaduna   Bauchi
GUINEA   Fouta   Bobo-Dioulasso   FASO   Bussa   Zungeru   Bukuru   Jos
BISSAU   Djalon   Bawku   Garniaga   Nikki   N I G E R I A   Yola
Bissau   GUINEA   Gambaga   Parakou   Ilorin   Baro   Garoua
Bissagos Is.   Kindia   Kankan   Kong   Tamale   Ogbomosho   Benue
Kankari   G   u   Oyo   Iwo   Oshogbo   Ngaoundéré
Conakry   SIERRA LEONE   Bouaké   GHANA   Ife   Lokoja   CENT
Freetown   Bo   IVORY   Kumasi   Abeokuta   Ibadan   Enugu   Adamawa
Pendembu   COAST   Pto. Novo   Lagos   Benin   Highlands
Sherbro I.   LIBERIA   Daloa   Abidjan   Lome   City   Onitsha   CAMEROON
Monrovia   Buchanan   Bingerville   Cotonou   Forcados   Aba   Cameroon
Grand   Sekondi-   Cape Coast   Bight of   Benin   Port Harcourt   Calabar   Bang
C. Palmas   Bassam   Takoradi   Elmina   Benin   Akassa   Buea   Ngkongsomba
Grand Cess   Accra   Bioko   Douala   Yaoundé
Malabo
EQUATORIAL   Kribi
Gulf   of   Guinea   Principé   GUINEA   Bata
SÃO TOMÉ   Mbini
& PRINCIPÉ   Libreville
São Tomé   Equator   Booué
GABON   Mbandaka
Annobon   C. Lopez   Ogoue   Moanda
Franceville   L. Mai
Tchibanga   Ndombe
Zaire (Congo)   Kwa

m
4000
3000
2000
1000
400
200
0
0   0
200
m

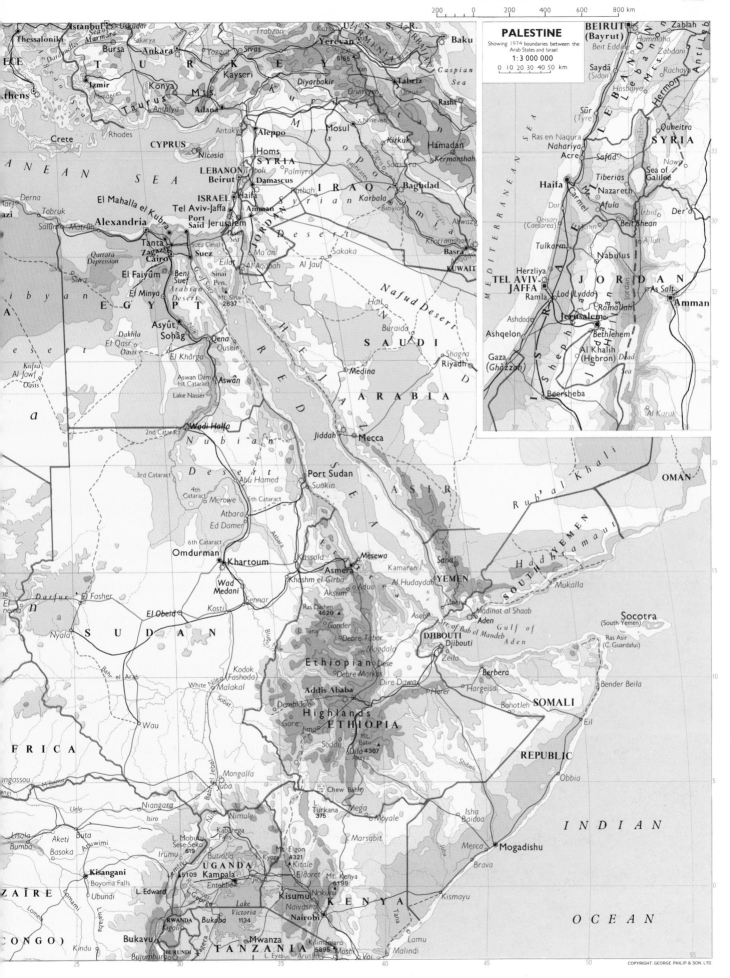

PALESTINE
Showing 1974 boundaries between the
Arab States and Israel
1 : 3 000 000
0 10 20 30 40 50 km

200   0   200   400   600   800 km

Thessaloniki
Istanbul   Üsküdar
Bursa   Ankara   Yozgat   Sivas
Marmara   Sakarya   Trabzon
TURKEY   Yerevan
İzmir   Konya   Kayseri
ECE   Taurus   Diyarbakir   Tabriz
thens   MTS.   Antalya   Adana
Crete   Rhodes
Nicosia
CYPRUS   Antakya   Aleppo   Mosul   Kirkuk
Homs   Nineveh   Hamadan   Baku
A N E A N   S E A   SYRIA   Kermanshah
Derna   LEBANON   Palmyra
Beirut   Damascus   IRAQ   Baghdad   Caspian Sea
Tobruk   ISRAEL   Haifa   Karbala   Babylon
Salûm   Matrûh   Tel Aviv-Jaffa   Amman   Rasht
azi   El Mahalla el Kubra   Port   Ahwaz
Alexandria   Said   Jerusalem   JORDAN   Desert
Tanta   Zagazig   Ma'an   Sakaka   Khorramshahr
Qattara   Cairo   Suez Canal   Al Jauf   Basra
Depression   El Faiyûm   Beni   Sinai   Al 'Aqabah   KUWAIT
Suef   Pen.   Eilat   Hail   Nafud Desert
Siwa   El Minya   Arabian   Mt. Sinai   Buraida
i b y a n   E G Y P T   Desert   2637   SAUDI
Asyût   Sohâg   Qena   Shagra
Dakhla   Qusair   Medina   Riyadh   ARABIA
El Qasr   Oasis   El Khârga
a   Aswan Dam   Aswân
1st Cataract   Mecca
Lake Nasser   Jiddah
Kufra   Wadi Halfa
Al Jawf   Nubian   ASIR   OMAN
Oasis   2nd Cataract   Rub' al Khali
Desert   Port Sudan
3rd Cataract   Abu Hamed   Suakin
4th   Merowe   6th Cataract
Cataract   Atbara
Ed Damer   SOUTH YEMEN   Socotra
6th Cataract   Kassala   Mesewa   Mukalla   (South Yemen)
Omdurman   Asmera   Kamaran I.   Ras Asir
Darfur   El Fasher   Khashm el Girba   Al Hudaydah   YEMEN   (C. Guardafui)
nena   Wad   Adua   Sana   Madinat al Shaab
Medani   Aksum   Aden   Gulf of   Aden   SOMALI
Nyala   SUDAN   Sennar   Ras Dashen   Mocha   DJIBOUTI   Berbera
El Obeid   Kosti   4620   Gonder   Djibouti   Hargeisa   Bender Beila
Kodok   L. Tana   Zeila   Harer   REPUBLIC
(Fashoda)   Debre Tabor   Dire Dawa   Bohotleh   Eil
Malakal   Magdala   Dese
White Nile   Sobat   Addis Ababa   Obbia
Highlands   Debre Markos
FRICA   Wau   ETHIOPIA   INDIAN
ngassou   Gore   Jima   Mt. Batu   Isha   Baidoa
ngi   Mongalla   Dila   4307   Shibeli   Merca   Mogadishu
Uele   Juba   Omo   Abaya   Brava
Niangara   Chew Bahir   OCEAN
Isiro   Nimule   Turkana   Mega   Marsabit   Kismayu
Lisala   Aketi   Buta   375   Moyale
Bumba   Kabarega   L. Mobutu   Falls
Basoka   Sese Seko   Butiaba   Mt. Elgon   Lamu
Kisangani   619   4321   Kitale   Mt. Kenya   Malindi
ZAIRE   Boyoma Falls   Kampala   Kyoga   Eldoret   5199
5109   UGANDA   Jinja   Nakuru   KENYA
CONGO)   L. Edward   L. George   Lake   Kisumu   Voi
RWANDA   Victoria   Naivasha   Nairobi
Bukavu   Kigali   Bukoba   1134
Kindu   BURUNDI   Mwanza   Kilimanjaro   Moshi
Bujumbura   TANZANIA   5895   Arusha   L. Eyasi

PALESTINE inset:
Zablah
BEIRUT   Hammana
(Bayrut)   Beit Eddine
Zabdani
LEBANON   Saydā   Anti Leb
(Sidon)   Hermon
Ras en Naqura   Rachaya
Nahariya   Quneitra
Acre   Safad   SYRIA
Haifa   Tiberias   Naw
Carmel   Nazareth   Sea of Galilee
Dor   Afula
Qeisari   Jenin   Beit Shean   Irbid   Der'a
(Caesarea)
Tulkarm   Ajlun
TEL AVIV-   Nabulus   JORDAN
JAFFA   Jordan   As Salt
Herzliya   Ramallah   Amman
Ramla   Lod (Lydda)
Ashdod   Jerusalem
Ashqelon   Bethlehem
Gaza   Al Khalil   Dead
(Ghazzah)   (Hebron)   Sea
Beersheba   Al Kurak

COPYRIGHT. GEORGE PHILIP & SON. LTD.

1:20 000 000

200   0   200   400   600   800 km

NIGERIA

CAMEROON

CENTRAL AFRICAN REPUBLIC

SUDAN

ETHIOPIA

SOMALI REP.

Cross
Cameroon Pk. 4070
B. of Biafra
Douala
Yaounde
Bioko
Bata
EQUATORIAL GUINEA
Libreville
C. Lopez
Ogowe
GABON
Franceville
Equator

Ubangi
Bangui
Bangassou
M. Bomu
Uele
Niangara
Lisala
Aketi
Buta
Basoko
Aruwimi
Isiro
Kisangani
Mbandaka
Ubundi
Lomami
Lualaba

Bahr el Jebel
Mongalla
Juba
Nimule
Wadelai
Kabarega Fall
Butiaba
L. Mobutu Sese Seko
Irumu
Semliki
5109
UGANDA
Kampala
Entebbe
Rwenzori
L. Edward
L. George
Kivu
Kigali
RWANDA
Bukavu
BURUNDI
Bujumbura

Oma
Chew Bahir (L. Stefanie)
L. Turkana
Marsabit
Mt. Elgon 4321
L. Kyoga
Kitale
Eldoret
Mt. Kenya 5199
Jinja
Kisumu
Nakuru
KENYA
Naivasha
Nairobi
Tana
Lamu
Malindi

CONGO
Zaire (Congo)
Kwa
Brazzaville
Pool Malebo
Kinshasa
Pointe Noire
Cabinda
Boma
Muanda
Matadi

ZAÏRE (CONGO)
Kindu
Sankuru
Ileba
Lusambo
Kananga
Kabinda
Lomela
Kasai
Lulua
Kamina
Sandoa
Luau

Kongolo
Kabalo
Kalemie
Luvua
Mpanda
L. Tanganyika
Kigoma
Tabora
Mwanza
Lake Victoria
Bukoba
Kagera
Mwanza
L. Eyasi
Arusha
L. Manyara
TANZANIA
Dodoma
Iringa
Morogoro

Kilimanjaro 5895
Moshi
Voi
Mombasa
Tanga
Pemba
Zanzibar
Bagamoyo
Dar-es-Salaam
Mafia
Kilwa

Luanda
Ambriz
Cuanza
Malanje
ANGOLA
Cuango
Kasai

Shaba
Bukama
Likasi
Lubumbashi
Kitwe
Ndola
L. Mweru
L. Bangweulu
Chambeshi
Luangwa
L. Rukwa
Mbala
Mbeya
Tukuyu
Karonga
Livingstonia
Manda
Ruvuma
Lindi
Mikindani
C. Delgado

Lobito
Benguela
Bié
Huambo
Plateau
Atlantic Ocean
Cubango
Cunene

ZAMBIA
Kafue
Kabwe
Lusaka
Kariba
Zambezi
Zumbo
Bassa Dam
Tete
Barotseland
Lealui
Mongu
Katue
Sesheke

Chipata
Lilongwe
MALAWI
Salima
Zomba
Blantyre
Limbe
Shire
Shirwa
Sena
Zambezi
Nampula
Mozambique
Quelimane
Chinde

Namibe
Gt. Fish Bay
C. Frio
Owambo
Cubango
Okavango
Etosha Pan
Otavi
Grootfontein

Livingstone
Victoria Falls
Hwange
ZIMBABWE
Gweru
Harare (Salisbury)
Mutare
Matabeleland
Bulawayo
Matopo Hills
Gt. Zimbabwe
Masvingo
Gwanda
West Nicholson
Beira
Sofala
Sabi
Zambezi
MOZAMBIQUE
Mozambique Channel

Swakopmund
Walvis Bay
Windhoek
Damaraland
NAMIBIA
Namaland
Lüderitz
Possession I.
Keetmanshoop
Karas Mts.
Hardap Dam
Nossob
Kalahari
Tropic of Capricorn

BOTSWANA
Botletle
Makgadikgadi Salt pan
Serowe
Shoshong
Palapye
Gaborone
Mafikeng
Molopo

Serule
Limpopo
Messina
Pietersburg
Olifants
Inhambane
Maputo
Delagoa Bay

TRANSVAAL
Pretoria
Brakpan
Springs
Krugersdorp
Johannesburg
Germiston
Vereeniging
Kroonstad
SWAZILAND
Barberton
Lydenburg

Namaland
Upington
Bushmanland
Orange
Kimberley
ORANGE FREE STATE
Bloemfontein
Vryburg
Vaal
Kroonstad

Mt. aux Sources 3299
Ladysmith
LESOTHO
Maseru
Drakensberg
NATAL
St. Lucia Bay
Pietermaritzburg
Durban
Thabana Ntlenyana 3482

Port Nolloth
SOUTH AFRICA
Calvinia
De Aar
Stormberg
Umtato
INDIAN OCEAN
Nuweveldberge
Karoo
Kompasberg 2504
Graaff-Reinet
William's Town
East London
Grahamstown

Cape Town
Table Mountain
C. of Good Hope
Paarl
Oudtshoorn
Swartberg
Mosselbaai
Agulhas
St. Helena Bay
Algoa Bay
Pt. Elizabeth

Projection: Sanson-Flamsteed's Sinusoidal
East from Greenwich

m
3000
2000
1000
400
200
0
200
m

MADAGASCAR
On the same scale as the main map

C. Bobraomby
Antsiranana
Nossi-Bé
Andoany
Vohimarina
2876
Tsaratanana
Andapa
Mahajanga
Marovoay
Besalampy
Maroantsetra
Maintirano
Mdevatanana
Fenoarivo
L. Alaotra
Ambatondrazaka
Toamasina
Belo-Tsiribihina
2643
Antananarivo
Antsirabe
Morondava
Mahanoro
Morombé
Fianarantsoa
Mangoro
Manjary
Ihosy
Manakara
Ankazoabo
Betroka
Farafangana
Toliara
Bekily
1956
Ambovombé
Tropic of Capricorn
Faradofay
C. Vohimena

1:20 000 000

COPYRIGHT. GEORGE PHILIP & SON. LTD

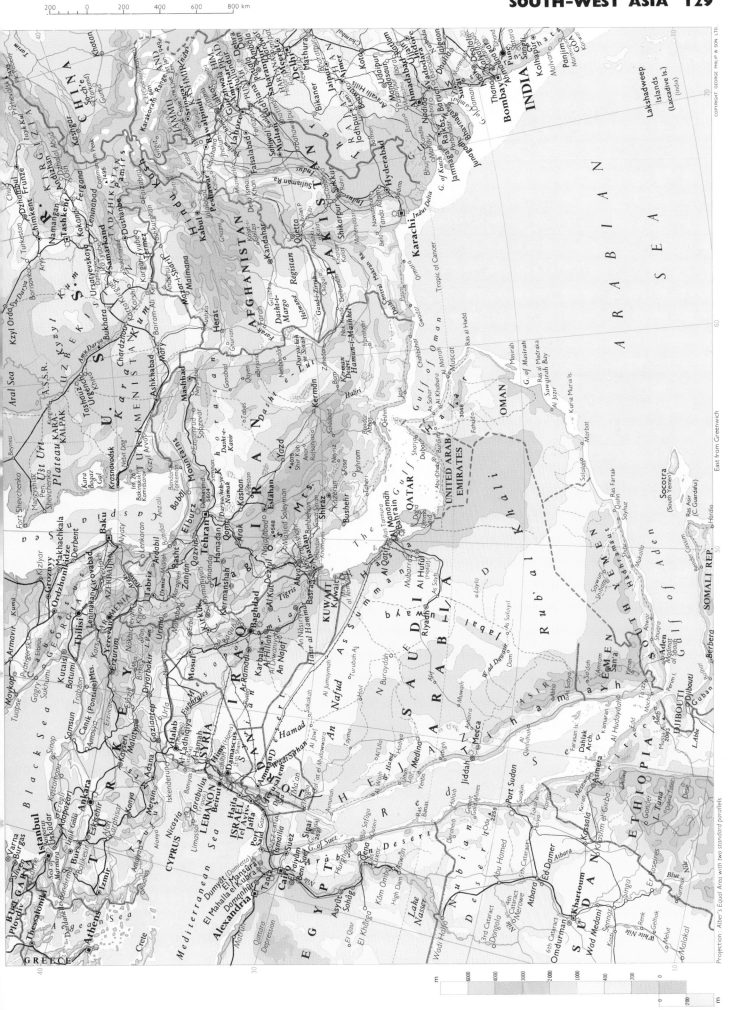

1:20 000 000

200   0   200   400   600   800 km

1:50 000 000

500   0   500   1000   1500   2000 km

ARCTIC OCEAN

PACIFIC OCEAN

Aleutian Is.

C. Dezhnev
Bering Str.

Kamchatka
Peninsula

Sea of
Okhotsk

Bering
Sea

Sredinny Ra.

Kurile Is.

Hokkaido

Bonin Is.

Guam
Caroline Is.
Palau Is.

New
Guinea

Australia

Arafura Sea

Timor
Flores
Bali

Celebes
Ceram
Banda Sea
Halmahera

Moluccas

Mindanao

Philippine
Is.

Luzon

Palawan
Kinabalu
Borneo

Celebes
Sea

Sulu
Sea

East
Java
Sea

Sunda Is.

Java Sea

Sumatra

Str. of Malacca

Malay
Peninsula

G. of
Thailand

Chao Phraya

Irrawaddy

Salween

Mekong

Hong (Red)

Si-kiang

Hainan

Formosa

East
China
Sea

Yellow
Sea

Ryukyu Is.

Shikoku
Kyushu

Korea
Str.

Sea of
Japan

Sikhote Alin Ra.

Sakhalin

Gydan Ra. (Kolyma)

Wrangel I.

New Siberian Is.

Kolyma

Indigirka

Verkhoyansk Range

Lena

Yana

Aldan

Stanovoy Ra.

Amur

Manchurian
Plain

Great Khingan Mts.

Great Plain of China

Hwang
(Yellow)

Plateau of
Mongolia

Koko
Nor

Altai

Sayan Mts.

Yablonovy Ra.

Selenga

Angara

Olenek

Lower Tunguska

Central Siberian Plateau

Yenisei

Ob

Irtysh

West Siberian Plain

Taimyr
Peninsula

Chelyuskin

Severnaya
Zemlya

Kara
Sea

Novaya Zemlya

Laptev Sea

Barents
Sea

Kola
Pen.

White
Sea

N. Dvina

Finland

Baltic Sea

Scandinavia

Svalbard

North Cape

Kolguyev

Greenland

Iceland

Arctic Circle

British Isles

North
Sea

Rhine

Elbe

Oder

Vistula

Danube

Carpathians

Adriatic Sea

Mediterranean Sea

Libyan Desert

Nile

Red Sea

Suez Canal

Cyprus

Anatolia

Taurus Mts.

Bosporus

Black Sea

Caucasus
5633

Dnepr

Don

Volga

Russian
Uplands

Central
Russian
Uplands

North European Plain

Ural Mountains

Ural

Tobol

Irtysh

L. Balkhash

Ili

Chu

Steppes

Caspian Sea

Aral
Sea

Syr Darya

Amu Darya

Turanian Plain

Elburz Mts.
Demavend
5604

Great Salt Desert

Plateau of Iran

The Gulf

G. of Oman

Arabian
Sea

Ar Rub' al Khali

Arabia

G. of Aden

Somali
Peninsula

Socotra

Ras Asir
(C. Guardafui)

Seychelles

Amirantes

INDIAN OCEAN

Equator

Chagos Arch.

Maldive Is.

Laccadive Is.

C. Comorin

Gulf of Monnar
Palk Strait

Ceylon

Eastern Ghats

Western Ghats

Deccan

Godavari
Krishna
Cauvery

Narmada

Yamuna

Ganges

Brahmaputra

Bay of
Bengal

Andaman Is.

Nicobar Is.

India

Thar

Sutlej

Indus

Sulaiman Ra.

Hindu Kush
Karakoram Ra.
7495

Pamir

Communism Pk.
7495

Tien Shan

Tarim Basin

Takla Makan

Lop Nor

Turfan Basin

Kunlun Shan

Plateau of
Tibet

Himalaya
Everest
8882

Tsangpo

China

Tsang

Belukha
4506

Syrian Desert

Mesopotamia

Tigris

Euphrates

Dead Sea

Sinai
Pen.

Arctic Circle

Tropic of Cancer

m   6000 4000 2000 1000 400 200 0

1:50 000 000

500   0   500   1000   1500   2000 km

COPYRIGHT GEORGE PHILIP & SON LTD

Projection: Bonne

P A C I F I C   O C E A N

O C E A N

N

Aleutian Is.

Bering Sea

Wrangel I.

Petropavlovsk

Sea of Okhotsk

Kuril Is.

Sakhalin

Khabarovsk

Komsomolsk

Vladivostok

Nikolayevsk

Sea of Japan

Sapporo
Hokkaido

J A P A N

Honshu

TOKYO
Yokohama
Osaka
Kyoto
Nagoya
Kitakyushu
Kyushu

N. KOREA
Pyongyang
SEOUL
S. KOREA
Pusan

Nagasaki

YELLOW Sea

To Sydney 4316
To San Francisco 4521
To Honolulu 3379
Bonin Is.
Guam (U.S.)

Tropic of Cancer

PHILIPPINES
Luzon
MANILA
Mindoro
Samar
Sulu Sea
Mindanao
Davao
Zamboanga
Sabah
Celebes Sea

New Guinea
Irian Jaya

Caroline Is.
Belau

Halmahera
Moluccas
Celebes
Ceram
Banda Sea

AUSTRALIA
Darwin
Thursday I.
Timor
Flores
Sumba

I N D O N E S I A
Borneo
Kuching
SARAWAK
BRUNEI
Java
Ujung Pandang
Surabaya
Jakarta
Sumatra

MALAYSIA
Kuala Lumpur
SINGAPORE
Str. of Malacca
Penang
PEN. MALAYSIA

South China Sea

SHANGHAI
Nanking
Wuhan
Soochow
Hangchow
Foochow
CANTON
HONG KONG (Br.)
Macau (Port.)
Hainan
Gulf of Tongking

VIETNAM
HANOI
Ho Chi Minh City
PHNOM PENH
CAMBODIA
LAOS
Vientiane

THAILAND
BANGKOK
Gulf of Thailand

BURMA
Mandalay
RANGOON
Irrawaddy
Salween

Gulf of Martaban

C H I N A

PEKING
Tientsin
Tsingtao
Shenyang (Mukden)
Changchun
Harbin
Manchuria
Sian
Lanchow
Chengtu
Chungking
Kunming
Siangtan
Hwang-ho
Yangtze Kiang

MONGOLIA
Ulan Bator
INNER MONGOLIA

CHINESE REPUBLIC
SINKIANG-UIGUR
Urumchi
Yarkand
Kashgar
Kuldja
Tarim

TIBET
Lhasa

NEPAL
KATMANDU

BHUTAN
BANGLADESH
Dacca

I N D I A
CALCUTTA
Lucknow
Kanpur
Varanasi (Benares)
Allahabad
Delhi
Agra
Hyderabad
BOMBAY
MADRAS
Pondicherry
Bangalore
Kozhikode (Calicut)
Goa
Godavari
Narmada
Ahmadabad

Bay of Bengal
Andaman Is. (India)
Nicobar Is. (India)
Calcutta to Singapore 1650

SRI LANKA
COLOMBO
Colombo to Fremantle 3120
MALDIVES
Lakshadweep Is. (India)

KASHMIR
PAKISTAN
ISLAMABAD
Lahore
Karachi
Quetta
Peshawar

AFGHANISTAN
KABUL
Kandahar
Herat

I R A N
TEHRAN
Esfahan
Shiraz
Mashhad
Tabriz
Bushire
Zahidan

OMAN
MUSCAT
Gulf of Oman
Gwadar
Kuria Muria Is.
UNITED ARAB EMIRATES
QATAR
BAHRAIN
The Gulf
KUWAIT

Arabian Sea

SAUDI ARABIA
RIYADH
MECCA
Medina
Aden to Melbourne 6445

YEMEN
SOUTH YEMEN
Socotra (South Yemen)

IRAQ
BAGHDAD
Tigris
Euphrates

SYRIA
DAMASCUS
Aleppo
LEBANON
BEIRUT
JORDAN
AMMAN
ISRAEL
Jerusalem
CYPRUS

TURKEY
ANKARA
Istanbul
Izmir
Erzurum

Black Sea
Batumi
TBILISI
YEREVAN
BAKU
Caspian Sea
Astrakhan

Mediterranean Sea

E G Y P T
CAIRO
Alexandria
Aswan
Nile
LIBYA

SUDAN
KHARTOUM
El Obeid
Port Sudan
Suakin

ETHIOPIA
ADDIS ABABA
Gondar

SOMALI REP
MOGADISHU
Obbia

DJIBOUTI
Red Sea

KENYA
NAIROBI
Mombasa
UGANDA
KAMPALA

TANZANIA
DAR ES SALAAM
RWANDA
BURUNDI
ZAIRE
ZAMBIA
MALAWI

SEYCHELLES
Amirantes
Equator

I N D I A N   O C E A N

U . S . S . R .

Arkhangelsk
Murmansk
White Sea
Barents Sea
Novaya Zemlya
Severnaya Zemlya
Kara Sea
Laptev Sea
New Siberian Is.
Severnaya

A R C T I C   O C E A N
Svalbard
ICELAND
Arctic Circle

MOSCOW
LENINGRAD
Volga
Dnieper
Don
Rostov
Orenburg
Sverdlovsk
Chelyabinsk
Magnitogorsk
Ufa
Ural Mts.
Ob
Tobolsk
Omsk
Novosibirsk
Tomsk
Kemerovo
Barnaul
Semipalatinsk
Krasnoyarsk
Irkutsk
L. Baikal
Chita
Kyakhta
Ulan-Ude
Yakutsk
Lena
Aldan
Lower Tunguska
Angara
Yenisei
Igarka
Irtysh

Alma Ata
Tashkent
Samarkand
Bukhara
Khiva
Krasnovodsk
Ashkhabad
Mary
Aral Sea
L. Balkhash
Syr Darya
Kokand

Baltic Sea
North Sea
E U R O P E
LONDON
PARIS
ROME
BERLIN
WARSAW
VIENNA
BUDAPEST
BELGRADE
Thessaloniki
ATHENS
ISTANBUL
Bucharest
Odessa
Danube
Rhine
Vistula
BRITISH ISLES

East from Greenwich

140   130   120   110   100   90   80   70   60   50   40

1:50 000 000

500   0   500   1000   1500   2000 km

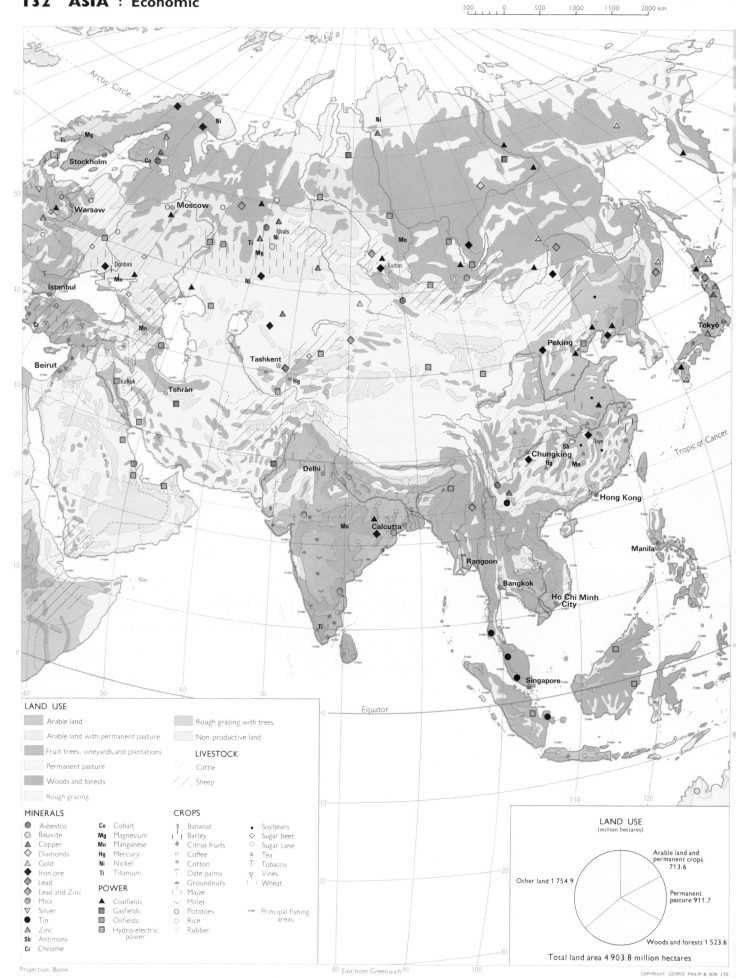

LAND USE

	Arable land		Rough grazing with trees
	Arable land with permanent pasture		Non-productive land
	Fruit trees, vineyards, and plantations		
	Permanent pasture		**LIVESTOCK**
	Woods and forests		Cattle
	Rough grazing		Sheep

MINERALS
- ◐ Asbestos
- ○ Bauxite
- ▲ Copper
- ◇ Diamonds
- △ Gold
- ◆ Iron ore
- ◈ Lead
- ◈ Lead and Zinc
- ● Mica
- ▽ Silver
- ● Tin
- △ Zinc
- **Sb** Antimony
- **Cr** Chrome

- **Co** Cobalt
- **Mg** Magnesium
- **Mn** Manganese
- **Hg** Mercury
- **Ni** Nickel
- **Ti** Titanium

POWER
- ▲ Coalfields
- ■ Gasfields
- ■ Oilfields
- ■ Hydro-electric power

CROPS
-) Bananas
- | Barley
- ♦ Citrus fruits
- ♣ Coffee
- ✳ Cotton
- ↑ Date palms
- ⚘ Groundnuts
- | Maize
- ⌣ Millet
- ○ Potatoes
- ○ Rice
- ▽ Rubber

- • Soybeans
- ◇ Sugar beet
- ◇ Sugar cane
- ▲ Tea
- T Tobacco
- ▽ Vines
- | Wheat

- ⊢ Principal fishing areas

LAND USE
(million hectares)

Other land 1 754.9

Arable land and permanent crops 713.6

Permanent pasture 911.7

Woods and forests 1 523.6

Total land area 4 903.8 million hectares

Projection: Bonne

East from Greenwich

COPYRIGHT GEORGE PHILIP & SON LTD

JANUARY TEMPERATURE
1:120 000 000

-20° -30° -30° -20° -10°
-30°
-10°
0°
10°
20°
Tropic of Cancer
Equator

JULY TEMPERATURE
1:120 000 000

Arctic Circle
10°
20°
Tropic of Cancer
30°
30°
Equator

C.
over 30°
20°– 30°
10°– 20°
0°– 10°
-10°– 0°
-20°–-10°
-30°–-20°
below –30°

20° Isotherms
in degrees Celsius
(reduced to Sea-Level)

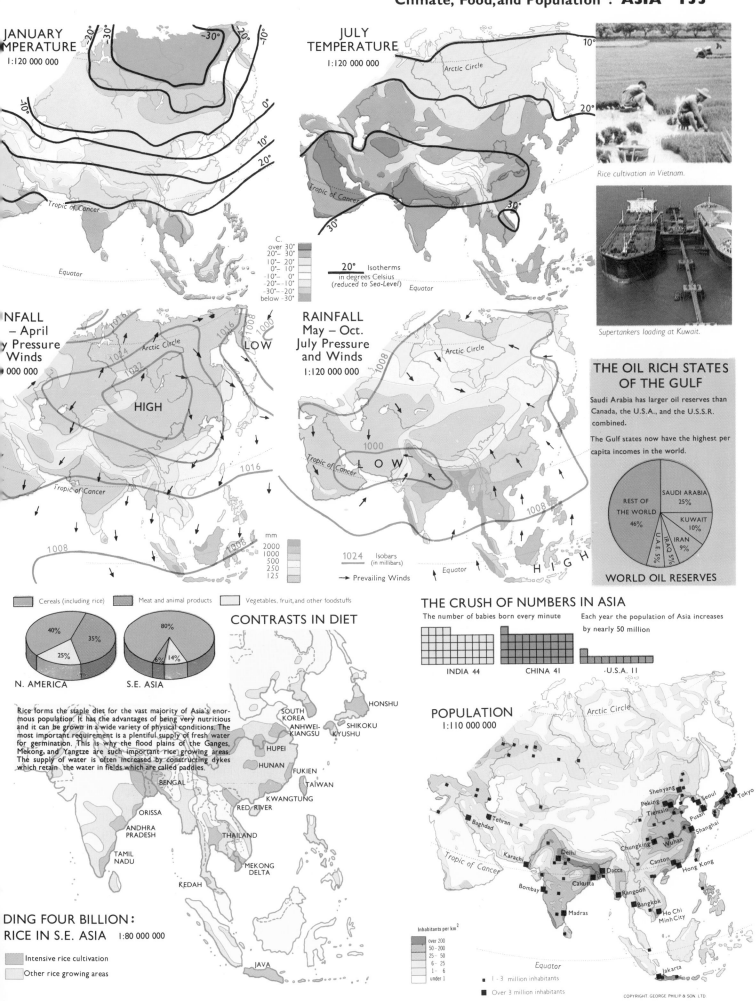

Rice cultivation in Vietnam.

Supertankers loading at Kuwait.

[RAI]NFALL
– April
[Dr]y Pressure
[and] Winds
[1:120] 000 000

Arctic Circle
1016
1024
1032
HIGH
LOW
1000
1016
Tropic of Cancer
1008

mm
2000
1000
500
250
125

RAINFALL
May – Oct.
July Pressure
and Winds
1:120 000 000

Arctic Circle
1008
1000
L O W
Tropic of Cancer
1008
H I G H
Equator

1024 Isobars
(in millibars)

→ Prevailing Winds

THE OIL RICH STATES OF THE GULF

Saudi Arabia has larger oil reserves than Canada, the U.S.A., and the U.S.S.R. combined.

The Gulf states now have the highest per capita incomes in the world.

REST OF THE WORLD 46%
SAUDI ARABIA 25%
KUWAIT 10%
IRAN 9%
IRAQ 5%
U.A.E. 5%

WORLD OIL RESERVES

Cereals (including rice) Meat and animal products Vegetables, fruit, and other foodstuffs

CONTRASTS IN DIET

40% 35% 25%
N. AMERICA

80% 6% 14%
S.E. ASIA

Rice forms the staple diet for the vast majority of Asia's enormous population. It has the advantages of being very nutritious and it can be grown in a wide variety of physical conditions. The most important requirement is a plentiful supply of fresh water for germination. This is why the flood plains of the Ganges, Mekong, and Yangtze are such important rice growing areas. The supply of water is often increased by constructing dykes which retain the water in fields which are called paddies.

SOUTH KOREA
HONSHU
ANHWEI-KIANGSU
SHIKOKU
KYUSHU
HUPEI
HUNAN
FUKIEN
BENGAL
TAIWAN
ORISSA
KWANGTUNG
RED RIVER
ANDHRA PRADESH
THAILAND
TAMIL NADU
MEKONG DELTA
KEDAH
JAVA

[FEE]DING FOUR BILLION: RICE IN S.E. ASIA 1:80 000 000

Intensive rice cultivation
Other rice growing areas

THE CRUSH OF NUMBERS IN ASIA

The number of babies born every minute

Each year the population of Asia increases by nearly 50 million

INDIA 44   CHINA 41   U.S.A. 11

POPULATION
1:110 000 000

Arctic Circle
Tropic of Cancer
Equator

Baghdad
Tehran
Shenyang
Peking
Seoul
Tokyo
Tientsin
Pusan
Karachi
Delhi
Chungking
Wuhan
Shanghai
Bombay
Dacca
Canton
Hong Kong
Calcutta
Rangoon
Madras
Bangkok
Ho Chi Minh City
Jakarta

Inhabitants per km²
over 200
50 – 200
25 – 50
6 – 25
1 – 6
under 1

■ 1 – 3 million inhabitants
■ Over 3 million inhabitants

1:20 000 000

200 0 200 400 600 800 km

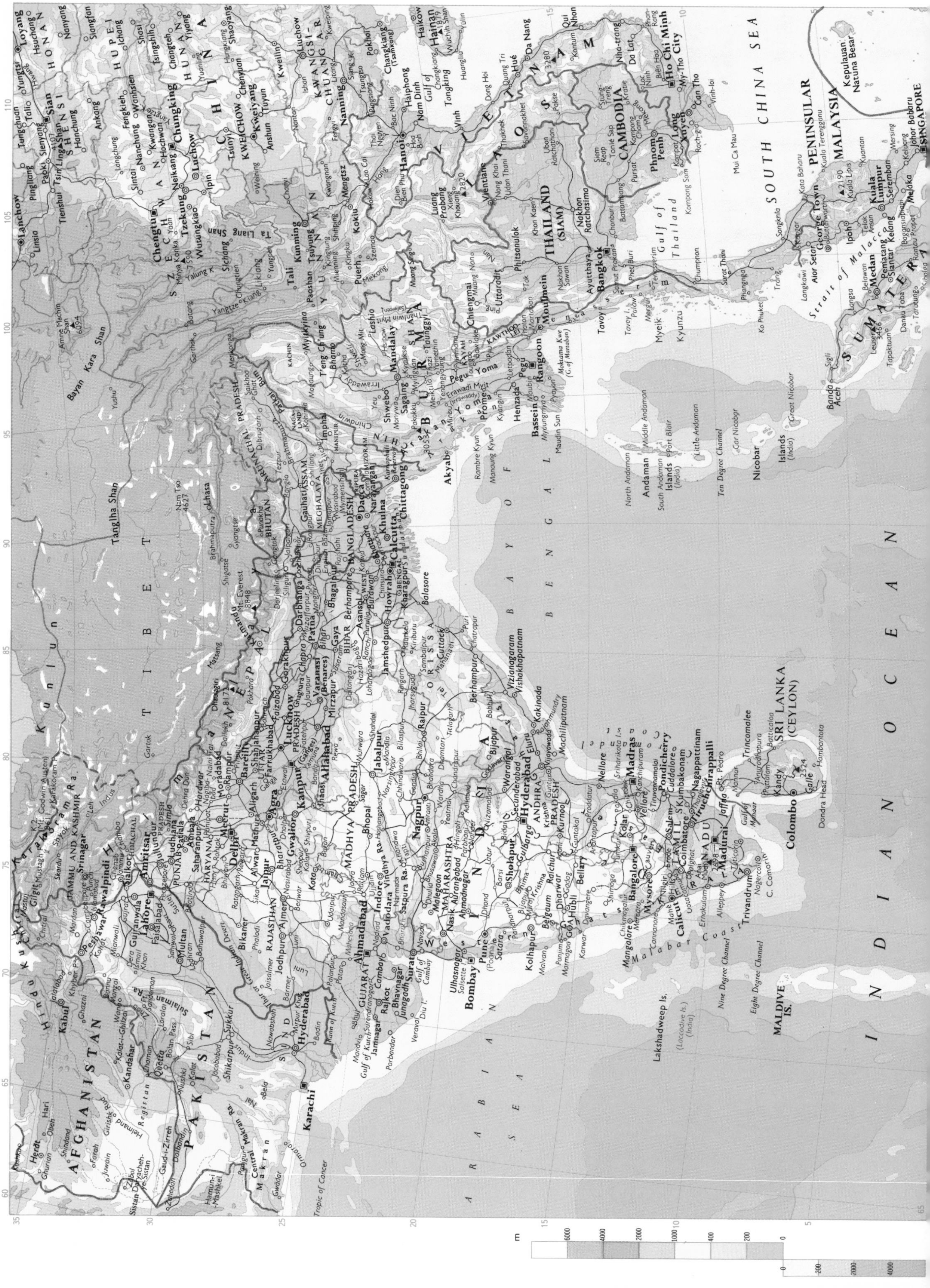

AFGHANISTAN
PAKISTAN
INDIA
TIBET
CHINA
NEPAL
BHUTAN
BANGLADESH
BURMA
THAILAND (SIAM)
LAOS
VIETNAM
CAMBODIA
SRI LANKA (CEYLON)
MALDIVE IS.
PENINSULAR MALAYSIA
SINGAPORE
SUMATERA
ARABIAN SEA
BAY OF BENGAL
INDIAN OCEAN
SOUTH CHINA SEA
Gulf of Thailand
Strait of Malacca
Tropic of Cancer
Andaman Islands (India)
Nicobar Islands (India)
Lakshadweep Is. (Laccadive Is.) (India)
Kabul
Karachi
Delhi
Bombay
Calcutta
Madras
Colombo
Rangoon
Bangkok
Hanoi
Lhasa
Kathmandu
Dacca
Mt. Everest 8848
m
6000
4000
2000
1000
400
200
0
200
2000
4000

1:20 000 000

200 0 200 400 600 800 km

PACIFIC OCEAN

Caroline Islands
(U.S. Trust Territory)

Belau

COPYRIGHT GEORGE PHILIP & SON LTD.

ARAFURA SEA

AUSTRALIA
Darwin
Van Diemen G.
Melville I.
Bathurst I.
Wessel Is.
C. Arnhem
JAYA
IRIAN
Vogelkop
Manokwari
Sorong
Waigeo
Schouten
Japen
Geelvink G.
Wokam
Kobroor
Aru Is.
Trangan
Selaru
Yamdena
Tanimbar Is.
Wetar
Leti
Alor
Pantar
Lomblen
Flores (Lesser Sunda Islands)
TIMOR SEA
Kupang
Ombai
Dili
Timor
Sawu Sea
Sawu
Roti

CERAM SEA
Seram
Ambon
Banda Is.
BANDA SEA
Buru
Namlea
Obi Is.
Mangole
Taliabu
Peleng
Bangai Arch.
Sula Is.

MOLUCCA SEA
Moluccas
Halmahera
Gebe
Ternate
Morotai
Manado
Gorontalo
G. of Tomini
SULAWESI (CELEBES)
Rantepao
Pare Pare
Str. of Makasar
Ujung Pandang (Makasar)
Selayar
Butung
Muna
Kendari
FLORES SEA
Flores
Sumbawa
Lombok
Bali
Sumba (Sandalwood)
Waingapu
Kangean Is.

CELEBES SEA
Talaud
Gt. Sangi
Sangi Arch.
C. S. Agustin
Davao Gulf
Davao
2965
Mindanao
Tinaca Point
Sarangani B.
Cotabato
Moro Gulf
Zamboanga
Basilan
Jolo
Sulu Arch.
SULU SEA
Sandakan
Tawau
Darvel B.
Sibuko B.
Tarakan
Kajan
Mahakam
Balikpapan
KALIMANTAN
BORNEO
Muller Ra.
Schwaner Ra.
Barito
Banjarmasin
Laut Laut
Little Laut Is.
Bawean

PHILIPPINE SEA

LUZON
Aparri
Looog
Baguio
2928
Dogupan
Quezon City
MANILA
Batangas
Manila B.
Mindoro
Lubang Is.
Polillo Is.
Lamon B.
Calamian Group
Mindoro Str.
Tablas
Sibuyan Str.
Panay
Iloilo
Masbate
Cebu
Bacolod
Negros
Bohol
Ozamiz
Cagayan
Bohol
Butuan
Surigao Str.
Surigao
Leyte
Tacloban
Samar
Catanduanes
Legaspi
Sorsogon
Naga

PHILIPPINES

Batan Is.
Bashi Channel
Babuyan Is.
Babuyan Chan.
TAIWAN (FORMOSA)
Bashi Channel

HONG KONG (Br.)
Kowloon
Victoria
Macau (Port.)
CHINA
Changkiang
Pakhoi
Pingsiang
Kiungchow Str.
Halkow
Hainan

SOUTH CHINA SEA
Paracel Is.
Spratly
Amboyna
Con Son Is.
N. Natuna Is.
S. Natuna Is.
Anambas Is.
Natuna Is.
N. Bunguran Is.

VIETNAM
Hanoi
Haiphong
G. of Tongking
Thanh Hoa
Vinh
Ha Tinh
Quang Tri
Hué (Tourane)
Da-Nang
An Nhon
Qui Nhon
Nha Trang
Phan Rang
Phan Thiet
HO CHI MINH CITY (SAIGON)
Go Cong
Can-Tho
Point Bai Bung

LAOS
Louang Prabang
Vientiane
Pakse
2257
Phu Loi

CAMBODIA
PHNOM PENH
Battambang
Kompong Som
Kompong Cham
Kratié
Kg. Cham
Long-Xuyen
Tonle Sap
Phanom Dang Raek

THAILAND (SIAM)
BANGKOK
Ayutthaya
Nakhon Ratchasima (Khorat)
Nakhon Sawan
Chanthaburi
Ubon
Udon Thani
Tak (Raheng)
Phitsanulok
Chiangmai
Uttaradit
Mekong
Gulf of Thailand
Isthmus of Kra
Champon
2180
Chumphon
Nakhon Si Thammarat
Songkhla (Singora)
Trang
Phuket
Kota Bharu
Kuala Terengganu
Kuala Trengganu

BURMA
RANGOON
Bassein
Prome
Yamethin
Taungoo
Toungoo
Moulmein
Amherst
Tavoy
Mergui
Mergui Arch.
Martaban
G. of Martaban
Mouths of Irrawaddy
Ramree I.
Cheduba I.

ANDAMAN SEA
Middle Andaman
Andaman Islands (India)
Pt. Blair
Little Andaman
Ten Degree Channel
Nicobar Islands (India)
Car Nicobar
Great Nicobar

MALAYSIA
Kuala Lumpur
George Town
Penang
Butterworth
Taiping
Ipoh
PEN. MALAYSIA
Telok Anson
Port Kelang (Port Swettenham)
Kelang
Malacca
Muar
Johor Baharu
SINGAPORE
Pulau Tioman
Berhala Str.
Pulau Bintan
Riau Arch.
Lingga Arch.
Bangka
Beliton
Pangkalpinang
Manggar
Karimata
Karimata Str.
Pontianak
Kapuas
Kuching
Sibu
Kapit
SARAWAK
BRUNEI
Kota Kinabalu (Jesselton)
Labuan
Victoria
SABAH
Kinabalu
Miri
Trab Besar Tama Abu Ra.

SUMATRA
Banda Aceh (Kutaraja)
Medan
Tebingtinggi
Pematangsiantar
Sibolga
Tapanuli
Nias
Batu Is.
Siberut
Mentawai Is.
Pagai
Sipora
Padang
Bukit Tinggi
3805
Kerinci
Sawahlunto
Pakanbaru
Jambi
Bogan Siapiapi
Rupat
Tanjungbalai
Bengkulu
Teluk Betung
Palembang
Musi
Bangka Str.
Sunda Str.

SOUTH CHINA SEA

INDONESIA
JAKARTA
Bogor
BANDUNG
3428
Cirebon
Tegal
Pekalongan
Semarang
Cilacap
Yogyakarta
Surakarta
Magelang
Madiun
Kediri
SURABAYA
Madura
Malang
Blitar
3726
Denpasar
JAVA
Greater Sunda Islands
Nusa Tenggara (Lesser Sunda Islands)

INDIAN OCEAN

Christmas I. (Austral.)
Cocos or Keeling Is. (Austral.)
Enggano

Equator

East from Greenwich

Projection: Bonne

m
4 000
2 000
1 000
400
200
0
m

1:20 000 000

200   0   200   400   600   800 km

UNION OF SOVIET SOCIALIST REPUBLICS

U.S.S.R.

MONGOLIA

INNER MONGOLIA

SINKIANG UIGUR (Autonomous Region)

Dzungaria

Takla Makan

Tarim

Kunlun Shan

Altyn Tagh

Nan Shan

TSINGHAI

TIBET (Autonomous Region)

Tangla Shan

NEPAL

BHUTAN

BANGLADESH

INDIA

BURMA

THAILAND (SIAM)

LAOS

VIETNAM

ASSAM

KASHMIR

JAMMU & KASHMIR

KAZAKH S.S.R.

KIRGIZ S.S.R.

SZECHWAN

YUNNAN

KWEICHOW

KWANGSI

KWANGTUNG

HUNAN

KIANGSI

FUKIEN

CHEKIANG

KIANGSU

ANHWEI

HUPEI

HONAN

SHANSI

SHENSI

KANSU

HOPEI

SHANTUNG

NORTH KOREA

SOUTH KOREA

JAPAN

TAIWAN (Formosa)

PHILIPPINES

RYUKYU

EAST CHINA SEA

SOUTH CHINA SEA

YELLOW SEA

BAY OF BENGAL

Khabarovsk
Blagoveshchensk
Vladivostok
HARBIN
Tsitsihar
Hailar
Ulanhot
Ulaanbaatar (Ulan Bator)
Huhehot
Paotow
Tatung
PEKING
TIENTSIN
TSINGTAO
TSINAN
TAIYUAN
SIAN
Lanchow
Sining
LHASA
Kathmandu
Dacca
CALCUTTA
Patna
Varanasi
Lucknow
Allahabad
Kanpur
Dehra Dun
Bareilly
Mandalay
Rangoon
HANOI
Haiphong
VIENTIANE
Kunming
CHUNGKING
CHENGTU
Kweiyang
Kweilin
NANNING
Canton
HONG KONG
Macau
Kowloon
Victoria
Swatow
Amoy
Foochow
Wenchow
NANCHANG
Changsha
Hengyang
WUHAN
Hankow
Ichang
NANKING
SHANGHAI
Hangchow
Ningpo
Soochow
Wusih
Chinkiang
Hwainan
Pengpu
Hsuchow
Kaifeng
Chengchow
Loyang
Sian
PYONGYANG
SEOUL
Inchon
Pusan
Taegu
Taejon
Kwangju
Mokpo
Fukuoka
Nagasaki
Sasebo
Taipei
Chilung (Keelung)
Kaohsiung
Tainan
Taichung

m 6000 4000 3000 2000 1500 1000 400 200 0 200 2000 4000 6000

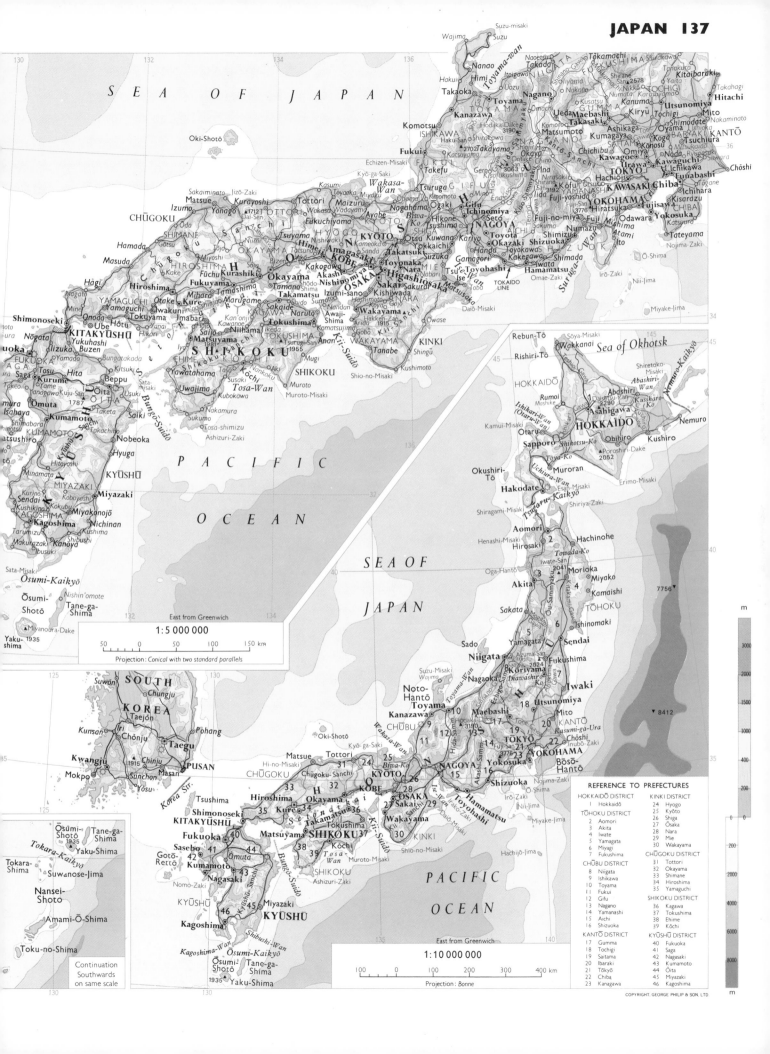

1 : 35 000 000

200 0 200 400 600 800 1000 1200 1400 km

1:40 000 000

400   0   400   800   1200   1600 km

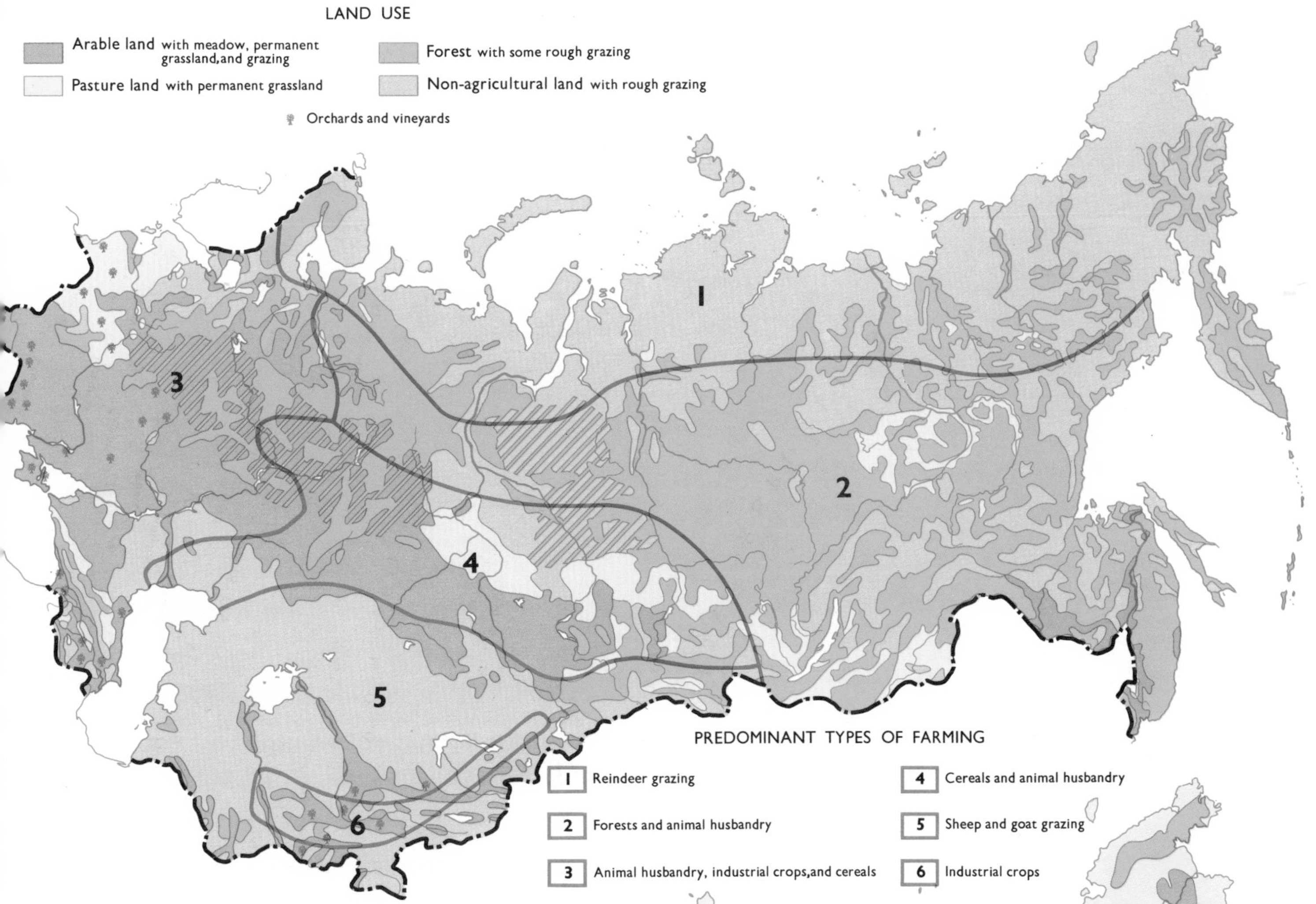

LAND USE

Arable land with meadow, permanent grassland, and grazing

Pasture land with permanent grassland

Forest with some rough grazing

Non-agricultural land with rough grazing

Orchards and vineyards

1

2

3

4

5

6

PREDOMINANT TYPES OF FARMING

1 Reindeer grazing

2 Forests and animal husbandry

3 Animal husbandry, industrial crops, and cereals

4 Cereals and animal husbandry

5 Sheep and goat grazing

6 Industrial crops

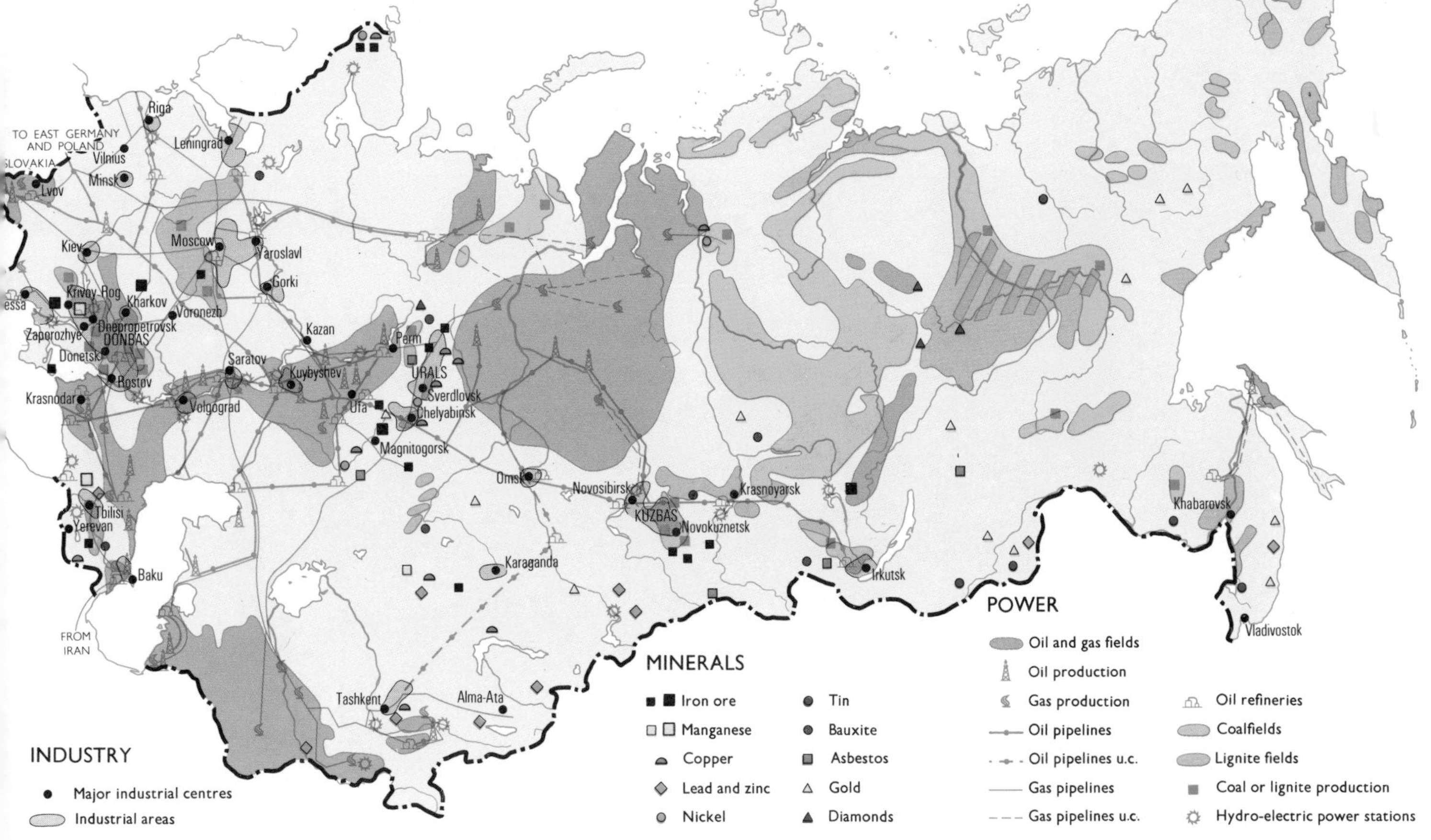

Riga
TO EAST GERMANY AND POLAND
SLOVAKIA
Leningrad
Vilnius
Lvov
Minsk
Kiev
Moscow
Yaroslavl
Gorki
essa
Krivoy Rog
Kharkov
Voronezh
Zaporozhye
Dnepropetrovsk
Kazan
Perm
DONBAS
Saratov
URALS
Donetsk
Kuybyshev
Sverdlovsk
Krasnodar
Rostov
Ufa
Chelyabinsk
Volgograd
Magnitogorsk
Omsk
Novosibirsk
Krasnoyarsk
Tbilisi
KUZBAS
Yerevan
Novokuznetsk
Irkutsk
Baku
Khabarovsk
FROM IRAN
Karaganda
Vladivostok
Tashkent
Alma-Ata

INDUSTRY

● Major industrial centres

Industrial areas

MINERALS

■■ Iron ore

□ □ Manganese

◠ Copper

◆ Lead and zinc

● Nickel

● Tin

● Bauxite

■ Asbestos

△ Gold

▲ Diamonds

POWER

Oil and gas fields

Oil production

Gas production

Oil pipelines

Oil pipelines u.c.

Gas pipelines

Gas pipelines u.c.

Oil refineries

Coalfields

Lignite fields

■ Coal or lignite production

Hydro-electric power stations

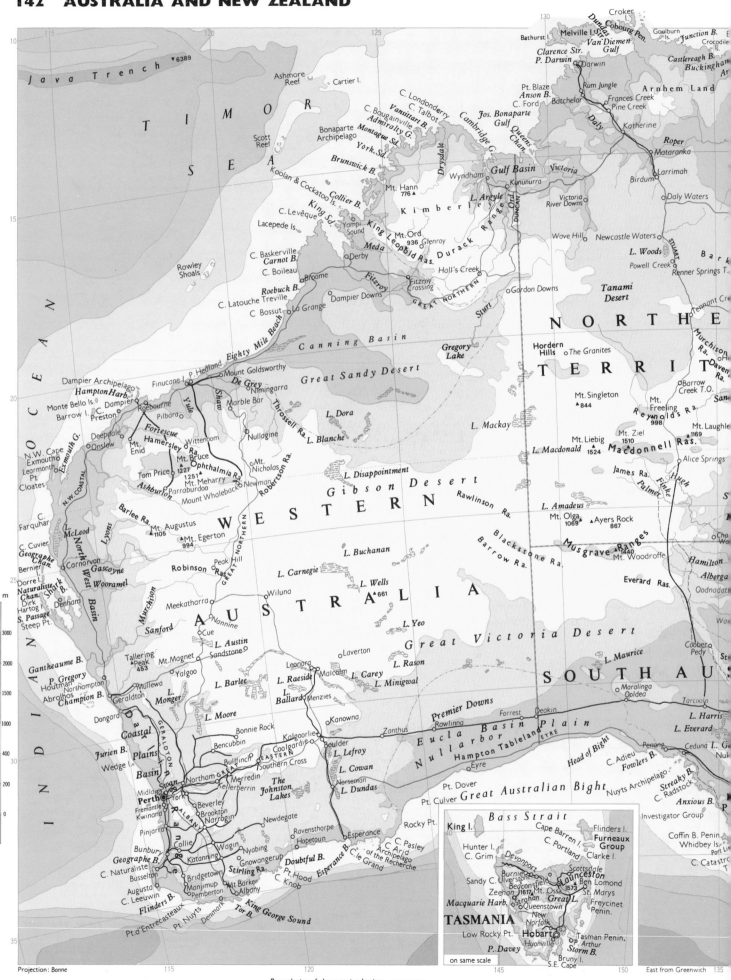

Java Trench ▼6389

T I M O R   S E A

Ashmore Reef   Cartier I.

C. Londonderry
C. Talbot
Vansittart B.
C. Bougainville
Admiralty G.
Montague Sd.
York Sd.
Brunswick B.

Scott Reef

Bonaparte Archipelago
Koolan & Cockatoo Is.
Collier B.
King Sd.
C. Lévêque
Lacepede Is.

Mt. Hann 776 ▲

C. Baskerville
Carnot B.
C. Boileau

Yampi Sound
Mt. Ord 936 ▲
Meda
Derby
Glenroy

Roebuck B.
Broome
Fitzroy
Fitzroy Crossing
Hall's Creek

C. Latouche Treville
C. Bossut   La Grange
Dampier Downs

Gordon Downs

Eighty Mile Beach

C A N N I N G   B A S I N

Gregory Lake

Rowley Shoals

Dampier Archipelago
Hampton Harb.
Monte Bello Is.
Barrow I.
Dampier
Preston
Roebourne

Finucane I.
P. Hedland
Mount Goldsworthy
De Grey
Nimingarra
Shaw
Marble Bar

Great Sandy Desert

Hordern Hills
The Granites

N O R T H E
T E R R I T

Pilbara
Fortescue Ra.
Hamersley Ra.
Mt. Enid
Mt. Bruce 1227
Ophthalmia Ra.

N.W. Cape
Exmouth G.
Exmouth
Learmonth
Pt. Cloates

Deepdale
Onslow

Tom Price
Mt. Meharry 1251
Parraburdoo
Ashburton
Mount Whaleback
Newman

Nullagine
Mt. Nicholas
Robertson Ra.

Throssell Ra.
L. Blanche
L. Dora

L. Disappointment

G i b s o n   D e s e r t

Rawlinson Ra.

L. Mackay
L. Macdonald
L. Amadeus

Mt. Singleton 844
Reynolds Ra.
Mt. Freeling 998
Mt. Liebig 1524
Mt. Ziel 1510
Macdonnell Ras.
Mt. Laughle 1169
Alice Springs
James Ra.
Hugh
Palmer
Flinke

W E S T E R N

Barlee Ra.
Mt. Augustus 1105
Mt. Egerton 994

C. Farquhar
C. Cuvier
Geographe Chan.
Bernier
Dorre I.
Naturaliste Chan.
Dirk Hartog
S. Passage
Steep Pt.
Denham

L. McLeod
Carnarvon
Gascoyne
Wooramel
North West Basin
Lyons
Murchison

Peak Hill
Robinson Ras.

Mt. Olga 1069
Mt. Woodroffe 1440
Ayers Rock 867
Musgrave Ranges
Everard Ras.

Blackstone Ra.
Barrow Ra.

A U S T R A L I A

L. Buchanan
L. Carnegie
L. Wells 661
L. Yeo

Meekatharra
Wiluna

L. Maurice

S O U T H   A U S

Gantheaume B.
P. Gregory
Houtman Abrolhos
Northampton
Champion B.
Geraldton
Dongara

Sanford
Nannine
Cue

Tallering Peak 453
Mt. Magnet
Yalgoo

Mullewa
L. Austin
Sandstone
L. Barlee
L. Moore
L. Monger

G r e a t   V i c t o r i a   D e s e r t

Leonora
Laverton
L. Rason

Malcolm
L. Carey
L. Minigwal
L. Raeside
L. Ballard
Menzies
Kanowna

Coober Pedy

Maralinga
Ooldea
Tarcoola

Premier Downs
Rawlinna
Forrest
Deakin

L. Harris
L. Everard

Bonnie Rock
Bencubbin
Kalgoorlie
Boulder
Coolgardie
L. Lefroy
L. Cowan
L. Dundas

Zanthus

E u c l a   B a s i n
N u l l a r b o r   P l a i n
Hampton Tableland

Eyre
Eyre

Penong
Ceduna
Nuyts Archipelago

Coastal
Plains
Basin

Jurien B.
Wedge I.

L. Moore
Bullfinch
Southern Cross
Merredin
Kellerberrin
The Johnston Lakes
Norseman

Great Australian Bight

Pt. Dover
Pt. Culver

Head of Bight
C. Adieu
Fowlers B.
C. Radstock
Streaky B.
Anxious B.

Midland
Swan
Perth
Fremantle
Kwinana
York
Northam
Beverley
Brookton
Narrogin

Newdegate
Ravensthorpe
Hopetoun

Rocky Pt.

Pinjarra
Bunbury
Geographe B.
Busselton
C. Naturaliste
Augusta
C. Leeuwin
Flinders B.

Collie
Katanning
Bridgetown
Manjimup
Pemberton

Wagin
Nyabing
Gnowangerup
Stirling Ra.
Mt. Barker
Albany
Denmark
Tor B.

Doubtful B.
Pt. Hood

Esperance
C. Pasley
C. Arid
Archipelago of the Recherche
C. le Grand
C. Knob
Esperance B.

King George Sound
Pt. Nuyts
Pt. d'Entrecasteaux

N O R T H E R N   T E R R I T O R Y

Wyndham
Kununurra
L. Argyle
Ord
Kimberley
King Leopold Ras.
Durack Range

Gulf Basin
Victoria
River Downs
Victoria
Wave Hill
Newcastle Waters
L. Woods
Powell Creek
Renner Springs
Tanami Desert
Tennant Cre
Barrow Creek T.O.
Daven Ra.
Barkly

Jos. Bonaparte Gulf
Cambridge G.
Drysdale
Queens Chan.

P. Darwin
Darwin
Pt. Blaze
Batchelor
Anson B.
Batchelor
Rum Jungle
Frances Creek
Pine Creek
Katherine
Daly
Roper
Mataranka
Larrimah
Birdum
Daly Waters

Clarence Str.
Bathurst
Melville I.
Van Diemen Gulf
Dundas
Cobourg Pen.
Croker
Goulburn Is.
Junction B.
Crocodile
Castlereagh B.
Buckingham

Arnhem Land

Gordon Downs

STUART

I N D I A N   O C E A N

m
3000
2000
1500
1000
400
200
0
0
200
2000
4000
6000
m

Projection: Bonne

115   120   125

Boundaries of the artesian basins — — —

East from Greenwich   130   135

B a s s   S t r a i t

King I.
Hunter I.
C. Grim
Low Rocky Pt.
P. Davey

Cape Barren I.
C. Portland
Devonport
Burnie
Ulverstone
Sandy C.
Zeehan
Macquarie Harb.
Queenstown

Flinders I.
Furneaux Group
Clarke I.

Scottsdale
Beaconsfield
Launceston
Ben Lomond
St. Marys
Freycinet Penin.
Great L.
Mt. Ossa 1617
Strahan
New Norfolk
Huonville
Hobart
Bruny I.
S.E. Cape

Mt. Olympus 1573

Coffin B. Penin.
Whidbey Is.
Investigator Group
Port

Tasman Penin.
Pt. Arthur
Storm B.

T A S M A N I A

on same scale   145   150

PAPUA NEW GUINEA
1:16 000 000
100 50 0   100   200 km

Admiralty Islands
Mussau I.
Lorengau
Manus I.
New
Hanover
Kavieng
Tabar Is.
Bismarck Archipelago
New
Ireland
Lihir
Group
Nuguria
Is.
Schouten Is.
Wewak
Manam I.
Karkar I.
Madang
Long I.
Umboi I.
Vitu Is.
St. George's Channel
Rabaul
Tanga Is.
Feni Is.
Green I.
Kilinailau Is.
Buka I.
Sepik
Ramu
Mt. Wilhelm
4508
Goroka
Vitiaz Strait
Dampier Strait
Kimbe
Bay
Nakanai Mts.
Bougainville I. Balbi
2743
Shortland I.
Mt. Capella
3993
Central Range
New
Mount
Hagen
Mt. Bangeta
4121
Lae
Huon
Gulf
Bulolo
New Britain
Solomon Sea
Great
Papuan
Plateau
Chambri
Lake
Guinea
Kikori
Strickland
Lake
Murray
Fly
Baimuru
Gulf of
Papua
Daru
Kiwai I.
Saibai I.
Torres Strait
Cape York
Mt. Victoria
4035
Owen Stanley Range
Port
Moresby
Popondetta
Goodenough I.
Fergusson I.
Normanby I.
D'Entrecasteaux
Islands
Trobriand Is.
Woodlark I.
Misima I.
Basilaki I.
Louisiade
Archipelago
Rossel I.
Tagula I.
Coral Sea

NEW ZEALAND
1:25 000 000
100 0   100 200 300km

C. Maria van Diemen
North C.
Whangarei
Kaipara
Harb.
Hauraki Gulf
Gt. Barrier I.
Auckland
Hamilton
Thames
Bay of Plenty
Rotorua
East C.
Tasman Sea
NORTH ISLAND
New Plymouth
Mt. Egmont
2518
L. Taupo
Ruapehu
2796
Mahia Pen.
Gisborne
Hawke B.
Napier
Hastings
Wanganui
Palmerston N.
C. Farewell
Nelson
Blenheim
Wellington
Greymouth
Hokitika
Cook Strait
C. Palliser
SOUTH ISLAND
Mt. Cook 3764
Canterbury
Plains
Bank's Pen.
Christchurch
PACIFIC
OCEAN
Doubtful
Sd.
Timaru
Waitaki
Oamaru
West C.
Te Anau
Dunedin
Foveaux Strait
Invercargill
Stewart I.
South West C.

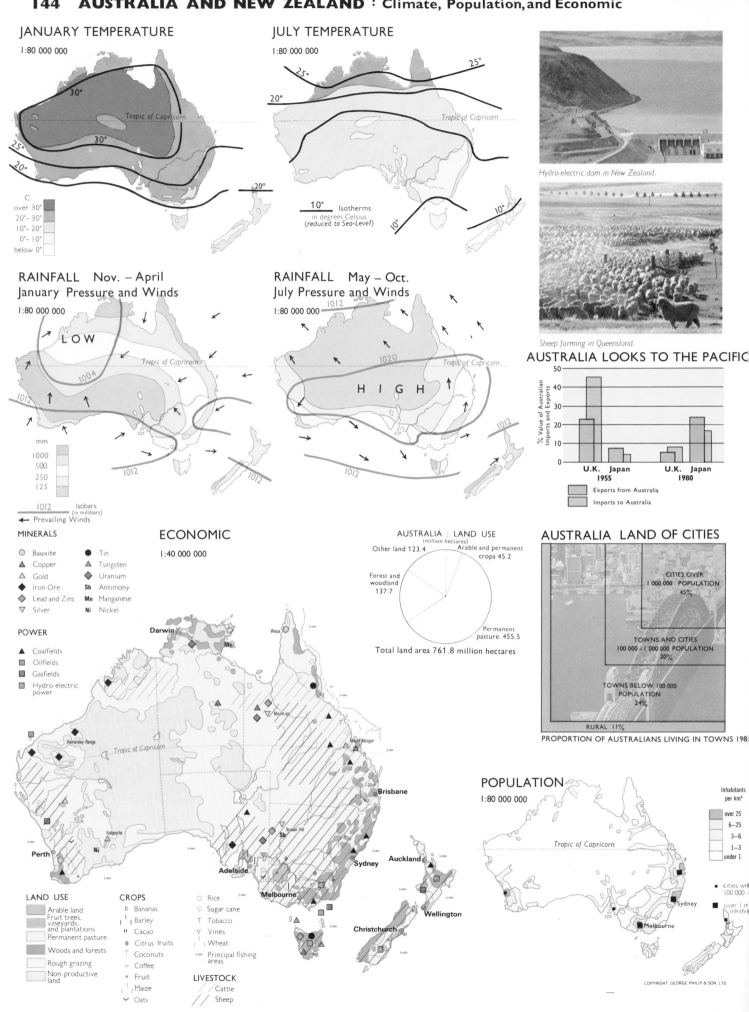

JANUARY TEMPERATURE
1:80 000 000

30°
Tropic of Capricorn
30°
25°
20°

C.
over 30°
20°–30°
10°–20°
0°–10°
below 0°

JULY TEMPERATURE
1:80 000 000

25°
20°
Tropic of Capricorn
20°
10°
10°

10° Isotherms
in degrees Celsius
(reduced to Sea-Level)

Hydro-electric dam in New Zealand.

Sheep farming in Queensland.

RAINFALL Nov. – April
January Pressure and Winds
1:80 000 000

LOW
1004
Tropic of Capricorn
1012
1012
1012

mm
1000
500
250
125

1012 Isobars
(in millibars)
← Prevailing Winds

RAINFALL May – Oct.
July Pressure and Winds
1:80 000 000

1012
1020
Tropic of Capricorn
HIGH
1012
1012
1012

AUSTRALIA LOOKS TO THE PACIFIC

% Value of Australian Imports and Exports

50
40
30
20
10
0

U.K. 1955   Japan   U.K. 1980   Japan

Exports from Australia
Imports to Australia

MINERALS
- ◎ Bauxite
- △ Copper
- △ Gold
- ◆ Iron Ore
- ◇ Lead and Zinc
- ▽ Silver
- ● Tin
- △ Tungsten
- ◇ Uranium
- **Sb** Antimony
- **Mn** Manganese
- **Ni** Nickel

POWER
- ▲ Coalfields
- ▪ Oilfields
- ▪ Gasfields
- ▪ Hydro-electric power

ECONOMIC
1:40 000 000

Darwin
Weipa
Mn
Hamersley Range
Mount Isa
Mount Morgan
Tropic of Capricorn
Kalgoorlie
Ni
Perth
Broken Hill
Sb
Brisbane
Adelaide
Sydney
Melbourne
Auckland
Wellington
Christchurch

AUSTRALIA : LAND USE
(million hectares)

Other land 123.4
Arable and permanent crops 45.2
Forest and woodland 137.7
Permanent pasture 455.5

Total land area 761.8 million hectares

AUSTRALIA LAND OF CITIES

CITIES OVER 1 000 000 POPULATION 45%

TOWNS AND CITIES 100 000 - 1 000 000 POPULATION 20%

TOWNS BELOW 100 000 POPULATION 24%

RURAL 11%

PROPORTION OF AUSTRALIANS LIVING IN TOWNS 198

LAND USE
- Arable land
- Fruit trees, vineyards, and plantations
- Permanent pasture
- Woods and forests
- Rough grazing
- Non-productive land

CROPS
- ⅅ Bananas
- | Barley
- ๐ Cacao
- ◆ Citrus fruits
- ⌘ Coconuts
- ๐ Coffee
- · Fruit
- ı Maize
- ⌄ Oats
- ○ Rice
- ◇ Sugar cane
- T Tobacco
- ▽ Vines
- ⊢ Wheat
- ⊢ Principal fishing areas

LIVESTOCK
- ⁄⁄ Cattle
- ⁄⁄ Sheep

POPULATION
1:80 000 000

Tropic of Capricorn
Sydney
Melbourne

Inhabitants per km²
over 25
6–25
3–6
1–3
under 1

▪ cities wi 500 000
■ over 1 m inhabit

COPYRIGHT. GEORGE PHILIP & SON LTD

AIR DISTANCES IN CANADA
(in kilometres)

	Calgary	Edmonton	Halifax	Montréal	Ottawa	Québec	Regina	Saint John	St. John's	Sudbury	Thunder Bay	Toronto	Vancouver	Whitehorse	Windsor	Winnipeg
Edmonton	246															
Halifax	3742	3679														
Montréal	3003	2967	804													
Ottawa	2877	2848	953	151												
Québec	3102	3047	646	234	368											
Regina	661	690	3099	2348	2219	2456										
Saint John	3556	3497	192	614	764	456	2911									
St. John's	4321	4216	880	1613	1766	1407	3718	1036								
Sudbury	2456	2433	1351	484	423	716	1798	1159	2112							
Thunder Bay	1791	1779	1997	1222	1090	1351	1131	1806	2695	667						
Toronto	2687	2687	1287	506	363	731	2026	1103	2122	340	909					
Vancouver	687	809	4426	3679	3550	3784	1332	4239	5005	3128	2461	3343				
Whitehorse	1677	1527	4836	4239	4147	4260	2196	4674	5167	3765	3169	4064	1484			
Windsor	2539	2567	1589	819	676	1044	1886	1407	2433	515	839	313	3173	4001		
Winnipeg	1191	1187	2574	1816	1688	1929	532	2385	3220	1266	600	1502	1863	2627	1386	
Yellowknife	1262	1018	3742	3178	3098	3182	1462	3585	4067	2738	2201	3057	1571	1103	3040	1742

	Bahrain	Buenos Aires	Cairo	Cape Town	Caracas	Delhi	Hong Kong	Honolulu	Lagos	London	Los Angeles	Mexico	Miami	Moscow	Nairobi	New York	Peking	Perth	Rio de Janeiro	Singapore	Sydney	Tokyo	Wellington
Toronto	10725	9093	9233	13129	3873	11631	12569	7465	8948	5704	3492	3247	1988	7462	12183	574	10552	18115	8336	15047	15772	10316	14194
Vancouver	11595	11298	10835	16454	6692	11131	10339	4349	11938	7575	1738	3942	4500	8180	14356	3928	8486	14804	11207	12811	12492	7555	11738

AIR DISTANCES FROM
VANCOUVER AND TORONTO
(in kilometres)

Projection centered on Vancouver
5000 km Distance from Vancouver

All distances are great circle routes
(the shortest possible route between two places).

Projection centered on Toronto
5000 km Distance from Toronto

These two pages give temperature and precipitation statistics for Canadian stations. They are arranged by province and alphabetically. The elevation of each station, in metres above sea-level, is stated beneath each name. The average monthly precipitation, in millimetres, and the average monthly temperatures, in degrees Celsius, are given. To the extreme right, the average yearly precipitation, the average yearly temperature and the annual range of temperature (the difference between the warmest and coldest months) are also stated. Additionally the amount of the total precipitation falling as rain is given (in italics) and the number of days in which snow fell (snowfall exceeding 2 mm in depth).

T = Trace

Owing to rounding of monthly figures, they may not add up to give yearly or average figures.

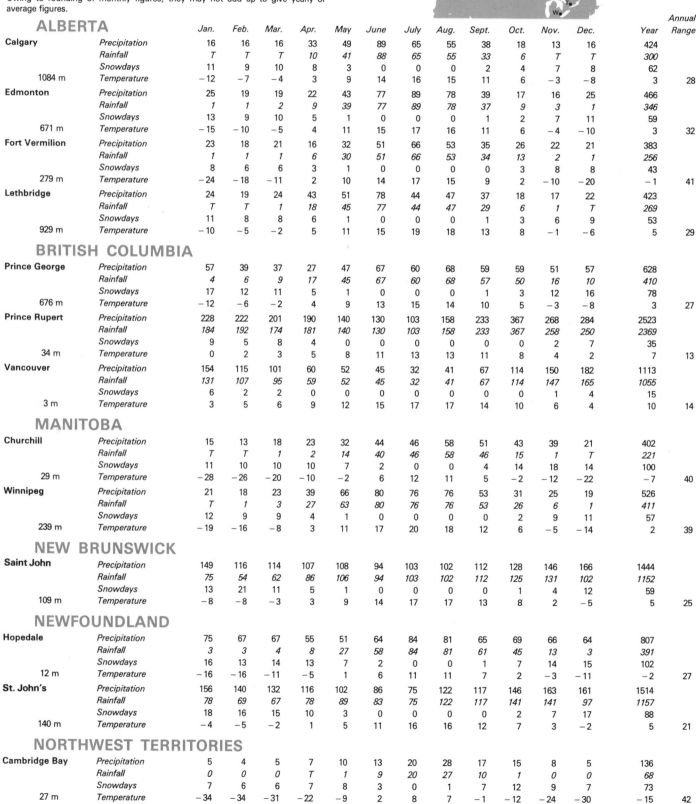

ALBERTA		Jan.	Feb.	Mar.	Apr.	May	June	July	Aug.	Sept.	Oct.	Nov.	Dec.	Year	Annual Range
Calgary	Precipitation	16	16	16	33	49	89	65	55	38	18	13	16	424	
	Rainfall	*T*	*T*	*T*	*10*	*41*	*88*	*65*	*55*	*33*	*6*	*T*	*T*	*300*	
	Snowdays	11	9	10	8	3	0	0	0	2	4	7	8	62	
1084 m	Temperature	−12	−7	−4	3	9	14	16	15	11	6	−3	−8	3	28
Edmonton	Precipitation	25	19	19	22	43	77	89	78	39	17	16	25	466	
	Rainfall	*1*	*1*	*2*	*9*	*39*	*77*	*89*	*78*	*37*	*9*	*3*	*1*	*346*	
	Snowdays	13	9	10	5	1	0	0	0	1	2	7	11	59	
671 m	Temperature	−15	−10	−5	4	11	15	17	16	11	6	−4	−10	3	32
Fort Vermilion	Precipitation	23	18	21	16	32	51	66	53	35	26	22	21	383	
	Rainfall	*1*	*1*	*1*	*6*	*30*	*51*	*66*	*53*	*34*	*13*	*2*	*1*	*256*	
	Snowdays	8	6	6	3	1	0	0	0	0	3	8	8	43	
279 m	Temperature	−24	−18	−11	2	10	14	17	15	9	2	−10	−20	−1	41
Lethbridge	Precipitation	24	19	24	43	51	78	44	47	37	18	17	22	423	
	Rainfall	*T*	*T*	*1*	*18*	*45*	*77*	*44*	*47*	*29*	*6*	*1*	*T*	*269*	
	Snowdays	11	8	8	6	1	0	0	0	1	3	6	9	53	
929 m	Temperature	−10	−5	−2	5	11	15	19	18	13	8	−1	−6	5	29

BRITISH COLUMBIA

		Jan.	Feb.	Mar.	Apr.	May	June	July	Aug.	Sept.	Oct.	Nov.	Dec.	Year	Annual Range
Prince George	Precipitation	57	39	37	27	47	67	60	68	59	59	51	57	628	
	Rainfall	*4*	*6*	*9*	*17*	*45*	*67*	*60*	*68*	*57*	*50*	*16*	*10*	*410*	
	Snowdays	17	12	11	5	1	0	0	0	1	3	12	16	78	
676 m	Temperature	−12	−6	−2	4	9	13	15	14	10	5	−3	−8	3	27
Prince Rupert	Precipitation	228	222	201	190	140	130	103	158	233	367	268	284	2523	
	Rainfall	*184*	*192*	*174*	*181*	*140*	*130*	*103*	*158*	*233*	*367*	*258*	*250*	*2369*	
	Snowdays	9	5	8	4	0	0	0	0	0	0	2	7	35	
34 m	Temperature	0	2	3	5	8	11	13	13	11	8	4	2	7	13
Vancouver	Precipitation	154	115	101	60	52	45	32	41	67	114	150	182	1113	
	Rainfall	*131*	*107*	*95*	*59*	*52*	*45*	*32*	*41*	*67*	*114*	*147*	*165*	*1055*	
	Snowdays	6	2	2	0	0	0	0	0	0	0	1	4	15	
3 m	Temperature	3	5	6	9	12	15	17	17	14	10	6	4	10	14

MANITOBA

		Jan.	Feb.	Mar.	Apr.	May	June	July	Aug.	Sept.	Oct.	Nov.	Dec.	Year	Annual Range
Churchill	Precipitation	15	13	18	23	32	44	46	58	51	43	39	21	402	
	Rainfall	*T*	*T*	*1*	*2*	*14*	*40*	*46*	*58*	*46*	*15*	*1*	*T*	*221*	
	Snowdays	11	10	10	10	7	2	0	0	4	14	18	14	100	
29 m	Temperature	−28	−26	−20	−10	−2	6	12	11	5	−2	−12	−22	−7	40
Winnipeg	Precipitation	21	18	23	39	66	80	76	76	53	31	25	19	526	
	Rainfall	*T*	*1*	*3*	*27*	*63*	*80*	*76*	*76*	*53*	*26*	*6*	*1*	*411*	
	Snowdays	12	9	9	4	1	0	0	0	0	2	9	11	57	
239 m	Temperature	−19	−16	−8	3	11	17	20	18	12	6	−5	−14	2	39

NEW BRUNSWICK

		Jan.	Feb.	Mar.	Apr.	May	June	July	Aug.	Sept.	Oct.	Nov.	Dec.	Year	Annual Range
Saint John	Precipitation	149	116	114	107	108	94	103	102	112	128	146	166	1444	
	Rainfall	*75*	*54*	*62*	*86*	*106*	*94*	*103*	*102*	*112*	*125*	*131*	*102*	*1152*	
	Snowdays	13	21	11	5	1	0	0	0	0	1	4	12	59	
109 m	Temperature	−8	−8	−3	3	9	14	17	17	13	8	2	−5	5	25

NEWFOUNDLAND

		Jan.	Feb.	Mar.	Apr.	May	June	July	Aug.	Sept.	Oct.	Nov.	Dec.	Year	Annual Range
Hopedale	Precipitation	75	67	67	55	51	64	84	81	65	69	66	64	807	
	Rainfall	*3*	*3*	*4*	*8*	*27*	*58*	*84*	*81*	*61*	*45*	*13*	*3*	*391*	
	Snowdays	16	13	14	13	7	2	0	0	1	7	14	15	102	
12 m	Temperature	−16	−16	−11	−5	1	6	11	11	7	2	−3	−11	−2	27
St. John's	Precipitation	156	140	132	116	102	86	75	122	117	146	163	161	1514	
	Rainfall	*78*	*69*	*67*	*78*	*89*	*83*	*75*	*122*	*117*	*141*	*141*	*97*	*1157*	
	Snowdays	18	16	15	10	3	0	0	0	0	2	7	17	88	
140 m	Temperature	−4	−5	−2	1	5	11	16	16	12	7	3	−2	5	21

NORTHWEST TERRITORIES

		Jan.	Feb.	Mar.	Apr.	May	June	July	Aug.	Sept.	Oct.	Nov.	Dec.	Year	Annual Range
Cambridge Bay	Precipitation	5	4	5	7	10	13	20	28	17	15	8	5	136	
	Rainfall	*0*	*0*	*0*	*T*	*1*	*9*	*20*	*27*	*10*	*1*	*0*	*0*	*68*	
	Snowdays	7	6	6	7	8	3	0	1	7	12	9	7	73	
27 m	Temperature	−34	−34	−31	−22	−9	2	8	7	−1	−12	−24	−30	−15	42

NOVA SCOTIA

		Jan.	Feb.	Mar.	Apr.	May	June	July	Aug.	Sept.	Oct.	Nov.	Dec.	Year	Annual Range
Halifax	Precipitation	125	124	102	93	101	81	91	104	82	112	148	124	1282	
	Rainfall	75	61	60	79	99	81	91	104	82	111	137	87	1066	
	Snowdays	10	10	9	4	0	0	0	0	0	0	2	8	43	
32 m	Temperature	−3	−3	0	6	10	15	18	19	16	11	6	0	8	21

ONTARIO

		Jan.	Feb.	Mar.	Apr.	May	June	July	Aug.	Sept.	Oct.	Nov.	Dec.	Year	Annual Range
Ottawa	Precipitation	55	55	59	65	68	80	85	85	80	68	74	73	846	
	Rainfall	15	13	30	61	67	80	85	85	80	67	58	28	668	
	Snowdays	13	11	8	1	0	0	0	0	0	1	5	13	52	
79 m	Temperature	−11	−10	−3	6	13	18	21	19	15	9	2	−8	6	32
Thunder Bay	Precipitation	41	28	45	51	73	77	75	83	89	55	53	42	712	
	Rainfall	2	2	14	35	69	77	75	83	89	52	25	4	527	
	Snowdays	13	10	10	5	1	0	0	0	0	1	9	12	61	
199 m	Temperature	−15	−13	−6	3	9	14	18	16	11	6	−3	−11	2	33
Timmins	Precipitation	56	46	59	49	70	90	90	90	91	69	79	64	852	
	Rainfall	3	1	13	28	64	89	90	90	91	57	28	6	560	
	Snowdays	18	15	12	7	2	0	0	0	1	6	16	19	96	
295 m	Temperature	−17	−16	−8	1	9	15	17	16	10	5	−4	−14	1	34
Toronto	Precipitation	50	46	61	70	66	67	71	77	64	62	63	65	762	
	Rainfall	21	21	37	62	66	67	71	77	64	61	55	36	637	
	Snowdays	12	10	8	2	0	0	0	0	0	0	4	11	47	
173 m	Temperature	−7	−6	1	6	12	18	21	20	16	9	3	−4	7	28
Windsor	Precipitation	55	50	72	83	70	89	83	84	67	57	65	73	849	
	Rainfall	28	29	52	78	70	89	83	84	67	57	54	46	738	
	Snowdays	12	9	7	2	0	0	0	0	0	0	5	10	45	
190 m	Temperature	−5	−4	1	8	14	20	22	21	17	11	4	−2	9	27

PRINCE EDWARD ISLAND

		Jan.	Feb.	Mar.	Apr.	May	June	July	Aug.	Sept.	Oct.	Nov.	Dec.	Year	Annual Range
Charlottetown	Precipitation	117	97	95	82	84	80	84	88	86	106	121	129	1169	
	Rainfall	43	33	32	54	81	80	84	88	86	104	97	59	841	
	Snowdays	15	13	12	6	1	0	0	0	0	1	5	15	68	
55 m	Temperature	−7	−8	−3	2	9	15	18	18	14	8	3	−4	5	25

QUEBEC

		Jan.	Feb.	Mar.	Apr.	May	June	July	Aug.	Sept.	Oct.	Nov.	Dec.	Year	Annual Range
Fort George	Precipitation	28	21	30	24	37	52	86	73	78	76	68	54	628	
	Rainfall	T	1	5	10	31	51	86	73	76	57	13	5	408	
	Snowdays	8	7	7	5	2	0	0	0	0	4	12	10	55	
7 m	Temperature	−23	−22	−16	−6	2	9	12	11	8	2	−5	−16	−4	35
Inoucdjouac	Precipitation	10	9	9	15	23	35	54	65	59	46	40	23	387	
	Rainfall	0	0	T	2	13	31	54	65	54	24	3	T	246	
	Snowdays	8	7	7	8	8	3	0	0	3	11	18	13	86	
5 m	Temperature	−25	−25	−21	−11	−2	4	9	9	5	0	−7	−18	−7	34
Montréal	Precipitation	72	65	74	74	66	82	90	92	88	76	81	87	946	
	Rainfall	24	15	37	64	64	82	90	92	88	74	61	33	723	
	Snowdays	16	12	9	3	0	0	0	0	0	1	6	15	62	
36 m	Temperature	−10	−9	−3	6	13	18	21	20	15	9	2	−7	6	31
Québec	Precipitation	90	78	82	73	87	110	117	117	119	91	97	114	1174	
	Rainfall	17	11	26	55	86	110	117	117	119	86	63	29	836	
	Snowdays	17	14	11	4	0	0	0	0	0	1	9	17	73	
73 m	Temperature	−12	−11	−5	3	11	16	19	18	13	7	0	−9	4	31
Schefferville	Precipitation	47	43	42	45	49	74	97	98	83	76	66	49	769	
	Rainfall	1	0	2	6	24	66	97	96	64	32	9	2	398	
	Snowdays	16	14	14	12	10	2	0	0	6	15	18	17	124	
522 m	Temperature	−23	−22	−15	−7	1	9	13	11	5	−1	−9	−19	−5	36
Sept Îles	Precipitation	96	80	83	78	84	90	97	104	112	97	100	105	1125	
	Rainfall	8	9	14	46	78	90	97	104	112	95	49	18	711	
	Snowdays	15	12	11	7	1	0	0	0	0	3	9	14	72	
55 m	Temperature	−14	−13	−7	0	6	12	15	14	9	4	−3	−11	1	29

SASKATCHEWAN

		Jan.	Feb.	Mar.	Apr.	May	June	July	Aug.	Sept.	Oct.	Nov.	Dec.	Year	Annual Range
Regina	Precipitation	17	16	18	24	46	80	53	45	37	19	14	17	384	
	Rainfall	T	1	2	14	44	80	53	45	35	11	1	1	287	
	Snowdays	13	10	9	4	1	0	0	0	1	2	8	10	58	
577 m	Temperature	−18	−14	−8	3	11	16	19	18	12	5	−5	−13	2	37
Saskatoon	Precipitation	18	16	18	21	40	59	54	38	32	17	15	20	349	
	Rainfall	T	T	1	12	38	59	54	38	31	8	3	1	245	
	Snowdays	12	10	9	4	1	0	0	0	1	3	8	11	59	
501 m	Temperature	−19	−15	−9	3	11	16	19	17	11	5	−6	−14	2	38

YUKON

		Jan.	Feb.	Mar.	Apr.	May	June	July	Aug.	Sept.	Oct.	Nov.	Dec.	Year	Annual Range
Dawson	Precipitation	17	16	10	10	21	39	47	44	28	29	22	25	306	
	Rainfall	T	0	T	2	19	39	47	44	25	6	T	T	183	
	Snowdays	9	10	7	4	1	0	0	0	1	9	11	13	65	
320 m	Temperature	−31	−24	−15	−2	8	14	16	13	7	−4	−17	−26	−5	47

Source: *Canadian Climatic Normals 1951-1980: Environment Canada*

These four pages give temperature and precipitation statistics for over 80 stations, which are arranged by listing the continents and the places within each continent in alphabetical order. The elevation of each station, in metres above mean sea level, is stated beneath its name. The average monthly temperature, in degrees Celsius, and the average monthly precipitation, in millimetres, are given. To the right, the average yearly rainfall, the average yearly temperature, and the annual range of temperature (the difference between the warmest and the coldest months) are also stated.

AFRICA

		Jan.	Feb.	Mar.	Apr.	May	June	July	Aug.	Sept.	Oct.	Nov.	Dec.	Year	Annual Range
Addis Ababa, Ethiopia															
	Precipitation	201	206	239	102	28	<3	0	<3	3	25	135	213	1 151	
2 450 m	Temperature	19	20	20	20	19	18	18	19	21	22	21	20	20	4
Cairo, Egypt															
	Precipitation	5	5	5	3	3	<3	0	0	<3	<3	3	5	28	
116 m	Temperature	13	15	18	21	25	28	28	28	26	24	20	15	22	15
Cape Town, South Africa															
	Precipitation	15	8	18	48	79	84	89	66	43	31	18	10	508	
17 m	Temperature	21	21	20	17	14	13	12	13	14	16	18	19	17	9
Casablanca, Morocco															
	Precipitation	53	48	56	36	23	5	0	<3	8	38	66	71	404	
50 m	Temperature	13	13	14	16	18	20	22	23	22	19	16	13	18	10
Johannesburg, South Africa															
	Precipitation	114	109	89	38	25	8	8	8	23	56	107	125	709	
1 665 m	Temperature	20	20	18	16	13	10	11	13	16	18	19	20	16	10
Khartoum, Sudan															
	Precipitation	<3	<3	<3	<3	3	8	53	71	18	5	<3	0	158	
390 m	Temperature	24	25	28	31	33	34	32	31	32	32	28	25	29	9
Kinshasa, Zaire															
	Precipitation	135	145	196	196	158	8	3	3	31	119	221	142	1 354	
325 m	Temperature	26	26	27	27	26	24	23	24	25	26	26	26	25	4
Lagos, Nigeria															
	Precipitation	28	46	102	150	269	460	279	64	140	206	69	25	1 836	
3 m	Temperature	27	28	29	28	28	26	26	25	26	26	28	28	27	4
Lusaka, Zambia															
	Precipitation	231	191	142	18	3	<3	<3	0	<3	10	91	150	836	
1 277 m	Temperature	21	22	21	21	19	16	16	18	22	24	23	22	21	8
Monrovia, Liberia															
	Precipitation	31	56	97	216	516	973	996	373	744	772	236	130	5 138	
23 m	Temperature	26	26	27	27	26	25	24	25	25	25	26	26	26	3
Nairobi, Kenya															
	Precipitation	38	64	125	211	158	46	15	23	31	53	109	86	958	
1 820 m	Temperature	19	19	19	19	18	16	16	16	18	19	18	18	18	3
Tananarive, Madagascar															
	Precipitation	300	279	178	53	18	8	8	10	18	61	135	287	1 356	
1 372 m	Temperature	21	21	21	19	18	15	14	15	17	19	21	21	19	7
Timbuktu, Mali															
	Precipitation	<3	<3	3	<3	5	23	79	81	38	3	<3	<3	231	
301 m	Temperature	22	24	28	32	34	35	32	30	32	31	28	23	29	13
Tunis, Tunisia															
	Precipitation	64	51	41	36	18	8	3	8	33	51	48	61	419	
66 m	Temperature	10	11	13	16	19	23	26	27	25	20	16	11	18	17
Walvis Bay, Namibia															
	Precipitation	<3	5	8	3	3	<3	<3	3	<3	<3	<3	<3	23	
7 m	Temperature	19	19	19	18	17	16	15	14	14	15	17	18	18	5

AMERICA, NORTH

		Jan.	Feb.	Mar.	Apr.	May	June	July	Aug.	Sept.	Oct.	Nov.	Dec.	Year	Annual Range
Anchorage, Alaska, U.S.A.															
	Precipitation	20	18	15	10	13	18	41	66	66	56	25	23	371	
40 m	Temperature	−11	−8	−5	2	7	12	14	13	9	2	−5	−11	2	25
Cheyenne, Wyo., U.S.A.															
	Precipitation	10	15	25	48	61	41	53	41	31	25	13	13	376	
1 871 m	Temperature	−4	−3	1	5	10	16	19	19	14	7	1	−2	7	23
Chicago, Ill., U.S.A.															
	Precipitation	51	51	66	71	86	89	84	81	79	66	61	51	836	
251 m	Temperature	−4	−3	2	9	14	20	23	22	19	12	5	−1	10	27
Churchill, Man., Canada															
	Precipitation	15	13	18	23	32	44	46	58	51	43	39	21	402	
13 m	Temperature	−28	−26	−20	−10	−2	6	12	11	5	−2	−12	−22	−7	40

		Jan.	Feb.	Mar.	Apr.	May	June	July	Aug.	Sept.	Oct.	Nov.	Dec.	Year	Annual range
Edmonton, Alta., Canada															
	Precipitation	25	19	19	22	43	77	89	78	39	17	16	25	466	
676 m	Temperature	−15	−10	−5	4	11	15	17	16	11	6	−4	−10	3	32
Honolulu, Hawaii, U.S.A.															
	Precipitation	104	66	79	48	25	18	23	28	36	48	64	104	643	
12 m	Temperature	23	18	19	20	22	24	25	26	26	24	22	19	22	8
Houston, Tex., U.S.A.															
	Precipitation	89	76	84	91	119	117	99	99	104	94	89	109	1 171	
12 m	Temperature	12	13	17	21	24	27	28	29	26	22	16	12	21	17
Kingston, Jamaica															
	Precipitation	23	15	23	31	102	89	38	91	99	180	74	36	800	
34 m	Temperature	25	25	25	26	26	28	28	28	27	27	26	26	26	3
Los Angeles, Calif., U.S.A.															
	Precipitation	79	76	71	25	10	3	<3	<3	5	15	31	66	381	
95 m	Temperature	13	14	14	16	17	19	21	22	21	18	16	14	17	9
Mexico City, Mexico															
	Precipitation	13	5	10	20	53	119	170	152	130	51	18	8	747	
2 309 m	Temperature	12	13	16	18	19	19	17	18	18	16	14	13	16	7
Miami, Fla., U.S.A.															
	Precipitation	71	53	64	81	173	178	155	160	203	234	71	51	1 516	
8 m	Temperature	20	20	22	23	25	27	28	28	27	25	22	21	24	8
Montréal, Que., Canada															
	Precipitation	72	65	74	74	66	82	90	92	88	76	81	87	946	
57 m	Temperature	−10	−9	−3	−6	13	18	21	20	15	9	2	−7	6	31
New York, N.Y., U.S.A.															
	Precipitation	94	97	91	81	81	84	107	109	86	89	76	91	1 092	
96 m	Temperature	−1	−1	3	10	16	20	23	23	21	15	7	2	8	24
St. Louis, Mo., U.S.A.															
	Precipitation	58	64	89	97	114	114	89	86	81	74	71	64	1 001	
173 m	Temperature	0	1	7	13	19	24	26	26	22	15	8	2	14	26
San Francisco, Calif., U.S.A.															
	Precipitation	119	97	79	38	18	3	<3	<3	8	25	64	112	561	
16 m	Temperature	10	12	13	13	14	15	15	15	17	16	14	11	14	7
San José, Costa Rica															
	Precipitation	15	5	20	46	229	241	211	241	305	300	145	41	1 798	
1 146 m	Temperature	19	19	21	21	22	21	21	21	21	20	20	19	20	2
Vancouver, B.C., Canada															
	Precipitation	154	115	101	60	52	45	32	41	67	114	150	182	1113	
14 m	Temperature	3	5	6	9	12	15	17	17	14	10	6	4	10	14
Washington, D.C., U.S.A.															
	Precipitation	86	76	91	84	94	99	112	109	94	74	66	79	1 064	
22 m	Temperature	1	2	7	12	18	23	25	24	20	14	8	3	13	24

AMERICA, SOUTH

		Jan.	Feb.	Mar.	Apr.	May	June	July	Aug.	Sept.	Oct.	Nov.	Dec.	Year	Annual range
Antofagasta, Chile															
	Precipitation	0	0	0	<3	<3	3	5	3	<3	3	<3	0	13	
94 m	Temperature	21	21	20	18	16	15	14	14	15	16	18	19	17	7
Buenos Aires, Argentina															
	Precipitation	79	71	109	89	76	61	56	61	79	86	84	99	950	
27 m	Temperature	23	23	21	17	13	9	10	11	13	15	19	22	16	14
Caracas, Venezuela															
	Precipitation	23	10	15	33	79	102	109	109	107	109	94	46	836	
1 042 m	Temperature	19	19	20	21	22	21	21	21	21	21	20	20	21	3
Lima, Peru															
	Precipitation	3	<3	<3	<3	5	5	8	8	8	3	3	<3	41	
120 m	Temperature	23	24	24	22	19	17	17	16	17	18	19	21	20	8
Manaus, Brazil															
	Precipitation	249	231	262	221	170	84	58	38	46	107	142	203	1 811	
44 m	Temperature	28	28	28	27	28	28	28	28	29	29	29	28	28	2
Paraná, Brazil															
	Precipitation	287	236	239	102	13	<3	3	5	28	127	231	310	1 582	
260 m	Temperature	23	23	23	23	23	21	21	22	24	24	24	23	23	3
Quito, Ecuador															
	Precipitation	99	112	142	175	137	43	20	31	69	112	97	79	1 115	
2 879 m	Temperature	15	15	15	15	15	14	14	15	15	15	15	15	15	1
Rio de Janeiro, Brazil															
	Precipitation	125	122	130	107	79	53	41	43	66	79	104	137	1 082	
61 m	Temperature	26	26	25	24	22	21	21	21	21	22	23	25	23	5
Santiago, Chile															
	Precipitation	3	3	5	13	64	84	76	56	31	15	8	5	358	
520 m	Temperature	21	20	18	15	12	9	9	10	12	15	17	19	15	12

ASIA

		Jan.	Feb.	Mar.	Apr.	May	June	July	Aug.	Sept.	Oct.	Nov.	Dec.	Year	Annual range
Bahrain															
	Precipitation	8	18	13	8	<3	0	0	0	0	0	18	18	81	
5 m	Temperature	17	18	21	25	29	32	33	34	31	28	24	19	26	16
Bangkok, Thailand															
	Precipitation	8	20	36	58	198	160	160	175	305	206	66	5	1 397	
2 m	Temperature	26	28	29	30	29	29	28	28	28	28	26	25	28	5
Beirut, Lebanon															
	Precipitation	191	158	94	53	18	3	<3	<3	5	51	132	185	892	
34 m	Temperature	14	14	16	18	22	24	27	28	26	24	19	16	21	14
Bombay, India															
	Precipitation	3	3	3	<3	18	485	617	340	264	64	13	3	1 809	
11 m	Temperature	24	24	26	28	30	29	27	27	27	28	27	26	27	6
Calcutta, India															
	Precipitation	10	31	36	43	140	297	325	328	252	114	20	5	1 600	
6 m	Temperature	20	22	27	30	30	30	29	29	29	28	23	19	26	11
Colombo, Sri Lanka															
	Precipitation	89	69	147	231	371	224	135	109	160	348	315	147	2 365	
7 m	Temperature	26	26	27	28	28	27	27	27	27	27	26	26	27	2
Harbin, China															
	Precipitation	5	5	10	23	43	94	112	104	46	33	8	5	488	
160 m	Temperature	−18	−15	−5	6	13	19	22	21	14	4	−6	−16	3	40
Ho Chi Minh City, Vietnam															
	Precipitation	15	3	13	43	221	330	315	269	335	269	114	56	1 984	
9 m	Temperature	26	27	29	30	29	28	28	28	27	27	27	26	28	4
Jakarta, Indonesia															
	Precipitation	300	300	211	147	114	97	64	43	66	112	142	203	1 798	
8 m	Temperature	26	26	27	27	27	27	27	27	27	27	27	26	27	1
Hong Kong															
	Precipitation	33	46	74	137	292	394	381	361	257	114	43	31	2 162	
33 m	Temperature	16	15	18	22	26	28	28	28	27	25	21	18	23	13
Kabul, Afghanistan															
	Precipitation	31	36	94	102	20	5	3	3	<3	15	20	10	338	
1 815 m	Temperature	−3	−1	6	13	18	22	25	24	20	14	7	3	12	28
Karachi, Pakistan															
	Precipitation	13	10	8	3	3	18	81	41	13	<3	3	5	196	
4 m	Temperature	19	20	24	28	30	31	30	29	28	28	24	20	26	12
New Delhi, India															
	Precipitation	23	18	13	8	13	74	180	172	117	10	3	10	640	
218 m	Temperature	14	17	23	28	33	34	31	30	29	26	20	15	25	20
Shanghai, China															
	Precipitation	48	58	84	94	94	180	147	142	130	71	51	36	1 135	
7 m	Temperature	4	5	9	14	20	24	28	28	23	19	12	7	16	24
Singapore															
	Precipitation	252	173	193	188	173	173	170	196	178	208	254	257	2 413	
10 m	Temperature	26	27	28	28	28	28	28	27	27	27	27	27	27	2
Tehran, Iran															
	Precipitation	46	38	46	36	13	3	3	3	3	8	20	31	246	
1 220 m	Temperature	2	5	9	16	21	26	30	29	25	18	12	6	17	28
Tokyo, Japan															
	Precipitation	48	74	107	135	147	165	142	152	234	208	97	56	1 565	
6 m	Temperature	3	4	7	13	17	21	25	26	23	17	11	6	14	23
Ulan Bator, Mongolia															
	Precipitation	<3	<3	3	5	10	28	76	51	23	5	5	3	208	
1 325 m	Temperature	−26	−21	−13	−1	6	14	16	14	8	−1	−13	−22	−3	42

AUSTRALIA, NEW ZEALAND, and ANTARCTICA

		Jan.	Feb.	Mar.	Apr.	May	June	July	Aug.	Sept.	Oct.	Nov.	Dec.	Year	Annual range
Alice Springs, Australia															
	Precipitation	43	33	28	10	15	13	8	8	8	18	31	38	252	
579 m	Temperature	29	28	25	20	15	12	12	14	18	23	26	28	21	17
Christchurch, New Zealand															
	Precipitation	56	43	48	48	66	66	69	48	46	43	48	56	638	
10 m	Temperature	16	16	14	12	9	6	6	7	9	12	14	16	11	10
Darwin, Australia															
	Precipitation	386	312	254	97	15	3	<3	3	13	51	119	239	1 491	
30 m	Temperature	29	29	29	29	28	26	25	26	28	29	30	29	28	5
Mawson, Antarctica															
	Precipitation	11	30	20	10	44	180	4	40	3	20	0	0	362	
14 m	Temperature	0	−5	−10	−14	−15	−16	−18	−18	−19	−13	−5	−1	−11	18

		Jan.	Feb.	Mar.	Apr.	May	June	July	Aug.	Sept.	Oct.	Nov.	Dec.	Year	Annual Range
Melbourne, Australia															
	Precipitation	48	46	56	58	53	53	48	48	58	66	58	58	653	
35 m	Temperature	20	20	18	15	13	10	9	11	13	14	16	18	15	11
Perth, Australia															
	Precipitation	8	10	20	43	130	180	170	149	86	56	20	13	881	
60 m	Temperature	23	23	22	19	16	14	13	13	15	16	19	22	18	10
Sydney, Australia															
	Precipitation	89	102	127	135	127	117	117	76	73	71	73	73	1 181	
42 m	Temperature	22	22	21	18	15	13	12	13	15	18	19	21	17	10

EUROPE and U.S.S.R.

		Jan.	Feb.	Mar.	Apr.	May	June	July	Aug.	Sept.	Oct.	Nov.	Dec.	Year	Annual Range
Archangel, U.S.S.R.															
	Precipitation	31	19	25	29	42	52	62	56	63	63	47	41	530	
13 m	Temperature	−16	−14	−9	0	7	12	15	14	8	2	−4	−11	0	31
Athens, Greece															
	Precipitation	62	37	37	23	23	14	6	7	15	51	56	71	402	
107 m	Temperature	10	10	12	16	20	25	28	28	24	20	15	11	18	18
Berlin, Germany															
	Precipitation	46	40	33	42	49	65	73	69	48	49	46	43	603	
55 m	Temperature	−1	0	4	9	14	17	19	18	15	9	5	1	9	20
Istanbul, Turkey															
	Precipitation	109	92	72	46	38	34	34	30	58	81	103	119	816	
114 m	Temperature	5	6	7	11	16	20	23	23	20	16	12	8	14	18
Kazalinsk, U.S.S.R.															
	Precipitation	10	10	13	13	15	5	5	8	8	10	13	15	125	
63 m	Temperature	−12	−11	−3	6	18	23	25	23	16	8	−1	−7	7	37
Lisbon, Portugal															
	Precipitation	111	76	109	54	44	16	3	4	33	62	93	103	708	
77 m	Temperature	11	12	14	16	17	20	22	23	21	18	14	12	17	12
London, U.K.															
	Precipitation	54	40	37	37	46	45	57	59	49	57	64	48	593	
5 m	Temperature	4	5	7	9	12	16	18	17	15	11	8	5	11	14
Malaga, Spain															
	Precipitation	61	51	62	46	26	5	1	3	29	64	64	62	474	
33 m	Temperature	12	13	15	17	19	29	25	26	23	20	16	13	18	17
Moscow, U.S.S.R.															
	Precipitation	39	38	36	37	53	58	88	71	58	45	47	54	624	
156 m	Temperature	−13	−10	−4	6	13	16	18	17	12	6	−1	−7	4	31
Odessa, U.S.S.R.															
	Precipitation	57	62	30	21	34	34	42	37	37	13	35	71	473	
64 m	Temperature	−3	−1	2	9	15	20	22	22	18	12	9	1	10	25
Omsk, U.S.S.R.															
	Precipitation	15	8	8	13	31	51	51	51	28	25	18	20	318	
85 m	Temperature	−22	−19	−12	−1	10	16	18	16	10	1	−11	−18	−1	40
Palma de Mallorca, Spain															
	Precipitation	39	34	51	32	29	17	3	25	55	77	47	40	449	
10 m	Temperature	10	11	12	15	17	21	24	25	23	18	14	11	17	15
Paris, France															
	Precipitation	56	46	35	42	57	54	59	64	55	50	51	50	619	
75 m	Temperature	3	4	8	11	15	18	20	19	17	12	7	4	12	17
Rome, Italy															
	Precipitation	71	62	57	51	46	37	15	21	63	99	129	93	744	
17 m	Temperature	8	9	11	14	18	22	25	25	22	17	13	10	16	17
Shannon, Irish Republic															
	Precipitation	94	67	56	53	61	57	77	79	86	86	96	117	929	
2 m	Temperature	5	5	7	9	12	14	16	16	14	11	8	6	10	11
Stavanger, Norway															
	Precipitation	93	56	45	70	49	84	93	118	142	129	125	126	1 130	
85 m	Temperature	1	1	3	6	10	13	15	15	13	9	6	3	8	14
Stockholm, Sweden															
	Precipitation	43	30	25	31	34	45	61	76	60	48	53	48	554	
44 m	Temperature	−3	−3	−1	5	10	15	18	17	12	7	3	0	7	21
Verkhoyansk, U.S.S.R.															
	Precipitation	5	5	3	5	8	23	28	25	13	8	8	5	134	
100 m	Temperature	−50	−45	−32	−15	0	12	14	9	2	−15	−38	−48	−17	64
Warsaw, Poland															
	Precipitation	27	32	27	37	46	69	96	65	43	38	31	44	555	
110 m	Temperature	−3	−3	2	7	14	17	19	18	14	9	3	0	8	22

Province area

Province or Territory	Total Area including Freshwater		Land Area	
	km²	percentage of Canada Total %	km²	percentage of Canada Total %
Newfoundland	404 517	4.1	370 485	4.0
Prince Edward I.	5 657	0.1	5 657	0.1
Nova Scotia	55 491	0.6	52 841	0.6
New Brunswick	73 436	0.7	72 092	0.8
Quebec	1 540 680	15.5	1 356 791	14.8
Ontario	1 068 582	10.8	891 194	9.7
Manitoba	650 087	6.6	548 495	6.0
Saskatchewan	651 900	6.6	570 269	6.2
Alberta	661 185	6.7	644 389	7.0
British Columbia	948 596	9.6	930 528	10.2
Yukon Territory	482 515	4.9	478 034	5.2
Northwest Terr.	3 379 684	34.1	3 246 390	35.4
CANADA	**9 922 330**		**9 167 165**	

Canada Year Book 1980-81

Population of Canada, 1851-1981

Census year	Population No.	Increase during intercensal period		Average annual rate of population growth %
		No.	%	
1851	2 436 297			
1861	3 229 633	793 336	32.6	2.9
1871	3 689 257	459 624	14.2	1.3
1881	4 324 810	635 553	17.2	1.6
1891	4 833 239	508 429	11.8	1.1
1901	5 371 315	538 076	11.1	1.1
1911	7 206 643	1 835 328	34.2	3.0
1921	8 787 949	1 581 306	21.9	2.0
1931	10 376 786	1 588 837	18.1	1.7
1941	11 506 655	1 129 869	10.9	1.0
1951[1]	14 009 429	2 502 774	21.8	1.7
1956	16 080 791	2 071 362	14.8	2.8
1961	18 238 247	2 157 456	13.4	2.5
1966	20 014 880	1 776 633	9.7	1.9
1971	21 568 311	1 553 431	7.8	1.5
1976	22 992 604	1 424 293	6.6	1.3
1981	24 343 180	1 350 576	5.9	1.2

[1]Includes Newfoundland for the first time.   Canada Year Book 1980-81.   1981 Census of Canada 92-901

Provincial population, 1971-2000

	Canada	N.W.T.	Y.T.	B.C.	Alta.	Sask.	Man.	Ont.	Que.	N.B.	N.S.	P.E.I.	Nfld.
													thousands
Census 1971	**21 568**	35	18	2 185	1 628	926	988	7 703	6 028	635	789	112	522
Census 1976	**22 993**	43	22	2 467	1 838	921	1 022	8 265	6 234	677	829	118	558
Census 1981	**24 343**	46	23	2 745	2 238	968	1 026	8 625	6 438	696	847	123	568
Estimate 1984	**25 082**	49	22	2 863	2 349	1 003	1 054	8 917	6 540	712	868	125	579
Projected 2000													
High probability	**30 723**	87	44	3 811	2 806	968	1 180	11 788	7 579	779	929	132	619
Low probability	**27 939**	64	33	3 104	3 044	1 203	1 166	10 086	6 523	883	1 004	161	669

Canada Year Book 1980-81.   1981 Census of Canada 92-901.   Population Projections for Canada and the Provinces 1976-2001 91-520

Provincial components of total population, 1921-1981

	Canada *thousands*	N.W.T.	Y.T.	B.C.	Alta.	Sask.	Man.	Ont.	Que.	N.B.	N.S.	P.E.I.	Nfld.
													percentage
1921	**8 787**	0.1	0.05	6.0	6.7	8.6	6.9	33.4	26.9	4.4	6.0	1.0	—
1931	**10 376**	0.1	0.04	6.7	7.1	8.9	6.7	33.1	27.7	3.9	4.9	0.8	—
1941	**11 506**	0.1	0.04	7.1	6.9	7.8	6.3	32.9	29.0	4.0	5.0	0.8	—
1951	**14 009**	0.1	0.06	8.3	6.7	5.9	5.5	32.8	28.9	3.7	4.6	0.7	2.6
1961	**18 238**	0.1	0.08	8.9	7.3	5.1	5.1	34.2	28.8	3.3	4.0	0.6	2.5
1971	**21 568**	0.2	0.08	10.1	7.5	4.3	4.5	35.7	27.9	2.9	3.7	0.5	2.4
1981	**24 343**	0.2	0.1	11.3	9.2	4.0	4.2	35.4	26.4	2.9	3.5	0.5	2.3

Average annual rate of population change, 1921-1981

	Canada	N.W.T.	Y.T.	B.C.	Alta.	Sask.	Man.	Ont.	Que.	N.B.	N.S.	P.E.I.	Nfld.
													percentage
1921-31	**1.68**	1.39	0.24	2.85	2.21	2.0	1.39	1.58	1.99	0.51	−0.21	−0.1	—
1931-41	**1.04**	2.58	1.76	1.65	0.84	−0.29	0.42	0.99	1.49	1.14	1.20	0.77	—
1941-51	**1.99**	2.92	6.17	3.60	1.68	−0.74	0.64	1.96	1.99	1.22	1.07	0.35	—
1951-61	**2.67**	3.70	4.84	3.41	3.55	1.07	1.73	3.10	2.63	1.49	1.38	0.61	2.39
1961-71	**1.69**	4.23	2.34	2.98	2.03	0.01	0.70	2.14	1.37	0.60	0.68	0.65	1.32
1971-81	**1.22**	2.76	2.35	2.31	3.24	0.44	0.38	1.14	0.66	0.93	0.71	0.94	0.84

Canada Year Book 1980-81.   1981 Census of Canada 92-901

Age distribution of the population, 1971-1981

Age Group	Number thousand 1981	Percentage of total population 1971	1976	1981
0-4	**1 783**	8.4	7.5	7.3
5-9	**1 777**	10.4	8.2	7.3
10-14	**1 921**	10.7	9.9	7.9
15-19	**2 315**	9.8	10.3	9.5
20-24	**2 344**	8.8	9.3	9.6
25-29	**2 178**	7.3	8.7	9.0
30-34	**2 039**	6.1	7.1	8.4
35-39	**1 630**	5.9	5.8	6.7
40-44	**1 338**	5.9	5.5	5.5
45-49	**1 255**	5.7	5.4	5.2
50-54	**1 244**	4.9	5.3	5.1
55-59	**1 180**	4.4	4.4	4.9
60-64	**979**	3.6	3.9	4.0
65-69	**844**	2.9	3.1	3.5
70-74	**633**	2.1	2.3	2.6
75-79	**433**	1.5	1.6	1.8
80-84	**257**	0.9	1.0	1.1
85-89	**131**	0.5	0.5	0.5
90+	**63**	0.2	0.2	0.3

Canada Year Book 1980-81.   1981 Census of Canada 92-901

Density of population, 1956-1981

	Population per km² 1956	1966	1976	1981
Newfoundland	1.1	1.3	1.5	1.5
Prince Edward I.	17.6	19.2	20.9	21.7
Nova Scotia	13.2	14.3	15.9	16.0
New Brunswick	7.7	8.6	9.4	9.7
Quebec	3.4	4.3	4.6	4.7
Ontario	6.1	7.8	9.3	9.7
Manitoba	1.6	1.8	1.9	1.9
Saskatchewan	1.5	1.7	1.6	1.7
Alberta	1.7	2.3	2.9	3.5
British Columbia	1.5	2.0	2.7	2.9
Yukon Territory	0.02	0.03	0.04	0.04
Northwest Terr.	0.01	0.01	0.01	0.01
Canada	**1.8**	**2.2**	**2.5**	**2.6**

Canada Year Book 1980-81

Birth rates, 1951-1982

births per thousand population

	Canada	N.W.T.	Y.T.	B.C.	Alta.	Sask.	Man.	Ont.	Que.	N.B.	N.S.	P.E.I.	Nfld.
Av. 1951-55	**28.0**	40.1	43.0	25.1	30.6	27.5	26.4	26.1	30.0	31.0	27.5	27.2	34.1
Av. 1961-65	**24.1**	45.9	34.9	21.5	26.5	24.4	23.4	23.5	24.0	25.8	24.7	25.7	31.8
Av. 1971-75	**16.0**	30.9	22.7	15.2	17.8	16.9	17.4	15.9	14.4	18.1	16.7	17.3	22.5
Av. 1980	**15.5**	30.2	22.2	15.2	19.1	17.6	15.5	14.4	15.4	15.0	14.5	15.7	17.8
Av. 1982	**15.1**	28.9	22.1	15.3	19.4	18.1	15.6	14.3	14.0	15.0	14.5	15.7	16.1

Death rates, 1951-1982

deaths per thousand population

	Canada	N.W.T.	Y.T.	B.C.	Alta.	Sask.	Man.	Ont.	Que.	N.B.	N.S.	P.E.I.	Nfld.
Av. 1951-55	**8.5**	17.1	9.4	9.8	7.4	7.6	8.4	9.0	8.0	8.6	8.8	9.2	7.6
Av. 1961-65	**7.7**	9.8	6.0	8.9	6.9	7.8	8.1	8.1	6.9	7.8	8.4	9.3	6.6
Av. 1971-75	**7.4**	6.1	5.4	8.0	6.5	8.4	8.3	7.5	7.0	7.8	8.5	8.2	6.1
Av. 1980	**7.2**	5.5	6.0	7.3	6.1	7.9	8.2	7.3	6.9	7.5	8.2	8.3	5.8
Av. 1982	**7.1**	4.9	5.0	7.4	5.6	8.4	8.2	7.3	6.7	7.4	8.1	8.0	5.9

Canada Year Book 1980-81.   Births and Deaths 84-204

Migration to, and from, Canada 1966-1981

		Canada	N.W.T.	Y.T.	B.C.	Alta.	Sask.	Man.	Ont.	Que.	N.B.	N.S.	P.E.I.	Nfld.
Immigrants	1966-71	**890 340**	653	332	116 353	59 890	14 324	35 730	474 710	166 749	5 840	10 626	811	4 322
Emigrants	1966-71	**472 400**	800	300	38 500	23 700	15 700	15 100	180 400	144 100	20 300	17 300	2 400	13 800
Immigrants	1971-76	**841 022**	896	475	131 840	61 671	10 238	31 762	451 399	127 470	8 646	10 812	1 209	4 604
Emigrants	1971-76	**357 200**	→	→	51 900	26 300	9 100	12 500	163 300	82 100	3 400	4 900	400	3 500
Immigrants	1976-81	**598 389**	632	357	89 623	70 447	12 622	26 807	278 806	102 252	5 673	7 397	1 020	2 753
Emigrants	1976-81	**371 655**	406	468	51 691	17 790	9 604	8 416	163 880	103 624	5 510	6 739	970	4 557

1981 Census of Canada 91-208

City population, 1976-1981

	thousands 1976	1981	% change
Alberta			
Calgary	471	593	26
Edmonton	556	657	18
Lethbridge	47	54	15
Medicine Hat	41	50	20
British Columbia			
Chilliwack	38	41	11
Courtenay	29	35	20
Kamloops	59	65	10
Kelowna	65	77	19
Nanaimo	49	58	19
Port Alberni	32	33	1
Powell River	20	19	−1
Prince George	60	68	13
Prince Rupert	17	18	7
Terrace	30	32	8
Trail	22	23	4
Vancouver	1 166	1 268	9
Vernon	37	42	15
Victoria	218	233	7
Manitoba			
Flin Flon	10	10	−4
Portage la Prairie	20	21	3
Thompson	17	14	−17
Winnipeg	578	585	1
New Brunswick			
Bathurst	24	24	3
Campbellton	16	16	−1
Edmundston	21	22	5
Fredericton	62	64	5
Moncton	96	98	3
Oromocto	14	14	-1
Saint John	113	114	1
Newfoundland			
Carbonear	13	13	4
Corner Brook	32	32	0
Grand Falls	15	15	−4
Labrador City	16	15	−7
St. John's	145	155	7
Nova Scotia			
Halifax	268	278	4
Kentville	19	21	9
New Glasgow	39	39	2
Sydney	89	88	−1
Sydney Mines	36	35	0
Truro	38	40	4

	thousands 1976	1981	% change
Ontario			
Barrie	55	61	12
Belleville	43	46	7
Brantford	83	88	7
Brockville	35	36	2
Chatham	45	47	4
Cobourg	20	20	0
Cornwall	53	53	1
Fergus	11	12	3
Guelph	75	79	5
Haileybury	14	13	−4
Hamilton	529	542	2
Hawkesbury	11	11	0
Kenora	16	16	−4
Kingston	114	115	1
Kitchener	272	288	6
Leamington	20	21	6
Lindsay	16	17	6
London	270	284	5
Midland	33	34	3
North Bay	57	57	0
Orillia	31	31	0
Oshawa	135	154	14
Ottawa-Hull	693	718	4
Owen Sound	27	27	2
Pembroke	23	22	−1
Petawawa	14	13	−8
Peterborough	84	86	2
St. Catharines-Ngra	302	304	1
Sarnia	81	84	3
Sault-Ste. Marie	85	87	2
Smiths Falls	15	15	2
Stratford	28	28	2
Sudbury	157	150	−5
Thunder Bay	119	121	2
Toronto	2 803	2 999	7
Trenton	39	39	1
Windsor	248	246	−1
Prince Edward Island			
Charlottetown	42	45	8
Summerside	15	15	−3

	thousands 1976	1981	% change
Quebec			
Asbestos	15	14	−4
Baie-Comeau	29	29	2
Chicoutimi-Jonquière	129	135	5
Cornwall	53	53	1
Dolbeau	14	15	11
Drummondville	53	55	4
Granby	43	46	7
Hawkesbury	11	11	0
Joliette	33	35	4
La Tuque	14	14	−1
Lachute	18	18	−2
Magog	17	18	7
Montréal	2 803	2 828	1
Ottawa-Hull	693	718	4
Québec	542	576	6
Rimouski	34	38	10
Rivière-du-Loup	19	21	10
Rouyn	30	29	−4
St.-Georges	17	19	14
St.-Hyacinthe	45	47	6
St.-Jean-sur-Richelieu	56	61	8
St.-Jérôme	41	44	6
Salaberry-de-Valleyfield	39	40	3
Sept-Îles	32	30	−5
Shawinigan	63	63	−1
Sherbrooke	111	117	6
Sorel	44	47	6
Thetford Mines	34	35	3
Trois-Rivières	106	112	5
Val-d'Or	22	24	7
Victoriaville	33	36	10
Saskatchewan			
Flin Flon	10	10	−4
Moose Jaw	35	36	4
North Battleford	17	19	10
Prince Albert	35	38	9
Regina	151	164	9
Saskatoon	134	154	15
Swift Current	16	17	3

The population totals are those of the Census Metropolitan Areas and the Census Agglomerations. These are for the built-up and labour-market areas of the cities and are not necessarily related to the population within the legal boundary of a city or town.

1981 Census of Canada, 93-901−93-912

Urban and rural population, 1981

	Canada	N.W.T.	Y.T.	B.C.	Alta.	Sask.	Man.	Ont.	Que.	N.B.	N.S.	P.E.I.	Nfld.
	thousands												
Rural Population	**5 907**	24	8	605	510	405	295	1 578	1 445	343	381	78	235
Percentage Rural	**24.3%**	52.2%	34.8%	22.0%	22.8%	41.8%	28.8%	18.3%	22.4%	49.3%	45.0%	63.4%	41.4%
Urban Population	**18 436**	22	15	2 139	1 728	563	731	7 047	4 994	353	467	45	333
Percentage Urban	**75.7%**	47.8%	65.2%	78.0%	77.2%	58.2%	71.2%	81.7%	77.6%	50.7%	55.0%	36.6%	58.6%

1981 Census of Canada 92-901

Place of birth, 1981

Province of residence	Province of birth N.W.T.	Y.T.	B.C.	Alta.	Sask.	Man.	Ont.	Que.	N.B.	N.S.	P.E.I.	*thousands* Nfld.
Northwest Territory	**26**	0.2	1	3	2	3	3	1	0.5	0.8	0.1	0.7
Yukon Territory	0.2	**7**	3	3	2	1	3	0.7	0.3	0.4	0.1	0.3
British Columbia	2	4	**1 255**	205	202	130	173	53	17	28	4	9
Alberta	4	2	80	**1 195**	195	87	171	48	19	28	6	14
Saskatchewan	0.9	0.3	12	29	**746**	42	29	6	2	3	0.8	1
Manitoba	0.4	0.2	9	13	49	**727**	46	9	4	6	0.7	3
Ontario	1	1	46	47	75	92	**5 644**	314	80	119	19	70
Quebec	0.8	0.1	6	7	6	10	134	**5 603**	50	14	3	8
New Brunswick	—	0.1	2	2	1	2	24	21	**571**	28	6	6
Nova Scotia	0.1	0.1	4	4	3	3	36	13	24	**684**	8	19
Prince Edward I.	—	—	0.4	0.6	0.3	0.3	5	2	3	5	**98**	0.9
Newfoundland	—	—	0.6	0.6	0.3	0.7	10	3	2	6	0.6	**530**
Of people living in Canada, no. born in province	35	15	1 420	1 509	1 282	1 098	6 278	6 075	773	924	145	662
Of people living in province, born in province %	57	30	46	54	78	72	66	88	83	81	81	94

1981 Census of Canada 92-913

Population born outside Canada, 1981

	Canada	N.W.T.	Y.T.	B.C.	Alta.	Sask.	Man.	Ont.	Que.	N.B.	N.S.	P.E.I.	*thousands* Nfld.
Born outside Canada	**3 867**	3	3	632	365	84	146	2 026	526	28	42	5	10
Percentage of population foreign born	**16.8**	6.5	13.0	23.3	16.5	8.8	14.4	23.7	8.3	4.1	5	4.1	1.8
Born in:—													
U.S.A.	**312**	0.3	0.6	63	44	17	11	109	40	11	11	2	0.2
Caribbean	**174**	—	—	6	7	1	4	111	44	—	1	—	—
Europe		2	2	389	225	54	99	1 444	325	14	24	2	6
U.K.	**885**	1	1	185	82	19	30	497	43	8	14	1	4
Italy	**387**	0.1	—	23	12	1	5	256	89	0.3	1	—	—
W. Germany	**164**	0.2	0.2	32	22	4	8	78	14	2	2	0.3	0.4
Poland	**149**	—	—	14	19	6	13	75	20	—	1	—	—
U.S.S.R.	**129**	—	—	15	15	8	14	63	13	0.2	0.3	—	—
France	**56**	—	—	4	3	0.5	1	10	37	0.3	0.5	—	—
Africa	**103**	—	—	13	11	1	2	41	33	—	1	—	—
Asia	**543**	0.3	0.2	134	62	10	22	243	64	2	4	0.3	1

1981 Census of Canada 92-913

Population by mother-tongue, 1981

	Canada	% of Canada's population	N.W.T.	Y.T.	B.C.	Alta.	Sask.	Man.	Ont.	Que.	N.B.	N.S.	P.E.I.	*thousands* Nfld.
English	14 918	61.3	25	20	2 249	1 811	771	736	6 679	706	453	793	115	560
Percentage of total speaking English	61.3		54.3	87.0	82.0	80.9	79.6	71.7	77.4	11.0	65.1	93.6	93.5	98.6
French	6 249	25.6	1	0.6	46	62	26	53	476	5 307	234	36	6	3
European languages	2 444	10.0	1	1	288	272	138	190	1 210	325	5	11	1	1
Italian	529	2.2	—	—	31	16	1	6	339	134	1	1	—	—
German	523	2.1	—	1	93	91	60	75	175	24	1	2	—	—
Ukrainian	292	1.2	—	—	27	68	45	59	82	11	—	1	—	—
Greek	123	0.5	—	—	6	3	1	2	65	44	—	1	—	—
Asian languages	555	2.3	—	—	149	64	10	20	235	67	2	4	—	2
Chinese	224	0.9	—	—	76	29	5	6	89	15	1	1	—	1
Amerindian	146	0.6	18	—	7	27	24	25	16	24	1	3	—	1

1981 Census of Canada 92-902

Provincial farm statistics, 1981

	Canada	B.C.	Alta.	Sask.	Man.	Ont.	Que.	N.B.	N.S.	P.E.I.	Nfld.
Total land area '000ha	922 097	89 307	63 823	57 011	54 771	91 743	135 781	7 157	5 284	566	37 164
Total farm area '000ha	65 889	2 179	19 109	25 947	7 616	6 039	3 779	438	466	283	33
% Farm area/Total area	7%	2%	30%	46%	14%	7%	3%	6%	9%	50%	—
Total number of farms	318 361	20 012	58 056	67 318	29 442	82 448	48 144	4 063	5 045	3 154	679
Average farm size ha	207	109	329	385	259	73	79	108	92	89	49
Improved farm land '000ha	46 122	946	12 525	19 684	5 504	4 516	2 360	192	178	203	11
Of improved land:—											
% land under crops	67%	60%	67%	60%	80%	80%	74%	68%	63%	78%	46%
% pasture	10%	28%	13%	5%	6%	15%	19%	22%	26%	18%	40%
% summer fallow	21%	7%	18%	34%	11%	1%	2%	3%	3%	1%	3%
% other improved land	2%	5%	2%	1%	3%	4%	5%	7%	8%	3%	11%
Unimproved farm land '000ha	19 768	1 232	6 583	6 263	2 112	1 521	1 419	246	288	80	23
Of unimproved land % woodland	18%	17%	8%	5%	12%	49%	75%	82%	84%	81%	25%
Value of:—											
Machinery & equipment '000$	17 444	693	4 362	4 917	1 824	3 462	1 733	142	150	149	12
Livestock & poultry '000$	103 275	572	2 504	1 403	792	2 522	1 512	85	114	72	10
Land & buildings '000$	9 585	7 261	29 961	25 048	7 836	25 299	6 224	441	633	479	94
All agricultural products sold, million $	15 832	799	3 265	3 078	1 445	4 692	2 032	154	199	140	28

1981 Census of Canada, 96-901

Farms with sales greater than $2 500 classified by type of farm, 1981

	Canada	B.C.	Alta.	Sask.	Man.	Ont.	Que.	N.B.	N.S.	P.E.I.	Nfld.
Total number of farms	318 361	20 012	58 056	67 318	29 442	82 448	48 144	4 063	5 045	3 154	679
Number of farms with sales >$2 500	271 604	13 597	51 164	64 342	26 517	68 960	38 184	2 702	3 169	2 585	384
Percentage of farms with sales >$2 500	85%	68%	88%	95%	90%	84%	79%	66%	63%	82%	56%
Number of farms in each category:—											
Dairy	41 905	1 345	2 743	1 623	1 803	12 841	19 161	773	830	768	58
Cattle	60 139	4 558	16 098	7 057	5 679	19 567	4 930	723	946	547	34
Pigs	12 301	347	1 402	632	1 011	4 984	3 331	117	196	255	26
Poultry	5 438	850	622	243	409	1 886	1 121	102	126	26	53
Wheat	55 780	185	7 378	41 096	6 105	692	300	8	11	5	—
Small grains[1]	52 086	684	16 493	10 162	8 533	14 016	2 021	45	47	85	—
Field crops[2]	7 722	623	1 122	287	498	3 190	1 008	438	74	462	20
Fruit and vegetables	10 269	2 815	76	28	88	4 335	2 107	231	449	53	87
Miscellaneous speciality	11 640	1 550	1 574	444	592	3 768	3 085	166	322	88	51

1 = All other grains except wheat.   2 = All crops, except cereals.   1981 Census of Canada, 96-917

Livestock and dairy produce, 1950-1983

Product	1950	1960	1970	1980	1981	1982	1983
Cattle '000 head	8 343	11 337	12 826	12 126	12 166	12 088	11 618
Milk cows '000 head	3 119	2 965	2 389	1 773	1 764	1 777	1 742
Milk '000t	6 762	8 049	8 176	7 692	7 920	8 025	8 100
Creamery butter '000t	119	145	159	103	113	123	104
Cheddar cheese '000t	44	49	76	107	101	89	99
Concentrated milk products '000t	128	278	173	157	132	156	147
Eggs '000 dozen	293 727	435 606	490 705	494 556	496 234	493 559	504 804
Eggs per 100 layers	14 963	19 319	20 872	23 618	24 093	24 419	24 865

Historical Statistics of Canada 11-516E.   Canadian Statistical Review 11-003E

Areas, production and exports of major crops, 1930-1982

Crop	Year	Area '000 ha	Yield kg/ha	Production '000t	Exports '000t
Wheat	1930	10 080	1 136	11 449	7 041
	1940	11 630	1 264	14 703	6 293
	1950	11 057	1 148	12 697	6 559
	1960	9 934	1 420	14 109	9 615
	1970	5 054	1 785	9 025	11 847
	1980	11 209	1 721	19 292	16 262
	1981	12 427	1 996	24 802	18 447
	1982	12 595	2 193	27 620	21 368
Oats	1930	5 368	1 216	6 526	64
	1940	4 979	1 179	5 869	364
	1950	4 528	1 368	6 196	317
	1960	3 895	1 578	6 146	94
	1970	2 786	1 954	5 445	80
	1980	1 451	2 006	2 911	45
	1981	1 561	2 043	3 188	48
	1982	1 653	2 284	3 776	58
Barley	1930	2 251	1 307	2 943	58
	1940	1 758	1 291	2 270	279
	1950	2 636	1 384	3 648	454
	1960	2 776	1 518	4 213	1 388

Crop	Year	Area '000 ha	Yield kg/ha	Production '000t	Exports '000t
	1970	4 006	2 219	8 891	1 932
	1980	4 687	2 431	11 394	3 236
	1981	5 476	2 506	13 724	5 722
	1982	5 190	2 712	14 074	4 368
Flaxseed	1930	236	546	129	10
	1940	159	497	79	—
	1950	238	529	126	77
	1960	1 017	563	573	317
	1970	1 341	908	1 218	473
	1980	555	796	442	565
	1981	465	1 005	468	448
	1982	627	1 191	747	435
Rapeseed	1960	309	815	252	306
	1970	1 639	999	1 637	504
	1980	2 080	1 194	2 483	1 372
	1981	1 401	1 311	1 837	1 359
	1982	1 717	1 231	2 114	1 271

Historical Statistics of Canada 11-516E.   Statistics Canada 22-007, 22-201.   FAO Trade Yearbook 1981

Principal wheat producers of the world

Country	1971				1981			
	Production '000 t	% of world total	Exports '000 t	% of world total	Production '000 t	% of world total	Exports '000 t	% of world total
U.S.S.R.	92 804	28%	5 773	10%	88 000	19%	2 396	2%
U.S.A.	40 034	12%	19 096	34%	76 026	17%	45 107	43%
China	29 687	9%	1	—	57 003	12%	4	—
India	20 687	6%	26	—	36 460	8%	49	—
Canada	**13 901**	**4%**	**11 488**	**20%**	**24 519**	**5%**	**18 447**	**18%**
France	14 112	4%	4 453	8%	22 782	5%	14 828	14%
Turkey	11 423	3%	—	—	17 074	4%	451	—
Australia	9 014	3%	7 310	13%	16 400	4%	10 676	10%
Pakistan	6 796	2%	—	—	11 340	3%	—	—
World	327 922	100%	56 811	100%	458 195	100%	105 120	100%

FAO Production Yearbook, 1981.   FAO Trade Yearbook, 1981.   UN Statistical Yearbook, 1981

Agricultural land use in Canada, 1951-1981

	Unit	1951	1961	1971	1981
Total farm area	'000ha	**69 619**	**69 020**	**67 867**	**65 889**
Percentage of total land area in farming	%	7.7%	7.6%	7.5%	7.1%
Number of farms	No.	**623 091**	**480 903**	**366 128**	**318 361**
Average farm size	ha	112	144	185	207
Area of improved farmland	'000ha	**38 741**	**41 361**	**43 256**	**46 122**
Improved land under crops	%	64%	60%	64%	67%
Improved pasture	%	10%	10%	10%	10%
Improved summer fallow	%	23%	27%	25%	21%
Other improved land	%	3%	3%	1%	2%
Area of unimproved farmland	'000ha	**30 878**	**27 659**	**24 608**	**19 768**
Unimproved woodland	%	30%	25%	19%	18%
Other unimproved land	%	70%	75%	81%	82%

1961, 1971, 1981 Census of Canada, Statistics Canada 96-901

Quantities of fish landed in marine and inland areas, 1930-1982

Year	Marine Fishing Areas t	Inland Fishing Areas t
1930	188 073	15 067
1940	418 284	13 388
1950	534 783	21 463
1960	610 552	18 581
1970	942 541	12 171
1980	1 279 726	54 297
1981	1 348 921	49 956
1982	1 331 400	57 948

Historical Statistics of Canada 11-516E.   FAO Yearbook of Fishery Statistics 1982

Forested areas and wood volumes by province

	Area of forest land	Area of productive forest land	% productive forest	Volume of wood cut
	'000 km²	'000 km²	%	million m³
Newfoundland	142	85	60%	464
Prince Edward I.	3	3	100%	33
Nova Scotia	41	29	71%	219
New Brunswick	65	62	95%	516
Quebec	940	849	90%	4 929
Ontario	807	426	53%	3 599
Manitoba	349	139	40%	745
Saskatchewan	178	89	50%	608
Alberta	349	234	67%	1 501
British Columbia	633	515	81%	9 731
Yukon Territory	242	67	28%	255
Northwest Terr.	615	143	23%	446
CANADA	**4 364**	**2 641**	**61%**	**23 046**

Statistics Canada 25-202

Lumber production and external trade, 1930-1982

Year	Softwood production	Hardwood production	Total production	Total exports
	'000 m³	'000 m³	'000 m³	'000 $
1930	8 757	649	9 406	39 689
1940	10 239	687	10 926	69 803
1950	14 411	1 055	15 466	291 121
1960	17 861	1 045	18 906	346 300
1970	24 235	1 041	25 276	663 775
1980	43 441	1 472	44 913	3 350 409
1981	39 237	980	40 217	2 989 706
1982	36 364	1 088	37 452	2 889 143

Statistics Canada 25-202

Volume of wood cut by type of product, 1978 & 1982

'000 m³

	Canada	N.W.T. & Y.T.	B.C.	Alta.	Sask.	Man.	Ont.	Que.	N.B.	N.S.	P.E.I.	Nfld.
Logs & bolts[1] 1978	**111 536**	113	74 951	3 817	1 614	640	8 255	18 576	2 265	974	71	261
1982	**88 869**	42	56 178	4 259	1 382	527	7 634	15 787	2 061	784	68	147
Pulpwood 1978	**38 832**	—	—	2 351	974	937	10 605	13 096	5 947	2 968	45	1 909
1982	**31 084**	—	—	1 175	898	790	10 222	10 316	3 956	1 943	48	1 736
Other round wood[2] 1978	**1 344**	17	213	249	119	93	139	396	93	11	6	8
1982	**1 390**	14	53	147	122	57	113	793	62	11	9	9
Total industrial wood 1978	**151 712**	130	75 164	6 417	2 707	1 670	18 999	32 068	8 305	3 953	122	2 178
1982	**121 343**	56	56 231	5 581	2 402	1 374	17 969	26 896	6 079	2 738	125	1 892
Fuelwood 1978	**4 138**	37	[3]	102	156	133	1 189	2 011	204	204	37	110
1978	**5 673**	105	[3]	133	124	124	1 809	2 237	241	263	150	487
Total 1978	**155 895**	**167**	**75 164**	**6 519**	**2 863**	**1 804**	**20 188**	**34 079**	**8 509**	**4 157**	**159**	**2 288**
1982	**127 016**	**161**	**56 231**	**5 714**	**2 526**	**1 494**	**19 778**	**29 133**	**6 320**	**3 001**	**275**	**2 379**

(1) Logs and bolts refers to felled wood in its natural state, with no bark removed.   (2) Roundwood refers to all felled wood in its natural state with or without bark. It may be impregnated, shaped or pointed.

(3) Included in logs and bolts category.   Logging Industry of Canada, Statistics Canada, 25-202

Production and exports of wood pulp and paper, 1930-1982

Year	PRODUCTION '000t				EXPORTS '000t			
	Total pulp	Groundwood	Total paper	Newsprint	Total pulp	Groundwood	Total paper	Newsprint
1930	3 283	2 072	2 655	2 266	689	190	2 153	2 116
1940	4 800	2 998	3 918	3 179	970	185	3 166	2 942
1950	7 687	4 455	6 180	4 825	1 675	225	4 643	4 480
1960	10 397	5 335	8 095	6 068	2 360	213	5 888	5 616
1970	16 609	6 940	11 252	7 996	5 063	251	8 266	7 340
1980	20 687	7 748	13 385	8 368	7 244	311	9 744	7 707
1981	20 572	8 085	13 956	8 933	6 756	274	9 748	7 987
1982	18 514	7 214	12 473	7 785	6 122	272	8 874	7 078

Groundwood is obtained by grinding or milling rounds or chips of wood into their fibres.   Historical Statistics of Canada 11-503E.   Statistics Canada 25-202

Supply and disposal of coal, 1930-1982

million t

		1930	1940	1950	1960	1970	1980	1981	1982
Supply:	Production	14.9	17.6	18.5	10.8	16.6	36.7	40.1	42.8
	Imports	18.8	17.4	27.0	13.6	18.9	15.6	15.0	15.4
Disposal:	Domestic use	33.0	34.5	45.1	23.5	31.1	37.3	38.4	41.4
	Exports	0.6	0.5	0.4	0.8	4.4	15.3	15.8	16.0

Statistics Canada 26-206; Historical Statistics of Canada 11-516E

Supply and disposal of crude oil, 1960-1982

'000 m³

		1960	1965	1970	1975	1980	1981	1982
Supply:	Production	36 498	50 814	80 207	91 661	89 522	80 342	79 463
	Imports	21 187	22 926	33 127	47 892	32 230	29 546	19 661
	Total supply	**57 676**	**73 740**	**113 334**	**139 553**	**121 752**	**109 888**	**99 124**
Disposal:	Deliveries to Refineries	46 778	56 056	74 285	98 095	109 802	100 776	86 199
	Exports	10 731	17 144	38 867	40 849	11 939	9 462	12 397

The Crude Petroleum and Natural Gas Industry, 26-213

Supply and disposal of natural gas, 1960-1982

million m³

		1960	1965	1970	1975	1980	1981	1982
Supply:	Production	15 895	29 667	51 790	69 347	69 835	67 857	69 289
	Imports	153	503	308	290	3	3	5
	[1]Other receipts	704	491	2 035	3 641	5 537	4 410	5 143
	Total supply	**16 752**	**30 661**	**54 133**	**73 278**	**75 375**	**72 270**	**74 437**
Disposal:	Sales	10 509	16 243	26 006	37 559	43 264	42 897	43 901
	Exports	4 788	11 472	22 096	26 839	22 563	21 584	22 198
	Pipeline uses	515	1 568	3 203	3 546	2 849	2 855	2 060
	[2]Deliveries	940	1 378	2 828	5 334	6 699	4 934	6 278

1 = From distributor storage, or liquified petroleum gas for gas enrichment.　　2 = Direct deliveries for industrial consumption or distributor storage.

Supply and disposal of electrical energy, 1965-1982

million mWh

	1965	1970	1975	1980	1981	1982
Supply:						
Hydro-Generation	117.1	156.7	202.4	251.2	263.4	255.3
Thermal-Generation	27.2	48.0	70.9	116.1	116.7	121.5
Total Generation	144.3	204.7	273.4	367.3	380.1	376.8
Total Imports	3.6	3.2	3.9	2.9	1.5	2.8
Total Supply	**147.8**	**207.9**	**277.4**	**370.2**	**381.6**	**379.7**
Disposal:						
Domestic & Farm use	29.7	43.4	64.1	92.4	95.1	99.3
Pulp & Paper Industry	21.3	25.2	25.2	32.8	33.2	32.1
Mineral Industry	7.4	11.8	15.3	20.6	21.8	20.1
Commercial use	23.9	39.7	65.1	75.2	77.3	79.5
Other Industries	48.5	64.3	68.4	86.6	90.6	84.5
Losses unaccounted for	13.3	17.8	27.8	32.3	28.4	29.9
Total Exports	3.7	5.6	11.4	30.3	35.4	34.2
Total Disposal	**147.8**	**207.9**	**277.4**	**370.2**	**381.6**	**379.6**

Statistics Canada 57-202

Generation of electrical energy, 1982 *percentage*

	Hydro Generation	Thermal Generation Steam	Nuclear	Internal Combustion	Gas Turbine	% of Total Canadian Energy Generated
Canada	68	22	10	—	—	100
N.W.T.	50	—	—	50	—	—
Y.T.	80	—	—	20	—	—
B.C.	95	4	—	1	—	13
Alta.	6	89	—	—	5	7
Sask.	24	75	—	—	1	3
Man.	99	1	—	—	—	5
Ont.	34	32	33	—	1	29
Que.	100	—	—	—	—	27
N.B.	31	66	3	—	—	2
N.S.	16	84	—	—	—	2
P.E.I.	—	100	—	—	—	—
Nfld.	97	3	—	—	—	12

Mineral production in Canada, 1950-1982

	1950	1960	1970	1980	1981	1982
Metallic Minerals						
Cobalt '000 kg	265	1 619	2 110	2 118	2 080	1 274
Copper '000 kg	239 685	398 489	610 274	716 363	691 328	612 455
Gold '000 g	125 902	131 232	68 295	50 620	52 034	64 735
Iron Ore '000 t	3 663	21 896	53 151	49 068	49 551	33 198
Lead '000 kg	150 316	186 561	353 060	251 627	268 556	272 187
Magnesium '000 kg	—	6 612	9 392	9 252	—	—
Molybdenum '000 kg	47	349	15 319	11 889	12 850	13 961
Nickel '000 kg	112 181	194 595	277 488	184 802	160 247	88 581
Platinum '000 g	3 544	13 721	13 665	12 776	11 902	7 105
Silver '000 kg	658	964	1 254	1 070	1 129	1 314
Tungsten '000 kg	129	314	1 691	4 007	2 515	3 030
Uranium '000 kg	—	11 568	3 725	6 739	7 507	7 643
Zinc '000 kg	284 153	369 106	1 135 705	883 697	911 178	965 607
Non-Metallic Minerals						
Asbestos '000 t	889	1 136	1 689	1 323	1 122	834
Gypsum '000 t	3 725	5 289	6 420	7 336	7 025	5 987
Peat Moss '000 t	76	189	325	466	462	487
Potash '000 t	—	—	3 475	7 201	6 549	5 309
Quartz '000 t	1 759	2 297	3 290	2 252	1 765	1 784
Salt '000 t	873	3 368	5 445	7 423	7 240	7 940
Sodium Sulphate '000 t	133	217	499	481	535	547
Structural Materials						
Clay Products $	—	—	—	108 453	119 116	95 993
Cement '000 t	2 977	5 880	8 073	10 274	10 145	8 426
Lime '000 t	1 142	1 554	1 703	2 554	2 555	2 197
Sand & Gravel '000 t	74 265	195 147	205 898	276 452	260 134	216 274
Stone '000 t	—	—	—	103 366	85 091	59 181

Mineral Production of Canada, Statistics Canada 26-202.   Historical Statistics of Canada

Value of mineral production, 1972 and 1982

by province as a percentage of total Canadian production

	1972						1982				
	Metallic Minerals	Non-Metallic Minerals	Fuels	Structural Materials	Total		Metallic Minerals	Non-Metallic Minerals	Fuels	Structural Materials	Total
CANADA mil. $	**2952.4**	**513.5**	**2 367.6**	**569.7**	**6 403.2**	**CANADA mil. $**	**6874.2**	**1979.3**	**23 038.4**	**1 729.6**	**33 837.0**
Yukon	3%	3%	—	—	2%	Yukon Territory	2%	—	—	—	—
Northwest Territory	4%	—	—	—	2%	Northwest Terr.	6%	—	—	2%	1%
British Columbia	14%	5%	8%	12%	11%	British Columbia	17%	5%	6%	10%	8%
Alberta	—	4%	81%	8%	30%	Alberta	—	28%	87%	18%	63%
Saskatchewan	1%	29%	10%	2%	6%	Saskatchewan	4%	35%	6%	3%	7%
Manitoba	9%	—	—	6%	5%	Manitoba	5%	1%	—	4%	2%
Ontario	42%	9%	—	41%	24%	Ontario	33%	7%	—	35%	9%
Quebec	15%	42%	—	24%	12%	Quebec	18%	18%	—	21%	6%
New Brunswick	3%	—	—	2%	2%	New Brunswick	6%	1%	—	3%	1%
Nova Scotia	—	4%	1%	3%	1%	Nova Scotia	—	4%	1%	3%	1%
Prince Edward I.	—	—	—	—	—	Prince Edward I.	—	—	—	—	—
Newfoundland	9%	4%	—	2%	5%	Newfoundland	9%	1%	—	1%	2%
Total for Canada	46%	8%	37%	9%	100%	Total for Canada	21%	6%	68%	5%	100%

Mineral Production of Canada, Statistics Canada 26-202

Value of mineral production, 1982

million $

Minerals	Canada	Y.T.	N.W.T.	B.C.	Alta.	Sask.	Man.	Ont.	Que.	N.B.	N.S.	P.E.I.	Nfld.
Cobalt	39	—	—	—	—	—	10	28	—	—	—	—	—
Copper	1 195	15	—	548	—	10	95	309	185	26	—	—	7
Gold	968	40	91	115	—	4	26	300	386	3	—	—	2
Iron Ore	1 201	—	—	20	—	—	—	181	428	—	—	—	572
Iron Remelt	104	—	—	—	—	—	—	104	—	—	—	—	—
Lead	197	26	46	61	—	—	1	4	—	59	—	—	1
Molybdenum	159	—	—	155	—	—	—	—	4	—	—	—	—
Nickel	601	—	—	—	—	—	17	429	—	—	—	—	—
Platinum	82	—	—	—	—	—	—	82	—	—	—	—	—
Silver	415	30	16	158	—	2	8	111	18	73	—	—	1
Uranium	837	—	—	—	—	248	—	589	—	—	—	—	—
Zinc	1 036	59	229	81	—	5	34	280	72	247	—	—	30
Total Metals	**6 834**	**170**	**382**	**1 138**	**—**	**269**	**191**	**2 313**	**1 197**	**408**	**—**	**—**	**613**
Asbestos	365	—	—	57	—	—	—	—	298	—	—	—	10
Gypsum	47	—	—	5	—	—	2	5	—	—	31	—	3
Potash	631	—	—	—	—	631	—	—	—	—	—	—	—
Peat	54	—	—	3	7	1	8	1	17	16	2	—	—
Quartz	32	—	—	—	3	1	2	8	—	—	—	—	1
Salt	157	—	—	—	15	19	—	88	—	—	—	—	—
Sodium Sulphate	47	—	—	—	7	44	—	—	—	—	—	—	—
Sulphur in smelter gas	42	—	—	12	—	—	—	15	11	2	—	—	—
Sulphur elemental	570	—	—	16	551	—	—	2	—	—	—	—	—
Total Non-metals	**1 945**	**—**	**—**	**93**	**583**	**696**	**12**	**119**	**326**	**18**	**33**	**—**	**14**
Coal	1 294	—	—	620	410	74	—	—	—	25	166	—	—
Natural Gas	7 262	—	20	366	6 808	27	—	41	—	—	—	—	—
Natural Gas By-products	2 302	—	—	36	2 259	7	—	—	—	—	—	—	—
Petroleum—Crude	12 180	—	15	330	10 538	1 192	90	15	—	—	—	—	—
Total Fuels	**23 038**	**—**	**35**	**1 352**	**20 015**	**1 300**	**90**	**56**	**—**	**25**	**166**	**—**	**—**
Clay Products	96	—	—	6	11	3	2	52	14	2	5	—	1
Cement	674	—	—	69	164	22	25	20	148	17	18	—	6
Lime	142	—	—	7	10	—	5	90	27	4	—	—	—
Sand & Gravel	555	1	41	75	130	21	28	157	66	8	17	2	9
Stone	263	—	1	22	3	—	12	100	107	12	5	—	2
Total Structural Materials	**1 730**	**1**	**42**	**179**	**318**	**46**	**72**	**419**	**362**	**43**	**45**	**2**	**18**

Mineral Production of Canada, Statistics Canada 26-202

Employees, salaries and value added by region for all manufacturing, 1961-1981

	1961				1971				1981		
	Number of Employees	Salaries and Wages	Value Added[1]		Number of Employees	Salaries and Wages	Value Added[1]		Number of Employees	Salaries and Wages	Value Added[1]
	'000	million $	million $		'000	million $	million $		'000	million $	million $
Canada	**1 352.4**	**5 701.0**	**10 948.9**	**Canada**	**1 628.1**	**12 128.1**	**23 184.6**	**Canada**	**1 853.3**	**37 090.0**	**78 251.7**
Atlantic Provinces	62.3	211.6	405.9	Atlantic Provinces	75.4	445.1	766.4	Atlantic Provinces	91.6	1 625.5	3 083.3
Quebec	452.5	1 775.7	3 331.6	Quebec	508.6	3 459.0	6 406.2	Quebec	525.8	9 843.6	21 199.5
Ontario	638.8	2 859.7	5 553.2	Ontario	800.0	6 326.5	12 537.2	Ontario	911.8	18 460.4	39 887.8
Prairie Provinces	95.3	383.1	769.5	Prairie Provinces	114.8	798.4	1 562.2	Prairie Provinces	165.0	3 279.9	7 202.9
British Columbia	103.5	470.9	888.7	British Columbia	129.3	1 099.1	1 912.6	British Columbia	159.1	3 880.6	6 878.2

Statistics Canada 31-203, 1961, 1971, 1981.   [1] Value added is the value of manufactured goods shipped less the cost of materials and fuel used.

Manufacturing activities of leading industries ranked by value of shipments of goods of own manufacture, 1981

CANADA	Establishments	Value of Shipments million $	Value Added[1] million $
1 Petroleum Refining	40	19 958	2 623
2 Pulp & Paper Mills	144	11 619	5 406
3 Motor Vehicle Manufacture	21	11 403	1 893
4 Slaughtering & Meat Processing	501	7 603	1 244
5 Iron & Steel Mills	33	7 000	2 737
6 Miscellaneous Machinery Manufacture	1 301	5 825	2 949
7 Sawmills & Planing Mills	1 313	4 973	1 828
8 Dairy Produce Industry	416	4 883	1 106
9 Motor Vehicle Parts & Accessories	344	4 358	2 030
10 Metal Stamping & Pressing	701	3 390	1 191

BRITISH COLUMBIA			
1 Sawmills & Planing	342	3 031	1 046
2 Pulp & Paper Mills	23	2 610	1 163
3 Petroleum Refining	7	1 841	218
4 Smelting & Refining	4	607	311
5 Veneer & Plywood Mills	28	544	226
6 Fish Products Industry	52	440	165
7 Miscellaneous Machinery Manufacture	144	432	240
8 Dairy Produce Industry	26	383	92
9 Slaughtering & Meat Processing	41	377	90
10 Shipbuilding & Repair	21	284	178

ALBERTA			
1 Petroleum Refining	6	2 787	68
2 Slaughtering & Meat Processing	64	1 816	189
3 Industrial Chemicals (Organic)	7	828	398
4 Miscellaneous Machinery Manufacture	135	637	213
5 Steel Pipe & Tuse Mills	4	365	90
6 Dairy Produce Industry	34	347	80
7 Feed Industry	72	267	46
8 Publishing & Printing	73	226	163
9 Ready Mix Concrete Manufacture	75	222	84
10 Pulp & Paper Mills	5	212	97

SASKATCHEWAN			
1 Slaughtering & Meat Processing	32	320	52
2 Agricultural Implements Industry	30	158	87
3 Feed Industry	23	69	15
4 Publishing & Printing	52	67	48
5 Fabricated Structural Metals Industry	9	54	32
6 Ready Mix Concrete Manufacture	39	49	18
7 Breweries	4	40	25
8 Sawmills & Planing Mills	12	39	14
9 Soft Drink Manufacture	12	38	21
10 Bakeries	61	31	17

MANITOBA			
1 Slaughtering & Meat Processing	32	509	87
2 Agricultural Implements Industry	25	395	227
3 Dairy Produce Industry	31	158	39
4 Metal Stamping & Pressing	30	146	44
5 Aircraft & Aircraft Parts	10	136	86
6 Men's Clothing Manufacture	37	127	62
7 Womens Clothing Manufacture	21	126	72
8 Commercial Printing	85	116	63
9 Feed Industry	33	113	18
10 Miscellaneous Food Processing	16	97	26

ONTARIO	Establishments	Value of Shipments million $	Value Added[1] million $
1 Motor Vehicle Manufacture	10	9 336	1 442
2 Petroleum Refining	10	7 062	1 256
3 Iron & Steel Mills	22	5 610	2 260
4 Motor Vehicle Parts & Accessories	266	4 217	2 016
5 Miscellaneous Machinery Manufacture	689	3 560	1 747
6 Pulp & Paper Mills	36	2 848	1 274
7 Slaughtering & Meat Processing	181	2 675	541
8 Industrial Chemicals (Organic)	21	1 897	488
9 Miscellaneous Food Processing	130	1 842	759
10 Metal Stamping & Pressing	338	1 720	675

QUEBEC			
1 Pulp & Paper Mills	56	4 102	2 010
2 Dairy Produce Industry	112	1 946	456
3 Smelting & Refining	12	1 758	958
4 Slaughtering & Meat Processing	130	1 747	249
5 Aircraft & Aircraft Parts	44	1 265	898
6 Metal Stamping & Processing	161	1 097	309
7 Miscellaneous Machinery Manufacture	254	1 039	568
8 Feed Industry	223	989	133
9 Commercial Printing	805	968	499
10 Sawmills & Planing Mills	411	966	429

NEW BRUNSWICK			
1 Pulp & Paper Mills	11	847	308
2 Fish Produce Industry	59	173	57
3 Sawmills & Planing Mills	80	157	45
4 Dairy Produce Industry	10	67	24
5 Soft Drinks Manufacture	8	45	17
6 Bakeries	27	43	23
7 Publishing & Printing	18	32	23
8 Miscellaneous Machine Manufacture	13	30	10
9 Feed Industry	6	29	4
10 Miscellaneous Food Processing	7	27	4

NOVA SCOTIA			
1 Fish Produce Industry	92	432	135
2 Pulp & Paper Mills	5	378	220
3 Dairy Produce Industry	15	136	34
4 Feed Industry	13	65	6
5 Shipbuilding & Repair	14	62	30
6 Publishing & Printing	17	50	37
7 Sawmills & Planing Mills	96	48	24
8 Bakeries	42	37	19
9 Fruit & Vegetable Canners & Preserves	8	37	19
10 Communications Equipment & Manuf.	8	32	20

PRINCE EDWARD ISLAND			
1 Dairy Produce Industry	12	58	12
2 Fish Produce Industry	19	50	17
3 Fertilizer Manufacture	5	15	3

NEWFOUNDLAND			
1 Fish Produce Industry	84	340	163
2 Pulp & Paper Mills	3	351	197
3 Publishing & Printing	8	21	16
4 Bakeries	11	17	9
5 Ready-Mix Concrete Manufacture	9	16	7

Statistics Canada 31-203.   [1] Value added refers to the value of manufactured goods shipped less the costs of materials and fuel used.

Canadian communications, 1982

	Canada	Y.T.	N.W.T.	B.C.	Alta.	Sask.	Man.	Ont.	Que.	N.B.	N.S.	P.E.I.	Nfld.
Road vehicles '000	14 310	19	18	2 074	1 787	687	670	5 060	2 826	372	535	68	190
Trucks '000	3 239	11	10	591	460	294	187	1 067	294	99	147	17	56
Rail track length, km	65 828	93	209	7 292	9 269	12 385	6 430	15 366	8 322	2 629	1 968	407	1 458
Oil pipeline length, km	36 377	0	0	2 689	19 099	8 185	2 033	3 584	699	0	0	0	0
over 500 mm diameter, km	7 958	0	0	835	2 880	1 952	720	1 348	223	0	0	0	0
Telephones '000	16 802		46	1 982	1 841	681	748	6 142	4 077	411	533	73	268
telephones/100 persons	69		64	71	79	69	72	70	63	58	62	59	47

Road motor vehicles 53-219, Railway transport 52-207, Oil pipeline transport 55-201, Telephone Statistics 56-203

Goods carried by rail

million t

Wheat	24.5
Coal	18.7
Potassium muriate	7.9
Barley	7.2
Lumber	5.5
Pulpwood	4.9
Sulphur	4.6
Wood pulp	4.3
Newsprint paper	4.1
Gypsum	3.9

Commodity origin and destination, Statistics Canada 52-214
Road Transport 53-006
International seaborne shipping port statistics 54-211

Goods carried by road

million t

Crude non-metallic minerals	22.9
Petroleum & coal products	13.6
Non-metallic—basic products	10.6
Crude wood materials	9.5
Wood—fabricated	8.3
General & Unclassified	6.5
Dairy products	6.0
Iron & steel plus alloys	5.7
Coal & crude petroleum	5.5
Special industry machinery	4.8
Other foods	4.8
Cereal grains	3.4
Chemicals	3.2

International cargo handled at Canadian ports

'000 t

Port	Total Cargo	Loaded	Container	Unloaded	Container
Vancouver	45 962	42 769	684	2 119	389
Port Cartier	19 103	17 260	0	1 842	0
Sept Iles	14 122	13 083	0	1 039	0
Montreal	9 372	4 589	1 604	1 793	1 385
Halifax	7 239	2 785	778	3 100	575
Quebec	7 164	6 319	1	843	0
St. John's	5 905	1 436	576	3 639	254
Nanticoke	5 554	20	0	5 533	0
Baie Comeau	5 159	3 638	0	1 521	0
Hamilton	4 762	921	2	3 839	99
Port Alfred	3 324	371	0	2 953	79
Thunder Bay	3 119	2 972	0	146	0
Sault Ste. Marie	3 012	270	0	2 742	0

Coastal cargo, 1982

'000 t

		Province of loading								
Province of unloading	Total	N.W.T.	B.C.	Man.	Ont.	Que.	N.B.	N.S.	P.E.I.	Nfld.
Newfoundland	2 159	—	—	—	87	694	305	851	—	221
Prince Edward I.	411	—	—	—	6	53	83	269	—	—
Nova Scotia	2 607	—	29	4	185	1 139	897	276	—	77
New Brunswick	1 499	—	—	—	24	973	24	466	6	7
Quebec	23 258	0.4	18	—	15 431	6 418	434	806	26	124
Ontario	12 425	0.1	—	—	9 866	2 475	20	45	—	19
Manitoba	—	—	—	—	—	—	—	—	—	—
British Columbia	23 374	—	23 374	—	—	—	—	—	—	—
Northwest Terr.	147	—	—	15	—	126	6	—	—	—
Total	65 882	0.5	23 421	19	25 601	11 881	1 769	2 712	32	447

Coastwise Shipping Statistics, Statistics Canada 54-210

Canadian airports

Top fifteen by number of passengers

	'000 Passengers	Of which domestic '000	Cargo '000 kg		'000 Passengers	Of which domestic '000	Cargo '000 kg
Toronto	12 240	4 595	167 619	Mirabel Int.	1 071	—	62 349
Vancouver	5 858	2 885	66 850	Edmonton Mun.	789	789	2 139
Montréal Int.	5 433	2 299	28 075	Regina	587	437	1 924
Calgary	3 797	2 269	27 590	Saskatoon	560	419	2 010
Edmonton Int.	2 033	2 004	24 952	Victoria	532	431	1 251
Winnipeg	2 032	1 230	22 999	St. John's	511	385	7 043
Ottawa	1 804	1 353	4 849	Québec	473	374	1 314
Halifax	1 531	808	14 470				

Air carrier traffic at Canadian airports 51-203

Railway commodity origin and destination

'000t

Origin	Total	Marine exports	U.S. by rail	N.W.T.	B.C.	Alta.	Sask.	Man.	Ont.	Que.	N.B.	N.S.	P.E.I.	Nfld.
Newfoundland	209	—	24	0	—	—	—	—	2	11	—	1	0	170
Prince Edward I.	145	0	0	0	—	—	—	1	100	43	—	0	—	1
Nova Scotia	4 911	1 271	269	0	9	14	3	19	71	139	147	2 925	9	35
New Brunswick	2 993	714	243	0	6	6	—	23	216	431	1 183	76	50	47
Quebec	14 678	1 085	4 864	2	282	335	81	226	2 386	4 754	411	187	11	56
Ontario	32 231	3 814	5 654	4	979	1 601	368	948	13 611	3 863	608	642	49	89
Manitoba	8 598	4 847	551	—	190	329	421	963	772	425	27	67	4	2
Saskatchewan	28 702	19 452	4 069	0	672	227	483	570	2 774	324	49	60	20	3
Alberta	33 679	20 467	4 391	231	2 214	2 555	344	487	2 318	555	44	59	4	13
British Columbia	24 329	12 316	3 497	14	4 282	1 392	136	260	1 638	689	51	38	2	14
Northwest Terr.	336	59	—	0	265	1	0	10	0	—	0	0	0	0
U.S. by rail	9 734	608	3 339	3	828	660	130	149	2 803	1 077	83	45	2	7
Maritime import	2 917	0	445	—	85	311	29	57	1 301	635	11	41	0	2
Total	163 464	64 633	27 346	254	9 812	7 431	1 995	3 712	27 991	12 944	2 615	4 141	152	438

Canadian international trade, 1983

million $

	Imports, 1983	Exports, 1983
Total	**75 694**	**88 426**
Principal trading areas		
U.S.A.	54 203	64 461
U.K.	1 811	2 446
Other E.E.C.	4 140	4 184
Japan	4 410	4 734
Other O.E.C.D.	2 093	1 578
Other American	3 825	2 758
Others	5 213	8 266

Exports—Principal countries, 1983

Exports to	million $	% of total	% variation 82/81	83/82
U.S.A.	64 461	72.9	+4	+15
Japan	4 734	5.4	+2	+4
U.K.	2 446	2.7	−19	−8
U.S.S.R.	1 762	2.0	+11	−15
China	1 605	1.8	+21	+31
W. Germany	1 156	1.3	−4	−6
Netherlands	953	1.1	−12	−8
Belgium—Lux.	696	0.8	−7	−10
France	627	0.7	−28	−11
Brazil	598	0.7	−22	+13

Imports—Principal countries, 1983

Imports from	million $	% of total	% variation 82/81	83/82
U.S.A.	54 203	71.6	−12	+13
Japan	4 410	5.8	−13	+25
U.K.	1 811	2.4	−20	−5
W. Germany	1 576	2.1	−14	+14
Mexico	1 079	1.4	−5	+8
Venezuela	1 014	1.3	−24	+44
Taiwan	926	1.2	−9	+40
France	841	1.1	—	−4
Hong Kong	821	1.1	−1	+23
Italy	798	1.1	+3	+10

Exports—Principal commodities, 1983

million $

Live animals	340
Food, Feed, Beverages & Tobacco	10 076
Meat & Fish	2 247
Cereals	5 991
Wheat	4 648
Crude Materials, Inedible	14 387
Metal ores & Scrap	2 897
Iron ore	972
Copper ore	476
Nickel ore	337
Zinc ore	282
Crude Petroleum	3 457
Natural gas	3 958
Coal	1 313
Fabricated Materials, Inedible	29 989
Wood & Paper	12 935
Lumber	3 896
Wood pulp	3 057
Newsprint	4 005
Textiles	227
Chemicals	4 345
Petroleum & Coal Products	2 815
Iron & Steel	1 634
Non Ferrous	5 416
Aluminium	1 744
Copper	696
Nickel	497
Electricity	1 228
Industrial Machinery	2 367
Agricultural Machinery	551
Transport Equipment	23 732
Cars	9 537
Trucks	4 204
Engines	1 549
Parts	5 749
Other Equipment & tools	2 761

Imports 65-203, Exports 65-202

Imports—Principal commodities, 1983

million $

Live animals	132
Food, Feed, Beverages & Tobacco	4 871
Fruit & Veg.	1 880
Coffee	401
Raw Sugar	201
Crude Materials, Inedible	7 201
Metal ores & Scrap	1 650
Coal	840
Crude Petroleum	3 274
Fabricated Materials, Inedible	14 009
Wood & Paper	1 199
Textiles	1 479
Chemicals	4 393
Iron & Steel	1 176
Non Ferrous	2 054
General Purpose Machinery	2 168
Special Industry Machinery	3 136
Agricultural Machinery	1 513
Transport Equipment	22 598
Cars	6 212
Other equipment & tools	11 323

Land use categories are shown as a percentage of land area for each country. Inland waters are not included. Arable land includes land under temporary and permanent crops. Forest and woodland is land under natural or planted trees whether productive or not. Other land includes unused but potentially productive land, built-up areas, parks, roads, wasteland, and any other land not included in other categories. The total land area of each country is given in the Population of Countries table.

Country	Arable	Permanent Pasture	Forest & Woodland	Other Land
Afghanistan	12	46	4	38
Albania	27	20	45	8
Algeria	3	15	2	80
Angola	3	23	43	31
Argentina	13	52	22	13
Australia	5	60	14	21
Austria	19	25	40	16
Bangladesh	69	4	16	11
Belgium	27	21	21	31
Belize	3	2	44	51
Benin	17	4	35	44
Bhutan	2	5	69	24
Bolivia	3	25	52	20
Botswana	1	76	2	21
Brazil	9	19	68	4
Brunei	2	1	79	18
Bulgaria	38	18	35	9
Burkina Faso	10	36	26	28
Burma	15	1	49	35
Burundi	51	36	2	11
Cambodia	17	3	76	4
Cameroon	15	18	54	13
Canada	5	3	35	57
Central African Rep.	3	5	64	28
Chad	3	36	16	45
Chile	7	16	21	56
China	11	31	13	45
Colombia	6	29	50	15
Congo	2	29	63	6
Costa Rica	10	41	34	15
Cuba	28	22	17	33
Cyprus	47	10	18	25
Czechoslovakia	41	13	37	9
Denmark	62	6	12	20
Djibouti	—	11	—	89
Dominican Republic	26	31	13	30
Ecuador	9	14	52	25
Egypt	3	—	—	97
El Salvador	35	29	7	29
Equatorial Guinea	8	4	61	27
Ethiopia	13	41	24	22
Fiji	13	3	65	19
Finland	8	1	76	15
France	34	24	27	15
French Guiana	—	—	82	18
Gabon	2	18	78	2
Gambia	27	16	21	36
Germany, East	47	12	28	13
Germany, West	31	19	30	20
Ghana	12	15	38	35
Greece	30	40	20	10
Greenland	—	1	—	99
Guatemala	17	8	41	34
Guinea	6	12	43	39
Guinea-Bissau	10	46	38	6
Guyana	3	6	83	8
Haiti	33	18	4	45
Honduras	16	30	36	18
Hong Kong	8	1	13	78
Hungary	58	14	18	10
Iceland	—	23	1	76
India	57	4	23	16
Indonesia	11	7	67	15
Iran	10	27	11	52
Iraq	13	9	3	75
Irish Republic	14	70	5	11
Israel	21	40	6	33
Italy	42	17	22	19
Ivory Coast	13	9	29	49
Jamaica	25	19	28	28
Japan	13	2	68	17
Jordan	15	1	1	83
Kenya	4	7	4	85
Korea, North	19	—	75	6
Korea, South	22	1	67	10

Country	Arable	Permanent Pasture	Forest & Woodland	Other Land
Kuwait	—	8	—	92
Laos	4	3	56	37
Lebanon	34	1	7	58
Lesotho	10	66	—	24
Liberia	4	2	39	55
Libya	1	7	—	92
Luxembourg	25	31	19	25
Madagascar	6	58	23	13
Malawi	25	20	46	9
Malaysia	13	—	68	19
Mali	1	25	7	67
Malta	44	—	—	56
Mauritania	—	38	15	47
Mauritius	58	4	31	7
Mexico	12	39	25	24
Mongolia	1	79	9	11
Morocco	19	28	12	41
Mozambique	4	56	20	20
Namibia	1	64	13	22
Nepal	17	13	33	37
Netherlands	25	34	9	32
New Zealand	2	53	26	19
Nicaragua	10	42	37	11
Niger	3	8	2	87
Nigeria	33	23	16	28
Norway	3	—	27	70
Oman	—	5	—	95
Pakistan	26	6	4	64
Papua New Guinea	1	—	71	28
Paraguay	5	39	52	4
Peru	3	21	55	21
Philippines	33	3	41	23
Poland	49	13	28	10
Portugal	39	6	38	17
Puerto Rico	16	38	20	26
Romania	46	19	28	7
Rwanda	40	18	11	31
Saudi Arabia	1	39	1	59
Senegal	27	30	28	15
Sierra Leone	24	31	29	16
Singapore	13	—	5	82
Somali Rep.	2	46	14	38
South Africa	11	66	4	19
Spain	41	21	31	7
Sri Lanka	33	7	37	23
Sudan	5	24	20	51
Surinam	1	—	96	3
Swaziland	11	64	6	19
Sweden	7	2	64	27
Switzerland	11	40	26	23
Syria	31	45	3	21
Tanzania	6	39	47	8
Thailand	35	1	30	34
Togo	26	4	30	40
Trinidad & Tobago	31	2	45	22
Tunisia	30	16	3	51
Turkey	37	12	26	25
Uganda	29	25	30	16
United Arab Emirates	—	2	—	98
U.S.S.R.	11	17	41	31
United Kingdom	29	47	9	15
United States	21	26	31	22
Uruguay	11	82	3	4
Venezuela	4	20	39	37
Vietnam	18	15	32	35
Western Samoa	20	—	70	10
Yemen, North	14	36	8	42
Yemen, South	1	27	7	65
Yugoslavia	31	25	36	8
Zaïre	3	4	78	15
Zambia	7	47	27	19
Zimbabwe	7	13	61	19

Source: F.A.O. Production Yearbook 1982

Country	Area in thousands of square km	Population in thousands	Density of population per sq. km.	Capital Population in thousands
Afghanistan	647	16 786	26	Kabul (1036)
Albania	29	2 858	99	Tiranë (198)
Algeria	2 382	20 293	9	Algiers (1 503)
Angola	1 247	7 452	6	Luanda (475)
Argentina	2 767	28 432	10	Buenos Aires (9 927)
Australia	7 687	15 175	2	Canberra (220)
Austria	84	7 571	90	Vienna (1 516)
Bangladesh	144	92 619	643	Dacca (3 459)
Belgium	31	9 845	318	Brussels (995)
Belize	23	171	7	Belmopan (3)
Benin	113	3 618	32	Porto-Novo (132)
Bhutan	47	1 355	29	Thimphu (60)
Bolivia	1 099	5 916	5	Sucre (63) La Paz (635)
Botswana	600	859	1	Gaborone (60)
Brazil	8 512	126 806	15	Brasilia (1 306)
Brunei	6	250	42	Bandar Seri Begawan (58)
Bulgaria	111	9 107	82	Sofia (1 052)
Burma	677	37 065	55	Rangoon (2 276)
Burundi	28	4 460	159	Bujumbura (157)
Cambodia	181	6 981	39	Phnom Penh (400)
Cameroon	475	8 865	19	Yaoundé (314)
Canada	9 976	24 625	2	Ottawa (718)
Central African Rep.	623	2 405	4	Bangui (302)
Chad	1 284	4 643	4	Ndjamena (303)
Chile	757	11 487	15	Santiago (3 831)
China	9 597	1 020 673	106	Peking (9 231)
Colombia	1 139	28 776	25	Bogota (2 855)
Congo	342	1 621	5	Brazzaville (422)
Costa Rica	51	2 324	46	San José (265)
Cuba	115	9 782	85	Havana (1 924)
Cyprus	9	645	72	Nicosia (161)
Czechoslovakia	128	15 369	120	Prague (1 184)
Denmark	43	5 118	119	Copenhagen (1 382)
Djibouti	22	332	15	Djibouti (150)
Dominican Republic	49	5 744	117	Santo Domingo (1 103)
Ecuador	284	8 945	31	Quito (844)
Egypt	1 001	44 673	45	Cairo (5 074)
El Salvador	21	4 999	238	San Salvador (366)
Equatorial Guinea	28	381	14	Rey Malabo (37)
Ethiopia	1 222	32 775	27	Addis Abeba (1 277)
Fiji	18	658	37	Suva (68)
Finland	337	4 824	14	Helsinki (483)
France	547	54 221	99	Paris (9 863)
French Guiana	91	64	1	Cayenne (39)
Gabon	268	563	2	Libréville (186)
Gambia	11	635	58	Banjul (109)
Germany, East	108	16 864	156	East Berlin (1 158)
Germany, West	249	61 638	248	Bonn (288)
Ghana	239	12 244	51	Accra (738)
Greece	132	9 793	74	Athens (3 027)
Greenland	2 176	52	0.02	Godthåb (10)
Guatemala	109	7 699	71	Guatemala (793)
Guinea	246	5 285	21	Conakry (526)
Guinea-Bissau	36	594	17	Bissau (109)
Guyana	215	922	4	Georgetown (187)
Haiti	28	5 201	186	Port-au-Prince (888)
Honduras	112	3 955	35	Tegucigalpa (473)
Hong Kong	1	5 233	5 233	Hong Kong (1 184)
Hungary	93	10 702	115	Budapest (2 060)
Iceland	103	236	2	Reykjavik (84)
India	3 288	711 664	216	Delhi (5 729)
Indonesia	2 027	153 032	75	Jakarta (4 576)
Iran	1 648	40 240	24	Tehran (4 496)
Iraq	435	13 997	32	Baghdad (2 969)
Irish Republic	70	3 483	50	Dublin (525)
Israel	21	4 022	192	Jerusalem (407)
Italy	301	56 276	187	Rome (2 831)
Ivory Coast	322	8 568	27	Abidjan (850)
Jamaica	11	2 253	205	Kingston (671)
Japan	372	118 449	318	Tokyo (8 349)
Jordan	98	3 489	36	Amman (649)
Kenya	583	17 864	31	Nairobi (835)
Korea, North	121	18 747	155	Pyongyang (1 500)
Korea, South	98	39 331	401	Seoul (8 367)

Country	Area in thousands of square km	Population in thousands	Density of population per sq. km.	Capital Population in thousands
Kuwait	18	1 562	87	Kuwait (775)
Laos	237	3 902	16	Vientiane (90)
Lebanon	10	2 739	274	Beirut (702)
Lesotho	30	1 409	47	Maseru (45)
Liberia	111	2 113	19	Monrovia (204)
Libya	1 760	3 224	2	Tripoli (551)
Luxembourg	3	357	119	Luxembourg (79)
Madagascar	587	9 233	16	Antananarivo (400)
Malawi	118	6 267	53	Lilongwe (103)
Malaysia	330	14 765	45	Kuala Lumpur (938)
Mali	1 240	7 342	6	Bamako (419)
Malta	0.3	360	1 200	Valletta (14)
Mauritania	1 031	1 730	2	Nouakchott (135)
Mauritius	2	983	492	Port Louis (146)
Mexico	1 973	73 011	37	Mexico (14 750)
Mongolia	1 565	1 764	1	Ulan Bator (419)
Morocco	447	21 667	48	Rabat (597)
Mozambique	783	11 052	14	Maputo (384)
Namibia	824	852	1	Windhoek (61)
Nepal	141	15 020	107	Katmandu (210)
Netherlands	41	14 310	349	Amsterdam (936)
New Zealand	269	3 158	12	Wellington (321)
Nicaragua	130	2 918	22	Managua (608)
Niger	1 267	5 646	4	Niamey (130)
Nigeria	924	82 392	89	Lagos (1 477)
Norway	324	4 115	13	Oslo (624)
Oman	212	948	4	Muscat (25)
Pakistan	804	87 125	108	Islamabad (77)
Panama	76	2 043	27	Panama (655)
Papua New Guinea	462	3 094	7	Port Moresby (123)
Paraguay	407	3 370	8	Asunción (602)
Peru	1 285	18 790	15	Lima (4 601)
Philippines	300	50 740	169	Manila (1 479)
Poland	313	36 227	116	Warsaw (1 612)
Portugal	92	10 056	109	Lisbon (818)
Puerto Rico	9	3 952	439	San Juan (1 086)
Romania	238	22 638	95	Bucharest (2 090)
Rwanda	26	5 276	203	Kigali (90)
Saudi Arabia	2 150	9 684	5	Riyadh (667)
Senegal	196	5 968	30	Dakar (799)
Sierra Leone	72	3 672	51	Freetown (214)
Singapore	0.6	2 472	4 120	Singapore (2 443)
Somali Republic	638	5 116	8	Mogadishu (400)
South Africa	1 221	31 008	25	Pretoria (563) Cape Town (1 107)
Spain	505	37 935	75	Madrid (3 159)
Sri Lanka	66	15 189	230	Colombo (1 412)
Sudan	2 506	19 451	8	Khartoum (561)
Surinam	163	407	2	Paramaribo (151)
Swaziland	17	585	34	Mbabane (23)
Sweden	450	8 325	19	Stockholm (1 387)
Switzerland	41	6 478	158	Berne (289)
Syria	185	9 660	52	Damascus (1 156)
Taiwan	36	18 458	513	Taipei (2 271)
Tanzania	945	19 111	20	Dar-es-Salaam (757)
Thailand	514	48 450	94	Bangkok (4 871)
Togo	56	2 747	49	Lomé (247)
Trinidad and Tobago	5	1 202	240	Port of Spain (66)
Tunisia	164	6 672	41	Tunis (944)
Turkey	781	46 312	59	Ankara (2 204)
Uganda	236	14 057	60	Kampala (332)
United Arab Emirates	84	790	9	Abu Dhabi (449)
U.S.S.R.	22 402	269 994	12	Moscow (8 203)
United Kingdom	245	55 782	228	London (6 696)
United States	9 363	232 057	25	Washington (3 061)
*Upper Volta	274	6 360	23	Ouagadougou (173)
Uruguay	178	2 947	17	Montevideo (1 173)
Venezuela	912	14 714	16	Caracas (2 849)
Vietnam	330	56 205	170	Hanoi (2 571)
Western Samoa	3	159	53	Apia (32)
Yemen, North	195	6 077	31	Sana (448)
Yemen, South	288	2 093	7	Aden (285)
Yugoslavia	256	22 646	88	Belgrade (775)
Zaire	2 345	26 377	11	Kinshasa (2 242)
Zambia	753	6 163	8	Lusaka (641)
Zimbabwe	391	7 540	19	Harare (686)

* Renamed Burkina Faso

The population figures used are from censuses or more recent estimates and are given in thousands for towns and cities over 500 000. Where possible the population of the metropolitan areas is given e.g. Greater London, Greater New York, etc.

AFRICA

ALGERIA (1974)
Algiers 1 503

EGYPT (1976)
Cairo 5 074
Alexandria 2 314
El Giza 1 230

ETHIOPIA (1980)
Addis Abeba 1 277

GUINEA (1972)
Conakry 526

IVORY COAST (1976)
Abidjan 850

LIBYA (1973)
Tripoli 551

MOROCCO (1973)
Casablanca 1 753
Rabat-Salé 596

NIGERIA (1975)
Lagos 1 477
Ibadan 847

SENEGAL (1976)
Dakar 799

SOUTH AFRICA (1970)
Johannesburg 1 441
Cape Town 698
Durban 737
Pretoria 545

TANZANIA (1978)
Dar-es-Salaam 757

TUNISIA (1976)
Tunis 944

ZAIRE (1975)
Kinshasa 2 242

ZAMBIA (1980)
Lusaka 641

ZIMBABWE (1981)
Harare 686

ASIA

AFGHANISTAN (1979)
Kabul 1 036

BANGLADESH (1982)
Dacca 3 459
Chittagong 1 388
Khulna 623

BURMA (1977)
Rangoon 2 276

CAMBODIA (1981)
Phnom Penh 400

CHINA (1970)
Shanghai *(1982)* 11 860
Peking *(1982)* 9 231
Tientsin *(1982)* 7 746
Shenyang 2 800
Wuhan 2 560
Canton 2 500
Chungking 2 400
Nanking 1 750
Harbin 1 670
Luta 1 650
Sian 1 600
Lanchow 1 450
Taiyuan 1 350
Tsingtao 1 300
Chengtu 1 250
Changchun 1 200
Kunming 1 100
Tsinan 1 100
Fushun 1 080
Anshan 1 050
Chengchow 1 050
Hangchow 960
Tangshan 950
Paotow 920
Tzepo 850
Changsha 825
Shihkiachwang 800
Tsitsihar 760
Soochow 730
Kirin 720
Suchow 700
Foochow 680
Nanchang 675
Kweiyang 660
Wusih 650
Hofei 630
Hwainan 600
Penki 600
Loyang 580
Nanning 550
Huhehot 530
Sining 500
Wulumuchi 500

HONG KONG (1981)
Kowloon 2 450
Hong Kong 1 184
Tsuen Wan 599

INDIA (1981)
Calcutta 9 194
Bombay 8 243
Delhi 5 729
Madras 4 289
Bangalore 2 922
Ahmadabad 2 548
Hyderabad 2 546
Pune 1 686
Kanpur 1 639
Nagpur 1 302
Jaipur 1 015
Lucknow 1 008
Coimbatore 920
Patna 919
Surat 914
Madurai 908
Indore 829
Varanasi 797
Jabalpur 757
Agra 747
Vadodara 744
Cochin 686
Dhanbad 678
Bhopal 671
Jamshedpur 670
Allahabad 650
Ulhasnagar 649
Tiruchchirapalli 610
Ludhiana 606
Srinagar 606
Vishakhapatnam 604
Amritsar 595
Gwalior 556
Calicut 546
Vijawada 543
Meerut 537
Dharwad 527
Trivandrum 520
Salem 519
Solapur 515
Jodhpur 506
Ranchi 503

INDONESIA (1971)
Jakarta 4 576
Surabaya 1 556
Bandung 1 202
Semarang 647
Medan 636
Palembang 583

IRAN (1976)
Tehran 4 496
Esfahan 672
Mashhad 670
Tabriz 599

IRAQ (1970)
Baghdad 2 969

ISRAEL (1981)
Tel Aviv-Jaffa 335

JAPAN (1980)
Tōkyō 8 349
Yokohama 2 774
Osaka 2 648
Nagoya 2 088
Kyōto 1 473
Sapporo 1 402
Kōbe 1 367
Fukuoka 1 089
Kitakyūshū 1 065
Kawasaki 1 041
Hiroshima 899
Sakai 810
Chiba 746
Sendai 665
Okayama 546
Kumamoto 526
Amagasaki 524
Higashiōsaka 522
Kagoshima 505

KOREA, NORTH (1970)
Pyongyang 1 500
Chongjin 265

KOREA, SOUTH (1980)
Seoul 8 367
Pusan 3 160
Taegu 1 607
Inchon 1 085
Kwangju 728
Taejon 652

KUWAIT (1975)
Kuwait 775

LEBANON (1980)
Beirut 702

MALAYSIA (1980)
Kuala Lumpur 938

PAKISTAN (1972)
Karachi 3 499
Lahore 2 165
Faisalabad 822
Hyderabad 628
Rawalpindi 615
Multan 542

PHILIPPINES (1975)
Manila 1 479
Quezon City 957

SAUDI ARABIA (1974)
Riyadh 667
Jedda 561

SINGAPORE (1981)
Singapore 2 443

SRI LANKA (1981)
Colombo 1 412

SYRIA (1979)
Damascus 1 156
Aleppo 919

TAIWAN (1981)
Taipei 2 271
Kaohsiung 1 227
Taichung 607
Tainan 595

THAILAND (1979)
Bangkok 4 871

TURKEY (1980)
Istanbul 2 854
Ankara 2 204
Izmir 754
Adana 569

VIETNAM (1973-79)
Ho Chi Minh City 3 420
Hanoi 2 571
Haiphong 1 279

AUSTRALASIA

AUSTRALIA (1981)
Sydney 3 205
Melbourne 2 723
Brisbane 1 029
Adelaide 932
Perth 899

NEW ZEALAND (1981)
Auckland 770

EUROPE

AUSTRIA (1981)
Vienna 1 516

BELGIUM (1983)
Brussels 989

BULGARIA (1980)
Sofia 1 052

CZECHOSLOVAKIA (1982)
Prague 1 184

DENMARK (1981)
Copenhagen 1 382

FINLAND (1979)
Helsinki 893

FRANCE (1975)
Paris 9 863
Lyon 1 152
Marseille 1 004
Lille 929
Bordeaux 591

GERMANY, EAST (1981)
East Berlin 1 158
Leipzig 562
Dresden 517

GERMANY, WEST (1980)
West Berlin 1 896
Hamburg 1 645
München 1 299
Cologne 977
Essen 648
Frankfurt am Main 629
Dortmund 608
Düsseldorf 590
Stuttgart 581
Duisburg 558
Bremen 555
Hannover 535

GREECE (1981)
Athens 3 027
Thessaloniki 707

HUNGARY (1980)
Budapest 2 060

IRISH REPUBLIC (1981)
Dublin 525

ITALY (1981)
Rome 2 831
Milano 1 635
Napoli 1 211
Torino 1 104
Genova 760
Palermo 700

NETHERLANDS (1983)
Rotterdam 1 025
Amsterdam 936
s'Gravenhage 674

NORWAY (1980)
Oslo 624

POLAND (1981)
Warsaw 1 612
Lódz 843
Kraków 723
Wroclaw 622
Poznań 558

PORTUGAL (1981)
Lisbon 818
Oporto 330

ROMANIA (1980)
Bucharest 2 090

SPAIN (1981)
Madrid 3 159
Barcelona 1 753
Valencia 745
Sevilla 646
Zaragoza 572
Malaga 502

SWEDEN (1980)
Stockholm 1 387
Göteborg 693

SWITZERLAND (1982)
Zürich 705

U.S.S.R. (1981)
Moskva 8 203
Leningrad 4 676
Kiyev 2 248
Tashkent 1 858
Kharkov 1 485
Gorkiy 1 367
Novosibirsk 1 343
Minsk 1 333
Sverdlovsk 1 239
Kuybyshev 1 238
Dnepropetrovsk 1 100
Tbilisi 1 095
Odessa 1 072
Chelyabinsk 1 055
Yerevan 1 055
Baku 1 046
Omsk 1 044
Donetsk 1 040
Perm 1 018
Kazan 1 011
Ufa 1 009
Alma-Ata 975
Rostov 957
Volgograd 948
Saratov 873
Riga 850
Krasnoyarsk 820
Zaporozhye 812
Voronezh 809
Lvov 688
Krivoy Rog 663
Yaroslavl 608
Karaganda 583
Krasnodar 581
Novokuznetsk 581
Ustinov 574
Irkutsk 568
Vladivostok 565
Frunze 552
Barnaul 549
Khabarovsk 545
Kishinev 539
Togliatti 533
Tula 521
Zhdanov 511
Dushanbe 510
Vilnius 503
Penza 500

UNITED KINGDOM (1981)
London 6 696
Birmingham 920
Glasgow 762
Liverpool 510

YUGOSLAVIA (1971)
Belgrade 775
Zagreb 602

NORTH AMERICA

CANADA (1981)
Toronto 2 999
Montréal 2 828
Vancouver 1 268
Ottawa 718
Edmonton 657
Calgary 593
Winnipeg 585
Québec 576
Hamilton 542

COSTA RICA (1978)
San José 563

CUBA (1981)
Havana 1 924

DOMINICAN REPUBLIC (1978)
Santo Domingo 1 103

GUATEMALA (1979)
Guatemala City 793

HAITI (1982)
Port-au-Prince 888

JAMAICA (1980)
Kingston 671

MEXICO (1979)
Mexico City 14 750
Guadalajara 2 468
Netzahualcóyotl 2 331
Monterrey 2 019
Puebla de Zaragoza 711
Ciudad Juárez 625
León de los Aldamas 625

NICARAGUA (1979)
Managua 608

PANAMA (1981)
Panama 655

PUERTO RICO (1980)
San Juan 1 086

UNITED STATES OF AMERICA (1980)
New York 16 121
Los Angeles 11 498
Chicago 7 870
Philadelphia 5 548
San Francisco 5 180
Detroit 4 618
Boston 3 448
Houston 3 101
Washington 3 061
Dallas 2 975
Cleveland 2 834
Miami 2 644
St. Louis 2 356
Pittsburgh 2 264
Baltimore 2 174
Minneapolis-St Paul 2 114
Seattle 2 093
Atlanta 2 030
San Diego 1 817
Cincinnati 1 660
Denver 1 621
Milwaukee 1 570
Tampa 1 569
Phoenix 1 509
Kansas City 1 327
Indianapolis 1 306
Portland (Or.) 1 243
Buffalo 1 243
New Orleans 1 187
Providence 1 096
Columbus (Ohio) 1 093
San Antonio 1 072
Sacramento 1 014
Dayton 1 014
Rochester 971
Salt Lake City 936
Memphis 913
Louisville 906
Nashville-Davidson 851
Birmingham 847
Oklahoma 834
Greensboro 827
Norfolk 807
Albany (N.Y.) 795
Toledo 792
Honolulu 763
Jacksonville (Fla.) 738
Hartford 726
Orlando 700
Tulsa 689
Syracuse 643
Scranton 640
Charlotte 637
Allentown 635
Richmond 632
Grand Rapids 602
Omaha 570
Greenville 569
West Palm Beach 577
Austin 537
Tucson 531
Springfield (Mass.) 531
Youngstown 531
Raleigh 531
Flint 522
Fresno 515

SOUTH AMERICA

ARGENTINA (1980)
Buenos Aires 9 927
Córdoba 982
Rosario 955
Mendoza 597
La Plata 560

BOLIVIA (1970)
La Paz 720

BRAZIL (1980)
São Paulo 8 732
Rio de Janeiro 5 539
Belo Horizonte 1 937
Salvador 1 502
Recife 1 433
Fortaleza 1 307
Brasilia 1 306
Pôrto Alegre 1 221
Nova Iguaçu 1 184
Curitiba 943
Belém 934
Goiânia 680
Duque de Caxias 666
São Gonçalo 660
Santo André 634
Campinas 587

CHILE (1982)
Santiago 3 831

COLOMBIA (1973)
Bogotá 2 855
Medellin 1 159
Cali 990
Barranquilla 692

ECUADOR (1981)
Guayaquil 1 169
Quito 844

PARAGUAY (1978)
Asunción 602

PERU (1981)
Lima 4 601

URUGUAY (1975)
Montevideo 1 173

VENEZUELA (1979)
Caracas 2 849
Maracaibo 874

Country I = Imports E = Exports		Total trade (million U.S. $)	Primary Comms. as a % of total trade	Manuf'd Goods as a % of total trade	Fuels as a % of total trade	Growth rate % 1970-1980
Afghanistan	I	839	17	82	23	17.3
	E	705	79	15	18	23.4
Algeria	I	10 891	27	73	3	24.0
	E	9 164	100	1	2	29.8
Angola	I	680	22	78	1	8.4
	E	666	91	9	1	5.2
Argentina	I	5 081	28	72	13	16.9
	E	7 518	76	24	18	16.1
Australia*	I	24 187	22	77	14	16.3
	E	22 002	70	27	15	15.1
Austria	I	19 559	32	68	19	17.6
	E	15 690	14	86	25	16.9
Bahamas	I	7 014	94	6	91	35.5
	E	6 546	96	4	98	53.5
Bahrain	I	3 730	67	33	62	29.2
	E	3 789	90	11	58	28.6
Bangladesh	I	2 300	68	31	19	19.9
	E	769	32	68	65	17.4
Barbados	I	550	37	63	17	15.2
	E	257	36	63	49	16.8
Belgium-Lux.	I	58 007	39	58	21	16.7
	E	52 392	23	73	23	15.3
Benin	I	312	29	71	10	19.5
	E	27	88	8	40	-2.9
Bolivia	I	496	21	80	2	16.1
	E	832	62	39	2	15.3
Brazil	I	21 884	62	48	37	21.4
	E	19 551	59	38	48	21.5
Brunei	I	599	20	78	1	19.5
	E	4 068	100	0	0	41.0
Bulgaria*	I	10 600	—	—	16	17.5
	E	10 500	33	66	19	16.4
Burma	I	408	17	83	8	7.5
	E	380	94	6	12	14.0
Burundi	I	214	29	70	26	20.2
	E	88	97	3	11	10.4
Cameroon	I	1 205	22	78	10	17.5
	E	998	82	18	14	15.2
Canada*	I	55 064	24	75	12	15.6
	E	68 498	43	56	12	14.3
Chad	I	46	31	69	14	-4.0
	E	10	92	8	39	-1.0
Chile	I	3 529	42	57	20	19.1
	E	3 822	28	72	18	11.1
China	I	18 625	42	52	2	800
	E	22 380	47	42	23	950
Colombia	I	5 478	28	71	14	17.9
	I	3 095	72	27	25	14.3
Congo	I	431	35	65	7	18.7
	E	955	92	8	3	36.5
Costa Rica	I	887	26	70	15	17.5
	E	872	66	28	24	16.2
Cuba	I	6 293	33	48	10	13.1
	E	5 536	94	0	11	18.1
Cyprus	I	1 249	40	60	22	15.1
	E	565	44	55	43	16.1
Czechoslovakia*	I	15 499	43	56	23	13.6
	E	15,734	13	87	23	13.1
Denmark	I	17 162	41	57	24	13.4
	E	15 527	43	58	27	15.1
Dominican Rep.*	I	1 248	53	48	33	16.2
	E	768	81	19	48	15.0
Ecuador	I	2 130	12	87	2	21.1
	E	60	97	3	2	26.6
Egypt	I	9 078	43	57	3	24.6
	E	3 120	87	13	8	14.0
El Salvador	I	883	23	77	8	14.9
	E	646	72	28	10	12.0
Ethiopia	I	787	27	73	17	14.2
	E	404	98	2	24	10.7
Fiji	I	515	40	56	22	17.8
	E	285	96	3	61	14.8
Finland	I	13 387	42	57	31	16.5
	E	13 132	25	75	31	17.8
France	I	115 405	44	56	29	18.2
	E	92 268	25	75	34	17.1
Gabon	I	674	22	78	2	23.2
	E	821	98	2	1	32.0
Germany, East*	I	21 743	—	—	—	13.8
	E	20 196	8	91	—	14.3
Germany, West	I	155 856	43	55	25	16.8
	E	176 428	12	86	23	16.1
Ghana	I	1 106	33	65	17	10.1
	E	1 063	95	6	18	9.7
Greece	I	10 023	39	61	22	14.7
	E	4 297	42	57	46	18.7
Guatemala	I	1 362	46	54	38	18.1
	E	1173	71	29	68	14.1
Guyana	I	283	28	63	16	12.0
	E	256	78	22	16	11.3
Haiti	I	266	40	60	13	19.9
	E	226	49	51	15	15.3
Honduras	I	949	27	73	16	16.5
	E	760	88	13	20	16.2
Hong Kong	I	23 554	25	74	8	19.0
	E	20 985	7	92	9	19.3
Hungary	I	8 825	34	66	17	12.5
	E	8 795	34	65	17	12.8
Iceland	I	942	30	70	17	18.7
	E	685	83	17	19	17.8
India	I	13 941	50	51	33	19.0
	E	7 960	41	59	43	16.2
Indonesia	I	16 858	29	71	13	26.0
	E	22 293	95	5	9	31.5
Iran	I	12 250	20	80	0	22.1
	E	17 610	99	1	0	18.5
Iraq	I	4 213	15	85	0	30.2
	E	10 878	100	1	0	33.4
Ireland	I	9 699	31	67	15	18.98
	E	8 064	38	58	20	20.1
Israel	I	7 848	42	58	26	16.7
	E	4 901	18	82	36	19.9
Italy	I	86 213	56	44	35	17.6
	E	73 490	16	84	41	17.1
Ivory Coast	I	2 184	44	55	22	18.0
	E	2 288	90	10	21	16.6
Jamaica	I	1 470	54	46	33	9.8
	E	820	94	6	51	10.0
Japan	I	131 932	77	22	52	20.2
	E	138 911	3	97	48	20.6
Jordan	I	3 241	40	63	17	29.6
	E	737	61	39	61	27.9
Kenya	I	1 585	36	64	28	15.1
	E	954	87	13	56	13.0
Korea, South	I	24 251	55	45	30	26.4
	E	21 853	9	91	37	34.2
Kuwait	I	6 969	17	82	1	26.5
	E	10 890	90	10	0	26.4
Lebanon	I	1 701	40	60	8	17.0
	E	436	21	79	33	11.9
Liberia	I	477	51	49	27	11.1
	E	531	98	1	25	8.5
Libya	I	8 382	22	78	1	23.8
	E	13 951	100	0	0	29.0
Madagascar	I	600	26	74	15	14.8
	E	402	94	6	26	10.3

Country I = Imports E = Exports		Total trade (million U.S. $)	Primary Comms. * as a % of total trade	Manuf'd Goods as a % of total trade	Fuels as a % of total trade	Growth rate % 1970- 1980
Malawi	I	314	21	79	10	13.9
	E	259	94	4	16	15.2
Malaysia	I	13 132	34	65	17	21.9
	E	12 884	75	24	18	19.8
Mali	I	365	41	54	11	25.3
	E	155	87	12	54	18.2
Malta	I	938	34	66	14	16.4
	E	497	7	93	29	24.8
Mauritania	I	273	41	58	8	15.2
	E	179	99	1	8	10.2
Mauritius	I	463	39	61	10	19.8
	E	362	88	11	11	16.0
Mexico	I	15 042	25	75	6	23.7
	E	21 006	59	41	12	28.1
Morocco	I	4 315	47	54	25	18.3
	E	2 062	70	30	47	14.9
Mozambique	I	278	24	77	8	-2.2
	E	129	97	2	17	-2.7
Netherlands	I	62 583	46	53	26	15.6
	E	66 322	49	50	25	17.4
Neths. Antilles	I	6771	88	12	83	21.5
	E	6054	98	2	98	21.5
New Caledonia	I	367	50	50	28	5.3
	E	265	20	78	33	5.4
New Zealand	I	5 752	29	71	20	14.8
	E	5 524	76	24	21	14.7
Nicaragua	I	883	37	63	21	17.2
	E	448	86	14	43	10.2
Niger	I	462	42	58	15	21.9
	E	448	98	2	17	27.3
Nigeria	I	20 821	21	78	2	29.3
	E	16 667	99	1	1	34.0
Norway	I	15 479	27	73	14	14.0
	E	17 595	61	38	13	19.8
Pakistan	I	5 381	49	51	28	18.6
	E	2 552	47	51	55	13.5
Panama	I	1 569	39	61	29	14.2
	E	309	90	10	91	10.4
Papua New Guinea*	I	1 017	33	63	11	13.8
	E	753	93	2	9	21.2
Paraguay*	I	631	37	63	21	20.7
	E	375	89	10	26	14.9
Peru	I	3 803	26	74	2	15.3
	E	3 255	59	41	2	12.0
Philippines	I	7 946	41	46	30	18.0
	E	4 852	53	25	45	15.8
Poland*	I	10 248	47	53	20	14.2
	E	11 208	21	79	23	12.7
Portugal	I	9 313	47	53	24	16.4
	E	4 111	29	70	58	14.3
Reunion	I	804	38	60	10	15.5
	E	69	88	11	72	6.9
Romania*	I	12 458	25	72	7	18.3
	E	12 610	29	69	6	19.1
Rwanda	I	243	36	65	8	23.7
	E	76	98	0	19	11.8
Saudi Arabia	I	40 654	17	83	1	42.9
	E	79 123	99	1	0	42.6
Senegal	I	861	48	51	19	14.6
	E	442	77	23	37	9.6
Sierra Leone	I	311	39	61	14	13.9
	E	153	45	55	28	6.0
Singapore	I	28 167	46	53	34	24.6
	E	20 788	43	50	44	26.7
Somalia	I	144	36	64	6	19.8
	E	317	96	3	11	16.4
South Africa*	I	21 006	11	88	1	9.9
	E	12 502	41	49	1	18.2
Spain	I	31 535	62	38	43	19.1
	E	20 522	27	73	67	21.7
Sri Lanka	I	1 771	46	53	25	15.0
	E	1 015	78	22	45	10.6
Sudan	I	1 285	41	59	19	16.9
	E	499	99	1	58	7.6
Sweden	I	27 570	36	64	25	13.7
	E	26 803	18	81	25	14.0
Switzerland	I	28 670	24	76	12	13.1
	E	26 024	5	95	13	14.3
Syria	I	4 028	31	69	7	27.2
	E	2 026	92	8	12	23.6
Tanzania	I	1 140	36	64	21	14.3
	E	566	86	14	48	7.3
Thailand	I	8 573	40	56	30	20.3
	E	6 490	66	32	44	23.1
Togo	I	435	36	64	8	18.9
	E	208	85	16	18	12.8
Trinidad & Tobago	I	3 697	52	48	37	17.2
	E	3 072	92	8	30	20.5
Tunisia	I	3 287	42	58	21	24.7
	E	1 959	66	34	31	25.4
Turkey	I	8 753	52	48	44	23.1
	E	5 701	62	38	83	20.8
Uganda	I	293	10	90	2	-0.3
	E	345	96	4	1	1.0
U.S.S.R.*	I	77 793	31	65	4	18.1
	E	86 949	50	37	4	18.0
United Kingdom	I	99 656	35	64	14	15.1
	E	96 994	14	83	14	16.4
United States	I	254 884	43	55	31	19.1
	E	212 275	29	67	37	16.4
† Upper Volta	I	338	43	57	16	19.2
	E	75	85	15	70	13.9
Uruguay	I	1 042	49	51	31	21.4
	E	1 023	70	30	42	16.2
Venezuela*	I	12 823	21	79	1	18.5
	E	16 512	96	4	1	18.6
Yemen, North	I	1 853	36	64	7	50.0
	E	23	49	47	—	22.6
Yemen, South	I	1 527	—	—	—	15.3
	E	779	—	—	—	3.1
Yugoslavia	I	14 057	40	60	24	16.7
	E	10 713	18	82	35	18.6
Zaire	I	480	28	71	10	2.1
	E	569	29	70	11	-1.6
Zambia*	I	831	23	77	14	8.6
	E	1 059	3	97	16	3.4
Zimbabwe	I	1 204	8	68	24	8.0
	E	1 129	53	45	2	11.0

† Renamed Burkina Faso

Source: U.N. Monthly Bulletin of Statistics and U.N. Yearbook of International Trade Statistics, 1981

Primary Commodities refer to sections 0-4 of the Standard International Trade Classification (Revised) and Manufactured Goods include sections 5-8. These, together with a nominal amount of miscellaneous products make up the total trade. Fuels are included in the Primary Commodities and Manufactured Goods categories, but have also been separated out. All the trade values used in the compilation of this table are at current prices. Unless otherwise stated imports are in terms of c.i.f. transaction values and exports f.o.b. transaction values. The latest figures available have been used and these are usually for 1982, or at least for a year in the period 1975-1981.

* = Imports f.o.b.

Country or Dependency	Total G.D.P. million $	G.D.P per capita $	Annual average change %	Origin of G.D.P. % Agricultural	Origin of G.D.P. % Mining and Mf'g
Afghanistan	2 809	200	4.1	63	20
Algeria	31 359	1 724	—	7	40
Angola	2 701	432	—	—	—
Argentina	36 749	1 448	2.5	9	27
Australia	148 064	10 127	3.4	6	27
Austria	76 975	10 250	3.7	4	27
Bangladesh	12 683	145	6.2	48	8
Belgium	119 105	12 080	3.2	2	26
Belize	116	757	3.3	21	13
Benin	747	221	2.2	44	6
Bhutan	104	90	—	—	—
Bolivia	5 507	983	5.2	16	24
Botswana	608	800	12.5	12	31
Brazil	248 592	2 021	9.2	10	27
Brunei	4 864	21 148	—	1	83
Bulgaria	34 000*	3 820*	4.7	19	48
Burma	4 299	133	3.0	47	11
Burundi	899	212	3.7	51	9
Cambodia	1 192	147	2.2	41	17
Cameroon	4 934	612	—	31	12
Canada	253 379	10 584	4.2	4	23
Central African Rep.	397	193	1.3	32	15
Chad	693	172	—	41.4	16.4
Chile	4 952	485	0.8	7	27
China	328 000	320	5.6	—	—
Colombia	33 509	1 237	5.8	23	23
Congo	879	602	—	8	46
Costa Rica	4 036	1 860	6.1	23	20
Cuba	9 097	990	2.5	4	43
Cyprus	2 103	3 338	1.5	9	18
Czechoslovakia	137 200*	8 970*	4.9	7	61
Denmark	66 377	12 964	2.9	5	17
Djibouti	105	493	—	5.2	7.6
Dominican Republic	5 496	1 041	7.8	18	19
Ecuador	11 368	1 361	8.0	12	29
Egypt	17 821	435	8.0	22	27
El Salvador	3 388	715	4.8	23	15
Equatorial Guinea	82	257	—	—	—
Ethiopia	2 669	97	2.5	45	10
Fiji	997	1 609	5.2	21	12
Finland	49 893	10 438	2.9	8	25
France	651 893	12 137	3.7	4	27
Gabon	2 925	5 417	—	6	49
Gambia	146	256	—	56	3
Germany, East	162 900*	9 750*	4.5	9	74
Germany, West	818 977	13 304	2.6	2	40
Ghana	4 594	465	-0.7	61	9
Greece	40 148	4 182	4.7	16	19
Guatemala	7 853	1 082	5.9	25	16
Guinea	573	130	—	43	8
Guinea-Bissau	110	208	—	—	—
Guyana	504	647	3.9	21	25
Haiti	1 419	283	4.1	31	19
Honduras	2 554	692	4.1	25	16
Hong Kong	21 618	4 264	7.4	1	26
Hungary	63 700*	5 950*	5.8	14	49
Iceland	2 855	12 413	4.8	—	—
India	159 837	241	3.6	32	17
Indonesia	69 802	472	7.6	25	36
Iran	52 649	1 577	8.8	17	21
Iraq	19 293	1 620	8.7	7	60
Irish Republic	17 825	5 243	4.6	6	35
Israel	21 019	5 431	6.7	6	27
Italy	393 954	6 907	2.9	6	33
Ivory Coast	7 714	1 014	8.6	27	11
Jamaica	1 419	1 554	1.7	8	29
Japan	1 036 159	8 873	4.6	3	32
Jordan	2 906	897	—	6	16
Kenya	6 992	426	4.7	28	12
Korea, South	60 655	1 616	10.3	17	30
Kuwait	23 330	18 086	2.5	0	67

Country or Dependency	Total G.D.P. million $	G.D.P per capita $	Annual average change %	Origin of G.D.P. % Agricultural	Origin of G.D.P. % Mining and Mf'g
Laos	300	91	—	—	—
Lebanon	3 438	1 293	—	9	13
Lesotho	148	124	—	26	12
Liberia	945	505	2.3	16	24
Libya	19 971	7 289	10.8	2	53
Luxembourg	3 509	9 723	2.6	2	31
Madagascar	2 095	253	—	32	19
Malawi	1 011	178	12.3	38	13
Malaysia	15 472	1 194	9.2	24	22
Mali	507	87	—	27	4
Malta	1 136	3 156	3.5	3	32
Mauritania	544	353	0.7	25	18
Mauritius	1 082	1 127	5.2	12	13
Mexico	121 333	1 749	5.2	8	28
Morocco	12 426	657	6.4	14	23
Mozambique	3 272	356	—	—	—
Nepal	1 763	129	2.7	63	4
Netherlands	167 656	11 857	3.1	4	26
New Zealand	21 378	6 896	—	11	24
Nicaragua	2 133	889	4.9	25	21
Niger	736	160	—	50	14
Nigeria	50 170	717	7.7	23	29
Norway	57 400	14 034	4.6	4	31
Oman	5 285	5 938	—	2	64
Pakistan	27 960	339	4.8	26	16
Panama	3 391	1 843	3.4	10	10
Papua New Guinea	2 594	823	7.8	36	18
Paraguay	4 448	1 449	8.3	28	17
Peru	19 239	1 085	3.1	9	37
Philippines	35 481	733	6.3	23	28
Poland	178 000*	4 960*	7.2	30	42
Portugal	17 795	1 816	4.5	9	30
Puerto Rico	14 653	4 260	3.7	2	37
Romania	94 700*	4 230*	10.2	15	58
Rwanda	1 163	230	1.5	46	17
Saudi Arabia	73 062	8 845	10.4	1	58
Senegal	2 403	513	1.8	18	28
Sierra Leone	932	283	1.5	30	11
Singapore	10 982	4 595	8.4	1	30
Somali Republic	492	157	—	—	—
South Africa	79 970	2 639	2.6	7	41
Spain	197 044	5 300	4.2	7	24
Sri Lanka	4 176	283	5.8	27	18
Sudan	5 310	338	3.9	37	8
Suriname	739	1 999	—	10	27
Swaziland	356	699	—	20	18
Sweden	123 664	14 881	2	3	22
Switzerland	101 493	15 933	0.3	6	40
Syria	12 905	1 437	10.4	18	23
Tanzania	4 354	263	5.0	46	9
Thailand	32 902	698	7.1	24	22
Togo	1 002	406	—	27	15
Trinidad & Tobago	4 921	4 279	4.6	2	42
Tunisia	8 728	1 370	7.9	14	25
Turkey	50 076	1 161	6.9	21	26
Uganda	2 567	222	-0.1	73	6
U.S.S.R.	1 587 000*	5 930*	3.7	15	51
United Kingdom	523 256	9 352	2.1	2	26
United States	2 587 000	11 363	3.2	3	27
† Upper Volta	826	126	—	37	11
Uruguay	9 864	3 401	3.1	7	22
Venezuela	60 028	4 315	5.5	6	39
Vietnam	—	—	2.8	29	7
Western Samoa	50*	320*	—	—	—
Yemen (North)	1 135	215	—	61	3
Yemen (South)	290	176	4.6	19	27
Yugoslavia	51 800*	2 300*	5.9	13	41
Zaire	3 785	168	0.3	26	16
Zambia	3 837	658	1.0	16	26
Zimbabwe	3 833	538	8.0	16	29

The Gross Domestic Product (G.D.P.) is a measure of a country's total production of goods and services. For comparison national currencies have been converted to U.S. dollars. Owing to difficulties in the use of exchange rates and individual national methods of calculation of G.D.P., the figures must be used cautiously. For countries where the G.D.P. figure was not available, Gross National Product (G.N.P.) figures are given which are a measure of the total value of goods and services produced in a given country together with its imports from abroad. For communist countries the Net Material Product (N.M.P.) is given. This is not strictly comparable with the G.D.P., it is the total value of goods and services but excludes many of the latter, for example, public administration, defense costs and professional services. The figures quoted are usually for 1980 or at least for a year in the period 1975-80 and the annual rate of change is from 1970-79.

*Gross National Product Figures

† Renamed Burkina Faso

The index is divided into two parts for ease of access. The first part gives place names in Canada and the second part names of places from the rest of the world.

The number in dark type which follows each name in the index refers to the page number where that feature or place will be found.

The geographical co-ordinates which follow the place name are sometimes only approximate but are close enough for the place name to be located.

An open square □ signifies that the name refers to an administrative division of a country while a solid square ■ follows the name of a country.

Rivers have been indexed to their mouth or to where they join another river. All rivers are followed by the symbol ↝.

The alphabetical order of names composed of two or more words is governed primarily by the first word and then by the second. This is an example of the rule:

> *East Tawas*
> *Eastbourne*
> *Easter Is.*
> *Eastern Ghats*
> *Eastleigh*

Names composed of a proper name (*Mexico*) and a description (*Gulf of*) are positioned alphabetically by the proper name. If the same word occurs in the name of a town and a geographical feature, the town name is listed first followed by the name or names of the geographical features

Names beginning with M', Mc are all indexed as if they were spelled Mac.

Names composed of the definite article (*Le, La, Les, L'*) and a proper name are usually alphabetized by the proper name.

> *Havre, Le*
> *Spezia, La*
> *Wash, The*

If the same place name occurs twice or more in the index and the places are in different countries, they will be followed by the country names and the latter in alphabetical order.

> *Boston, U.K.*
> *Boston, U.S.A.*

If the same place name occurs two or more times in the index and all are in the same country, each is followed by the name of the administrative subdivision in which it is located. The names are placed in the alphabetical order of the subdivisions. For example:

> *Aberdeen, Ohio, U.S.A.*
> *Aberdeen, S. Dak., U.S.A.*
> *Aberdeen, Wash., U.S.A.*

If there is a mixture of these situations, the primary order is fixed by the alphabetical sequence of the countries and the secondary order by that of the country subdivisions.

> *Bedford, U.K.*
> *Bedford, Ind., U.S.A.*
> *Bedford, Pa., U.S.A.*

Below is a list of abbreviations used in the index.

A.S.S.R. – *Autonomous Soviet Socialist Republic*
Ala. – *Alabama*
Arch. – *Archipelago*
Ariz. – *Arizona*
Ark. – *Arkansas*
B. – *Baie, Bahia, Bay, Boca, Bucht, Bugt*
B.C. – *British Columbia*
Br. – *British*
C. – *Cabo, Cap, Cape*
Calif. – *California*
Chan. – *Channel*
Col. – *Colombia*
Colo. – *Colorado*
Conn. – *Connecticut*
Cord. – *Cordillera*
D.C. – *District of Columbia*
Del. – *Delaware*
Dep. – *Dependency*
Des. – *Desert*
Dist. – *District*
Dom. Rep. – *Dominican Republic*
E. – *East*
Fd. – *Fjord*
Fed. – *Federal, Federation*

Fla. – *Florida*
Fr. – *France, French*
G. – *Golfe, Golfo, Gulf, Guba,*
Ga. – *Georgia*
Gt. – *Great*
Hts. – *Heights*
I.(s) – *Ile, Ilha, Insel, Isla Island(s)*
Ill. – *Illinois*
Ind. – *Indiana*
K. – *Kap, Kapp*
Kans. – *Kansas*
Ky. – *Kentucky*
L. – *Lac, Lacul, Lago, Lagoa, Lake, Limni, Loch, Lough*
La. – *Louisiana*
Ld. – *Land*
Mad. P. – *Madhya Pradesh*
Man. – *Manitoba*
Mass. – *Massachusetts*
Md. – *Maryland*
Mich. – *Michigan*
Minn. – *Minnesota*
Miss. – *Mississippi*
Mo. – *Missouri*
Mont. – *Montana*

Mt.(s) – *Mont, Monta, Monti, Muntii, Montaña, Mount, Mountain(s)*
Mys. – *Mysore*
N. – *North, Northern*
N.B. – *New Brunswick*
N.C. – *North Carolina*
N.Dak. – *North Dakota*
N.H. – *New Hampshire*
N.J. – *New Jersey*
N. Mex – *New Mexico*
N.S. – *Nova Scotia*
N.S.W. – *New South Wales*
N.W.T. – *North West Territories*
N.Y. – *New York*
N.Z. – *New Zealand*
Nat. Park – *National Park*
Nebr. – *Nebraska*
Neth. – *Netherlands*
Nev. – *Nevada*
Nfld. – *Newfoundland*
Nic. – *Nicaragua*
Nig. – *Nigeria*
Okla. – *Oklahoma*
Ont. – *Ontario*
Oreg. – *Oregon*

P. – *Pass, Passo, Pasul,*
P.E.I. – *Prince Edward Island*
Pa. – *Pennsylvania*
Pak. – *Pakistan*
Pass. – *Passage*
Pen. – *Peninsula*
Pk. – *Peak*
Plat. – *Plateau*
Prov. – *Province, Provincial*
Pt. – *Point*
Pta. – *Ponta, Punta*
Pte. – *Pointe*
Qué. – *Québec*
R. – *Rio, River*
R.S.F.S.R. – *Russian Soviet Federative Socialist Republic*
Ra.(s) – *Range(s)*
Rep. – *Republic*
Res. – *Reserve, Reservoir*
S. – *South*
S. Africa – *South Africa*
S.C. – *South Carolina*
S. Dak. – *South Dakota*
S.S.R. – *Soviet Socialist Republic*

Sa. – *Serra, Sierra*
Sask. – *Saskatchewan*
Scot. – *Scotland*
Sd. – *Sound*
Sp. – *Spain, Spanish*
St. – *Saint*
Str. – *Strait, Stretto*
Tenn. – *Tennessee*
Terr. – *Territory*
Tex. – *Texas*
U.K. – *United Kingdom*
U.S.A. – *United States of America*
U.S.S.R. – *Union of Soviet Socialist Republics*
Ut. P. – *Uttar Pradesh*
Va. – *Virginia*
Vic. – *Victoria*
Vt. – *Vermont*
Wash. – *Washington*
W. – *West*
W. Va. – *West Virginia*
Wis. – *Wisconsin*
Wyo. – *Wyoming*
Yug. – *Yugoslavia*
Yukon T. – *Yukon Territory*

In the index, each place name is followed by its geographical co-ordinates which allow the reader to find the place on the map. These co-ordinates give the latitude and the longitude of a particular place.

The latitude (or parallel) is the distance of a point north or south of the Equator measured as an angle with the center of the earth. The Equator is latitude 0°, the North Pole is 90° N, and the South Pole 90° S. On a globe, the lines could be drawn as concentric circles parallel to the Equator, decreasing in diameter from the Equator until they become a point at the poles. On the maps, these lines of latitude are usually represented as lines running across the map from East to West in smooth curves. They are numbered on the sides of the map. North of the Equator the numbers increase northwards, to the south they increase southwards. The degree interval between them depends on the scale of the map. On a large scale map (for example 1:2 500 000), the interval is one degree, but on a small scale map, (for example, 1:50 000 000) the interval will be ten degrees.

Lines of longitude (or meridians) cut the latitude lines at right angles on the globe and intersect with one another at the poles. Longitude is measured by an angle at the center of the earth between it & the meridian of origin (0°), which runs through Greenwich, G.B. It may be a measurement

East or West of this line from 0° to 180° in each direction. The longitude line of 180° runs North – South through the Pacific Ocean. On a particular map, the interval between the lines of longitude is always the same as that between the lines of latitude. Normally, the meridians are drawn vertically. They are numbered in the top and bottom margins and a note states East or West from Greenwich.

The unit of measurement for latitude and longitude is the degree, and it is subdivided into 60 minutes. An index entry states the position of a place in degrees and minutes, a space being left between the degrees and minutes. The latitude is followed by N(orth) or S(outh) and the longitude by E(ast) or W(est).

The diagrams below illustrate how the reader has to estimate the required distance from the nearest line of latitude or longitude. In the case of the first diagram, there is one degree, or 60 minutes between the lines and so to find the position of Moncton an estimate has to be made, 7 parts of 60 north of the 46 degree latitude line and 51 parts of 60, or 51 minutes west of the 64 degree longitude line. In the case of the second diagram, it is a little more difficult to estimate since there are 10 degrees between the lines. In the example of Anchorage, the reader has to estimate 1 degree 10 minutes north of 60° and 9° 50 minutes west of 140°.

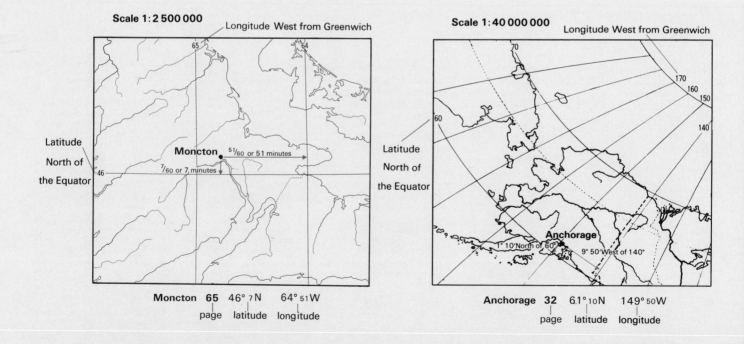

CANADA INDEX

bamasagi L. 75 50 28N 87 15W
bbey 78 50 44N 108 45W
bbotsford 85 49 5N 122 20W
berdeen 78 52 20N 106 8W
berfoyle 73 43 28N 80 9W
bernethy 78 50 45N 103 25W
bingdon 73 43 5N 79 41W
bitau → 77 59 53N 109 3W
bitau L. 77 60 27N 107 15W
bitibi → 75 51 3N 80 55W
bitibi L. 60 48 40N 79 40W
cadia 83 50 58N 114 4W
cadia Valley 81 51 8N 110 13W
cme 81 51 33N 113 30W
cton 73 43 38N 80 3W
cton Vale 67 45 39N 72 34W
dams → 85 51 25N 119 27W
dams L. 85 51 10N 119 40W
delaide Pen. 87 68 15N 97 30W
dlavik Is. 62 55 2N 57 45W
dmiral 78 49 43N 108 1W
dmiral's Beach 63 47 1N 53 39W
dmiralty I. 87 69 25N 101 10W
dmiralty Inlet 87 72 30N 86 0W
dvocate Harbour 65 45 20N 64 47W
gassiz 85 49 14N 121 46W
gawa → 75 47 23N 84 40W
gincourt 72 43 47N 79 17W
gnes L. 74 48 15N 91 20W
guanish 64 50 14N 62 2W
guanus → 64 50 13N 62 5W
iguebelle, Parc 66 48 30N 78 45W
illik 62 55 11N 59 18W
ilsa Craig 70 43 8N 81 33W
inslie, L. 65 46 8N 61 11W
ir Force I. 87 67 58N 74 5W
irdrie 81 51 18N 114 2W
iyansh 76 55 17N 129 2W
jax 71 43 50N 79 1W
kimiski I. 60 52 50N 81 30W
klavik 86 68 12N 135 0W
kpatok I. 62 60 25N 68 8W
kron 75 48 55N 84 7W
Alameda 79 49 16N 102 17W
Alaska Highway 76 60 0N 130 0W
Albanel 67 48 53N 72 27W
Albanel, L. 62 50 55N 73 12W
Albany → 60 52 17N 81 31W
Albert Canyon 85 51 8N 117 41W
Albert Park 82 50 24N 104 38W
Alberta □ 76 54 40N 115 0W
Alberta Beach 80 53 40N 114 21W
Alberton, Ont. 73 43 11N 80 5W
Alberton, P.E.I. 65 46 50N 64 0W
Albreda 85 52 35N 119 10W
Alcantara L. 77 60 57N 108 9W
Aldershot, N.S. 65 45 6N 64 31W
Aldershot, Ont. 69 43 18N 79 51W
Alert 87 83 2N 60 0W
Alert Bay 84 50 30N 126 55W
Alex Graham, Mt. 85 52 4N 122 52W
Alexander Arch. 76 57 0N 135 0W
Alexandra Falls 76 60 29N 116 18W
Alexandria, B.C. 85 52 35N 122 27W
Alexandria, Ont. 71 45 19N 74 38W
Alexis → 62 52 33N 56 8W
Alexis Creek 84 52 10N 123 20W
Algonquin Prov. Park 71 45 50N 78 30W
Alhambra 81 52 20N 114 40W
Alice 71 45 47N 77 14W
Alice Arm 76 55 29N 129 31W
Alida 79 49 25N 101 55W
Alix 81 52 24N 113 11W
Allan 78 51 53N 106 4W
Allanburg 73 43 5N 79 12W
Allanwater 74 50 14N 90 10W
Allard, L. 64 50 32N 63 31W
Allardville 65 47 28N 65 29W
Alliance 81 52 26N 111 47W
Alliford Bay 84 53 12N 131 58W
Allison Harbour 84 51 2N 127 29W
Alliston 70 44 9N 79 52W
Alluviaq, Fj. 62 59 27N 65 10W
Alma, N.B. 65 45 36N 64 57W
Alma, Ont. 73 43 44N 80 30W
Alma, Que. 67 48 35N 71 40W
Alma, 60 43 25N 84 40W
Almonte 71 45 14N 76 12W
Alpena 60 45 6N 83 24W
Alsask 78 51 21N 109 59W
Alta Lake 85 50 10N 123 0W
Alta Vista 69 45 23N 75 40W
Altario 81 51 55N 110 9W
Alton 73 43 54N 80 5W
Altona, Man. 79 49 6N 97 33W
Altona, Ont. 73 43 58N 79 12W
Alvena 78 52 31N 106 1W
Alvinston 70 42 49N 81 52W
Amadjuak 87 64 0N 72 39W
Amadjuak L. 87 65 0N 71 8W
Amaranth 79 50 36N 98 43W
Amery 77 56 34N 94 3W
Amet Sound 65 45 47N 63 10W
Amherst 65 45 48N 64 8W
Amherst I. 71 44 8N 76 43W
Amherstburg 70 42 6N 83 6W
Amisk 81 52 33N 111 4W
Amisk L. 77 54 35N 102 15W
Amos 66 48 35N 78 5W
Amqui 64 48 28N 67 27W
Amund Ringnes I. 87 78 20N 96 25W
Amundsen Gulf 86 71 0N 124 0W
Amyot 75 48 29N 84 57W
Anacortes 76 48 30N 122 40W
Anahim Lake 84 52 28N 125 18W
Anama Bay 79 51 58N 98 4W
Anaunethad L. 77 60 55N 104 25W
Ancaster 69 43 13N 79 59W
Ancienne-Lorette 69 46 48N 71 21W
Anderson → 86 69 42N 129 0W
Anderson L. 85 50 37N 122 25W
Andover 65 46 45N 67 42W
Andreville 67 47 41N 69 44W
Andrew 80 53 53N 112 21W
Aneroid 78 49 43N 107 18W
Ange-Gardien, L. 69 45 22N 72 57W
Angers 66 45 31N 75 29W
Angikuni L. 77 62 0N 100 0W
Angliers 66 47 33N 79 14W
Angoon 76 57 40N 134 40W
Anguille Mts. 63 48 0N 59 11W
Angus 70 44 19N 79 53W
Angusville 79 50 44N 101 1W
Ann Arbor 60 42 17N 83 45W
Annacis I. 88 49 10N 122 57W
Annaheim 78 52 19N 104 49W
Annapolis Royal 65 44 44N 65 32W
Annieopsquotch Mts. 63 48 20N 57 30W
Annieville 88 49 11N 122 55W
Annonciation, L' 66 46 25N 74 55W
Anola 79 49 53N 96 38W
Anse, L' 60 46 47N 88 28W
Anse-au-Clair, L' 63 51 25N 57 5W
Anse au Loup, L' 63 51 32N 56 50W
Anticosti, Î. d' 64 49 30N 63 0W
Antigonish 65 45 38N 61 58W
Antler, 79 49 34N 101 27W
Antler, 77 48 58N 101 18W
Antler → 79 49 8N 101 0W
Apohaqui 65 45 42N 65 36W
Apostle Is. 60 47 0N 90 30W
Apple Hill 71 45 13N 74 46W
Appleby 69 43 23N 79 46W
Apsley 71 44 45N 78 6W
Ara L. 75 50 33N 87 28W
Arbor Vitae 74 48 54N 94 18W
Arborfield 78 53 6N 103 39W
Arborg 79 50 54N 97 13W
Arcadia 65 43 50N 66 4W
Archerwill 78 52 26N 103 51W
Arcola 79 49 40N 102 30W
Arctic Bay 87 73 1N 85 7W
Arctic Red River 86 67 15N 134 0W
Ardbeg 70 45 38N 80 5W
Arden, Man. 79 50 17N 99 16W
Arden, Ont. 71 44 43N 76 56W
Ardmore 80 54 20N 110 29W
Ardoise, L' 65 45 37N 60 45W
Argentia 63 47 18N 53 58W
Argyle 79 50 11N 97 27W
Arichat 65 45 31N 61 1W
Ariss 73 43 35N 80 22W
Aristazabal I. 84 52 40N 129 10W
Arkell 73 43 32N 80 10W
Arkona 70 43 4N 81 50W
Arlington 76 48 11N 122 4W
Armadale 72 43 50N 79 15W
Armagh 67 46 41N 70 32W
Armidale 65 44 37N 63 38W
Armstrong, B.C. 85 50 25N 119 10W
Armstrong, Ont. 74 50 18N 89 4W
Arnaud → 62 59 59N 69 46W
Arnot 77 55 56N 96 41W
Arnprior 71 45 26N 76 21W
Arntfield 66 48 12N 79 15W
Arran 79 51 53N 101 43W
Arrandale 76 54 57N 130 0W
Arrow Park 85 50 6N 117 57W
Arrowhead 85 50 40N 117 55W
Arrowwood 81 50 44N 113 9W
Arsenault L. 77 55 6N 108 32W
Arthur 73 43 50N 80 32W
Arthurette 65 46 47N 67 29W
Artillery L. 77 63 9N 107 52W
Arundel 66 45 58N 74 37W
Arvert, L. 64 52 18N 61 45W
Arvida 67 48 25N 71 14W
Arvilla 80 53 59N 114 0W
Asbestos 61 45 47N 71 58W
Ashcroft 85 50 40N 121 20W
Ashern 79 51 11N 98 21W
Asheweig → 60 54 17N 87 12W
Ashgrove 73 43 36N 79 53W
Ashland, Maine, 61 46 34N 68 26W
Ashland, Wis., 60 46 40N 90 52W
Ashmont 80 54 7N 111 35W
Ashuanipi, L. 64 52 45N 66 15W
Aspen 65 45 18N 62 3W
Aspen Grove 85 49 57N 120 37W
Asquith 78 52 8N 107 13W
Assigny, L. 64 52 0N 65 20W
Assiniboia 78 49 40N 105 59W
Assiniboine → 79 49 53N 97 8W
Astorville 70 46 11N 79 17W
Athabasca 80 54 45N 113 20W
Athabasca → 77 58 40N 110 50W
Athabasca, L. 77 59 15N 109 15W
Athens 71 44 38N 75 57W
Atherley 70 44 37N 79 20W
Atholville 65 47 59N 66 43W
Aticonipi, L. 64 51 52N 59 22W
Atikokan 74 48 45N 91 37W
Atikonak → 64 52 51N 65 16W
Atikonak L. 64 52 40N 64 32W
Atlin 76 59 31N 133 41W
Atlin, L. 76 59 26N 133 45W
Attawapiskat 60 52 56N 82 24W
Attawapiskat → 60 52 57N 82 18W
Attawapiskat, L. 60 52 18N 87 54W
Attercliffe 73 42 59N 79 36W
Attikamagen L. 62 55 0N 66 30W
Attwood → 74 51 15N 88 30W
Atwood 70 43 40N 81 1W
Au Sable → 60 44 25N 83 20W
Au Sable Pt. 60 46 40N 86 10W
Aubry L. 86 67 23N 126 30W
Auden 75 50 14N 87 53W
Audley 73 43 54N 79 1W
Augusta 61 44 20N 69 46W
Augustines, L. des 66 47 37N 75 56W
Aulneau Pen. 74 49 23N 94 29W
Aurora 73 44 0N 79 28W
Ausable → 70 43 19N 81 46W
Austin Chan. 87 75 35N 103 25W
Auteuil 68 45 38N 73 46W
Auteuil, L. d' 64 50 38N 61 17W
Avalon Pen. 63 47 30N 53 20W
Avola 85 51 45N 119 19W
Avondale 63 47 25N 53 12W
Avonlea 78 50 0N 105 0W
Avonmore 71 45 10N 74 58W
Axel Heiberg I. 87 80 0N 90 0W
Ayer's Cliff 67 45 10N 72 3W
Aylen L. 71 45 37N 77 51W
Aylmer, Ont. 70 42 46N 80 59W
Aylmer, Que. 69 45 24N 75 51W
Aylmer L. 86 64 0N 110 8W
Aylsham 78 53 12N 103 49W
Ayr 73 43 17N 80 27W
Azilda 70 46 33N 81 6W
Azure L. 85 52 23N 120 3W

Babine 76 55 22N 126 37W
Babine → 76 55 45N 127 44W
Babine L. 76 54 48N 126 0W
Baccalieu I. 63 48 8N 52 48W
Back → 86 65 10N 104 0W
Back Bay 65 45 3N 66 52W
Bad Axe 60 43 48N 82 59W
Bad Heart 80 55 30N 118 18W
Baddeck 65 46 6N 60 45W
Badger 63 49 0N 56 4W
Badger's Quay 63 49 7N 53 35W
Baffin □ 87 70 0N 80 0W
Baffin B. 87 72 0N 64 0W
Baffin I. 87 68 0N 75 0W
Bagotville 67 48 22N 70 54W
Baie Comeau 64 49 12N 68 10W
Baie-des-Sables 64 48 43N 67 54W
Baie-du-Poste 67 50 24N 73 56W
Baie-du-Renard 64 49 17N 61 50W
Baie-St-Paul 67 47 28N 70 32W
Baie-Ste-Anne 65 47 3N 64 58W
Baie-Ste-Catherine 67 48 6N 69 44W
Baie-Ste-Claire 64 49 54N 64 30W
Baie Trinité 64 49 25N 67 20W
Baie Verte, N.B. 65 46 1N 64 6W
Baie Verte, Nfld. 63 49 55N 56 12W
Baieville 67 46 8N 72 43W
Baird Pen. 87 68 55N 76 4W
Baker, L. 87 64 0N 96 0W
Baker Lake 87 64 20N 96 3W
Baker Mt. 76 48 50N 121 49W
Baker's Dozen Is. 62 56 45N 78 45W
Bala 70 45 1N 79 37W
Balcarres 78 50 50N 103 35W
Baldock L. 77 56 33N 97 57W
Baldur 79 49 23N 99 15W
Balgonie 78 50 29N 104 16W
Ballinafad 73 43 42N 80 1W
Balmertown 74 51 4N 93 41W
Balmoral 79 50 15N 97 19W
Balsam 73 43 59N 79 4W
Bamfield 84 48 45N 125 10W
Bancroft 71 45 3N 77 51W
Banff 81 51 10N 115 34W
Banff Nat. Park 81 51 30N 116 15W
Bangor 61 44 48N 68 42W
Banks I., B.C. 84 53 20N 130 0W
Banks I., N.W.T. 86 73 15N 121 30W
Bannockburn 71 44 39N 77 33W
Bar Harbor 61 44 15N 68 20W
Barachois-de-Malbaie. 64 48 37N 64 17W
Barachois Pond Prov. Park 63 48 28N 58 15W
Baraga 60 46 49N 88 29W
Baralzon L. 77 60 0N 98 3W
Baranof I. 76 57 0N 135 10W
Barbara L. 75 49 20N 87 47W
Barbeau Pk. 87 81 54N 75 1W
Barbel, L. 64 51 55N 68 13W
Barclay 74 49 47N 92 43W
Bardoux, L. 64 51 9N 67 50W
Baring, C. 86 70 0N 117 30W
Bark L. 71 45 27N 77 51W
Barkley Sound 84 48 50N 125 10W
Barlow L. 77 62 0N 103 0W
Barnes Icecap 87 70 0N 73 15W
Barnet 88 49 17N 122 55W
Barnston I. 88 49 12N 122 42W
Barnwell 81 49 46N 112 15W
Barons 81 50 0N 113 5W
Barraute 66 48 26N 77 38W
Barrhead 80 54 10N 114 24W
Barrie 70 44 24N 79 40W
Barriefield 71 44 14N 76 28W
Barrière 85 51 12N 120 7W
Barrington L. 77 56 55N 100 15W
Barrington Passage 65 43 30N 65 38W
Barrow Str. 87 74 20N 95 0W
Barrows 79 52 50N 101 27W
Barry's Bay 71 45 29N 77 41W
Bartlett, L. 76 63 5N 118 20W
Bartletts Harbour 63 50 57N 57 0W
Bartonville 69 43 14N 79 48W
Bashaw 81 52 35N 112 58W
Basin L. 78 52 38N 105 17W
Baskatong, Rés. 60 46 46N 75 50W
Bass River 65 45 25N 63 47W
Bassano 81 50 48N 112 20W
Bastille, L. 64 51 46N 61 11W
Batchawana B. 75 46 53N 84 30W
Batchawana Bay 75 46 55N 84 37W
Bath, N.B. 65 46 31N 67 36W
Bath, Ont. 71 44 11N 76 47W
Bath, 61 43 50N 69 49W
Bathurst 61 47 37N 65 43W
Bathurst, C. 86 70 34N 128 0W
Bathurst I. 87 76 0N 100 30W
Bathurst Inlet 86 66 50N 108 1W
Batiscan 67 46 30N 72 15W
Batiscan → 67 46 16N 72 15W
Batiscan, L. 67 47 22N 71 55W
Battle 81 52 58N 110 52W
Battle → 78 52 43N 108 15W
Battle Harbour 62 52 16N 55 35W
Battleford 78 52 45N 108 15W
Bauld, C. 63 51 38N 55 26W
Bawlf 81 52 55N 112 28W
Bay Bulls 63 47 19N 52 50W
Bay City 60 43 35N 83 51W
Bay de Verde 63 48 5N 52 54W
Bay L'Argent 63 47 33N 54 54W
Bay Roberts 63 47 36N 53 16W
Bayfield, 70 43 34N 81 42W
Bayfield, 60 46 50N 90 48W
Bays, L. of 70 45 15N 79 4W
Bayside 71 44 7N 77 30W
Baysville 70 45 9N 79 7W
Bazin → 66 47 29N 75 22W
Beach Grove 88 49 2N 123 3W
Beachburg 71 45 44N 76 51W
Beachville 70 43 5N 80 49W
Beaconia 79 50 25N 96 31W
Beaconsfield 68 45 26N 73 50W
Beale, C. 84 48 47N 125 13W
Beamsville 70 43 12N 79 28W
Bear L., Alta. 80 55 9N 119 4W
Bear L., B.C. 76 56 10N 126 52W
Bear L., Man. 77 55 8N 96 0W
Bear River 65 44 34N 65 39W
Beardmore 75 49 36N 87 57W
Béarn 66 47 17N 79 20W
Bearskin Lake 60 53 58N 91 2W
Beatton → 76 56 15N 120 45W
Beatton River 76 57 26N 121 20W
Beatty 78 52 54N 104 48W
Beauceville 67 46 13N 70 46W
Beauchûne, L. 66 46 35N 78 55W
Beaufort Sea 86 72 0N 140 0W
Beauharnois 68 45 20N 73 52W
Beauharnois □ 68 45 15N 74 0W
Beauharnois, Canal de 68 45 19N 73 54W
Beaulac 67 45 50N 71 23W
Beaulieu 69 46 51N 71 8W
Beaulieu → 76 62 3N 113 11W
Beaumont, Alta. 80 53 21N 113 25W
Beaumont, Nfld. 63 49 37N 55 41W
Beauport 69 46 52N 71 11W
Beaupré 67 47 3N 70 54W
Beauséjour 79 50 5N 96 35W
Beauval 77 55 9N 107 37W
Beaver →, B.C. 76 59 52N 124 20W
Beaver →, Ont. 60 55 55N 87 48W
Beaver →, Sask. 77 55 26N 107 45W
Beaver Brook Station 65 47 8N 65 36W
Beaver Creek 86 63 0N 141 0W
Beaver Hill L. 77 54 5N 94 50W
Beaver I. 60 45 40N 85 31W
Beaverdell 85 49 27N 119 6W
Beaverhill L., Alta. 80 53 27N 112 32W
Beaverhill L., N.W.T. 77 63 2N 104 22W
Beaverlodge 80 55 11N 119 29W
Beavermouth 85 51 32N 117 23W
Beaverstone → 60 54 59N 89 25W
Beaverton 70 44 26N 79 9W
Beddington Cr. → 83 51 9N 114 3W
Bedford, N.S. 65 44 44N 63 40W
Bedford, Que. 67 45 7N 72 59W
Bedford Basin 65 44 42N 63 38W
Beebe Plain 67 45 1N 72 9W
Beechey Hd. 85 48 10N 123 30W
Beechy 78 50 53N 107 24W
Beeton 70 44 5N 79 47W
Beetz, L. 64 50 34N 62 42W
Beiseker 81 51 23N 113 32W
Bélanger 68 45 36N 73 43W
Belanger → 79 53 27N 97 41W
Belbutte 78 53 22N 107 49W
Belcher Chan. 87 77 15N 95 0W
Belcher Is. 62 56 15N 78 45W
Belcourt 66 48 24N 77 21W
Belfast 61 44 30N 69 0W
Belfountain 73 43 48N 80 1W
Belize Inlet 84 51 8N 127 20W
Bell → 66 49 48N 77 38W
Bell I., Nfld. 63 47 38N 52 58W
Bell I., Nfld. 63 50 46N 55 35W
Bell-Irving → 76 56 12N 129 5W
Bell L. 74 49 48N 90 58W
Bell Peninsula 87 63 50N 82 0W
Bella Bella 84 52 10N 128 10W
Bella Coola 84 52 25N 126 40W
Bellburns 63 50 20N 57 32W
Belle Isle 63 51 57N 55 25W
Belle Isle, Str. of 63 51 30N 56 30W
Belle River 70 42 18N 82 43W
Bellechasse□ 69 46 47N 71 14W
Belledune 61 47 55N 65 50W
Belleoram 63 47 31N 55 25W
Belleterre 66 47 25N 78 41W
Belleville 71 44 10N 77 23W
Bellevue 81 49 35N 114 22W
Bellin 62 60 0N 70 0W
Bellingham 76 48 45N 122 27W
Belliveau Cove 65 44 23N 66 4W
Bells Corners 71 45 19N 75 50W
Bellsite 79 52 35N 101 4W
Belly → 81 49 46N 113 2W
Belmont, Man. 79 49 25N 99 27W
Belmont, N.S. 65 45 25N 63 23W
Belmont, Ont. 70 42 53N 81 5W
Belmont Park 85 48 27N 123 27W
Beloeil 67 45 34N 73 12W
Belot, L. 86 66 53N 126 16W
Belwood 73 43 47N 80 19W
Belwood, L. 73 43 46N 80 20W
Bendale 72 43 46N 79 14W
Bengough 78 49 25N 105 10W
Beniah L. 76 63 23N 112 17W
Bennett 76 59 56N 134 53W
Benny 70 46 47N 81 38W
Benoit's Cove 63 49 1N 58 7W
Benson 78 49 27N 103 1W
Bentley 81 52 28N 114 4W
Berens → 79 52 25N 97 2W
Berens I. 79 52 18N 97 18W
Berens River 79 52 25N 97 0W
Beresford 65 47 42N 65 42W
Bereziuk, L. 60 54 0N 76 18W
Berland → 80 54 0N 116 50W
Bermen, L. 62 53 35N 68 55W
Bernard L. 70 45 45N 79 23W
Bernier B. 87 71 5N 88 15W
Bernierville 67 46 6N 71 34W
Berry Cr. → 81 50 50N 111 37W
Berthierville 67 46 5N 73 10W
Bertrand 65 47 45N 65 4W
Berwick, N.B. 65 45 47N 65 36W
Berwick, N.S. 65 45 3N 64 44W
Berwyn 80 56 9N 117 44W
Besnard L. 77 55 25N 106 0W
Bethany 71 44 11N 78 34W
Bethesda 73 43 58N 79 21W
Bethune 78 50 43N 105 13W
Betsiamites 67 48 56N 68 40W
Betsiamites → 67 48 56N 68 38W
Bewdley 71 44 5N 78 19W
Bibby I. 77 61 55N 93 0W
Bic 67 48 20N 68 41W
Bic, Île du 67 48 24N 68 52W
Biche, L. la 80 54 50N 112 3W
Biche, La → 76 59 57N 123 50W
Bickerton West 65 45 6N 61 44W
Biddeford 61 43 30N 70 28W
Bienfait 78 49 10N 102 50W
Bienville, L. 62 55 5N 72 40W
Big → 62 54 50N 58 55W
Big B. 62 55 43N 60 35W

Charlevoix 60 45 19N 85 14W
Charlo 65 47 59N 66 17W
Charlotte L. 84 52 12N 125 19W
Charlottetown 65 46 14N 63 8W
Charlton I. 62 52 0N 79 20W
Charny 69 46 43N 71 15W
Charron L. 79 52 44N 95 15W
Chase 85 50 50N 119 41W
Chasm 85 51 13N 121 30W
Châteauguay 68 45 23N 73 45W
Châteauguay □ 68 45 11N 73 45W
Châteauguay → 68 45 23N 73 45W
Châteauguay, L. 62 56 26N 70 3W
Châteauguay-Centre 68 45 21N 73 45W
Châteauvert, L. 67 47 39N 73 56W
Chatham, N.B. 65 47 2N 65 28W
Chatham, Ont. 70 42 24N 82 11W
Chatham Head 65 47 0N 65 33W
Chatham Reach 88 49 15N 122 44W
Chatham Str. 76 57 0N 134 40W
Chats, L. des 71 45 30N 76 20W
Chatsworth 70 44 27N 80 54W
Chaudière → 67 46 45N 71 17W
Chauvin 81 52 45N 110 10W
Chavigny, L. 62 58 12N 75 8W
Cheam View 85 49 15N 121 40W
Cheboygan 60 45 38N 84 29W
Checleset B. 84 50 5N 127 35W
Chedabucto B. 65 45 25N 61 8W
Chedoke 69 43 14N 79 53W
Cheepash → 75 51 3N 80 59W
Cheepay → 75 51 25N 83 26W
Cheeseman L. 74 49 27N 89 20W
Chef, R. du → 67 49 21N 73 25W
Chelan, L. 76 48 5N 120 30W
Chelsea 69 45 30N 75 47W
Cheltenham 73 43 45N 79 55W
Chemainus 85 48 55N 123 42W
Chénéville 66 45 53N 75 3W
Chenil, L. 64 51 51N 59 41W
Cherhill 80 53 49N 114 41W
Cherry Creek 85 50 43N 120 40W
Cherryville 85 50 15N 118 37W
Cherrywood 72 43 52N 79 8W
Cheslatta 84 53 48N 125 48W
Cheslatta L. 84 53 49N 125 20W
Chesley 70 44 17N 81 5W
Chester 65 44 33N 64 15W
Chesterfield Inlet 87 63 30N 90 45W
Chesterville 71 45 6N 75 14W
Chesuncook L. 61 46 0N 69 10W
Chéticamp 65 46 37N 60 59W
Chetwynd 76 55 45N 121 36W
Chewelah 76 48 17N 117 43W
Chezacut 84 52 24N 124 1W
Chibougamau 67 49 56N 74 24W
Chibougamau → 66 49 42N 75 57W
Chibougamau, Parc
Prov. de 67 49 15N 73 45W
Chibougamau L. 67 49 50N 74 20W
Chic-Chocs, Mts. 64 48 55N 66 0W
Chic-Chocs, Parc
Prov. des 64 48 55N 66 20W
Chichagof I. 76 58 0N 136 0W
Chicobi, L. 66 48 53N 78 30W
Chicoutimi 61 48 28N 71 5W
Chicoutimi, Parc
Prov. de 67 48 30N 70 20W
Chidley C. 62 60 23N 64 26W
Chiefs Pt. 70 44 41N 81 18W
Chignecto, Cape 65 45 20N 64 57W
Chignecto B. 65 45 30N 64 40W
Chigoubiche, L. 67 49 7N 73 30W
Chilako → 84 53 53N 122 57W
Chilanko → 84 52 7N 123 41W
Chilanko Forks 84 52 7N 124 5W
Chilco 84 54 3N 123 49W
Chilcotin → 85 51 44N 122 23W
Chilko → 84 52 0N 123 40W
Chilko, L. 84 51 20N 124 10W
Chilliwack 85 49 10N 121 54W
Chinchaga → 80 58 53N 118 20W
Chinook 81 51 28N 110 59W
Chinook Valley 80 56 29N 117 39W
Chip L. 80 53 40N 115 23W
Chipewyan L. 77 58 0N 98 27W
Chipman, Alta. 80 53 42N 112 38W
Chipman, N.B. 65 46 6N 65 53W
Chipman L. 75 49 58N 86 15W
Chippawa 73 43 5N 79 2W
Chiputneticook Lakes 65 45 37N 67 40W
Chisholm 80 54 55N 114 10W
Chitek 78 53 48N 107 45W
Chitek L., Man. 79 52 25N 99 25W
Chitek L., Sask. 78 53 45N 107 47W
Choelquoit L. 84 51 42N 124 12W
Choiceland 78 53 29N 104 29W
Chomedey 68 45 32N 73 45W
Christian I. 70 44 50N 80 12W
Christie B. 77 62 32N 111 10W
Christies Corners 73 43 16N 80 2W
Christina → 80 56 40N 111 3W
Christina, L. 85 49 3N 118 12W
Christopher Lake 78 53 32N 105 48W
Chu Chua 85 51 22N 120 10W
Chuchi L. 76 55 12N 124 30W
Churchbridge 79 50 54N 101 54W
Churchill 77 58 47N 94 11W
Churchill →, Man. 77 58 47N 94 12W
Churchill →, Nfld. 62 53 19N 60 10W
Churchill, C. 77 58 46N 93 12W
Churchill Falls 62 53 36N 64 19W
Churchill L., Ont. 74 50 50N 91 10W
Churchill L., Sask. 77 55 55N 108 20W
Churchill Pk. 76 58 10N 125 10W
Chute-aux-Outardes 67 49 7N 68 24W
Chute-des-Passes 67 49 52N 71 16W
City View, Ont. 69 45 21N 75 45W
City View, Sask. 82 50 28N 104 37W
Clairambault, L. 62 54 29N 69 0W
Claire 67 47 15N 68 40W
Claire, L. 76 58 35N 112 5W
Clairmont 80 55 16N 118 47W
Clandonald 80 53 34N 110 44W
Clanwilliam 79 50 22N 99 49W
Clapperton I. 70 46 0N 82 14W
Clappisons Corners 69 43 18N 79 55W
Clare 60 43 47N 84 45W
Claremont 73 43 58N 79 7W
Clarence Str. 76 55 40N 132 10W
Clarendon 65 45 29N 66 26W
Clarenville 63 48 10N 54 1W
Claresholm 81 50 0N 113 33W
Clark, Pt. 70 44 4N 81 45W
Clarke City 64 50 12N 66 38W
Clarke L. 78 54 24N 106 54W
Clark's Harbour 65 43 25N 65 38W
Clarkson 72 43 31N 79 37W
Claude 73 43 47N 79 54W
Clay L. 74 50 3N 93 30W
Clear → 80 56 11N 119 42W
Clear, L. 71 45 26N 77 12W
Clearwater 85 51 38N 120 2W
Clearwater →, Alta. 80 56 44N 111 23W
Clearwater →, Alta. 81 52 22N 114 57W
Clearwater →, B.C. 85 51 38N 120 3W
Clearwater Cr. → 76 61 36N 125 30W
Clearwater L. 85 52 15N 120 13W
Clearwater Prov. Park 79 54 0N 101 0W
Clementsport 65 44 40N 65 37W
Clermont 67 47 41N 70 14W
Climax 78 49 10N 108 20W
Clinton, B.C. 85 51 6N 121 35W
Clinton, Ont. 70 43 37N 81 32W
Clinton Colden L. 86 63 58N 107 27W
Clinton Creek 86 64 25N 140 37W
Clive 81 52 28N 113 27W
Clive L. 76 63 13N 118 54W
Clova 66 48 7N 75 22W
Clover Pt. 85 48 24N 123 21W
Cloverdale, B.C. 88 49 7N 122 44W
Cloverdale, N.B. 65 46 17N 67 22W
Cloyne 71 44 49N 77 11W
Cluculz L. 84 53 53N 123 33W
Clyde, Alta. 80 54 9N 113 39W
Clyde, Ont. 73 43 22N 80 14W
Clyde → 65 43 35N 65 27W
Clyde River, N.S. 65 43 38N 65 29W
Clyde River, N.W.T. 87 70 30N 68 30W
Coacoachou, L. 64 50 25N 60 14W
Coal → 76 59 39N 126 57W
Coal Creek 81 49 30N 114 59W
Coal Harbour 84 50 36N 127 35W
Coaldale 81 49 45N 112 35W
Coalhurst 81 49 45N 112 56W
Coalmont 85 49 32N 120 42W
Coast Mts. 84 55 0N 129 0W
Coaticook 67 45 10N 71 46W
Coats I. 87 62 30N 83 0W
Cobalt 60 47 25N 79 42W
Cobaz, L. 64 51 15N 60 21W
Cobden 71 45 38N 76 53W
Coboconk 71 44 39N 78 48W
Cobourg 71 43 58N 78 10W
Coburg I. 87 75 57N 79 26W
Cocagne 65 46 20N 64 37W
Cochenour 74 51 5N 93 48W
Cochrane, Alta. 81 51 11N 114 30W
Cochrane, Ont. 60 49 0N 81 0W
Cochrane → 77 59 0N 103 40W
Cockburn, C. 87 74 52N 79 24W
Cockburn I. 70 45 55N 83 22W
Cod I. 62 57 47N 61 47W
Coderre 78 50 11N 106 31W
Codette 78 53 16N 104 0W
Codroy 63 47 53N 59 24W
Codroy Pond 63 48 4N 58 52W
Coe Hill 71 44 52N 77 50W
Colborne 71 44 0N 77 53W
Cold L. 80 54 33N 110 5W
Cold Lake 80 54 27N 110 10W
Coldwater 70 44 42N 79 40W
Colebrook 88 49 6N 122 52W
Coleman 81 49 40N 114 30W
Coleraine 72 43 49N 79 41W
Coleville 78 51 43N 109 15W
Colinet 63 47 13N 53 33W
Colinton 80 54 37N 113 15W
College Bridge 65 45 59N 64 33W
College Heights 81 52 28N 113 45W
Collette 61 46 40N 65 30W
Colleymount 84 54 2N 126 19W
Collingwood 70 44 29N 80 13W
Collingwood Corner 65 45 37N 63 56W
Collins 74 50 17N 89 27W
Collinson Pen. 87 69 58N 101 24W
Colombier 67 48 52N 68 51W
Colonsay 78 51 59N 105 52W
Colquitz 85 48 29N 123 24W
Columbia, Mt. 85 52 8N 117 20W
Columbia L. 81 50 15N 115 52W
Columbus 73 43 59N 78 55W
Colville 76 48 33N 117 54W
Colville Lake 86 67 2N 126 7W
Colwood 85 48 26N 123 29W
Comber 70 42 14N 82 33W
Combermere 71 45 22N 77 37W
Come by Chance 63 47 51N 54 0W
Commanda 70 45 57N 79 36W
Commissaires, L. des 67 48 10N 72 16W
Commissioner I. 79 52 10N 97 16W
Committee B. 87 68 30N 86 30W
Comox 84 49 42N 124 55W
Compeer 81 51 52N 110 0W
Compton 67 45 14N 71 49W
Conception, La 66 46 9N 74 42W
Conception B. 63 47 45N 53 0W
Conche 63 50 55N 55 58W
Concord 72 43 48N 79 29W
Concrete 76 48 35N 121 49W
Condie Res. 82 50 34N 104 43W
Conestogo 73 43 32N 80 30W
Congnarauya 62 58 35N 68 1W
Coniston 70 46 29N 80 51W
Conklin 80 55 38N 111 5W
Connors 67 47 10N 68 52W
Conquest 78 51 32N 107 14W
Consecon 71 44 0N 77 31W
Consort 81 52 1N 110 46W
Consul 78 49 20N 109 30W
Contin L. 79 53 25N 95 10W
Contrecoeur 67 45 51N 73 14W
Contwoyto L. 86 65 42N 110 50W
Cooking L. 80 53 26N 113 2W
Cook's Harbour 63 51 36N 55 52W
Cookshire 67 45 25N 71 38W
Cooksville 72 43 36N 79 35W
Coombs 84 49 18N 124 25W
Copetown 73 43 14N 80 4W
Copp L. 76 60 14N 114 40W
Copper Cliff 70 46 28N 81 4W
Copper Hàrbor 60 47 31N 87 55W
Coppermine 86 67 50N 115 5W
Coppermine → 86 67 49N 116 4W
Coquitlam → 88 49 13N 122 48W
Coral Harbour 87 64 8N 83 10W
Cormack 63 49 18N 57 23W
Cormack L. 76 60 56N 121 37W
Cormorant 79 54 14N 100 35W
Cormorant L. 79 54 15N 100 50W
Corner Brook 63 48 57N 57 58W
Corning 78 49 58N 102 58W
Cornwall, Ont. 71 45 2N 74 44W
Cornwall, P.E.I. 65 46 14N 63 13W
Cornwall I. 87 77 37N 94 38W
Cornwallis I. 87 75 8N 95 0W
Coronach 78 49 7N 105 31W
Coronation 81 52 5N 111 27W
Coronation Gulf 86 68 25N 110 0W
Coronation I. 76 55 52N 134 20W
Corunna 70 42 53N 82 26W
Corvette, L. de la 62 53 25N 74 3W
Corwhin 73 43 31N 80 6W
Costebelle, L. 64 50 19N 62 23W
Côte-St-Luc 68 45 28N 73 40W
Coteau Landing 67 45 15N 74 13W
Cottam 70 42 8N 82 45W
Coudres, Île aux 67 47 24N 70 23W
Coulonge → 66 45 52N 76 46W
Coupeaux, L. 64 51 27N 63 58W
Courtenay 84 49 45N 125 0W
Courtice 73 43 55N 78 46W
Courtland 70 42 51N 80 38W
Courtright 70 42 49N 82 28W
Courville 69 46 53N 71 10W
Coutts 81 49 0N 111 57W
Couture, L. 62 60 7N 75 20W
Cove I. 70 45 17N 81 44W
Coventry L. 77 61 15N 106 15W
Cow Head 63 49 55N 57 48W
Cowan 79 52 5N 100 45W
Cowan L. 78 54 0N 107 15W
Cowansville 67 45 14N 72 46W
Cowichan L. 84 48 53N 124 17W
Cowley 81 49 34N 114 5W
Cox I. 84 50 48N 128 36W
Cox's Cove 63 49 7N 58 5W
Cracroft Is. 84 50 32N 126 25W
Craig 76 55 30N 133 5W
Craigflower 85 48 27N 123 26W
Craigmyle 81 51 40N 112 15W
Craik 78 51 3N 105 49W
Cranberry Portage 77 54 35N 101 23W
Cranbrook 81 49 30N 115 46W
Crane I. 67 47 4N 70 33W
Crane L. 78 50 5N 109 5W
Crane River 79 51 30N 99 14W
Crapaud 65 46 14N 63 30W
Crauford, C. 87 73 44N 84 51W
Craven 78 50 42N 104 49W
Craven, L. 62 54 20N 76 56W
Crean L. 78 54 5N 106 9W
Credit → 72 43 33N 79 35W
Crediton 70 43 17N 81 33W
Cree → 77 58 57N 105 47W
Cree L. 77 57 30N 106 30W
Creelman 78 49 49N 103 18W
Creemore 70 44 19N 80 6W
Cremona 81 51 33N 114 29W
Crescent Beach 88 49 3N 122 53W
Crescent Spur 85 53 34N 120 42W
Creston 81 49 10N 116 31W
Crete, La 76 58 11N 116 24W
Crimson Lake 81 52 27N 115 2W
Crimson Lake Prov.
Park 81 52 28N 114 54W
Crofton 85 48 52N 123 38W
Croix, La, L. 74 48 20N 92 15W
Croker, C. 70 44 58N 80 59W
Cromarty 77 58 3N 94 9W
Cromer 79 49 44N 101 14W
Crooked → 76 54 50N 122 54W
Crooked L. 63 48 24N 56 17W
Crooked River 78 52 51N 103 44W
Crosby 77 48 55N 103 18W
Cross Creek 65 46 19N 66 43W
Cross L. 77 54 45N 97 30W
Crossfield 81 51 25N 114 0W
Crow → 76 59 41N 124 20W
Crowsnest Pass 81 49 40N 114 40W
Cry L. 76 58 45N 129 0W
Crystal Bay 69 45 22N 75 51W
Crystal City 79 49 9N 98 57W
Cudworth 78 52 30N 105 44W
Cumberland, B.C. 84 49 40N 125 0W
Cumberland, Ont. 71 45 29N 75 24W
Cumberland House 79 53 58N 102 16W
Cumberland L. 79 54 3N 102 18W
Cumberland Pen. 87 67 0N 64 0W
Cumberland Sd. 87 65 30N 66 0W
Cumnock 73 43 46N 80 27W
Cumshewa Inlet 84 53 3N 131 50W
Cupar 78 50 57N 104 10W
Cushing, Mt. 76 57 35N 126 57W
Cusson, Pte. 62 60 23N 77 46W
Cut Bank 76 48 40N 112 15W
Cut Knife 78 52 45N 109 1W
Cutbank 78 51 18N 106 51W
Cutbank → 80 54 43N 118 32W
Cynthia 80 53 17N 115 25W
Cypress Hills 77 49 40N 109 30W
Cypress Hills Prov.
Park 78 49 40N 109 30W
Cypress River 79 49 34N 99 5W
Cyrville 69 45 25N 75 38W
Czar 81 52 27N 110 50W

Dalhousie 65 48 5N 66 26W
Dalhousie East 65 44 43N 64 48W
Dalhousie West 65 44 43N 65 13W
Dall I. 76 54 59N 133 25W
Dalmeny 78 52 20N 106 46W
Dalton 75 48 11N 84 1W
Daly L. 77 56 32N 105 39W
Damascus 73 43 55N 80 29W
Dana, Lac 62 50 53N 77 20W
Danforth, 72 43 43N 79 15W
Danforth, 61 45 39N 67 57W
Daniel's Harbour 63 50 13N 57 35W
Danielson Prov. Park 78 51 16N 106 50W
Danskin 84 53 59N 125 47W
Dark Cove 63 48 47N 54 13W
Darnley B. 86 69 30N 123 30W
Darrington 76 48 14N 121 37W
Dartmouth 65 44 40N 63 30W
Dartmouth → 64 48 53N 64 34W
Dasserat, L. 66 48 16N 79 25W
Daulnay 65 47 25N 65 28W
Dauphin 79 51 9N 100 5W
Dauphin L. 79 51 20N 99 45W
Davidson 78 51 16N 105 59W
Davis Inlet 62 55 50N 60 59W
Davis Str. 87 65 0N 58 0W
Davy L. 77 58 53N 108 18W
Dawson 86 64 10N 139 30W
Dawson B. 79 52 53N 100 49W
Dawson Creek 76 55 45N 120 15W
Dawson Inlet 77 61 50N 93 25W
Daysland 81 52 50N 112 20W
De Grau 63 48 29N 59 9W
De Morhiban, L. 64 51 50N 62 54W
Deacon 82 49 51N 96 56W
Deadwood L. 76 59 10N 128 30W
Dean → 84 52 49N 126 58W
Dean Chan. 84 52 30N 127 15W
Dearborn 60 42 18N 83 15W
Dease → 76 59 56N 128 32W
Dease Arm 86 66 52N 119 37W
Dease L. 76 58 40N 130 5W
Dease Lake 76 58 25N 130 6W
Debden 78 53 30N 106 50W
Debec 65 46 4N 67 41W
Debert 65 45 26N 63 28W
Debolt 80 55 12N 118 1W
Decelles, Rés. 66 47 42N 78 8W
Déception, B. 62 62 8N 74 41W
Deception L. 77 56 33N 104 13W
Deep B. 76 61 15N 116 35W
Deep Cove 88 49 20N 122 56W
Deer → 77 58 23N 94 13W
Deer, L. 63 49 6N 57 35W
Deer Lake, Nfld. 63 49 11N 57 27W
Deer Lake, Ont. 77 52 36N 94 20W
Deer Pond 63 48 30N 54 45W
Dégelis 67 47 30N 68 35W
Delaronde L. 78 54 3N 107 3W
Delburne 81 52 12N 113 14W
Delhi 70 42 51N 80 30W
Delia 81 51 38N 112 23W
Delisle 78 51 55N 107 8W
Deloraine 79 49 15N 100 29W
Delorme, L. 62 54 31N 69 52W
Delta □ 88 49 7N 123 0W
Delta Beach 79 50 11N 98 19W
Denbigh 71 45 8N 77 15W
Denman Island 84 49 33N 124 48W
Denzil 78 52 14N 109 39W
Departure Bay 84 49 13N 123 57W
Deroche 85 49 12N 122 4W
Derrynane 73 43 56N 80 35W
Derwent 80 53 41N 110 58W
Desbarats 70 46 20N 83 56W
Desbiens 67 48 25N 71 57W
Deschaillons 67 46 32N 72 7W
Deschambault 67 46 39N 71 56W
Descharme → 77 56 51N 109 13W
Deschênes 66 45 23N 75 48W
Deschênes, L. 69 45 22N 75 51W
Deseronto 71 44 12N 77 3W
Deskenatlata L. 76 60 55N 112 3W
Desmarais 80 55 56N 113 49W
Desmaraisville 66 49 32N 76 9W
Desméloizes 66 48 57N 79 29W
Desolation Sound
Prov. Marine Park 84 50 5N 124 25W
Destruction Bay 86 61 15N 138 48W
Detroit 60 42 23N 83 5W
Deux-Loutres, L. aux 64 51 31N 62 28W
Deux Montagnes 68 45 32N 73 53W
Deux Montagnes □ 68 45 40N 74 0W
Deux Montagnes, Lac
des 68 45 28N 73 59W
Devastation Chan. 84 53 40N 128 50W
Devenyns, L. 67 47 5N 73 50W
Devils Paw 76 58 47N 134 0W
Devon 80 53 24N 113 44W
Devon I. 87 75 10N 85 0W
Dewberry 80 53 35N 110 32W
Dezadeash L. 76 60 28N 136 58W
Diamond City 81 49 48N 112 51W
Diana B. 62 61 20N 70 0W
Didsbury 81 51 35N 114 10W
Diefenbaker L. 77 51 0N 106 55W
Dieppe 65 46 6N 64 45W
Digby 65 44 38N 65 50W
Digby Neck 65 44 30N 66 5W
Digges 77 58 40N 94 0W
Digges Is. 62 62 40N 77 50W
Dildo 63 47 34N 53 33W
Dilke 78 50 52N 105 15W
Dillon 77 55 56N 108 35W
Dillon → 77 55 56N 108 56W
Dingwall 65 46 54N 60 28W
Dinorwic 74 49 41N 92 30W
Dinorwic L. 74 49 37N 92 33W
Dinosaur Prov. Park 81 50 47N 111 30W
Dinsmore 78 51 20N 107 26W
Dionne, L. 64 49 26N 67 55W
Disko I. 87 69 30N 54 30W
Disraëli 67 45 54N 71 21W
Dixon Entrance 76 54 30N 132 0W
Dixonville 80 56 32N 117 40W
Dixville 67 45 4N 71 46W
Doaktown 65 46 33N 66 8W
Dobie → 74 51 41N 90 29W
Dodge L. 77 59 50N 105 36W
Dodsland 78 51 50N 108 45W
Dog → 74 48 32N 89 39W
Dog Creek 85 51 35N 122 14W
Dog L., Man. 79 51 2N 98 31W
Dog L., Ont. 74 48 48N 89 30W
Dog L., Ont. 75 48 17N 84 8W
Doig → 76 56 25N 120 40W
Dolbeau 67 48 53N 72 18W
Dollard 78 49 37N 108 35W
Dollard-des-Ormeaux 68 45 29N 73 49W
Dollarton 88 49 18N 122 57W
Dolphin and Union
Str. 86 69 5N 114 45W
Dome Creek 85 53 44N 121 1W
Dominion 65 46 13N 60 1W
Dominion, C. 87 65 30N 74 28W
Dominion City 79 49 9N 97 9W
Dominion L. 64 52 40N 61 45W
Don → 72 43 39N 79 21W
Don Mills 72 43 42N 79 21W
Don Pen. 84 52 25N 128 12W
Donald 85 51 29N 117 10W
Donalda 81 52 35N 112 34W
Donan 82 49 57N 97 6W
Donkin 65 46 11N 59 52W
Donnaconna 67 46 41N 71 41W
Donnelly 80 55 44N 117 6W
Donovans 63 47 32N 52 50W
Doran L. 77 61 13N 108 6W
Dorchester 65 45 54N 64 31W
Dorchester, C. 87 65 27N 77 27W
Dorchester Crossing 65 46 10N 64 34W
Doré, Le, L. =
Lillian L. 64 51 17N 61 23W
Doré L. 77 54 46N 107 17W
Doré Lake 77 54 38N 107 36W
Dorion, Ont. 74 48 47N 88 39W
Dorion, Que. 68 45 23N 74 3W
Dorset 71 45 14N 78 54W
Dorval 68 45 27N 73 44W
Dorval Airport 68 45 28N 73 44W
Dosquet 67 46 28N 71 32W
Doting Cove 63 49 27N 53 57W
Douglas, 71 45 31N 76 56W
Douglas, 76 58 23N 134 24W
Douglas Chan. 84 53 40N 129 20W
Douglas I. 88 49 13N 122 47W
Douglas Pt. 70 44 19N 81 37W
Douglas Prov. Park 78 51 3N 106 28W
Douglastown, N.B. 64 48 46N 64 24W
Douglastown, N.B. 65 47 1N 65 30W
Dover-Foxcroft 61 45 14N 69 14W
Dowager I. 84 52 25N 128 22W
Downeys 73 43 29N 80 14W
Downsview 72 43 43N 79 29W
Downton, Mt. 84 52 42N 124 52W
Doyles 63 47 50N 59 12W
Dozois, Rés. 66 47 30N 77 5W
Drake 78 51 45N 105 1W
Drayton 70 43 46N 80 40W
Drayton Valley 80 53 12N 114 58W
Dresden 70 42 35N 82 11W
Drinkwater 78 50 18N 105 8W

Drocourt CANADA Gil I.

Drocourt	**70**	45 46N	80 21W
Drowning →	**75**	50 54N	84 34W
Drumbo	**73**	43 16N	80 35W
Drumheller	**81**	51 25N	112 40W
Drummond	**65**	47 2N	67 41W
Drummond I.	**60**	46 0N	83 40W
Drummondville	**67**	45 55N	72 25W
Drumquin	**73**	43 32N	79 47W
Dryberry L.	**74**	49 33N	93 53W
Dryden	**74**	49 47N	92 50W
Du Gas, L.	**64**	51 55N	75 12W
Du Gué →	**62**	57 21N	70 45W
Dubawnt →	**77**	64 33N	100 6W
Dubawnt, L.	**77**	63 4N	101 42W
Duberger	**69**	46 49N	71 18W
Dubreuilville	**75**	48 21N	84 32W
Dubuc	**79**	50 41N	102 28W
Duchess	**81**	50 43N	111 55W
Duck Bay	**79**	52 10N	100 9W
Duck Lake	**78**	52 50N	106 16W
Duck Mt. Prov. Parks	**79**	51 45N	101 0W
Dufferin □	**73**	43 55N	80 15W
Duffin →	**72**	43 49N	79 2W
Dufrost, Pte.	**62**	60 4N	77 39W
Dugald	**82**	49 53N	96 51W
Duke I.	**76**	54 50N	131 20W
Duluth	**60**	46 48N	92 10W
Dumbell L.	**64**	52 28N	65 45W
Dumoine →	**66**	46 13N	77 51W
Dumoine L.	**66**	46 55N	77 55W
Dunbarton	**72**	43 50N	79 7W
Duncan	**85**	48 45N	123 40W
Duncan, L.	**62**	53 29N	77 58W
Duncan Dam	**85**	50 15N	116 56W
Duncan L.	**76**	62 51N	113 58W
Dunchurch	**70**	45 39N	79 51W
Dundalk	**70**	44 10N	80 24W
Dundarave	**88**	49 20N	123 10W
Dundas	**69**	43 17N	79 59W
Dundas I.	**76**	54 30N	130 50W
Dundas Pen.	**86**	74 50N	111 36W
Dundurn	**78**	51 49N	106 30W
Dundurn Camp	**78**	51 51N	106 34W
Dunedin →	**76**	59 30N	124 5W
Dungannon	**70**	43 51N	81 36W
Dungarvon →	**65**	46 49N	65 54W
Dunière, Parc Prov. de	**64**	48 45N	66 41W
Dunkley	**85**	53 17N	122 28W
Dunmore	**81**	49 58N	110 36W
Dunnville	**70**	42 54N	79 36W
Dunrankin →	**75**	48 47N	82 51W
Dunster	**85**	53 8N	119 50W
Dunvegan	**80**	55 55N	118 36W
Dunvegan L.	**77**	60 8N	107 10W
Dunville	**63**	47 16N	53 54W
Duparquet	**66**	48 30N	79 14W
Duparquet, L.	**66**	48 28N	79 16W
Dupuy	**66**	48 50N	79 21W
Durham	**70**	44 10N	80 49W
Durham □	**73**	43 57N	79 5W
Durham Bridge	**65**	46 7N	66 36W
Durocher, L.	**64**	50 52N	61 12W
Dusey →	**75**	51 11N	86 21W
Dutton	**70**	42 39N	81 30W
Duval	**78**	51 9N	104 59W
Duvernay	**68**	45 35N	73 40W
Dwight	**71**	45 20N	79 1W
Dyment	**74**	49 37N	92 18W
Dysart	**78**	50 57N	104 2W
Eabamet, L.	**75**	51 30N	87 46W
Eagle →	**62**	53 36N	57 26W
Eagle Cr. →	**78**	52 20N	107 30W
Eagle I.	**79**	53 40N	98 55W
Eagle L., B.C.	**84**	51 55N	124 23W
Eagle L., Ont.	**74**	49 42N	93 13W
Eagle L.,	**61**	46 23N	69 22W
Eagle Lake	**73**	45 8N	78 29W
Eagle River	**74**	49 47N	93 12W
Eaglehead L.	**74**	49 2N	89 12W
Eaglesham	**80**	55 47N	117 53W
Ear Falls	**74**	50 38N	93 13W
Earl Grey	**78**	50 57N	104 43W
Earls Cove	**84**	49 45N	124 0W
Earltown	**65**	45 35N	63 8W
East Angus	**67**	45 30N	71 40W
East Bay	**65**	46 1N	60 25W
East Broughton Station	**67**	46 14N	71 5W
East Chezzetcook	**65**	44 43N	63 14W
East Coulee	**81**	51 23N	112 27W
East Don →	**72**	43 39N	79 21W
East Harbour	**88**	49 22N	123 16W
East Humber →	**72**	43 48N	79 35W
East Kildonan	**82**	49 55N	97 5W
East Main = Eastmain	**62**	52 10N	78 30W
East Pine	**76**	55 48N	120 12W
East Pt.	**65**	46 27N	61 58W
East Thurlow I.	**84**	50 24N	125 25W
East Trout L.	**78**	54 22N	105 5W
East York	**72**	43 42N	79 20W
Eastcap Cr. →	**88**	49 27N	123 6W
Eastend	**78**	49 32N	108 50W
Eastern Passage	**65**	44 37N	63 30W
Easterville	**79**	53 8N	99 49W
Eastmain	**62**	52 10N	78 30W
Eastmain →	**62**	52 27N	78 26W
Eastman	**67**	45 18N	72 19W
Eastport	**61**	44 57N	67 0W
Eatonia	**78**	51 13N	109 25W
Eatonville	**67**	47 20N	69 41W
Eau-Claire, L. à l', Nfld.	**64**	52 36N	65 50W
Eau-Claire, L. à l', Que.	**62**	56 10N	74 25W
Eboulements, Les	**67**	47 28N	70 21W
Echo Bay, N.W.T.	**86**	66 5N	117 55W
Echo Bay, Ont.	**70**	46 29N	84 4W
Echoing →	**77**	55 51N	92 5W
Échouani, L.	**66**	47 46N	75 42W
Eckville	**81**	52 21N	114 22W
Eclipse Sd.	**87**	72 38N	79 0W
Écorce, L. de l'	**66**	47 5N	76 24W
Ecueils, Pte. aux	**62**	59 47N	77 50W
Ecum Secum	**65**	44 58N	62 8W
Edam	**78**	53 11N	108 46W
Edberg	**81**	52 47N	112 47W
Edehon L.	**77**	60 25N	97 15W
Eden	**79**	50 23N	99 28W
Eden L.	**77**	56 38N	100 15W
Eden Mills	**73**	43 35N	80 9W
Edgeley	**72**	43 48N	79 31W
Edgerton	**81**	52 45N	110 27W
Edgewater	**81**	50 42N	116 5W
Edgewood	**85**	49 47N	118 8W
Edmonds	**88**	49 13N	122 57W
Edmonton	**83**	53 30N	113 30W
Edmund L.	**77**	54 45N	93 17W
Edmundston	**65**	47 23N	68 20W
Edna Bay	**76**	55 55N	133 40W
Edson	**80**	53 35N	116 28W
Edward I.	**74**	48 22N	88 37W
Edzo	**76**	62 49N	116 4W
Eel River Crossing	**65**	48 1N	66 25W
Eganville	**71**	45 32N	77 5W
Egenolf L.	**77**	59 3N	100 0W
Egg L.	**77**	55 5N	105 30W
Eglington I.	**86**	75 48N	118 30W
Egmont	**84**	49 45N	123 56W
Egmont B.	**65**	46 29N	64 6W
Eholt	**85**	49 10N	118 34W
Eileen L.	**77**	62 16N	107 37W
Ekwan →	**60**	53 12N	82 15W
Ekwan Pt.	**60**	53 16N	82 7W
Elaho →	**84**	50 7N	123 23W
Elbow	**78**	51 7N	106 35W
Elbow →	**83**	51 3N	114 2W
Eldorado, Ont.	**71**	44 35N	77 31W
Eldorado, Sask.	**77**	59 35N	108 30W
Eldorado Park	**72**	43 39N	79 46W
Elfrida	**73**	43 10N	79 47W
Elgin, B.C.	**88**	49 4N	122 49W
Elgin, Man.	**79**	49 27N	100 16W
Elgin, N.B.	**61**	45 48N	65 10W
Elgin, Ont.	**71**	44 36N	76 13W
Elk →	**81**	49 11N	115 14W
Elk Island Nat. Park	**80**	53 35N	112 59W
Elk Lake	**60**	47 40N	80 25W
Elk Lakes Prov. Park	**81**	50 30N	115 10W
Elk Point	**80**	53 54N	110 55W
Elkford	**81**	49 52N	114 53W
Elkhorn	**79**	49 59N	101 14W
Elko	**81**	49 20N	115 10W
Ellef Ringnes I.	**87**	78 30N	102 2W
Ellerslie	**83**	53 26N	113 30W
Ellesmere I.	**87**	79 30N	80 0W
Elliot L.	**79**	52 54N	95 18W
Elliot Lake	**70**	46 25N	82 35W
Elliston	**63**	48 38N	53 3W
Ells →	**80**	57 18N	111 40W
Elm Grove	**82**	49 47N	96 49W
Elma	**79**	49 52N	95 55W
Elmira	**73**	43 36N	80 33W
Elmsdale	**65**	44 58N	63 30W
Elmvale	**70**	44 35N	79 52W
Elmworth	**80**	55 3N	119 37W
Elnora	**81**	51 59N	113 12W
Elora	**73**	43 41N	80 26W
Elphin	**71**	44 55N	76 37W
Elphinstone	**79**	50 32N	100 30W
Elrose	**78**	51 12N	108 0W
Elsa	**86**	63 55N	135 29W
Elsas	**75**	48 32N	82 55W
Elsona	**88**	49 12N	122 57W
Embarras Portage	**77**	58 27N	111 28W
Embro	**70**	43 9N	80 54W
Emeril	**62**	47 26N	75 47W
Emerson	**79**	49 0N	97 10W
Emo	**74**	48 38N	93 50W
Empress	**81**	50 57N	110 0W
Emsdale	**70**	45 32N	79 19W
Endako	**84**	54 6N	125 2W
Endeavour	**78**	52 10N	102 39W
Enderby	**85**	50 35N	119 10W
Enfield	**65**	44 56N	63 32W
Engemann L.	**77**	58 0N	106 55W
Englee	**63**	50 45N	56 5W
Englefeld	**78**	52 10N	104 39W
Englefield, C.	**87**	69 49N	85 34W
Englehart	**60**	47 49N	79 52W
Engler L.	**77**	59 8N	106 52W
English →, Ont.	**74**	49 12N	91 5W
English →, Ont.	**74**	50 35N	93 30W
English B.	**88**	49 17N	123 11W
English Harbour East	**63**	47 38N	54 54W
English River	**74**	49 14N	91 0W
Enilda	**80**	55 25N	116 18W
Ennadai	**77**	61 8N	100 53W
Ennadai L.	**77**	61 0N	101 0W
Ennotville	**73**	43 39N	80 20W
Enterprise	**76**	60 47N	115 45W
Entiako L.	**84**	53 13N	125 31W
Epiphanie, L'	**67**	45 51N	73 29W
Eramosa	**73**	43 37N	80 13W
Eric	**62**	51 56N	65 45W
Eric L.	**64**	51 55N	65 36W
Erie, L.	**70**	42 15N	81 0W
Erieau	**70**	42 16N	81 57W
Eriksdale	**79**	50 52N	98 7W
Erin	**73**	43 45N	80 7W
Erindale	**72**	43 32N	79 39W
Erlandson, L.	**62**	57 3N	68 28W
Erskine	**81**	52 20N	112 53W
Escoumins, Les	**67**	48 21N	69 24W
Esker	**62**	53 53N	66 25W
Eskimo Lakes	**86**	69 15N	132 17W
Eskimo Pt.	**77**	61 10N	94 15W
Esnagami L.	**75**	50 19N	86 51W
Esnagi L.	**75**	48 36N	84 33W
Espanola	**70**	46 15N	81 46W
Esperanza	**84**	49 52N	126 43W
Esperanza Inlet	**84**	49 51N	126 55W
Esquimalt	**85**	48 26N	123 25W
Essex	**70**	42 10N	82 49W
Essondale	**88**	49 14N	122 48W
Est, Î. de l'	**65**	47 37N	61 23W
Estcourt	**67**	47 28N	69 14W
Esterhazy	**79**	50 37N	102 5W
Estevan	**78**	49 10N	102 59W
Estevan Group	**84**	53 3N	129 38W
Estevan Sd.	**84**	53 5N	129 34W
Eston	**78**	51 8N	108 40W
Etamamu	**64**	50 18N	59 59W
Étang-du-Nord	**65**	47 22N	61 57W
Etawney L.	**77**	57 50N	96 50W
Etchemin →	**69**	46 46N	71 14W
Ethelbert	**79**	51 32N	100 25W
Etobicoke	**72**	43 42N	79 34W
Etobicoke Cr. →	**72**	43 35N	79 32W
Etolin I.	**76**	56 5N	132 20W
Étroits, Les	**67**	47 24N	68 54W
Etzikom	**81**	49 29N	111 6W
Eudistes, L. des	**64**	50 30N	65 15W
Eureka,	**87**	80 0N	85 56W
Eureka,	**76**	48 53N	115 6W
Eureka River	**80**	56 27N	118 44W
Eutsuk L.	**84**	53 20N	126 45W
Évain	**66**	48 14N	79 8W
Evans L.	**62**	50 50N	77 0W
Evansburg	**80**	53 36N	114 59W
Everrett Mts.	**87**	62 45N	67 12W
Everton	**73**	43 40N	80 9W
Exeter	**70**	43 21N	81 29W
Exploits, B. of	**63**	49 20N	55 0W
Exshaw	**81**	51 3N	115 9W
Eyeberry L.	**77**	63 8N	104 43W
Eyebrow	**78**	50 48N	106 9W
Eyehill Cr. →	**81**	52 14N	110 0W
Fabre	**66**	47 12N	79 22W
Fabreville	**68**	45 34N	73 51W
Faillon, L.	**66**	48 21N	76 39W
Fair Harbour	**84**	50 4N	127 10W
Fairfield Plain	**73**	43 3N	80 24W
Fairford	**79**	51 37N	98 38W
Fairport	**72**	43 49N	79 5W
Fairvale	**65**	45 25N	66 0W
Fairview, Alta.	**80**	56 5N	118 25W
Fairview, N.S.	**65**	44 40N	63 38W
Falcon I.	**74**	49 23N	94 45W
Falconbridge	**70**	46 35N	80 45W
Falher	**80**	55 44N	117 15W
Falkland	**73**	43 10N	80 26W
False Creek	**88**	49 15N	123 8W
Family L.	**79**	51 54N	95 27W
Fanny Bay	**84**	49 27N	124 48W
Fanshaw	**76**	57 11N	133 30W
Far Mt.	**84**	52 47N	125 20W
Faride, L.	**64**	50 58N	59 55W
Farmers Rapids	**69**	45 30N	75 45W
Farnham	**67**	45 17N	72 59W
Faro	**86**	62 11N	133 22W
Farrand, C.	**87**	71 45N	90 0W
Fatima	**65**	47 24N	61 53W
Fauquier, B.C.	**85**	49 52N	118 5W
Fauquier, Ont.	**75**	49 18N	82 3W
Faust	**80**	55 19N	115 38W
Favourable Lake	**60**	52 50N	93 39W
Fawcett	**80**	54 32N	114 5W
Fawn →	**60**	52 22N	88 20W
Fenelon Falls	**71**	44 32N	78 45W
Fenton	**60**	42 47N	83 44W
Fenwick	**73**	43 1N	79 22W
Fergus	**73**	43 43N	80 24W
Ferintosh	**81**	52 46N	112 58W
Ferland, Ont.	**74**	50 19N	88 27W
Ferland, Sask.	**78**	49 27N	106 57W
Ferme-Neuve	**66**	46 42N	75 27W
Fernie	**81**	49 30N	115 5W
Feronia	**70**	46 22N	79 19W
Ferryland	**63**	47 2N	52 53W
Feuilles →	**62**	58 47N	70 4W
Feuilles, B. aux	**62**	58 55N	69 20W
Field	**70**	46 31N	80 1W
Fife L.	**78**	49 14N	105 53W
File Axe, L.	**67**	50 18N	73 34W
Fillmore	**78**	49 50N	103 25W
Fils, L. du	**66**	46 37N	78 7W
Finch	**71**	45 11N	75 7W
Findlater	**78**	50 47N	105 24W
Finger L.	**84**	53 33N	124 18W
Finland	**74**	48 51N	93 55W
Finlay →	**76**	57 0N	125 10W
Finmark	**74**	48 35N	89 45W
Fire River	**75**	48 47N	83 21W
Firebag →	**80**	57 45N	111 21W
Firedrake L.	**77**	61 25N	104 30W
First Narrows	**88**	49 19N	123 8W
Firvale	**84**	52 27N	126 13W
Fish Cr. →	**83**	50 54N	114 1W
Fisher B.	**79**	51 35N	97 13W
Fisher Bay	**79**	51 29N	97 18W
Fisher Branch	**79**	51 5N	97 13W
Fisher Str.	**87**	63 15N	83 30W
Fishing L.	**79**	52 10N	95 24W
Fitz Hugh Sd.	**84**	51 40N	127 55W
Fitzgerald	**76**	59 51N	111 36W
Fitzwilliam I.	**70**	45 30N	81 45W
Five Islands	**65**	45 23N	64 6W
Flaherty I.	**62**	56 15N	79 15W
Flamboro Centre	**69**	43 22N	79 56W
Flanders	**74**	48 44N	92 5W
Flat →	**76**	61 51N	128 0W
Flat Bay	**63**	48 24N	58 36W
Flat L.	**80**	54 38N	112 54W
Flatbush	**80**	54 42N	114 9W
Flaxcombe	**78**	51 29N	109 36W
Fleming	**79**	50 4N	101 31W
Flesherton	**70**	44 16N	80 33W
Fleur de Lys	**63**	50 7N	56 8W
Fleur-de-May, L.	**64**	52 0N	65 5W
Flin Flon	**77**	54 46N	101 53W
Flint	**60**	43 5N	83 40W
Flint L.	**75**	49 52N	85 53W
Floradale	**73**	43 37N	80 35W
Florence	**65**	46 16N	60 16W
Flores I.	**84**	49 20N	126 10W
Flower Sta.	**71**	45 10N	76 41W
Flower's Cove	**63**	51 14N	56 46W
Foam Lake	**78**	51 40N	103 32W
Fogo	**63**	49 43N	54 17W
Fogo, C.	**63**	49 40N	54 0W
Fogo I.	**63**	49 40N	54 5W
Foins, L. aux	**66**	47 5N	78 11W
Foley I.	**87**	68 32N	75 5W
Foleyet	**75**	48 15N	82 25W
Fond-du-Lac	**77**	59 19N	107 12W
Fond-du-Lac →	**77**	59 17N	106 0W
Fontaine	**65**	46 51N	64 58W
Fontas →	**76**	58 14N	121 48W
Fonteneau, L.	**64**	51 55N	61 30W
Foothills	**81**	53 4N	116 47W
Fording	**81**	50 12N	114 52W
Foremost	**81**	49 26N	111 34W
Forest	**70**	43 6N	82 0W
Forest Grove	**85**	51 46N	121 5W
Forest Hill	**72**	43 42N	79 25W
Forestburg	**81**	52 35N	112 1W
Forestville	**67**	48 48N	69 2W
Forget	**78**	49 39N	102 52W
Forillon, Parc National	**64**	48 46N	64 12W
Fork River	**79**	51 31N	100 1W
Forsythe	**66**	48 14N	76 26W
Fort Albany	**60**	52 15N	81 35W
Fort Assiniboine	**80**	54 20N	114 45W
Fort Chipewyan	**77**	58 42N	111 8W
Fort-Coulonge	**66**	45 50N	76 45W
Fort Frances	**74**	48 36N	93 24W
Fort Fraser	**84**	54 4N	124 33W
Fort Garry	**82**	49 50N	97 9W
Fort George	**62**	53 50N	79 0W
Fort Good-Hope	**86**	66 14N	128 40W
Fort Hope	**75**	51 30N	88 0W
Fort Kent	**61**	47 12N	68 30W
Fort Langley	**85**	49 10N	122 35W
Fort Liard	**76**	60 14N	123 30W
Fort Mackay	**80**	57 12N	111 41W
Fort McKenzie	**62**	57 20N	69 0W
Fort Macleod	**81**	49 45N	113 30W
Fort McMurray	**80**	56 44N	111 7W
Fort McPherson	**86**	67 30N	134 55W
Fort Nelson	**76**	58 50N	122 44W
Fort Nelson →	**76**	59 32N	124 0W
Fort Norman	**86**	64 57N	125 30W
Fort Providence	**76**	61 3N	117 40W
Fort Qu'Appelle	**78**	50 45N	103 50W
Fort Resolution	**76**	61 10N	113 40W
Fort Ross	**87**	72 0N	94 14W
Fort Rouge	**82**	49 52N	97 9W
Fort Rupert, B.C.	**84**	50 42N	127 23W
Fort Rupert, Que.	**62**	51 30N	78 40W
Fort St. James	**76**	54 30N	124 10W
Fort St. John	**76**	56 15N	120 50W
Fort Saskatchewan	**80**	53 40N	113 15W
Fort Severn	**60**	56 0N	87 40W
Fort Simpson	**76**	61 45N	121 15W
Fort Smith	**76**	60 0N	111 51W
Fort Smith Region □	**86**	63 0N	120 0W
Fort Vermilion	**76**	58 24N	116 0W
Fort Whyte	**82**	49 49N	97 13W
Forteau	**62**	51 28N	56 58W
Fortin, L.	**64**	50 50N	67 46W
Fortune	**63**	47 4N	55 50W
Fortune B.	**63**	47 30N	55 22W
Fosheim Pen.	**87**	80 0N	85 0W
Fosston	**78**	52 12N	103 49W
Foster	**67**	45 17N	72 30W
Foster →	**77**	55 47N	105 49W
Fourchu	**65**	45 43N	60 17W
Fourmont, L.	**64**	52 5N	60 27W
Fournier, L.	**64**	51 33N	65 25W
Fox →	**77**	56 3N	93 18W
Fox Creek	**80**	54 24N	116 48W
Fox Valley	**78**	50 30N	109 25W
Foxe Basin	**87**	66 0N	77 0W
Foxe Chan.	**87**	65 0N	80 0W
Foxe Pen.	**87**	65 0N	76 0W
Foxville	**75**	50 4N	81 38W
Frances →	**76**	60 16N	129 10W
Frances L.	**76**	61 23N	129 30W
Francis	**78**	50 6N	103 52W
François	**63**	47 35N	56 45W
François L.	**84**	54 0N	125 30W
Frankford	**71**	44 12N	77 36W
Franklin B.	**86**	69 45N	126 0W
Franklin Mts.	**86**	65 0N	125 0W
Franklin River	**84**	49 7N	124 48W
Franklin Str.	**87**	72 0N	96 0W
Franquelin	**64**	49 18N	67 54W
Franz	**75**	48 25N	84 30W
Fraser →, B.C.	**85**	49 7N	123 11W
Fraser →, Nfld.	**62**	56 39N	62 10W
Fraser Lake	**84**	54 0N	124 50W
Fraserdale	**75**	49 55N	81 37W
Fraserwood	**79**	50 38N	97 13W
Frazer L.	**74**	49 15N	88 40W
Frederick Sd.	**76**	57 10N	134 0W
Fredericton	**65**	45 57N	66 40W
Fredericton Junc.	**65**	45 41N	66 40W
Freels, C.	**63**	49 15N	53 30W
Freelton	**73**	43 24N	80 2W
Freeman →	**80**	54 19N	114 47W
Freeport, N.S.	**65**	44 15N	66 20W
Freeport, Ont.	**73**	43 25N	80 25W
Frégate, L.	**60**	53 15N	74 45W
French →, Ont.	**70**	46 2N	80 34W
French →, Ont.	**75**	50 40N	80 59W
French River	**70**	46 2N	80 34W
Frenchman Butte	**78**	53 35N	109 38W
Frikson	**79**	50 30N	99 55W
Frobisher	**79**	49 12N	102 26W
Frobisher B.	**87**	62 30N	66 0W
Frobisher Bay	**87**	63 44N	68 31W
Frobisher L.	**77**	56 20N	108 15W
Frog L.	**80**	53 55N	110 20W
Frontier	**78**	49 12N	108 34W
Fruitland	**73**	43 13N	79 43W
Fruitvale	**85**	49 7N	117 33W
Fry L.	**74**	51 14N	91 19W
Fulford Harbour	**85**	48 47N	123 27W
Fulton	**73**	43 8N	79 40W
Fundy, B. of	**65**	45 0N	66 0W
Fundy Nat. Park	**65**	45 35N	65 10W
Fury and Hecla Str.	**87**	69 56N	84 0W
Gabarouse	**65**	45 50N	60 9W
Gabriola I.	**85**	49 9N	123 47W
Gagetown	**65**	45 46N	66 10W
Gagnon	**64**	51 50N	68 5W
Gagnon, L., N.W.T.	**77**	62 3N	110 27W
Gagnon, L., Que.	**66**	46 7N	75 7W
Gaillarbois, L.	**64**	52 0N	67 27W
Galahad	**81**	52 31N	111 56W
Galeton	**75**	51 8N	80 55W
Galissonnière, La, L.	**64**	51 25N	62 0W
Gambier I.	**85**	49 30N	123 23W
Gammon →	**79**	51 24N	95 44W
Gananoque	**71**	44 20N	76 10W
Gander	**63**	48 58N	54 35W
Gander →	**63**	49 16N	54 30W
Gander L.	**63**	48 58N	54 35W
Gang Ranch	**85**	51 33N	122 20W
Garde L.	**77**	62 50N	106 13W
Gardiner L.	**80**	57 32N	112 30W
Gardner Canal	**84**	53 27N	128 8W
Garibaldi, Mt.	**85**	49 51N	123 0W
Garibaldi Prov. Park	**85**	49 50N	122 40W
Garneau, L.	**64**	51 43N	63 22W
Garnish	**63**	47 14N	55 22W
Garry L.	**87**	65 58N	100 18W
Garson →	**77**	56 20N	110 1W
Garson L.	**80**	56 19N	110 2W
Gascons	**64**	48 11N	64 51W
Gaspé	**64**	48 52N	64 30W
Gaspé, Baie de	**64**	48 46N	64 17W
Gaspé, C. de	**64**	48 48N	64 7W
Gaspé, Pén. de	**64**	48 45N	65 40W
Gaspésie, Parc Prov. de la	**64**	48 55N	65 50W
Gataga →	**76**	58 35N	126 59W
Gateshead I.	**87**	70 36N	100 26W
Gatineau	**66**	45 29N	75 38W
Gatineau →	**69**	45 27N	75 42W
Gatineau, Parc de la	**66**	45 40N	76 0W
Gauer L.	**77**	57 0N	97 50W
Gaultois	**63**	47 36N	55 54W
Gaylord	**60**	45 1N	84 41W
Gayot, L.	**62**	55 43N	70 50W
Geary	**65**	45 46N	66 29W
Geikie →	**77**	57 45N	103 52W
Geikie I.	**74**	50 0N	88 35W
Gem	**81**	50 57N	112 11W
Genesee	**80**	53 21N	114 20W
George →, Que.	**61**	58 49N	66 10W
George →, Que.	**62**	49 21N	67 59W
George B.	**65**	45 45N	61 45W
George River = Port Nouveau-Québec	**62**	58 30N	65 59W
Georgetown, Ont.	**73**	43 40N	79 56W
Georgetown, P.E.I.	**65**	46 13N	62 24W
Georgia, Str. of	**84**	49 25N	124 0W
Georgian B.	**70**	45 15N	81 0W
Georgina I.	**70**	44 22N	79 17W
Geraldton	**75**	49 44N	86 59W
Germain, Grand L.	**64**	51 12N	66 41W
Germansen Landing	**76**	55 43N	124 40W
Gerrard	**85**	50 30N	117 17W
Gethsémani	**62**	50 13N	60 40W
Ghost River	**74**	50 12N	91 30W
Gibbons	**80**	53 50N	113 20W
Gibsons	**85**	49 24N	123 32W
Giffard	**69**	46 51N	71 12W
Gift Lake	**80**	55 53N	115 49W
Gil I.	**84**	53 12N	129 15W

Gilbert, Mt. CANADA Isle L.

Gilbert, Mt. 84 50 52N 124 16W
Gilbert Plains 79 51 9N 100 28W
Gilford I. 84 50 40N 126 30W
Gillam 77 56 20N 94 40W
Gillies Bay 84 49 42N 124 29W
Gilmour 71 44 48N 77 37W
Gimli 77 50 40N 97 0W
Girardville 67 49 0N 72 32W
Girouxville 80 55 45N 117 20W
Gisborne L. 63 47 48N 54 49W
Gjoa Haven 87 68 38N 95 53W
Glace Bay 65 46 11N 59 58W
Glacier B. 76 58 30N 136 10W
Glacier Nat. Park 85 51 15N 117 30W
Glacier Peak Mt. 76 48 7N 121 7W
Glacier Str. 87 76 12N 79 15W
Gladmar 78 49 10N 104 27W
Gladstone 79 50 13N 98 57W
Gladys L. 76 59 50N 133 0W
Glaslyn 78 53 22N 108 21W
Glen Almond 66 45 42N 75 29W
Glen Cross 73 43 59N 80 3W
Glen Ewen 79 49 12N 102 1W
Glen Morris 73 43 16N 80 21W
Glen Williams 73 43 40N 79 55W
Glenavon 78 50 12N 103 8W
Glenboro 79 49 33N 99 17W
Glencairn 82 50 26N 104 33W
Glenchristie 73 43 28N 80 17W
Glencoe 70 42 45N 81 43W
Glendale, Alta. 83 51 2N 114 9W
Glendale, N.S. 65 45 49N 61 18W
Glendon 80 54 15N 111 10W
Gleneagle 69 45 32N 75 48W
Glenella 79 50 33N 99 11W
Glenmoor Res. 83 50 59N 114 8W
Glenwood, Alta. 81 49 21N 113 31W
Glenwood, Nfld. 63 49 0N 54 58W
Glovertown 61 48 40N 54 3W
Gobles 73 43 9N 80 34W
Godbout 64 49 20N 67 38W
Godbout → 64 49 19N 67 36W
Goderich 70 43 45N 81 41W
Godham 87 60 55N 60 40W
Gods → 77 56 22N 92 51W
Gods L. 77 54 40N 94 15W
Goéland, L. au 66 49 50N 76 48W
Gogama 75 47 35N 81 43W
Gold River 84 49 46N 126 3 E
Golden 85 51 20N 117 59W
Golden Ears Prov. Park 85 49 30N 122 25W
Golden Hinde 84 49 40N 125 44W
Golden Lake 71 45 34N 77 21W
Golden Prairie 78 50 13N 109 37W
Goldfields 77 59 28N 108 29W
Goldsand L. 77 57 2N 101 8W
Good Hope Mt. 84 51 9N 124 10W
Good Spirit L. 78 51 34N 102 40W
Gooderham 71 44 54N 78 21W
Goodeve 78 51 4N 103 10W
Goodsoil 77 54 24N 109 13W
Goodwater 78 49 24N 103 42W
Goodwood 65 44 37N 63 40W
Goose → 62 53 20N 60 35W
Goose Bay 62 53 15N 60 20W
Goose Cove 63 51 18N 55 38W
Goose I. 84 51 57N 128 26W
Goose L. 79 54 28N 101 30W
Gordon 82 50 0N 97 21W
Gordon Hd. 85 48 29N 123 18W
Gordon L., Alta. 80 56 30N 110 25W
Gordon L., N.W.T. 76 63 5N 113 11W
Gordonville 73 43 54N 80 33W
Gore Bay 70 45 57N 82 28W
Gormley 73 43 56N 79 23W
Goschen I. 84 53 48N 130 33W
Goshen 65 45 23N 61 59W
Gough L. 81 52 2N 112 28W
Gouin, Rés. 66 48 35N 74 40W
Goulais → 75 46 43N 84 27W
Goulds 63 47 29N 52 46W
Govan 78 51 20N 105 0W
Goyelle, L. 64 50 47N 60 45W
Gracefield 66 46 6N 76 3W
Graham 74 49 20N 90 30W
Graham → 76 56 31N 122 17W
Graham I., B.C. 84 53 40N 132 30W
Graham I., N.W.T. 87 77 25N 90 30W
Graham L. 80 56 35N 114 33W
Grahamdale 79 51 23N 98 30W
Grainland 78 50 59N 106 33W
Granby 67 45 25N 72 45W
Granby → 85 49 2N 118 27W
Grand → 73 42 51N 79 34W
Grand Bank 63 47 6N 55 48W
Grand Bay 65 45 18N 66 12W
Grand Bend 70 43 19N 81 45W
Grand Bruit 63 47 40N 58 14W
Grand Calumet, Île du 66 45 44N 76 41W
Grand Centre 80 54 25N 110 13W
Grand Coulee 78 50 26N 104 49W
Grand Falls 65 48 56N 55 40W
Grand Forks 85 49 0N 118 30W
Grand Harbour 65 44 41N 66 46W
Grand I., 79 52 51N 100 0W
Grand I., 60 46 30N 86 40W
Grand L., N.B. 65 45 57N 66 7W
Grand L., Nfld. 62 53 40N 60 30W
Grand L., Nfld. 63 49 0N 57 30W
Grand Lac Victoria 60 47 35N 77 35W
Grand Le Pierre 63 47 41N 54 47W
Grand Manan I. 65 44 45N 66 52W
Grand Marais, 74 47 45N 90 25W
Grand Marais, 60 46 39N 85 59W
Grand Mère 67 46 36N 72 40W
Grand Piles 67 46 40N 72 40W
Grand Portage 60 47 58N 89 41W
Grand Rapids 79 53 12N 99 19W
Grand Valley 73 43 54N 80 19W
Grand View 79 51 10N 100 42W
Grande, La → 62 53 50N 79 0W
Grande-Anse 65 47 48N 65 11W
Grande Baie 67 48 19N 70 52W
Grande Baleine, R. de la → 62 55 16N 77 47W
Grande Cache 80 53 53N 119 8W
Grande-Cascapédia 64 48 15N 65 54W
Grande-Entrée 65 47 30N 61 40W
Grande Pointe 79 49 46N 97 3W
Grande Prairie 80 55 10N 118 50W
Grande-Rivière 64 48 26N 64 30W
Grande-Vallée 64 49 14N 65 8W
Grandes-Bergeronnes 67 48 16N 69 35W
Grandmesnil, L. 64 51 19N 67 33W
Grandoe Mines 76 56 29N 129 54W
Granet, L. 66 47 47N 77 31W
Granite Pt. 63 50 31N 56 17W
Granville L. 77 56 18N 100 30W
Gras, L. de 86 64 30N 110 30W
Grass → 77 56 3N 96 33W
Grass River Prov. Park 77 54 40N 100 50W
Grasset, L. 66 49 55N 78 10W
Grassie 73 43 9N 79 37W
Grassy Lake 81 49 49N 111 43W
Gravelbourg 78 49 50N 106 35W
Gravenhurst 70 44 52N 79 20W
Grayling 60 44 40N 84 42W
Grayling → 76 59 21N 125 0W
Grayson 78 50 45N 102 40W
Greasy L. 76 62 55N 122 12W
Great Bear → 86 65 0N 124 0W
Great Bear L. 86 65 30N 120 0W
Great Burnt L. 63 48 20N 56 20W
Great Central 84 49 20N 125 10W
Great Central L. 84 49 22N 125 10W
Great Duck I. 70 45 40N 82 57W
Great Falls 79 50 27N 96 1W
Great Harbour Deep 63 50 25N 56 32W
Great I. 77 58 53N 96 35W
Great Slave L. 76 61 23N 115 38W
Greely Fd. 87 80 30N 85 0W
Green → 65 47 18N 68 9W
Green B. 63 49 45N 55 55W
Green Cr. → 69 45 28N 75 34W
Green Lake 78 54 17N 107 47W
Green Park 73 43 52N 80 27W
Green River 73 43 53N 79 11W
Greenbush 77 48 46N 96 10W
Greenfields 73 43 18N 80 29W
Greenough Pt. 70 44 58N 81 26W
Greenville 61 45 30N 69 32W
Greenwater L. 74 48 34N 90 26W
Greenwater Lake 78 52 30N 103 31W
Greenwater Lake Prov. Park 78 52 32N 103 30W
Greenwood, B.C. 85 49 10N 118 40W
Greenwood, Ont. 73 43 56N 79 3W
Grenfell 78 50 30N 102 56W
Grenville 66 45 37N 74 36W
Grenville Chan. 84 53 40N 129 46W
Gretna 79 49 1N 97 34W
Grey → 63 47 34N 57 6W
Grey, Pt. 88 49 16N 123 16W
Grey Is. 63 50 50N 55 35W
Grey Res. 63 48 20N 56 30W
Grey River 63 47 35N 57 6W
Gribbell I. 84 53 23N 129 0W
Griffith 71 45 15N 77 10W
Griffith I. 70 44 50N 80 55W
Grimsby 73 43 12N 79 34W
Grimsby Beach 73 43 12N 79 32W
Grimshaw 80 56 10N 117 40W
Grindstone I. 71 44 43N 76 14W
Grise Fiord 87 76 25N 82 57W
Groais I. 63 50 55N 55 35W
Gronlid 78 53 6N 104 28W
Gros C. 76 61 59N 113 32W
Gros-Morne 64 49 15N 65 34W
Gros Morne Nat. Park 63 49 40N 57 50W
Grosse Isle 79 50 4N 97 27W
Grosses-Roches 64 48 57N 67 5W
Groswater B. 62 54 20N 57 40W
Grouard Mission 80 55 33N 116 9W
Groundhog → 75 48 45N 82 58W
Grovedale 80 55 3N 118 52W
Grundy Prov. Pk. 70 45 58N 80 30W
Grunthal 79 49 24N 96 51W
Guadeloupe, La 67 45 57N 70 56W
Guéguen, L. 66 48 6N 77 13W
Guelph 73 43 35N 80 20W
Guernsey 78 51 53N 105 11W
Guigues 66 47 28N 79 26W
Guilford 61 45 12N 69 25W
Guillaume-Delisle, L. 62 56 15N 76 17W
Guines, L. 64 52 8N 61 25W
Gull → 74 49 45N 89 0W
Gull L. 81 52 34N 114 0W
Gull Lake 78 50 10N 108 29W
Gunisao → 79 53 56N 97 53W
Gunisao L. 79 53 33N 96 15W
Guysborough 65 45 23N 61 30W
Gypsum Pt. 76 61 53N 114 35W
Gypsumville 79 51 45N 98 40W
Habay 76 58 50N 118 44W
Hafford 78 52 43N 107 21W
Hagensborg 84 52 23N 126 32W
Hagersville 73 42 58N 80 3W
Haileybury 60 47 30N 79 38W
Haines Junction 76 60 45N 137 30W
Halbrite 78 49 30N 103 33W
Haldimand-Norfolk □ 73 42 57N 79 50W
Half Island Cove 65 45 21N 61 12W
Halfway → 76 56 12N 121 32W
Haliburton 71 45 3N 78 30W
Halifax 65 44 38N 63 35W
Halkirk 81 52 17N 112 9W
Hall Beach 87 68 46N 81 12W
Hall Pen. 87 63 30N 66 0W
Hallebourg 75 49 40N 83 31W
Halliday L. 77 61 21N 108 56W
Hallock 77 48 47N 97 0W
Halton □ 69 43 30N 79 53W
Hamber Prov. Park 85 52 20N 118 0W
Hamilton 69 43 15N 79 50W
Hamilton Beach 69 43 17N 79 47W
Hamilton Harbour 69 43 18N 79 50W
Hamilton Inlet 61 54 0N 57 30W
Hamilton Sound 63 49 35N 54 15W
Hamilton-Wentworth □ 69 43 15N 79 49W
Hamiota 79 50 11N 100 38W
Hampden 63 49 33N 56 51W
Hampstead 65 45 37N 66 5W
Hampton, N.B. 65 45 32N 65 51W
Hampton, Ont. 71 43 58N 78 45W
Hanceville 85 51 55N 123 2W
Hancock 60 47 10N 88 40W
Handel 78 52 4N 108 42W
Haney 85 49 12N 122 40W
Hanlan 72 43 39N 79 39W
Hanley 78 51 38N 106 26W
Hanmer 70 46 39N 80 56W
Hanna 81 51 40N 111 54W
Hannah 77 48 58N 98 42W
Hannah B. 60 51 40N 80 0W
Hannon 69 43 11N 79 50W
Hanover 70 44 9N 81 2W
Hant's Harbour 63 48 1N 53 16W
Hantsport 65 45 4N 64 11W
Happy Valley 62 53 15N 60 20W
Harbor Beach 60 43 50N 82 38W
Harbour Breton 63 47 29N 55 50W
Harbour Grace 63 47 40N 53 22W
Harcourt 65 46 27N 65 15W
Hardisty 81 52 40N 111 18W
Hardwicke I. 84 50 27N 125 50W
Hardwicke Island 84 50 26N 125 55W
Hardwood Ridge 65 46 10N 66 1W
Hare B. 63 51 15N 55 45W
Hare Bay 63 48 51N 54 1W
Harley 73 43 4N 80 29W
Harmon L. 74 49 56N 90 13W
Harmony 73 43 54N 78 50W
Haro Str. 85 48 30N 123 15W
Harp L. 62 55 5N 61 50W
Harricana → 66 50 56N 79 32W
Harrington Harbour 64 50 31N 59 30W
Harris 78 51 44N 107 35W
Harris Pt. 70 43 6N 82 9W
Harrisburg 73 43 14N 80 13W
Harrison, C. 62 54 55N 57 55W
Harrison Hot Springs 85 49 18N 121 47W
Harrison L. 85 49 33N 121 50W
Harriston 70 43 57N 80 53W
Harrisville 60 44 40N 83 19W
Harrow 70 42 2N 82 55W
Harrowsmith 71 44 24N 76 40W
Hartell 81 50 36N 114 14W
Hartland 65 46 20N 67 32W
Hartley Bay 84 53 25N 129 15W
Hartney 79 49 30N 100 35W
Harty 75 49 29N 82 41W
Harvey 65 45 43N 67 1W
Hastings 71 44 18N 77 57W
Hastings Road 88 49 16N 122 56W
Hatchet L. 77 58 36N 103 40W
Hattonford 80 53 46N 115 42W
Haultain → 77 55 51N 106 46W
Hauterive 67 49 10N 68 16W
Have, La → 65 44 14N 64 20W
Havelock, N.B. 65 46 2N 65 24W
Havelock, Ont. 71 44 26N 77 53W
Havre-Aubert 65 47 12N 61 56W
Havre Aubert, Î. 65 47 13N 61 57W
Havre-aux-Maisons, Î. 65 47 25N 61 47W
Havre-St.-Pierre 64 50 18N 63 33W
Hawarden 78 51 25N 106 36W
Hawk Junction 75 48 5N 84 38W
Hawk Lake 74 49 48N 93 59W
Hawkes Bay 63 50 36N 57 10W
Hawkesbury 60 45 37N 74 37W
Hawkesbury I. 84 53 37N 129 3W
Hay → 76 60 50N 116 26W
Hay, C. 86 74 25N 113 0W
Hay Cove 65 45 45N 60 44W
Hay I. 70 44 53N 80 58W
Hay L. 76 58 50N 118 50W
Hay Lakes 81 53 12N 113 2W
Hay River 76 60 51N 115 44W
Hayes → 77 57 3N 92 12W
Hays 81 50 6N 111 48W
Haysboro 83 50 59N 114 5W
Hazelmere 88 49 2N 122 43W
Hazelton 76 55 20N 127 42W
Hazenmore 78 49 42N 107 8W
Hazlet 78 50 24N 108 36W
Head of Bay d'Espoir 63 47 56N 55 45W
Head of St. Margarets Bay 65 44 41N 63 55W
Headingley 82 49 53N 97 24W
Hearne B. 77 60 10N 99 10W
Hearne L. 76 62 20N 113 10W
Hearst 75 49 40N 83 41W
Heart's Content 63 47 54N 53 27W
Heath Pt. 64 49 8N 61 40W
Heath Steele 65 47 17N 66 5W
Heatherton, N.S. 65 45 35N 61 47W
Heatherton, Nfld. 63 48 17N 58 45W
Hebert 78 50 30N 107 10W
Hebron, N.S. 65 43 53N 66 5W
Hebron, Nfld. 62 58 5N 62 30W
Hebron Fd. 62 58 9N 62 45W
Hecate I. 84 51 42N 128 0W
Hecate Str. 84 53 10N 130 30W
Hecla I. 79 51 10N 96 43W
Hedley 85 49 22N 120 4W
Hedley B. 86 73 0N 108 0W
Heisler 81 52 41N 112 13W
Helene L. 78 53 33N 108 12W
Hemford 65 44 30N 64 47W
Hemmingford 67 45 3N 73 35W
Henderson, Mt. 84 54 16N 128 4W
Hendrix Lake 85 52 5N 120 48W
Henley Harbour 63 52 2N 55 51W
Henrietta Maria C. 60 55 9N 82 20W
Henry Kater, C. 87 69 8N 66 30W
Henryville 67 45 8N 73 11W
Hensall 70 43 26N 81 30W
Hepworth 70 44 37N 81 9W
Herbert Inlet 84 49 20N 125 58W
Hereford, Mt. 67 45 5N 71 36W
Hereward 73 43 50N 80 19W
Heriot Bay 84 50 7N 125 13W
Hermitage 63 47 33N 55 56W
Heron Bay 75 48 40N 86 25W
Hérons, Île aux 68 45 25N 73 35W
Herring Cove 65 44 34N 63 34W
Herschel 78 51 38N 108 21W
Herschel, I. 86 69 35N 139 5W
Hespeler 73 43 26N 80 19W
Hewett, C. 87 70 16N 67 45W
Hibben I. 84 53 0N 132 18W
Hickmans Harbour 63 48 6N 53 44W
High I., Nfld. 61 56 40N 61 10W
High I., Nfld. 62 52 28N 55 40W
High Level 76 58 31N 117 8W
High Prairie 80 55 30N 116 30W
High River 81 50 30N 113 50W
Highland Creek 72 43 47N 79 10W
Highland Park 83 51 6N 114 4W
Highridge 80 54 3N 114 8W
Highrock L. 77 57 5N 105 32W
Hilda 81 50 28N 110 3W
Hilden 65 45 18N 63 18W
Hill Island L. 77 60 30N 109 50W
Hill Spring 81 49 17N 113 38W
Hillhurst 83 51 3N 114 7W
Hillmond 78 53 26N 109 41W
Hillsborough B. 65 46 8N 63 5W
Hillsburgh 73 43 47N 80 9W
Hillsdale 82 50 25N 104 37W
Hillsport 75 49 27N 85 34W
Hilton Beach 70 46 15N 83 53W
Hinds L. 63 48 58N 57 0W
Hines Creek 80 56 20N 118 40W
Hinton 80 53 26N 117 34W
Hitchcock 78 49 14N 103 7W
Hixon 85 53 25N 122 35W
Hjalmar L. 77 61 33N 109 25W
Hoare B. 87 65 17N 62 30W
Hobson L. 85 52 35N 120 15W
Hodges Hill 63 49 4N 55 53W
Hodgeville 78 50 7N 106 58W
Hodgson 79 51 13N 97 36W
Hogeland 77 48 51N 108 40W
Holberg 84 50 40N 128 0W
Holden 80 53 13N 112 11W
Holdfast 78 50 58N 105 25W
Holinshead L. 74 49 39N 89 40W
Holman 86 70 44N 117 44W
Holton 62 54 31N 57 12W
Holyrood 63 47 27N 53 8W
Homathko → 84 51 0N 124 56W
Home B. 87 68 40N 67 10W
Homer 73 43 10N 79 11W
Homestead 80 55 31N 119 22W
Hondo 80 55 4N 114 2W
Honey Harbour 70 44 52N 79 49W
Honguedo, Détroit d' 64 49 15N 64 0W
Hooker L. 74 50 35N 91 1W
Hope, B.C. 85 49 25N 121 25 E
Hope, Ont. 72 43 53N 79 31W
Hope I., B.C. 84 50 55N 127 53W
Hope I., Ont. 70 44 55N 80 11W
Hopedale 62 55 28N 60 13W
Hopes Advance, C. 62 61 4N 69 34W
Hopewell 65 45 29N 62 42W
Hopewell Cape 65 45 51N 64 35W
Horn → 76 61 30N 118 1W
Horn Mts. 76 62 15N 119 15W
Hornaday → 86 69 19N 123 48W
Hornby 73 43 34N 79 50W
Hornell L. 76 62 20N 119 25W
Hornepayne 75 49 14N 84 48W
Hornings Mills 70 44 9N 80 12W
Horse Is. 63 50 15N 55 50W
Horsefly 85 52 20N 121 25W
Horsefly L. 85 52 25N 121 0W
Horseshoe Bay 88 49 22N 123 17W
Horton → 86 69 56N 126 52W
Horwood 63 49 27N 54 32W
Horwood, L. 75 48 5N 82 20W
Hotchkiss → 80 57 2N 117 28W
Hottah L. 86 65 4N 118 30W
Houghton 60 47 9N 88 39W
Houlton 61 46 5N 67 50W
Houston 76 54 25N 126 39W
Howard L. 77 62 15N 105 57W
Howe I. 71 44 16N 76 17W
Howe Sd. 85 49 35N 123 15W
Howell 60 42 38N 83 56W
Howick 67 45 11N 73 51W
Howley 63 49 12N 57 2W
Hubbard 78 51 8N 103 22W
Hubbards 65 44 38N 64 4W
Hubbart Pt. 77 59 21N 94 41W
Hudson 74 50 6N 92 9W
Hudson Bay 79 52 51N 102 23W
Hudson Str. 87 62 0N 70 0W
Hudson's Hope 76 56 0N 121 54W
Hudwin L. 79 53 12N 95 41W
Hull 71 45 25N 75 44W
Humber 73 43 54N 79 49W
Humber → 72 43 38N 79 28W
Humber B. 72 43 38N 79 28W
Humber Bay 72 43 38N 79 27W
Humboldt 78 52 15N 105 9W
Hundred and Fifty Mile House 85 52 7N 121 57W
Hundred Mile House 85 51 38N 121 18W
Hunter, C. 87 71 42N 72 30W
Hunter I. 84 51 55N 128 0W
Huntingdon 67 45 6N 74 10W
Huntsville 70 45 20N 79 14W
Hupel 85 50 37N 118 44W
Huron, L. 70 45 0N 83 0W
Hussar 81 51 3N 112 41W
Hutte Sauvage, L. de la 62 56 15N 64 45W
Huttonsville 73 43 38N 79 48W
Hyas 79 51 54N 102 16W
Hyde In. 87 75 2N 80 0W
Hyland → 76 59 52N 128 12W
Hymers 74 48 18N 89 43W
Hythe 80 55 20N 119 33W

Ian L. 84 53 50N 132 45W
Iberville 67 45 19N 73 17W
Iberville, Lac D' 62 55 55N 73 15W
Iberville, Mt. d' 62 58 50N 63 50W
Icy Str. 76 58 20N 135 30W
Igloolik 87 69 20N 81 49W
Ignace 74 49 30N 91 40W
Igornachoix Bay 63 50 40N 57 25W
Île-à-la Crosse 77 55 27N 107 53W
Île-à-la-Crosse, Lac 77 55 40N 107 45W
Île-Bizard 68 45 29N 73 53W
Île-Cadieux 68 45 25N 74 1W
Île d'Orleans, Chenal de l' 69 46 58N 71 0W
Île-Perrot 68 45 23N 73 57W
Île-Perrot-Sud 68 45 21N 73 54W
Îles, L. des 66 46 20N 75 18W
Ilford 77 56 4N 95 35W
Illukotat → 62 60 48N 78 11W
Imperial 78 51 21N 105 28W
Indian Arm 88 49 23N 122 53W
Indian Cabins 76 59 52N 117 40W
Indian Harbour 62 54 27N 57 13W
Indian Head 78 50 30N 103 41W
Indian L. 74 50 14N' 94 5W
Ingersoll 70 43 4N 80 55W
Inglewood 73 43 47N 79 56W
Ingomar 65 43 34N 65 22W
Ingonish 65 46 42N 60 18W
Ingonish Beach 65 46 38N 60 25W
Inkerman 65 47 40N 64 49W
Inklin 76 58 56N 133 5W
Inklin → 76 58 50N 133 10W
Innerkip 70 43 13N 80 42W
Innetalling I. 62 56 0N 79 0W
Innisfail 81 52 0N 113 57W
Innisfree 80 53 22N 111 32W
Inoucdjouac 62 58 25N 78 15W
Intata Reach 84 53 38N 125 30W
Inuvik 86 68 16N 133 40W
Inuvik □ 86 70 0N 130 0W
Invermay 78 51 48N 103 9W
Invermere 81 50 30N 116 2W
Inverness 65 46 15N 61 19W
Inwood 79 50 30N 97 30W
Ioco 88 49 18N 122 53W
Iona 65 45 58N 60 48W
Ione 76 48 44N 117 29W
Irma 81 52 55N 111 14W
Iron Bridge 70 46 17N 83 14W
Iron Springs 81 49 56N 112 41W
Ironside 69 45 27N 75 45W
Ironwood 60 46 30N 90 10W
Iroquois 71 44 51N 75 19W
Iroquois Falls 60 48 46N 80 41W
Irvine 81 49 57N 110 16W
Isachsen 87 78 47N 103 30W
Ishpeming 60 46 30N 87 40W
Iskut → 76 56 45N 131 49W
Island → 76 60 25N 121 12W
Island Falls, 75 49 35N 81 20W
Island Falls, 61 46 0N 68 16W
Island L. 77 53 47N 94 25W
Island Pond 63 48 25N 56 23W
Islands, B. of 63 49 11N 58 15W
Islay 80 53 24N 110 33W
Isle aux Morts 63 47 35N 59 0W
Isle L. 80 53 38N 114 44W

Isle Pierre CANADA Lord's Cove

Isle Pierre	84	53 57N	123 16W
Isle Verte, L'	67	48 1N	69 20W
Isles, L. des	74	49 10N	89 40W
Islington	72	43 38N	79 32W
Issoudun	67	46 35N	71 38W
Itomamo, L.	67	49 11N	70 28W
Ituna	78	51 10N	103 24W
Ivanhoe L.	77	60 25N	106 30W
Ivugivik	62	62 24N	77 55W
Jaab L.	75	51 10N	82 58W
Jackfish L.	78	53 9N	108 29W
Jackman	61	45 35N	70 17W
Jackson's Arm	63	49 52N	56 47W
Jacobs	74	50 15N	89 50W
Jacques-Cartier →	67	46 40N	71 45W
Jacques Cartier, Dét. de	62	50 0N	63 30W
Jacques-Cartier, L.	67	47 35N	71 13W
Jacques-Cartier, Mt.	64	48 57N	66 0W
Jacquet River	65	47 55N	66 0W
Jakobshavn	87	68 0N	51 0W
James B.	75	51 30N	80 0W
James River	65	45 35N	62 7W
Jameson, C.	87	72 5N	74 14W
Jan L.	77	54 56N	102 55W
Jansen	78	51 54N	104 45W
Jarvis	70	42 53N	80 6W
Jarvis River	74	48 7N	89 21W
Jasper, Alta.	81	52 55N	118 5W
Jasper, Ont.	71	44 50N	75 56W
Jasper Nat. Park	81	52 50N	118 8W
Jean Marie River	76	61 32N	120 38W
Jeanette L.	74	51 5N	92 5W
Jeanne-d'Arc	69	45 32N	75 38W
Jedway	84	52 17N	131 14W
Jellicoe	75	49 40N	87 30W
Jemseg	65	45 50N	66 7W
Jennings →	76	59 38N	132 5W
Jerome	75	47 37N	82 14W
Jerrobert	78	51 56N	109 8W
Jerseyside	63	47 16N	53 58W
Jerseyville	73	43 12N	80 7W
Jervis Inlet	84	50 0N	123 57W
Jesus, Île	68	45 35N	73 45W
Joe Batt's Arm	63	49 44N	54 10W
Joffre, Mt.	81	50 32N	115 13W
Joggins	65	45 42N	64 27W
Jogues	75	49 36N	83 45W
Johnson's Crossing	76	60 29N	133 18W
Johnstone Str.	84	50 28N	126 0W
Joir →	64	51 59N	60 12W
Joliette	67	46 3N	73 24W
Joliette, Parc. Prov. de	67	46 30N	74 0W
Jones Sound	87	76 0N	85 0W
Jonesport	61	44 32N	67 38W
Jonquière	67	48 27N	71 14W
Jordan, L.	65	44 5N	65 14W
Jordan Falls	65	43 49N	65 14W
Jordan Harbour	73	43 11N	79 23W
Joseph, L., Nfld.	64	52 45N	65 18W
Joseph, L., Ont.	70	45 10N	79 44W
Joseph, Petit lac	64	52 36N	65 5W
Joussard	80	55 22N	115 50W
Joy B.	62	61 30N	72 0W
Juan de Fuca Str.	84	48 15N	124 0W
Juan Perez Sd.	84	52 32N	131 30W
Jubilee L.	63	48 3N	55 11W
Jude I.	63	47 15N	54 49W
Judique	65	45 52N	61 30W
Julian L.	62	54 25N	77 57W
Juniper	65	46 33N	67 13W
Jupiter →	64	49 29N	63 37W
Juskatla	84	53 37N	132 18W
Kabinakagami →	75	50 25N	84 20W
Kabinakagami L.	75	48 54N	84 25W
Kaegudeck L.	63	48 7N	55 12W
Kagaki L.	74	49 13N	93 52W
Kagawong L.	70	45 54N	82 15W
Kagianagami L.	75	50 57N	87 50W
Kagiano L.	75	49 16N	86 26W
Kahniah →	76	58 15N	120 55W
Kaipokok B.	62	54 54N	59 47W
Kakabeka Falls	74	48 24N	89 37W
Kakisa →	76	61 3N	118 10W
Kakisa L.	76	60 56N	117 43W
Kakwa →	80	54 37N	118 28W
Kaladar	71	44 37N	77 5W
Kalkaska	60	44 44N	85 11W
Kamilukuak, L.	77	62 22N	101 40W
Kaminak L.	77	62 10N	95 0W
Kaministikwia	74	48 32N	89 35W
Kamloops	85	50 40N	120 20W
Kamloops L.	85	50 45N	120 40W
Kamouraska	67	47 34N	69 52W
Kamsack	79	51 34N	101 54W
Kamuchawie L.	77	56 18N	101 59W
Kanaaupscow	62	54 2N	76 30W
Kanaaupscow →	62	53 39N	77 9W
Kanairiktok →	62	55 2N	60 18W
Kanata	71	45 20N	75 59W
Kane Basin	87	79 1N	73 0W
Kaniapiskau →	62	56 40N	69 30W
Kaniapiskau L.	62	54 10N	69 55W
Kapikotongwa →	75	50 39N	86 43W
Kapiskau →	60	52 47N	81 55W
Kaposvar Cr. →	78	50 31N	101 55W
Kapuskasing	75	49 25N	82 30W
Kapuskasing →	75	49 49N	82 0W
Kasba L.	77	60 20N	102 10W
Kashabowie	74	48 40N	90 26W
Kaskattama →	77	57 3N	90 4W
Kaslo	85	49 55N	116 55W
Kasmere L.	77	59 34N	101 10W
Katimik L.	79	52 53N	99 21W
Kawagama L.	71	45 18N	78 45W
Kawene	74	48 45N	91 15W
Kawinawl	79	52 50N	99 30W
Kearney	70	45 33N	79 13W
Kechika →	76	59 41N	127 12W
Kedgwick	65	47 40N	67 20W
Keeley L.	77	54 54N	108 8W
Keene	71	44 15N	78 10W
Keewatin,	74	49 46N	94 34W
Keewatin,	87	47 23N	93 0W
Keewatin □	77	63 20N	95 0W
Keewatin →	77	56 29N	100 46W
Keezhik L.	74	51 45N	88 30W
Keg River	76	57 54N	117 55W
Kégashka, L.	64	50 20N	61 25W
Kegaska	64	50 9N	61 18W
Keglo, B.	62	58 40N	66 0W
Keith Arm	86	64 20N	122 15W
Kejimkujik Nat. Park	65	44 25N	65 25W
Kellett C.	86	72 0N	126 0W
Kellett Str.	86	75 45N	117 30W
Kelligrews	63	47 30N	53 1W
Kelliher	78	51 16N	103 44W
Kelowna	85	49 50N	119 25W
Kelsey Bay	84	50 25N	126 0W
Kelvin I.	74	49 51N	88 40W
Kelvington	78	52 10N	103 30W
Kelwood	79	50 37N	99 28W
Kemano	84	53 35N	128 0W
Kempt, L.	67	47 25N	74 22W
Kemptown	65	45 28N	63 5W
Kemptville	71	45 0N	75 38W
Kenaston	78	51 30N	106 17W
Kennebecasis →	65	45 19N	66 4W
Kennedy, B.C.	88	49 10N	122 53W
Kennedy, Sask.	79	50 1N	102 21W
Kennedy, Mt.	86	81 2N	78 55W
Kennedy I.	84	54 3N	130 11W
Kennedy L.	84	49 3N	125 32W
Kennetcook	65	45 11N	63 44W
Keno Hill	86	63 57N	135 18W
Kénogami	67	48 25N	71 15W
Kenogami →	75	51 6N	84 28W
Kénogami, L.	67	48 20N	71 23W
Kenora	74	49 47N	94 29W
Kensington	65	46 28N	63 34W
Kent Junction	65	46 35N	65 20W
Kent Pen.	86	68 30N	107 0W
Kentville	65	45 6N	64 29W
Kenville	79	52 0N	101 20W
Keremeos	85	49 13N	119 50W
Kerrobert	77	52 0N	109 11W
Kersley	85	52 49N	122 25W
Kesagami →	60	51 40N	79 45W
Kesagami L.	60	50 23N	80 15W
Keswick	70	44 15N	79 28W
Kettle →, B.C.	85	48 41N	118 7W
Kettle →, Man.	77	56 40N	89 34W
Kettle Falls	76	48 41N	118 2W
Kettle Pt.	70	43 13N	82 1W
Keweenaw B.	60	46 56N	88 23W
Key Harbour	70	45 50N	80 45W
Khedive	78	49 37N	104 31W
Kicking Horse Pass	85	51 28N	116 16W
Kiglapait Mts.	62	57 6N	61 22W
Kikino	80	54 27N	112 8W
Kikkatla	84	53 47N	130 25W
Kilbride, Nfld.	63	47 32N	52 45W
Kilbride, Ont.	73	43 25N	79 56W
Kildala Arm	84	53 50N	128 29W
Killala L.	75	49 5N	86 32W
Killaloe Sta.	71	45 33N	77 25W
Killaly	78	50 45N	102 50W
Killam	81	52 47N	111 51W
Killarney, Man.	79	49 10N	99 40W
Killarney, Ont.	70	45 55N	81 30W
Killarney Prov. Park	70	46 2N	81 35W
Killdeer	78	49 6N	106 22W
Killinek I.	62	60 24N	64 37W
Kilmar	66	45 46N	74 37W
Kimberley	81	49 40N	115 59W
Kimbo	73	43 7N	79 36W
Kimiwan L.	80	55 45N	116 55W
Kimsquit	84	52 45N	126 57W
Kinaskan L.	76	57 38N	130 8W
Kinbasket L.	85	52 0N	118 10W
Kincaid	78	49 40N	107 0W
Kincardine	70	44 10N	81 40W
Kindersley	78	51 30N	109 10W
King City	73	43 56N	79 32W
King George Is.	62	57 20N	78 25W
King I.	84	52 10N	127 40W
King William I.	87	69 10N	97 25W
Kingcome Inlet	84	50 56N	126 29W
Kinghorn	72	43 55N	79 34W
King's Point	63	49 35N	56 11W
Kingsey Falls	67	45 51N	72 4W
Kingsgate	81	49 1N	116 11W
Kingsmere L.	78	54 6N	106 27W
Kingston, N.S.	65	44 59N	64 57W
Kingston, Ont.	71	44 14N	76 30W
Kingsville	70	42 2N	82 45W
Kinistino	78	52 57N	105 2W
Kinkora	65	46 19N	63 36W
Kinmount	71	44 48N	78 45W
Kinnaird	85	49 17N	117 39W
Kinoje →	60	52 8N	81 25W
Kinoje Lakes	75	51 35N	81 48W
Kinsale	73	43 56N	79 2W
Kinushseo →	60	55 15N	83 45W
Kinuso	80	55 20N	115 25W
Kiosk	71	46 6N	78 53W
Kipahigan L.	77	55 20N	101 55W
Kipawa	66	46 47N	78 59W
Kipawa, Parc de	66	47 0N	78 50W
Kipawa L.	66	46 50N	79 0W
Kipling	78	50 6N	102 38W
Kippens	63	48 33N	58 38W
Kirkfield	71	44 34N	78 59W
Kirkfield Park	82	49 53N	97 17W
Kirkland	68	45 27N	73 52W
Kirkland Lake	60	48 9N	80 2W
Kirkwall	73	43 21N	80 10W
Kisbey	78	49 39N	102 40W
Kiskatinaw →	76	56 8N	120 10W
Kiskitto L.	79	54 16N	98 30W
Kiskittogisu L.	79	54 13N	98 20W
Kississing L.	77	55 10N	101 20W
Kitchener	73	43 27N	80 29W
Kitikmeot □	86	70 0N	110 0W
Kitimat	84	54 3N	128 38W
Kitimat Arm	84	53 55N	128 42W
Kitimat Ranges	84	54 0N	129 15W
Kitscoty	80	53 20N	110 20W
Kittertoksoak, I.	62	58 50N	65 50W
Kivitoo	87	67 56N	64 52W
Klappan →	76	58 0N	129 43W
Klawak	76	55 35N	133 0W
Kleczkowski, L.	64	50 48N	63 27W
Kleena Kleene	84	52 0N	124 59W
Kleinburg	72	43 50N	79 38W
Kleindale	84	49 38N	123 58W
Klinaklini →	84	51 21N	125 40W
Klondike	86	64 0N	139 26W
Klotz, L.	62	60 32N	73 40W
Kluane L.	86	61 15N	138 40W
Knee L., Man.	77	55 3N	94 45W
Knee L., Sask.	77	55 51N	107 0W
Knewstubb L.	84	53 33N	124 55W
Knight Inlet	84	50 45N	125 40W
Knowlton	67	45 13N	72 31W
Knox, C.	84	54 11N	133 5W
Koartac	62	60 55N	69 40W
Kogaluk →	62	56 12N	61 44W
Kokanee Glacier Prov. Park	85	49 47N	117 10W
Koocanusa, L.	81	49 20N	115 15W
Kootenay L.	85	49 45N	116 50W
Kootenay Nat. Park	81	51 0N	116 0W
Kopka →	74	50 4N	89 1W
Kormack	75	47 38N	82 59W
Koroc →	62	58 50N	65 50W
Kosciusko I.	76	56 0N	133 40W
Kotaneelee →	76	60 11N	123 42W
Kotcho L.	76	59 7N	121 12W
Kouchibouguac Nat. Park	65	46 50N	65 20W
Kovic, B.	62	61 35N	77 36W
Kowkash	75	50 20N	87 12W
Kruzof I.	76	57 10N	135 40W
Krydor	78	52 47N	107 4W
Kugaluk, B.	62	59 10N	78 40W
Kugong I.	62	56 18N	79 50W
Kukukus L.	74	49 47N	91 41W
Kunghit I.	84	52 6N	131 3W
Kuroki	78	51 52N	103 29W
Kusawa L.	76	60 20N	136 13W
Kuujjuaq	62	58 6N	68 15W
Kwadacha →	76	57 28N	125 38W
Kwataboahegan →	75	51 9N	80 50W
Kwinitsa	84	54 19N	129 22W
Kyle	78	50 50N	108 2W
Kynoch Inlet	84	52 45N	128 0W
Kyuquot	84	50 3N	127 25W
Laberge, L.	76	61 11N	135 12W
Labrador, Coast of □	61	53 20N	61 0W
Labrador City	64	52 57N	66 55W
Labrieville	67	49 18N	69 34W
Lac Allard	64	50 33N	63 24W
Lac-au-Saumon	64	48 25N	67 22W
Lac-aux-Sables	67	46 51N	72 24W
Lac Bouchette	67	48 16N	72 11W
Lac Carré	67	46 7N	74 29W
Lac-des-Écorces	66	46 34N	75 22W
Lac du Bonnet	79	50 15N	96 4W
Lac Édouard	67	47 40N	72 16W
Lac-Etchemin	67	46 24N	70 30W
Lac La Biche	80	54 45N	111 58W
Lac la Hache	85	51 49N	121 27W
Lac la Martre	86	63 8N	117 16W
Lac-Meach	69	45 32N	75 51W
Lac-Mégantic	67	45 35N	70 53W
Lac-Rémi	66	46 1N	74 46W
Lac-St-Charles	69	46 54N	71 23W
Lac-Ste-Marie	66	45 57N	75 57W
Lac Seul, Res.	74	50 25N	92 30W
Lachine	68	45 30N	73 40W
Lachute	67	45 39N	74 21W
Laclu	74	49 46N	94 41W
Lacolle	67	45 5N	73 22W
Lacombe	81	52 30N	113 44W
Ladner	88	49 5N	123 4W
Lady Ann Str.	87	75 40N	79 50W
Ladysmith	84	49 0N	123 49W
Laferte →	76	61 53N	117 44W
Laflamme →	66	49 17N	77 9W
Lafleche	78	49 45N	106 40W
Laforce	66	47 32N	78 44W
Laidlaw	85	49 20N	121 36W
Laird	78	52 43N	106 35W
Lake Alma	78	49 9N	104 12W
Lake Cowichan	84	48 49N	124 3W
Lake Harbour	87	62 50N	69 50W
Lake Hill	85	48 28N	123 22W
Lake Lenore	78	52 24N	104 59W
Lake Louise	81	51 30N	116 10W
Lake River	60	54 30N	82 31W
Lake St. Peter	71	45 18N	78 2W
Lake Superior Prov. Park	75	47 45N	84 45W
Lake View	72	43 34N	79 33W
Lakefield	71	44 25N	78 16W
Lakeview, Ont.	69	45 21N	75 50W
Lakeview, Sask.	82	50 25N	104 38W
Lakitusaki →	60	54 21N	82 25W
Lamaline	63	46 52N	55 49W
Lambeth	70	42 54N	81 18W
Lambton	67	45 50N	71 5W
Lambton, C.	86	71 5N	123 9W
Lambton Mills	72	43 39N	79 31W
Lamèque	65	47 45N	64 38W
Lamming Mills	85	53 20N	120 15W
Lamont	80	53 46N	112 50W
Lampman	78	49 25N	102 50W
Lamprey	77	58 33N	94 8W
Lanark	71	45 1N	76 22W
Lancaster	71	45 10N	74 30W
Lancaster Sd.	87	74 13N	84 0W
Lancer	78	50 48N	108 53W
Landis	78	52 12N	108 27W
Landrienne	66	48 30N	77 50W
Lang Bay	84	49 45N	124 21W
Langara I.	84	54 14N	133 1W
Langenburg	79	50 51N	101 43W
Langford	85	48 27N	123 29W
Langham	78	52 22N	106 58W
Langlade	63	46 50N	56 20W
Langley	85	49 7N	122 39W
Langruth	79	50 23N	98 40W
Langstaff	72	43 50N	79 25W
Lanigan	78	51 51N	105 2W
Lanoraie	67	45 58N	73 13W
Lansdowne	71	44 24N	76 1W
Lansdowne House	60	52 14N	87 53W
Lansing	72	43 45N	79 25W
Lanz I.	84	50 49N	128 41W
Lanzville	84	49 15N	124 5W
Lapeer	60	43 3N	83 20W
Larder Lake	60	48 5N	79 40W
Laredo Sd.	84	52 30N	128 53W
Lark Harbour	63	49 6N	58 23W
Larrys River	65	45 13N	61 23W
Larus L.	74	51 17N	94 40W
Lasalle	68	45 26N	73 38W
Lashburn	78	53 10N	109 40W
Lasqueti	84	49 30N	124 21W
Lasqueti I.	84	49 29N	124 16W
Last Mountain L.	78	51 5N	105 14W
Latchford	60	47 20N	79 50W
Latulipe	66	47 26N	79 2W
Laurel	73	43 57N	80 13W
Laurentian Plat.	62	52 0N	70 0W
Laurentides, Parc Prov. des	67	47 45N	71 15W
Laurie L.	77	56 35N	101 57W
Laurier	79	50 53N	99 33W
Laurier-Station	67	46 32N	71 38W
Laurierville	67	46 18N	71 39W
Laurium	60	47 14N	88 26W
Lauzon	69	46 48N	71 10W
Laval	68	45 35N	73 45W
Laval-des-Rapides	68	45 33N	73 42W
Laval-Ouest	68	45 33N	73 52W
Laval-sur-le-Lac	68	45 32N	73 52W
Lavaltrie	67	45 53N	73 17W
Lavant Sta.	71	45 3N	76 42W
Laverlochère	66	47 26N	79 18W
Lavieille, L.	71	45 51N	78 14W
Lavillètte	65	47 16N	65 18W
Lavoy	80	53 27N	111 52W
Lawn	63	46 57N	55 35W
Lawrence Station	65	45 26N	67 11W
Lawrencetown	65	44 53N	65 10W
Leach I.	75	47 28N	84 57W
Leader	78	50 50N	109 30W
Leaf L.	79	53 1N	102 8W
Leamington	70	42 3N	82 36W
Leaside	72	43 42N	79 22W
Leask	78	53 5N	106 45W
Lebel-sur-Quévillon	66	49 3N	76 59W
Leduc	80	53 15N	113 30W
Leech L.	78	51 5N	102 28W
Lefebvre	67	47 12N	69 49W
Lefroy	70	44 16N	79 34W
Legal	80	53 55N	113 35W
Légère	65	47 25N	64 56W
Leitrim	69	45 20N	75 36W
Lejeune	67	47 46N	68 34W
Leland Lakes	77	60 0N	110 59W
Lemberg	78	50 44N	103 12W
Lemieux	67	46 18N	72 7W
Lemieux, L.	66	50 19N	74 38W
Lemieux Is.	87	63 40N	64 20W
Lemoine, L.	66	48 0N	78 0W
Lennoxville	67	45 22N	71 51W
Lenore L.	78	52 30N	104 59W
Leoville	78	53 39N	107 33W
Lepellé →	62	59 58N	72 24W
Lepreau	65	45 10N	66 28W
Leroy	78	52 0N	104 44W
Leroy, L.	62	55 10N	67 15W
Léry	68	45 21N	73 48W
Leslieville	81	52 23N	114 36W
Lesser Slave L.	80	55 30N	115 25W
Lesser Slave Lake Prov. Park	80	55 26N	114 49W
Lester B. Pearson International Airport	72	43 42N	79 38W
Lestock	78	51 19N	103 59W
Lethbridge, Alta.	83	49 45N	112 45W
Lethbridge, Nfld.	63	48 22N	53 52W
Levack	70	46 38N	81 23W
Lévis	69	46 48N	71 9W
Levis, L.	76	62 37N	117 58W
Lewis Hills	63	48 48N	58 30W
Lewisporte	63	49 15N	55 3W
Lewisville	65	46 6N	64 46W
Liard →	76	61 51N	121 18W
Liberty	78	51 8N	105 26W
Liddon Gulf	86	75 3N	113 0W
Lièvre →	66	45 31N	75 26W
Likely	85	52 37N	121 35W
Lillian L.	64	51 17N	61 23W
Lillooet	85	50 44N	121 57W
Lillooet →	85	49 15N	121 57W
Lillooet L.	85	50 18N	122 35W
Limages	66	45 20N	75 16W
Limbour	69	45 29N	75 45W
Limehouse	73	43 38N	79 58W
Limerick	78	49 39N	106 16W
Limestone →	77	56 31N	94 7W
Limestone B.	79	53 50N	98 53W
Limoges	71	45 20N	75 15W
Linaria	80	54 19N	114 8W
Lincoln,	73	43 10N	79 29W
Lincoln,	61	45 27N	68 29W
Lincolnville	65	45 30N	61 33W
Lindell Beach	85	49 2N	122 1W
Linden	81	51 36N	113 28W
Lindsay	71	44 22N	78 43W
Linière	67	46 4N	70 32W
Link L.	84	52 25N	127 40W
Lintlaw	78	52 4N	103 14W
Linton, Ont.	73	43 56N	79 40W
Linton, Que.	67	47 15N	72 16W
Linwood	70	43 35N	80 43W
Lion's Head	70	44 58N	81 15W
Lipton	78	50 54N	103 51W
Listowel	70	43 44N	80 58W
Little Abitibi →	75	50 29N	81 32W
Little Bay	63	49 36N	55 57W
Little Bow →	81	49 53N	112 29W
Little Burnt Bay	63	49 29N	55 5W
Little Cadotte →	80	56 41N	117 6W
Little Churchill →	77	57 30N	95 22W
Little Corners	73	43 20N	80 17W
Little Current	70	45 55N	82 0W
Little Current →	75	50 57N	84 36W
Little Dover	65	45 15N	61 3W
Little Fort	85	51 26N	120 13W
Little Grand Rapids	79	52 0N	95 29W
Little Narrows	65	45 59N	60 59W
Little Pic →	75	48 48N	86 37W
Little Quill L.	78	51 55N	104 5W
Little Rouge →	72	43 48N	79 8W
Little Smoky →	80	54 44N	117 11W
Little White →	70	46 23N	83 20W
Lively	70	46 26N	81 9W
Liverpool	65	44 5N	64 41W
Liverpool, C.	87	73 38N	78 6W
Liverpool Bay	86	70 0N	128 0W
Lloyd L.	77	57 22N	108 57W
Lloydminster	78	53 17N	110 0W
Lloyds →	63	48 35N	57 15W
Lloydtown	73	43 59N	79 42W
Lochdale	88	49 17N	122 58W
Loche, La	77	56 29N	109 26W
Lockeport	65	43 47N	65 4W
Lodgepole	81	53 6N	115 19W
Logan, Mount	64	48 53N	66 38W
Logan I.	74	50 7N	88 27W
Logan Pass	76	48 41N	113 44W
Loggieville	65	47 4N	65 23W
Logy Bay	63	47 38N	52 40W
Lomond	81	50 24N	112 36W
London	70	42 59N	81 15W
Londonderry	65	45 29N	63 36W
Lone Butte	85	51 33N	121 12W
Lone Pine	80	54 18N	115 7W
Lone Rock	78	53 3N	109 53W
Lonely I.	70	45 34N	81 28W
Long Beach	84	49 1N	125 40W
Long Branch	72	43 35N	79 32W
Long Cr. →	78	49 7N	102 59W
Long I., N.W.T.	62	54 50N	79 20W
Long I., Nfld.	63	47 34N	55 59W
Long L., Alta.	80	54 22N	112 46W
Long L., Ont.	75	49 30N	86 50W
Long Lake	65	44 36N	63 38W
Long Pt., Man.	79	53 2N	98 25W
Long Pt., Nfld.	63	48 47N	58 46W
Long Pt., Ont.	70	42 35N	80 2W
Long Point B.	70	42 40N	80 10W
Long Range Mts.	63	49 30N	57 30W
Long Reach	65	45 28N	66 5W
Longlac	75	49 45N	86 25W
Longlegged L.	74	50 46N	94 8W
Longue-Pointe-de-Mingan	64	50 16N	64 9W
Longueuil	67	45 32N	73 30W
Longview	81	50 32N	114 10W
Lookout, C.	60	55 18N	83 56W
Loon →, Alta.	80	57 8N	115 3W
Loon →, Man.	77	55 53N	101 59W
Loon Lake	78	54 2N	109 10W
Lord Selkirk	82	49 56N	97 11W
Lord's Cove	63	46 53N	55 40W

Loreburn CANADA Moose Mountain Cr.

Loreburn	78	51 13N	106 36W
Lorette	79	49 44N	96 52W
Loretteville	69	46 51N	71 21W
Lorne	65	47 53N	66 8W
Lorne Park	72	43 32N	79 36W
Lorraine	68	45 41N	73 47W
Lorrainville	66	47 21N	79 23W
Lott Cr. →	83	51 0N	114 13W
Lougheed	81	52 44N	111 33W
Lougheed I.	86	77 26N	105 6W
Louis Creek	85	51 8N	120 7W
Louis XIV, Pte.	62	54 37N	79 45W
Louisbourg	65	45 55N	60 0W
Louisbourg Nat. Historic Park	65	45 58N	60 20W
Louisdale	65	45 36N	61 4W
Louise I.	84	52 55N	131 50W
Louiseville	67	46 20N	72 56W
Loups Marins, Lacs des	62	56 30N	73 45W
Lourdes	63	48 39N	59 0W
Lourdes-du-Blanc-Sablon	63	51 24N	57 12W
Love	78	53 29N	104 10W
Loverna	78	51 40N	110 0W
Low	66	45 50N	76 0W
Low, C.	87	63 7N	85 18W
Low L.	62	55 54N	67 5W
Lowe Farm	79	49 21N	97 35W
Lower Arrow L.	85	49 40N	118 5W
Lower Capilano	88	49 19N	123 7W
Lower Manitou L.	74	49 15N	93 0W
Lower Nicola	85	50 12N	120 54W
Lower Post	76	59 58N	128 30W
Lower West Pubnico	65	43 38N	65 48W
Lower Wood Harbour	65	43 31N	65 44W
Lowther	75	49 32N	83 2W
Lubicon L.	80	56 23N	115 56W
Lubicon Lake	80	56 22N	115 52W
Lucan	70	43 11N	81 24W
Lucerne	85	52 52N	118 33W
Luceville	67	48 32N	68 22W
Luck L.	78	51 5N	107 5W
Lucknow	70	43 57N	81 31W
Lucky Lake	78	50 59N	107 8W
Ludlow	65	46 29N	66 21W
Lulu I.	88	49 10N	123 5W
Lumsden, Nfld.	63	49 19N	53 37W
Lumsden, Sask.	78	50 39N	104 52W
Lund	84	49 59N	124 45W
Lundar	79	50 42N	98 2W
Lundbreck	81	49 35N	114 10W
Lunenburg	65	44 22N	64 18W
Luscar	81	53 4N	117 24W
Luseland	78	52 5N	109 24W
Luther, L.	73	43 56N	80 26W
Lyal I.	70	44 57N	81 24W
Lyell I.	84	52 40N	131 35W
Lymburn	80	55 21N	119 47W
Lynden	73	43 14N	80 9W
Lynn Canal	76	58 50N	135 20W
Lynn Cr. →	88	49 18N	123 2W
Lynn Creek	88	49 20N	123 2W
Lynn Lake	77	56 51N	101 3W
Lynnmour	88	49 19N	123 3W
Lynx L.	77	62 25N	106 15W
Lyster	67	46 22N	71 37W
Lytton	85	50 13N	121 31W
Ma-Me-O Beach	81	52 58N	113 59W
Mabel L.	85	50 35N	118 43W
Maberly	71	44 50N	76 32W
Mabou	65	46 4N	61 29W
McAdam	65	45 36N	67 20W
Macalister	85	52 27N	122 24W
Macamic	66	48 45N	79 0W
Macaulay Pt.	85	48 25N	123 24W
McAuley	79	50 16N	101 23W
McBride	85	53 20N	120 19W
McCallum	63	47 38N	56 14W
Maccan	65	45 43N	64 15W
McCauley I.	84	53 40N	130 15W
McClelland L.	80	57 29N	111 20W
McClintock	77	57 50N	94 10W
McClure Str.	86	75 0N	119 0W
McCreary	79	50 46N	99 29W
McCusker →	77	55 32N	108 39W
McDame	76	59 44N	128 59W
Macdiarmid	74	49 26N	88 8W
Macdougall L.	87	66 0N	98 27W
MacDowell L.	60	52 15N	92 45W
Macdun	78	49 19N	103 16W
Maces Bay	65	45 6N	66 29W
McFarlane →	77	59 12N	107 58W
MacGregor	79	49 57N	98 48W
McGregor →	76	55 10N	122 0W
McGregor L.	81	50 25N	112 52W
Machias	61	44 40N	67 28W
Machichi →	77	57 3N	92 6W
McIntosh	74	49 57N	93 36W
McIntosh L.	77	55 45N	105 0W
McIntyre B.	84	54 5N	132 0W
Mackay	80	53 39N	115 35W
Mackay →	80	57 10N	111 38W
McKay L.	75	49 37N	86 25W
McKellar	70	45 30N	79 55W
Mackenzie	76	55 20N	123 5W
Mackenzie →	86	69 10N	134 20W
Mackenzie Bay	86	69 0N	137 30W
Mackenzie Highway	76	58 0N	117 15W
Mackenzie King I.	86	77 45N	111 0W
McKenzie L.	78	54 12N	102 30W
Mackenzie Mts.	86	64 0N	130 0W
Mackinaw City	60	45 47N	84 44W
Macklin	78	52 20N	109 56W
McLean	78	50 31N	104 4W
Maclean Str.	87	77 30N	103 30W
McLennan	80	55 42N	116 50W
McLeod →	80	54 9N	115 42W
MacLeod, B.	77	62 53N	110 0W
MacLeod Lake	76	54 58N	123 0W
M'Clintock Chan.	86	72 0N	102 0W
McLure	85	51 2N	120 13W
McMorran	78	51 19N	108 42W
McMurray = Fort McMurray	80	56 44N	111 7W
McNabs I	65	44 37N	63 32W
MacNutt	79	51 5N	101 36W
Macoun L.	77	56 32N	103 40W
MacTier	70	45 8N	79 47W
Madame I.	65	45 30N	60 58W
Madawaska	71	45 30N	77 55W
Madawaska →	71	45 27N	76 21W
Maddox Cove	63	47 28N	52 42W
Madeira Park	84	49 37N	124 0W
Madeleine →	64	49 15N	65 19W
Madeleine, Îs. de la	65	47 30N	61 40W
Madeleine-Centre	64	49 15N	65 22W
Madoc	71	44 30N	77 28W
Madsen	74	50 58N	93 55W
Mafeking	79	52 40N	101 10W
Magaguadavic	65	45 42N	67 12W
Magaguadavic →	65	45 7N	66 54W
Magaguadavic L.	65	45 43N	67 12W
Magnetawan	70	45 40N	79 39W
Magog	67	45 18N	72 9W
Magpie	64	50 19N	64 30W
Magpie →, Ont.	75	47 56N	84 50W
Magpie →, Que.	64	50 19N	64 27W
Magpie L.	64	51 0N	64 41W
Magrath	81	49 25N	112 50W
Maguse L.	77	61 40N	95 10W
Maguse Pt.	77	61 20N	93 50W
Mahatta River	84	50 22N	127 47W
Mahone Bay	61	44 30N	64 20W
Mahood Falls	85	51 50N	120 38W
Mahood L.	85	51 50N	120 23W
Maicasagi →	66	49 58N	76 33W
Maidstone	78	53 5N	109 20W
Maillardville	88	49 15N	122 52W
Main-à-Dieu	65	46 0N	59 51W
Main Brook	63	51 11N	56 1W
Main Centre	78	50 35N	107 21W
Maine □	61	45 20N	69 0W
Maisonnette	65	47 49N	65 0W
Maitland	65	45 19N	63 30W
Maitland Bridge	65	44 27N	65 12W
Major	78	51 52N	109 37W
Makkovik	62	55 10N	59 10W
Makokibatan L.	75	51 17N	87 20W
Malachi	74	49 56N	94 59W
Malartic	66	48 9N	78 9W
Malartic, L.	66	48 15N	78 5W
Malbaie, La	67	47 40N	70 10W
Malcolm I.	84	50 38N	127 0W
Maligne L.	81	52 40N	117 31W
Mallaig	80	54 13N	111 22W
Mallorytown	71	44 29N	75 53W
Malton	72	43 42N	79 38W
Malvern	72	43 48N	79 14W
Mameigwess L., Ont.	60	52 35N	87 50W
Mameigwess L., Ont.	74	49 34N	91 49W
Manawan L.	77	55 24N	103 14W
Mancelona	60	44 54N	85 5W
Manchester L.	77	61 28N	107 29W
Manicouagan →	67	49 30N	68 30W
Manicouagan, Rés.	62	51 5N	68 40W
Manigotagan	79	51 6N	96 18W
Manigotagan L.	79	50 52N	95 37W
Manito L.	78	52 43N	109 43W
Manitoba □	79	55 30N	97 0W
Manitoba, L.	79	51 0N	98 45W
Manitou, Man.	79	49 15N	98 32W
Manitou, Que.	64	50 18N	65 15W
Manitou →	64	50 18N	65 15W
Manitou I.	60	47 22N	87 30W
Manitou L., Ont.	70	45 51N	82 0W
Manitou L., Que.	62	50 55N	65 17W
Manitoulin I.	70	45 40N	82 30W
Manitouwadge	75	49 8N	85 48W
Manitowaning	70	45 46N	81 49W
Maniwaki	66	46 23N	75 58W
Mankota	78	49 25N	107 5W
Manlius	82	50 0N	97 2W
Mannheim	73	43 24N	80 33W
Manning	80	56 53N	117 39W
Manning Park	85	49 4N	120 47W
Manning Prov. Park	85	49 5N	120 45W
Mannville	80	53 20N	111 10W
Manor	79	49 36N	102 5W
Manotick	71	45 13N	75 41W
Manouane, L., Que.	62	50 45N	70 45W
Manouane, L., Que.	67	47 33N	74 6W
Manseau	67	46 22N	72 0W
Mansel I.	62	62 0N	80 0W
Manson Creek	76	55 37N	124 32W
Manton	60	44 23N	85 25W
Manuels	65	47 3N	64 59W
Many Island L.	81	50 8N	110 3W
Manyberries	81	49 24N	110 42W
Maple	72	43 51N	79 31W
Maple Bay	85	48 48N	123 37W
Maple Creek	78	49 55N	109 29W
Maple Grove	68	45 19N	73 50W
Maples, The	73	43 52N	80 10W
Marathon	75	48 44N	86 23W
Marblehead	85	50 15N	116 58W
Marbleton	67	45 37N	71 35W
Marceau, L.	64	51 25N	66 41W
Marcelin	78	52 55N	106 47W
Marconi	82	49 55N	97 6W
Marden	73	43 36N	80 18W
Marengo	78	51 29N	109 47W
Margaree Forks	65	46 20N	61 5W
Margaret Bay	84	51 20N	126 35W
Margaret L.	76	58 56N	115 25W
Margo	78	51 49N	103 20W
Marguerite	85	52 30N	122 25W
Maria	64	48 10N	65 59W
Marian L.	76	63 0N	116 15W
Maricourt	62	56 34N	70 49W
Marie L.	80	54 38N	110 18W
Marieville	67	45 26N	73 10W
Markdale	70	44 19N	80 39W
Markerville	81	52 7N	114 10W
Markham	72	43 52N	79 16W
Markham L.	77	62 30N	102 35W
Markstay	70	46 29N	80 32W
Marlbank	71	44 26N	77 6W
Marmion L.	74	48 55N	91 20W
Marmora	71	44 28N	77 41W
Marquette,	79	50 4N	97 44W
Marquette,	60	46 30N	87 21W
Marquette, L.	67	48 54N	73 54W
Marsden	78	52 51N	109 49W
Marshall	78	53 11N	109 47W
Marsoui	64	49 13N	66 4W
Marsville	73	43 50N	80 13W
Marten River	70	46 44N	79 49W
Martensville	78	52 17N	106 40W
Martre, L., La	86	63 0N	118 0W
Marwayne	80	53 32N	110 20W
Mary Frances L.	77	63 19N	106 13W
Maryen, L.	64	51 20N	60 28W
Maryfield	79	49 50N	101 35W
Maryhill	73	43 32N	80 23W
Mary's Harbour	62	52 18N	55 51W
Marystown	63	47 10N	55 10W
Marysville, B.C.	81	49 35N	116 0W
Marysville, N.B.	65	45 59N	66 35W
Mascouche	68	45 45N	73 36W
Mascouche →	68	45 41N	73 37W
Maskinongé	67	46 14N	73 1W
Masset	84	54 2N	132 10W
Masset Inlet	84	53 43N	132 20W
Massey	70	46 12N	82 5W
Masson	66	45 32N	75 25W
Massueville	67	45 55N	72 56W
Mastigouche, Parc	67	46 33N	73 41W
Matachewan	60	47 56N	80 39W
Matagami	66	49 45N	77 34W
Matagami, L.	66	49 50N	77 40W
Matamec, L.	64	50 21N	65 58W
Matane	64	48 50N	67 33W
Matane →	64	48 50N	67 35W
Matane, Parc Prov. de	64	48 40N	67 0W
Matapédia	65	48 0N	66 59W
Matapédia, L.	64	48 35N	67 35W
Matawin →	67	46 54N	72 56W
Matawin, Rés.	67	46 46N	73 50W
Matchi-Manitou, L.	66	48 0N	77 4W
Matheson Island	79	51 45N	96 56W
Matinenda L.	70	46 22N	82 57W
Mattagami →	75	50 43N	81 29W
Mattagami L.	75	47 54N	81 35W
Mattawa	60	46 20N	78 45W
Mattawamkeag	61	45 30N	68 21W
Mattawitchewan →	75	49 52N	83 12W
Mattice	75	49 40N	83 20W
Maugerville	65	45 52N	66 27W
Maunoir, L.	86	67 30N	124 55W
Mauricie, Parc Nat. de la	67	46 45N	73 0W
Mavillette	65	44 6N	66 11W
Maxhamish L.	76	59 50N	123 17W
Maxville	71	45 17N	74 51W
Mayerthorpe	80	53 57N	115 8W
Mayfair	78	52 58N	107 36W
Mayland	81	51 3N	114 0W
Maymont	78	52 34N	107 42W
Mayne	85	48 52N	123 17W
Mayo	86	63 38N	135 57W
Mayson L.	77	57 55N	107 10W
Mazenod	78	49 52N	106 13W
Mazhabong L.	75	46 58N	82 30W
Meacham	78	52 6N	105 45W
Meachen	81	49 38N	116 17W
Meadow L.	78	54 7N	108 26W
Meadow Lake	78	54 10N	108 26W
Meadow Lake Prov. Park	77	54 27N	109 0W
Meaford	70	44 36N	80 35W
Meaghers Grant	65	44 55N	63 15W
Mealy Mts.	61	53 10N	58 0W
Meander River	76	59 2N	117 42W
Meares I.	84	49 12N	125 50W
Meath Park	78	53 27N	105 22W
Mecatina, Little →	64	52 0N	60 15W
Mécatina, Petit-→	64	50 40N	59 30W
Méchins, Les	64	48 59N	66 59W
Medicine Hat	83	50 0N	110 45W
Medley	80	54 25N	110 16W
Medstead	78	53 19N	108 5W
Meductic	65	46 0N	67 29W
Medway →	65	44 8N	64 36W
Mégantic, L.	67	45 32N	70 53W
Mégantic, Mt.	67	45 28N	71 9W
Mégiscane →	66	48 29N	75 38W
Mégiscane, L.	66	48 35N	75 55W
Meighen I.	87	80 0N	99 30W
Mékinac, L.	67	47 3N	72 41W
Meldrum Bay	70	45 56N	83 6W
Meldrum Creek	85	52 6N	122 21W
Mélèzes →	62	57 40N	69 29W
Melfort	78	52 50N	104 37W
Melita	79	49 15N	101 0W
Mellen	60	46 19N	90 36W
Melochville	68	45 19N	73 56W
Melville	78	50 55N	102 50W
Melville, L.	62	53 30N	60 0W
Melville I.	86	75 30N	112 0W
Melville Pen.	87	68 0N	84 0W
Melvin →	76	59 11N	117 31W
Memphrémagog, L.	67	45 8N	72 17W
Ménascouagama, L.	64	51 13N	61 52W
Mendham	78	50 46N	109 40W
Menihek	62	54 28N	56 36W
Menihek L.	62	54 0N	67 0W
Ménistouc, L.	64	52 52N	66 29W
Meota	78	53 2N	108 27W
Merasheen I.	63	47 25N	54 15W
Mercier	68	45 19N	73 45W
Mercoal	80	53 10N	117 5W
Mercy C.	87	65 0N	63 30W
Merigomish	65	45 38N	62 26W
Merivale	69	45 19N	75 43W
Merrickville	71	44 55N	75 50W
Merritt	85	50 10N	120 45W
Merry I.	62	55 29N	77 31W
Mersey →	65	44 2N	64 43W
Merton	73	43 25N	79 44W
Merville	84	49 48N	125 3W
Mervin	78	53 20N	108 53W
Mesgouez, L.	62	51 20N	75 0W
Mesilinka →	76	56 6N	124 30W
Mess Cr. →	76	57 55N	131 14W
Messine	66	46 14N	76 2W
Metaline Falls	76	48 52N	117 22W
Meteghan	65	44 11N	66 10W
Methy L.	77	56 28N	109 30W
Métis-sur-Mer	64	48 40N	67 59W
Metlakatla	76	55 10N	131 33W
Meyronne	78	49 39N	106 50W
Mica Creek	85	52 2N	118 35W
Michikamau L.	61	54 20N	63 10W
Michipicoten	75	47 55N	84 55W
Michipicoten B.	75	47 53N	84 53W
Michipicoten I.	75	47 40N	85 40W
Micmac Lake	65	44 41N	63 33W
Midale	78	49 25N	103 20W
Middle Church	82	49 59N	97 4W
Middle Lake	78	52 29N	105 18W
Middle Musquodoboit	65	45 3N	63 9W
Middleton	65	44 57N	65 4W
Middlewood	65	44 14N	64 34W
Midland, Man.	82	49 54N	97 11W
Midland, Ont.	70	44 45N	79 50W
Midland,	60	43 37N	84 17W
Midnapore	83	50 55N	114 5W
Midway	85	49 1N	118 48W
Miette Hotsprings	80	53 8N	117 46W
Mikkwa →	80	58 25N	114 46W
Milden	78	51 29N	107 32W
Mildmay	70	44 3N	81 7W
Milestone	78	49 59N	104 31W
Milford Station	65	45 3N	63 26W
Milk →	81	49 0N	110 33W
Milk River	81	49 10N	112 5W
Mill Cove	65	44 43N	63 40W
Mill Cr. →	83	53 33N	113 29W
Mill Village	65	44 9N	64 39W
Millbridge	71	44 41N	77 36W
Millbrook	71	44 10N	78 29W
Mille Îles, R. des →	68	45 42N	73 32W
Mille Lacs, L. des	74	48 45N	90 35W
Millerand	65	47 13N	61 59W
Millertown	63	48 49N	56 33W
Millet	81	53 6N	113 28W
Millgrove	69	43 20N	79 58W
Milliken	72	43 49N	79 18W
Millinocket	61	45 45N	68 45W
Mills L.	76	61 30N	118 20W
Millstream	65	48 2N	67 2W
Milltown, N.B.	65	45 10N	67 18W
Milltown, Nfld.	63	47 54N	55 46W
Millville	65	46 8N	67 12W
Milnesville	73	43 55N	79 16W
Milo	81	50 34N	112 53W
Milot	67	48 54N	71 49W
Milton, N.S.	65	44 4N	64 45W
Milton, Ont.	73	43 31N	79 53W
Milton Heights	73	43 31N	79 56W
Milverton	70	43 34N	80 55W
Mimico Cr. →	72	43 37N	79 30W
Miminegash	65	46 53N	64 14W
Miminiska L.	74	51 35N	88 37W
Mimosa	73	43 44N	80 13W
Minago →	79	54 33N	98 59W
Minaki	74	49 59N	94 40W
Minas Basin	65	45 20N	64 12W
Minas Channel	65	45 15N	64 45W
Mindemoya	70	45 44N	82 10W
Minden	71	44 55N	78 43W
Mine, L.	64	50 51N	64 43W
Mine Centre	74	48 45N	92 37W
Minegan, Îles de	64	50 12N	63 35W
Mingan	64	50 20N	64 0W
Mingan →	64	50 18N	63 59W
Minipi, L.	64	52 25N	60 45W
Miniss L.	74	50 48N	90 50W
Minitonas	79	52 5N	101 2W
Mink L.	76	61 54N	117 40W
Minnedosa	79	50 14N	99 50W
Minnitaki L.	74	49 57N	92 10W
Minstrel Island	84	50 37N	126 18W
Minto	65	46 5N	66 5W
Minto, L.	62	57 13N	75 0W
Minton	78	49 10N	104 35W
Miquelon	66	49 25N	76 27W
Miquelon, I.	63	47 1N	56 20W
Mira	65	46 2N	59 58W
Mira →	65	46 2N	59 58W
Mirabel Airport	68	45 41N	74 2W
Miramichi, Little S.W. →	65	46 58N	65 40W
Miramichi, N.W. →	65	46 57N	65 50W
Miramichi, S.W. →	65	46 58N	65 38W
Miramichi B.	65	47 15N	65 0W
Mirond L.	77	55 6N	102 47W
Mirror	81	52 30N	113 7W
Miscou Centre	65	47 57N	64 34W
Miscou I.	65	47 57N	64 31W
Miscouche	65	46 26N	63 52W
Misehkow →	74	51 26N	89 11W
Missanabie	75	48 20N	84 6W
Missinaibi →	75	50 43N	81 29W
Missinaibi L.	75	48 23N	83 40W
Missinaibi Lake Prov. Park	75	48 25N	83 30W
Mission City	85	49 10N	122 15W
Missipuskiow →	78	53 53N	103 18W
Missisa L.	60	52 20N	85 7W
Missisicabi →	62	51 14N	79 31W
Mississagi →	70	46 15N	83 9W
Mississagi Prov. Park	70	46 30N	82 40W
Mississauga	72	43 32N	79 35W
Mississippi L.	71	45 5N	76 10W
Mistake B.	77	62 8N	93 0W
Mistanipisipou →	64	51 32N	61 50W
Mistaouac, L.	66	49 25N	78 41W
Mistassibi →	67	48 53N	72 13W
Mistassibi Nord-Est. →	67	49 31N	71 56W
Mistassini	67	48 53N	72 12W
Mistassini →	67	48 42N	72 20W
Mistassini, Parc. Prov. de	67	50 20N	74 0W
Mistassini L.	62	51 0N	73 30W
Mistastin L.	61	55 57N	63 20W
Mistatim	78	52 52N	103 22W
Misty L.	77	58 53N	101 40W
Mitchell	70	43 28N	81 12W
Mitchell Corners	73	43 35N	78 53W
Mitchell I.	88	49 12N	123 5W
Mitchell L.	85	52 52N	120 37W
Mitchinamécus, Rés.	66	47 19N	75 9W
Moberly →	76	56 12N	120 55W
Moffat	73	43 31N	80 3W
Moira →	71	44 21N	77 24W
Moisie	64	50 12N	66 1W
Moisie →	64	50 14N	66 5W
Mojikit L.	74	50 40N	88 15W
Molson L.	79	54 22N	96 40W
Monarch	81	49 48N	113 7W
Monarch Mt.	76	51 55N	125 57W
Monashee Prov. Park	85	50 30N	118 15W
Monck	73	43 58N	80 29W
Moncouche, L.	67	48 45N	70 42W
Moncton	65	46 7N	64 51W
Mondonac, L.	67	47 24N	73 58W
Mongolia	73	43 56N	79 13W
Monitor	81	51 58N	110 34W
Monkstown	63	47 35N	54 26W
Monkton	70	43 35N	81 5W
Monmouth Mt.	84	51 0N	123 47W
Mono Mills	73	43 57N	79 58W
Mono Road Station	73	43 51N	79 51W
Mont-Carmel	67	47 26N	69 52W
Mont-Joli	67	48 37N	68 10W
Mont Laurier	66	46 35N	75 30W
Mont-Louis	64	49 15N	65 44W
Mont-Royal	68	45 31N	73 39W
Mont St-Pierre	64	49 13N	65 49W
Mont-Tremblant	66	46 13N	74 36W
Mont Tremblant Prov. Park	67	46 30N	74 30W
Montague	65	46 10N	62 39W
Montcerf	66	46 32N	76 3W
Montcevelles, L.	64	51 7N	60 38W
Montebello	66	45 40N	74 55W
Montgomery	83	51 4N	114 10W
Monticello	73	43 59N	80 24W
Montmagny	67	46 58N	70 34W
Montmartre	78	50 14N	103 27W
Montmorency	69	46 53N	71 11W
Montmorency →	69	46 53N	71 7W
Montréal	68	45 31N	73 34W
Montreal →	75	47 14N	84 39W
Montréal, Île de	68	45 30N	73 40W
Montreal I.	75	47 19N	84 44W
Montreal L.	78	54 20N	105 45W
Montreal Lake	78	54 3N	105 46W
Montréal-Nord	68	45 36N	73 38W
Montreuil, L.	66	50 12N	77 40W
Montrose, B.C.	85	49 5N	117 35W
Montrose, Ont.	73	43 3N	79 8W
Monts, Pte. des	64	49 20N	67 12W
Moonbeam	75	49 20N	82 10W
Moore Pt.	72	43 48N	79 3W
Moores Mill	65	45 18N	67 17W
Moose →	75	51 20N	80 25W
Moose Creek	71	45 15N	74 58W
Moose Factory	75	51 16N	80 32W
Moose Heights	85	53 4N	122 31W
Moose Hill	74	48 15N	89 29W
Moose I.	79	51 42N	97 10W
Moose Jaw	78	50 24N	105 30W
Moose Jaw →	78	50 34N	105 18W
Moose L.	79	53 46N	100 8W
Moose Lake	79	53 43N	100 20W
Moose Mountain Cr. →	78	49 13N	102 12W

Moose Mountain Prov. Park CANADA Oyster River

Moose Mountain Prov. Park 79 49 48N 102 25W
Moose River 75 50 48N 81 17W
Moosehead L. 61 45 34N 69 40W
Moosomin 79 50 9N 101 40W
Moosonee 45 51 17N 80 39W
Morden 79 49 15N 98 10W
Morell 65 46 25N 62 42W
Moresby I. 84 52 30N 131 40W
Morice → 84 54 12N 127 5W
Morice L. 84 53 50N 127 40W
Morin-Heights 67 45 54N 74 15W
Morinville 80 53 49N 113 41W
Morrin 81 51 40N 112 47W
Morris 79 49 25N 97 22W
Morris → 79 49 21N 97 21W
Morris L. 65 44 39N 63 30W
Morrisburg 71 44 55N 75 7W
Morriston 73 43 27N 80 7W
Morse 78 50 25N 107 3W
Morson 74 49 6N 94 19W
Mortlach 78 50 27N 106 4W
Moses Inlet 84 51 47N 127 23W
Mosher 75 48 42N 84 12W
Mosley Cr. → 84 51 18N 124 50W
Mosquito B. 62 61 10N 78 0W
Mossbank 78 49 56N 105 56W
Mossy → 78 54 5N 102 58W
Mothe, La, Rés. 67 48 46N 71 9W
Motte, L. la 66 48 20N 78 2W
Mouchalagane → 62 50 56N 68 41W
Mould Bay 86 76 12N 119 25W
Mount Albert 70 44 8N 79 19W
Mount Assiniboine Prov. Park 81 50 53N 115 39W
Mount Brydges 70 42 54N 81 29W
Mount Carleton Prov. Park 65 47 25N 66 55W
Mount Carmel 63 47 9N 53 29W
Mount Clemens 60 42 35N 82 50W
Mount Dennis 72 43 41N 79 29W
Mount Desert I. 61 44 15N 68 25W
Mount Edgecumbe 76 57 8N 135 22W
Mount Forest 70 43 59N 80 43W
Mount Hamilton 69 43 14N 79 51W
Mount Hope 69 43 9N 79 55W
Mount Moriah 63 48 58N 58 2W
Mount Pearl 63 47 31N 52 47W
Mount Pleasant, Alta. 83 51 4N 114 5W
Mount Pleasant, Ont. 73 43 5N 80 19W
Mount Pleasant, 60 43 35N 84 47W
Mount Revelstoke Nat. Park 85 51 5N 118 30W
Mount Robson 76 52 56N 119 15W
Mount Robson Prov. Park 85 53 0N 119 0W
Mount Royal 82 50 27N 104 40W
Mount Seymour Prov. Park 88 49 24N 122 55W
Mount Stewart 65 46 22N 62 52W
Mount Tolmie 85 48 28N 123 20W
Mount Uniacke 65 44 54N 63 50W
Mount Vernon, 73 43 6N 80 24W
Mount Vernon, 76 48 25N 122 20W
Mountain Park 81 52 50N 117 15W
Mountain View 81 49 8N 113 36W
Muchalat Inlet 84 49 38N 126 15W
Mud B. 88 49 5N 122 53W
Muddy L. 78 52 19N 109 6W
Mudjatik → 77 56 1N 107 36W
Muenster 78 52 12N 105 0W
Mukutawa → 79 53 10N 97 24W
Mulgrave 65 45 38N 61 31W
Muncho Lake 76 59 0N 125 50W
Mundare 80 53 35N 112 20W
Munising 60 46 25N 86 39W
Munroe L. 77 59 13N 98 35W
Munson 81 51 34N 112 45W
Murchison I. 74 50 0N 88 21W
Murdochville 64 48 58N 65 30W
Murdock 82 49 56N 97 4W
Muriel L. 80 54 9N 110 40W
Murphy L. 85 52 3N 121 15W
Murray → 76 56 11N 120 45W
Murray Harbour 65 46 0N 62 28W
Murray River 65 46 1N 62 37W
Murtle L. 85 52 8N 119 38W
Musgrave Harbour 63 49 27N 53 58W
Mushaboom 65 44 51N 62 32W
Muskeg → 76 60 20N 123 20W
Muskeg L. 74 49 0N 90 2W
Muskeg River 80 53 55N 118 39W
Muskoka, L. 70 45 0N 79 25W
Muskwa →, Alta. 80 56 15N 113 48W
Muskwa →, B.C. 76 58 47N 122 48W
Muskwa L. 80 56 9N 114 38W
Musquanousse, L. 64 50 22N 61 5W
Musquaro 64 50 10N 61 3W
Musquaro, L. 62 50 38N 61 5W
Musquash 65 45 11N 66 19W
Musquodoboit Harbour 65 44 50N 63 9W
Mussel Inlet 84 52 53N 128 7W
Muzon C. 76 54 40N 132 40W
Myrnam 80 53 40N 111 14W
Mystery Lake 80 54 10N 114 55W

Nabisipi → 62 50 14N 62 13W
Nachicapau, L. 62 56 40N 68 5W
Nachvak Fd. 62 59 3N 63 45W
Nackawic 65 45 59N 67 17W
Nacmine 81 51 28N 112 47W
Nadern Harb. 84 54 0N 132 36W
Nadina → 84 53 58N 126 30W
Nadina L. 84 53 53N 127 2W
Nagagami → 75 49 40N 84 40W
Nagagami L. 75 49 25N 85 1W
Nagagamisis L. 75 49 28N 84 40W
Nagas Pt. 84 52 12N 131 22W
Nagasin L. 75 47 48N 83 37W
Nahanni Butte 76 61 2N 123 31W
Nahanni Nat. Park 76 61 15N 125 0W
Nahlin 76 58 55N 131 38W
Naicam 78 52 30N 104 30W
Naikoon Prov. Park 84 53 55N 131 55W
Nain 62 56 34N 61 40W
Nairn 70 46 20N 81 35W
Nakina, B.C. 76 59 12N 132 52W
Nakina, Ont. 75 50 10N 86 40W
Nakusp 85 50 20N 117 45W
Namakan L. 74 48 27N 92 35W
Namew L. 79 54 14N 101 56W
Namu 84 51 52N 127 50W
Namur 66 45 54N 74 56W
Nanaimo 84 49 10N 124 0W
Nanika L. 84 53 47N 127 38W
Nanisivik 87 73 2N 84 33W
Nansen Sd. 87 81 0N 91 0W
Nanton 81 50 21N 113 46W
Naococane L. 62 52 50N 70 45W
Napanee 71 44 15N 77 0W
Napartokh B. 62 58 1N 62 19W
Napierville 67 45 11N 73 25W
Napierville □ 68 45 10N 73 30W
Napinka 79 49 19N 100 50W
Narraway → 80 55 44N 119 55W
Nash Creek 65 47 56N 66 6W
Nashwaak Bridge 65 46 14N 66 37W
Nashwaaksis 65 45 59N 66 38W
Naskaupi → 62 53 47N 60 51W
Nass → 76 55 0N 129 40W
Nastapoka → 62 56 55N 76 33W
Nastapoka, Is. 62 56 55N 76 50W
Natal 81 49 43N 114 51W
Natalkuz L. 84 53 36N 125 20W
Natashquan 64 50 14N 61 46W
Natashquan → 64 50 7N 61 50W
Natashquan-Est → 64 51 20N 61 40W
Natashquan Pt. 64 50 8N 61 40W
Nation → 76 55 30N 123 32W
Naubinway 60 46 7N 85 27W
Naughton 70 46 24N 81 12W
Navin 82 49 51N 97 0W
Nazko 84 53 1N 123 37W
Nazko → 84 53 7N 123 34W
Nechako → 85 53 30N 122 44W
Nechako Res. 84 53 42N 127 30W
Neepawa 79 50 15N 99 30W
Negaunee 60 46 30N 87 36W
Neguac 65 47 15N 65 5W
Neidpath 78 50 12N 107 20W
Neilburg 78 52 50N 109 38W
Neil's Harbour 65 46 48N 60 20W
Nejanilini L. 77 59 33N 97 48W
Nelson, B.C. 85 49 30N 117 20W
Nelson, Ont. 69 43 23N 79 50W
Nelson → 77 54 33N 98 2W
Nelson Forks 76 59 30N 124 0W
Nelson House 77 55 47N 98 51W
Nelson L. 77 55 48N 100 7W
Nelson-Miramichi 65 46 59N 65 34W
Nemegosenda L. 75 48 0N 83 7W
Nemeiben L. 77 55 20N 105 20W
Némiscachingue, L. 66 47 25N 74 30W
Némiscau 62 51 18N 76 54W
Némiscau, L. 62 51 25N 76 40W
Neoskweskau 62 51 52N 74 17W
Nepisiguit → 65 47 37N 65 38W
Neptune 78 49 22N 104 4W
Néret L. 62 54 45N 70 44W
Nestaocano → 67 49 38N 73 28W
Nestor Falls 74 49 7N 93 56W
Netherby 73 42 57N 79 8W
Nettilling L. 87 66 30N 71 0W
Neudorf 78 50 43N 103 1W
Neufchâtel 69 46 51N 71 23W
Neustadt 70 44 5N 81 0W
Neville 78 49 58N 107 39W
New Brigden 81 51 42N 110 29W
New Brunswick □ 61 46 50N 66 30W
New Carlisle 65 48 1N 65 20W
New Denmark 65 47 2N 67 38W
New Denver 85 50 0N 117 25W
New Dundee 73 43 21N 80 31W
New Durham 73 43 3N 80 34W
New Germany 65 44 33N 64 43W
New Glasgow 65 45 35N 62 36W
New Hamburg 70 43 23N 80 42W
New Harbour 65 45 13N 61 29W
New Hazelton 76 55 20N 127 30W
New Liskeard 60 47 31N 79 41W
New Norway 81 52 52N 112 57W
New Richmond 64 48 15N 65 45W
New Ross 65 44 44N 64 27W
New Sarepta 80 53 16N 113 8W
New Toronto 72 43 36N 79 30W
New Waterford 65 46 13N 60 4W
New Westminster 85 49 13N 122 55W
New World I. 63 49 35N 54 40W
Newberry 60 46 20N 85 32W
Newboro L. 71 44 38N 76 20W
Newbrook 80 54 24N 112 57W
Newburgh 71 44 19N 76 52W
Newcastle 65 47 1N 65 38W
Newcastle Bridge 65 46 5N 66 3W
Newell, L. 81 50 26N 111 55W
Newfoundland 61 48 30N 56 0W
Newfoundland □ 61 53 0N 58 0W
Newgate 81 49 2N 115 12W
Newhalem 76 48 41N 121 16W
Newmarket 70 44 3N 79 28W
Newport, Ont. 73 43 6N 80 14W
Newport, 64 48 16N 64 45W
Newport, 76 48 11N 117 2W
Newton 88 49 8N 122 51W
Newton Brook 72 43 48N 79 24W
Newtown 63 49 12N 53 31W
Niagara □ 73 43 15N 79 4W
Niagara → 73 43 16N 79 3W
Niagara Falls 73 43 7N 79 5W
Niagara-on-the-Lake 73 43 15N 79 4W
Nicola 85 50 12N 120 40W
Nicola L. 85 50 10N 120 32W
Nicolet 67 46 17N 72 35W
Nicomekl → 88 49 3N 122 52W
Nigel I. 84 50 53N 127 43W
Nimpkish → 84 50 34N 126 58W
Nimpkish L. 84 50 25N 126 59W
Nimpo L. 84 52 20N 125 10W
Ninemile 76 56 0N 130 7W
Ninette 79 49 24N 99 38W
Nioman 62 50 25N 66 5W
Nipawin 78 53 20N 104 0W
Nipawin Prov. Park 78 54 0N 104 37W
Nipekamew → 78 54 59N 104 52W
Nipigon 74 49 0N 88 17W
Nipigon, L. 74 49 50N 88 30W
Nipigon B. 75 48 53N 87 50W
Nipin → 77 55 46N 108 35W
Nipishish L. 62 54 12N 60 45W
Nipisi L. 80 55 47N 114 57W
Nipissing L. 70 46 20N 80 0W
Nipissis → 62 50 30N 66 5W
Nipissis, L. 64 51 2N 66 10W
Nipisso, L. 64 50 52N 65 50W
Nipper's Harbour 63 49 48N 55 52W
Niskibi → 60 56 29N 88 9W
Nisutlin → 76 60 14N 132 34W
Nitchequon 62 53 10N 70 58W
Nith → 70 43 12N 80 23W
Nitinat 84 48 56N 124 29W
Nitinat L. 84 48 45N 124 45W
Niverville 79 49 36N 97 3W
Nobel 70 45 25N 80 6W
Nobleford 81 49 53N 113 3W
Nobleton 73 43 54N 79 40W
Noel 65 45 18N 63 45W
Noelville 70 46 8N 80 26W
Noirclair, L. 64 50 38N 60 23W
Noire → 66 45 54N 76 57W
Nokomis 78 51 35N 105 0W
Nokomis L. 77 57 0N 103 0W
Noman L. 77 62 15N 108 55W
Nominingue 66 46 24N 75 2W
Nominingue, L. 66 46 26N 74 59W
Nonacho L. 77 61 42N 109 40W
Noonan 77 48 51N 102 59W
Nootka 84 49 38N 126 38W
Nootka I. 84 49 32N 126 42W
Noranda 66 48 20N 79 0W
Nord, Grand L. du 64 50 54N 67 6W
Nord, Petit L. du 64 50 50N 67 10W
Nordegg 81 52 29N 116 5W
Norembega 60 48 59N 80 43W
Norman Wells 86 65 17N 126 51W
Normandin 67 48 49N 72 31W
Norman's Cove 63 47 33N 53 40W
Normanview 82 50 28N 104 40W
Normétal 66 49 0N 79 22W
Norquay 79 51 53N 102 5W
Norris Arm 63 49 5N 55 15W
Norris Point 63 49 31N 57 53W
North → 62 57 30N 61 50W
North Aulatsivik I. 62 59 46N 64 5W
North Battleford 78 52 50N 108 17W
North Bay 70 46 20N 79 30W
North Belcher Is. 62 56 50N 79 50W
North Bend 85 49 50N 121 27W
North Buck L. 80 54 41N 112 32W
North Burnaby 88 49 17N 123 0W
North C. 65 47 2N 60 20W
North Caribou L. 60 52 50N 90 40W
North Channel 70 46 0N 83 0W
North French → 75 51 10N 80 50W
North Gower 71 45 8N 75 43W
North Grant 65 45 40N 62 2W
North Hatley 67 45 17N 71 58W
North Head, N.B. 65 44 46N 66 45W
North Head, Nfld. 63 47 29N 52 38W
North Henik L. 77 61 45N 97 40W
North Knife → 77 58 53N 94 45W
North Lonsdale 88 49 20N 123 4W
North Magnetic Pole 87 77 18N 101 48W
North Nahanni → 76 62 15N 123 20W
North Pt. 65 47 5N 64 0W
North Portal 79 49 0N 102 33W
North Ram → 81 52 16N 114 38W
North Rustico 65 46 27N 63 19W
North Saskatchewan → 78 53 15N 105 5W
North Seneca 73 43 7N 79 56W
North Star 80 56 51N 117 38W
North Sydney 65 46 12N 60 15W
North Thompson → 85 50 40N 120 20W
North Twin I. 62 53 20N 80 0W
North Twin L. 63 49 16N 55 56W
North Vancouver 85 49 25N 123 3W
North Wabiskaw L. 80 56 0N 113 55W
North West River 62 53 30N 60 10W
North West Territories □ 86 67 0N 110 0W
North York 72 43 46N 79 30W
Northern Indian L. 77 57 20N 97 20W
Northern Light, L. 74 48 15N 90 39W
Northmount 72 43 46N 79 24W
Northport 65 45 56N 63 52W
Northumberland Str. 65 46 20N 64 0W
Northwest Gander → 63 48 55N 55 2W
Norton 65 45 38N 65 42W
Norway House 79 53 59N 97 50W
Norwegian B. 87 77 30N 90 0W
Norwich 70 42 59N 80 36W
Norwood 71 44 23N 77 59W
Nose Cr. → 83 51 3N 114 1W
Notigi Dam 77 56 40N 99 10W
Notikewin → 80 57 2N 117 38W
Notre-Dame 65 46 18N 64 46W
Notre-Dame, Les 64 48 10N 68 0W
Notre Dame B. 63 49 45N 55 30W
Notre Dame de Koartac = Koartac 62 60 55N 69 40W
Notre-Dame-de-la-Doré 67 48 43N 72 39W
Notre-Dame-de-l'Île-Perrot 68 45 23N 73 56W
Notre Dame de Lourdes 79 49 32N 98 33W
Notre-Dame-des-Bois 67 45 24N 71 4W
Notre-Dame-des-Laurentides 69 46 55N 71 18W
Notre Dame d'Ivugivic = Ivugivik 62 62 24N 77 55W
Notre-Dame-du-Bon-Conseil 67 46 0N 72 21W
Notre Dame du Lac, Ont. 70 46 18N 80 11W
Notre Dame du Lac, Que. 67 47 36N 68 48W
Notre-Dame-du-Laus 66 46 5N 75 37W
Notre-Dame-du-Nord 66 47 36N 79 30W
Notre-Dame-du-Portage 67 47 46N 69 37W
Nottawasaga B. 70 44 35N 80 15W
Nottaway → 62 51 22N 78 55W
Nottingham I. 87 63 20N 77 55W
Nottingham Island 87 63 6N 77 50W
Notukeu Cr. → 78 49 56N 106 29W
Nouveau Comptoir 62 53 0N 78 49W
Nouveau-Québec 62 56 0N 71 0W
Nouvelle 65 48 8N 66 19W
Nouvelle → 65 48 7N 66 19W
Nouvelle France, C. de 62 62 27N 73 42W
Nova Scotia □ 61 45 10N 63 0W
Nova Zembla I. 87 72 11N 74 50W
Novar 70 45 27N 79 15W
Noyes I. 76 55 30N 133 40W
Nueltin L. 77 60 30N 99 30W
Nugssuaq Pen. 87 70 30N 53 0W
Nulki L. 84 53 55N 124 7W
Nunaksaluk I. 62 55 49N 60 20W
Nungesser L. 74 51 28N 93 30W
Nut L. 78 52 22N 103 42W
Nutak 62 57 28N 61 59W
Nuvuk Is. 62 62 24N 78 3W
Nyarling → 76 60 41N 113 23W

Oak Bay, B.C. 85 48 26N 123 18W
Oak Bay, N.B. 65 45 14N 67 12W
Oak Bluff 82 49 46N 97 19W
Oak Hill 65 45 20N 67 20W
Oak Lake 79 49 46N 100 38W
Oak Point 79 50 30N 98 1W
Oak Ridges 73 43 57N 79 28W
Oak River 79 50 8N 100 26W
Oakbank 79 49 57N 96 51W
Oakland 73 43 2N 80 20W
Oakville 73 43 27N 79 41W
Oakville → 73 43 27N 79 41W
Oba 75 49 4N 84 7W
Oba L. 75 48 40N 84 16W
Obakamiga L. 75 49 9N 85 9W
Obalski, L. 66 48 43N 77 58W
Obamsca, L. 66 50 24N 78 16W
Obatanga Prov. Park 75 48 20N 85 10W
Obed 80 53 30N 117 10W
Obedjwan 66 48 40N 74 56W
Obonga L. 74 49 57N 89 22W
Observatory Inlet 76 55 10N 129 54W
Ocean Falls 84 52 18N 127 48W
Ocean Park 88 49 2N 122 52W
Ochre River 79 51 4N 99 47W
Odei → 77 56 6N 96 54W
Odessa, Ont. 71 44 17N 76 43W
Odessa, Sask. 78 50 17N 103 47W
Ogahalla 75 50 6N 85 51W
Ogascanane, L. 66 47 5N 78 25W
Ogden 83 51 0N 114 0W
Ogema 78 49 35N 104 55W
Ogilvie Mts. 86 65 0N 140 0W
Ogoki 75 51 38N 85 58W
Ogoki → 75 51 38N 85 57W
Ogoki L. 75 50 50N 87 10W
Ogoki Res. 74 50 45N 88 15W
Ohsweken 73 43 4N 80 7W
Oil Springs 70 42 47N 82 7W
Okak 62 57 33N 61 58W
Okak Is. 62 57 30N 61 30W
Okanagan L. 85 50 0N 119 30W
Okanagan Mission 85 49 45N 119 30W
Okanagan Mountain Prov. Park 85 49 45N 119 30W
Okanogan 76 48 6N 119 43W
Old Chelsea 69 45 30N 75 49W
Old Crow 86 67 30N 140 5 E
Old Fort → 77 58 36N 110 24W
Old Perlican 63 48 5N 53 1W
Old Town 61 45 0N 68 41W
Old Wives L. 78 50 5N 106 0W
Oldman → 81 49 57N 111 42W
Olds 81 51 50N 114 10W
O'Leary 65 46 42N 64 13W
Olga, L. 66 49 47N 77 15W
Oliver 85 49 13N 119 37W
Oliver L. 77 56 56N 103 22W
Olomane → 62 50 14N 60 37W
Omemee 71 44 18N 78 33W
Omineca → 76 56 3N 124 16W
Ommanney B. 87 73 0N 101 0W
Onakawana 75 50 36N 81 27W
Onaman → 75 49 59N 88 0W
Onaman L. 75 50 0N 87 26W
Onanole 79 50 37N 99 58W
Onaping 70 46 37N 81 25W
Onaping → 70 46 37N 81 18W
Onaping L. 75 47 3N 81 30W
Onatchiway, L. 67 49 3N 71 5W
Onion Lake 78 53 43N 110 0W
Onondaga 73 43 7N 80 7W
Onoway 80 53 42N 114 12W
Ontario □ 60 52 0N 88 10W
Ontario, L. 71 43 40N 78 0W
Ontonagon 60 46 52N 89 19W
Oona River 84 53 57N 130 16W
Ootsa L. 84 53 50N 126 2W
Ootsa Lake 84 53 50N 126 5W
Opasatica, L. 66 48 5N 79 18W
Opasatika 75 49 30N 82 50W
Opasatika → 75 50 25N 82 25W
Opasatika L. 75 49 4N 83 6W
Opasquia 77 53 16N 93 34W
Opataca, L. 66 50 22N 74 55W
Opawica, L. 66 49 35N 75 55W
Opémisca, L. 66 49 56N 74 52W
Opeongo L. 71 45 42N 78 23W
Opheim 77 48 52N 106 30W
Opinaca → 62 52 15N 78 2W
Opinaca L. 62 52 39N 76 20W
Opiscoteo, L. 62 53 10N 68 10W
Opiskotish, L. 62 53 10N 67 50W
Opocopa, L. 64 52 38N 66 35W
Orangeville 73 43 55N 80 5W
Orillia 70 44 40N 79 24W
Orléans, Î. d' 69 46 54N 70 58W
Ormiston 78 49 44N 105 24W
Ormstown 67 45 8N 74 0W
Oromocto 65 45 54N 66 29W
Oromocto, L. 65 45 36N 67 0W
Orono 71 43 59N 78 37W
Oroville 76 48 58N 119 30W
Orsainville 69 46 51N 71 14W
Osawin → 75 49 45N 85 19W
Osborne Corners 73 43 13N 80 16W
Osgoode 71 45 8N 75 36W
Oshawa 71 43 50N 78 50W
Oskélanéo 66 48 5N 75 15W
Osler 78 52 22N 106 33W
Osnaburgh L. 74 51 12N 90 9W
Osoyoos 85 49 0N 119 30W
Osoyoos L. 85 49 0N 119 27W
Ospika → 76 56 20N 124 0W
Ospringe 73 43 42N 80 7W
Ossokmanuan L. 62 53 25N 65 0W
Ostaboningue, L. 66 47 9N 78 53W
O'Sullivan L. 75 50 25N 87 2W
Otelnuk L. 62 56 9N 68 12W
Otish, Mts. 62 52 22N 70 30W
Otoskwin → 60 52 13N 88 6W
Otosquen 79 53 17N 102 1W
Ottawa 71 45 27N 75 42W
Ottawa → = Outaouais → 67 45 27N 74 8W
Ottawa-Carleton □ 69 45 23N 75 40W
Ottawa International Airport 69 45 19N 75 40W
Ottawa Is. 87 59 35N 80 10W
Otter L. 77 55 35N 104 39W
Otter Rapids, Ont. 75 50 11N 81 39W
Otter Rapids, Sask. 77 55 38N 104 44W
Otterville 70 42 55N 80 36W
Ouareau, L., Rés. 67 46 17N 74 9W
Ouasiemsca → 67 49 0N 72 30W
Ouest, Pte. 64 49 52N 64 40W
Oustic 73 43 42N 80 15W
Outaouais → 67 45 27N 74 8W
Outardes 67 50 20N 69 10W
Outardes → 67 49 24N 69 30W
Outer I. 62 51 10N 58 35W
Outlook, 78 51 30N 107 0W
Outlook, 77 48 53N 104 46W
Outremount 68 45 31N 73 37W
Overflowing → 79 53 8N 101 5W
Owen Sound 70 44 35N 80 55W
Owikeno L. 84 51 40N 126 50W
Owl → 77 57 51N 92 44W
Owosso 60 43 0N 84 10W
Oxbow 79 49 14N 102 10W
Oxford 65 45 44N 63 52W
Oxford L. 77 54 51N 95 37W
Oyama 85 50 7N 119 22W
Oyen 81 51 22N 110 28W
Oyster River 84 49 53N 125 7W

Pabos Mills CANADA Republic

Pabos Mills	64	48 19N	64 42W
Pacific	76	54 48N	128 28W
Pacific Rim Nat. Park	84	48 40N	124 45W
Packenham	71	45 22N	76 25W
Pacquet	63	50 0N	55 53W
Paddockwood	78	53 30N	105 30W
Padle	87	62 10N	97 5W
Padloping Island	87	67 0N	62 50W
Pagwa River	75	50 2N	85 14W
Pagwachuan →	75	50 12N	84 43W
Paimpont, L.	64	50 28N	61 34W
Paint Hills = Nouveau Comptoir	62	53 0N	78 49W
Paint I.	77	55 28N	97 57W
Paisley	70	44 18N	81 16W
Paix, Îles de la	68	45 20N	73 51W
Pakashkan L.	74	49 21N	90 15W
Pakenham	66	45 18N	76 18W
Pakowi L.	81	49 20N	111 0W
Pakwash L.	74	50 45N	93 30W
Palermo	73	43 26N	79 47W
Palgrave	73	43 57N	79 50W
Palmarolle	66	48 40N	79 12W
Palmerston	70	43 50N	80 51W
Palomar	75	48 10N	82 16W
Panache, L.	70	46 15N	81 20W
Pangmar	78	49 39N	104 40W
Panny →	80	57 8N	114 51W
Papineau-Labelle, Parc Prov.	66	46 10N	75 15W
Papineauville	66	45 37N	75 1W
Paradis	66	48 15N	76 35W
Paradise →	62	53 27N	57 19W
Paradise Hill	78	53 32N	109 28W
Paradise Valley	81	53 2N	110 17W
Parent	66	47 55N	74 35W
Parent, Lac	66	48 31N	77 1W
Parham	71	44 39N	76 43W
Paris	73	43 12N	80 25W
Park Royal	88	49 20N	123 8W
Parker	73	43 46N	80 35W
Parkerview	78	51 21N	103 18W
Parkhill	70	43 15N	81 38W
Parks L.	75	49 27N	87 38W
Parkside	78	53 10N	106 33W
Parksville	84	49 20N	124 21W
Parrsboro	65	45 30N	64 25W
Parry, C.	87	70 20N	123 38W
Parry Is.	86	77 0N	110 0W
Parry Sound	70	45 20N	80 0W
Parsnip →	76	55 10N	123 2W
Parson	85	51 5N	116 37W
Parsons Pond, Nfld.	63	49 59N	57 37W
Parsons Pond, Nfld.	63	50 2N	57 43W
Partridge →	75	51 19N	80 18W
Partridge Pt.	63	50 10N	56 10W
Pasadena	63	49 1N	57 36W
Pasfield L.	77	58 24N	105 20W
Paspébiac	65	48 3N	65 17W
Pass Island	63	47 30N	56 12W
Passage Pt.	86	73 29N	115 16W
Pasteur, L.	64	50 13N	66 58W
Patrick's Cove	63	47 3N	54 7W
Patrie, La	67	45 24N	71 15W
Patten	61	45 59N	68 28W
Patterson	72	43 54N	79 28W
Paul I.	62	56 30N	61 20W
Paul-Sauvé, L.	66	50 15N	78 20W
Paulatuk	86	69 25N	124 0W
Payne Bay = Bellin	62	60 0N	70 0W
Peace →	76	59 0N	111 25W
Peace Point	76	59 7N	112 27W
Peace River	80	56 15N	117 18W
Peachland	85	49 47N	119 45W
Pearl	74	48 40N	88 40W
Pearse I.	76	54 52N	130 14W
Peel □	72	43 45N	79 47W
Peel →	86	67 0N	135 0W
Peerless L.	80	56 37N	114 40W
Peerless Lake	80	56 40N	114 35W
Peers	80	53 40N	116 0W
Peggy's Cove	65	44 30N	63 55W
Pékans →	64	52 12N	66 49W
Pelee, Pt.	70	41 54N	82 31W
Pelee I.	70	41 47N	82 40W
Pelham	73	43 3N	79 21W
Pelham Union	73	43 5N	79 23W
Pélican, L.	62	59 47N	73 35W
Pelican L.	79	52 28N	100 20W
Pelican Narrows	77	55 10N	102 56W
Pelican Rapids	79	52 45N	100 42W
Pelletier Sta.	67	47 33N	69 26W
Pelly	79	51 52N	101 56W
Pelly →	86	62 47N	137 19W
Pelly Bay	87	68 38N	89 50W
Pelly Crossing	86	62 49N	136 34W
Pelly L.	86	66 0N	102 0W
Pelly Pt.	88	49 7N	123 12W
Pemberton	85	50 25N	122 50W
Pembina	77	48 58N	97 15W
Pembina →, Alta.	80	54 45N	114 17W
Pembina →, Man.	79	49 0N	98 12W
Pembroke	71	45 50N	77 7W
Penetanguishene, Nfld.	63	47 36N	52 45W
Penetanguishene, Ont.	70	44 50N	79 55W
Penhold	81	52 8N	113 52W
Pennant	78	50 32N	108 14W
Penniac	65	46 2N	66 34W
Penny	85	53 51N	121 20W
Penny Highland	87	67 19N	66 20W
Penny Str.	87	76 30N	97 0W
Pense	78	50 25N	104 59W
Pentecôte →	64	49 46N	67 10W
Pentecôte, L.	64	49 53N	67 20W
Penticton	85	49 30N	119 38W
Pentland Corners	73	43 40N	80 30W
Penylan L.	77	61 50N	106 20W
Percé	64	48 31N	64 13W
Perdue	78	52 4N	107 33W
Péribonca →	62	48 45N	72 5W
Péribonca, L.	67	50 1N	71 10W
Peribonka	67	48 46N	72 3W
Perow	76	54 35N	126 10W
Perrot, Île	68	45 22N	73 57W
Perry River	87	67 43N	102 14W
Perth, N.B.	65	46 44N	67 42W
Perth, Ont.	71	44 55N	76 15W
Petawawa	71	45 54N	77 17W
Peter Pond L.	77	55 55N	108 44W
Peterbell	75	48 36N	83 21W
Peterborough	71	44 20N	78 20W
Peters, L.	62	59 41N	70 53W
Petersburg	76	56 50N	133 0W
Petersfield	79	50 18N	96 58W
Petit-Cap	64	48 3N	64 30W
Petit-de-Grat	65	45 30N	60 58W
Petit Étang	65	46 39N	60 58W
Petit Lac Manicouagan	64	51 25N	67 40W
Petit-Mécatina, I. du	62	50 30N	59 25W
Petit-Rocher	65	47 46N	65 43W
Petitcodiac	65	45 57N	65 11W
Petite Baleine →	62	56 0N	76 45W
Petite-Cascapédia, Parc Prov. de la	64	48 30N	65 45W
Petite-Rivière	67	47 20N	70 33W
Petite Rivière Bridge	65	44 14N	64 27W
Petite Saguenay	67	48 15N	70 4W
Petitsikapau, L.	62	54 37N	66 25W
Petoskey	60	45 22N	84 57W
Petrolia	70	42 54N	82 9W
Petty Harbour Long Pond	63	47 31N	52 58W
Phelps L.	77	59 15N	103 15W
Philipsburg	67	45 2N	73 5W
Piapot	78	49 59N	109 8W
Piashti, L.	64	50 29N	62 52W
Pic →	75	48 36N	86 18W
Pic I.	75	48 43N	86 37W
Piccadilly	63	48 34N	58 55W
Pickerel L.	74	48 40N	91 25W
Pickering	72	43 52N	79 2W
Pickering Beach	72	43 50N	78 59W
Pickle Lake	74	51 30N	90 12W
Picton	71	44 1N	77 9W
Pictou	65	45 41N	62 42W
Pictou I.	65	45 49N	62 33W
Picture Butte	81	49 55N	112 45W
Pie I.	74	48 15N	89 6W
Pierceland	78	54 20N	109 46W
Pierrefonds	68	45 29N	73 52W
Pierreville	67	46 4N	72 49W
Pierson	79	49 11N	101 15W
Pigeon L., Alta.	81	53 1N	114 2W
Pigeon L., Ont.	71	44 27N	78 30W
Pikwitonei	77	55 35N	97 9W
Pilot Butte	78	50 28N	104 25W
Pilot Mound	79	49 15N	98 54W
Pin-Blanc, L.	66	46 45N	78 8W
Pinawa	79	50 9N	95 50W
Pincher Creek	81	49 30N	113 57W
Pinchi L.	76	54 38N	124 30W
Pincourt	68	45 23N	74 0W
Pine →	77	58 50N	105 38W
Pine, C.	63	46 37N	53 32W
Pine Dock	79	51 38N	96 48W
Pine Falls	79	50 34N	96 11W
Pine Grove	72	43 48N	79 35W
Pine Pass	76	55 25N	122 42W
Pine Point	76	60 50N	114 28W
Pine Portage	74	49 20N	88 26W
Pine Ridge	82	50 0N	96 50W
Pine River	79	51 45N	100 30W
Pineview	85	53 50N	122 38W
Pink →	77	56 50N	103 50W
Pins, Pte. aux	70	42 15N	81 51W
Pinware	63	51 37N	56 42W
Pinware →	63	51 39N	56 42W
Pipestone →	60	52 53N	89 23W
Pipestone Cr. →	79	49 38N	100 15W
Pipmuacan, Rés.	67	49 45N	70 30W
Pistol B.	77	62 25N	92 37W
Pistolet B.	63	51 35N	55 45W
Pitt →	88	49 13N	122 46W
Pitt I.	84	53 30N	129 50W
Pitt L.	85	49 25N	122 32W
Pitt Meadows	88	49 13N	122 42W
Pivabiska →	75	50 13N	82 52W
Placentia	63	47 20N	54 0W
Placentia B.	63	47 0N	54 40W
Plaine, La	68	45 47N	73 46W
Plamondon	80	54 51N	112 32W
Plaster Rock	65	46 53N	67 22W
Playgreen L.	79	54 0N	98 15W
Pleasant Bay	61	46 51N	60 48W
Pleasantdale	78	52 35N	104 30W
Pledger L.	75	50 53N	83 42W
Plenty	78	51 47N	108 38W
Plessisville	67	46 14N	71 47W
Pletipi L.	62	51 44N	70 6W
Plevna	71	44 58N	76 59W
Plonge, Lac la	77	55 8N	107 20W
Plum Coulee	79	49 11N	97 45W
Plumas	79	50 23N	99 5W
Plunkett	78	51 55N	105 27W
Plympton	65	44 30N	65 55W
Pocatière, La	67	47 22N	70 2W
Pogamasing	75	46 55N	81 50W
Poile, La	63	47 41N	58 24W
Point Edward	70	43 0N	82 30W
Point L.	86	65 15N	113 4W
Point Leamington	63	49 20N	55 24W
Point Pelee Nat. Park	70	41 57N	82 31W
Point Pleasant	65	44 37N	63 34W
Point Sapin	65	46 58N	64 50W
Pointe-à-la-Frégate	64	49 12N	64 55W
Pointe-à-Maurier	64	50 20N	59 48W
Pointe au Baril Sta.	70	45 35N	80 23W
Pointe-au-Pic	67	47 38N	70 9W
Pointe-aux-Anglais	64	49 41N	67 10W
Pointe-aux-Outardes	67	49 3N	68 26W
Pointe-aux-Trembles	67	45 40N	73 30W
Pointe-Calumet	68	45 30N	73 58W
Pointe-Claire	68	45 26N	73 50W
Pointe-des-Cascades	68	45 20N	73 58W
Pointe du Bois	79	50 18N	95 33W
Pointe-Gatineau	71	45 28N	75 42W
Pointe-Lebel	67	49 10N	68 12W
Pointe-Parent	64	50 8N	61 47W
Pointe Verte	65	47 51N	65 46W
Poisson-Blanc, L. du	66	46 0N	75 45W
Poltimore	66	45 47N	75 43W
Ponask, L.	60	54 0N	92 41W
Ponass L.	78	52 16N	103 58W
Poncheville, L.	66	50 10N	76 55W
Pond Inlet	87	72 40N	77 0W
Ponds, I. of	62	53 27N	55 52W
Ponoka	81	52 42N	113 40W
Ponsonby	73	43 38N	80 22W
Pont-Rouge	67	46 45N	71 42W
Pont-Viau	68	45 34N	73 41W
Ponteix	78	49 46N	107 29W
Pontiac	60	42 40N	83 20W
Pontiac, Parc	66	46 30N	76 30W
Ponton →	76	58 27N	116 11W
Pontypool	71	44 6N	78 38W
Pooley I.	84	52 45N	128 15W
Poplar →, Man.	79	53 0N	97 19W
Poplar →, N.W.T.	76	61 22N	121 52W
Poplar Point	79	50 4N	97 59W
Poplarfield	79	50 53N	97 36W
Porcher I.	84	53 50N	130 30W
Porcupine	75	48 30N	81 11W
Porcupine →	77	59 11N	104 46W
Porcupine Plain	78	52 36N	103 15W
Port Alberni	84	49 40N	124 50W
Port Alfred	67	48 18N	70 53W
Port Alice	84	50 20N	127 25W
Port au Choix	63	50 43N	57 22W
Port au Port	63	48 33N	58 43W
Port au Port B.	63	48 40N	58 50W
Port Austin	60	44 3N	82 59W
Port Blandford	63	48 20N	54 10W
Port Burwell	70	42 40N	80 48W
Port Carling	70	45 7N	79 35W
Port-Cartier	64	50 2N	66 50W
Port-Cartier-Ouest	64	50 1N	66 52W
Port Clements	84	53 40N	132 10W
Port Colborne	70	42 50N	79 10W
Port Coquitlam	85	49 15N	122 45W
Port Credit	72	43 33N	79 35W
Port Dalhousie	73	43 13N	79 16W
Port-Daniel, Parc Prov. de	64	48 11N	64 58W
Port Dover	70	42 47N	80 12W
Port Dufferin	65	44 55N	62 23W
Port Edward	84	54 12N	130 10W
Port Elgin, N.B.	65	46 3N	64 5W
Port Elgin, Ont.	60	44 25N	81 25W
Port Greville	65	45 24N	64 33W
Port Guichon	88	49 5N	123 7W
Port Hammond	88	49 12N	122 39W
Port Hardy	84	50 41N	127 30W
Port Harrison = Inoucdjouac	62	58 25N	78 15W
Port Hastings	65	45 39N	61 24W
Port Hawkesbury	65	45 36N	61 22W
Port Hood	65	46 0N	61 32W
Port Hope	71	43 56N	78 20W
Port Howe	65	45 51N	63 45W
Port Huron	60	43 0N	82 28W
Port Kells	88	49 10N	122 42W
Port Loring	70	45 55N	80 0W
Port Lorne	65	44 57N	65 16W
Port McNeill	84	50 35N	127 5W
Port Mann	88	49 12N	122 49W
Port Medway	65	44 8N	64 35W
Port Mellon	85	49 32N	123 31W
Port-Menier	64	49 51N	64 15W
Port Moody	85	49 17N	122 51W
Port Mouton	65	43 58N	64 50W
Port Nelson, Man.	77	57 3N	92 36W
Port Nelson, Ont.	69	43 20N	79 46W
Port Nouveau-Québec	62	58 30N	65 59W
Port Perry	71	44 6N	78 56W
Port Radium = Echo Bay	86	66 5N	117 55W
Port Renfrew	84	48 30N	124 20W
Port Robinson	73	43 2N	79 13W
Port Rowan	70	42 40N	80 30W
Port Royal	65	44 43N	65 36W
Port Sanilac	60	43 26N	82 33W
Port Saunders	63	50 40N	57 18W
Port Severn	70	44 48N	79 43W
Port Simpson	76	54 30N	130 20W
Port Stanley	70	42 40N	81 10W
Port Wallace	65	44 42N	63 33W
Port Weller East	73	43 14N	79 13W
Port Whitby	73	43 51N	78 56W
Portage B.	79	51 33N	98 50W
Portage La Prairie	79	49 58N	98 18W
Porter L., N.W.T.	77	61 41N	108 5W
Porter L., Sask.	77	56 20N	107 20W
Porthill	76	49 0N	116 30W
Portland,	71	44 42N	76 12W
Portland,	61	43 40N	70 15W
Portland Creek Pond	63	50 11N	57 32W
Portland Prom.	62	58 40N	78 33W
Portneuf	69	46 43N	71 55W
Portneuf →	67	48 38N	69 5W
Portneuf, Parc Prov. de	67	47 10N	72 25W
Poste-de-la-Baleine	62	55 17N	77 45W
Pottageville	73	43 59N	79 37W
Pouce Coupé	76	55 40N	120 10W
Pouch Cove	63	47 46N	52 46W
Poulin-de-Courval, L.	67	48 52N	70 27W
Poutrincourt, L.	67	49 11N	74 7W
Povungnituk	62	60 2N	77 10W
Povungnituk →	62	60 3N	77 15W
Povungnituk, B.	62	60 0N	77 30W
Povungnituk, Mts. de	62	61 22N	75 5W
Powassan	70	46 5N	79 25W
Powell L.	84	50 2N	124 25W
Powell River	84	49 50N	124 35W
Prairies, R. des →	68	45 42N	73 29W
Preeceville	78	51 57N	102 40W
Preissac, L.	66	48 20N	78 20W
Prelate	78	50 51N	109 24W
Premier	76	56 4N	129 56W
Prescott	71	44 45N	75 30W
Prescott I.	84	54 6N	130 37W
Presque Isle	61	46 40N	68 0W
Preston	73	43 23N	80 21W
Price	64	48 36N	68 7W
Price I.	84	52 23N	128 41W
Priest L.	76	48 30N	116 55W
Priestly	76	54 8N	125 20W
Primrose L.	77	54 55N	109 45W
Prince	78	52 58N	108 23W
Prince Albert	78	53 15N	105 50W
Prince Albert Nat. Park	78	54 0N	106 25W
Prince Albert Pen.	86	72 30N	116 0W
Prince Albert Sd.	86	70 25N	115 0W
Prince Alfred C.	86	74 20N	124 40W
Prince Charles I.	86	67 47N	76 12W
Prince Edward I. □	65	46 20N	63 20W
Prince Edward Island Nat. Pk.	65	46 26N	63 12W
Prince Edward Pt.	71	43 56N	76 52W
Prince George	85	53 55N	122 50W
Prince Gustav Adolf Sea	86	78 30N	107 0W
Prince of Wales I.,	87	73 0N	99 0W
Prince of Wales I.,	76	55 30N	133 0W
Prince of Wales Str.	86	73 0N	117 0W
Prince Patrick I.	86	77 0N	120 0W
Prince Regent Inlet	87	73 0N	90 0W
Prince Rupert	84	54 20N	130 20W
Princess Margaret Range	87	80 30N	92 0W
Princess Royal Chan.	84	53 0N	128 31W
Princess Royal I.	84	53 0N	128 40W
Princeton, B.C.	85	49 27N	120 30W
Princeton, Ont.	73	43 10N	80 32W
Princeville	67	46 10N	71 53W
Principe Chan.	84	53 28N	130 0W
Procter	85	49 37N	116 57W
Prophet →	76	58 48N	122 40W
Prøven	87	72 10N	55 8W
Providence Bay	70	45 41N	82 15W
Provost	81	52 25N	110 20W
Prud'homme	78	52 20N	105 54W
Pugwash	65	45 51N	63 40W
Pukaskwa →	75	48 0N	85 53W
Pukaskwa Nat. Park	75	48 20N	86 0W
Pukatawagan	77	55 45N	101 20W
Punnichy	78	51 23N	104 18W
Puntzi L.	84	52 12N	124 2W
Puslinch	73	43 26N	80 5W
Puslinch, L.	73	43 25N	80 16W
Putahow L.	77	59 54N	100 40W
Puyjalon, L.	64	50 30N	63 25W
Quadra I.	84	50 10N	125 15W
Qualicum Beach	84	49 22N	124 26W
Qu'Appelle	78	50 33N	103 53W
Qu'Appelle →	78	50 26N	101 19W
Quarryville	65	46 50N	65 47W
Quathiaski Cove	84	50 3N	125 12W
Quatsino	84	50 30N	127 40W
Quatsino Sd.	84	50 25N	127 58W
Québec	69	46 52N	71 13W
Quebec □	61	50 0N	70 0W
Queen Charlotte	84	53 15N	132 2W
Queen Charlotte Is.	84	53 20N	132 10W
Queen Charlotte Mts.	84	53 5N	132 15W
Queen Charlotte Str.	84	51 0N	128 0W
Queen Elizabeth Is.	87	76 0N	95 0W
Queen Maud G.	86	68 15N	102 30W
Queens Sd.	84	51 57N	128 20W
Queensborough	88	49 12N	122 56W
Queenston	73	43 10N	79 3W
Queenstown	65	45 41N	66 7W
Quesnel	85	53 0N	122 30W
Quesnel →	85	52 58N	122 29W
Quesnel L.	85	52 30N	121 20W
Quetico Prov. Park	74	48 30N	91 45W
Quévillon, L.	66	49 4N	76 57W
Quick	76	54 36N	126 54W
Quidi Vidi	63	47 35N	52 41W
Quiet L.	76	61 5N	133 5W
Quilchena	85	50 10N	120 30W
Quill Lake	78	52 4N	104 15W
Quinton	78	51 23N	104 24W
Quinze, L. des	66	47 35N	79 5W
Quyon	66	45 31N	76 14W
Raanes Pen.	87	78 30N	85 45W
Rabbit →	76	59 41N	127 12W
Rabbit Lake	78	53 8N	107 46W
Rabbitskin →	76	61 47N	120 42W
Race, C.	63	46 40N	53 5W
Racine L.	75	48 2N	83 20W
Radisson	78	52 30N	107 20W
Radium Hot Springs	81	50 35N	116 2W
Radville	78	49 30N	104 15W
Radway	80	54 4N	112 57W
Rae	76	62 50N	116 3W
Rae Isthmus	87	66 40N	87 30W
Rainbow Lake	76	58 30N	119 23W
Rainy →	74	48 43N	94 29W
Rainy L.	74	48 42N	93 10W
Rainy River	74	48 43N	94 29W
Raleigh	63	51 34N	55 44W
Ralston	81	50 15N	111 10W
Ram →, Alta.	81	52 23N	115 25W
Ram →, N.W.T.	76	62 1N	123 41W
Rama	78	51 46N	103 0W
Ramah	62	58 52N	63 15W
Ramah B.	62	58 52N	63 13W
Ramea	63	47 31N	57 23W
Ramea Is.	63	47 31N	57 22W
Ramore	60	48 30N	80 25W
Ramsay I.	84	52 33N	131 23W
Ramsayville	69	45 23N	75 34W
Ramsey	75	47 25N	82 20W
Ramsey L.	75	47 13N	82 15W
Rancheria →	76	60 13N	129 7W
Random I.	63	48 8N	53 44W
Ranfurly	80	53 25N	111 41W
Ranger L.	75	46 52N	83 35W
Rankin Inlet	87	62 30N	93 0W
Ranoke	75	50 26N	81 35W
Raper, C.	87	69 44N	67 6W
Rapid →	76	59 15N	129 5W
Rapid City	79	50 7N	100 2W
Rapide-Blanc	67	47 48N	73 2W
Rapide-Mascouche	68	45 46N	73 40W
Rapide-Sept	66	47 46N	78 19W
Rapides des Joachims	66	46 13N	77 43W
Rat →	79	49 35N	97 10W
Rat River	76	61 7N	112 36W
Rats, R. aux →	67	48 53N	72 14W
Ratz, Mt.	76	57 23N	132 12W
Rawdon	67	46 3N	73 40W
Ray, C.	63	47 33N	59 15W
Rayleigh	85	50 49N	120 17W
Raymond	81	49 30N	112 35W
Raymore	78	51 25N	104 31W
Read Island	86	69 12N	114 31W
Reading	73	43 50N	80 13W
Red →	79	50 24N	96 48W
Red Bay	63	51 44N	56 25W
Red Deer	81	52 20N	113 50W
Red Deer →, Alta.	81	50 58N	110 0W
Red Deer →, Man.	79	52 53N	101 1W
Red Deer L., Alta.	81	52 43N	113 2W
Red Deer L., Man.	79	52 55N	101 20W
Red I.	63	47 23N	54 10W
Red Indian L.	63	48 35N	57 0W
Red L.	74	51 3N	93 49W
Red Lake	74	51 3N	93 49W
Red Lake Road	74	49 59N	93 25W
Red Pass	85	53 0N	119 0W
Red River Floodway	82	49 50N	96 57W
Red Rock, B.C.	85	53 42N	122 40W
Red Rock, Ont.	74	48 55N	88 15W
Red Sucker L.	77	54 9N	93 40W
Redberry L.	78	52 45N	107 14W
Redcliff	81	50 10N	110 50W
Redditt	74	49 59N	94 24W
Redknife →	76	61 14N	119 22W
Redonda Bay	84	50 17N	124 57W
Redonda Is.	84	50 15N	124 50W
Redrock Pt.	76	62 11N	115 2W
Redvers	79	49 35N	101 40W
Redwater	80	53 55N	113 6W
Redwillow →	80	55 2N	119 18W
Reed, L	77	54 38N	100 30W
Regent Park	82	50 28N	104 39W
Regina	78	50 27N	104 35W
Regina Beach	78	50 47N	105 0W
Reid L.	78	50 0N	108 9W
Reid Lake	84	53 58N	123 6W
Reindeer →	77	55 36N	103 11W
Reindeer I.	79	52 30N	98 0W
Reindeer L.	77	57 15N	102 15W
Reinland	79	49 2N	97 52W
Reliance	77	63 0N	109 20W
Remi Lake Prov. Park	75	49 30N	82 15W
Rémigny	66	47 46N	79 12W
Renata	85	49 27N	118 7W
Rencontre East	63	47 38N	55 12W
Renews	63	46 56N	52 56W
Renfrew	71	45 30N	76 40W
Renison	75	50 58N	81 7W
Rennell Sd.	84	53 23N	132 35W
Rennie	79	49 51N	95 33W
Rennison I.	84	52 50N	129 20W
Repentigny	67	45 44N	73 28W
Republic	60	46 25N	87 59W

Repulse Bay	**87**	66 30N	86 30W
Reserve	**78**	52 28N	102 39W
Resolute	**87**	74 42N	94 54W
Resolution I.	**45**	61 30N	65 0W
Restigouche →	**65**	47 50N	67 0W
Reston	**79**	49 33N	101 6W
Revelstoke	**85**	51 0N	118 10W
Revillagigedo I.	**76**	55 50N	131 20W
Rexdale	**72**	43 43N	79 33W
Rexton	**65**	46 39N	64 52W
Reynolds	**79**	49 40N	95 55W
Rhein	**79**	51 25N	102 15W
Ribstone Cr. →	**81**	52 52N	110 5W
Rice L.	**71**	44 12N	78 10W
Riceton	**78**	50 7N	104 19W
Rich, C.	**70**	44 43N	80 38W
Rich Valley	**80**	53 51N	114 21W
Richan	**74**	49 59N	92 49W
Richards I.	**86**	68 0N	135 0W
Richards L.	**77**	59 10N	107 10W
Richardson	**82**	50 23N	104 27W
Richardson →	**77**	58 25N	111 14W
Richardson Mts.	**86**	68 20N	135 45W
Riche, Pte.	**63**	50 42N	57 25W
Richibucto	**65**	46 42N	64 54W
Richmond, Ont.	**71**	45 11N	75 50W
Richmond, Que.	**67**	45 40N	72 9W
Richmond □	**88**	49 9N	123 7W
Richmond Hill	**72**	43 52N	79 27W
Richmound	**78**	50 27N	109 45W
Richvale	**72**	43 51N	79 26W
Rideau →	**69**	45 27N	75 42W
Rideau Canal	**69**	44 53N	76 0W
Ridge →	**75**	50 25N	84 20W
Ridgedale	**78**	53 0N	104 10W
Ridgetown	**70**	42 26N	81 52W
Riding Mt. Nat. Park.	**79**	50 50N	100 0W
Rigaud	**67**	45 29N	74 18W
Rigolet	**62**	54 10N	58 23W
Rimbey	**81**	52 35N	114 15W
Rimouski	**67**	48 27N	68 30W
Rimouski →	**67**	48 27N	68 32W
Rimouski, Parc Prov. de	**67**	48 0N	68 15W
Rimouski-Est	**67**	48 28N	68 31W
Ringwood	**73**	43 58N	79 17W
Riondel	**85**	49 46N	116 51W
Riou L.	**77**	59 7N	106 25W
Ripley	**70**	44 4N	81 35W
Ripon	**66**	45 45N	75 10W
Ritchie L.	**64**	52 58N	66 1W
River Hébert	**65**	45 42N	64 23W
River John	**65**	45 45N	63 3W
River Jordan	**84**	48 26N	124 3W
River of Ponds	**63**	50 32N	57 24W
River of Ponds L.	**63**	50 30N	57 20W
River Valley	**70**	46 35N	80 11W
Rivercrest	**79**	50 0N	97 3W
Riverhead	**63**	46 58N	53 31W
Riverhurst	**78**	50 55N	106 50W
Riverport	**65**	44 18N	64 20W
Rivers	**79**	50 2N	100 14W
Rivers, L. of the	**78**	49 49N	105 44W
Rivers Inlet	**84**	51 42N	127 15W
Riverside-Albert	**65**	45 42N	64 45W
Riverton	**79**	51 1N	97 0W
Riverview Heights	**65**	46 4N	64 48W
Rivière-à-la-Chaloupe	**64**	50 17N	65 6W
Rivière-à-Pierre	**67**	46 59N	72 11W
Rivière-au-Renard	**64**	48 59N	64 23W
Rivière-aux-Rats	**67**	47 13N	72 53W
Rivière-Bersimis	**67**	48 56N	68 42W
Rivière-de-la-Chaloupe	**64**	49 8N	62 32W
Rivière-des-Prairies	**68**	45 39N	73 33W
Rivière-du-Loup	**67**	47 50N	69 30W
Rivière-Ouelle	**67**	47 26N	70 1W
Rivière-Pentecôte	**64**	49 57N	67 1W
Rivière-Pigou	**64**	50 16N	65 35W
Rivière-Portneuf	**67**	48 38N	69 6W
Rivière-St-Jean	**64**	50 17N	64 19W
Rivière-Ste-Marguerite	**64**	50 8N	66 37W
Rivière Verte	**65**	47 19N	68 9W
Rivierre-au-Tonnère	**64**	50 16N	64 47W
Robb	**80**	53 13N	116 58W
Robe-Noire, L. de la	**64**	50 42N	62 42W
Robert's Arm	**63**	49 29N	55 49W
Roberts Bank Superport	**88**	49 1N	123 9W
Roberts Creek	**85**	49 26N	123 38W
Robertsonville	**67**	46 9N	71 13W
Robertville	**65**	47 42N	65 46W
Roberval	**67**	48 32N	72 15W
Roblin	**79**	51 14N	101 21W
Roblin Park	**82**	49 52N	97 17W
Robsart	**78**	49 23N	109 17W
Robson, Mt.	**85**	53 10N	119 10W
Rocanville	**79**	50 23N	101 42W
Roche Percée	**78**	49 4N	102 48W
Rochebaucourt	**66**	48 41N	77 30W
Rocher River	**76**	61 23N	112 44W
Roches →	**64**	50 2N	66 55W
Rochester	**80**	54 22N	113 27W
Rock →	**76**	60 7N	127 7W
Rock Creek	**85**	49 4N	119 0W
Rock Island	**67**	45 26N	73 34W
Rockcliffe Park	**69**	45 27N	75 41W
Rockglen	**78**	49 11N	105 57W
Rockingham	**65**	44 41N	63 39W
Rockland,	**71**	45 33N	75 17W
Rockland,	**61**	44 6N	69 6W
Rockton	**73**	43 17N	80 7W
Rockway	**73**	43 6N	79 20W
Rockwood	**73**	43 37N	80 8W
Rocky →	**81**	53 8N	117 59W
Rocky Harbour	**63**	49 36N	57 55W
Rocky Island L.	**75**	46 55N	83 0W
Rocky Lane	**76**	58 31N	116 22W
Rocky Mountain House	**81**	52 22N	114 55W
Rocky Mts.	**76**	55 0N	121 0W
Rockyford	**81**	51 14N	113 10W
Roddickton	**63**	50 51N	56 8W
Roderick I.	**84**	52 38N	128 22W
Rodney	**70**	42 34N	81 41W
Roes Welcome Sd.	**87**	65 0N	87 0W
Roger, L.	**66**	47 50N	78 59W
Rogers City	**60**	45 25N	83 49W
Rogersville	**65**	46 44N	65 26W
Roggan	**62**	54 25N	79 32W
Roggan L.	**62**	54 8N	77 50W
Rohault, L.	**67**	49 23N	74 20W
Roland	**79**	49 22N	97 56W
Rolla	**77**	48 50N	99 36W
Rollet	**66**	47 55N	79 15W
Rolling Hills	**81**	50 13N	111 46W
Romaine →	**62**	50 18N	63 47W
Rondeau Prov. Park	**70**	42 19N	81 51W
Ronge, L. la	**77**	55 6N	105 17W
Ronge, La	**77**	55 5N	105 20W
Roosevelt, Mt.	**76**	58 26N	125 20W
Roosville	**81**	49 0N	115 3W
Rorketon	**79**	51 24N	99 35W
Rosalind	**81**	52 47N	112 27W
Rose Blanche	**63**	47 38N	58 45W
Rose Harbour	**84**	52 15N	131 10W
Rose Pt.	**84**	54 11N	131 39W
Rose Valley	**78**	52 19N	103 49W
Roseau	**77**	48 51N	95 46W
Rosebud →	**81**	51 25N	112 38W
Rosedale	**85**	49 10N	121 48W
Roseisle	**79**	49 30N	98 20W
Rosemary	**81**	50 46N	112 5W
Rosemère	**68**	45 38N	73 48W
Rosemont	**82**	50 27N	104 39W
Rosetown	**78**	51 35N	107 59W
Ross River	**86**	62 30N	131 30W
Rossburn	**79**	50 40N	100 49W
Rosseau	**70**	45 16N	79 39W
Rosseau L.	**70**	45 10N	79 35W
Rosser	**82**	49 59N	97 27W
Rossignol, L., N.S.	**65**	44 12N	65 10W
Rossignol, L., Que.	**62**	52 43N	73 40W
Rossland	**85**	49 6N	117 50W
Rossmore	**71**	44 8N	77 23W
Rossport	**75**	48 50N	87 30W
Rosthern	**78**	52 40N	106 20W
Rothesay	**65**	45 23N	66 0W
Rouge →, Ont.	**72**	43 48N	79 7W
Rouge →, Que.	**66**	45 17N	74 10W
Rouge Hill	**72**	43 48N	79 8W
Rouleau	**78**	50 10N	104 56W
Round Hill, Alta.	**81**	53 10N	112 38W
Round Hill, N.S.	**65**	44 46N	65 24W
Round L., Nfld.	**63**	51 15N	56 32W
Round L., Ont.	**71**	45 38N	77 30W
Round Pond	**63**	48 11N	56 0W
Round Valley	**80**	53 21N	114 57W
Routhierville	**64**	48 11N	67 9W
Rouvray, L.	**67**	49 18N	70 49W
Rouyn	**66**	48 20N	79 0W
Rowan L.	**74**	49 18N	93 32W
Rowatt	**82**	50 20N	104 37W
Rowley I.	**87**	69 6N	77 52W
Roxboro	**68**	45 31N	73 48W
Roxton Falls	**67**	45 34N	72 31W
Royal Oak	**85**	48 29N	123 23W
Ruel	**75**	47 15N	81 28W
Ruisseau-Vert	**67**	49 4N	68 28W
Rummelhardt	**73**	43 27N	80 34W
Rumsey	**81**	51 51N	112 48W
Rupert →	**62**	51 29N	78 45W
Rupert B.	**62**	51 35N	79 0W
Rupert House = Fort Rupert	**62**	51 30N	78 40W
Rusagonis	**65**	45 48N	66 37W
Rush L.	**75**	47 47N	82 11W
Rush Lake	**78**	50 24N	107 24W
Rushoon	**63**	47 21N	54 55W
Russell	**77**	50 50N	101 20W
Russell I.	**87**	74 0N	98 25W
Russell L., Man.	**77**	56 15N	101 30W
Russell L., N.W.T.	**76**	63 5N	115 44W
Rutledge →	**77**	61 4N	112 0W
Rutledge L.	**77**	61 33N	110 47W
Rutter	**70**	46 6N	80 40W
Ryans B.	**62**	59 35N	64 3W
Ryckman	**69**	43 15N	79 54W
Rycroft	**80**	55 45N	118 40W
Ryley	**80**	53 17N	112 26W
Saanich	**85**	48 28N	123 22W
Sable, C.	**65**	43 29N	65 38W
Sable I.	**61**	44 0N	60 0W
Sable River	**65**	43 51N	65 3W
Sables, R. aux →	**70**	46 13N	82 3W
Sabourin, L.	**66**	47 58N	77 41W
Sachigo →	**60**	55 6N	88 58W
Sachigo, L.	**60**	53 50N	92 12W
Sachs Harbour	**86**	71 59N	125 15W
Sackville	**65**	45 54N	64 22W
Sacré-Coeur-de-Jésus	**67**	48 14N	69 48W
Saganaga L.	**74**	48 14N	90 52W
Saganash L.	**75**	49 4N	82 35W
Saginaw	**60**	43 26N	83 55W
Saginaw B.	**60**	43 50N	83 40W
Saglek B.	**62**	58 30N	63 0W
Saglek Fd.	**62**	58 29N	63 15W
Saglouc	**62**	62 14N	75 38W
Saguenay →	**67**	48 22N	71 0W
Sahtaneh →	**76**	59 2N	122 28W
St-Adalbert	**67**	46 51N	69 53W
St-Agapitville	**67**	46 34N	71 26W
St. Alban's	**63**	47 51N	55 50W
St. Albert	**80**	53 37N	113 32W
St-Alexandre	**67**	47 41N	69 38W
St-Alexis-des-Monts	**67**	46 28N	73 8W
St-Ambroise	**67**	48 33N	71 20W
St-Anaclet	**67**	48 29N	68 26W
St-André	**65**	47 8N	67 45W
St-André-Avellin	**66**	45 43N	75 3W
St-André-Est	**67**	45 34N	74 20W
St. Andrews, N.B.	**65**	45 7N	67 5W
St. Andrews, Nfld.	**63**	47 45N	59 15W
St-Anicet	**67**	45 8N	74 22W
St. Ann B.	**65**	46 22N	60 25W
St. Annes	**79**	49 40N	96 39W
St. Anns	**73**	43 5N	79 30W
St-Anselme, N.B.	**65**	46 4N	64 43W
St-Anselme, Que.	**67**	46 37N	70 58W
St. Anthony, N.B.	**65**	46 22N	64 45W
St. Anthony, Nfld.	**63**	51 22N	55 35W
St-Antoine	**68**	45 46N	73 59W
St-Antonin	**67**	47 46N	69 29W
St-Apolline	**67**	46 48N	70 12W
St. Arthur	**65**	47 33N	67 46W
St-Aubert	**67**	47 11N	70 13W
St-Augustin	**68**	45 38N	73 59W
St-Augustin →	**62**	51 16N	58 40W
St-Augustin, L.	**69**	46 45N	71 23W
St-Augustin-de-Desmaures	**69**	46 45N	71 30W
St-Augustin-Saguenay	**63**	51 13N	58 38W
St-Barthélémy	**67**	46 11N	73 8W
St-Basile	**65**	47 21N	68 14W
St-Basile-Sud	**67**	46 45N	71 49W
St. Benedict	**78**	52 34N	105 23W
St. Boniface	**79**	49 53N	97 5W
St. Brendan's	**63**	48 52N	53 40W
St. Bride's	**63**	46 56N	54 10W
St. Brieux	**78**	52 38N	104 54W
St-Bruno	**67**	48 28N	71 39W
St-Casimir	**67**	46 40N	72 8W
St. Catharines	**73**	43 10N	79 15W
St-Césaire	**67**	45 25N	73 0W
St. Charles	**82**	49 53N	97 19W
St-Charles	**69**	46 46N	70 57W
St-Charles →	**69**	46 49N	71 13W
St-Charles, L.	**69**	46 55N	71 23W
St-Chrysostôme	**67**	45 6N	73 46W
St. Clair, L.	**70**	42 30N	82 45W
St. Claude	**79**	49 40N	98 20W
St-Clet	**67**	45 21N	74 13W
St-Coeur de Marie	**67**	48 39N	71 43W
St-Côme	**67**	46 16N	73 47W
St-Constant	**68**	45 22N	73 37W
St-Croix	**65**	45 34N	67 26W
St. Croix →	**65**	45 5N	67 6W
St-Cyrille-de-L'Islet	**67**	47 2N	70 17W
St-David-de-l'Auberivière	**69**	46 47N	71 12W
St. David's, Nfld.	**63**	48 12N	58 52W
St. David's, Ont.	**73**	43 10N	79 6W
St-Donat-de-Montcalm	**67**	46 19N	74 13W
St-Eleanors	**65**	46 25N	63 49W
St. Elias, Mt.	**76**	60 14N	140 50W
St. Elias Mts.	**86**	60 33N	139 28W
St-Éloi	**67**	48 2N	69 14W
St-Élouthère	**67**	47 30N	69 15W
St-Émile	**69**	46 52N	71 20W
St-Éphrem-de-Tring	**67**	46 2N	70 59W
St-Étienne-de-Beauharnois	**68**	45 15N	73 55W
St-Étienne-de-Beaumont	**69**	46 50N	71 1W
St. Eugène	**71**	45 30N	74 28W
St-Eusèbe	**67**	47 33N	68 55W
St. Eustache	**79**	49 59N	97 47W
St-Eustache	**68**	45 33N	73 54W
St-Fabien	**67**	48 18N	68 52W
St-Félicien	**67**	48 40N	72 25W
St-Félix-de-Valois	**67**	46 10N	73 26W
St-Félix-du-Cap-Rouge	**69**	46 45N	71 22W
St-Francis, L.	**67**	45 10N	74 22W
St-François, Que.	**67**	46 48N	70 49W
St-François, Que.	**68**	45 40N	73 35W
St-François →	**67**	46 7N	72 55W
St-François, L.	**67**	45 10N	74 22W
St-François-du-Lac	**67**	46 5N	72 50W
St. François Xavier	**79**	49 55N	97 32W
St-Fulgence	**67**	48 27N	70 54W
St-Gabriel-de-Brandon	**67**	46 17N	73 24W
St-Gabriel-de-Gaspé	**64**	48 31N	64 32W
St-Gabriel-de-Rimouski	**67**	48 25N	68 10W
St-Gabriel-Ouest	**69**	47 2N	71 35W
St-Gédéon	**67**	48 30N	71 46W
St-Gédéon-de-Beauce	**67**	45 45N	70 40W
St. George, N.B.	**65**	45 11N	66 50W
St. George, Ont.	**73**	43 15N	80 15W
St. George, C.	**63**	48 30N	59 16W
St. George's	**63**	48 26N	58 31W
St-Georges	**67**	46 8N	70 40W
St. George's B.	**63**	48 24N	58 53W
St-Georges-de-Cacouna	**67**	47 55N	69 30W
St-Georges-Ouest	**67**	46 7N	70 40W
St-Gérard	**67**	45 46N	71 25W
St-Germain-de-Grantham	**67**	45 50N	72 34W
St-Godefroi	**65**	48 5N	65 6W
St-Guillaume-d'Upton	**67**	45 53N	72 46W
St-Henri	**69**	46 42N	71 4W
St-Hilarion	**67**	47 34N	70 24W
St-Honoré	**67**	48 32N	71 5W
St-Hubert-de-Témiscouata	**67**	47 49N	69 9W
St-Hyacinthe	**67**	45 40N	72 58W
St-Ignace	**65**	46 42N	65 5W
St. Ignace	**60**	45 53N	84 43W
St. Ignace I.	**75**	48 45N	88 0W
St-Isidore	**68**	45 20N	73 42W
St-Isidore-Jonction	**68**	45 21N	73 38W
St. Jacobs	**73**	43 32N	80 33W
St-Jacques, N.B.	**65**	47 26N	68 23W
St-Jacques, Que.	**67**	45 57N	73 34W
St. James-Assiniboia	**79**	49 54N	97 15W
St-Janvier	**68**	45 42N	73 56W
St-Jean	**67**	45 20N	73 20W
St-Jean →, Que.	**62**	50 17N	64 20W
St-Jean →, Que.	**64**	48 46N	64 26W
St-Jean, L.	**67**	48 40N	72 0W
St. Jean Baptiste	**79**	49 15N	97 20W
St-Jean-Baptiste-de-Restigouche	**65**	47 46N	67 13W
St-Jean-Chrysostôme	**69**	46 43N	71 12W
St-Jean-de-Boischatel	**69**	46 54N	71 9W
St-Jean-de-Dieu	**67**	48 0N	69 3W
St-Jean-Port-Joli	**67**	47 15N	70 13W
St-Jérôme, Que.	**67**	48 26N	71 53W
St-Jérôme, Que.	**68**	45 47N	74 0W
St-Joachim	**67**	47 4N	70 50W
St-Joachim-de-Tourelle	**64**	49 9N	66 25W
St. John,	**65**	45 20N	66 8W
St. John,	**77**	48 58N	99 40W
St. John →	**65**	45 15N	66 4W
St. John, C.	**63**	50 0N	55 32W
St. John, L.	**63**	48 23N	54 41W
St. John B.	**63**	50 55N	57 9W
Saint John Harbour	**65**	45 15N	66 2W
St. John I.	**63**	50 49N	57 14W
St. Johns, Man.	**82**	49 55N	97 7W
St. John's, Nfld.	**63**	47 35N	52 40W
St. John's Airport	**63**	47 6N	52 45W
St. John's B.	**63**	47 34N	52 38W
St. John's East	**63**	47 38N	52 42W
St. John's North	**63**	47 33N	52 49W
St. John's South	**63**	47 30N	52 43W
St. Joseph, I.	**70**	46 12N	83 58W
St. Joseph, L.	**74**	51 10N	90 35W
St-Joseph-de-Beauce	**67**	46 18N	70 53W
St-Joseph-de-la-Rivière-Bleue	**67**	47 26N	69 3W
St-Joseph-de-Sorel	**67**	46 2N	73 7W
St-Joseph-du-Lac	**68**	45 32N	74 0W
St-Jovite	**66**	46 8N	74 38W
St-Jude	**67**	45 46N	72 59W
St-Justine	**67**	46 24N	70 21W
St. Laurent	**79**	50 25N	97 58W
St-Laurent	**68**	45 30N	73 40W
St-Laurent d'Orléans	**69**	46 51N	71 1W
St. Lawrence	**63**	46 54N	55 23W
St. Lawrence →	**61**	49 30N	66 0W
St. Lawrence, Gulf of	**61**	48 25N	62 0W
St. Lazare	**79**	50 27N	101 18W
St-Léolin	**65**	47 46N	65 10W
St-Léon-le-Grand	**64**	48 23N	67 30W
St. Leonard	**65**	47 12N	67 58W
St-Léonard	**68**	45 35N	73 35W
St-Léonard-de-Portneuf	**67**	46 53N	71 55W
St. Lewis →	**62**	52 26N	56 11W
St Louis	**65**	46 53N	64 8W
St. Louis	**78**	52 55N	105 49W
St-Louis →	**68**	45 19N	73 53W
St-Louis, L.	**68**	45 24N	73 48W
St-Louis, Mts	**62**	46 13N	73 36W
St-Louis-de-Kent	**65**	46 44N	64 58W
St-Louis-de-Pintendre	**69**	46 45N	71 8W
St-Louis-de-Terrebonne	**68**	45 42N	73 47W
St-Luc	**67**	45 22N	73 18W
St-Luc-de-Matane	**64**	48 48N	67 28W
St-Ludger	**67**	45 45N	70 42W
St. Lunaire-Griquet	**63**	51 31N	55 28W
St-Magloire	**67**	46 35N	70 17W
St. Malo	**79**	49 19N	96 57W
St. Margarets	**65**	46 54N	65 11W
St-Martin	**68**	45 35N	73 44W
St. Martin L.	**79**	51 40N	98 30W
St. Martins	**65**	45 22N	65 34W
St. Mary →	**81**	49 37N	115 38W
St. Mary B.	**61**	46 50N	53 50W
St. Mary Res.	**81**	49 20N	113 11W
St. Marys	**70**	43 20N	81 10W
St. Mary's, C.	**63**	46 50N	54 12W
St. Mary's Alpine Prov. Park	**81**	49 50N	116 25W
St. Marys Bay	**65**	44 25N	66 10W
St-Maurice →	**67**	46 21N	72 31W
St-Maurice, Parc Prov. du	**67**	47 5N	73 15W
St-Michel, Que.	**68**	45 34N	73 37W
St-Michel, Que.	**69**	46 52N	70 55W
St-Michel-des-Saints	**67**	46 41N	73 55W
St-Nazaire	**67**	45 44N	72 37W
St-Nicolas	**69**	46 42N	71 24W
St-Noël	**64**	48 35N	67 50W
St. Norbert	**79**	49 46N	97 9W
St-Octave-de l'Aveniro	**64**	49 0N	66 33W
St-Omer	**67**	47 3N	69 43W
St-Ours	**67**	45 53N	73 9W
St-Pacome	**67**	47 24N	69 58W
St-Pamphile	**67**	46 58N	69 48W
St. Pascal	**67**	47 32N	69 48W
St-Patrice, L.	**66**	46 22N	77 20W
St. Paul	**80**	54 0N	111 17W
St-Paul →	**62**	51 27N	57 42W
St. Paul, I.	**65**	47 12N	60 9W
St-Paul-de-Montmigny	**67**	46 44N	70 22W
St-Paul-du-Nord	**67**	48 34N	69 14W
St-Paulin	**67**	46 25N	73 1W
St. Pauls	**63**	49 52N	57 49W
St. Peters, N.S.	**65**	45 40N	60 53W
St. Peters, P.E.I.	**65**	46 25N	62 35W
St-Philemon	**67**	46 41N	70 27W
St-Pie	**67**	45 30N	72 54W
St. Pierre	**79**	49 26N	96 59W
St Pierre	**63**	46 46N	56 12W
Saint-Pierre, I.	**63**	46 47N	56 11W
St-Pierre, L., Que.	**67**	50 8N	68 26W
St-Pierre, L., Que.	**67**	46 12N	72 52W
St-Pierre et Miquelon □	**63**	46 55N	56 10W
St-Prime	**67**	48 35N	72 20W
St. Quentin	**65**	47 30N	67 23W
St-Raphaël	**67**	46 48N	70 45W
St-Raymond	**67**	46 54N	71 50W
St-Rédemptueur	**69**	46 42N	71 17W
St-Rémi	**68**	45 16N	73 37W
St-Roch	**67**	47 18N	70 12W
St-Romuald	**69**	46 46N	71 20W
St-Rose	**68**	45 37N	73 47W
St-Sauveur	**65**	47 32N	65 20W
St-Sébastien	**67**	45 47N	70 58W
St-Siméon	**67**	47 51N	69 54W
St-Siméon-de-Bonaventure	**65**	48 5N	65 36W
St-Simon-de-Rimouski	**67**	48 12N	69 3W
St. Stephen	**65**	45 16N	67 17W
St. Thomas	**70**	42 45N	81 10W
St-Timothée	**68**	45 18N	74 2W
St-Tite	**67**	46 45N	72 34W
St-Tite-des-Caps	**67**	47 8N	70 47W
St-Ulric	**64**	48 47N	67 42W
St-Urbain	**67**	47 33N	70 32W
St-Vianney	**64**	48 37N	67 25W
St. Victor	**78**	49 26N	105 52W
St-Vincent-de-Paul	**68**	45 37N	73 39W
St. Vincent's	**63**	46 48N	53 38W
St. Vital	**82**	49 51N	97 7W
St. Walburg	**78**	53 39N	109 12W
St-Yvon	**64**	49 10N	64 48W
St. Marys →	**65**	45 2N	61 53W
Ste-Adèle	**67**	45 57N	74 7W
Ste. Agathe	**79**	49 34N	97 11W
Ste-Agathe	**67**	46 23N	71 25W
Ste-Agathe-des-Monts	**67**	46 3N	74 17W
Ste-Angèle-de-Mérici	**64**	48 32N	68 5W
Ste. Anne, L.	**80**	53 42N	114 25W
Ste-Anne, L.	**64**	50 0N	67 42W
Ste Anne de Beaupré	**67**	47 2N	70 58W
Ste-Anne-de-Bellevue	**68**	45 24N	73 57W
Ste-Anne-de-Madawaska	**65**	47 15N	68 2W
Ste-Anne-des-Monts	**64**	49 8N	66 30W
Ste-Anne-des-Plaines	**68**	45 47N	73 49W
Ste-Anne-du-Lac	**66**	46 48N	75 25W
Ste-Blandine	**67**	48 22N	68 28W
Ste-Claire	**67**	46 36N	70 51W
Ste-Croix	**67**	46 38N	71 44W
Ste-Dorothée	**68**	45 32N	73 49W
Ste-Famille	**67**	46 58N	70 58W
Ste-Félicité	**64**	48 54N	67 20W
Ste-Florence	**64**	48 16N	67 14W
Ste-Foy	**69**	46 47N	71 17W
Ste-Françoise	**67**	48 6N	69 4W
Ste-Geneviève	**68**	45 29N	73 52W
Ste-Marguerite →	**62**	50 9N	66 36W
Ste-Marie de la Madeleine	**67**	46 26N	71 0W
Ste-Marthe-de-Gaspé	**64**	49 12N	66 10W
Ste-Marthe-sur-le-Lac	**68**	45 32N	73 57W
Ste-Martine	**68**	45 15N	73 48W
Ste-Monique	**67**	48 44N	71 51W
Ste-Pudentienne	**67**	45 28N	72 40W
Ste. Rose du lac	**79**	51 4N	99 30W
Ste-Sabine	**67**	45 15N	73 2W
Ste-Thècle	**67**	46 49N	72 31W
Ste-Thérèse	**68**	45 38N	73 51W
Ste-Thérèse-de-Lisieux	**69**	46 56N	71 12W
Ste-Thérèse-Ouest	**68**	45 37N	73 50W
Sairs, L.	**66**	46 49N	78 26W
Sakami, L.	**62**	53 15N	77 0W
Salaberry-de-Valleyfield	**67**	45 15N	74 8W
Salem	**73**	43 42N	80 27W
Salisbury	**65**	46 2N	65 3W
Salisbury I.	**87**	63 30N	77 0W
Sally's Cove	**63**	49 44N	57 56W
Salmo	**85**	49 10N	117 20W
Salmon →, B.C.	**76**	54 3N	122 40W
Salmon →, N.B.	**65**	46 6N	65 56W
Salmon →, Que.	**64**	49 25N	62 25W
Salmon Arm	**85**	50 40N	119 15W
Salmon Res.	**63**	48 5N	56 0W
Salmon River	**65**	44 3N	66 10W
Salt →	**76**	60 0N	112 25W
Saltair	**84**	48 57N	123 46W
Saltcoats	**79**	51 5N	102 15W
Saltery Bay	**84**	49 47N	124 10W
Salvador	**78**	52 10N	109 32W

Sambro	65	44 28N	63 36W
San Clara	79	51 29N	101 26W
Sand →	80	54 23N	111 2W
Sand L.	74	50 10N	94 35W
Sandbank L.	75	51 8N	82 41W
Sandfly L.	77	55 43N	106 6W
Sandhill	73	43 50N	79 52W
Sandspit	84	53 14N	131 49W
Sandusky	60	43 26N	82 50W
Sandwich B.	62	53 40N	57 15W
Sandy →	62	55 30N	68 21W
Sandy Cove	63	51 21N	56 40W
Sandy L., Alta.	80	53 47N	114 2W
Sandy L., Nfld.	63	49 15N	57 0W
Sandy L., Ont.	60	53 2N	93 0W
Sandy Lake	60	53 0N	93 15W
Sandy Narrows	77	55 5N	103 4W
Sandy Point	65	43 42N	65 19W
Sandybeach L.	74	49 49N	92 21W
Sangudo	80	53 50N	114 54W
Sanmaur	67	47 54N	73 47W
Sardis	85	49 8N	121 58W
Sarles	77	48 58N	99 0W
Sarnia	70	42 58N	82 23W
Sarre, La	66	48 45N	79 15W
Sasaginnigak L.	79	51 36N	95 39W
Saseginaga, L.	66	47 6N	78 35W
Saskatchewan □	77	54 40N	106 0W
Saskatchewan →	79	53 37N	100 40W
Saskatchewan Landing Prov. Park	78	50 38N	107 59W
Saskatoon	82	52 10N	106 38W
Saturna	85	48 47N	123 11W
Saubosq, L.	64	51 30N	64 53W
Saugeen →	70	44 30N	81 22W
Saulnierville	65	44 16N	66 8W
Sault-au-Moulton	67	48 33N	69 15W
Sault aux Cochons →	67	48 44N	69 4W
Sault Ste. Marie	70	46 30N	84 20W
Sault Ste. Marie	60	46 27N	84 22W
Saumur, L.	64	51 16N	62 49W
Sauvage, L.	66	50 6N	74 30W
Savant L.	74	50 16N	90 44W
Savant Lake	74	50 14N	90 40W
Savona	85	50 45N	120 50W
Sawyerville	67	45 20N	71 34W
Sayabec	64	48 35N	67 41W
Scandia	81	50 20N	112 0W
Scarborough	72	43 45N	79 12W
Scatarie I.	65	46 0N	59 44W
Sceptre	78	50 51N	109 15W
Schefferville	62	54 48N	66 50W
Schreiber	75	48 45N	87 20W
Schuler	81	50 20N	110 6W
Schumacher	75	48 30N	81 16W
Scie, La	63	49 57N	55 36W
Scotland	73	43 1N	80 22W
Scotstown	67	45 32N	71 17W
Scott	78	52 22N	108 50W
Scott Chan.	84	50 45N	128 30W
Scott Inlet	87	71 0N	71 0W
Scott Is.	84	50 48N	128 40W
Scott-Jonction	67	46 30N	71 4W
Scott L.	77	59 55N	106 18W
Scugog, L.	71	44 10N	78 55W
Sea I.	88	49 12N	123 10W
Seaforth	70	43 35N	81 25W
Seager Wheeler L.	78	54 17N	103 31W
Seahorse L.	64	52 12N	65 48W
Seal →	77	58 50N	97 30W
Seal Cove, N.B.	65	44 39N	66 51W
Seal Cove, Nfld.	63	47 29N	56 4W
Seal Cove, Nfld.	63	49 57N	56 22W
Seal L.	62	54 20N	61 30W
Searchmont	75	46 47N	84 3W
Searle	82	49 51N	97 15W
Seba Beach	80	53 35N	114 47W
Sebewaing	60	43 45N	83 27W
Sebringville	70	43 24N	81 4W
Sechelt	84	49 25N	123 42W
Second Narrows	88	49 18N	123 2W
Sedgewick	81	52 48N	111 41W
Sedley	78	50 10N	104 0W
Seeley's Bay	71	44 29N	76 14W
Seine →	82	49 54N	97 19W
Selkirk, Man.	79	50 10N	96 55W
Selkirk, Ont.	70	42 49N	79 56W
Selkirk I.	79	53 20N	99 6W
Selkirk Mts.	76	51 15N	117 40W
Selwyn L.	77	60 0N	104 30W
Semans	78	51 25N	104 44W
Semiahmoo B.	88	49 1N	122 50W
Sénécal, L.	64	52 5N	63 20W
Senneterre	66	48 25N	77 15W
Senneville	68	45 27N	73 57W
Separation Point	62	53 37N	57 25W
Sept-Îles	62	50 13N	66 22W
Sequart L.	64	52 26N	63 47W
Sérigny →	62	56 47N	66 0W
Serpentine →	88	49 5N	122 51W
Seton L.	85	50 42N	122 8W
Seton Portage	85	50 42N	122 17W
Setting L.	77	55 0N	98 38W
Seven Islands B.	62	59 25N	63 45W
Seven Sisters	76	54 56N	128 10W
Seven Sisters Falls	79	50 7N	96 2W
Seventy Mile House	85	51 18N	121 23W
Severn →	60	56 2N	87 36W
Severn L.	60	53 54N	90 48W
Sewell	84	53 47N	132 16W
Sexsmith	80	55 21N	118 47W
Seymour	88	49 18N	123 1W
Seymour, Mt.	88	49 24N	122 57W
Seymour Arm	85	51 15N	118 57W
Seymour Heights	88	49 19N	123 0W
Seymour Inlet	84	51 3N	127 0W
Seymour L.	88	49 27N	122 57W
Shabogamo L.	62	53 15N	66 30W
Shabuskwia L.	74	51 15N	89 0W
Shakespeare I.	74	49 38N	88 25W
Shalalth	85	50 43N	122 13W
Shallow Lake	70	44 36N	81 5W
Shamattawa	77	55 51N	92 5W
Shamattawa →	60	55 1N	85 23W
Shamrock	78	50 10N	106 37W
Shannon L.	75	49 48N	83 24W
Sharbot Lake	71	44 46N	76 41W
Sharpe L.	77	54 5N	93 40W
Shaunavon	78	49 35N	108 25W
Shawanaga	70	45 31N	80 17W
Shawinigan	67	46 35N	72 50W
Shawinigan Sud	67	46 31N	72 45W
Shawville	66	45 36N	76 30W
Shebandowan	74	48 38N	90 4W
Shediac	65	46 14N	64 32W
Sheet Harbour	65	44 56N	62 31W
Sheffield	73	43 19N	80 12W
Sheffield L.	63	49 20N	56 34W
Sheguiandah	70	45 54N	81 55W
Sheho	78	51 35N	103 13W
Sheila	65	47 29N	64 55W
Shelburne, N.S.	65	43 47N	65 20W
Shelburne, Ont.	70	44 4N	80 15W
Sheldrake	62	50 20N	64 51W
Shell Lake	78	53 19N	107 2W
Shellbrook	78	53 13N	106 24W
Shelley	85	54 0N	122 37W
Shellmouth	79	50 56N	101 29W
Shepard	83	50 57N	113 55W
Sherbrooke	67	45 28N	71 57W
Sheridan	72	43 31N	79 40W
Sheridan L.	85	51 31N	120 54W
Sherman	88	49 21N	123 14W
Sherridon	77	55 8N	101 5W
Sherwood	77	48 59N	101 36W
Sherwood Park	83	53 31N	113 19W
Sheslay	76	58 17N	131 52W
Sheslay →	76	58 48N	132 5W
Shethanei L.	77	58 48N	97 50W
Shibogama L.	60	53 35N	88 15W
Shilo	79	49 49N	99 38W
Shingleton	60	46 25N	86 33W
Shippegan	65	47 45N	64 45W
Shippegan I.	65	47 50N	64 38W
Shoal L.	74	49 33N	95 1W
Shoal Lake	79	50 30N	100 35W
Shoals Prov. Park	75	47 50N	83 50W
Shubenacadie	65	45 5N	63 24W
Shuswap L.	85	50 55N	119 3W
Sibley Prov. Park	74	48 30N	88 45W
Sicamous	85	50 49N	119 0W
Sideburned L.	75	47 45N	83 15W
Sidney, B.C.	85	48 39N	123 24W
Sidney, Man.	79	49 54N	99 4W
Sifton	79	51 21N	100 8W
Sifton Pass	76	57 52N	126 15W
Signal Hill	63	47 35N	52 41W
Sigutlat L.	84	52 57N	126 12W
Sikkani Chief →	76	57 47N	122 15W
Silcox	77	57 12N	94 10W
Sillery	69	46 46N	71 15W
Silver Islet	74	48 20N	88 45W
Silver Ridge	79	50 48N	98 52W
Silver Star Prov. Park	85	50 23N	119 5W
Silver Water	70	45 52N	82 52W
Silvertip Mt.	85	49 10N	121 13W
Silverton	85	49 57N	117 21W
Simard, L.	66	47 40N	78 40W
Simcoe	70	42 50N	80 20W
Simcoe, L.	70	44 25N	79 20W
Simmie	78	49 56N	108 6W
Simmons	69	45 26N	75 49W
Simmons Pen.	87	76 40N	89 7W
Simonette →	80	55 9N	118 15W
Simonhouse	79	54 26N	101 23W
Simpson	78	51 27N	105 27W
Simpson I.	75	48 46N	87 41W
Simpson Pen.	87	68 34N	88 45W
Simpsons Corners	73	43 46N	80 18W
Sinclair Mills	76	54 5N	121 40W
Sinclair Pass	81	50 40N	115 58W
Sintaluta	78	50 29N	103 27W
Sioux Lookout	74	50 10N	91 50W
Sioux Narrows	74	49 25N	94 10W
Sipiwesk L.	77	55 5N	97 35W
Sir Francis Drake, Mt.	84	50 49N	124 48W
Sir Sandford, Mt.	85	51 40N	117 52W
Sisipuk L.	77	55 45N	101 50W
Skagway	76	59 23N	135 20W
Skeena →	84	54 9N	130 5W
Skeena Mts.	76	56 40N	128 30W
Skidegate	84	53 15N	132 1W
Skihist, Mt.	85	50 12N	121 54W
Skowhegan	61	44 49N	69 40W
Skownan	79	51 58N	99 35W
Slate Is.	75	48 40N	87 0W
Slave →	76	61 18N	113 39W
Slave Lake	80	55 17N	114 43W
Slave Pt.	76	61 11N	115 56W
Slemon L.	76	63 13N	116 4W
Slocan	85	49 48N	117 28W
Slocan L.	85	49 50N	117 23W
Smalltree L.	77	61 0N	105 0W
Smeaton	78	53 30N	104 49W
Smiley	78	51 38N	109 29W
Smith	80	55 10N	114 0W
Smith →	76	59 34N	126 30W
Smith Arm	86	66 15N	123 0W
Smith I.	62	54 13N	58 18W
Smith Pen.	87	77 12N	78 50W
Smithers	76	54 45N	127 10W
Smiths Cove	65	44 37N	65 42W
Smiths Falls	71	44 55N	76 0W
Smithville	73	43 6N	79 33W
Smoky →	80	56 10N	117 21W
Smoky Falls	75	50 4N	82 10W
Smoky Lake	80	54 10N	112 30W
Smooth Rock Falls	75	49 17N	81 37W
Smoothrock L.	74	50 30N	89 30W
Smoothstone L.	77	54 40N	106 50W
Snake L.	77	55 32N	106 35W
Snaring	81	53 5N	118 4W
Snelgrove	73	43 44N	79 49W
Snipe L.	80	55 7N	116 47W
Snow Lake	77	54 52N	100 3W
Snowbird L.	77	60 45N	103 0W
Snowdrift	77	62 24N	110 44W
Snowdrift →	77	62 24N	110 44W
Snowflake	79	49 3N	98 39W
Snyder	73	42 57N	79 3W
Sointula	84	50 38N	127 0W
Solina	73	43 58N	78 47W
Sombra	70	42 43N	82 29W
Somerset	79	49 25N	98 39W
Somerset I.	87	73 30N	93 0W
Sonningdale	78	52 23N	107 44W
Sonora	65	45 4N	61 54W
Sonora I.	84	50 22N	125 15W
Sooke	85	48 13N	123 43W
Sop's Arm	63	49 46N	56 56W
Sorel	67	46 0N	73 10W
Soscumica, L.	66	50 15N	77 27W
Soucy	66	48 10N	75 30W
Soulanges, Canal de	68	45 20N	73 58W
Sounding Cr. →	81	52 6N	110 28W
Sounding L.	81	52 8N	110 29W
Souris, Man.	77	49 40N	100 20W
Souris, P.E.I.	65	46 21N	62 15W
Souris →	79	49 40N	99 34W
South Aulatsivik I.	62	56 45N	61 30W
South Baymouth	70	45 33N	82 1W
South Bentinck Arm	84	52 7N	126 47W
South Branch	63	47 55N	59 2W
South Brook	63	49 26N	56 5W
South Burnaby	88	49 13N	123 0W
South East Passage	65	44 36N	63 28W
South Gillies	74	48 14N	89 42W
South Hd.	63	49 9N	58 22W
South Heart →	80	55 34N	116 11W
South Henik, L.	77	61 30N	97 30W
South Knife →	77	58 55N	94 37W
South Nahanni →	76	61 3N	123 21W
South Nation →	71	45 34N	75 6W
South Porcupine	75	48 30N	81 12W
South River	70	45 52N	79 23W
South Saskatchewan →	78	53 15N	105 5W
South Seal →	77	58 48N	98 8W
South Thompson →	85	50 40N	120 20W
South Twin I.	62	53 7N	79 52W
South Twin L.	63	49 16N	55 47W
South Wabasca L.	80	55 55N	113 45W
South West Port Moulton	65	43 54N	64 49W
South Westminster	88	49 12N	122 53W
Southampton, N.S.	65	45 35N	64 15W
Southampton, Ont.	70	44 30N	81 25W
Southampton I.	87	64 30N	84 0W
Southbank	84	54 2N	125 46W
Southdate	65	44 40N	63 34W
Southend	77	56 19N	103 22W
Southern Indian L.	77	57 10N	98 30W
Southey	78	50 56N	104 30W
Sovereign	78	51 31N	107 43W
Sowden L.	74	49 32N	91 12W
Spalding	78	52 20N	104 30W
Spaniard's Bay	63	47 38N	53 20W
Spanish	70	46 12N	82 20W
Spanish →	70	46 11N	82 19W
Sparwood	81	49 44N	114 53W
Spatsizi →	76	57 42N	128 7W
Spear, C.	63	47 31N	52 37W
Speed →	73	43 23N	80 22W
Speers	78	52 43N	107 34W
Spence Bay	87	69 32N	93 32W
Spencerville	71	44 51N	75 33W
Spences Bridge	85	50 25N	121 20W
Sperling	79	49 30N	97 42W
Spirit River	80	55 45N	118 50W
Spiritwood	78	53 24N	107 33W
Split L.	77	56 8N	96 15W
Spragge	70	46 15N	82 40W
Sprague	79	49 2N	95 38W
Sprigg's Pt.	63	47 33N	52 40W
Spring Coulee	81	49 20N	113 3W
Spring Valley	78	49 56N	105 24W
Springbrook	73	43 39N	79 47W
Springdale	63	49 30N	56 6W
Springfield, Man.	82	49 56N	96 56W
Springfield, N.S.	65	44 38N	64 52W
Springfield, Ont.	70	42 50N	80 56W
Springhill	61	45 40N	64 4W
Springhouse	85	51 56N	122 7W
Springside	78	51 21N	102 44W
Springvale	69	43 13N	79 59W
Springwater	78	51 58N	108 23W
Sproat L.	84	49 17N	125 2W
Spruce Grove	80	53 32N	113 55W
Spruce I.	79	53 5N	100 40W
Spruce Woods Prov. Park	79	49 43N	99 5W
Sprucedale	70	45 29N	79 28W
Spryfield	65	44 37N	63 37W
Spuzzum	85	49 37N	121 23W
Squamish	85	49 45N	123 10W
Squamish →	85	49 45N	123 8W
Square Islands	62	52 47N	55 47W
Squatec	67	47 53N	68 43W
Squaw Rapids	78	53 41N	103 21W
Stamford	73	43 8N	79 6W
Standard	81	51 7N	112 59W
Stanley, N.B.	65	46 20N	66 44W
Stanley, Sask.	77	55 24N	104 22W
Star City	78	52 50N	104 20W
Starbuck	79	49 46N	97 37W
Stave Falls	85	49 13N	122 22W
Stave L.	85	49 22N	122 17W
Stavely	81	50 10N	113 38W
Stayner	70	44 25N	80 5W
Steele, Mt.	86	61 6N	140 23W
Steen River	76	59 40N	117 12W
Steensby Inlet	87	70 15N	78 35W
Steep Rock	79	51 30N	98 48W
Stefansson I.	86	73 20N	105 45W
Steinbach	79	49 32N	96 40W
Stellarton	65	45 32N	62 30W
Stephens I.	84	54 10N	130 45W
Stephenville	63	48 31N	58 35W
Stephenville Crossing	63	48 30N	58 26W
Stettler	81	52 19N	112 40W
Stevens	75	49 33N	85 49W
Stevenson L.	79	53 55N	96 0W
Steveston	88	49 8N	123 11W
Stewart, B.C.	76	55 56N	129 57W
Stewart, N.W.T.	86	63 19N	139 26W
Stewart Valley	78	50 36N	107 48W
Stewiacke	65	45 9N	63 22W
Stickney	65	46 23N	67 34W
Stikine →	76	56 40N	132 30W
Stirling, Alta.	81	49 30N	112 30W
Stirling, Ont.	71	44 18N	77 33W
Stittsville	71	45 15N	75 55W
Stockholm	79	50 39N	102 18W
Stokes Bay	70	45 0N	81 28W
Stoneham	67	47 0N	71 22W
Stoner	85	53 38N	122 40W
Stonewall	79	50 10N	97 19W
Stoney Creek	69	43 14N	79 45W
Stony L., Man.	77	58 51N	98 40W
Stony L., Ont.	71	44 30N	78 0W
Stony Mountain	79	50 5N	97 13W
Stony Plain	80	53 32N	114 0W
Stony Rapids	77	59 16N	105 50W
Storkerson B.	86	72 56N	124 50W
Stormy L.	74	49 23N	92 18W
Stouffville	73	43 58N	79 15W
Stoughton	78	49 40N	103 0W
Stout, L.	77	52 0N	94 40W
Strachan, Mt.	88	49 25N	123 12W
Stranraer	78	51 43N	108 29W
Strasbourg	78	51 4N	104 55W
Stratford	70	43 23N	81 0W
Strathcona Prov. Park	84	49 38N	125 40W
Strathmore	81	51 5N	113 18W
Strathnaver	85	53 20N	122 33W
Strathroy	70	42 58N	81 38W
Stratton	74	48 41N	94 10W
Strawberry Hill	88	49 8N	122 53W
Streetsville	72	43 35N	79 42W
Strome	81	52 48N	112 4W
Strongfield	78	51 20N	106 35W
Stroud	70	44 19N	79 37W
Struthers	75	48 41N	85 51W
Stryker	76	48 40N	114 44W
Stuart →	76	54 0N	123 35W
Stuart L.	76	54 30N	124 30W
Stull, L.	77	54 24N	92 34W
Stupart →	77	56 0N	93 25W
Sturgeon →, Alta.	83	53 46N	113 10W
Sturgeon →, Ont.	70	46 35N	80 11W
Sturgeon →, Sask.	78	53 12N	105 52W
Sturgeon B.	79	52 0N	97 50W
Sturgeon Cr. →	82	49 52N	97 16W
Sturgeon Falls	70	46 25N	79 57W
Sturgeon L., Alta.	80	55 6N	117 32W
Sturgeon L., Ont.	71	44 28N	78 43W
Sturgeon L., Ont.	74	50 0N	90 45W
Sturgeon L., Ont.	74	48 29N	91 38W
Sturgis	78	51 56N	102 36W
Success	78	50 28N	108 6W
Sud, Pte.	64	49 3N	62 14W
Sud-Ouest, Pte. du	64	49 23N	63 36W
Sudbury	70	46 30N	81 0W
Suffield	81	50 12N	111 10W
Sugar L.	85	50 24N	118 30W
Sugarloaf Head	63	47 37N	52 39W
Suggi L.	78	54 22N	102 47W
Sugluk = Saglouc	62	62 14N	75 38W
Sukunka →	76	55 45N	121 15W
Sullivan, B.C.	88	49 7N	122 48W
Sullivan, Que.	66	48 7N	77 50W
Sullivan Bay	84	50 55N	126 50W
Sullivan L.	81	52 0N	112 0W
Sulphur Pt.	76	60 56N	114 48W
Sultan	75	47 36N	82 47W
Summerford	63	49 29N	54 47W
Summerland	85	49 32N	119 41W
Summerside, Nfld.	63	48 59N	57 59W
Summerside, P.E.I.	65	46 24N	63 47W
Summerville, Nfld.	63	48 27N	53 33W
Summerville, Ont.	72	43 37N	79 34W
Summit Lake	76	54 20N	122 40W
Sunbury	88	49 9N	122 59W
Sunderland	71	44 16N	79 4W
Sundown	79	49 6N	96 16W
Sundre	81	51 49N	114 38W
Sundridge	70	45 45N	79 25W
Sunny Corner	65	46 57N	65 49W
Sunnybrae	65	45 24N	62 30W
Sunnyside	63	47 51N	53 55W
Sunwapta Pass	81	52 13N	117 10W
Superior	60	46 45N	92 5W
Superior, L.	75	47 40N	87 0W
Surprise, L.	66	49 20N	74 55W
Surprise L.	76	59 40N	133 15W
Surrey	88	49 12N	122 51W
Surrey □	88	49 9N	122 46W
Surrey Centre	88	49 7N	122 45W
Sussex	65	45 45N	65 37W
Sustut →	76	56 20N	127 30W
Sutton, Ont.	70	44 18N	79 22W
Sutton, Que.	67	45 6N	72 37W
Sutton →	60	55 15N	83 45W
Sverdrup Chan.	87	79 56N	96 25W
Sverdrup Is.	87	79 0N	97 0W
Swan →, Alta.	80	55 30N	115 18W
Swan →, Man.	79	52 30N	100 45W
Swan Hills	80	54 42N	115 24W
Swan L.	79	52 30N	100 40W
Swan River	79	52 10N	101 16W
Swansea	72	43 38N	79 28W
Swastika	60	48 7N	80 6W
Swift Current, Nfld.	63	47 53N	54 12W
Swift Current, Sask.	78	50 20N	107 45W
Swiftcurrent →	78	50 38N	107 44W
Swindle, I.	84	52 30N	128 35W
Sydenham →	70	42 33N	82 25W
Sydney	65	46 7N	60 7W
Sydney L.	74	50 41N	94 25W
Sydney Mines	65	46 18N	60 15W
Sydney River	65	46 7N	60 13W
Sylvan L.	81	52 21N	114 10W
Sylvan Lake	81	52 20N	114 3W
Sylvania	78	52 42N	104 0W
Sylvester	80	55 0N	119 41W
Tabatière, La	63	50 50N	58 58W
Taber	81	49 47N	112 8W
Table B.	62	53 40N	56 25W
Tachick L.	84	53 57N	124 12W
Tadoule, L.	77	58 36N	98 20W
Tadoussac	67	48 11N	69 42W
Tagish	76	60 19N	134 16W
Tagish L.	76	60 10N	134 20W
Tahsis	84	49 55N	126 40W
Takiyuak L.	86	65 30N	113 5W
Takla L.	76	55 15N	125 45W
Takla Landing	76	55 30N	125 50W
Taku →	76	58 30N	133 50W
Takysie Lake	84	53 53N	125 53W
Talbot L.	79	54 0N	99 55W
Taltson →	76	61 24N	112 46W
Taltson L.	77	61 30N	110 15W
Talunkwan I.	84	52 50N	131 45W
Tamworth	71	44 29N	77 0W
Tangier	65	44 48N	62 42W
Tansley	73	43 25N	79 48W
Tantallon	79	50 32N	101 50W
Tanu I.	84	52 46N	131 40W
Tanzilla →	76	58 8N	130 43W
Tapleytown	69	43 11N	79 44W
Tara	70	44 28N	81 9W
Tarbert	73	43 56N	80 20W
Taschereau	66	48 40N	78 40W
Taseko →	84	52 4N	123 9W
Taseko L.	84	51 15N	123 35W
Tassialuk, L.	62	59 3N	74 0W
Tasu	84	52 45N	132 5W
Tasu Sd.	84	52 47N	132 2W
Tatamagouche	65	45 43N	63 18W
Tathlina L.	76	60 33N	117 39W
Tatinnai L.	77	60 55N	97 40W
Tatla L.	84	52 0N	124 20W
Tatlayoko L.	84	51 35N	124 24W
Tatnam, C.	77	57 16N	91 0W
Tatton	85	51 43N	121 22W
Tatuk, L.	84	53 32N	124 14W
Taunton	73	43 56N	78 49W
Tavistock	70	43 19N	80 50W
Tawas City	60	44 16N	83 31W
Taylor	76	56 13N	120 40W
Tazin →	77	60 26N	110 45W
Tazin L.	77	59 44N	108 42W
Tchentlo L.	76	55 15N	125 0W
Tecumseh	70	42 19N	82 54W
Tee Lake	66	46 40N	79 0W
Teepee Creek	80	55 22N	118 24W
Teeswater	70	43 59N	81 17W
Telegraph Cove	84	50 32N	126 50W
Telegraph Cr. →	76	58 0N	131 10W
Telkwa	76	54 41N	127 5W
Temiscamie →	62	50 59N	73 5W
Témiscaming	66	46 44N	79 5W
Témiscamingue, L.	66	47 10N	79 25W
Temperance Vale	65	46 4N	67 15W
Temperanceville	72	43 56N	79 28W
Templeman, Mt.	85	50 42N	117 12W
Templeton	69	45 29N	75 35W
Ten Mile L.	63	51 6N	56 42W
Tent L.	77	62 25N	107 54W
Terence Bay	65	44 28N	63 43W
Terra Cotta	73	43 43N	79 56W
Terra Nova	63	48 30N	54 13W
Terra Nova →	63	48 40N	54 0W
Terra Nova Nat. Park	63	48 33N	53 58W
Terrace	76	54 30N	128 35W
Terrace Bay	75	48 47N	87 5W
Terrasse-Vaudreuil	68	45 24N	73 59W
Terrebonne	68	45 42N	73 38W

WORLD INDEX

Barranquilla WORLD Coral Sea

Barranquilla 104 11 0N 74 50W
Barreiras 105 12 8S 45 0W
Barrow-in-Furness 114 54 8N 3 15W
Barstow 97 34 58N 117 2W
Bartlesville 95 36 50N 95 58W
Basle 118 47 35N 7 35E
Basra 129 30 30N 47 50E
Bass Str. 142 39 15S 146 30E
Basse-Terre 98 16 0N 61 40W
Bassein 134 19 26N 72 48E
Batabanó, G. of 99 22 30N 82 30W
Batan I. 135 20 30N 121 50E
Bath 114 51 22N 2 22W
Bathurst 142 33 25S 149 31E
Baton Rouge 95 30 30N 91 5W
Bauru 105 22 10S 49 0W
Bavaria □ 118 49 7N 11 30E
Bay City 92 43 35N 83 51W
Bayeux 116 49 17N 0 42W
Bayonne 117 43 30N 1 28W
Baytown 95 29 42N 94 57W
Beagle, Canal 106 55 0S 68 30W
Béarn 117 43 8N 0 36W
Beauce, Plaine de la 116 48 10N 1 45E
Beaufort Sea 89 72 0N 140 0W
Beaumont 95 30 5N 94 8W
Beauvais 116 49 25N 2 8E
Beersheba 127 31 15N 34 48E
Beira 128 19 50S 34 52E
Beirut 127 33 53N 35 31E
Békéscsaba 119 46 40N 21 5E
Belém 105 1 20S 48 30W
Belfast 114 54 35N 5 56W
Belfort 116 47 38N 6 50E
Belgaum 134 15 55N 74 35E
Belgium ■ 116 50 30N 5 0E
Belgrade 119 44 50N 20 37E
Belize ■ 98 17 0N 88 30W
Belize City 98 17 25N 88 0W
Belle-Île 116 47 20N 3 10W
Belleville 94 38 30N 90 0W
Bellingham 96 48 45N 122 27W
Bellingshausen Sea 107 66 0S 80 0W
Belmopan 98 17 18N 88 30W
Beloit 94 42 35N 89 0W
Bemidji 94 47 30N 94 50W
Ben Nevis 114 56 48N 5 0W
Bend 96 44 2N 121 15W
Bengal, Bay of 130 15 0N 90 0E
Benghazi 127 32 11N 20 3E
Benguela 128 12 37S 13 25E
Beni Suef 127 29 5N 31 6E
Benin ■ 126 10 0N 2 0E
Benin, Bight of 126 5 0N 3 0E
Benin City 126 6 20N 5 31E
Bentinck I. 143 17 3S 139 35E
Beppu 137 33 15N 131 30E
Berbera 127 10 30N 45 2E
Bérgamo 118 45 42N 9 40E
Bergen 115 60 23N 5 20E
Bergerac 117 44 51N 0 30E
Berhampore 134 24 2N 88 27E
Bering Sea 89 58 0N 167 0E
Berkeley 96 37 52N 122 20W
Berlin 118 52 32N 13 24E
Bermuda ■ 99 32 45N 65 0W
Bern 118 46 57N 7 28E
Berre, Étang de 117 43 27N 5 5E
Berry 116 47 0N 2 0E
Bertoua 126 4 30N 13 45E
Berwick-upon-Tweed 114 55 47N 2 0W
Besançon 116 47 15N 6 0E
Beskids 119 49 35N 18 40E
Bessemer 93 33 25N 86 57W
Bethlehem, Jordan 127 31 43N 35 12E
Bethlehem, U.S.A. 92 40 39N 75 24W
Béthune 116 50 30N 2 38E
Beverly Hills 97 34 4N 118 29W
Béziers 117 43 20N 3 12E
Bhagalpur 134 25 10N 87 0E
Bhamo 134 24 15N 97 15E
Bharatpur 134 27 15N 77 30E
Bhatpara 134 22 50N 88 25E
Bhavnagar 134 21 45N 72 10E
Bhopal 134 23 20N 77 30E
Bhutan ■ 134 27 25N 90 30E
Biała Podlaska 119 52 4N 23 6E
Białystok 119 53 10N 23 10E
Biarritz 117 43 29N 1 33W
Biddeford 93 43 30N 70 28W
Biel 118 47 8N 7 14E
Bielefeld 118 52 2N 8 31E
Bielsko-Biała 119 49 50N 19 2E
Big Spring 95 32 10N 101 25W
Bighorn → 96 46 9N 107 28W
Bighorn Mts. 96 44 30N 107 30W
Bihar 134 25 5N 85 40E
Bijeljina 119 44 46N 19 17E
Bikaner 134 28 2N 73 18E
Bikini Atoll 140 12 0N 167 30E
Bilbao 117 43 16N 2 56W
Billings 96 45 43N 108 29W
Biloxi 95 30 24N 88 53W
Bingham Canyon 96 40 31N 112 10W
Binghamton 92 42 9N 75 54W
Bioko 126 3 30N 8 40E
Birdum 142 15 39S 133 13E
Birmingham, U.K. 114 52 30N 1 55W
Birmingham, U.S.A. 93 33 31N 86 50W
Biscay, B. of 108 45 0N 2 0W
Bismarck 94 46 49N 100 49W
Bismarck Arch. 143 2 30S 150 0E
Bismarck Sea 143 4 10S 146 50E
Bissagos 126 11 15N 16 10W
Bitola 121 41 5N 21 10E
Bitterroot Range 96 46 0N 114 20W
Biwa-Ko 137 35 15N 136 10E
Bizerte 126 37 15N 9 50E
Black Forest 118 48 0N 8 0E
Black Sea 138 43 30N 35 0E
Blackburn 114 53 44N 2 30W
Blackpool 114 53 48N 3 3W
Blanc, Mont 117 45 48N 6 50E
Blantyre 128 15 45S 35 0E
Blida 126 36 30N 2 49E
Blitar 135 8 5S 112 11E
Bloemfontein 128 29 6S 26 14E
Bloomington 94 40 27N 89 0W
Blue Mts., Oreg., U.S.A. 96 45 15N 119 0W
Blue Mts., Pa., U.S.A. 92 40 30N 76 30W
Blue Nile → 127 15 38N 32 31E
Blue Ridge Mts. 93 36 30N 80 15W
Blumenau 106 27 0S 49 0W
Bobo-Dioulasso 126 11 8N 4 13W
Boca, La 98 8 56N 79 30W
Boca Raton 93 26 21N 80 5W
Bochum 118 51 28N 7 12E
Bodensee 118 47 35N 9 25E
Bogalusa 95 30 50N 89 55W
Bogor 135 6 36S 106 48E
Bogota 104 4 34N 74 0W
Bohemia 118 50 0N 14 0E
Böhmerwald 118 49 30N 12 40E
Bohol 135 9 50N 124 10E
Boise 96 43 43N 116 9W
Bolivia ■ 104 17 6S 64 0W
Bologna 118 44 30N 11 20E
Bolton 114 53 35N 2 26W
Bolzano 118 46 30N 11 20E
Boma 128 5 50S 13 4E
Bombay 134 18 55N 72 50E
Bon, C. 126 37 1N 11 2E
Bonifacio 117 41 24N 9 10E
Bonifacio, Str. of 120 41 12N 9 15E
Bonn 118 50 43N 7 6E
Bonny, Bight of 126 3 30N 9 20E
Borås 115 57 43N 12 56E
Bordeaux 117 44 50N 0 36W
Borger 95 35 40N 101 20W
Borneo 135 1 0N 115 0E
Bornholm 115 55 10N 15 0E
Bosnia □ 119 44 0N 18 0E
Bosporus 129 41 10N 29 10E
Boston 92 42 20N 71 0W
Bothnia, G. of 115 63 0N 20 0E
Botletle → 128 20 10S 23 15E
Botoşani 119 47 42N 26 41E
Botswana ■ 128 22 0S 24 0E
Botucatu 105 22 55S 48 30W
Bouaké 126 7 40N 5 2W
Bougainville I. 143 6 0S 155 0E
Boulder 94 40 3N 105 10W
Boulogne-sur-Mer 116 50 42N 1 36E
Bounty I. 140 48 0S 178 30E
Bourbonnais 117 46 28N 3 0E
Bourges 116 47 9N 2 25E
Bournemouth 114 50 43N 1 53W
Bozeman 96 45 40N 111 0W
Bradenton 93 27 25N 82 35W
Bradford 114 53 47N 1 45W
Bragança 105 1 0S 47 2W
Brahmaputra → 134 24 2N 90 59E
Brăila 119 45 19N 27 59E
Branco → 104 1 20S 61 50W
Brandenburg 118 52 24N 12 33E
Brasil, Planalto 105 18 0S 46 30W
Brasília 105 15 47S 47 55E
Braşov 119 45 38N 25 35E
Bratislava 118 48 10N 17 7E
Brawley 97 32 58N 115 30W
Brazil ■ 104 10 0S 50 0W
Brazos → 95 28 53N 95 23W
Brazzaville 128 4 9S 15 12E
Breda 116 51 35N 4 45E
Bremen 118 53 4N 8 47E
Bremerhaven 118 53 34N 8 35E
Bremerton 96 47 30N 122 38W
Bréscia 118 45 33N 10 13E
Brest 116 48 24N 4 31W
Bridgeport 92 41 12N 73 12W
Bridgetown 98 13 0N 59 30W
Brigham City 96 41 30N 112 1W
Brighton 114 50 50N 0 9W
Bríndisi 121 40 39N 17 55E
Brisbane 143 27 25S 153 2E
Bristol, U.K. 114 51 26N 2 35W
Bristol, U.S.A. 93 36 36N 82 11W
Bristol Channel 114 51 18N 4 30W
British Antarctic Territory □ 107 66 0S 45 0W
British Isles 110 55 0N 4 0W
Brive-la-Gaillarde 117 45 10N 1 32E
Brno 118 49 10N 16 35E
Broken Hill 143 31 58S 141 29E
Brooks Ra. 88 68 40N 147 0W
Broome 142 18 0S 122 15E
Brownsville 95 25 56N 97 25W
Brownwood 95 31 45N 99 0W
Bruay-en-Artois 116 50 29N 2 33E
Bruges 116 51 13N 3 13E
Brunei ■ 135 4 50N 115 0E
Brunswick, Germany 118 52 17N 10 28E
Brunswick, U.S.A. 93 31 10N 81 30W
Brussels 116 50 51N 4 21E
Bryan 95 30 40N 96 27W
Brzeg 119 50 52N 17 30E
Bucaramanga 104 7 0N 73 0W
Bucharest 119 44 27N 26 10E
Budapest 119 47 29N 19 5E
Buenaventura 104 3 53N 77 4W
Buenos Aires 106 34 30S 58 20W
Buffalo 92 42 55N 78 50W
Bug → 119 52 31N 21 5E
Buga 104 4 0N 76 15W
Bujumbura 128 3 16S 29 18E
Bukoba 128 1 20S 31 49E
Bulawayo 128 20 7S 28 32E
Bulgaria ■ 121 42 35N 25 30E
Bully-les-Mines 116 50 27N 2 44E
Bundaberg 143 24 54S 152 22E
Bungo-Suidō 137 33 0N 132 15E
Buraydah 129 26 20N 44 8E
Burbank 97 34 9N 118 23W
Burgas 121 42 33N 27 29E
Burgenland □ 118 47 20N 16 20E
Burgos 117 42 21N 3 41W
Burgundy 116 47 0N 4 30E
Burkina Faso ■ 126 12 0N 1 0W
Burlington, N.C., U.S.A. 93 36 7N 79 27W
Burlington, Vt., U.S.A. 92 44 27N 73 14W
Burma ■ 134 21 0N 96 30E
Bursa 129 40 15N 29 5E
Buru 135 3 30S 126 30E
Burundi ■ 128 3 15S 30 0E
Būshehr 129 28 55N 50 55E
Bussum 116 52 16N 5 10E
Butte 96 46 0N 112 31W
Butung 135 5 0S 122 45E
Buzău 119 45 10N 26 50E
Bydgoszcz 119 53 10N 18 0E

Cabimas 104 10 23N 71 25W
Cabinet Mts. 96 48 0N 115 30W
Cabora Bassa Dam 128 15 20S 32 50E
Cachoeira do Sul 106 30 3S 52 53W
Cádiz 120 36 30N 6 20W
Caen 116 49 10N 0 22W
Cágliari 120 39 15N 9 6E
Caguas 99 18 14N 66 4W
Cahors 117 44 27N 1 27E
Caicos Is. 99 21 40N 71 40W
Cairns 143 16 57S 145 45E
Cairo, Egypt 127 30 1N 31 14E
Cairo, U.S.A. 95 37 0N 89 10W
Cajamarca 104 7 5S 78 28W
Calais 116 50 57N 1 56E
Călăraşi 119 44 12N 27 20E
Calcutta 134 22 36N 88 24E
Caldwell 96 43 45N 116 42W
Cali 104 3 25N 76 35W
Calicut 134 11 15N 75 43E
California □ 96 37 25N 120 0W
California, G. of 98 27 0N 111 0W
Callao 104 12 0S 77 0W
Camagüey 99 21 20N 78 0W
Camargue 117 43 34N 4 34E
Cambodia ■ 134 12 15N 105 0E
Cambrai 116 50 11N 3 14E
Cambrian Mts. 114 52 25N 3 52W
Cambridge, U.K. 114 52 13N 0 8E
Cambridge, U.S.A. 92 42 20N 71 8W
Camden, Ark., U.S.A. 95 33 40N 92 50W
Camden, N.J., U.S.A. 92 39 57N 75 7W
Cameroon ■ 126 6 0N 12 30E
Cameroun, Mt. 126 4 13N 9 10E
Camocim 105 2 55S 40 50W
Campeche 98 19 51N 90 32W
Campeche, G. of 98 19 30N 93 0W
Campina Grande 105 7 20S 35 47W
Campinas 105 22 50S 47 0W
Campo Grande 105 20 25S 54 40W
Campos 105 21 50S 41 20W
Can Tho 134 10 2N 105 46E
Canary Is. 126 28 30N 16 0W
Canberra 143 35 15S 149 8E
Candala 127 11 30N 49 58E
Canik Mts. 129 40 30N 38 0E
Cannes 117 43 32N 7 0E
Canning Basin 142 19 50S 124 0E
Cantabrian Mts. 120 43 0N 5 10W
Canterbury 114 51 17N 1 5E
Canterbury Plains 143 43 55S 171 22E
Cap-Haïtien 99 19 40N 72 20W
Cape Girardeau 95 37 20N 89 30W
Cape Province □ 128 32 0S 23 0E
Cape Town 128 33 55S 18 22E
Cape Verde Is. ■ 108 17 10N 25 20W
Cape York Peninsula 143 12 0S 142 30E
Capri 120 40 34N 14 15E
Caracas 104 10 30N 66 55W
Caratinga 105 19 50S 42 10W
Carbondale 95 37 45N 89 10W
Carcassonne 117 43 13N 2 20E
Cardiff 114 51 28N 3 11W
Cardigan B. 114 52 30N 4 30W
Caribbean Sea 99 15 0N 75 0W
Carinthia □ 118 46 52N 13 30E
Carlisle 114 54 54N 2 55W
Carlsbad 95 32 20N 104 14W
Carmel-by-the-Sea 97 36 38N 121 55W
Carmel Mt. 127 32 45N 35 3E
Carnegie, L. 142 26 5S 122 30E
Carolina 105 7 10S 47 30W
Caroline I. 141 9 15S 150 3W
Caroline Is. 140 8 0N 150 0E
Carpathians, Mts. 119 49 50N 21 0E
Carpentaria, G. of 143 14 0S 139 0E
Carson City 96 39 12N 119 46W
Cartagena, Colombia 104 10 25N 75 33W
Cartagena, Spain 120 37 38N 0 59W
Cartago 104 4 45N 75 55W
Carthage 95 37 10N 94 20W
Cartier I. 142 12 31S 123 29E
Caruaru 105 8 15S 35 55W
Carúpano 104 10 39N 63 15W
Casablanca 126 33 36N 7 36W
Cascade Ra. 96 47 0N 121 30W
Casiquiare → 104 2 1N 67 7W
Casper 96 42 52N 106 20W
Caspian Sea 138 43 0N 50 0E
Castellón de la Plana 117 39 58N 0 3W
Castres 117 43 37N 2 13E
Castries 98 14 0N 60 50W
Catalonia □ 117 41 40N 1 15E
Catamarca 106 28 30S 65 50W
Catánia 120 37 31N 15 4E
Catskill Mts. 92 42 15N 74 15W
Caucasus 110 43 0N 44 0E
Caucasus Mts. 138 42 50N 44 0E
Caviana, I. 105 0 10N 50 10W
Caxias 105 4 55S 43 20W
Caxias do Sul 106 29 10S 51 10W
Cayenne 105 5 0N 52 18W
Cayes, Les 99 18 15N 73 46W
Ceará □ 105 5 0S 40 0W
Cebu 135 10 18N 123 54E
Cedar Rapids 94 42 0N 91 38W
Celaya 98 20 31N 100 37W
Celebes Sea 135 3 0N 123 0E
Central, Cordillera 104 5 0N 75 0W
Central African Republic ■ 127 7 0N 20 0E
Central Siberian Plateau 138 65 0N 105 0E
Ceram Sea 135 2 30S 128 30E
Cesena 118 44 9N 12 14E
Ceuta 126 35 52N 5 18W
Chad ■ 126 15 0N 17 15E
Chad, L. 126 13 30N 14 30E
Chagos Arch. 130 6 0S 72 0E
Châlons-sur-Marne 116 48 58N 4 20E
Chambéry 117 45 34N 5 55E
Champagne 116 49 0N 4 40E
Champaign 94 40 8N 88 14W
Champlain, L. 92 44 30N 73 20W
Ch'angchih 136 36 11N 113 6E
Changchow, Fukien, China 136 24 32N 117 44E
Changchow, Shantung, China 136 36 55N 118 3E
Changchun 136 43 58N 125 19E
Changhua 136 24 2N 120 30E
Changkiakow 136 40 52N 114 45E
Changkiang 136 19 25N 108 57E
Changsha 136 28 12N 113 0E
Changteh 136 29 12N 111 43E
Channel Is. 116 49 30N 2 40W
Chaochow 136 23 45N 116 32E
Chari → 126 12 58N 14 31E
Charleroi 116 50 24N 4 27E
Charleston, S.C., U.S.A. 93 32 47N 79 56W
Charleston, W. Va., U.S.A. 92 38 24N 81 36W
Charleville 143 26 24S 146 15E
Charleville-Mézières 116 49 44N 4 40E
Charlotte 93 35 16N 80 46W
Charlotte Amalie 99 18 22N 64 56W
Charlotte Waters 142 25 56S 134 54E
Charlottenberg 118 59 54N 12 17E
Chartres 116 48 29N 1 30E
Chattahoochee → 93 30 43N 84 51W
Chattanooga 93 35 2N 85 17W
Chehalis 96 46 44N 122 59W
Cheju Do 136 33 29N 126 34E
Chełmźa 119 53 10N 18 39E
Cheltenham 114 51 55N 2 5W
Chelyabinsk 138 55 10N 61 24E
Chengchow 136 34 47N 113 46E
Chengteh 136 41 0N 117 55E
Chengtu 136 30 45N 104 0E
Chenyuan 136 27 0N 108 20E
Cherbourg 116 49 39N 1 40W
Chesapeake Bay 92 38 0N 76 12W
Chester 92 39 54N 75 20W
Chesterfield, Îles 143 19 52S 158 15E
Cheviot Hills 114 55 20N 2 30W
Chew Bahir 127 4 40N 36 50E
Cheyenne 94 41 9N 104 49W
Cheyenne → 94 44 40N 101 15W
Chiai 136 23 29N 120 25E
Chiang Mai 134 18 47N 98 59E
Chiba 137 35 30N 140 7E
Chicago 94 41 53N 87 40W
Chickasha 95 35 0N 98 0W
Chiclayo 104 6 42S 79 50W
Chico 96 39 45N 121 54W
Chihuahua 98 28 38N 106 5W
Chile ■ 106 35 0S 72 0W
Chillán 106 36 40S 72 10W
Chiloé, I. de 106 42 30S 73 50W
Chiltern Hills 114 51 44N 0 42W
Chilung 136 25 3N 121 45E
Chimbote 104 9 0S 78 35W
China ■ 136 30 0N 110 0E
Chincha Alta 104 13 25S 76 7W
Chinchow 136 41 10N 121 2E
Chinkiang 136 32 2N 119 29E
Chinwangtao 136 40 0N 119 31E
Chipata 128 13 38S 32 28E
Chiquinquira 104 5 37N 73 50W
Chita 138 52 0N 113 35E
Chittagong 134 22 19N 91 48E
Chivilcoy 106 34 55S 60 0W
Chŏnju 136 35 50N 127 4E
Chonos, Arch. de los 106 45 0S 75 0W
Chorzów 119 50 18N 18 57E
Christchurch 143 43 33S 172 47E
Christiansted 99 17 45N 64 42W
Christmas I. 135 10 30S 105 40E
Chuanchow 136 24 57N 118 31E
Chubut → 106 43 20S 65 5W
Chuchow 136 27 56N 113 3E
Chudskoye, L. 115 58 13N 27 30E
Chuhsien 136 35 31N 118 45E
Chula Vista 97 32 39N 117 8W
Chumatien 136 33 0N 114 4E
Chungking 136 29 30N 106 30E
Cicero 94 41 48N 87 48W
Ciénaga 104 11 1N 74 15W
Cienfuegos 99 22 10N 80 30W
Cincinnati 92 39 10N 84 26W
Cinto, Mt. 117 42 24N 8 54E
Cirebon 135 6 45S 108 32E
Citlaltépetl 98 19 0N 97 20W
Ciudad Bolívar 104 8 5N 63 36W
Ciudad Guayana 104 8 0N 62 30W
Ciudad Juárez 98 31 44N 106 29W
Ciudad Madero 98 22 16N 97 50W
Ciudad Obregón 98 27 29N 109 56W
Ciudad Victoria 98 23 44N 99 8W
Clarksdale 95 34 12N 90 33W
Clarksville 93 36 32N 87 20W
Clearwater 93 27 58N 82 45W
Clearwater, Mts. 96 46 20N 115 30E
Clermont-Ferrand 117 45 46N 3 4E
Cleveland 92 41 28N 81 43W
Clinton 94 41 50N 90 12W
Clipperton, I. 141 10 18N 109 13W
Cloncurry 143 20 40S 140 28E
Clovis 95 34 20N 103 10W
Cluj-Napoca 119 46 47N 23 38E
Clyde, Firth of 114 55 20N 5 0W
Coast Ranges 96 41 0N 123 0W
Coastal Plains Basin 142 30 10S 115 30E
Coatzacoalcos 98 18 9N 94 25W
Cochabamba 104 17 26S 66 10W
Cocos Is. 135 12 10S 96 55E
Cod, C. 91 42 8N 70 10W
Cœur d'Alene 96 47 45N 116 51W
Coffeyville 95 37 0N 95 40W
Coffs Harbour 143 30 16S 153 5E
Cognac 117 45 41N 0 20W
Coimbatore 134 11 2N 76 59E
Coleraine 114 55 8N 6 40W
Colima 98 19 14N 103 43W
Cologne 118 50 56N 6 58E
Colombia ■ 104 3 45N 73 0W
Colombo 134 6 56N 79 58E
Colón 98 9 20N 79 54W
Colorado □ 97 37 40N 106 0W
Colorado →, Argentina 106 39 50S 62 8W
Colorado →, U.S.A. 97 34 45N 114 40W
Colorado Plateau 97 36 40N 110 30W
Colorado Springs 94 38 55N 104 50W
Columbia, Mo., U.S.A. 94 38 58N 92 20W
Columbia, S.C., U.S.A. 93 34 0N 81 0W
Columbia, Tenn., U.S.A. 93 35 40N 87 0W
Columbia → 96 46 15N 124 5W
Columbia, District of □ 92 38 55N 77 0W
Columbia Basin 96 47 30N 118 30W
Columbus, Ga., U.S.A. 93 32 30N 84 58W
Columbus, Miss., U.S.A. 95 33 30N 88 26W
Columbus, Ohio, U.S.A. 92 39 57N 83 1W
Communism Pk. 138 38 40N 72 20E
Como 118 45 48N 9 5E
Comodoro Rivadavia 106 45 50S 67 40W
Comorin, C. 134 8 3N 77 40E
Comoro Is. ■ 123 12 10S 44 15E
Conakry 126 9 29N 13 49W
Concarneau 116 47 52N 3 56W
Concepción 106 36 50S 73 0W
Concepción del Uruguay 106 32 35S 58 20W
Concord, N.C., U.S.A. 93 35 28N 80 35W
Concord, N.H., U.S.A. 92 43 12N 71 30W
Concordia 106 31 20S 58 2W
Congo ■ 128 1 0S 16 0E
Congo Basin 122 0 10S 24 30E
Connecticut □ 92 41 40N 72 40W
Connecticut → 92 41 17N 72 21W
Connemara 114 53 29N 9 45W
Constanţa 119 44 14N 28 38E
Constantine 126 36 25N 6 42E
Cook, Mt. 143 43 36S 170 9E
Cook Is. 141 17 0S 160 0W
Coopers Cr. → 143 28 29S 137 46E
Cootamundra 143 34 36S 148 1E
Copenhagen 115 55 41N 12 34E
Copiapó 106 27 30S 70 20W
Coquimbo 106 30 0S 71 20W
Coracora 104 15 5S 73 45W
Coral Sea 140 15 0S 150 0E

Córdoba WORLD Guadalcanal

Córdoba **106** 31 20 S 64 10 W
Córdoba □ **120** 38 5 N 5 0 W
Corinth, G. of **121** 38 16 N 22 30 E
Cork **114** 51 54 N 8 30 W
Coromandel Coast **134** 12 30 N 81 0 E
Coronado **97** 32 45 N 117 9 W
Corpus Christi **95** 27 50 N 97 28 W
Corrientes **106** 27 30 S 58 45 W
Corse, C. **117** 43 1 N 9 25 E
Corsica **117** 42 0 N 9 0 E
Corsicana **95** 32 5 N 96 30 W
Corumbá **104** 19 0 S 57 30 W
Coruña, La **120** 43 20 N 8 25 W
Corvallis **96** 44 36 N 123 15 W
Costa Rica ■ **99** 10 0 N 84 0 W
Cotentin **116** 49 30 N 1 30 W
Cotonou **126** 6 20 N 2 25 E
Cotopaxi, Vol. **104** 0 40 S 78 30 W
Cotswold Hills **114** 51 42 N 2 10 W
Council Bluffs **94** 41 20 N 95 50 W
Coventry **114** 52 25 N 1 31 W
Covington **92** 39 5 N 84 30 W
Craiova **119** 44 21 N 23 48 E
Crato **105** 7 10 S 39 25 W
Crazy Mts. **96** 46 14 N 110 30 W
Crete **121** 35 15 N 25 0 E
Creus, C. **117** 42 20 N 3 19 E
Creusot, Le **116** 46 50 N 4 24 E
Crewe **114** 53 6 N 2 28 W
Criciúma **106** 28 40 S 49 23 W
Crimea **138** 45 0 N 34 0 E
Crosse, La **94** 43 48 N 91 13 W
Cruz Alta **106** 28 45 S 53 40 W
Cruz del Eje **106** 30 45 S 64 50 W
Cruzeiro do Sul **104** 7 35 S 72 35 W
Cuba ■ **99** 22 0 N 79 0 W
Cúcuta **104** 7 54 N 72 31 W
Cuenca **104** 2 50 S 79 9 W
Cuernavaca **98** 18 55 N 99 15 W
Cuiabá **105** 15 30 S 56 0 W
Culiacán **98** 24 48 N 107 24 W
Cumaná **104** 10 30 N 64 5 W
Cumberland **92** 39 40 N 78 43 W
Cumbrian Mts. **114** 54 30 N 3 0 W
Cunene → **128** 17 20 S 11 50 E
Curaçao **99** 12 10 N 69 0 W
Curicó **106** 34 55 S 71 20 W
Curitiba **106** 25 20 S 49 10 W
Cuttack **134** 20 25 N 85 57 E
Cuzco **104** 13 32 S 72 0 W
Cyprus ■ **121** 35 0 N 33 0 E
Cyrenaica **122** 27 0 N 23 0 E
Czechoslovakia ■ **118** 49 0 N 17 0 E
Częstochowa **119** 50 49 N 19 7 E

Da Lat **134** 11 56 N 108 25 E
Da Nang **134** 16 4 N 108 13 E
Dacca **134** 23 43 N 90 26 E
Dakar **126** 14 34 N 17 29 W
Dakhla Oasis **127** 25 30 N 28 50 E
Dalby **143** 27 10 S 151 17 E
Dallas **95** 32 50 N 96 50 W
Dalton **93** 34 47 N 84 58 W
Damaraland **128** 21 0 S 17 0 E
Damascus **129** 33 30 N 36 18 E
Dampier **142** 20 41 S 116 42 E
Dampier Arch. **142** 20 38 S 116 32 E
Danube → **119** 45 20 N 29 40 E
Danville **93** 36 40 N 79 20 W
Dar es Salaam **128** 6 50 S 39 12 E
Darbhanga **134** 26 15 N 85 55 E
Dardanelles **121** 40 0 N 26 0 E
Darién, G. of **99** 9 0 N 77 0 W
Darjeeling **134** 27 3 N 88 18 E
Darling → **143** 34 4 S 141 54 E
Darling Ra. **142** 32 30 S 116 0 E
Darmstadt **118** 49 51 N 8 40 E
Dartmoor **114** 50 36 N 4 0 W
Darwin **142** 12 25 S 130 51 E
Dasht-e Lūt **129** 31 30 N 58 0 E
Daugavpils **115** 55 53 N 26 32 E
Dauphiné **117** 45 15 N 5 25 E
Davao **135** 7 0 N 125 40 E
Davenport **94** 41 30 N 90 40 W
Davis Str. **89** 65 0 N 58 0 W
Davos **118** 46 48 N 9 49 E
Dayton **92** 39 45 N 84 10 W
Daytona Beach **93** 29 14 N 81 0 W
De Aar **128** 30 39 S 24 0 E
Dead Sea **127** 31 30 N 35 30 E
Death Valley **97** 36 19 N 116 52 W
Debre Markos **127** 10 20 N 37 40 E
Debre Tabor **127** 11 50 N 38 26 E
Debrecen **119** 47 33 N 21 42 E
Decatur, Ala., U.S.A. **93** 34 35 N 87 0 W
Decatur, Ill., U.S.A. **94** 39 50 N 89 0 W
Deccan **130** 18 0 N 79 0 E
Dej **119** 47 10 N 23 52 E
Delano **97** 35 48 N 119 13 W
Delaware □ **92** 39 0 N 75 40 W
Delaware → **92** 39 20 N 75 25 W
Delft **116** 52 1 N 4 22 E
Delgado, C. **128** 10 45 S 40 40 E
Delhi **134** 28 38 N 77 17 E
Dembidolo **127** 8 34 N 34 50 E
Den Helder **116** 52 57 N 4 45 E
Denmark ■ **115** 55 30 N 9 0 E
Denmark Str. **89** 66 0 N 30 0 W
Denton **95** 33 12 N 97 10 W
Denver **94** 39 45 N 105 0 W
Derby **114** 52 55 N 1 28 W
Derryveagh Mts. **114** 55 0 N 8 40 W
Des Moines **94** 41 35 N 93 37 W
Des Moines → **94** 40 23 N 91 25 W
Dese **127** 11 5 N 39 40 E
Dessau **118** 51 49 N 12 15 E
Detroit **92** 42 23 N 83 5 W
Deventer **116** 52 15 N 6 10 E
Dezfūl **129** 32 20 N 48 30 E
Diamantina **105** 18 17 S 43 40 W
Dieppe **116** 49 54 N 1 4 E
Dijon **116** 47 20 N 5 0 E
Dîmbovița → **119** 44 14 N 26 13 E
Dinan **116** 48 28 N 2 2 W
Dinosaur National Monument **96** 40 30 N 108 58 W
Dire Dawa **127** 9 35 N 41 45 E
Dirk Hartog I. **142** 25 50 S 113 5 E
Disappointment L. **142** 23 20 S 122 40 E
Diyarbakir **129** 37 55 N 40 18 E
Djibouti **127** 11 30 N 43 5 E
Djibouti ■ **127** 12 0 N 43 0 E
Dnepropetrovsk **138** 48 30 N 35 0 E
Dnieper → **138** 46 30 N 32 18 E
Dodecanese **121** 36 35 N 27 0 E
Dodge City **95** 37 42 N 100 0 W
Dodoma **128** 6 8 S 35 45 E
Dominica ■ **98** 15 20 N 61 20 W
Dominican Rep. ■ **99** 19 0 N 70 30 W
Don → **138** 47 4 N 39 18 E
Donegal **114** 54 39 N 8 8 W
Donegal B. **114** 54 30 N 8 35 W
Donetsk **138** 48 0 N 37 45 E
Dordogne → **117** 45 2 N 0 36 W
Dordrecht **116** 51 48 N 4 39 E
Dorohoi **119** 47 56 N 26 30 E
Dortmund **118** 51 32 N 7 28 E
Dothan **93** 31 10 N 85 25 W
Douai **116** 50 21 N 3 4 E
Douala **126** 4 0 N 9 45 E
Douglas, U.K. **114** 54 9 N 4 29 W
Douglas, U.S.A. **97** 31 21 N 109 30 W
Dover **114** 51 7 N 1 19 E
Dover, Str. of **116** 51 0 N 1 30 E
Drakensberg **128** 31 0 S 28 0 E
Dresden **118** 51 2 N 13 45 E
Dreux **116** 48 44 N 1 23 E
Drina → **121** 44 53 N 19 21 E
Drogheda **114** 53 45 N 6 20 W
Dronning Maud Land **107** 72 30 S 12 0 E
Dubai **129** 25 18 N 55 20 E
Dublin, Ireland **114** 53 20 N 6 18 W
Dublin, U.S.A. **93** 32 30 N 82 34 W
Dubrovnik **121** 42 39 N 18 6 E
Duisburg **118** 51 27 N 6 42 E
Duluth **94** 46 48 N 92 10 W
Dumfries **114** 55 4 N 3 37 W
Dun Laoghaire **114** 53 17 N 6 9 W
Duncan **95** 34 25 N 98 0 W
Dundalk **114** 54 1 N 6 25 W
Dundee **114** 56 29 N 3 0 W
Dunedin **143** 45 50 S 170 33 E
Dunkirk **116** 51 2 N 2 20 E
Durango □ **98** 24 50 N 104 50 W
Durazno **106** 33 25 S 56 31 W
Durban **128** 29 49 S 31 1 E
Durham **93** 36 0 N 78 55 W
Durmitor **121** 43 10 N 19 0 E
Dushanbe **138** 38 33 N 68 48 E
Düsseldorf **118** 51 15 N 6 46 E
Dyersburg **95** 36 2 N 89 20 W
Dzungaria **136** 44 10 N 88 0 E

East China Sea **136** 30 5 N 126 0 E
East Germany ■ **118** 52 0 N 12 0 E
East Indies **130** 0 0 120 0 E
East London **128** 33 0 S 27 55 E
East Orange **92** 40 46 N 74 13 W
East St. Louis **94** 38 37 N 90 4 W
East Siberian Sea **138** 73 0 N 160 0 E
Easter Islands **141** 27 0 S 109 0 W
Eastern Ghats **134** 14 0 N 78 50 E
Eau Claire **94** 44 46 N 91 30 W
Ebro → **117** 40 43 N 0 54 E
Ecuador ■ **104** 2 0 S 78 0 W
Edinburg **95** 26 22 N 98 10 W
Edinburgh **114** 55 57 N 3 12 W
Edward, L. **128** 0 25 S 29 40 E
Edwards Plat. **95** 30 30 N 101 5 W
Égadi, Ísole **120** 37 55 N 12 16 E
Egypt ■ **127** 28 0 N 31 0 E
Eighty Mile Beach **142** 19 30 S 120 40 E
Eindhoven **116** 51 26 N 5 30 E
El Aaiún **126** 27 9 N 13 12 W
El Centro **97** 32 50 N 115 40 W
El Djouf **126** 20 0 N 11 30 E
El Dorado, Ark., U.S.A. **95** 33 10 N 92 40 W
El Dorado, Kans., U.S.A. **95** 37 55 N 96 56 W
El Faiyûm **127** 29 19 N 30 50 E
El Fâsher **127** 13 33 N 25 26 E
El Ferrol **120** 43 29 N 8 15 W
El Khârga **127** 25 30 N 30 33 E
El Mahalla el Kubra **127** 31 0 N 31 0 E
El Minyâ **127** 28 7 N 30 33 E
El Obeid **127** 13 8 N 30 10 E
El Paso **97** 31 50 N 106 30 W
El Reno **95** 35 30 N 98 0 W
El Salvador ■ **98** 13 50 N 89 0 W
Elâzığ **129** 38 37 N 39 14 E
Elbe → **118** 53 50 N 9 0 E
Elbląg **119** 54 10 N 19 25 E
Elbrus **138** 43 21 N 42 30 E
Elgin **94** 42 0 N 88 20 W
Elgon, Mt. **128** 1 10 N 34 30 E
Elizabeth **92** 40 37 N 74 12 W
Elizabeth City **93** 36 18 N 76 16 W
Elizabethton **93** 36 20 N 82 13 W
Elko **96** 40 50 N 115 50 W
Ellesworth Land **107** 76 0 S 89 0 W
Elmhurst **94** 41 52 N 87 58 W
Eluru **134** 16 48 N 81 8 E
Ely **114** 52 24 N 0 16 E
Emāmrūd **129** 36 30 N 55 0 E
Emerald **143** 23 32 S 148 10 E
Emilia-Romagna □ **118** 44 33 N 10 40 E
Ems → **118** 52 37 N 9 26 E
Enderby Land **107** 66 0 S 53 0 E
Enewatak **140** 11 30 N 162 15 E
Engadin **118** 46 45 N 10 10 E
Enggano **135** 5 20 S 102 40 E
England □ **114** 53 0 N 2 0 W
Englewood **94** 39 40 N 105 0 W
English Channel **114** 50 0 N 2 0 W
Enid **95** 36 26 N 97 52 W
Enniskillen **114** 54 20 N 7 40 W
Enschede **116** 52 13 N 6 53 E
Ensenada **98** 31 52 N 116 37 W
Entebbe **128** 0 4 N 32 28 E
Entre Ríos □ **106** 30 30 S 58 30 W
Enugu **126** 6 20 N 7 30 E
Equatorial Guinea ■ **126** 2 0 S 8 0 E
Ereğli **129** 41 15 N 31 30 E
Erfurt **118** 50 58 N 11 2 E
Erg Chech **126** 50 59 N 11 0 E
Erie **92** 42 10 N 80 7 W
Erie, L. **92** 42 15 N 81 0 W
Erzurum **129** 39 57 N 41 15 E
Esbjerg **115** 55 29 N 8 29 E
Eşfahān **129** 33 0 N 53 0 E
Eskişehir **129** 39 50 N 30 35 E
Esmeraldas **104** 1 0 N 79 40 W
Esperance **142** 33 45 S 121 55 E
Espinhaço, Serra do **105** 17 30 S 43 30 W
Espírito Santo □ **105** 20 0 S 40 45 W
Essen **118** 51 28 N 6 59 E
Estonian S.S.R. □ **115** 58 30 N 25 30 E
Ethiopia ■ **127** 8 0 N 40 0 E
Ethiopian Highlands **122** 10 0 N 37 0 E
Etosha Pan **128** 18 40 S 16 30 E
Eufaula **93** 31 55 N 85 11 W
Eugene **96** 44 0 N 123 8 W
Euphrates → **129** 31 0 N 47 25 E
Eureka **96** 40 50 N 124 0 W
Europe **110** 50 0 N 20 0 E
Evanston **94** 42 0 N 87 40 W
Evansville **92** 38 0 N 87 35 W
Everest, Mt. **130** 28 5 N 86 58 E
Everett **96** 48 0 N 122 10 W
Everglades Nat. Park **93** 25 27 N 80 53 W
Évreux **116** 49 0 N 1 8 E
Évvoia **121** 38 30 N 24 0 E
Exeter **114** 50 43 N 3 31 W
Exmoor **114** 51 10 N 3 59 W
Eyasi, L. **128** 3 30 S 35 0 E
Eyre, L. **143** 29 30 S 137 26 E
Eyre Pen. **143** 33 30 S 137 17 E

Fairbanks **41** 64 50 N 147 50 W
Fairfield, Ala., U.S.A. **93** 33 30 N 87 0 W
Fairfield, Calif., U.S.A. **96** 38 14 N 122 1 W
Faisalabad **134** 31 30 N 73 5 E
Falkland Is. **106** 51 30 S 59 0 W
Falkland Is. Dependency □ **107** 57 0 S 40 0 W
Fall River **92** 41 45 N 71 5 W
Famagusta **121** 35 8 N 33 55 E
Farasan Is. **129** 16 45 N 41 55 E
Fargo **94** 46 52 N 96 40 W
Faroe Is. **110** 62 0 N 7 0 W
Fatshan **136** 23 0 N 113 4 E
Fayetteville, Ark., U.S.A. **95** 36 0 N 94 5 W
Fayetteville, N.C., U.S.A. **93** 35 0 N 78 58 W
F'Dérik **126** 22 40 N 12 45 W
Feather → **96** 38 47 N 121 36 W
Feira de Santana **105** 12 15 S 38 57 W
Fengkieh **136** 31 0 N 109 33 E
Fens, The **114** 52 45 N 0 2 E
Fenyang **136** 37 19 N 111 46 E
Ferrara **118** 44 50 N 11 36 E
Fès **126** 34 0 N 5 0 W
Fianarantsoa **128** 21 26 S 47 5 E
Figueras **117** 42 18 N 2 58 E
Fiji ■ **140** 17 20 S 179 0 E
Finisterre, C. **120** 42 50 N 9 19 W
Finland ■ **115** 63 0 N 27 0 E
Finland, G. of **115** 60 0 N 26 0 E
Fitzroy Crossing **142** 18 9 S 125 38 E
Flagstaff **97** 35 10 N 111 40 W
Flaming Gorge Res. **96** 41 15 N 109 30 W
Flanders **116** 51 10 N 3 15 E
Flathead L. **96** 47 50 N 114 0 W
Flensburg **118** 54 46 N 9 28 E
Flers **116** 48 47 N 0 33 W
Flinders → **143** 17 36 S 140 36 E
Flinders B. **142** 34 19 S 115 19 E
Flinders I. **142** 40 0 S 148 0 E
Flinders Ranges **143** 31 30 S 138 30 E
Flint **92** 43 5 N 83 40 W
Florence, Italy **118** 43 47 N 11 15 E
Florence, Ala., U.S.A. **93** 34 50 N 87 40 W
Florence, S.C., U.S.A. **93** 34 12 N 79 44 W
Flores **135** 8 35 S 121 0 E
Flores Sea **135** 6 30 S 124 0 E
Florianópolis **106** 27 30 S 48 30 W
Florida **106** 34 7 S 56 10 W
Florida □ **93** 28 30 N 82 0 W
Florida, Straits of **99** 25 0 N 80 0 W
Fly → **143** 8 25 S 143 0 E
Foix □ **117** 43 0 N 1 30 E
Folkestone **114** 51 5 N 1 11 E
Fond du Lac **94** 43 46 N 88 26 W
Fonseca, G. of **99** 13 10 N 87 40 W
Foochow **136** 26 2 N 119 25 E
Forlì **118** 44 14 N 12 2 E
Formentera **120** 38 43 N 1 27 E
Formosa **106** 26 15 S 58 10 W
Fort-de-France **98** 14 36 N 61 2 W
Fort Dodge **94** 42 29 N 94 10 W
Fort Lauderdale **93** 26 10 N 80 5 W
Fort Myers **93** 26 39 N 81 51 W
Fort Peck L. **96** 47 40 N 107 0 W
Fort Pierce **93** 27 29 N 80 19 W
Fort Scott **95** 37 50 N 94 40 W
Fort Smith **95** 35 25 N 94 25 W
Fort Wayne **92** 41 5 N 85 10 W
Fort Worth **95** 32 45 N 97 25 W
Fortaleza **105** 3 45 S 38 35 W
Forth, Firth of **114** 56 5 N 2 55 W
Fouta Djalon **126** 11 20 N 12 10 W
Franca **105** 20 33 S 47 30 W
France ■ **116** 47 0 N 3 0 E
Frankfurt am Main **118** 50 7 N 8 40 E
Franz Josef Land **138** 82 0 N 55 0 E
Fraser I. **143** 25 15 S 153 10 E
Fray Bentos **106** 33 10 S 58 15 W
Fredericksburg **92** 38 16 N 77 29 W
Freeport, Bahamas **99** 26 30 N 78 47 W
Freeport, U.S.A. **94** 42 18 N 89 40 W
Freetown **126** 8 30 N 13 17 W
Freiberg **118** 50 55 N 13 20 E
French Guiana ■ **105** 4 0 N 53 0 W
French Polynesia □ **141** 20 0 S 145 0 E
Fresnillo **98** 23 10 N 102 53 W
Fresno **97** 36 47 N 119 50 W
Frisian Is. **118** 53 30 N 6 0 E
Friuli-Venezia Giulia □ **118** 46 0 N 13 0 E
Frome, L. **143** 30 45 S 139 45 E
Front Range **96** 40 0 N 105 40 W
Frunze **138** 42 54 N 74 46 E
Fuchow **136** 27 50 N 116 14 E
Fuji-no-miya **137** 35 10 N 138 40 E
Fujisawa **137** 35 22 N 139 29 E
Fukui **137** 36 0 N 136 10 E
Fukuoka **137** 33 39 N 130 21 E
Fukushima **137** 37 44 N 140 28 E
Fukuyama **137** 34 35 N 133 20 E
Funabashi **137** 35 45 N 140 0 E
Funchal **126** 32 38 N 16 54 W
Furneaux Group **142** 40 10 S 147 50 E
Fürth **118** 49 29 N 11 0 E
Fushun **136** 41 50 N 123 55 E
Fusin **136** 42 12 N 121 33 E
Fyn **115** 55 20 N 10 30 E

Gabon ■ **128** 0 10 S 10 0 E
Gaborone **128** 24 45 S 25 57 E
Gadsden **93** 34 1 N 86 0 W
Gainesville, Fla., U.S.A. **93** 29 38 N 82 20 W
Gainesville, Ga., U.S.A. **93** 34 17 N 83 47 W
Gainesville, Tex., U.S.A. **95** 33 40 N 97 10 W
Galápagos **141** 0 0 89 0 W
Galați **119** 45 27 N 28 2 E
Galdhøpiggen **115** 61 38 N 8 18 E
Galesburg **94** 40 57 N 90 23 W
Galilee, Sea of **127** 32 53 N 35 18 E
Galveston **95** 29 15 N 94 48 W
Galway B. **114** 53 10 N 9 20 W
Gambia ■ **126** 13 25 N 16 0 W
Gambia → **126** 13 28 N 16 34 W
Gamboa **98** 9 8 N 79 42 W
Ganga → **134** 23 20 N 90 30 E
Gao **126** 16 15 N 0 5 W
Garden City **95** 38 0 N 100 45 W
Garonne → **117** 45 2 N 0 36 W
Gary **92** 41 35 N 87 20 W
Gascony **117** 43 45 N 0 20 E
Gastonia **93** 35 17 N 81 10 W
Gateshead **114** 54 57 N 1 37 W
Gatun **98** 9 16 N 79 55 W
Gatun, L. **98** 9 7 N 79 56 W
Gauhati **134** 26 10 N 91 45 E
Gävle **115** 60 40 N 17 9 E
Gaya **134** 24 47 N 85 4 E
Gaza **127** 31 30 N 34 28 E
Gaziantep **129** 37 6 N 37 23 E
Gdańsk **119** 54 22 N 18 40 E
Gdynia **119** 54 35 N 18 33 E
Geelong **143** 38 10 S 144 22 E
Gelsenkirchen **118** 51 30 N 7 5 E
Geneva **118** 46 12 N 6 9 E
Genk **116** 50 58 N 5 32 E
Genoa **118** 44 24 N 8 56 E
George, L. **128** 0 5 N 30 10 E
George Town **135** 5 25 N 100 15 E
Georgetown **104** 6 50 N 58 12 W
Georgia □ **93** 32 0 N 82 0 W
Georgian S.S.R. □ **138** 42 0 N 43 0 E
Gera **118** 50 53 N 12 11 E
Germiston **128** 26 15 S 28 10 E
Gerona **117** 41 58 N 2 46 E
Getafe **117** 40 18 N 3 44 W
Gettysburg **92** 39 47 N 77 18 W
Ghana ■ **126** 6 0 N 1 0 W
Ghat **126** 24 59 N 10 11 E
Ghent **116** 51 2 N 3 42 E
Gibraltar **120** 36 7 N 5 22 W
Gibraltar, Str. of **120** 35 55 N 5 40 W
Gibson Des. **142** 24 0 S 126 0 E
Gifu **137** 35 30 N 136 45 E
Gijón **120** 43 32 N 5 42 W
Gila → **97** 32 43 N 114 33 W
Gilgit **134** 35 50 N 74 15 E
Gippsland **143** 37 45 S 147 15 E
Girardot **104** 4 18 N 74 48 W
Gladstone **143** 33 15 S 138 22 E
Glasgow **114** 55 52 N 4 14 W
Glen Canyon Nat. Recreation Area **97** 37 30 N 111 0 W
Glendale **97** 34 7 N 118 18 W
Gliwice **119** 50 22 N 18 41 E
Głogów **118** 51 37 N 16 5 E
Gloucester **114** 51 52 N 2 15 W
Gniezno **119** 52 30 N 17 35 E
Gobi **130** 44 0 N 111 0 E
Goiana **105** 7 33 S 34 59 W
Goiás □ **105** 12 10 S 48 0 W
Golden Gate **96** 37 54 N 122 30 W
Goldsboro **93** 35 24 N 77 59 W
Gomel **138** 52 28 N 31 0 E
Gómez Palacio **98** 25 34 N 103 30 W
Gonaïves **99** 19 20 N 72 42 W
Good Hope, C. of **128** 34 24 S 18 30 E
Goondiwindi **143** 28 30 S 150 21 E
Gorakhpur **134** 26 47 N 83 23 E
Gorki **138** 56 20 N 44 0 E
Göteborg **115** 57 43 N 11 59 E
Gotland **115** 57 30 N 18 33 E
Gottwaldov **119** 49 14 N 17 40 E
Governador Valadares **105** 18 15 S 41 57 W
Goya **106** 29 10 S 59 10 W
Gozo **120** 36 0 N 14 13 E
Graham Land **107** 65 0 S 64 0 W
Grampian Mts. **114** 56 50 N 4 0 W
Gran Chaco **106** 25 0 S 61 0 W
Granada **120** 37 10 N 3 35 W
Grand Bahama **99** 26 40 N 78 30 W
Grand Bassam **126** 5 10 N 3 49 W
Grand-Bourg **98** 15 53 N 61 19 W
Grand Canyon **97** 36 3 N 112 9 W
Grand Cayman **99** 19 20 N 81 20 W
Grand Coulee Dam **96** 48 0 N 118 50 W
Grand Forks **94** 48 0 N 97 3 W
Grand Island **94** 40 59 N 98 25 W
Grand Rapids **92** 42 57 N 86 40 W
Grand Teton **96** 43 54 N 111 50 W
Grange, La **93** 33 4 N 85 0 W
Granite City **94** 38 45 N 90 3 W
Grasse **117** 43 38 N 6 56 E
Graz **118** 47 4 N 15 27 E
Great Abaco I. **99** 26 25 N 77 10 W
Great Australia Basin **143** 26 0 S 140 0 E
Great Australian Bight **142** 33 30 S 130 0 E
Great Barrier Reef **143** 18 0 S 146 50 E
Great Basin **96** 40 0 N 116 30 W
Great Britain **110** 54 0 N 2 15 W
Great Falls **96** 47 27 N 111 12 W
Great Plains **40** 47 0 N 105 0 W
Great Saint Bernard P. **118** 45 50 N 7 10 E
Great Salt Lake **96** 41 0 N 112 30 W
Great Salt Lake Desert **96** 40 20 N 113 50 W
Great Sandy Desert **142** 21 0 S 124 0 E
Great Smoky Mts. Nat. Park **93** 35 39 N 83 30 W
Great Victoria Des. **142** 29 30 S 126 30 E
Great Wall **136** 38 30 N 109 30 E
Greater Antilles **99** 17 40 N 74 0 W
Greater Sunda Is. **135** 7 0 S 112 0 E
Greece ■ **121** 40 0 N 23 0 E
Greeley **94** 40 30 N 104 40 W
Green → **97** 38 11 N 109 53 W
Green Bay **94** 44 30 N 88 0 W
Greenland □ **89** 66 0 N 45 0 W
Greenland Sea **89** 73 0 N 10 0 W
Greenock **114** 55 57 N 4 46 W
Greensboro **93** 36 7 N 79 46 W
Greenville, Ala., U.S.A. **93** 31 50 N 86 37 W
Greenville, Miss., U.S.A. **95** 33 25 N 91 0 W
Greenville, N.C., U.S.A. **93** 35 37 N 77 26 W
Greenville, S.C., U.S.A. **93** 34 54 N 82 24 W
Greenwood, Miss., U.S.A. **95** 33 30 N 90 4 W
Greenwood, S.C., U.S.A. **93** 34 13 N 82 13 W
Grenada ■ **98** 12 10 N 61 40 W
Grenadines **98** 12 40 N 61 20 W
Grenoble **117** 45 12 N 5 42 E
Grey Range **143** 27 0 S 143 30 E
Griffin **93** 33 17 N 84 14 W
Grimsby **114** 53 35 N 0 5 W
Gris Nez, C. **116** 50 52 N 1 35 E
Groningen **116** 53 15 N 6 35 E
Groote Eylandt **143** 14 0 S 136 40 E
Groznyy **138** 43 20 N 45 45 E
Grudziądz **119** 53 30 N 18 47 E
Guadalajara, Mexico **98** 20 40 N 103 20 W
Guadalajara, Spain **117** 40 37 N 3 12 W
Guadalcanal **143** 9 32 S 160 12 E

Guadarrama, Sierra de WORLD Leipzig

Guadarrama, Sierra de 117 41 0N 4 0W
Guadeloupe ■ 98 16 20N 61 40W
Guajira, Pen. de la 104 12 0N 72 0W
Gualeguay 106 33 10S 59 14W
Gualeguaychú 106 33 3S 59 31W
Guam 140 13 27N 144 45E
Guanajuato 98 21 1N 101 15W
Guantánamo 99 20 10N 75 14W
Guarapuava 106 25 20S 51 30W
Guatemala 98 14 40N 90 22W
Guatemala ■ 98 15 40N 90 30W
Guayaquil 104 2 15S 79 52W
Guayaquil, G. de 104 3 10S 81 0W
Guaymas 98 27 56N 110 54W
Guecho 117 43 21N 2 59W
Guernsey 116 49 30N 2 35W
Guinea ■ 126 10 20N 10 0W
Guinea, Gulf of 126 3 0N 2 30E
Gujranwala 134 32 10N 74 12E
Gulf, The 129 27 0N 50 0E
Gulf Basin 142 15 20S 129 0E
Guthrie 95 35 55N 97 30W
Gutiérrez Zamora 98 20 27N 97 5W
Guyana ■ 104 5 0N 59 0W
Guyenne 117 44 30N 0 40E
Gwalior 134 26 12N 78 10E
Györ 119 47 41N 17 40E

Haarlem 116 52 23N 4 39E
Hachinohe 137 40 30N 141 29E
Hachiōji 137 35 40N 139 20E
Hagen 118 51 21N 7 29E
Haifa 127 32 46N 35 0E
Haikow 136 20 0N 110 20E
Hailar 136 49 12N 119 37E
Hainan 134 19 0N 110 0E
Haiti ■ 99 19 0N 72 30W
Hakodate 137 41 45N 140 44E
Halberstadt 118 51 53N 11 2E
Halle 118 51 29N 12 0E
Halmahera 135 0 40N 128 0E
Hamada 137 34 56N 132 4E
Hamadān 129 34 52N 48 32E
Hamāh 129 35 5N 36 40E
Hamamatsu 137 34 45N 137 45E
Hamburg 118 53 32N 9 59E
Hamilton, Bermuda 99 32 15N 64 45W
Hamilton, N.Z. 143 37 47S 175 19E
Hamm 118 51 40N 7 49E
Hammerfest 115 70 39N 23 41E
Hammond 92 41 40N 87 30W
Hampton 92 37 4N 76 18W
Hampton Tableland 142 32 0S 127 0E
Hanchung 136 33 10N 107 2E
Hancock 94 45 26N 95 46W
Hangchow 136 30 12N 120 1E
Hanku 136 39 16N 117 50E
Hannibal 94 39 42N 91 22W
Hannover 118 52 23N 9 43E
Hanoi 134 21 5N 105 55E
Hantan 136 36 42N 114 30E
Harare 128 17 43S 31 2E
Harbin 136 45 48N 126 40E
Hardanger Fjord 115 60 15N 6 0E
Hardwar 134 29 58N 78 9E
Harlingen 95 26 20N 97 50W
Harney Basin 96 43 30N 119 0W
Harrisburg 92 40 18N 76 52W
Hartford 92 41 47N 72 41W
Harvey 94 41 40N 87 40W
Hasa 129 26 0N 49 0E
Hastings, U.K. 114 50 51N 0 36E
Hastings, U.S.A. 94 40 34N 98 22W
Hatteras, C. 93 35 10N 75 30W
Hattiesburg 95 31 20N 89 20W
Hatvan 119 47 40N 19 45E
Havana 99 23 8N 82 22W
Havre 96 48 34N 109 40W
Havre, Le 116 49 30N 0 5E
Hawaii □ 90 20 30N 157 0W
Hebron 127 31 32N 35 6E
Heidelberg 118 49 23N 8 41E
Heilbronn 118 49 8N 9 13E
Helena, Ark., U.S.A. 95 34 30N 90 35W
Helena, Mont., U.S.A. 96 46 40N 112 0W
Helsingborg 115 56 3N 12 42E
Helsinki 115 60 15N 25 3E
Henderson 93 36 20N 78 25W
Hengyang 136 26 51N 112 30E
Henzada 134 17 38N 95 26E
Herāt 129 34 20N 62 7E
Hercegovina □ 119 44 0N 18 0E
Herford 118 52 7N 8 40E
Hermosillo 98 29 4N 110 58W
's-Hertogenbosch 116 51 42N 5 17E
Hibbing 94 47 30N 93 0W
Hickory 93 35 46N 81 17W
Higashiōsaka 137 34 40N 135 37E
High Point 93 35 57N 79 58W
Hiiumaa 115 58 50N 22 45E
Hildesheim 118 52 9N 9 55E
Hilo 90 19 44N 155 5W
Hilversum 116 52 14N 5 10E
Himalaya, Mts. 130 29 0N 84 0E
Himeji 137 34 50N 134 40E
Ḩimş 129 34 40N 36 45E
Hindu Kush 129 36 0N 71 0E
Hiratsuka 137 35 19N 139 21E
Hirosaki 137 40 34N 140 28E
Hiroshima 137 34 24N 132 30E
Hispaniola 99 19 0N 71 0W
Hitachi 137 36 36N 140 39E
Ho Chi Minh City 134 10 58N 106 40E
Hobart 142 42 50S 147 21E
Hochwan 136 30 0N 106 15E
Hódmezövásárhely 119 46 28N 20 22E
Hofei 136 31 52N 117 15E
Hōfu 137 34 3N 131 34E
Hoggar, Mts. 126 23 0N 6 30E
Hokang 136 47 36N 130 28E
Hokkaidō □ 137 43 30N 143 0E
Holguín 99 20 50N 76 20W
Holyhead 114 53 18N 4 38W
Honduras ■ 98 14 40N 86 30W
Honduras, G. of 98 16 50N 87 0W
Hong Kong ■ 136 22 11N 114 14E
Honolulu 90 21 19N 157 52W
Honshū 137 36 0N 138 0E
Hood Mt. 96 45 24N 121 41W
Hoover Dam 97 36 0N 114 45W
Hoquiam 96 46 50N 123 55W
Horn, Cape 106 55 50S 67 30W
Horsham 143 36 44S 142 13E
Hot Springs 95 34 30N 93 0W
Houlton 93 46 5N 67 50W
Houston 95 29 50N 95 20W
Hovd 136 48 2N 91 37E
Howrah 134 22 37N 88 20E
Hrádec Králové 118 50 15N 15 50E
Hsiamen 136 24 30N 118 7E
Hsinchu 136 24 48N 120 58E
Hsüch'ang 136 34 1N 113 53E
Huacho 104 11 10S 77 35W
Huambo 128 12 42S 15 54E
Huancavelica 104 12 50S 75 5W
Huancayo 104 12 5S 75 12W
Huánuco 104 9 55S 76 15W
Huascarán 104 9 8S 77 36W
Huddersfield 114 53 38N 1 49W
Hudson → 92 40 42N 74 2W
Hue 134 16 30N 107 35E
Huelva 120 37 18N 6 57W
Huesca 117 42 8N 0 25W
Hughenden 143 20 52S 144 10E
Huhehot 136 40 52N 111 36E
Hull 114 53 45N 0 20W
Humaitá 104 7 35S 63 1W
Humber → 114 53 40N 0 10W
Humboldt → 96 40 2N 118 31W
Hunedoara 119 45 40N 22 50E
Hungary ■ 119 47 20N 19 20E
Hunsrück 118 49 30N 7 0E
Huntington 92 38 20N 82 30W
Huntsville 93 34 45N 86 35W
Huron, L. 92 45 0N 83 0W
Hwainan 136 32 44N 117 1E
Hwang-ho → 136 37 30N 118 50E
Hyderabad, India 134 17 22N 78 29E
Hyderabad, Pakistan 134 25 23N 68 24E
Hyères 117 43 8N 6 9E

Iaşi 119 47 10N 27 40E
Ibadan 126 7 22N 3 58E
Ibagué 104 4 20N 75 20W
Iberian Peninsula 110 40 0N 5 0W
Ibiá 105 19 30S 46 30W
Ibiza 120 38 54N 1 26E
Icá 104 14 0S 75 48W
Iceland ■ 89 65 0N 19 0W
Ichang 136 30 48N 111 29E
Ichihara 137 35 28N 140 5E
Ichikawa 137 35 44N 139 55E
Ichinomiya 137 35 18N 136 48E
Idaho □ 96 44 10N 114 0W
Idaho Falls 96 43 30N 112 1W
Ife 126 7 30N 4 31E
Iguaçu Falls 106 25 41S 54 26W
IJsselmeer 116 52 45N 5 20E
Ikaría 121 37 35N 26 10E
Iki 137 33 45N 129 42E
Île-de-France 116 49 0N 2 20E
Ilhéus 105 14 49S 39 2W
Illinois □ 94 40 15N 89 30W
Illinois → 94 38 55N 90 28W
Iloilo 135 10 45N 122 33E
Ilorin 126 8 30N 4 35E
Imperial Dam 97 32 50N 114 30W
Imphal 134 24 48N 93 56E
Inari, L. 115 68 54N 27 5E
Inchon 136 37 27N 126 40E
Independence, Kans., U.S.A. 95 37 10N 95 43W
Independence, Mo., U.S.A. 94 39 3N 94 25W
India ■ 134 20 0N 78 0E
Indian → 93 27 59N 80 34W
Indian Ocean 130 5 0S 75 0E
Indiana □ 92 40 0N 86 0W
Indianapolis 92 39 42N 86 10W
Indonesia ■ 135 5 0S 115 0E
Indore 134 22 42N 75 53E
Indus → 134 24 20N 67 47E
Inhambane 128 23 54S 35 30E
Ining 136 43 57N 81 20E
Inner Hebrides 114 57 0N 6 30W
Innsbruck 118 47 16N 11 23E
International Falls 94 48 36N 93 25W
Inverness 114 57 29N 4 12W
Iona 114 56 20N 6 25W
Ionian Is. 121 38 40N 20 0E
Ionian Sea 121 37 30N 17 30E
Íos 121 36 41N 25 20E
Iowa □ 94 42 18N 93 30W
Iowa City 94 41 40N 91 35W
Ipswich 114 52 4N 1 9E
Iquique 104 20 19S 70 5W
Iquitos 104 3 45S 73 10W
Iráklion 121 35 20N 25 12E
Iran ■ 129 33 0N 53 0E
Irapuato 98 20 41N 101 28W
Iraq ■ 129 33 0N 44 0E
Ireland ■ 114 53 0N 8 0W
Irian Jaya □ 135 4 0S 137 0E
Iriri → 105 3 52S 52 37W
Irish Sea 114 54 0N 5 0W
Irkutsk 138 52 18N 104 20E
Iron Gate 119 44 42N 22 30E
Ironwood 94 46 30N 90 10W
Irrawaddy → 134 15 50N 95 6E
Irtysh → 138 61 4N 68 52E
Ise 137 34 25N 136 45E
İskenderun 129 36 32N 36 10E
Israel ■ 127 32 0N 34 50E
İstanbul 129 41 0N 29 0E
Istria 118 45 10N 14 0E
Itabuna 105 14 48S 39 16W
Itaipu Dam 106 25 30S 54 30W
Itajaí 106 27 50S 48 39W
Italy ■ 120 42 0N 13 0E
Ituiutaba 105 19 0S 49 25W
Ivanovo 138 57 5N 41 0E
Ivory Coast ■ 126 7 30N 5 0W
Iwaki 137 37 4N 140 55E
Iwakuni 137 34 15N 132 8E
Iwo 126 7 39N 4 9E
Izmir 129 38 25N 27 8E
Izumi-sano 137 34 23N 135 18E

Jabalpur 134 23 9N 79 58E
Jackson, Miss., U.S.A. 95 32 20N 90 10W
Jackson, Tenn., U.S.A. 93 35 40N 88 50W
Jacksonville, Fla., U.S.A. 93 30 15N 81 38W
Jacksonville, Ill., U.S.A. 94 39 42N 90 15W
Jaén 120 37 44N 3 43W
Jaffna 134 9 45N 80 2E
Jahrom 129 28 30N 53 31E
Jaipur 134 27 0N 75 50E
Jakarta 135 6 9S 106 49E
Jamaica ■ 98 18 10N 77 30W
Jambi 135 1 38S 103 30E
James → 94 42 52N 97 18W
Jamestown, N. Dak., U.S.A. 94 46 54N 98 42W
Jamestown, N.Y., U.S.A. 92 42 5N 79 18W
Jammu & Kashmir □ 134 34 25N 77 0E
Jamshedpur 134 22 44N 86 12E
Janesville 94 42 39N 89 1W
Japan ■ 137 36 0N 136 0E
Japan, Sea of 137 40 0N 135 0E
Japurá → 104 3 8S 64 46W
Jarosław 119 50 2N 22 42E
Jarvis I. 141 0 15S 159 55W
Jasper 93 33 48N 87 16W
Jaú 105 22 10S 48 30W
Java 135 7 0S 110 0E
Java Sea 135 4 35S 107 15E
Jefferson City 94 38 34N 92 10W
Jequié 105 13 51S 40 5W
Jerez de la Frontera 120 36 41N 6 7W
Jersey 116 49 13N 2 7W
Jersey City 92 40 41N 74 8W
Jerusalem 127 31 47N 35 10E
Jiddah 129 21 29N 39 10E
João Pessoa 105 7 10S 34 52W
Jodhpur 134 26 23N 73 8E
Johannesburg 128 26 10S 28 2E
Johnson City 93 36 18N 82 21W
Johnstown 92 40 19N 78 53W
Joinvile 106 26 15S 48 55E
Joliet 94 41 30N 88 0W
Jonesboro 95 35 50N 90 45W
Jönköping 115 57 45N 14 10E
Joplin 95 37 0N 94 31W
Jordan ■ 127 31 0N 36 0E
Jordan → 127 31 48N 35 32E
Joseph Bonaparte G. 142 14 35S 128 50E
Juan de Fuca Str. 96 48 15N 124 0W
Juàzeiro 105 9 30S 40 30W
Juàzeiro do Norte 105 7 10S 39 18W
Juby, C. 126 28 0N 12 59W
Juiz de Fora 105 21 43S 43 19W
Juliaca 104 15 25S 70 10W
Jullundur 134 31 20N 75 40E
Jundiaí 106 24 30S 47 0W
Juneau 41 58 20N 134 20W
Junín 106 34 33S 60 57W
Jura, Mts. 117 46 40N 6 5E
Jutland 115 56 25N 9 30E

Kābul 129 34 28N 69 11E
Kaduna 126 10 30N 7 21E
Kagoshima 137 31 35N 130 33E
Kaieteur Falls 104 5 1N 59 10W
Kaifeng 136 34 49N 114 30E
Kainji Res. 126 10 1N 4 40E
Kaiserslautern 118 49 30N 7 43E
Kakegawa 137 34 45N 138 1E
Kakinada 134 16 57N 82 11E
Kakogawa 137 34 46N 134 51E
Kalahari 122 24 0S 21 30E
Kalamazoo 92 42 20N 85 35W
Kalgoorlie-Boulder 142 30 40S 121 22E
Kalimantan 135 0 0 114 0E
Kalinin 138 56 55N 35 55E
Kaliningrad 115 54 42N 20 32E
Kalispell 96 48 10N 114 22W
Kalisz 119 51 45N 18 8E
Kamchatka 138 57 0N 160 0E
Kampala 128 0 20N 32 30E
Kananga 128 5 55S 22 18E
Kanazawa 137 36 30N 136 38E
Kanchow 136 25 58N 114 55E
Kandahar 129 31 32N 65 30E
Kandy 134 7 18N 80 43E
Kangaroo I. 143 35 45S 137 0E
Kankakee 94 41 6N 87 50W
Kankan 126 10 23N 9 15W
Kannapolis 93 35 32N 80 37W
Kano 126 12 2N 8 30E
Kanpur 134 26 28N 80 20E
Kansas □ 94 38 40N 98 0W
Kansas City, Kans., U.S.A. 94 39 0N 94 40W
Kansas City, Mo., U.S.A. 94 39 3N 94 30W
Kaohsiung 136 22 35N 120 16E
Kara Kum 138 39 30N 60 0E
Kara Sea 138 75 0N 70 0E
Karachi 134 24 53N 67 0E
Karaganda 138 49 50N 73 10E
Karakoram Pass 136 35 33N 77 50E
Karakoram Ra. 134 35 30N 77 0E
Karbalā 129 32 36N 44 3E
Kariba Lake 128 16 40S 28 25E
Karl-Marx-Stadt 118 50 50N 12 55E
Karlskrona 115 56 10N 15 35E
Karlsruhe 118 49 3N 8 23E
Karnataka □ 134 13 15N 77 0E
Kárpathos 121 35 37N 27 10E
Kāshān 129 34 5N 51 30E
Kashgar 136 39 46N 75 52E
Kashing 136 30 45N 120 41E
Kassala 127 16 0N 36 0E
Kassel 118 51 19N 9 32E
Katanning 142 33 40S 117 33E
Katmandu 134 27 45N 85 20E
Katowice 119 50 17N 19 5E
Katsina 126 13 0N 7 32E
Kattegat 115 57 0N 11 20E
Kaunas 115 54 54N 23 54E
Kawagoe 137 35 55N 139 29E
Kawaguchi 137 35 52N 139 45E
Kawasaki 137 35 35N 139 42E
Kayes 126 14 25N 11 30W
Kayseri 129 38 45N 35 30E
Kazan 138 55 48N 49 3E
Kecskemét 119 46 57N 19 42E
Kediri 135 7 51S 112 1E
Kefallinía 121 38 20N 20 30E
Kelang 135 3 2N 101 26E
Kemerovo 138 55 20N 86 5E
Kemi 115 65 44N 24 34E
Kenitra 126 34 15N 6 40W
Kennewick 96 46 11N 119 2W
Kenosha 94 42 33N 87 48W
Kentucky □ 92 37 20N 85 0W
Kenya ■ 128 1 0N 38 0E
Kenya, Mt. 128 0 10S 37 18E
Kerala □ 134 11 0N 76 15E
Kérkira 121 39 38N 19 50E
Kermadec Is. 140 30 0S 178 15W
Kermān 129 30 15N 57 1E
Kermānshāh 129 34 23N 47 0E
Keweenaw Pen. 94 47 30N 88 0W
Khabarovsk 138 48 30N 135 5E
Khaniá 121 35 30N 24 4E
Kharagpur 134 22 20N 87 25E
Kharkov 138 49 58N 36 20E
Khartoum 127 15 31N 32 35E
Khíos 121 38 27N 26 9E
Khorāsān □ 129 34 0N 58 0E
Khorrāmshahr 129 30 29N 48 15E
Khulna 134 22 45N 89 34E
Khyber Pass 134 34 10N 71 8E
Kiamusze 136 46 45N 130 30E
Kiel 118 54 16N 10 8E
Kiel B. 118 54 20N 10 20E
Kielce 119 50 52N 20 42E
Kiev 138 50 30N 30 28E
Kikládhes 121 37 20N 24 30E
Kilimanjaro 128 3 7S 37 20E
Kilkenny 114 52 40N 7 17W
Killarney 114 52 2N 9 30W
Kilmarnock 114 55 36N 4 30W
Kimba 143 33 8S 136 23E
Kimberley, Australia 142 32 50S 141 4E
Kimberley, S. Africa 128 28 43S 24 46E
King I. 142 39 50S 144 0E
King Sd. 142 16 50S 123 20E
Kings Canyon National Park 97 37 0N 118 35W
Kingsport 93 36 33N 82 36W
Kingston 98 18 0N 76 50W
Kingstown 98 13 10N 61 10W
Kingsville 95 27 30N 97 53W
Kingtehchen 136 29 8N 117 21E
Kinshasa 128 4 20S 15 15E
Kinston 93 35 18N 77 35W
Kintyre 114 55 30N 5 35W
Kiribati ■ 140 1 0N 176 0E
Kirin 136 43 58N 126 31E
Kiritimati 141 1 58N 157 27W
Kirkūk 129 35 30N 44 21E
Kirov 138 58 35N 49 40E
Kiryū 137 36 24N 139 20E
Kisangani 128 0 35N 25 15E
Kishiwada 137 34 28N 135 22E
Kisi 136 45 21N 131 0E
Kiskörös 119 46 37N 19 20E
Kitakyūshū 137 33 50N 130 50E
Kíthira 121 36 9N 23 0E
Kitwe 128 12 54S 28 13E
Klagenfurt 118 46 38N 14 20E
Klamath Falls 96 42 20N 121 50W
Klamath Mts. 96 41 20N 123 0W
Knoxville 93 35 58N 83 57W
Kōbe 137 34 45N 135 10E
Koblenz 118 50 21N 7 36E
Kōchi 137 33 30N 133 35E
Kodiak I. 40 57 30N 152 45W
Kōfu 137 35 40N 138 30E
Kokiu 136 23 30N 103 0E
Kokomo 92 40 30N 86 6W
Kola Pen. 138 67 30N 38 0E
Kolar 134 13 12N 78 15E
Kolhapur 134 16 43N 74 15E
Kolo 119 52 14N 18 40E
Komárno 119 47 49N 18 5E
Komatsu 137 36 25N 136 30E
Kongmoon 136 22 35N 113 1E
Konya 129 37 52N 32 35E
Korea Strait 136 34 0N 129 30E
Körös → 119 46 43N 20 12E
Košice 119 48 42N 21 15E
Kota 134 25 14N 75 49E
Kowloon 136 22 20N 114 15E
Kraków 119 50 4N 19 57E
Krasnodar 138 45 5N 39 0E
Krasnoyarsk 138 56 8N 93 0E
Krefeld 118 51 20N 6 32E
Krivoy Rog 138 47 51N 33 20E
Krotoszyn 119 51 42N 17 23E
Krugersdorp 128 26 5S 27 46E
Kuala Lumpur 135 3 9N 101 41E
Kumagaya 137 36 9N 139 22E
Kumamoto 137 32 45N 130 45E
Kumasi 126 6 41N 1 38W
Kunlun Shan 136 36 0N 86 30E
Kuopio 115 62 53N 27 35E
Kurashiki 137 34 40N 133 50E
Kure 137 34 14N 132 32E
Kuria Maria Is. 129 17 30N 55 58E
Kuril Is. 138 45 0N 150 0E
Kurnool 134 15 45N 78 0E
Kursk 138 51 42N 36 11E
Kurume 137 33 15N 130 30E
Kushiro 137 43 0N 144 25E
Kuwait 129 29 30N 47 30E
Kuwait ■ 129 29 30N 47 30E
Kuybyshev 138 55 27N 78 19E
Kwangchow 136 23 10N 113 10E
Kwangju 136 35 9N 126 54E
Kwangsi-Chuang A.R. □ 136 24 0N 109 0E
Kweiyang 136 26 30N 106 35E
Kyle of Lochalsh 114 57 17N 5 43W
Kyoga, L. 128 1 35N 33 0E
Kyōto 137 35 0N 135 45E
Kyūshū 137 33 0N 131 0E
Kzyl Kum 138 42 0N 65 0E

Lackawanna 92 42 49N 78 50W
Ladoga, L. 138 61 15N 30 30E
Lafayette 95 30 18N 92 0W
Lagos 126 6 25N 3 27E
Lahore 134 31 32N 74 22E
Lajes 106 27 48S 50 20W
Lake Charles 95 30 15N 93 10W
Lake City 93 30 10N 82 40W
Lake Worth 93 26 36N 80 3W
Lakeland 93 28 0N 82 0W
Lakewood 92 41 28N 81 50W
Lakshadweep Is. 134 10 0N 72 30E
Lancaster 92 40 4N 76 19W
Lanchow 136 36 4N 103 44E
Landes, Les 117 44 20N 1 0W
Land's End 114 50 4N 5 43W
Langres, Plateau de 116 47 45N 5 3E
Languedoc 117 43 58N 4 0E
Lansing 92 42 47N 84 40W
Laos ■ 134 17 45N 105 0E
Lapland 115 68 7N 24 0E
Laptev Sea 138 76 0N 125 0E
Laramie 94 41 20N 105 38W
Laredo 95 27 34N 99 29W
Las Cruces 97 32 18N 106 50W
Las Palmas 126 28 7N 15 26W
Las Vegas 97 36 10N 115 5W
Lashio 134 22 56N 97 45E
Lassen Pk. 96 40 29N 121 31W
Latvian S.S.R. □ 115 56 50N 24 0E
Launceston 142 41 24S 147 8E
Laurel 95 31 41N 89 9W
Lausanne 118 46 32N 6 38E
Laut 135 4 45N 108 0E
Lawrence 94 39 0N 95 10W
Lawton 95 34 33N 98 25W
Leavenworth 94 39 25N 95 0W
Lebanon ■ 129 34 0N 36 0E
Lebanon Mts. 127 33 45N 35 45E
Leeds 114 53 48N 1 34W
Leeuwarden 116 53 15N 5 48E
Leeuwin, C. 142 34 20S 115 9E
Leeward Is., Atl. Oc. 98 16 30N 63 30W
Leeward Is., Pac. Oc. 141 16 0S 147 0W
Leghorn 120 43 32N 10 18E
Leicester 114 52 39N 1 9W
Leipzig 118 51 20N 12 23E

Nizhniy Tagil WORLD Rotterdam

Nizhniy Tagil **138** 57 55N 59 57 E
Nobeoka **137** 32 36N 131 41 E
Nogales, Mexico **98** 31 20N 110 56W
Nogales, U.S.A. **97** 31 33N 110 56W
Noirmoutier, Î. de **116** 46 58N 2 10W
Norfolk **92** 36 40N 76 15W
Norman **95** 35 12N 97 30W
Normandy **116** 48 45N 0 10 E
Normanton **143** 17 40 S 141 10 E
Norrköping **115** 58 37N 16 11 E
Norrland □ **115** 66 50N 18 0 E
North America **40** 40 0N 100 0W
North Atlantic Ocean **108** 30 0N 50 0W
North Bend **96** 43 28N 124 14W
North Cape **115** 71 15N 25 40 E
North Carolina □ **93** 35 30N 80 0W
North Channel **114** 55 0N 5 30W
North Dakota □ **94** 47 30N 100 0W
North European Plain **110** 55 0N 20 0 E
North I. **143** 38 0 S 175 0 E
North Korea ■ **136** 40 0N 127 0 E
North Minch **114** 58 5N 5 55W
North Platte **94** 41 10N 100 50W
North Platte → **94** 41 15N 100 45W
North Pole **89** 90 0N 0 0 E
North Rhine Westphalia □ **118** 51 55N 7 0 E
North Sea **110** 56 0N 4 0 E
North West Highlands **114** 57 35N 5 2W
North York Moors **114** 54 25N 0 50W
Northampton **114** 52 14N 0 54W
Northern Ireland □ **114** 54 45N 7 0W
Northern Territory □ **142** 16 0 S 133 0 E
Norway ■ **115** 63 0N 11 0 E
Norwegian Dependency □ **107** 66 0 S 15 0 E
Norwegian Sea **89** 66 0N 1 0 E
Norwich **114** 52 38N 1 17 E
Nottingham **114** 52 57N 1 10W
Nouâdhibou **126** 20 54N 17 0W
Nouakchott **126** 18 9N 15 58W
Novara **118** 45 27N 8 36 E
Novaya Zemlya **138** 75 0N 56 0 E
Novi Sad **119** 45 18N 19 52 E
Novokuznetsk **138** 53 45N 87 10 E
Novosibirsk **138** 55 0N 83 5 E
Nubian Desert **127** 21 30N 33 30 E
Nueva Rosita **98** 27 57N 101 13W
Nuevo Laredo **98** 27 30N 99 31W
Nullarbor **142** 31 28 S 130 55 E
Numazu **137** 35 7N 138 51 E
Nunivak **40** 60 0N 166 0W
Nuremburg **118** 49 26N 11 5 E
Nyíregyháza **119** 47 58N 21 47 E

Oahe L. **94** 45 30N 100 25W
Oahu **90** 21 30N 158 0W
Oak Park **94** 41 55N 87 45W
Oak Ridge **93** 36 1N 84 12W
Oakland **97** 37 50N 122 18W
Oaxaca de Juárez **98** 17 3N 96 43W
Ob → **138** 66 45N 69 30 E
Ob, G. of **138** 70 0N 73 0 E
Oberhausen **118** 51 28N 6 50 E
Obihiro **137** 42 56N 143 12 E
Ocala **93** 29 11N 82 5W
Occidental, Cordillera **104** 5 0N 76 0W
Oceanside **97** 33 13N 117 26W
October Revolution I. **138** 79 30N 97 0 E
Odawara **137** 35 20N 139 6 E
Odense **115** 55 22N 10 23 E
Oder → **118** 53 33N 14 38 E
Odessa, U.S.A. **95** 31 51N 102 23W
Odessa, U.S.S.R. **138** 46 30N 30 45 E
Odžak **119** 45 3N 18 18 E
Offenbach **118** 50 6N 8 46 E
Ogaden **127** 7 30N 45 30 E
Ogbomosho **126** 8 1N 4 11 E
Ogden **96** 41 13N 112 1W
Ogdensburg **92** 44 40N 75 27W
Ohio □ **92** 40 20N 14 10 E
Ohio → **92** 38 0N 86 0W
Ōita **137** 33 14N 131 36 E
Ojos del Salado, Cerro **106** 27 0 S 68 40W
Okanogan → **96** 48 6N 119 43W
Okayama **137** 34 40N 133 54 E
Okazaki **137** 34 57N 137 10 E
Okeechobee, L. **93** 27 0N 80 50W
Okefenokee Swamp **93** 30 50N 82 15W
Okhotsk, Sea of **138** 55 0N 145 0 E
Oki-Shotō **137** 36 5N 133 15 E
Okinawa-Jima **136** 26 32N 128 0 E
Oklahoma □ **95** 35 20N 97 30W
Oklahoma City **95** 35 25N 97 30W
Okmulgee **95** 35 38N 96 0W
Okushiri-Tō **137** 42 15N 139 30 E
Öland **115** 56 45N 16 38 E
Olavarría **106** 36 55 S 60 20W
Old Castile **117** 41 55N 4 0W
Oldenburg **118** 53 10N 8 10 E
Oléron, Île d' **117** 45 55N 1 15W
Olifants → **128** 24 5 S 31 20 E
Olomouc **118** 49 38N 17 12 E
Olsztyn **119** 53 48N 20 29 E
Olympia, Greece **121** 37 39N 21 39 E
Olympia, U.S.A. **96** 47 0N 122 58W
Olympic Mts. **96** 47 50N 123 45W
Olympus, Mt. **121** 40 6N 22 23 E
Omagh **114** 54 36N 7 20W
Omaha **94** 41 15N 96 0W
Oman ■ **129** 23 0N 58 0 E
Oman, G. of **129** 24 30N 58 30 E
Omdurmân **127** 15 40N 32 28 E
Ōmiya **137** 35 54N 139 38 E
Omsk **138** 55 0N 73 12 E
Ōmuta **137** 33 0N 130 26 E
Onega, L. **138** 62 0N 35 30 E
Onitsha **126** 6 6N 6 42 E
Ontario **97** 34 2N 117 40W
Ontario, L. **92** 43 40N 78 0W
Opole **119** 50 42N 17 58 E
Oporto **120** 41 8N 8 40W
Oradea **119** 47 2N 21 58 E
Oran **126** 35 45N 0 39W
Orange **95** 30 10N 93 50W
Orange → **128** 28 41 S 16 28 E
Orange Free State □ **128** 28 30 S 27 0 E
Orangeburg **93** 33 35N 80 53W
Oraya, La **104** 11 32 S 75 54W
Ordos **136** 39 25N 108 45 E
Ordzhonikidze **138** 43 0N 44 35 E
Örebro **115** 59 20N 15 18 E
Oregon □ **96** 44 0N 121 0W
Orel **138** 52 57N 36 3 E
Orenburg **138** 51 45N 55 6 E
Oriental, Cordillera **104** 6 0N 73 0W
Orinoco → **104** 9 15N 61 30W
Orissa □ **134** 20 0N 84 0 E
Orizaba **98** 18 51N 97 6W
Orkney Is. **114** 59 0N 3 0W
Orlando **93** 28 30N 81 25W
Orléanais **116** 48 0N 2 0 E
Orléans **116** 47 54N 1 52 E
Oruro **104** 18 0 S 67 9W
Ōsaka **137** 34 40N 135 30 E
Oshkosh **94** 41 27N 102 20W
Oshogbo **126** 7 48N 4 37 E
Osijek **119** 45 34N 18 41 E
Oslo **115** 59 55N 10 45 E
Osnabrück **118** 52 16N 8 2 E
Osorno **106** 40 25 S 73 0W
Ostend **116** 51 15N 2 50 E
Ostrava **119** 49 51N 18 18 E
Ostrów Wielkopolski **119** 51 36N 17 44 E
Ōsumi-Kaikyō **137** 30 55N 131 0 E
Ōsumi-Shotō **137** 30 30N 130 0 E
Oswego **92** 43 29N 76 30W
Ōtake **137** 34 12N 132 13 E
Otaru **137** 43 10N 141 0 E
Otranto, Str. of **121** 40 15N 18 40 E
Ōtsu **137** 35 0N 135 50 E
Ottumwa **94** 41 0N 92 25W
Ouachita Mts. **95** 34 50N 94 30W
Ouagadougou **126** 12 25N 1 30W
Ouessant, Île d' **116** 48 28N 5 6W
Oujda **126** 34 41N 1 55W
Oulu **115** 65 1N 25 29 E
Outer Hebrides **114** 57 30N 7 40W
Owen Falls **128** 0 30N 33 5 E
Owen Stanley Range **143** 8 30 S 147 0 E
Owyhee → **96** 43 46N 117 2W
Oxford **114** 51 45N 1 15W
Oxnard **97** 34 10N 119 14W
Oyama **137** 36 18N 139 48 E
Oyo **126** 7 46N 3 56 E
Oyonnax **117** 46 16N 5 40 E
Ozark Plateau **95** 37 20N 91 40W

Paarl **128** 33 45 S 18 56 E
Pacaraima, Sierra **104** 4 0N 62 30W
Pachuca de Soto **98** 20 7N 98 44W
Pacific Ocean **140** 10 0N 140 0W
Padang **135** 1 0 S 100 20 E
Padua **118** 45 24N 11 52 E
Paducah **92** 37 0N 88 40W
Painted Desert **97** 36 0N 111 30W
Paisley **114** 55 51N 4 27W
Paita **104** 5 11 S 81 9W
Pakanbaru **135** 0 30N 101 15 E
Pakhoi **136** 21 30N 109 10 E
Pakistan ■ **134** 30 0N 70 0 E
Palawan **135** 9 30N 118 30 E
Palembang **135** 3 0 S 104 50 E
Palermo **120** 38 8N 13 20 E
Palestine **95** 31 42N 95 35W
Palm Springs **97** 33 51N 116 35W
Palma de Mallorca **117** 39 35N 2 39 E
Palmer Land **107** 73 0 S 60 0W
Palmira **104** 3 32N 76 16W
Palmyra Is. **141** 5 52N 162 5W
Palo Alto **97** 37 25N 122 8W
Pamirs **130** 37 40N 73 0 E
Pamlico Sd. **93** 35 20N 76 0W
Pampa **95** 35 35N 100 58W
Pampa, La □ **106** 36 50 S 66 0W
Pamplona **117** 42 48N 1 38W
Panamá **98** 9 0N 79 25W
Panama ■ **99** 8 48N 79 55W
Panama Canal **98** 9 10N 79 37W
Panama City **93** 30 10N 85 41W
Panay **135** 11 10N 122 30 E
Pantelleria **120** 36 52N 12 0 E
Paoki **136** 34 25N 107 15 E
Paoting **136** 38 50N 115 30 E
Paotow **136** 40 45N 110 0 E
Papua, Gulf of **143** 9 0 S 144 50 E
Papua New Guinea ■ **143** 8 0 S 145 0 E
Pará □ **105** 3 20 S 52 0W
Paraguaná, Pen. de **104** 12 0N 70 0W
Paraguay ■ **106** 23 0 S 57 0W
Paraíba □ **105** 7 0 S 36 0W
Paramaribo **105** 5 50N 55 10W
Paraná **106** 31 45 S 60 30W
Paraná □ **106** 24 30 S 51 0W
Paraná → **106** 33 43 S 59 15W
Paranaguá **106** 25 30 S 48 30W
Parecis, Serra dos **104** 13 0 S 60 0W
Paris, France **116** 48 50N 2 20 E
Paris, U.S.A. **95** 33 40N 95 30W
Park Range **96** 40 0N 106 30W
Parkes **143** 33 9 S 148 11 E
Parma **118** 44 50N 10 20 E
Parnaíba **105** 2 54 S 41 47W
Parnaíba → **105** 3 0 S 41 50W
Pasadena, Calif., U.S.A. **97** 34 5N 118 9W
Pasadena, Tex., U.S.A. **95** 29 45N 95 14W
Pasco **96** 46 10N 119 0W
Passo Fundo **106** 28 10 S 52 20W
Pasto **104** 1 13N 77 17W
Patagonia **106** 45 0 S 69 0W
Paterson **92** 40 55N 74 10W
Patiala **134** 30 23N 76 26 E
Patkai Bum **134** 27 0N 95 30 E
Patna **134** 25 35N 85 12 E
Patos, Lag. dos **106** 31 20 S 51 0 E
Pátrai **121** 38 14N 21 47 E
Pau **117** 43 19N 0 25W
Paulista **105** 7 57 S 34 53W
Paulo Afonso **105** 9 21 S 38 15W
Pavia **118** 45 10N 9 10 E
Pawtucket **92** 41 51N 71 22W
Paysandú **106** 32 19 S 58 8W
Paz, La, Bolivia **104** 16 20 S 68 10W
Paz, La, Mexico **98** 24 10N 110 18W
Pearl Harbor **90** 21 20N 158 0W
Pecos → **95** 29 42N 102 30W
Pécs **119** 46 5N 18 15 E
Pegu **134** 17 20N 96 29 E
Pekalongan **135** 6 53 S 109 40 E
Pekin **94** 40 35N 89 40W
Peking **136** 39 55N 116 20 E
Pelée, Mt. **98** 14 48N 61 0W
Pelotas **106** 31 42 S 52 23W
Pelvoux, Massif de **117** 44 52N 6 20 E
Pematangsiantar **135** 2 57N 99 5 E
Pemba **128** 5 0 S 39 45 E
Penang **135** 5 25N 100 15 E
Pend Oreille, L. **96** 48 0N 116 30W
Pendleton **96** 45 35N 118 50W
Pengpu **136** 33 0N 117 25 E
Peninsular Malaysia □ **135** 4 0N 102 0 E
Penki **136** 41 20N 132 50 E
Pennines **114** 54 50N 2 20W
Pennsylvania □ **92** 40 50N 78 0W
Penong **142** 31 59 S 133 5 E
Pensacola **93** 30 30N 87 10W
Pentland Firth **114** 58 43N 3 10W
Penza **138** 53 15N 45 5 E
Peoria **94** 40 40N 89 40W
Perche **116** 48 31N 1 1 E
Pereira **104** 4 49N 75 43W
Pergamino **106** 33 52 S 60 30W
Périgueux **117** 45 10N 0 42 E
Perm **138** 58 0N 57 10 E
Pernambuco □ **105** 8 0 S 37 0W
Perpignan **117** 42 42N 2 53 E
Perth, Australia **142** 31 57 S 115 52 E
Perth, U.K. **114** 56 24N 3 27W
Perth Amboy **92** 40 31N 74 16W
Peru ■ **104** 8 0 S 75 0W
Pésaro **118** 43 55N 12 53 E
Peshawar **134** 34 2N 71 37 E
Peterborough **114** 52 35N 0 14W
Peterhead **114** 57 30N 1 49W
Petrópolis **105** 22 33 S 43 9W
Pforzheim **118** 48 53N 8 43 E
Phenix City **93** 32 30N 85 0W
Philadelphia **92** 40 0N 75 10W
Philippines ■ **135** 12 0N 123 0 E
Phitsanulok **134** 16 50N 100 12 E
Phnom Penh **134** 11 33N 104 55 E
Phoenix **97** 33 30N 112 10W
Phoenix Is. **141** 3 30 S 172 0W
Piacenza **118** 45 2N 9 42 E
Piauí □ **105** 7 0 S 43 0W
Picardy **116** 50 0N 2 15 E
Piedmont □ **118** 45 0N 7 30 E
Piedras Negras **98** 28 42N 100 31W
Pietermaritzburg **128** 29 35 S 30 25 E
Pietrosul **119** 47 35N 24 43 E
Pílos **121** 36 55N 21 42 E
Pindus Mts. **121** 40 0N 21 0 E
Pine Bluff **95** 34 10N 92 0W
Pingliang **136** 35 20N 106 40 E
Pingsiang **136** 27 43N 113 50 E
Pingtung **136** 22 36N 120 30 E
Piotrków Trybunalski **119** 51 23N 19 43 E
Piracicaba **105** 22 45 S 47 40W
Piraiévs **121** 37 57N 23 42 E
Pisa **118** 43 43N 10 23 E
Pisco **104** 13 50 S 76 12W
Pistóia **118** 43 57N 10 53 E
Pitcairn I. **141** 25 5 S 130 5W
Pittsburg **95** 37 21N 94 43W
Pittsburgh **92** 40 25N 79 55W
Piura **104** 5 15 S 80 38W
Plainview **95** 34 10N 101 40W
Plata, La **106** 35 0 S 57 55W
Plata, Río de la **106** 34 45 S 57 30W
Platte → **94** 39 16N 94 50W
Plauen **118** 50 29N 12 9 E
Pleven **121** 43 26N 24 37 E
Płock **119** 52 32N 19 40 E
Ploieşti **119** 44 57N 26 5 E
Plovdiv **121** 42 8N 24 44 E
Plymouth **114** 50 23N 4 9W
Plzen **118** 49 45N 13 22 E
Po → **118** 44 57N 12 4 E
Pocatello **96** 42 50N 112 25W
Poços de Caldas **105** 21 50 S 46 33W
Pointe-à-Pitre **98** 16 10N 61 30W
Pointe Noire **128** 4 48 S 11 53 E
Poitiers **116** 46 35N 0 20 E
Poland ■ **119** 52 0N 20 0 E
Pollensa **117** 39 54N 3 1 E
Pomona **97** 34 2N 117 49W
Ponca City **95** 36 40N 97 5W
Ponce **99** 18 1N 66 37W
Pondicherry **134** 11 59N 79 50 E
Ponta Grossa **106** 25 7 S 50 10W
Pontchartrain, L. **95** 30 12N 90 0W
Pontiac **92** 42 40N 83 20W
Pontianak **135** 0 3 S 109 15 E
Poopó, Lago de **104** 18 30 S 67 35W
Popayán **104** 2 27N 76 36W
Poplar Bluff **95** 36 45N 90 22W
Popocatépetl, Volcán **98** 19 2N 98 38W
Pori **115** 61 29N 21 48 E
Port Angeles **96** 48 7N 123 30W
Port Arthur **95** 30 0N 94 0W
Port-au-Prince **99** 18 40N 72 20W
Port-de-Paix **99** 19 50N 72 50W
Port Elizabeth **128** 33 58 S 25 40 E
Port Harcourt **126** 4 40N 7 10 E
Port Hedland **142** 20 25 S 118 35 E
Port Huron **92** 43 0N 82 28W
Port Moresby **143** 9 24 S 147 8 E
Port Nolloth **128** 29 17 S 16 52 E
Port of Spain **98** 10 40N 61 31W
Port Phillip B. **143** 38 10 S 144 50 E
Port Said **127** 31 16N 32 18 E
Port Sudan **127** 19 32N 37 9 E
Portland, Maine, U.S.A. **93** 43 40N 70 15W
Portland, Oreg., U.S.A. **96** 45 35N 122 40W
Pôrto Alegre **106** 30 5 S 51 10W
Pôrto Seguro **105** 16 26 S 39 5W
Portsmouth, U.K. **114** 50 48N 1 6W
Portsmouth, U.S.A. **92** 36 50N 76 20W
Portugal ■ **120** 40 0N 7 0W
Portugalete **117** 43 19N 3 4W
Posadas **106** 27 30 S 55 50W
Potomac → **92** 38 0N 76 23W
Potosí **104** 19 38 S 65 50W
Potow **136** 38 8N 116 31 E
Potsdam **118** 52 23N 13 4 E
Poughkeepsie **92** 41 40N 73 57W
Powder → **94** 46 47N 105 12W
Powell, L. **97** 37 25N 110 45W
Požarevac **119** 44 35N 21 18 E
Poznań **118** 52 25N 16 55 E
Prague **118** 50 5N 14 22 E
Prato **118** 43 53N 11 5 E
Přerov **119** 49 28N 17 27 E
Presidencia Roque Saenz Peña **106** 26 45 S 60 30W
Presidente Prudente **105** 22 5 S 51 25W
Presque Isle **93** 46 40N 68 0W
Preston **114** 53 46N 2 42W
Pretoria **128** 25 44 S 28 12 E
Prichard **93** 30 47N 88 5W
Principe, I. de **126** 1 37N 7 27 E
Pripyat Marshes **110** 52 0N 28 10 E
Prokopyevsk **138** 54 0N 86 45 E
Provence **117** 43 40N 5 46 E
Providence **92** 41 50N 71 28W
Provo **96** 40 16N 111 37W
Pruszków **119** 52 9N 20 49 E
Prydz B. **107** 69 0 S 74 0 E
Przemyśl **119** 49 50N 22 45 E
Puebla **98** 19 3N 98 12W
Pueblo **94** 38 20N 104 40W
Puente Alto **106** 33 32 S 70 35W
Puerto Cabello **104** 10 28N 68 1W
Puerto La Cruz **104** 10 13N 64 38W
Puerto Montt **106** 41 28 S 73 0W
Puerto Plata **99** 19 48N 70 45W
Puerto Rico **99** 11 5 S 67 38W
Puget Sd. **96** 47 15N 122 30W
Pullman **96** 46 49N 117 10W
Pune **134** 18 29N 73 57 E
Punjab □ **134** 31 0N 76 0 E
Puno **104** 15 55 S 70 3W
Punta Alta **106** 38 53 S 62 4W
Punta Arenas **106** 53 10 S 71 0W
Purus → **104** 3 42 S 61 28W
Pusan **136** 35 5N 129 0 E
Putumayo → **104** 3 7 S 67 58W
Puy-de-Dôme **117** 45 46N 2 57 E
Pyŏngyang **136** 39 0N 125 30 E
Pyrenees **110** 42 45N 0 18 E

Qatar ■ **129** 25 30N 51 15 E
Qattâra Depression **127** 29 30N 27 30 E
Qazvin **129** 36 15N 50 0 E
Qena **127** 26 10N 32 43 E
Qeshm **129** 26 55N 56 10 E
Qom **129** 34 40N 51 0 E
Queensland □ **143** 22 0 S 142 0 E
Quelimane **128** 17 53 S 36 58 E
Querétaro **98** 20 36N 100 23W
Quetta **134** 30 15N 66 55 E
Quezon City **135** 14 38N 121 0 E
Qui Nhon **134** 13 40N 109 13 E
Quillota **106** 32 54 S 71 16W
Quimper **116** 48 0N 4 9W
Quincy **94** 39 55N 91 20W
Quito **104** 0 15 S 78 35W
Quneitra **127** 33 7N 35 48 E

Rabat **126** 34 2N 6 48W
Racibórz **119** 50 7N 18 18 E
Racine **94** 42 41N 87 51W
Radom **119** 51 23N 21 12 E
Rafaela **106** 31 10 S 61 30W
Rainier, Mt. **96** 46 50N 121 50W
Raipur **134** 21 17N 81 45 E
Rajasthan □ **134** 26 45N 73 30 E
Rajkot **134** 22 15N 70 56 E
Raleigh **93** 35 47N 78 39W
Ramallah **127** 31 55N 35 10 E
Ramla **127** 31 55N 34 52 E
Rampur **134** 28 50N 79 5 E
Rancagua **106** 34 10 S 70 50W
Rangoon **134** 16 45N 96 20 E
Rapid City **94** 44 0N 103 0W
Rasht **129** 37 20N 49 40 E
Ravenna **118** 44 28N 12 15 E
Rawalpindi **134** 33 38N 73 8 E
Rawlins **96** 41 50N 107 20W
Ré, Île de **117** 46 12N 1 30W
Reading, U.K. **114** 51 27N 0 57W
Reading, U.S.A. **92** 40 20N 75 53W
Rebun-Tō **137** 45 23N 141 2 E
Recife **105** 8 0 S 35 0W
Red →, Minn., U.S.A. **94** 48 10N 97 0W
Red →, Tex., U.S.A. **95** 31 0N 91 40W
Red Sea **129** 25 0N 36 0 E
Redding **96** 40 30N 122 25W
Redlands **97** 34 0N 117 11W
Redwood City **97** 37 30N 122 15W
Regensburg **118** 49 1N 12 7 E
Réggio di Calábria **121** 38 7N 15 38 E
Réggio nell' Emilia **118** 44 42N 10 38 E
Reidsville **93** 36 21N 79 40W
Reims **116** 49 15N 4 0 E
Remscheid **118** 51 11N 7 12 E
Rennes **116** 48 7N 1 41W
Reno **96** 39 30N 119 50W
Republican → **94** 39 3N 96 48W
Resistencia **106** 27 30 S 59 0W
Réunion **122** 22 0 S 56 0 E
Reus **117** 41 10N 1 5 E
Reykjavík **89** 64 10N 21 57 E
Rheinland-Pfalz □ **118** 50 0N 7 0 E
Rhine → **118** 51 52N 6 20 E
Rhodope Mts. **121** 41 40N 24 20 E
Rhondda **114** 51 39N 3 30W
Rhône → **117** 43 28N 4 42 E
Riau Arch. **135** 0 30N 104 20 E
Ribeirão Prêto **105** 21 10 S 47 50W
Richland **96** 46 15N 119 15W
Richmond, Calif., U.S.A. **96** 37 58N 122 21W
Richmond, Va., U.S.A. **92** 37 33N 77 27W
Riga **115** 56 53N 24 8 E
Riga, G. of **115** 57 40N 23 45 E
Rijeka **118** 45 20N 14 21 E
Rímini **118** 44 3N 12 33 E
Rîmnicu Vîlcea **119** 45 9N 24 21 E
Rio Branco **104** 9 58 S 67 49W
Río Cuarto **106** 33 10 S 64 25W
Rio de Janeiro **105** 23 0 S 43 12W
Rio de Janeiro □ **105** 22 50 S 43 0W
Río Gallegos **106** 51 35 S 69 15W
Río Grande **106** 53 50 S 67 45W
Rio Grande → **95** 25 57N 97 9W
Rio Grande do Norte □ **105** 5 40 S 36 0W
Rio Grande do Sul □ **106** 30 0 S 53 0W
Ríobamba **104** 1 50 S 78 45W
Rioja, La **106** 29 20 S 67 0W
Rishiri-Tō **137** 45 11N 141 15 E
Rivera **106** 31 0 S 55 50W
Riverina **143** 29 45 S 120 40 E
Riverside **97** 34 0N 117 22W
Riyadh **129** 24 41N 46 42 E
Roanoke **92** 37 19N 79 55W
Robinson Crusoe I. **141** 33 38 S 78 52W
Rocha **106** 34 30 S 54 25W
Rochefort **117** 45 56N 0 57W
Rochelle, La **117** 46 10N 1 9W
Rochester, Minn., U.S.A. **94** 44 1N 92 28W
Rochester, N.Y., U.S.A. **92** 43 10N 77 40W
Rock Hill **93** 34 55N 81 2W
Rock Island **94** 41 30N 90 35W
Rock Sprs. **96** 41 40N 109 10W
Rockford **94** 42 20N 89 0W
Rockhampton **143** 23 22 S 150 32 E
Rocky Mount **93** 35 55N 77 48W
Rocky Mts. **40** 55 0N 121 0W
Ródhos **121** 36 15N 28 10 E
Romania ■ **119** 46 0N 25 0 E
Rome, Italy **120** 41 54N 12 30 E
Rome, U.S.A. **93** 34 20N 85 0W
Roncador, Serra do **105** 12 30 S 52 30W
Rondônia □ **104** 11 0 S 63 0W
Roraima □ **104** 2 0N 61 30W
Roraima, Mt. **104** 5 10N 60 40W
Rosario **106** 33 0 S 60 40W
Roseau **98** 15 20N 61 24W
Roseburg **96** 43 10N 123 20W
Roseville **96** 38 46N 121 17W
Ross Dependency □ **107** 70 0 S 170 5W
Rostock **118** 54 4N 12 9 E
Rostov **138** 47 15N 39 45 E
Roswell **95** 33 26N 104 32W
Roto **143** 33 0 S 145 30 E
Rotterdam **116** 51 55N 4 30 E

Tigris WORLD Zwoll

Tigris → 129 31 0N 47 25 E
Tihāmah 129 22 0N 39 0 E
Tijuana 98 32 32N 117 1W
Tilburg 116 51 31N 5 6 E
Timişoara 119 45 43N 21 15 E
Timor 135 9 0 S 125 0 E
Timor Sea 135 10 0 S 127 0 E
Tindouf 126 27 42N 8 10W
Tipperary 114 52 28N 8 10W
Tirana 121 41 18N 19 49 E
Tîrgu-Jiu 119 45 5N 23 19 E
Tîrgu Mureş 119 46 31N 24 38 E
Tiruchchirappalli 134 10 45N 78 45 E
Tisza → 119 46 8N 20 2 E
Titicaca, L. 104 15 30 S 69 30W
Titovo Užice 119 43 55N 19 50 E
Tlemcen 126 34 52N 1 21W
Toamasina 128 18 10 S 49 25 E
Tobago 98 11 10N 60 30W
Tobruk 127 32 7N 23 55 E
Tocantins → 105 1 45 S 49 10W
Togo ■ 126 6 15N 1 35 E
Tokaj 119 48 8N 21 27 E
Tokelau Is. 140 9 0 S 171 45W
Tokuno-Shima 137 27 56N 128 55 E
Tokushima 137 34 4N 134 34 E
Tokuyama 137 34 3N 131 50 E
Tōkyō 137 35 45N 139 45 E
Toledo, Spain 117 39 50N 4 2W
Toledo, U.S.A. 92 41 37N 83 33W
Toluca 98 19 20N 99 40W
Tombouctou 126 16 50N 3 0W
Tomini 135 0 10 S 122 0 E
Tomsk 138 56 30N 85 5 E
Tonawanda 92 43 0N 78 54W
Tonga ■ 140 19 50 S 174 30W
Tonga Trench 140 18 0 S 175 0W
Tongking, G. of 134 20 0N 108 0 E
Tongue → 94 46 24N 105 52W
Toowoomba 143 27 32 S 151 56 E
Topeka 94 39 3N 95 40W
Torne älv → 115 65 50N 24 12 E
Torrelavega 117 43 20N 4 5W
Torrens, L. 143 31 0 S 137 50 E
Torreón 98 25 33N 103 26W
Torres Strait 143 9 50 S 142 20 E
Tortosa 117 40 49N 0 31 E
Toruń 119 53 0N 18 39 E
Tottori 137 35 30N 134 15 E
Toulon 117 43 10N 5 55 E
Toulouse 117 43 37N 1 27 E
Touraine 116 47 20N 0 30 E
Tours 116 47 22N 0 40 E
Townshend, C. 143 22 18 S 150 30 E
Townsville 143 19 15 S 146 45 E
Toyama 137 36 40N 137 15 E
Toyama-Wan 137 37 0N 137 30 E
Toyohashi 137 34 45N 137 25 E
Toyonaka 137 34 50N 135 28 E
Toyota 137 35 3N 137 7 E
Trabzon 129 41 0N 39 45 E
Trafalgar, C. 120 36 10N 6 2W
Tralee 114 52 16N 9 42W
Transvaal □ 128 25 0 S 29 0 E
Transylvania 119 46 19N 25 0 E
Treinta y Tres 106 33 16 S 54 17W
Trelew 106 43 10 S 65 20W
Trenque Lauquen 106 36 5 S 62 45W
Trentino-Alto Adige □ 118 46 30N 11 0 E
Trento 118 46 5N 11 8 E
Trenton 92 40 15N 74 41W
Tres Arroyos 106 38 26 S 60 20W
Treviso 118 45 40N 12 15 E
Trier 118 49 45N 6 37 E
Trieste 118 45 39N 13 45 E
Trincomalee 134 8 38N 81 15 E
Trinidad, Bolivia 104 14 46 S 64 50W
Trinidad, U.S.A. 95 37 15N 104 30W
Trinidad, W. Indies 98 10 30N 61 15W
Trinidad & Tobago ■ 98 10 30N 61 20W
Trinity → 95 30 30N 95 0W
Trinity Mts. 96 40 20N 118 50W
Tripoli 126 32 49N 13 7 E
Tristan da Cunha 109 37 6 S 12 20W
Trivandrum 134 8 41N 77 0 E
Trondheim 115 63 36N 10 25 E
Troy, Ala., U.S.A. 93 31 50N 85 58W
Troy, N.Y., U.S.A. 92 42 45N 73 39W
Troyes 116 48 19N 4 3 E
Trujillo, Peru 104 8 6 S 79 0W
Trujillo, Venezuela 104 9 22N 70 38W
Tsinan 136 34 50N 105 40 E
Tsingkiang 136 27 50N 114 38 E
Tsingshih 136 29 43N 112 13 E
Tsingtao 136 36 0N 120 25 E
Tsining 136 35 30N 116 35 E
Tsitsihar 136 47 20N 124 0 E
Tsu 137 34 45N 136 25 E
Tsuchiura 137 36 5N 140 15 E
Tsugaru-Kaikyō 137 41 35N 141 0 E
Tuamotu Arch. 141 17 0 S 144 0W
Tubarão 106 28 30 S 49 0W
Tubuai Is. 141 25 0 S 150 0W
Tucson 97 32 14N 110 59W
Tucumcari 95 35 12N 103 45W
Tucuruí 105 3 42 S 49 44W
Tula 138 54 13N 37 38 E
Tulare 97 36 15N 119 26W
Tulcea 119 45 13N 28 46 E
Ţūlkarm 127 32 19N 35 2 E
Tulsa 95 36 10N 96 0W
Tulua 104 4 6N 76 11W
Tumaco 104 1 50N 78 45W
Tummo 126 22 45N 14 8 E
Tumucumaque, Serra 105 2 0N 55 0W
Tungchow 136 39 58N 116 50 E
Tungchuan 136 35 4N 109 2 E
Tunghwa 136 41 46N 126 0 E
Tunis 126 36 50N 10 11 E
Tunisia ■ 126 33 30N 9 10 E
Tunja 104 5 33N 73 25W
Tupelo 95 34 15N 88 42W
Turin 118 45 4N 7 40 E
Turkana, L. 128 3 30N 36 5 E
Turkey ■ 129 39 0N 36 0 E
Turkmen S.S.R. □ 138 39 0N 59 0 E
Turks Is. 99 21 20N 71 20W
Turku 115 60 30N 22 19 E
Turnu Măgurele 119 43 46N 24 56 E
Turnu-Severin 119 44 39N 22 41 E
Tuscaloosa 93 33 13N 87 31W
Tuvalu ■ 140 8 0 S 178 0 E
Tuxtla Gutiérrez 98 16 50N 93 10W
Tuyun 136 26 15N 107 32 E
Tuzla 119 44 34N 18 41 E
Twin Falls 96 42 30N 114 30W
Tyler 95 32 18N 95 18W
Tyrol □ 118 47 3N 10 43 E
Tyrrhenian Sea 120 40 0N 12 30 E
Tzekung 136 29 25N 104 30 E
Tzepo 136 36 28N 117 58 E

Uaupés → 104 0 2N 67 16W
Ubá 105 21 8 S 43 0W
Ube 137 33 56N 131 15 E
Uberaba 105 19 50 S 47 55W
Uberlândia 105 19 0 S 48 20W
Ucayali → 104 4 30 S 73 30W
Údine 118 46 5N 13 10 E
Ueda 137 36 24N 138 16 E
Ufa 138 54 45N 55 55 E
Uganda ■ 128 2 0N 32 0 E
Uinta Mts. 96 40 45N 110 30W
Újpest 119 47 32N 19 6 E
Ujung Pandang 135 5 10 S 119 20 E
Ukrainian S.S.R. □ 138 49 0N 32 0 E
Ulaanbaatar 136 47 55N 106 53 E
Ulan Ude 138 51 45N 107 40 E
Ulanhot 136 46 5N 122 1 E
Ulhasnagar 134 19 15N 73 10 E
Ulm 118 48 23N 10 0 E
Ulyanovsk 138 54 20N 48 25 E
Ulyasutay 136 47 56N 97 28 E
Umeå 115 63 45N 20 20 E
United Arab Emirates ■ 129 23 50N 54 0 E
United Kingdom ■ 111 55 0N 3 0W
United States of America ■ 90 37 0N 96 0W
Upper Austria □ 118 48 10N 14 0 E
Upper Volta ■ = Burkina Faso ■ 126 12 0N 1 0W
Ural Mts. 110 60 0N 59 0 E
Urawa 137 35 50N 139 40 E
Urbana 94 40 7N 88 12W
Urfa 129 37 12N 38 50 E
Urmia 129 37 40N 45 0 E
Urmia, L. 129 37 50N 45 30 E
Uruguaiana 106 29 50 S 57 0W
Uruguay ■ 106 32 30 S 56 30W
Uruguay → 106 34 12 S 58 18W
Ushuaia 106 54 50 S 68 23W
Üsküdar 129 41 0N 29 5 E
Uspallata, P. de 106 32 37 S 69 22W
Ust Urt Plat. 138 44 0N 55 0 E
Ústí nad Labem 118 50 41N 14 3 E
Ustinov 138 56 51N 53 14 E
Utah □ 96 39 30N 111 30W
Utica 92 43 5N 75 18W
Utrecht 116 52 5N 5 8 E
Utsunomiya 137 36 30N 139 50 E
Uttaradit 134 17 36N 100 5 E
Uyuni 104 20 28 S 66 47W
Uzbek S.S.R. □ 138 41 30N 65 0 E

Vaasa 115 63 6N 21 38 E
Vadodara 134 22 20N 73 10 E
Valdivia 106 39 50 S 73 14W
Valdosta 93 30 50N 83 20W
Valence 117 44 57N 4 54 E
Valencia 120 39 27N 0 23W
Valenciennes 116 50 20N 3 34 E
Valera 104 9 19N 70 37W
Valladolid 120 41 38N 4 43W
Vallejo 96 38 12N 122 15W
Valparaíso 106 33 2 S 71 40W
Van, L. 129 38 30N 43 0 E
Van Diemen G. 142 11 45 S 132 0 E
Vancouver 96 45 44N 122 41W
Vanderlin I. 143 15 44 S 137 2 E
Vänern 115 58 47N 13 30 E
Vannes 116 47 40N 2 47W
Vanuatu ■ 140 15 0 S 168 0 E
Varanasi 134 25 22N 83 0 E
Vardangar Fjord 115 70 3N 29 25 E
Varna 121 43 13N 27 56 E
Västerås 115 59 37N 16 38 E
Vättern 115 58 25N 14 30 E
Vega, La 99 19 20N 70 30W
Vellore 134 12 57N 79 10 E
Venado Tuerto 106 33 50 S 62 0W
Vendée □ 116 46 50N 1 35W
Venezuela ■ 104 8 0N 65 0W
Venice 118 45 27N 12 20 E
Ventura 97 34 16N 119 18W
Veracruz 98 19 10N 96 10W
Verdun 116 49 12N 5 24 E
Verkhoyansk Ra. 138 66 0N 129 0 E
Vermont □ 92 43 40N 72 50W
Vernon 95 34 10N 99 20W
Verona 118 45 27N 11 0 E
Vert, C. 126 14 45N 17 30W
Vesterålen 115 68 45N 15 0 E
Vesuvius, Mt. 120 40 50N 14 22 E
Vicenza 118 45 32N 11 31 E
Vichy 117 46 9N 3 26 E
Vicksburg 95 32 22N 90 56W
Victoria 95 28 50N 97 0W
Victoria □ 143 37 0 S 144 0 E
Victoria, L. 128 1 0 S 33 0 E
Victoria Falls 128 17 58 S 25 52 E
Viedma 106 40 50 S 63 0W
Vienna 118 48 12N 16 22 E
Vientiane 134 17 58N 102 36 E
Vierzon 116 47 13N 2 5 E
Vietnam ■ 134 19 0N 106 0 E
Vigo 120 42 12N 8 41W
Villa María 106 32 20 S 63 10W
Villaguay 106 32 0 S 59 0W
Villahermosa 98 17 59N 92 55W
Villefranche-sur-Saône 117 45 59N 4 43 E
Vilnius 115 54 38N 25 19 E
Viña del Mar 106 33 0 S 71 30W
Vinh 134 18 45N 105 38 E
Vire 116 48 50N 0 53W
Virgin Is. 99 18 40N 64 30W
Virginia □ 92 37 45N 78 0W
Virginia Beach 92 36 54N 75 58W
Vishakhapatnam 134 17 45N 83 20 E
Vitória, Brazil 105 20 20 S 40 22W
Vitória, Spain 117 42 50N 2 41W
Vitória da Conquista 105 14 51 S 40 51W
Vizianagaram 134 18 6N 83 30 E
Vladivostok 138 43 10N 131 53 E
Vogelkop 135 1 25 S 133 0 E
Volga → 138 48 30N 46 0 E
Volgograd 138 48 40N 44 25 E
Vólos 121 39 24N 22 59 E
Volta → 126 5 46N 0 41 E
Volta, L. 126 7 30N 0 15 E
Volta Redonda 105 22 31 S 44 5W
Vorarlberg □ 118 47 20N 10 0 E
Voronezh 138 51 40N 39 10 E
Vosges 116 48 20N 7 10 E

Wabash → 92 37 46N 88 2W
Waco 95 31 33N 97 5W
Wâd Medanî 127 14 28N 33 30 E
Waddenzee 116 53 6N 5 10 E
Wadi Halfa 127 21 53N 31 19 E
Waigeo 135 0 20 S 130 40 E
Wakasa-Wan 137 35 40N 135 30 E
Wakayama 137 34 15N 135 15 E
Wakkanai 137 45 28N 141 35 E
Wałbrzych 118 50 45N 16 18 E
Wales □ 114 52 30N 3 30W
Walla Walla 96 46 3N 118 25W
Wallachia 119 44 35N 25 0 E
Wallowa, Mts. 96 45 20N 117 30W
Walvis Bay 128 23 0 S 14 28 E
Wanhsien 136 36 45N 107 24 E
Warangal 134 17 58N 79 35 E
Warner Mts. 96 41 30 S 120 20W
Warrego → 143 30 24 S 145 21 E
Warrington 93 30 22N 87 16W
Warsaw 119 52 13N 21 0 E
Wasatch Ra. 96 40 30N 111 15W
Wash, The 114 52 58N 0 20 E
Washington 92 38 52N 77 0W
Washington □ 96 47 45N 120 30W
Washington Mt. 92 44 15N 71 18W
Waterford 114 52 16N 7 8W
Waterloo 94 42 27N 92 20W
Waterton Glacier Int. Peace Park 96 48 35N 113 40W
Watertown 92 43 58N 75 57W
Waterville 93 44 35N 69 40W
Watsonville 97 36 55N 121 49W
Wau 127 7 21 S 146 47 E
Waukegan 94 42 22N 87 54W
Waukesha 94 43 0N 88 15W
Wausau 94 44 57N 89 40W
Wauwatosa 94 43 6N 87 59W
Waxahachie 95 32 22N 96 53W
Waycross 93 31 12N 82 25W
Weald, The 114 51 7N 0 9 E
Weddell Sea 107 72 30 S 40 0W
Weifang 136 36 47N 119 10 E
Wellesley Is. 143 16 42 S 139 30 E
Wellington 143 41 19 S 174 46 E
Wellington, I. 106 49 30 S 75 0W
Wenatchee 96 47 30N 120 17W
Wenchow 136 28 0N 120 35 E
Weser → 118 53 33N 8 30 E
West Bengal □ 134 23 0N 88 0 E
West Germany ■ 118 52 0N 9 0 E
West Palm Beach 93 26 44N 80 3W
West Siberian Plain 138 62 0N 75 0 E
West Virginia □ 92 39 0N 81 0W
Western Australia □ 142 25 0 S 118 0 E
Western Ghats 134 14 0N 75 0 E
Western Sahara ■ 126 25 0N 13 0W
Western Samoa ■ 140 14 0 S 172 0W
Westerwald 118 50 39N 8 0 E
Wheeling 92 40 2N 80 41W
White →, Ark., U.S.A. 95 33 53N 91 3W
White →, Ind., U.S.A. 92 38 25N 87 44W
White Nile → 127 15 38N 32 31 E
White Russia □ 138 53 30N 27 0 E
White Sea 138 66 30N 38 0 E
Whitney, Mt. 97 36 35N 118 14W
Whyalla 143 33 2 S 137 30 E
Wichita 95 37 40N 97 20W
Wichita Falls 95 33 57N 98 30W
Wicklow Mts. 114 53 0N 6 30W
Wiesbaden 118 50 7N 8 17 E
Wight, I. of 114 50 40N 1 20W
Wilberforce, C. 143 11 54 S 136 35 E
Wilhelmshaven 118 53 30N 8 9 E
Wilkes Barre 92 41 15N 75 52W
Willemstad 99 12 5N 69 0W
Williamsburg 92 37 17N 76 44W
Williamsport 92 41 18N 77 1W
Williston 94 48 10N 103 35W
Wilmington, Del., U.S.A. 92 39 45N 75 32W
Wilmington, N.C., U.S.A. 93 34 14N 77 54W
Wilson 93 35 44N 77 54W
Wimmera 143 36 30 S 142 0 E
Wind River Range 96 43 0N 109 30W
Windhoek 128 22 35 S 17 4 E
Windsor 114 51 28N 0 36W
Windward Is., Atl. Oc. 98 13 0N 63 0W
Windward Is., Pac. Oc. 141 18 0 S 149 0W
Windward Passage 99 20 0N 74 0W
Winona 94 44 2N 91 39W
Winston-Salem 93 36 7N 80 15W
Winterthur 118 47 30N 8 44 E
Winton 143 22 24 S 143 3 E
Wisconsin □ 94 44 30N 90 0W
Wisła → 119 54 22N 18 55 E
Włocławek 119 52 40N 19 3 E
Wollongong 143 34 25 S 150 54 E
Wolverhampton 114 52 35N 2 6W
Woodland 96 38 40N 121 50W
Worcester, U.K. 114 52 12N 2 12W
Worcester, U.S.A. 92 42 14N 71 49W
Wrangel I. 89 71 0N 180 0 E
Wuchow 136 23 26N 111 19 E
Wuchung 136 38 4N 106 12 E
Wuhan 136 30 35N 114 15 E
Wuhu 136 31 18N 118 20 E
Wulumuchi 136 43 40N 87 50 E
Wuppertal 118 51 15N 7 8 E
Würzburg 118 49 46N 9 55 E
Wusih 136 31 30N 120 30 E
Wutunghliao 136 29 25N 104 0 E
Wyandotte 92 42 14N 83 13W
Wyndham 142 15 33 S 128 3 E
Wyoming □ 96 42 48N 109 0W

Xingu → 105 1 30 S 51 53W
Xique-Xique 105 10 50 S 42 40W

Yablonovy Ra. 138 53 0N 114 0 E
Yakima 96 46 42N 120 30W
Yaku-Shima 137 30 20N 130 30 E
Yakutsk 138 62 5N 129 50 E
Yamaguchi 137 34 10N 131 32 E
Yamdena 135 7 45 S 131 20 E
Yamma-Yamma, L. 143 26 16 S 141 20 E
Yangchuan 136 38 0N 113 29 E
Yangtze Kiang → 136 31 40N 122 0 E
Yaroslavl 138 57 35N 39 55 E
Yatsushiro 137 32 30N 130 40 E
Yazd 129 31 55N 54 27 E
Yazoo → 95 32 35N 90 50W
Yellow Sea 136 35 0N 123 0 E
Yellowstone → 94 47 58N 103 59W
Yellowstone National Park 96 44 35N 110 0W
Yemen ■ 129 15 0N 44 0 E
Yenisey → 138 71 50N 82 40 E
Yenki 136 43 12N 129 30 E
Yentai 136 37 30N 121 22 E
Yerevan 138 40 10N 44 31 E
Yeu, I. d' 116 46 42N 2 20W
Yilan 136 24 47N 121 44 E
Yinchwan 136 38 30N 106 20 E
Yingkow 136 40 43N 122 9 E
Yiyang 136 28 45N 112 16 E
Yogyakarta 135 7 49 S 110 22 E
Yokkaichi 137 35 0N 136 38 E
Yokohama 137 35 27N 139 28 E
Yokosuka 137 35 20N 139 40 E
Yonago 137 35 25N 133 19 E
Yonkers 92 40 57N 73 51W
York, U.K. 114 53 58N 1 7W
York, U.S.A. 92 39 57N 76 43W
York, C. 143 10 42 S 142 31 E
Yorke Pen. 143 34 50 S 137 40 E
Yosemite National Park 97 38 0N 119 30W
Youngstown 92 41 7N 80 41W
Yuba City 96 39 12N 121 37W
Yucatán □ 98 20 50N 89 0W
Yugoslavia ■ 121 44 0N 20 0 E
Yukon → 41 65 30N 150 0W
Yuma 97 32 45N 114 37W
Yungtsi 136 34 50N 110 25 E
Yutze 136 37 45N 112 45 E

Zabrze 119 50 18N 18 50 E
Zacatecas 98 22 47N 102 35W
Zagreb 118 45 50N 16 0 E
Zagros Mts. 129 33 45N 47 0 E
Zahlah 127 33 52N 35 50 E
Zaïre ■ 128 3 0 S 23 0 E
Zaïre → 128 6 4 S 12 24 E
Zambezi → 128 18 55 S 36 4 E
Zambia ■ 128 15 0 S 28 0 E
Zamboanga 135 6 59N 122 3 E
Zamora de Hidalgo 98 19 59N 102 16W
Zanesville 92 39 56N 82 2W
Zanjan 129 36 40N 48 35 E
Zanzibar 128 6 12 S 39 12 E
Zaouiet Reggane 126 26 32N 0 3 E
Zaporozhye 138 47 50N 35 10 E
Zaria 126 11 0N 7 40 E
Zhdanov 138 47 5N 37 31 E
Zilina 119 49 12N 18 42 E
Zimbabwe ■ 128 20 0 S 30 0 E
Zion Nat. Park 97 37 25N 112 50W
Zomba 128 15 22 S 35 19 E
Zrenjanin 119 45 22N 20 23 E
Zürich 118 47 22N 8 32 E
Zwickau 118 50 43N 12 30 E
Zwolle 116 52 31N 6 6 E

The Earth from Space

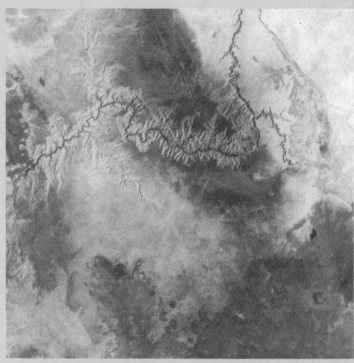

1. NORTH CAPE (NORWAY)
The area lies well north of the Arctic Circle and is made up of peaked and ridged mountains with strings of islands jutting into the sea. It is a landscape of sparse vegetation, forests, and bare rock, with little agriculture.

2. GRAND CANYON (U.S.A.)
The Colorado River is shown here flowing through the Grand Canyon in Arizona, which at this point is 1.5km deep and 20km wide. The reddish area distinguishes the Kaibab Plateau, an area over 2700m high, on which higher precipitation permits vegetation growth.

A Landsat satellite launched and controlled by NASA in the USA travels around the earth at a height of 917km, and "photographs" every point of the world once every 18 days. The view from the satellite is broken into four component bands of the spectrum, bands 4, 5, 6, and 7, converted into electrical signals and transmitted

3. TAKLA MAKAN DESERT (CHINA)
Snow cover spreads over the marshland around the Tarim River in the north-east and onto the desert sand dunes. It is not easy to appreciate the size of the dunes from this image; individual dune ridges are 1.5-3km wide and extend 8-32km.

4. MISSISSIPPI DELTA (U.S.A.)
The blue coloring of the farmland in this area is caused by extensive flooding of the Mississippi River. The large quantity of sediment transported by the river flows into the Gulf of Mexico building up the delta and appearing as a light blue mass in the sea.

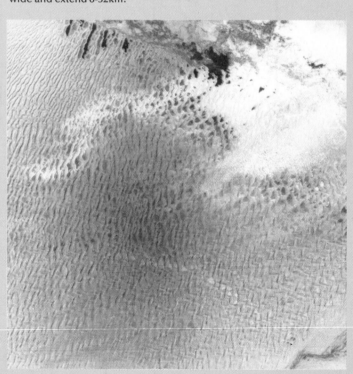

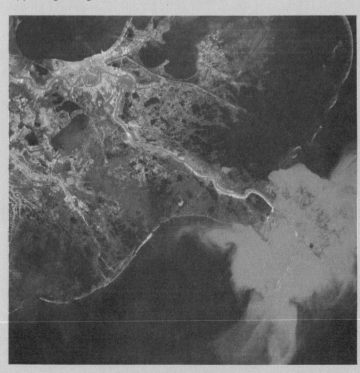